THE BROOKINGS QUARTERLY ECONOMETRIC MODEL
OF THE UNITED STATES

THE BROOKINGS
QUARTERLY ECONOMETRIC
MODEL OF THE UNITED STATES

Edited by

JAMES S. DUESENBERRY, *Harvard University*

GARY FROMM, *The Brookings Institution*

LAWRENCE R. KLEIN, *University of Pennsylvania*

EDWIN KUH, *Massachusetts Institute of Technology*

1965

RAND McNALLY & COMPANY - CHICAGO

NORTH-HOLLAND PUBLISHING COMPANY - AMSTERDAM

Published by:

RAND McNALLY & COMPANY – CHICAGO

Sole distributors outside the United States and Canada:
NORTH-HOLLAND PUBLISHING COMPANY – AMSTERDAM

Library of Congress Catalog Card Number 65–18589

PRINTED IN THE NETHERLANDS

PREFACE

This volume has an unusually long history and reflects the work of many hands. For good or ill, it is the result of collective and sponsored research. The papers presented here are the response, after a long distributed lag, to a stimulus provided by the Social Science Research Council (SSRC). In early 1959, Mr. Paul Webbink, on behalf of the SSRC, arranged a conference on research on the stability of the American economy. At the conference held at Ann Arbor in June, 1959, there was general agreement that econometric models should play a central role in the analysis of business-cycle problems and stabilization policies. It was also agreed that econometric models tend to become rapidly obsolete unless there is some arrangement to adjust the equations to data revisions and new research results. The need for larger-scale models with more detail than previously used was generally recognized.

After the Ann Arbor conference, the SSRC established a committee on economic stability. That committee approved the proposal for the development of a larger-scale econometric model to be sponsored by the SSRC; Professor James S. Duesenberry and Professor Lawrence R. Klein were appointed co-chairmen of the project. During 1960–61, the committee discussed the broad outlines of the model and drew up a list of potential participants. The National Science Foundation provided an initial grant of $ 125 000.

It was agreed from the outset that the model should build on the experience of economists who had worked on particular sectors of the economy or particular types of economic activity. A rough sketch of the whole model was prepared which indicated the major variables which had to be explained in each sector or type of activity. Those who agreed to participate were asked to prepare papers reviewing the empirical literature in their assigned area and to suggest tentative sets of equations for their sectors. The papers were presented at a conference held at Dartmouth College in August, 1961.

The Dartmouth Conference was a unique experience for all of us. We were housed in Dartmouth dormitories for three weeks, and many of the participants brought their families. The conference was much more than a

paper-reading exercise. Each participant presented his results in the regular
sessions, but the discussions went on through breakfast, lunch, dinner, and
on into the night. Research assistants and computational facilities were
available, and many suggestions were tested before the conference was
over. The sessions produced useful suggestions for the individual sectors
and brought out previously unforeseen problems in delineation of the
structure of the model linkages between sectors, in and even in the form of
the system. The participants were asked to complete their work, taking
into account the suggestions made at the conference, and to report by
the summer of 1962.

A second two-week conference was held at Dartmouth in August, 1962.

Its sessions were notable for the cooperative spirit shown by the participants. Most of the papers were completed in time, and all at the conference
tried to contribute to the construction of the complete model rather than
to show off their own sectors. Most of the participants had nearly completed
their empirical work, and by the end of the conference, we felt that we had
most of the pieces of the model.

The two Dartmouth conferences were outstandingly successful. We owe
a debt of gratitude to Paul Webbink and the SSRC for support in arranging
the innumerable details of the care and feeding of economists [1]). Dartmouth
College was generous and cooperative in providing its facilities. We are
also grateful for the warm welcome we received from the members of the
Dartmouth faculty.

After the 1962 conference, those who had given papers were asked to
tidy up their empirical work and to prepare final drafts. To the surprise
of the editors, most of the papers were received in good time, and the
long process of editorial work and of assembling the equations into a
coherent model was begun.

The National Science Foundation made a second grant of $ 248,000
to the Brookings Institution for continued work on the model for a three-
year period beginning September, 1963. The project now is guided by
James Duesenberry, Gary Fromm, Lawrence Klein, and Edwin Kuh and
has as additional members of an advisory committee (of which Professor
Duesenberry is chairman) Edward F. Denison, Robert A. Gordon, Bert
G. Hickman, Arthur Okun, Guy Orcutt, and Henri Theil.

At Brookings, a small staff, headed by Gary Fromm, performed the la-

---

[1]) A full list of participants and a more complete accounting of the achievements of
the conferences are given in two reports in *Items*, Vol. XVI (September, 1962) 37–40.

borious and vital tasks of unifying the notation used by the various contributors to the volume, reconciling diverse data sources (sometimes for the same concept) used by the different specialists, and making a large number of separate presentations generally consistent with one another. It might be noted that, generally, in lists of symbols and in theoretical manipulations, all monetary variables appear as if in current dollars. In estimated equations, the distinction between current and constant dollars is made explicit. Major theoretical and estimated equations are numbered consecutively by chapter. This system is modified slightly in chapter 18, which contains the complete model.

Since the completion of the papers presented here, work on the model has continued. A great deal of effort has gone into removing various incompatibilities (cf. pp. 734–736), into preparing the model for complete system solutions, and into the development of simulation programs suitable for use with large–scale models. Summer workshops on the model were held at M.I.T. in 1964 and at Brookings in 1965. Research by specialists at several universities has also been sponsored. These efforts, and those of members of the project staff, have resulted in additional papers on various sectors and the model as a whole. It is expected that this research will be published in another volume in the near future.

The Brookings staff has also been constructing a consistent and replicable set of data and arranging a system for keeping it up to date. Testing the individual equations for stability of parameters in different time periods and for accuracy of forecasts also has been accomplished. Complete model solutions and simulations are now being processed. Many of the latter were suggested by government and university economists invited as participants in a research conference to design simulation experiments, held during May, 1965.

The continuing research program will, of course, lead to substantial revision of the model, so that the system described here will be superseded shortly after it is published. That is in line with our original objectives. We do not hope to produce once and for all a fixed model of the American economy. We hope to bring together in a continually revised model all tested research results in the field of aggregate economics. The resulting model must be continually adjusted to take account of the evolution of the economy and of new research findings.

Our progress has been aided by innumerable individuals and organizations. The great debt owed to Paul Webbink and the SSRC and the financial support of the National Science Foundation have already been cited.

Special mention also should be made of the encouragement and assistance of the Federal Reserve Board, the International Monetary Fund, and the Office of Business Economics of the U. S. Department of Commerce. This volume benefited immeasurably, too, from the painstaking efforts of James A. Craig in checking for consistency in variable units and equation parameters, in verifying data and equation specifications, and in assisting in the preparation of the variable notation and final manuscripts. Alix Ryckoff typed several chapters and many of the equations in others; C. S. Raman helped with the indexing. Other economists and groups are cited throughout the volume by each author. To all who assisted in this venture, we are extremely grateful.

August 1965 The Editors

TABLE OF CONTENTS

PREFACE V

TABLE OF CONTENTS IX

LIST OF TABLES XI

LIST OF FIGURES XV

I. INTRODUCTION

1. Introduction: The research strategy and its application, JAMES
   S. DUESENBERRY AND LAWRENCE R. KLEIN   3

II. PRODUCER INVESTMENT DECISIONS

2. Anticipations and investment behavior, DALE W. JORGENSON . .   35
3. Realization of investment anticipations, ROBERT EISNER   95
4. Factors influencing investment in inventories, PAUL G. DARLING
   AND MICHAEL C. LOVELL 131
5. Business anticipatory demand: An analysis of business orders,
   1948-1962, MANORANJAN DUTTA. 163

III. CONSUMER EXPENDITURE DECISIONS

6. Nonbusiness construction, SHERMAN J. MAISEL 179
7. Consumption regressions with quarterly data, DANIEL B. SUITS AND
   GORDON R. SPARKS 203

IV. INCOME DISTRIBUTION, PRICE AND WAGE DETERMINATION AND LABOR FORCE

8. Income distribution and employment over the business cycle,
   EDWIN KUH. 227
9. Prices and wages, CHARLES L. SCHULTZE AND JOSEPH L. TRYON . . 281
10. The labor force and marriages as endogenous factors, STANLEY
    LEBERGOTT 335

V. SUBSECTORS: FOREIGN TRADE AND AGRICULTURE

11. The foreign sector, RUDOLF R. RHOMBERG AND LORETTE BOISSON-
    NEAULT 375
12. A submodel of the agricultural sector, KARL A. FOX 409

VI. MONETARY AND FISCAL SECTORS

13. A model of financial behavior, FRANK DE LEEUW 465
14. Government revenues and expenditures, ALBERT ANDO, E. CARY
    BROWN AND EARL W. ADAMS, JR 533

VII. ESTIMATION, SIMULATION, AGGREGATION AND THE COMPLETE MODEL

15. Dynamic structure and estimation in economy-wide econometric
    models, FRANKLIN M. FISHER 589
16. Validation and application of macroeconomic models using
    computer simulation, CHARLES C. HOLT 637
17. Price and output aggregation in the Brookings econometric
    model, FRANKLIN M. FISHER, LAWRENCE R. KLEIN AND YOICHI
    SHINKAI 653
18. The complete model: A first approximation, GARY FROMM AND
    LAWRENCE R. KLEIN 681

KEY TO ABBREVIATIONS 739

AUTHOR INDEX 765

SUBJECT INDEX 770

LIST OF TABLES

2.1 Unrestricted estimates of regression coefficients   61
2.2 Restricted estimates of regression coefficients   63
2.3 Estimates of regression coefficients: total regulated   67
2.4 Estimates of regression coefficients: all other   69
2.5 Goodness of fit statistics, fitted, naive and forecasting models   70
2.6 Average lag between changes in demand for capital and actual investment
     expenditure.   76
2.7 Time form of lagged response   81
2.8 Response of demand for capital to changes in market conditions and the tax
     structure   88

3.1 Estimated equations with sales realizations and profits changes   104
3.2 Estimated equations with sales changes and profits changes   105
3.3 Structural equations with sales realizations and profits changes (trans-
     formations from table 3.1)   106
3.4 Structural equations with sales changes and profits changes (transforma-
     tions from table 3.2).   107
3.5 Estimated equations with changes in sales and unfilled orders of machinery   109
3.6 Estimated equations with changes in sales, profits and unfilled orders of
     machinery   110
3.7 Structural equations with changes in sales and unfilled orders of machinery
     (transformations from table 3.5)   112
3.8 Structural equations with changes in sales, profits and unfilled orders of
     machinery (transformations from table 3.6)   114
3.9 Errors in anticipations versus errors in predictions from structural equations
     with sales realizations and profits changes: manufacturing, 1949: 3 to 1960:
     4; nondurables 1953: 4 to 1960: 4   115
3.10 Errors in anticipations versus errors in predictions from structural equations
     with sales changes and profits changes: durables, nondurables utilities and
     commercial, 1949: 1 to 1960: 4   116
3.11 Forecasts of 1961: means of errors in anticipations and predictions   117
3.12 Forecasts of 1961: totals in manufacturing and all sectors; capital expenditures,
     anticipations and predictions using structural equations with sales changes
3.13 Forecasts of 1962 and 1963: durable manufacturing   118
3.14 Forecasts of 1962 and 1963: nondurable manufacturing   120
3.15 Forecasts of 1962 and 1963: public utilities   122
3.16 Forecasts of 1962 and 1963: commercial   122
3.17 Forecasts of 1962 and 1963: total durables, nondurables, public utilities and
     commercial.   123

3.18 Comparison of forecasts using change-in-profit variables 125

4.1 Comparison of cyclical changes in business inventory investment and in goods output (GNP less services and construction) during the postwar period 132
4.2 Durable manufacturing inventory regressions 138
4.3 Nondurable manufacturing inventory regressions 141
4.4 Inventory investment regressions: combined wholesale and retail trade (less autos), 1951 through 1960 151
4.5 Inventory investment regressions: selected components of trade, 1951 through 1960 154
4.6 Manufacturing regression variables, data sources and adjustments 157
4.7 Trade regression variables, data sources and adjustments 158
4.8 Coefficients of simple correlation between pairs of variables used in regressions for combined wholesale and retail trade 159

5.1 New orders equations for durable and nondurable manufacturing 166
5.2 New orders equations for two-digit manufacturing industries 170

6.1 GNP expenditures for nonbusiness construction 179
6.2 Nonbusiness construction equations 180
6.3 The housing stock and its utilization in the United States on April 1, 1960 . 190

7.1 Consumer expenditure equations 208
7.2 Squared multiple correlation coefficients for first differences and levels . . . 217
7.3 Summary of regression equations (1948: 1–1960: 4) 218
7.4 Stock of cars 220
7.5 Liquid asset holdings, beginning of quarter, seasonally adjusted (billions of 1954 dollars) 222

8.1 Distribution of gross private nonfarm national income shares 229
8.2 Distribution of net private nonfarm national income shares 229
8.3 Distribution of charges against corporate gross product 230
8.4 Change in shares of private nonfarm national income 231
8.5 Cyclical changes in gross factor income 232
8.6 Proportion of nonproduction workers in total employment 241
8.7 Lag weights for employment equations 247
8.8 Elasticities and reaction coefficients 248
8.9 Employment functions 249
8.10 Covariance components of error variances: employment explained by output and capital stock 251
8.11 Covariance components of error variances: employment explained by output, capital stock, lagged employment, per cent change in output 252
8.12 Production worker hour demand functions 255
8.13 Reaction coefficients and target hours/week from production worker hour equations 257

8.14 Lag weights for production worker hour equations 258
8.15 Final least squares estimates for hours and employment functions 259
8.16 Error variance analysis: manufacturing. 263
8.17 Normalized covariance matrix of total employment error 266
8.18 Ratio of gross entrepreneurial income to gross product originating 268
8.19 Price indexes related to inventory valuation 273

9.1 Price regressions for nonagricultural production sectors, 1948: 2–1960: 4 . . 292
9.2 Price regressions for nonagricultural production sectors using first differences
     between quarters one year apart: 1949: 1–1960: 4 295
9.3 Price regressions for global aggregates: 1948: 1–1960: 2 297
9.4 Price regressions for individual industries, 1948: 2–1960: 4 298
9.5 Price regressions for individual industries using value-added price as dependent
     variable: 1949: 2–1960: 4 303
9.6 Final price equations 308
9.7 Wage regressions for nonagricultural production sectors, 1950: 1–1960: 4 . . 318
9.8 Wage equations 327
9.9 Wage rate increases for alternative adjustment parameters 329
9.10 Equilibrium wage change for given unemployment levels, profit share and
     price level 330

10.1 Participation rates for married women: April, 1940 338
10.2 Correlations of female labor force participation rates and unemployment . 341
10.3 Correlation coefficients of specified variables and labor force participation
     rates for females aged 20 and over 349
10.4 Labor force participation rate equations for females aged 20 and over . . . 350
10.5 Labor force participation equations for females aged 20 and over 353
10.6 Labor force participation rate equations for females aged 14 to 19 and 14 and
     over 355
10.7 Labor force participation rate equations for males aged 20 and over and 14
     to 19 356
10.8 Marriages and key variables: zero order correlations 366
10.9 Marriage and marriage rate equations 370

11.1 Imports of finished goods and services, including food 382
11.2 Imports of unfinished goods 383
11.3 Exports of goods and services 384
11.4 Imports of finished goods and services, excluding food 385
11.5 Imports of food 386
11.6 Exports of goods 387
11.7 Foreign trade elasticities: aggregate import and export equations 388
11.8 Test of forecasting efficiency of aggregate import and export equations, four
     quarters of 1962 391
11.9 Imports of crude materials (adjusted) 394
11.10 Per capita imports of crude foodstuffs (adjusted) 396
11.11 Per capita imports of manufactured foodstuffs (adjusted) 397
11.12 Imports of semimanufactures (adjusted) 398
11.13 Imports of finished manufactures (adjusted) 399

11.14 Foreign trade elasticities: commodity group import equations 400
11.15 Test of forecasting efficiency of commodity group import equations, four
   quarters of 1962 402

12.1 Determination of farm prices 415
12.2 Food expenditures and quantities purchased: logarithmic regressions upon
   family income, urban families, U.S., spring 1948 419
12.3 Price and income elasticities of demand at retail: percentage change in
   quantities demanded resulting from one per cent changes in prices or income,
   1955-1957 (after Brandow) 420
12.4 Determination of farm income and expenditures 436
12.5 Determination of farm prices, farm income and expenditures 450
12.6 Change in quantities of inputs per unit of total farm output and changes in
   prices of inputs, United States, 1940 to 1960 452

13.1 Final equations. 476
13.2 Quarterly changes in the public's holdings of currency 490
13.3 Quarterly changes in the public's holdings of demand deposits 491
13.4 Quarterly changes in the public's holdings of time deposits 492
13.5 Quarterly changes in savings and insurance claims 495
13.6 Quarterly changes in household holdings of U.S. securities 496
13.7 Quarterly changes in business holdings of U.S. securities 497
13.8 Term structure relationships 501
13.9 Net borrowing by households 504
13.10 Net borrowing by business 505
13.11 Changes in bank holdings of U.S. securities· 509
13.12 Changes in member bank borrowing and excess reserves 510
13.13 Quarterly changes in the average rate of private loans and investments . . . 514
13.14 Annual changes in the yield on time deposits 516
13.15 Changes in nonbank finance holdings of U.S. securities 520
13.16 Changes in nonbank finance holdings of private securities 521
13.17 Prediction errors, 1961–1962 525

14.1 Government revenues and expenditures 535
14.2 Excise tax functions 544

17.1 Consolidated input coefficient matrix, I–A 664
17.2 Ratios of sector gross outputs to GNP originating by industries, 1947 . . . 665
17.3 1947 values of implicit deflators of GNP originating by sectors 665
17.4 Computed sector final demands 665
17.5 Coefficients of final demand conversion 666
17.6 Weights for price conversion 675

18.1 Gross national product or expenditure 728
18.2 National income, by type of income 730
18.3 Relation of gross national product, national income, personal income, and
   disposable income 732

LIST OF FIGURES

1.1   Condensed flow diagram of Brookings-SSRC Econometric Model   24
1.2   Preliminary ordering of causal structure   28

2.1   Sequence of intermediate stages   39

6.1   Flow diagram for non-business construction   184
6.2   Relationships between housing starts and the independent variables   196

7.1   Actual and calculated automobile demand   211
7.2   Index of consumer attitudes and deviation of disposable income from trend (1953–1961)   213

8.1   Labor productivity in nondurable manufacturing   237
8.2   Labor productivity in durable manufacturing   238
8.3   Durable manufacturing production worker employment equation   244
8.4   Durable manufacturing production worker hours equation   254

9.1   Unemployment and aggregate excess demand for labor   313

12.1   Illustration of causal ordering of farm price determination   412
12.2   Pork prices: 1947–1962   434
12.3   Year to year changes in pork prices   435
12.4   Internal mechanism of the cattle cycle   446
12.5   Internal mechanism of the hog cycle   446

13.1   Changes in the public's holding of demand deposits and selected explanatory variables   473
13.2   Changes in the public's holdings of time deposits and selected explanatory variables   474
13.3   The term structure of U.S. security rates   502
13.4   Calculated values based on simultaneous estimation, 1955–1962   528

17.1   Actual and computed indexes for price conversion   674

PART I

Introduction

CHAPTER 1

INTRODUCTION:
THE RESEARCH STRATEGY AND ITS APPLICATIONS

Contents

1.1. Model characteristics and research strategy   5
1. Special sector detail. 2. Degree of aggregation. 3. Econometric model
building as a cumulative and collective process. 4. Providing a place to
put things.

1.2. Applications of the model   9
1. Policy simulation. 2. Business cycle and growth theories. 3. Forecasting.

1.3. Econometric research by committee   14

1.4. The flow chart of the system   22

1.5. Some problems of statistical method.   23

1.6. Some problems of short time series   29

1.7. Progress and plans   31

References   32

INTRODUCTION:
THE RESEARCH STRATEGY AND ITS APPLICATION

JAMES S. DUESENBERRY

Harvard University, Cambridge, Massachusetts

and

LAWRENCE R. KLEIN

University of Pennsylvania, Philadelphia, Pennsylvania

The papers presented here are the first fruits of a collective effort to increase our knowledge of the structure of the American economy. Each paper can stand on its own merits as a piece of independent research. But the articles represent more than a collection of essays. The work presented here, taken as a whole, constitutes a complete model which "explains" the variations in *GNP* and its major components, as well as major price movements, employment, and wage rates.

The general outline of the model reflects a consensus on the part of the participants—a general agreement on the best set of working hypotheses about the nature of the economy. Naturally each participant has some reservations about the validity of various elements in the model, and in all cases those reservations apply to his own contributions, as well as to those of other participants. Nonetheless, there is a general agreement on the broad outline of the model.

In the last few years empirical research in economics has advanced rapidly. A great deal has been learned about the behavior of business investment, consumption, inventory investment and so on. The model presented here incorporates not only the contributions of the authors but of others on whose work they built. But, while much has been done, much more remains to be done. This model presents only the first stage of a continuing effort. As it develops, the model will incorporate the results of new research from all sources and should reflect, to a progressively greater degree, whatever agreement there may be on the structure of the economy.

The development of a large-scale econometric model integrating empirical work in many fields is a natural outgrowth of the development of economics.

In the past thirty years there has been a rapid increase in the amount and quality of empirical work in economics. And, in turn, the need for empirical research is inherent in the nature of economics.

The questions economists ask are questions about quantities—prices, outputs, incomes—and the relations among them. So-called "literary" economics does not use mathematics or statistics. It is nonetheless an analysis of relationships among variables which are, in principle, capable of numerical measurement or ordering.

Many questions of economic policy turn on the relative magnitudes of the parameters in some relationship, or set of relationships, among economic variables. The goals of economic policy are usually stated, albeit somewhat vaguely, in terms of the numerical rate of growth of *GNP*, the price level, the rate of unemployment and the numerical state of the balance of payments. Discussion of measures to achieve those goals involves judgments about the response of various economic magnitudes to previous policy actions.

Some interesting questions in economics may be answered from a knowledge of one or two economic relationships viewed in isolation. But most economists are convinced that many changes in policy or in other exogenous factors will have not only a direct effect in one sector of the economy, but will also have secondary or indirect effects on many other sectors.

We must view the economy as a system of quantitative relationships. Those relationships may be more or less persistent in time, but they may be disturbed in a variety of ways. Yet, however that may be, it is important to find out as much as we can about the quantitative characteristics of the economic system.

We certainly need a quantitative specification of the relations among economic variables which make our economy a system instead of a set of unrelated random processes. Such a quantitative specification is an econometric model (regardless of the methods used to estimate the parameters).

The task before us is a difficult one. Some of the more vexing difficulties in the model-building are discussed below. And it is undoubtedly true that we have a great deal to learn. The equations presented here must be taken as very tentative statements about the structure of our economy. If an econometric model is used unwisely, if econometricians present themselves as witch doctors with computers, econometric models can be dangerous. But any method of economic analysis can be misused.

The need for quantitative knowledge of our economic system is great, but we cannot learn enough about it to solve all the problems of stabilization. We may never know as much as we should like to know. But in the twenty-five years since Tinbergen's pioneering in econometric model-building a great deal of progress has been made. The amount and quality of data for model-building purposes have increased enormously and statistical technique has advanced rapidly. Computation problems which a few years ago seemed appalling in magnitude are coming under control.

There has also been substantial progress in the investigation of a wide variety of aspects of the economic structure. The fact that controversy ranges over the relative importance of capacity utilization and cash flow in determining investment, or over alternative formulations of the consumption function, shows that we have much to learn. But the fact that the controversies are empirical, and the amount and quality of the work being done in connection with those controversies, suggest healthy progress. In this case, heat may generate some light.

When we consider the increase in the number of economists doing empirical work and in the facilities for doing it, we must view our present position as a beginning and not as an end. And the usefulness of econometric models must be judged not only by the results of those now available but by their potential for systematically linking and bringing out the implications of theoretical and empirical work now going forward.

1.1. Model characteristics and research strategy

In its basic form our model is similar to its predecessors. Its structure depicts the economy as a set of interrelated dynamic processes involving production, generation and distribution of incomes, price and wage determination, and purchases of goods and services by households, businesses and governments. A central role in these processes is played by the mutual feedback between production, income payments and purchases of goods and services. The rate of production at any time in any sector is strongly influenced by current and recent past sales; production rates are a major determinant of income flows; and income flows are major determinants of product sales. That system of interactions forms the core of all econometric models and it dominates their form. If one did not believe that the production-income-expenditures-production sequence was of great importance the form of econometric models would be very different. The dynamic elements in our model, as in others, come from three sources: (1) lagged relationships and rate of change variables; (2) relationships including stock variables where the stocks are cumulants of flows generated by the model; (3) changing exogenous variables and random shocks.

In general the method of building a complete econometric model can be described in terms of the following steps: (1) Decide upon the outputs of the model, i.e., the variables which the model is supposed to explain or predict. (2) For each output variable decide (tentatively) upon an equation involving other variables which purport to explain the behavior of the dependent variable. The decision may be based on a mixture of theoretical considerations and prior empirical work of all sorts (not merely regression work, but survey work, historical material, qualitative interviews, or anything else that lends conviction to the chosen equation). (3) The variables entering the equations explaining the output variables must be classified into (a) other current or lagged endogenous variables already included in the system, (b) endogenous variables not yet explained, (c) variables which are to be regarded as exogenous to the system. (4) Equations similar to those in (2) must be developed for the endogenous variables not yet explained. (5) This process has to be continued until every variable is explained by some combination of endogenous variables already explained and exogenous variables.

All the equations must then be estimated by methods which take account, as well as possible, of simultaneous equation bias, collinearity, serial correlation and other statistical pitfalls. Our procedures for dealing with those problems are discussed in section 1.3. The fitted equations must then be tested by forecasting (or backcasting) on data outside those used in fitting and for consistency of parameters with all types of information external to the model.

1.1.1. Special sector detail

In its very broadest outlines and in the purposes for which we hope to employ it, our model does not differ in any essential way from its predecessors. It may appear that we have merely constructed a larger, more detailed version of the same kind of thing that has been done before. The Brookings-SSRC econometric model is very much larger than any other econometric model; it does have a more detailed sector breakdown. But we hope that we have not been victims of the fallacy that "bigger is better". Nor have we enlarged the number of sectors in the model in order to display the power of computing machines. The relatively large size of the model reflects the purposes we have in mind and the methods used to develop the model.

We have given a more detailed treatment than usual to six aspects of the economy, viz., (1) agriculture, (2) foreign trade, (3) housing, (4) money and finance, (5) government, (6) demography. The reasons for giving special attention to those sectors are fairly obvious, but it may be worth while to spell them out.

The agriculture, housing, monetary and government sectors, and to some extent the foreign trade sector, are very largely influenced by government policy measures. For reasons given above we want to have explicit parameters in the model to reflect the influence of those measures.

In the case of demographic variables, such as marriage rates, household formation and labor force participation rates, there are responses to economic conditions which have not usually been considered in econometric models.

Housing and agriculture, though they are producing sectors whose contribution to *GNP* is not so very much greater than that of some of the other producing sectors, are very different from them. Rather special institutional factors play an important role in those sectors. The relations between changes in aggregate demand and production are qualitatively different from those applicable to other sectors.

Similarly the monetary sector is not only important quantitatively, but it also has a complex structure of its own which must be spelled out in considerable detail if monetary factors are to be treated realistically.

The government sector is of special importance because of the large number of policy instruments associated with taxation and expenditure. In addition, some aspects of government expenditure as well as of revenue are responsive to changing economic conditions in a regular way. In order to separate out those parts of government expenditure which should be treated as endogenous it is necessary to describe the government sector in considerable detail.

1.1.2. Degree of aggregation

There is always some question as to the appropriate degree of disaggregation of producing sectors of the economy, particularly in manufacturing. In principle one could disaggregate down to the four-digit manufacturing industry level or even farther. It has sometimes been suggested that we should work with company data, or even with establishment data. Certainly it is true that every establishment has its own production function and every firm its own law of price, wage and investment determination. Any higher level of aggregation involves some lack of precision because of variation in the internal composition of the aggregates used. Moreover, direct knowledge of the impact of technical change or legislation often comes to us in the form of information about particular products or plants or companies.

On the other hand, a very fine disaggregation poses many problems. When the unit of observation is very small the "noise-to-signal ratio" becomes very high. A systematic influence which affects the behavior of all firms in the same way may be of considerable importance in the aggregate. Yet its influence on each individual firm may be so swamped by other factors specific to the firm (and canceling each other in the aggregate) that it cannot be detected or, if detected, cannot be measured with any reliability. The computational problems raised by the use of a very large number of sectors are obvious.

Initially our model will be fitted with seven producing sectors: agriculture, durable manufacturing, nondurable manufacturing, regulated industries (transport, communication, utilities), contract construction, trade and a residual sector. This is necessary partly because data are not yet available for a more refined breakdown. But in addition, we need to solve many problems of estimation and of testing models with a limited degree of disaggregation before grappling with larger models.

Ultimately, we hope to structure a larger model in such a way as to permit a good deal of flexibility in the choice of a level of aggregation for a specific purpose. This enlarged model could use as many as thirty-two producing sectors, of which twenty would be two-digit manufacturing industries.

For some purposes it may be desirable to disaggregate further. If we should discover a particularly large change in the composition of output within one of the sectors, whose subdivisions respond differently, it would be useful to subdivide it. It may also prove desirable to change the degree of time disaggregation by using monthly data in some equations to give a more precise specification of the lag structure.

By presenting the model in terms of a relatively large number of sectors we hope to encourage those who work with the model, or its descendants, in the future to use a level of disaggregation which is appropriate to the problem in hand.

The features outlined above differentiate the sectoral scope of our model from its predecessors. It also differs from its predecessors in the way it has been constructed and in our hopes for its future.

1.1.3. *Econometric model building as a cumulative and collective process*

In the U.S., at least, econometric models of the economy have been constructed by single individuals or very small groups. A small group can hardly do justice to the task of providing a quantitative description of the American economy. Certain short cuts are necessary to make the task manageable. Moreover, on controversial issues any small group model is likely to reflect certain ways of looking at things which are not generally accepted. Even when those crotchets are relatively unimportant they detract from the acceptance of the model. Of course, a collectively produced model may have its own problems—a camel is a horse designed by a committee. But whatever the defects of collective efforts, there must be an initial consensus for econometric work to become cumulative. Econometric models rapidly become obsolete as data are revised and the economy evolves. They need to be continually revised if they are to be used. But beyond that, real improvement requires continuous effort on the part of a large number of econometricians. It is our hope that the Brookings-SSRC econometric model will represent a fairly widely accepted set of views as to the nature of the economy. If there is some degree of consensus on that point it may become worth while for a large number of workers to criticize and improve the model. In that way econometric model building can become a cumulative process.

1.1.4. *Providing a place to put things*

Our economy consists of a myriad of diverse parts which we group together in various ways for research purposes. Much of the knowledge produced by economic research is knowledge about rather fine-grained sectors of the economy. And much more could be produced if the producers had any place to put it. But knowledge about small subsectors of the economy is often sterile unless it can be used either (a) as illustration, confirmation, disproof or modification of some general principle of economic theory or (b) in some larger context. We hope that by providing a model with a relatively high degree of disaggregation and some flexibility it will be possible to make more direct and fruitful use of research about small subsectors of the economy.

1.2. *Applications of the model*

An econometric model can be used to give quantitative answers to a host of specific questions—forecasting, simulation of the effects of policy actions, simulation of business cycle theories—but the procedure for obtaining those answers from a given model is the same for a variety of applications. The model consists of a large set of equations describing hypotheses about the interrelations among a number of economic variables. The variables in the system fall into three classes: (1) endogenous variables, which are explained by the model; (2) exogenous policy variables, which are not explained by the model but are subject to legislative or administrative control, e.g., tax rates; (3) other exogenous variables.

The equations of the model can be solved and presented as a set of reduced form equations in which each endogenous variable at time t can be expressed as a function of current and lagged values of the exogenous variables and lagged values of the endogenous variables.

Suppose we are interested in the implications of the model for time period t. The reduced form equations contain lagged values of exogenous and endogenous variables for several time periods $t-1, t-2$, etc. These are taken as historically given. The set of lagged values relevant for the reduced form equations for period t is called the set of initial conditions.

To obtain values of the endogenous variables for period t we must specify (1) the initial conditions for period t and (2) the values of the exogenous variables for period t. Given those data we can compute the numerical values of endogenous variables for period t from the reduced form equations.

If we also wish to consider period $t+1$, we use the values of endogenous variables for period t as part of the initial conditions for $t+1$. We must specify a new set of values for the exogenous variables for $t+1$ and compute a new numerical solution for endogenous variables for it. The process can be repeated indefinitely in that manner.

Applications of the model differ in the way in which the initial conditions and exogenous variables are specified. For a one-quarter forecast, for, say, the first quarter of 1964, the initial conditions are the historical values of the variables for periods prior to the beginning of 1964. The exogenous variables are independent predictions of the values of those variables which will, in fact, rule from the first quarter of 1964.

For a forecast of more than one quarter the initial conditions are the same as in the previous case and the nonpolicy exogenous variables are also unconditional predictions. But the policy exogenous variables may be predicted by some rule of behavior imputed to policy makers.

In simulation experiments we try to find what the model implies as to the consequences of various combinations of (1) initial conditions, (2) specified sequences of policy actions or specified rules for formation of policy, and (3) specified sequences of values of nonpolicy exogenous variables.

For example, suppose we were to follow the rule of balancing the budget at full employment and some rule for formation of monetary policy. Then we can ask: Under what combinations of initial conditions and movement of nonpolicy exogenous variables would we achieve full employment?

Since our equations are subject to error, a full examination of the properties of the model requires the use of random shock or Monte Carlo simulation. The error terms in the equations constitute a set of exogenous variables which we assume are determined by random processes. In a random shock simulation we proceed as before except that we add to each equation for each period a random variable drawn from a distribution defined by the estimated variance-covariance matrix. We repeat the process many times. We then study the distribution of outcomes of a forecast or of one of the simulations described above.

Another procedure is to work out forecasts or simulations with alternative sets of values for the parameters of the equations. This procedure is called *sensitivity analysis*, since we try to ascertain the sensitivity of the model's properties to variations of its parameters.

With those general procedures in mind we can consider policy simulation, cycle and growth analysis, and forecasting in more detail.

1.2.1. Policy simulation

Many policy issues turn upon judgments as to the magnitude and speed of effect of alternative policy measures on certain variables in the economic system. Interest attaches not only to the direct effect of policy actions at the point of impact, so to speak, but on the whole chain of repercussions through the system set off by a policy action. An econometric model is obviously an ideal instrument for evaluating the total impact of alternative policy measures—provided, of course, that the parameter estimates are reasonably correct.

Many policy instruments influence more than one target variable, and it may often happen that a movement of a policy instrument which affects one target variable in a desirable way has an adverse effect on another. We may, therefore, consider policy formation as the simultaneous choice of a set of values for policy instruments to achieve a set of values for target variables. If we have to deal with an exactly specified and static system, it is simple enough in principle. We have only to calculate the values for the policy instrument variables which maximize some "objective function" (subject to appropriate constraints) of the target variables. Unfortunately the real problem is much more difficult. We deal with a dynamic system which is subject to disturbances and whose parameters are not exactly known.

Formally, the problem of making decisions for some well-defined systems subject to uncertainty can be dealt with—there is a large literature on statistical decision theory—but in practice the problem of making the correct choices from a large complicated model is an enormous one.

We propose to make an extended set of policy-simulation experiments with our model. In those experiments we shall explore the consequences of a variety of systems of formulating policy (i.e., of systematic ways of responding to signals). Programs for these simulation experiments have been developed by Professor Charles Holt. Since we know that the system is subject to random disturbance and that our parameter estimates are subject to error, we shall give particular attention to the risks involved in following alternative decision rules and to the tradeoffs between improvement in the expected value of the outcomes and the variance of the outcomes.

Experiments of the type we have just described can of course be performed with any model. But if we intend to perform experiments of that sort we must have a model with explicit policy parameters. Thus, governments do not control tax revenues as such but instead make decisions about tax rates, and we shall need tax rate parameters explicitly in the model. Moreover, the government has available a large number of policy instruments. For accuracy and to permit realistic discussion of policy in terms of the model it is desirable to use explicit parameters for all the more important policy instruments.

1.2.2. Business cycle and growth theories

In the past twenty-five years or so a great many mathematical business cycle models have been developed. In these models the economy is described by equations involving lagged variables, derivatives, or cumulants of variables in the model. If the system is fairly simple, its dynamic properties can be analyzed to see what kinds of behavior—e.g., exponential growth, damped or exploding cycles—will be produced by alternative sets of values for the parameters. To succeed in that type of analysis it is necessary to make drastic simplifications in the specification of the model. Otherwise the analysis becomes unmanageable or leads only to the conclusion that anything can happen.

If, however, the parameters of the model are numerically specified it is possible to get results by simulation on a much more complex and (hopefully) realistic model. Moreover, one can study the dynamic properties of the model when it is subjected to different patterns of movement of the exogenous variables or to random shocks or both.

It will be recalled that Tinbergen's original objective was to test business cycle theories. More recently, the dynamic properties of the Klein-Goldberger model have been analyzed by Irma Adelman, Frank Adelman, and John Cornwall [1, 2].

The investigation of the cycle and growth properties of our economy is not merely an academic exercise. It is obviously important to know, for example, what combination of tax rates and government expenditures is consistent with a satisfactory rate of growth of demand. It is equally important to know what movements of tax and expenditure parameters will do to the relative rates of growth of demand, labor supply, actual capacity and productivity.

In the area of cycles it is of more than academic interest to know whether our economy is subject to an endogenously generated cycle. Would cycles occur if the exogenous variables of the system moved smoothly? Would they occur if the exogenous variables moved smoothly except for random shocks? Can major depressions occur as a result of the working of the systematic elements in the system? Or must we account for them by reference to *ad hoc* "shocks" such as financial crises?

Realistic answers to those questions can only be obtained by the use of a numerically and accurately specified model.

1.2.3. Forecasting

Many people think of econometric models as primarily tools for forecasting. As we have already indicated, there are other, and perhaps more important, uses for econometric models. We have noted the many difficulties to be faced in the construction of econometric models. Those difficulties reveal themselves most sharply when we try to forecast.

In the present state of knowledge it is inevitable that forecasts, however made, will be subject to error. Our data, particularly in the case of stocks of capital of all kinds but elsewhere as well, are inaccurate. Our seasonal adjustment and deflation procedures leave much to be desired. The most complex model we conceive of using will still leave out of account a myriad of factors influencing economic behavior. The effect of these variables will to some extent wash out, but the variance of their net effect may still be substantial. And the "disturbances" produced by those variables may be serially correlated in time and correlated across the sectors. The accuracy of parameter estimates is limited by the evolution of our economy. As technology, institutional arrangements, tastes and managerial techniques change, the relationships represented by our equations will inevitably shift. Without going into all the problems posed by that fact and all the possible ways of dealing with them, it may be asserted that the evolution of our economic system does limit the extent to which past responses can be used to predict future ones. The problems of identification, bias, serial correlation of errors, collinearity and misspecification impose further inherent limitations on the accuracy of parameter estimates. Various kinds of nonlinearities, such as response thresholds or backlogs of "investment opportunities", produced by one set of variables whose exploitation is triggered by another are often not adequately accounted for in our models. Those phenomena are difficult to investigate because they may operate infrequently.

Though those points do not exhaust the catalogue of difficulties faced by the econometric forecaster, they are sufficient to make one wonder that econometric forecasting has any success at all. Only a few econometric models have been used for forecasting over an extended period. In spite of all the difficulties of forecasting they have produced forecasts substantially better than naive forecasts and substantially better than those of most *ad hoc* forecasters.

But the case for the usefulness of econometric models in forecasting does not rest entirely, or perhaps even mainly, on the record of past success. Naive forecast methods are, almost by definition, difficult to improve. Econometric models can be improved. Some of the specific ways in which we may hope to improve on the performance of existing models are discussed below. But no one, and least of all the makers of the present models, will doubt that there are real possibilities of improving the performance of existing models.

1.3. Econometric research by committee

The division of responsibility within this model-building project has perhaps not been unique, but it has been unusual. Many experts on parts of the economy have been called in. Their research stories will be separately told in the chapters to follow, but now we may give a preview of their separate contributions. At the end, we shall try to put all the parts together into a consistent model.

Whether this method of research works or not depends on the newness of insight given by expert treatment—treatment that would not have been discernible to the one-man investigator of many model-building projects. It also depends on whether the separate contributions form a disjointed whole or whether they can be welded together into a single consistent system.

Let us first briefly consider each of the contributions to see what new insights have emerged from each as a result of expert investigation.

D. B. Suits and G. R. Sparks   Consumption research since the *General Theory* first concentrated on the aggregate consumption function. Next we followed the traditional breakdown of the national product accounts into durables, nondurables and services. Suits and Sparks have shown the separate significance of car demand in durables and of food demand in nondurables. In car demand, they have shown the significance of stocks and the possible use of consumer buying plans. While research along these lines was being pursued by other workers in studies of specific demand, Suits and Sparks have added new dimensions to disaggregated treatment of consumer demand in complete models of the whole economy.

S. J. Maisel   An important part of Maisel's contribution has been his explicit treatment of starts, a forward variable often referred to in economic analysis, and the proper integration of this variable with construction expenditures. Starts are endogenously explained, as well as unit dwelling value. The phasing-in of *value* of starts to construction outlays according to the pattern actually used by the Department of Commerce is a procedure that may well have escaped the attention of someone less familiar with this market. The intimate knowledge of accounting and demographic identities in this market and the assignment of proper roles to financial conditions and to demographic requirements are other contributions that arose from the sector specialization applied by Maisel to an explanation of housing demand behavior.

P. Darling and M. Lovell   The role of orders and backlogs in the explanation of manufacturing inventory behavior was beginning to come to light in a few earlier econometric investigations. These results were amplified and solidified in the work of Darling and Lovell. In addition, they brought out the strategic significance of government military orders and capacity utilization in durable inventories for manufacturing. These particular variables are not used in our final formulation, but they may be brought back into the expanded model being contemplated. The split into manufacturing durables, manufacturing nondurables and trade inventories is also a disaggregation that may not have been thought to be worth while by the nonspecialist. The general approach of stock adjustment mechanism in manufacturing and trade inventories used by Darling and Lovell is not new but it is carefully applied by them in a wide range of inventory calculations.

M. Dutta   The endogenous explanation of orders like those of housing starts and other forward-looking variables of this model is the task of Dutta's research. The variable used most successfully in equations of inventory demand is unfilled orders (or its change) and the variable explained in Dutta's equations is new orders. A modified use of the accounting identity between new orders, unfilled orders and sales is an important contribution in his chapter. This identity holds in seasonally unadjusted undeflated terms, while the consistent model is uniformly estimated from adjusted deflated data. Therefore, equations have to be developed by Dutta to convert the elements of the accounting identity to those used throughout the model.

R. Eisner   Since we have committed ourselves to the use of anticipatory data where possible and useful within the model, we have need for a systematic exploration, such as Eisner has made, to see how investment intentions data can be most efficiently used within the model. We know that the accurate prediction of investment is going to be crucial in applications of our model, and Eisner has been able to show through his construction of realization equations how to transform intentions into predictors of actual investment—more reliable for prediction than the mechanized extrapolation of recorded intentions into predictions of actual investment. His equations explain why, in an economic sense, predictions and actual investment do not coincide. His extrapolations beyond the fitted sample give encouragement to the belief that we have an efficient method of predicting actual from anticipated investment.

D. Jorgenson   Eisner's equations are useful by themselves for predicting investment ahead by one or two quarters, but we do not have quarterly investment anticipations farther in advance than two quarters on a regular basis [1]). Jorgenson is the first researcher, to our knowledge, to try to explain investment anticipations so that more distant extrapolations can be made. He makes a very careful analysis of the theoretical structure of investment functions and the time shape of the lags involved. Both Jorgenson and Eisner have been able to carry out statistical investment research for the economy as a whole on a detailed sector basis by quarters, and this is surely an empirical job that could be done only by a specialist in the analysis of investment behavior. Many of their quarterly series are the only ones available in this kind of research.

R. Rhomberg and L. Boissonneault   Foreign trade elasticities and other parameters have been debated for some time on the empirical level, and several research workers have reached pessimistic conclusions about the possibility of making reliable estimates. The research of Rhomberg for this project has established plausible estimates of U.S. import and export functions with reasonably high price elasticity estimates and reasonably low ones where each seems appropriate. His estimate of the American export equation and associated elasticities is of extreme importance in throwing light on crucial matters of trade policy. Also, he has done much to isolate the extreme influence of the Korean War period on U.S. trade.

A. Ando, E. C. Brown and E. Adams   The task of much applied work in econometrics has been to expand the scope of endogeneity. We have already gone over some of this ground in discussing the work of Maisel, Dutta, Eisner and Jorgenson in which anticipatory variables are generated by equations within the model. In an interrelated social system, very little activity is purely exogenous—surely less than we classify as exogenous in practice. In most macroeconomic analysis, we place all government receipts and expenditures in the exogenous category. In the application of econometric models, but not in their statistical estimation, it has often been recognized that tax receipts and transfer payments are not exogenous—they are related to aggregate activity variables. This has been a small concession to the reality of the situation in the government sector, but Ando, Brown and Adams have made the first comprehensive review of the econometrics of the government sector. They have managed to develop an endogenous explanation of

---

[1]) We have a set of *annual* anticipations in the spring [OBE-SEC] and autumn [McGraw-Hill].

many nondefense expenditures on goods and services, most transfer payments and most receipts. By their careful study and intimate knowledge of government fiscal accounts, they have related their equations to specific variables that appear elsewhere in the model, thus giving us, for the first time, a good system of feedback from the private to the public sector. This has influenced our equation system's method of parameter estimation by removing from the exogenous or predetermined group of variables such old favorites as personal tax receipts, corporate tax receipts, or total government expenditures on goods and services. These are all endogenous, or partly so, and we now use variables like income tax *rates* and defense expenditures as the genuine exogenous variables of the model for purposes of estimation.

The thoroughness and detail of this part of our model have given us better understanding of the public sector and enable us to identify true policy parameters and variables. Thinking has been advanced measurably but we still have to rely on simple empirical relationships in some cases, and so all variables that we should like to have classified as endogenous cannot yet be made so.

E. Kuh   Production functions and factor income payments outside agriculture are estimated in the work of Kuh. Property and interest income had to be properly tied by him to other studies dealing with the determination of interest rates and other related variables. He also dealt with the division between corporate retentions and dividends and between corporate and noncorporate income. This work followed along lines that had been developed in previous econometric studies, but Kuh's treatment of interest is novel. Apart from the important step of deriving production functions by different industrial sectors on a comprehensive basis, Kuh has broken new ground in the separate treatment of employment and hours for each producing sector. Especially significant has been his distinction between production and other (overhead) employees. In his separate equations for these two groups, he brings out the differences in their relation to capital.

Rentier income has generally been lumped with all nonwage income or treated separately in a purely mechanical way, i.e., as a trend or simple autoregression. Kuh, however, has shown explicitly how this type of property income is related to the capital base (housing stock, fixed investment stock, consumer credit, etc.) and to the rates of interest. He has also given us an equation for the inventory valuation adjustment, an important concept related to price change and profit valuation.

C. L. Schultze and J. Tryon   Two important developments have grown out of the specialized work of Schultze and Tryon in the explanation of wage rates and prices. In the first place, they immediately recognized the need for an entirely new set of data if they were to develop their equations on an industrial sector basis. It is through their work that the whole project has been supplied with comprehensive quarterly series of *GNP* by industry of origin, employment, wages, prices and other related variables for each of the seven sectors of the model and eventually for all two-digit manufacturing industries. This is a remarkable and valuable body of data not previously available.

In the second place, they have developed a model of price determination that promises to give a satisfactory econometric treatment of price levels. Most previous model work has gone further in the successful explanation of real activity than in price levels and current money values. They explain price by markup equations at the industrial origin of production. They explain manufacturing price (durable and nondurable), public utility price, etc. This appears to be far more promising than the synthetic explanation of various *GNP* deflators by direct methods.

Their work on wage determination is comprehensive in coverage and introduces promising specific variables, but it generally follows established lines of analysis in this field. It does, however, give much industrial sector detail.

K. Fox   When we examined all our accounting identities in the model, we discovered that farm income was unexplained but necessary for the closure of the system. Karl Fox, who was already serving as a specialist on input-output applications within the project, agreed to devote his expert knowledge of agricultural economics to explanation of the farm sector, giving a generating mechanism for farm income. In other models of the aggregative economy (e.g., Klein-Goldberger annual model), farm income is treated in a simple pair of equations expressing: (1) net farm receipts as a function of nonagricultural income, the farm-nonfarm price ratio and agricultural exports and (2) the agricultural price level as a function of the nonfarm price level. This formulation has proved to be inadequate. Fox has been able to delineate the main sources of farm gross receipts, to link these with food consumption in the model's treatment of consumer demand and to explain farm expenses. He found it important to explain the marketing margin between farmer and retail food distributor, and he handled the difficult problems of integrating agricultural support payments of government into the formation of net income. Farm inventories were not covered in the inventory section of the model; therefore he provides explanations of this variable. He provides a pure autoregressive equation for farm investment in buildings and equipment, but this equation is not used in the final model of the whole system.

S. Lebergott   Rather than follow the *simpliste* explanation of labor supply as exogenous (sociological or demographic in nature), we consistently followed the objective of broadening the scope of endogeneity in the model by seeking expert analysis of the labor force. We recognized, moreover, that short-run fluctuations in labor supply have a perplexing and significant bearing on the count of unemployed. Lebergott formulated a strategic sex-age decomposition of the labor force that brings out clearly some of the volatile groups on the supply side—working wives, semiretired people and student-age people. He was also led into an investigation of the marriage rate to account for the labor force status of females. The marriage rate is significant in Maisel's housing market model, and linkage was provided between the two sector studies.

F. de Leeuw   Money must be important in our money economy, yet models that have been constructed have often (not always) found weak linkage between the money and real economies. This weak linkage has probably discouraged more careful and elaborate analysis of the monetary sector. Recent advances in data collection in the Flow of Funds tables and discovery of some strong monetary influences in capital formation and elsewhere, due to wider movements in money market rates since 1952, led us to devote greater energy and resources to the monetary sector. De Leeuw's intimate knowledge of the banking system, federal finance and other institutions in the money market have enabled him to produce a model with careful treatment of money supply, usually assumed exogenous, and demand for cash by main groups within the economy. A feature of his submodel is that it brings the main instruments of monetary policy into explicit display within the model. It links long-term and short-term loan markets, and it treats time deposits separately from other elements of the money supply.

K. Fox and J. Babcock (later supplemented by F. M. Fisher, L. R. Klein and Y. Shinkai): In the first planning stages of this new project, we set aside one study to explore the possible uses of input-output analysis, not knowing specifically how this technique would fit in with our work but feeling intuitively that it must be important. Fox reported on this afterward at our first summer seminar, where we relied on the technique of ideas by free association to work out a definite role for the essential use of input-output in our model. It is not clear how this idea would have been developed in the absence of our seminar method of associating ideas among co-operating specialists. Schultze's approach to explanation of price levels was quickly seen to lie in the construction of several price mark-up equations for each producing sector of the system. This is the economic stage of price formation. On the other hand, we have *GNP* price deflators in our model, and each of these is a different composite of producers' prices. Jorgenson, Fisher, Fox, Babcock and others suggested and worked out the method of establishing input-output weights for converting producers' prices into final *GNP* composite prices. Babcock and Fox consolidated the large 1947 tableau into an input-output table of sectors in our model and made some preliminary final demand regressions for establishing the weights called for in the theoretical setup of Fisher. Klein and Shinkai carried this work further and report the empirical findings in their chapter. They show how the computed *GNP* deflators compare with the published ones and how they can be made to agree closely on an up-to-date basis.

F. Fisher   A model as complicated as ours and as large gives rise to many specific statistical problems. Fisher gave advice on many statistical procedures that were to be followed in sample selection and data treatment. Since the model grew to such large proportions, he found it important to develop methods for recursive or near-recursive systems in order to simplify the estimation procedures. His work on block recursive systems has been very helpful in designing the estimates and in choosing predetermined variables to be used at each stage of the estimation process. In addition, Fisher contributed importantly, as mentioned above, to the development of the input-output sector in this model.

C. Holt   It has not been our aim simply to build a model. We want one that can be used, and we want to use it in significant problems. To use the model (in forecasting, simulation, policy formation), we have to test it and solve it algebraically, but that is difficult because of the non-linearities contained in the system. Even if the system were fully linear, its size would make solution difficult. Holt has been able to show how to find the greatest possible amount of recursiveness in the model's structure. That simplifies the solution. He has also shown how to deal with nonlinearities. His technical know-how in computer methods has been important in the applications part (potential and actual) of the whole project.

When all of these pieces of research are put together, it can be readily seen that the accomplishment of group research is large in volume—larger than any one individual could have managed. Probably any one of the studies could have been developed by another research worker; they are not unique contributions in this respect, but it is certain that no single individual or small team could have uncovered so many interesting and revealing relationships in a single model in a time span of three years. Clearly, our method has the advantage of bringing forth expert knowledge, subtle relationships and a large volume of intricate detail. Also, the experts are in a position to know the main lines of policy and the variables that would bring out their effects. There are disadvantages, however, and these have to do with the problems of co-ordinating diverse points of view and separate calculations.

In order to achieve uniformity and coherence within our system, we had to establish rules of conformity. All data series were tied, wherever possible, to the conceptual scheme of the U.S. Department of Commerce, National Income Division. All series were adjusted for seasonal variation by standard methods. We had many parameters to be estimated within this system and did not want to burden ourselves with additional estimates of seasonal parameters. In our first summer meetings, much time was devoted to trimming individual sector estimates so that they were not unduly large and detailed or improperly related to the rest of the system. Specialists were urged to use explanatory variables that occurred elsewhere in the system.

The main purpose of the sector specialists' research was to open new ideas in model building. In coordinating their work, we were free to choose among their contributions in a way that fitted together for the system as a whole. It will be seen in the final consistent model that has grown out of this project that we have built what seems to be a plausible interrelated system. Once their new ideas have been put forward and new leads for research established together with the pertinent data series, a small research team can maintain and follow up the same kind of work. Thus, the experts have produced the ideas that have been molded into a new complete system capable of being extended beyond the sample values at hand.

1.4. The flow chart of the system

The preceding section sketches the main parts of the model, as contributed by each specialist. A view of the entire system can be seen in the accompanying flow chart. This is a rough working picture of the system. It does not give as much detail as the actual equations, which come later.

On the right we have the *GNP* components, which are fed by the main demand decisions of the economy—consumption, investment, government and foreign. These demands feed back to stimulate orders and more inventories or they work through our input-output mechanism with our final demand regressions and determine the composition of sector outputs. These determine sector labor requirements and with wage-price determination in the left center boxes make up a large part of factor incomes. Another part comes from the money market box. These incomes become disposable through the tax-transfer boxes and feed back into the investment decision, but that will only supplement the output requirements of investment and the capital market facilities in investment planning. Residential investment decisions, like consumption, are fed through population, through the capital market and through disposable income.

This diagram gives only a general picture of the workings of the model. For example, the tax functions of the model will in fact be highly specific among various excises, state and local taxes, federal income taxes and other categories. For purposes of the flow diagram, however, much of this detail need not be included to show simply the main lines of causation and extent of feedback.

1.5. Some problems of statistical method

On an exploratory basis, nearly every equation discussed above and implied in the flow diagram has been estimated as a single-equation-least-squares regression. This was the natural way to start, but most of the equations contained some amount of simultaneity among endogenous variables, and statistically consistent methods of estimation must be used for equation systems. First, each equation of the model was estimated, usually in several experimental forms, by separate least-squares regressions from a homogeneous body of data. We then re-estimated equations that were not already in reduced form by consistent methods. These calculations are described in chapter 18. Where national income accounts data were involved, we followed the uniform rule of using series based on the concepts of the U.S. Department of Commerce, seasonally adjusted at annual rates, by quarters, 1948–1960. This whole body of data is now placed in a central file for continuing work on the model.

Obtaining consistent estimates for this large system of equations is a

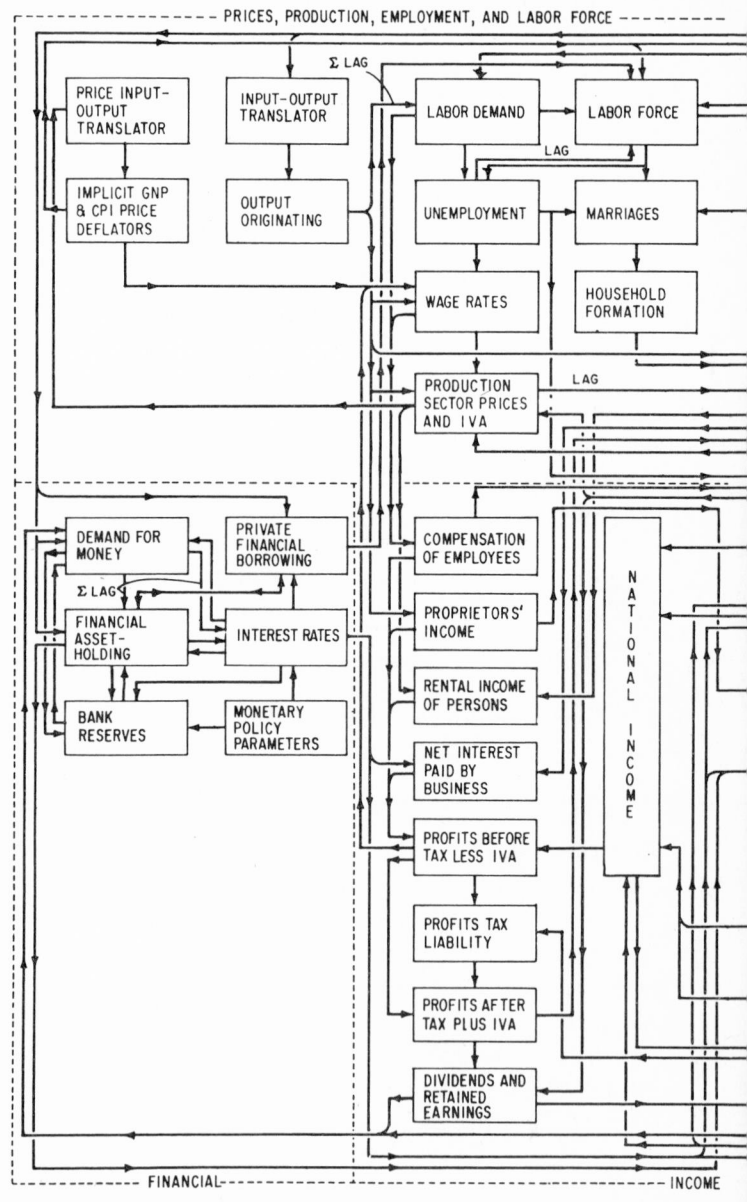

Figure 1.1. Condensed flow diagram

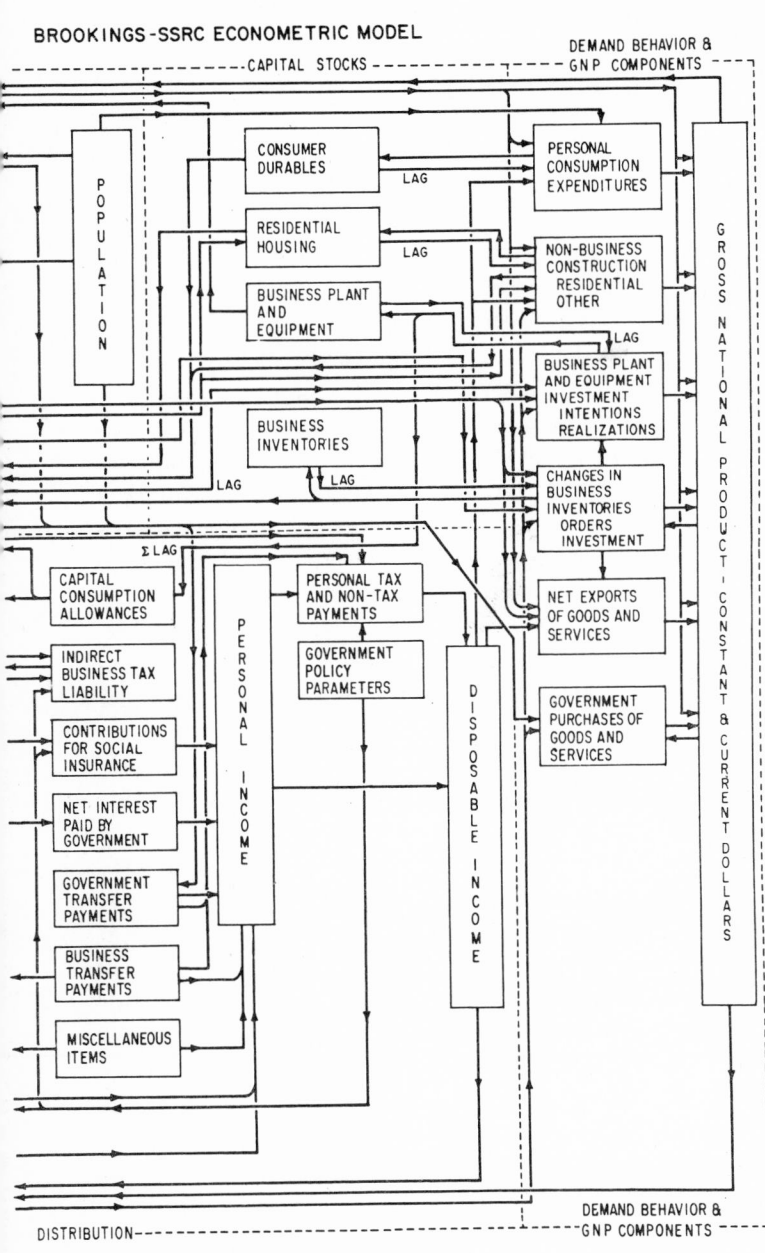

Brookings-SSRC Econometric Model.

formidable computing problem. The fairly aggregative version, as we have outlined it here, will have upward of a hundred and fifty equations, and as far as we know this is larger than any other estimated by consistent methods. Systems of thirty-five equations and many smaller systems have been estimated by two-stage-least-squares and limited-information-maxi-mum-likelihood methods. Full-information-maximum-likelihood estimates have been obtained for fifteen-equation models.

A real problem in the present case is the paucity of degrees of freedom. An essential first step in computation by the well-known consistent methods involves the regression of each endogenous variable on the whole set of predetermined variables in the entire system—lagged endogenous and exogenous variables. In a system as large as ours, with at most sixty quarterly observations available, there will not be enough degrees of freedom to esti-mate a single reduced-form regression for the whole system. Counting lag variables, we shall have more than sixty predetermined variables. But even if we did formally have enough observations to make these massive reduced-form regressions, we should run head-on into the problem of multicolli-nearity, for the predetermined variables in our system are far from being mutually independent. There are many similar trends in population, techni-cal progress functions, capital stocks, money balances and other slow-moving variables. Some of the predetermined variables may also have similar cycles.

In models of substantial size that have been estimated by two-stage-least squares or limited-information methods we have frequently had to divide the sets of equations into blocks and estimate each block with a separate, smaller set of predetermined variables, for it can be shown that consistency remains in estimating a particular equation, even if predetermined variables in the system but not in the particular equation are not included in the re-duced-form regressions. The usual practice is to select an approximately ortho-gonal subset for each bloc that leaves an adequate number of degrees of freedom. Similar trends and cycles should not be found among the pre-determined variables contained within a block.

There is an obvious element of personal choice in this procedure, but it has worked well in practice, and the effects of this personal choice can be made negligible in most cases. An alternative procedure may be that sug-gested recently by Dutch econometricians—to use as an orthogonal subset principal components of predetermined variables that are free of personal choice. Our computing programs are not immediately adaptable to this procedure, although they could be so changed. It may be noted in passing

Introduction: The research strategy and its application

that the multicollinearity and degrees-of-freedom problems of limited-information methods are also present in full-information methods; moreover, full-information methods do not lend themselves to separate block treatment in general. Also, they must be completely linear models for the programs being used today—in parameters *and* variables—and our system is highly nonlinear. The existing programs for full-information calculations on one of the largest machines available would not allow for enough capacity in its present form to cope with our hundred-equation model, nor would there be enough degrees of freedom to cope with all the predetermined variables. Furthermore, subdivision into blocks is not possible in full-information computing except under special probability assumptions.

We are therefore left with the problem of obtaining two-stage-least-squares and limited-information estimates without having too many and too highly interrelated predetermined variables. One of our main considerations preparatory to consistent estimation of the system as a whole is to take advantage of its recursive structure. In many publications Herman Wold has stressed the simplicity of estimation procedure and ease of causal interpretation in fully recursive systems; i.e., systems in which the Jacobian determinant formed from the matrix of linear coefficients of endogenous variables can be made triangular [3]. Triangularity of this matrix and mutual independence of structural disturbances lead to a series of single-equation-least-squares regressions as full-information estimates. Without independence of disturbances we may still find simple consistent estimates from a special kind of single-equation-least-square regressions.

Our system is not fully recursive, i.e., the Jacobian is not triangular. In our quarterly consumption functions we have lags, but there is a nontrivial effect of current quarterly income on current quarterly consumption. The same is true of inventory change, housing and so on throughout the model. Franklin Fisher, however, has stressed an analogous property that may help us. His method is described more fully in chapter 15. Instead of having a fully recursive system, we have what Fisher calls a block-recursive system. Such a system has matrices of nonzero elements in the main diagonal and below. Above the main diagonal of matrices are zero matrices. It appears as

$$
\begin{bmatrix}
(A) & 0 & 0 & \cdots\cdots & 0 \\
(B) & (C) & 0 & \cdots\cdots & 0 \\
(D) & (E) & (F) & 0\cdots\cdots & 0 \\
\vdots & \multicolumn{4}{c}{\cdots\cdots\cdots\cdots\cdots} \\
(G) & \multicolumn{3}{c}{\cdots\cdots\cdots\cdots} & (H)
\end{bmatrix}
$$

The terms in parentheses are entire matrices. Within a matrix there is simultaneous interdependence, and the sectors are arrayed so that those in the topmost rows are interdependent with sectors in the same position but not with those below. Lag relationships are not shown in this matrix of simultaneous interdependences.

Until the lag structure of the model is precisely specified, we cannot finally make an array of the type discussed, but we might proceed as follows: (1) On the basis of exploratory estimates, make such an array. (2) Using principles to be outlined below in connection with an array, make consistent estimates. (3) If necessary, revise the judgments about the lag structure. (4) On the basis of the revised lag structure, again make consistent estimates. Pragmatically speaking, it will probably not be necessary to make more than one such revision.

A preliminary ordering of our causal structure gives the following layout:

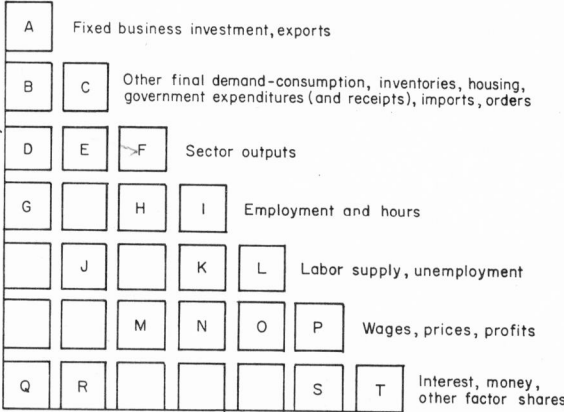

Figure 1.2. Preliminary ordering of causal structure.

Our system is highly interdependent, and this array is only approximate. In order to achieve as much triangularity as possible in the array, we have neglected some relatively minor effects. It will be seen below that our fixed-investment functions depend only on lag variables; therefore, they belong at the head of the recursive ordering. But exports depend, in addition to an external variable such as world demand, on domestic prices which come much lower in the ordering. This is the sense in which the above array is only approximate.

The second block contains all the elements of final demand besides fixed investment; hence it is quite large. When final aggregate demand is determined, we use input-output methods to allocate it among sectors to determine industry outputs. Production functions are then transformed, as Kuh has in fact done in his chapter, to determine labor requirements, given sector capital and output variables determined at a previous stage. Next we determine labor market conditions and go from these to wages, prices and profits. Since all factor shares are not determined until the next block is reached, these would have to be gross profits before interest and rental income. Finally, we complete the system with the equations of the money market to determine interest rates, deposits and interest income.

In order to keep this exposition compact, we have not tried to make the recursive ordering by individual equations. Instead we have done it by functional groups of equations. In practice, our recursive ordering will have to be more detailed, considering the lag and exogenous structure of each individual equation of the model.

Within each of these major blocks, we shall try to make consistent estimates of the individual equations by two-stage-least-squares or limited-information methods, following rules suggested by Fisher. Purely exogenous variables within each block will certainly be used as predetermined variables in making the consistent estimates for each equation in a given block. Lagged endogenous variables within a block will contribute little toward explanation because they are usually highly serially correlated with the endogenous variables within the block. We could regress these lagged endogenous variables on lagged exogenous variables and use the computed values as predetermined variables. Lagged endogenous variables from outside blocks may be used, but this should be done sparingly. Exogenous variables from outside blocks may be used. If disturbances between blocks are independent, we may treat endogenous variables from the higher blocks in the array as predetermined variables. If we do not make the independence assumption, we may use computed values of such endogenous variables as predetermined variables.

Using this block-recursive scheme, we still have the old problems of degrees of freedom and multicollinearity, but we have an advantage in that the degree of interdependence is reduced, and we may not have to use many variables outside a given block to obtain good consistent estimates for the constituent equations of each block.

1.6. Some problems of short time series

At the outset of our study we decided to limit ourselves to the quarterly economic history of the postwar period, seasonally adjusted. We chose to use adjusted data because we deal with such a large complicated system having an enormous number of parameters (in terms of experience in this kind of research) that we did not want to carry the added burden of estimating seasonal parameters as well, even though we may prefer the use of explicit seasonal variables to prior adjustment of data.

In this fairly short span of time, 1948–1962, there have been at least two major disturbances—the Korean War and the steel strike of 1959. In several particular equations, these events cause serious aberrations in the data. We could omit these periods from our sample; we could include them with dummy variables (e.g., one during Korean quarters and zero at all other times); or we could simply include them on an equal footing with all other sample observations. Tentatively we have followed the last course in most cases. If there was clear evidence that a relationship had been distorted by such major events, we have included a dummy variable. New orders, for example, were seriously affected by stockpiling decisions for basic materials during the Korean period, and we would probably have poor estimates unless we gave special treatment to relevant quarters in 1950–1951. Preliminary estimates of an affected relationship, say by the single-equation-least-squares method, were examined for residual variation. If the residual was large in the abnormal period and if this appeared to affect the parameter estimates, we considered giving special treatment to the relationship in question. In some of the separate chapters, special attention is paid to important unique events for estimation of equations, and the final composite model contains a number of "dummy" variables to account for such instances.

In applied econometric work it is often necessary to decide whether the last few observations from the sample should be withheld and to see if a truncated sample estimate extrapolates well into the period for which data are withheld. Our position here is clear. We are not rich in data. We need all the good observations we can find to meet our degrees-of-freedom problems. But our estimation problem is large and time-consuming. By using data through 1961 for all calculations made in 1963, we shall have used up the sample of reliable data. Data for 1962 are likely to be subject to substantial revision during this period. By the time we are ready to test the model, and surely during the time-consuming period of testing, more and more quarterly data will have become available, so that in a very short time we shall have plenty of observations for testing by extrapolation.

1.7. Progress and plans

For the more aggregative type of model considered (sectors are agriculture, durable manufactures, nondurable manufactures, regulated industries, trade, construction and a residual group) data have been collected and equations estimated by single-equation-least-squares and consistent methods. A number of special series had to be prepared on a quarterly basis for this work; they are now complete and gathered in a central file.

The model that we have estimated is to be tested by extrapolation, forecasting experiments and simulation calculations. As a result of these tests, there will undoubtedly be further revisions. This is to be a living model. As new ideas come up from these tests, as our a priori view of the functioning of the economy changes and as new data become available, we shall recompute estimates of the model. These re-estimates will all be done by consistent methods. We hope to make continuous applications of the model to problems of theory and policy.

This is a model in which changes in detail can be readily made. Just as it contains a fairly elaborate agricultural submodel, it can be made to contain other submodels. Potentially much can be done to elaborate the inventory-orders subsections. We might build series on inventories by stage of fabrication for more detailed elucidation. The foreign sector can always be subdivided and extended to cover more balance-of-payments items. Indeed, the whole financial sector admits of nearly unlimited expansion and refinement. All components of final demand can potentially be further subdivided for more detail.

Apart from these obvious refinements, each of which might add another dozen equations or so, we are already preparing for a much larger model. We could keep approximately present detail on the side of final demand and factor payments but subdivide the producing sector into all two-digit manufacturing industries and corresponding residual sector groups. In all, we plan to have a model with approximately 32 sectors on the production side. Thus we shall have 32 wage rate equations, 32 production functions, 32 hours worked equations, 32 price equations, and 32 final demand regressions. These changes alone will add approximately 150 equations to an already large model. Corresponding to these changes on the side of production, we shall make similar decompositions on the side of final demand. We would want 32 investment functions in order to build up 32 series on capital stock for the 32 production functions. We would also need 32 depreciation equations. The final demand regressions will be improved if we make these and similar decompositions of other types of final demand. Foreign trade, consumption and inventories will probably be further decomposed.

It is thus clear that a requirement of explicit treatment of more production sectors will enlarge the system by more than a few equations. We shall probably end up with a system of approximately 300 to 400 equations. This is a very large system in terms of present technologies and research resources; therefore it cannot be estimated in full for another year or two, at least. However, many single least-squares regressions can be made for component parts. Ultimately, we aim for a large system of the 32-sector magnitude, but for the near future we shall concentrate on estimation of a seven-sector model with the type of final demand detail shown in our flow diagram. Even that is a major research task and a large step ahead of previous trials.

REFERENCES

1. ADELMAN, IRMA, and ADELMAN, F. L. The Dynamic Properties of the Klein-Goldberger Model, *Econometrica* 27 (October, 1959) 569–625.
2. CORNWALL, JOHN. Economic Implications of the Klein-Goldberger Model, *Review of Economics and Statistics* 41 (May, 1959) 154–161.
3. STROTZ, R. H., and WOLD, H. O. A. Recursive vs. Nonrecursive Systems: An Attempt at Synthesis, *Econometrica* 28 (April, 1960) 417–427.

PART II

Producer Investment Decisions

CHAPTER 2

ANTICIPATIONS AND INVESTMENT BEHAVIOR

Contents

2.1. Introduction.   35

2.2. The theory and econometrics of investment behavior   43

2.3. Problems of measurement   55

2.4. Tests of the theory   59

2.5. Structure of the investment process   78

References   89

ANTICIPATIONS AND INVESTMENT BEHAVIOR

DALE W. JORGENSON

University of California, Berkeley, California

2.1. Introduction

The purpose of this study is to develop a theory of investment behavior encompassing both actual and anticipated investment expenditures. As a point of departure we divide the investment process into separate stages. The first stage of the process is a change in the demand for capital services. Subsequent to an alteration in demand for capital services, architectural and engineering plans must be drawn up, cost estimates prepared, funds appropriated and funds committed through the issuing of orders for equipment or the letting of contracts for construction. Actual investment expenditure is the final stage in the investment process. Only after a given investment project has passed through each of the intermediate stages can actual investment expenditure take place.

To formalize the relationship between successive stages of the investment process, we first observe that transitions between any two stages are distributed over time. For example, given a change in demand for capital services, completion of the resulting architectural and engineering plans is distributed over time. The simplest assumption about the distribution of transitions between two successive stages is that the distribution is concentrated at a single point. For example, it might happen that the transition between changes in the demand for capital services and the drawing up of architectural and engineering plans always requires exactly six months. A more general and more useful hypothesis is that for changes in demand for capital in the current period, a certain proportion of transitions to the planning stage is completed in the current period, a certain proportion in the following period, and so on. This assumption includes that in which all transitions are concentrated at a single point in time as a special case. In the example, the proportion of plans completed in six months would be unity and the proportion completed at any other point of time would be zero.

Looking at the relationship between successive stages of the investment process from the opposite time perspective, we can describe this relationship by saying that each stage lags behind the preceding stage. For example, the drawing up of architectural and engineering plans lags behind changes in the demand for fixed capital. A certain proportion of plans completed in the current period is due to changes in demand for capital in the current period, a certain proportion to changes in the previous period, and so on. From this point of view, where transitions are concentrated at a single point in time, the lag is fixed. In the example given above, the lag between changes in demand for capital and the drawing up of plans is fixed at six months.

As it stands, the assumption that transitions between any two stages of the investment process are distributed over time is not sufficiently restrictive to be of much help in the study of investment behavior. Virtually any conceivable investment behavior is consistent with this hypothesis. Accordingly, we adopt the further assumption that the proportion of transitions between any two successive stages of the investment process depends only on the time elapsed between the two stages and not on the actual time at which either stage of the process occurs. This assumption is the fundamental working hypothesis of this study; it is the basis of the whole analysis of the investment process which follows. Although the implications of this hypothesis seem clear enough, it should be pointed out explicitly that we assume that the response to a downward change in the demand for capital services has the same distribution over time as a response to an upward change.

As a second working hypothesis, we assume that transitions between any two successive stages are distributed independently of the time required for transition from preceding stages to the first of the two stages. For example, given the appropriation of funds for an investment project, the distribution over time of commitments of these funds is independent of the time elapsed between the preparation of cost estimates and the appropriation of funds. The chief advantage of this assumption is the simplicity it gives to the analysis of the investment process. Given the distribution over time of transitions between any pair of successive stages, it is possible to derive the distribution over time of transitions between any pair of stages by straightforward computation. This assumption is easily tested, and so no further a priori justification for the assumption seems necessary at this point.

In this study we treat anticipated investment expenditures as a special kind of intermediate stage of the investment process. In the quarterly investment survey of the Office of Business Economics and the Securities and Exchange Commission, anticipated investment expenditures are reported for one quarter in advance and for two quarters in advance. The conventional hypothesis about anticipated investment and actual investment is that actual investment lags one-quarter anticipated investment by exactly one-quarter with some random variation; similarly, actual investment lags two quarters anticipated investment by exactly two quarters, again with some random variation. This hypothesis is the basis for the current reporting of anticipated investment expenditures [1]); after the anticipations data have been adjusted for seasonal variation and for "bias" the forecast of actual investment for the current quarter is taken to be equal to last quarter's one-quarter anticipated investment. This forecasting scheme is highly successful [2]); nevertheless, there are a number of facts which suggest that it might be improved upon.

First, an immediate implication of the hypothesis that actual investment lags behind one-quarter anticipated investment by exactly one quarter is that the seasonal pattern in one quarter anticipated investment should lead that in actual investment by one quarter; but this implication is refuted by the facts [3]). Second, if differences between anticipated investment and actual investment can be shown to depend on certain "explanatory" variables, the hypothesis cannot be correct. Modigliani and Weingartner [45] [4]), Eisner [7–13] and Okun [50] have presented evidence that certain explanatory variables do have some effect in explaining differences between actual and anticipated investment, and so the second implication of the hypothesis is refuted by the facts.

At this point a number of alternative lines of attack may be suggested. First, the relationships between explanatory variables and differences between

---

[1]) Anticipated investment expenditures are reported quarterly. Each quarterly report contains actual expenditures on depreciable assets during the previous quarter together with anticipated investment expenditures for the two quarters to follow. Quarterly reports are published, currently, in the March, June, September, and December issues of the *Survey of Current Business* [59].

[2]) For appraisals of the OBE-SEC Investment Survey as a forecasting scheme, see Foss and Natrella [16, 17], Friend and Bronfenbrenner [18, 19], Levine [37], Nassimbene and Teeter [47], Natrella [48], Okun [50] and Theil [56].

[3]) See Nassimbene and Teeter [47].

[4]) See also the comment by Anderson [1] and the reply by Modigliani and Weingartner [46].

actual and anticipated investment expenditure obtained by Modigliani and others might be made the basis of a forecasting procedure. This has been proposed by Modigliani and Cohen [44]; the explanatory relationship is called a "realization function". The realization function itself is used to forecast actual investment expenditures, given anticipated investment and the values of the explanatory variables. A second line of attack on the problem, which is adopted here, is to assume that investment expenditures lag behind anticipations but that the lag is distributed over time. This hypothesis includes the conventional view of anticipated investment as a forecast as a special case. In the conventional view the lag is concentrated at exactly one quarter for one-quarter anticipations and at two quarters for two-quarter anticipations. At the same time our hypothesis is much simpler than the "realization function" approach. We assume that, given anticipated investment expenditure, a certain proportion of the anticipated investment will result in actual investment in the same period, a certain proportion will result in actual investment in the following period, and so on. Similarly, we assume that given an initial change in the demand for capital stock a certain proportion of the change will result in anticipated investment in the same period, a certain proportion will result in anticipated investment in the following period, and so on.

Schematically, a sequence of intermediate stages might be represented as in the accompanying diagram. The variable t_1 is the lag between initiation of an investment project and appropriation of funds for the project, the variable t_2 is the lag between appropriations and the letting of contracts, and so on. In this schematic representation the distribution of transitions from one stage to the next is concentrated at a single value of time—$t_1, t_2 \ldots t_5$. In the following analysis we adopt the more general assumption that completions of each successive stage are distributed over time or, to use an alternative terminology, that each stage lags behind its predecessor and that the lag is distributed over time.

Up to this point we have discussed only the time pattern of the relationship between successive stages of the investment process. But each of the stages, including actual investment expenditures, depends ultimately on changes in the demand for capital services. The problem remaining is to devise an explanation for changes in the demand for capital services. Our objective in this study is to base the explanation of changes in the demand for capital services on the neoclassical theory of optimal capital accumulation.

The objective of explaining investment behavior on the basis of the neoclassical theory of optimal accumulation of capital cannot be described as novel. In fact, this objective was adopted at the very outset of econometric studies of investment behavior in Tinbergen's pioneering monograph, *Statistical Testing of Business Cycle Theories* [57]. Subsequently, a similar objective was adopted first by Roos [51, 52] and later by Klein [31]. In these early studies of investment behavior, the theory of optimal capital accumulation was employed mainly to provide a list of explanatory variables for regressions with investment as the variable to be explained. The rate of interest and the price of investment goods were used as explanatory variables along with other variables, such as profits, output, changes in output, and so on.

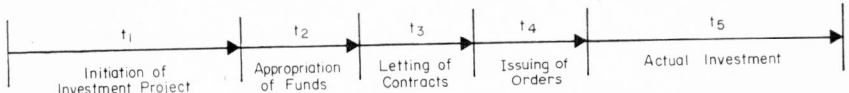

Figure 2.1 Sequence of intermediate stages.

By and large the early attempts to base the study of investment on the neoclassical theory of capital were unsuccessful. A naively positivistic interpretation of the results of these studies can lead only to the conclusion that the theory is inconsistent with the facts. This interpretation seems to have been adopted at the outset of almost all recent studies of investment behavior [5]. The objective of current research appears to be to combine or "synthesize" various essentially *ad hoc* descriptive generalizations about investment into one over-all descriptive generalization. Examples of descriptive generalizations studied in the current literature would include the "capacity" principle and the "profits" or "liquidity" principle. The central feature of the neoclassical theory of optimal capital accumulation—the response of demand for capital to changes in factor prices or the price of output—is almost entirely absent from the recent literature on investment behavior.

The synthesis of various descriptive generalizations about investment behavior has much to commend it as an objective of research. If the decision to abandon the original objective—explanation of investment behavior on the basis of the neoclassical theory of capital—were based on a straightforward confrontation of the theory with the available evidence, it would

---

[5]) The sole exception appears to be in the work of Zvi Griliches; see, for example, his paper on investment in farm tractors [22].

be fruitless to continue to strive to attain this objective, whatever its esthetic appeal. Given the unattainability of a sound theoretical explanation of investment behavior that is consistent with the observed facts, it would be wise to attempt to reconcile the various alternative descriptive generalizations about investment.

Unfortunately, the naively positivistic argument that the neoclassical theory has been found to be inconsistent with the observed facts will not withstand critical scrutiny. First, none of the tests of the neoclassical theory reported in the early literature on investment behavior was based on a fully rigorous statement of that theory. Little attention was paid to the precise way in which the rate of interest and the price of capital goods enter the demand for capital services. Both variables enter only through the *user cost* of capital services [6]), that is, through the implicit rental of the services of capital. There is no effect of the price of capital goods except in combination with the rate of interest and vice versa; furthermore, the combination required is not a simple additive or multiplicative combination of the two variables. The user cost of capital services also depends on the rate of depreciation and the tax structure, including the rate of taxation of business income and the proportion of each component of user cost which may be charged against income for tax purposes.

A second important defect in the early attempts to test the neoclassical theory is that the lag between changes in the demand for capital services and actual investment expenditure was assumed to be fixed or to be distributed over time in a very simple way. These tests were carried out prior to the important contributions of Chenery [3] and Koyck [34] to the analysis of distributed lags and investment behavior. Taking the "flexible accelerator" of Chenery and Koyck as a point of departure, the relationships studied by Tinbergen, Roos and Klein were not correctly formulated with regard to the lag structure between changes in demand for capital services and actual investment expenditures. On this basis alone the results of the early tests of the neoclassical theory are vitiated; these tests depend in an essential way on the correct specification of the entire relationship between investment and the set of explanatory variations, including correct specification of the lag structure.

In the course of this study, we derive a theory of investment behavior

---

[6]) The most complete discussion of the concept of *user cost* is that of Lewis [38, especially pp. 33–45]; see also Keynes [30, pp. 66–73], Lerner [36], Lutz and Lutz [39] and Scott [53].

based on the neoclassical theory of optimal capital accumulation which includes the flexible accelerator as a special case. This theory provides an opportunity to test the neoclassical theory as an explanation of demand for capital services. By providing a wide range of possible lag patterns between changes in demand for capital services and actual investment expenditures, including the flexible accelerator, we are able to overcome the most important defect of previous attempts to test the neoclassical theory.

We then attempt to provide a rigorous formulation of the theory of demand for capital services as determined by the optimal accumulation of capital. We take the maximization of an intertemporal utility function as the criterion for optimal accumulation of capital. Under certain well-known conditions [7]) the problem of maximization of an intertemporal utility function can be solved in two stages: (1) A production plan is chosen to maximize the net worth of the productive enterprise. (2) Consumption is allocated over time to maximize utility subject to net worth. The production plan includes levels of output and levels of all inputs, including the input of capital services. Capital stock is accumulated or decumulated to provide an optimal level of capital services. This view of the optimal accumulation of capital originated with I. Fisher [15]. To summarize, we take the demand for capital services to be determined so as to maximize net worth of the productive enterprise. This formulation necessarily includes a detailed analysis of the effects of the tax structure—especially the taxation of business income—on demand for capital. We assume that the lag between changes in demand for capital services and the resulting investment expenditures is distributed over time, as outlined above.

One determinant of the level of investment expenditures is changes in demand for capital services. We will call such expenditures investment for expansion of capital. A second determinant of the level of investment expenditures is the need for replacement of previously acquired capital goods. The need for replacement represents reduction of the capacity of capital stock in the current period to produce a flow of capital services in the following period. We will use the term investment for replacement of capital to represent expenditures undertaken to maintain the capacity of capital stock in the current period to produce a flow of capital services in

---

[7]) Derivation of the criterion of maximization of the present value of net worth from maximization of an intertemporal utility function was first discussed by Fisher [15]; Fisher's analysis of the problem has been revived and elaborated by Hirshleifer [25] and Bailey [2].

the following period. We assume that the need for replacement investment generated by the previous acquisition of capital goods is distributed over time; replacement investment lags behind previous investment, including investment both for expansion and for replacement of capital. A particular form of this relationship is based on the geometric distribution of replacements over time. This form leads to the hypothesis that replacement investment is proportional to capital stock. The geometric form of the distribution of replacements over time can be derived as an asymptotic approximation for any distribution of times for replacement of capital goods and for any initial age distribution of the capital stock; the proposition holds for constant, growing or declining capital stock, provided only that growth or decay takes place at a constant rate (in a probabilistic sense) [8]).

The principal alternative hypothesis on the form of the distribution of replacements over time, given an initial investment, is that the distribution for the stock as a whole should follow the distribution for individual elements of the stock; a number of studies of the distribution of replacements of particular types of equipment or buildings have been made [9]). In principle, one could attempt to determine the distribution of replacements for aggregates from the distribution of replacements for each type of capital good in the aggregate. However, a simple indirect test of this alternative hypothesis can be made; for any distribution of replacements for the aggregate— except the geometric distribution—one would expect to observe an "echo effect" of the bunching of replacements of the aggregate at lags corresponding to points of relatively high density in the distribution of replacements for individual types of equipment The only systematic investigation of the "echo effect" reported in the literature, that of Meyer and Kuh [43, pp. 91–94], shows no evidence for such an effect.

Replacement projects, like projects for expansion of capital, take time for completion. To complete the theory of investment behavior, the distribution over time of replacement of new equipment, given retirement of the old, is required. Since the plant and equipment to be replaced are continued in service until replacement occurs, we assume that the lag between demand for capital for replacement and the acquisition of new capital goods is zero.

---

[8]) In a probabilistic sense, constant growth takes place if each investment is the progenitor of a sequence of additional investments; each of the additional investments is taken to be proportional to the initial investment, where the proportions remain fixed over time.

[9]) A recent summary of research on lifetimes of capital equipment is given by Marston, Winfrey, and Hempstead [42]. A very important earlier discussion is that of Kurtz [35].

This implies that the distribution of completions of each of the intermediate stages is concentrated at zero for replacement investment.

In the following section we take up in greater detail the three parts of the theory of investment behavior outlined above: demand for capital services, distribution of completions of investment projects for expansion of capital over time and distribution of replacement of capital goods over time. Subsequently, we discuss problems of measurement of the variables entering the theory of investment behavior. Finally, we present a number of empirical tests of the theory along with an analysis of new evidence on the time form of lagged response to changes in the long-run demand for capital services.

2.2. *The theory and econometrics of investment behavior*

We begin the discussion of the theory of investment behavior by considering the demand for capital that results from maximization of net worth under standard neoclassical conditions of production: (1) Levels of each output, of each variable input and of the services of each capital input are constrained by a production function. (2) For each capital input, the rate of change of capital stock is equal to investment less replacement. It will be assumed that replacement is proportional to capital stock; justification for this assumption is given below. For simplicity, the following analysis will be confined to a production process with a single output, a single variable input and a single capital input. The theoretical framework is easily extended to an arbitrary number of outputs and inputs. In view of the importance of direct taxation of business income in the U.S., a relatively detailed representation of the tax structure is required for a precise definition of net worth. The critical problem in the definition of business income for tax purposes is the treatment of the various charges for capital services, including depreciation, cost of capital and capital gain or loss. We will represent the proportion of each of these charges which may be deducted from income for tax purposes as a separate offset against revenue less outlay on current account [10]).

Where X, L and I represent levels of output, variable input and investment in capital stock, and p, s and q represent the corresponding prices, the difference between revenue and outlay on both current and capital account

---

[10]) Many of the symbols in this chapter, which are defined as they are introduced, differ from the standard symbols used in all other chapters. The statistical equations in section 2.4 are, however, written using standard symbols.

in period t, say $Z(t)$, is given by the expression: [11])

$$Z(t) = pX - sL - qI. \tag{2.1}$$

To represent the tax structure, let $u(t)$ be the rate of taxation of net income, defined for tax purposes; further, let $v(t)$, $w(t)$ and $x(t)$ represent the proportions of depreciation, cost of capital and capital loss which may be charged against revenue less outlay on current account in measuring income for tax purposes. Finally, let δ represent the rate of depreciation (replacement), r the cost of capital and $-\dot{q}/q$ the rate of capital loss. Where K is the stock of capital, the amount of direct tax assessed in period t, say $T(t)$, is given by the expression:

$$T(t) = u(t) \left[pX - sL - q \left\{ v(t)\delta + w(t)r - x(t)\frac{\dot{q}}{q} \right\} K \right]. \tag{2.2}$$

Net worth, say NW, is defined as the discounted integral of revenue less outlay on both current and capital account less direct taxes:

$$NW = \int_0^\infty e^{-rt}[Z(t) - T(t)]dt. \tag{2.3}$$

Net worth is maximized subject to two constraints. First, for capital input the rate of change of capital stock is equal to investment less replacement. Under the assumption that replacement is proportional to capital stock, this constraint takes the form:

$$\dot{K} = I - \delta K, \tag{2.4}$$

where $\dot{K}$ is the time rate of change of capital stock. Second, levels of output and input are constrained by a production function:

$$F(X, L, K) = 0; \tag{2.5}$$

it may be noted that capital services, not capital stock, are an input to the productive process. Implicitly, capital stock is multiplied by a factor representing the rate of service per period of time; in the representation (2.5) of the production function, this factor is normalized at unity. If this conven-

---

[11]) In this section time is taken to be a continuous parameter. For example, $u(t)$ is a function of time, defined for any real value of the parameter t. In the sections below time will be taken to be a discrete parameter. For example, u_t will be a function of time, defined for any integer value of the parameter t. The essential results of this section hold for continuous and discrete time; continuous time is used in this section to simplify the presentation.

tion is kept in mind, no confusion need arise from the use of the same symbol to represent both capital stock and the services of this stock. The production function is assumed to be twice-differentiable with positive marginal rates of substitution between inputs and positive marginal productivities of both inputs. Furthermore, it is assumed that the function is strictly convex.

To maximize net worth (2.3), subject to the constraints (2.4) and (2.5), we maximize the Lagrangian expression:

$$\mathscr{L} = \int_0^\infty \{e^{-rt}[Z(t) - T(t)] + l_0(t)F(X, L; K) + l_1(t)[\dot{K} - I + \delta K]\}dt$$

$$= \int_0^\infty f(t)dt. \tag{2.6}$$

The Euler necessary conditions for a maximum may be written:

$$\frac{\partial f}{\partial X} = e^{-rt}[1 - u(t)]p + l_0(t)\frac{\partial F}{\partial X} = 0,$$

$$\frac{\partial f}{\partial L} = -e^{-rt}[1 - u(t)]s + l_0(t)\frac{\partial F}{\partial L} = 0.$$

$$\frac{\partial f}{\partial I} = -e^{-rt}q - l_1(t) = 0, \tag{2.7}$$

$$\frac{\partial f}{\partial K} - \frac{d}{dt}\frac{\partial f}{\partial \dot{K}} = e^{-rt}u(t)q\left\{v(t)\delta + w(t)r - x(t)\frac{\dot{q}}{q}\right\}$$

$$+ l_0(t)\frac{\partial F}{\partial K} + l_1(t)\delta - \frac{d}{dt}l_1(t) = 0$$

and also

$$\frac{\partial f}{\partial l_0} = F(X, L; K) = 0,$$

$$\frac{\partial f}{\partial l_1} = \dot{K} - I + \delta K = 0. \tag{2.8}$$

Solving (2.7) for $l_1(t)$:

$$l_1(t) = -e^{-rt}q;$$

using this expression for $l_1(t)$, the Euler condition for capital input may be written:

$$l_0(t)\frac{\partial F}{\partial K} = e^{-rt}q \left\{[1-uv]\delta+[1-uw]r-[1-ux]\frac{\dot{q}}{q}\right\}.$$

Combining this condition with the Euler condition for output, we obtain the usual marginal productivity condition:

$$\frac{\partial X}{\partial K} = \frac{q\left\{\left[\frac{1-uv}{1-u}\right]\delta+\left[\frac{1-uw}{1-u}\right]r-\left[\frac{1-ux}{1-u}\right]\frac{\dot{q}}{q}\right\}}{p}. \qquad (2.9)$$

The marginal productivity of the input of capital services is equal to the ratio of the price of capital services to the price of output. Following terminology which has become fairly standard in the literature [12]), we will call the price of capital services the *user cost* of capital.

User cost is a shadow price or accounting price that arises from the fact that firms own capital stock from which they derive capital services. For optimal accumulation of capital the firm should charge itself an implicit rental equal to the user cost of capital services at each point of time and should then maximize profit in the usual way. To simplify notation, we will introduce a symbol for user cost, say c:

$$c = q\left[\left[\frac{1-uv}{1-u}\right]\delta+\left[\frac{1-uw}{1-u}\right]r-\left[\frac{1-ux}{1-u}\right]\frac{\dot{q}}{q}\right], \qquad (2.10)$$

so that the marginal productivity condition (2.9) may be written:

$$\frac{\partial X}{\partial K} = \frac{c}{p}.$$

If there is no lag in the completion of investment projects, the level of investment, like the levels of output, current input, and capital input, is determined from the necessary conditions (2.7) and (2.8). In particular, output and the level of both types of input are determined from marginal productivity conditions and the production function; investment is determined from the constraint that the rate of change of capital stock is equal to investment less replacement. In the theory of investment behavior described below, it is assumed that time is required for the completion of new investment projects; this implies that the actual level of capital stock on hand may differ from that which would be obtained by a solution of the set of equations consisting of the two marginal productivity conditions

---

[12]) See footnote 6 and the references listed there.

and the production function. We assume that, given the actual level of capital stock, output and current input and the production function and given the resulting levels of output and current input, the desired level of capital stock is determined by the marginal productivity condition for capital input. The level of capital actually held is determined by the constraint (2.8). Equality between actual and desired levels of capital stock is replaced by an equality between the level of capital stock which is desired and the level actually held plus the backlog of uncompleted investment projects for the expansion of capital stock.

To represent this theory of investment more formally, let the proportion of investment projects initiated in period t and completed in period $t+\tau$ be μ_τ. The distribution of completions over time may be described by a sequence of non-negative numbers:

$$\mu_0, \mu_1 \ldots \tag{2.11}$$

The sum of all such numbers is, of course, unity:

$$\sum_{\tau=0}^{\infty} \mu_\tau = 1. \tag{2.12}$$

We refer here to investment projects for the expansion of capacity; the level of such investment projects at time t will be denoted IE_t. At each point of time investment for the expansion of capital is a weighted average of the level of projects initiated in all previous periods; where IN_t is the level of projects initiated in period t:

$$IE_t = \mu_0 IN_t + \mu_1 IN_{t-1} + \ldots \tag{2.13}$$

To condense notation for weighted averages of this kind, we introduce the lag operator, θ, defined as:

$$\theta a_t = a_{t-1}$$

for any sequence $\{a_\tau\}$. The weighted average (2.13) may be rewritten in the form:

$$IE_t = \mu(\theta)IN_t,$$

where $\mu(\theta)$ is a power series in the lag operator:

$$\mu(\theta) = \mu_0 + \mu_1 \theta + \mu_2 \theta^2 + \ldots$$

We have described the distributed lag relationship between investment for expansion of capacity and new project starts. We turn next to the mechanism for the initiation of investment projects for expansion. In each period new projects are initiated until the backlog of uncompleted projects at the beginning of the period is equal to the difference between desired capital stock, which we will denote K_{t-1}^E, and actual capital stock at the beginning of the period, K_{t-1}. The proportion of projects initiated during the preceding period but not completed at the beginning of the current period is $(1-\mu_0-\mu_1)$ and so on. The backlog of uncompleted projects at the beginning of the current period is the sum of the uncompleted portions of all projects already under way:

$$IN_t+(1-\mu_0)IN_{t-1}+(1-\mu_0-\mu_1)IN_{t-2}+ \ldots$$

The mechanism determining the level of new starts in the current period, IN_t, is that the backlog of uncompleted projects must be equal to the difference between desired and actual capital stock:

$$IN_t+(1-\mu_0)IN_{t-1}+(1-\mu_0-\mu_1)IN_{t-2}+ \ldots = K_t^E-K_{t-1}. \qquad (2.14)$$

An immediate implication of this mechanism is that current capital stock plus the backlog of uncompleted projects will bring actual capital stock up to the desired level.

The mechanism for the determination of new investment projects may be rewritten in the form:

$$K_t^E-K_{t-1} = \frac{1-\theta\mu(\theta)}{1-\theta}IN_t,$$

where:

$$\frac{1}{1-\theta} = 1+\theta+\theta^2+ \ldots$$

Using the fact that:

$$[1-\theta]K_{t-1} = IE_{t-1} = \theta\mu(\theta)IN_t,$$

we find that the mechanism may be expressed in the simple form:

$$IN_t = K_t^E-K_{t-1}^E. \qquad (2.15)$$

New investment starts in each period are equal to the period-to-period change in desired capital stock. From (2.15) and the distributed lag function (2.13), the expression for investment for expansion of capital may be derived:

$$IE_t = \mu(\theta)[K_t^E-K_{t-1}^E].$$

If new investment projects are initiated so that the backlog of projects is equal to the difference between desired and actual capital stock in each period, investment for expansion is a distributed lag function of period-to-period changes in desired capital stock.

The theory of investment for expansion of capital is easily generalized to include stages of the investment process intermediate between the initiation of investment projects and actual investment expenditures. Appropriations of funds, letting of contracts, issuing of orders for equipment and anticipations of investment expenditures are examples of such intermediate stages. We assume that the completions of each stage, given the previous stage, are distributed over time. Let the proportion of investment projects initiated in period t for which the first stage is completed in period $t+\tau$ be $v_{1\tau}$. The distribution of completions over time may be described by a sequence of non-negative numbers:

$$v_{10}, v_{11} \ldots \tag{2.16}$$

The sum of all such numbers is, of course, unity:

$$\sum_{\tau=0}^{\infty} v_{1\tau} = 1. \tag{2.17}$$

Similarly, the distribution of completions of the second stage over time, given completion of the first, may be described by a sequence $\{v_{2\tau}\}$ and so on.

Second, let $IE_{1_t}, IE_{2_t} \ldots IE_{m_t}$ represent the levels of investment for expansion of capital at each of m intermediate stages. The initiation of investment projects may be interpreted as stage 0 and actual investment expenditure as stage $m+1$. At each point of time the level of completions of each stage of the process of investment for the expansion of capital is a weighted average of the level of completions of the previous stage in all previous periods. Using the notation for the lag operator introduced above:

$$
\begin{aligned}
IE_{1_t} &= v_1(\theta)IN_t, \\
IE_{2_t} &= v_2(\theta)IE_{1_t}, \\
&\cdots\cdots\cdots\cdots \\
IE_{m+1_t} &= v_{m+1}(\theta)IE_{m_t},
\end{aligned} \tag{2.18}
$$

where, for example, $v_1(\theta)$ is a power series in the lag operator:

$$v_1(\theta) = v_{10} + v_{11}\theta + v_{12}\theta^2 + \ldots$$

We assume that transitions between any two successive stages are distributed independently of the time required for transition from preceding stages to the first of the two stages. This implies that the distribution of completions of the transition between any pair of stages is the convolution of the distributions of completions of each stage between the first of the pair and the last, given the previous stage in the sequence. For example, the distribution of completions of the second stage, given the initiation of new investment projects, is the convolution of the distribution of completions of the first stage given the initiation of new investment projects and the distribution of completions of the second stage given completion of the first. This implies that the level of completions of the second stage is a weighted average of new investment starts:

$$IE_{2_t} = v_2(\theta)v_1(\theta)IN_t. \tag{2.19}$$

A similar relationship holds between the level of completions of any intermediate stage and the level of completions of any previous stage. The appropriate weighted average may be derived from the convolution of the distributions of completions of each stage between the first of the pair and the last. In particular, the weighted average of (2.13) may be derived from the weighted averages (2.18) as follows:

$$\prod_{j=0}^{m+1} v_j(\theta) = \mu(\theta).$$

This and similar relationships between the distributions of completions of successive stages provide powerful tests of the consistency of the empirical results from each part of the investment process.

Up to this point, we have discussed investment expenditures generated by the expansion of capital stock; we turn now to investment for replacement of previously acquired capital goods. Let the proportion of investment goods acquired in period t and replaced in period $t+\tau$ be ρ_τ. The distribution of replacements over time may be described by a sequence of non-negative numbers:

$$\rho_0, \rho_1 \ldots, \tag{2.20}$$

where:

$$\sum_{\tau=0}^{\infty} \rho_\tau = 1. \tag{2.21}$$

Replacement investment, say IR_t, is a weighted average of past gross investment, say I_t:

$$IR_t = \rho(\theta)I_t, \tag{2.22}$$

where $\rho(\theta)$ is a power series in the lag operator:

$$\rho(\theta) = \rho_0 + \rho_1\theta + \rho_2\theta^2 + \ldots$$

Capital stock at the end of the period is the sum of past investment net of replacement:

$$K_t = \sum_{\tau=0}^{\infty} \left[I_{t-\tau} - IR_{t-\tau} \right] = \frac{1-\rho(\theta)}{1-\theta} I_t. \tag{2.23}$$

Using (2.22) and (2.23), replacement investment may be expressed as a function of past values of capital stock:

$$IR_t = \frac{\rho(\theta)[1-\theta]}{1-\rho(\theta)} K_t. \tag{2.24}$$

We assume that the distribution of replacements over time is geometric, beginning with the period following that in which the investment is made. The justification for the use of this distribution of replacements in empirical work is that replacement, unlike expansion of capacity, is a recurrent event. An initial increase in capacity generates replacements distributed over time; but each replacement generates a new set of replacements. This process repeats itself indefinitely. The appropriate model for replacement investment is not the distribution over time of the replacements for a single investment but rather the distribution over time of the infinite stream of replacements generated by a single investment. It is a fundamental result of renewal theory that the distribution of replacements for such an infinite stream approaches a constant fraction of capital stock for (almost) any distribution of replacements over time and for any initial age distribution of capital stock. This result holds for a constant stock and for a growing stock as well. But this is precisely the relationship between replacement and capital stock for the geometric distribution of replacements over time for a single investment. To demonstrate this we observe that for a geometric distribution of replacements over time the power series in the lag operator $\rho(\theta)$ takes the form:

$$\rho(\theta) = \delta\theta + \delta(1-\delta)\theta^2 + \dots \tag{2.25}$$

The expression (2.23) for capital stock reduces to:

$$K_t = I_t + (1-\delta)K_{t-1}; \tag{2.26}$$

the expression (2.24) for replacement investment reduces to:

$$IR_t = \delta K_{t-1}. \tag{2.27}$$

To complete the theory of investment behavior, it is necessary to combine the theory of investment for expansion of capital with the theory of replacement investment. First, gross investment is the sum of the two types of

investment:

$$I_t = IE_t + IR_t. \tag{2.28}$$

Combining this identity with expression (2.27), giving replacement investment as a constant fraction of capital stock, and with the distributed lag function derived from the relationships (2.13) and (2.15), giving investment for expansion of capital as a distributed lag function of past changes in desired capital stock, we obtain:

$$I_t = \mu(\theta)[K_t^E - K_{t-1}^E] + \delta K_{t-1}, \tag{2.29}$$

which is the complete theory of investment behavior.

This theory of investment behavior is easily extended to intermediate stages of the investment process. At each intermediate stage gross investment is the sum of expansion and replacement components. We assume that there is no delay between retirement of previously acquired capital goods and replacement investment; the level of replacement investment at each of the intermediate stages is equal to the level of actual expenditure for replacement investment, IR_t. Let $I_{1_t}, I_{2_t} \ldots I_{m_t}$ represent the levels of gross investment at each of m intermediate stages. From (2.27) and the distributed lag functions (2.18) we obtain:

$$I_{1_t} = v_1(\theta)[K_t^E - K_{t-1}^E] + \delta K_{t-1},$$
$$I_{2_t} = v_2(\theta)[I_{1_t} - \delta K_{t-1}] + \delta K_{t-1}, \tag{2.30}$$
$$\ldots \ldots \ldots \ldots \ldots \ldots \ldots \ldots$$
$$I_t = v_{m+1}(\theta)[I_{m_t} - \delta K_{t-1}] + \delta K_{t-1}.$$

These relationships may be further combined so that gross investment at any intermediate stage may be expressed as a function of capital stock and investment for expansion at any preceding stage and ultimately of past changes in desired capital stock.

The flexible accelerator of Chenery [3] and Koyck [34] is a special case of the theory of investment behavior (2.29); this special case is obtained by assuming that the distribution of actual investment expenditures, given new investment starts, is geometric. To show this, we observe that the mechanism for the generation of new investment starts (2.14) and the distributed lag function (2.13) imply that:

$$IE_t = \frac{[1-\theta]\mu(\theta)}{1-\theta\mu(\theta)}[K_t^E - K_{t-1}].$$

Now, suppose that the sequence $\{\mu_\tau\}$ declines geometrically; then:

$$\mu(\theta) = \frac{1-l}{1-l\theta} \; ;$$

hence,

$$IE_t = [1-l][K_t^E - K_{t-1}],$$

which is the familiar flexible accelerator.

For empirical implementation of the theory of investment behavior outlined above, it is necessary, first, to choose a particular form for the production function (2.5). We will take the form to be Cobb-Douglas [13]):

$$X = AK^\alpha L^\beta, \tag{2.31}$$

where strict convexity of the production function requires diminishing returns to scale, that is, $\alpha + \beta < 1$. For the Cobb-Douglas production function, the marginal productivity condition (2.9) may be represented in the form:

$$\frac{\partial X}{\partial K} = \alpha \frac{X}{K} = \frac{c}{p}. \tag{2.32}$$

Taking output as determined by the production function and the marginal productivity condition for current input, given the actual level of capital stock, desired capital is obtained from (2.32) as follows:

$$K^E = \alpha \frac{pX}{c}. \tag{2.33}$$

Second, it is necessary to choose a particular form for the distributed lag functions (2.13) and (2.18). We take the form to be general Pascal [14]); a distributed lag function is a member of the class of general Pascal distributed lag functions if, and only if, the function may be written with finite lags in both independent and dependent variables. This condition is precisely equivalent to the condition that the power series $\mu(\theta)$ is rational, that is,

$$\mu(\theta) = \frac{\gamma(\theta)}{\omega(\theta)}, \tag{2.34}$$

---

[13]) A summary of studies of the Cobb-Douglas production function is given in Douglas's presidential address to the American Economic Association [5]. Properties of the "Cobb-Douglas" form of the production function are described in Wicksell's article on the choice of optimum durability of capital [61]. Wicksell's work antedates that of Cobb and Douglas.

[14]) See [29].

where $\gamma(\theta)$ and $\omega(\theta)$ are polynomials in the lag operator θ:

$$\gamma(\theta) = \gamma_0 + \gamma_1 \theta + \ldots + \gamma_k \theta^k,$$
$$\omega(\theta) = \omega_0 + \omega_1 \theta + \ldots + \omega_l \theta^l;$$

without loss of generality we may normalize the coefficient ω_0 at unity.

The general Pascal distributed lag function includes the distributed lag functions previously discussed in the literature—by I. Fisher [15], Koyck [34], and Solow [54]—as special cases. In particular, the geometric distributed lag function discussed by Koyck is the special case in which there is a single lagged value of the independent variable; the polynomial $\omega(\theta)$ is of first degree. Also, the general Pascal distributed lag function has two properties which are of significance in the present context. It is possible to approximate an arbitrary distributed lag function to any desired degree of accuracy by a member of the general Pascal class. Further, the convolution of any two general Pascal distributed lag functions is a general Pascal distributed lag function. Provided the distributed lag function between any two successive stages of the investment process has the general Pascal form, the distributed lag function between any stage and any subsequent stage whatever has the general Pascal form.

To illustrate the specific form of the theory of investment behavior (2.29) under the additional restrictions (2.33) and (2.34), we may rewrite (2.29) in the form:

$$I_t = \frac{\gamma(\theta)}{\omega(\theta)} \left[\alpha \frac{p_t X_t}{c_t} - \alpha \frac{p_{t-1} X_{t-1}}{c_{t-1}} \right] + \delta K_{t-1}.$$

Multiplying both sides by $\omega(\theta)$ we obtain:

$$\omega(\theta)[I_t - \delta K_{t-1}] = \gamma(\theta) \left[\alpha \frac{p_t X_t}{c_t} - \alpha \frac{p_{t-1} X_{t-1}}{c_{t-1}} \right].$$

As an example, we take the polynomials $\omega(\theta)$ and $\gamma(\theta)$ to be of first degree. Then:

$$[1 + \omega_1 \theta][I_t - \delta K_{t-1}] = [\gamma_0 + \gamma_1 \theta] \left[\alpha \frac{p_t X_t}{c_t} - \alpha \frac{p_{t-1} X_{t-1}}{c_{t-1}} \right],$$

which may be written:

$$I_t = \alpha \gamma_0 \left[\frac{p_t X_t}{c_t} - \frac{p_{t-1} X_{t-1}}{c_{t-1}} \right] + \alpha \gamma_1 \left[\frac{p_{t-1} X_{t-1}}{c_{t-1}} - \frac{p_{t-2} X_{t-2}}{c_{t-2}} \right],$$

$$- \omega_1 [I_{t-1} - \delta K_{t-2}] + \delta K_{t-1}. \quad (2.35)$$

For two alternative stochastic specifications of the general Pascal distributed lag function, a consistent estimator of the parameters of the function may be derived by well-known statistical methods based on the principle of minimum chi-squared [15]. First, an error or random term may be added to equation (2.35); where the error corresponding to period t is denoted ε_t, we will suppose that the error satisfies the hypotheses:

$$E(\varepsilon_t) = 0, \qquad (t = 1 \ldots n),$$
$$E(\varepsilon_t \varepsilon_s) = \delta_{ts} \sigma^2, \qquad (t, s = 1 \ldots n), \tag{2.36}$$

where δ_{ts} is the Kronecker delta. Further, it will be assumed that the independent variables in (2.35) may be taken as fixed. Under these hypotheses the ordinary least squares estimator of the parameters $\gamma_1, \gamma_2 \ldots \gamma_k$ and ω_1, $\omega_2 \ldots \omega_l$ is consistent [6, 33, 41]. If the second of the two hypotheses (2.36) is not satisfied, the least squares estimator is not, in general, consistent [23, 40]. This stochastic specification may be called the error in equation specification of the general Pascal distributed lag function. The error in equation specification is employed in the empirical work reported below. An alternative stochastic specification is that an error term satisfying the conditions (2.36) may be added to the distributed lag function (2.29). This stochastic specification may be called the errors in variables specification of the general Pascal distributed lag function. A consistent estimator may be obtained by applying weighted least squares to the resulting linear structural relation [16].

As it stands, the relationship (2.35) is not identified under either errors in variables or error in equation specifications. However, the restriction (2.12):

$$\sum_{\tau=0}^{\infty} \mu_\tau = 1,$$

may be employed to obtain an estimate of the parameter α; given this estimate, estimates of the remaining parameters may be obtained from the regression function or linear structural relation corresponding to (2.35). Under restriction (2.12), the relation (2.35) is exactly identified.

2.3. *Problems of measurement*

The problems of preparing data for empirical implementation of the theory

---

[15] For a discussion of estimation based on the principle of minimum chi-squared, see Neyman [49], Ferguson [14] and Chiang [4].

[16] For further discussion of this point, see [29]; see also Klein [32].

of investment behavior outlined in the preceding section can be divided into three parts: (1) measurement of investment and capital stock, (2) measurement of output and income, and (3) measurement of user cost. The over-all framework for the study is provided by the OBE-SEC Investment Survey. This survey provides data on investment expenditures and anticipated investment expenditures on a quarterly basis since 1947; a special industrial classification based on a two-digit breakdown of the Standard Industrial Classification is used for the OBE-SEC Investment Survey. All other data used in this study—data on capital stock, output, income, interest rates, and so on—have been derived on a quarterly basis since 1947 (where the data are available) for the industrial classification used in the OBE-SEC Investment Survey. In this paper results are reported for four industrial groups; these groups with the corresponding SIC industry groups are the following:

OBE-SEC INDUSTRY	SIC INDUSTRY
total durables	19, 24, 25, 32–39
total nondurables	20–23, 26–31
total regulated	40–42, 44–49
all other	divisions B, C, F, G, H

Results for the subindustries within each of these groups for which data are reported in the OBE-SEC survey will be presented elsewhere. It should be noted that the OBE-SEC survey covers all business, except for agriculture, forestry, fishing, banking, insurance carriers, real estate, medical services, legal services and nonprofit organizations. The all other sector combines the industry groups, trade and residual industries used in the other studies reported in this volume, except that industries excluded from the OBE-SEC survey are by necessity excluded from the all other sector in the results reported here [17]).

There are two distinct problems in the preparation of data on investment and capital stock: reduction of investment expenditures at various stages of the investment process to constant prices and calculation of capital stock and replacement investment, given data on investment in constant prices.

Reduction of investment expenditures to constant prices is made difficult

[17]) A general description of the OBE-SEC Investment Survey is provided by Nassimbene and Teeter [47]. The industry classification employed in the OBE-SEC Survey is based on the Standard Industrial Classification [55].

by the fact that conventional price indexes for producers' durable equipment and nonresidential construction are based on the prices of inputs to the equipment or construction industries rather than the prices of the output of these industries. Despite the presence of a serious upward bias in conventional price indexes for producers' durable equipment and nonfarm nonresidential construction, price indexes of the conventional type are used to convert investment expenditures in current prices to constant prices in this study. This procedure is made necessary by the absence of an alternative body of data on the prices of investment goods. To be more specific, separate price indexes for investment goods were prepared for manufacturing and for regulated and other industries. For each of the two groups, the price index of investment goods is a weighted average of the implicit deflators for producers' durables and for nonfarm, nonresidential construction from the U.S. National Product Accounts. The weights are derived from estimates of investment in constant prices from the OBE Capital Goods Study. In that study investment data are presented annually; to derive an appropriate set of weights for a quarterly index of the price of investment goods in each sector, the corresponding annual weights were interpolated linearly [18]).

To calculate capital stock and replacement investment, given data on investment in constant prices, it is necessary to adopt an explicit model for replacement. Under the assumption that replacement is a constant fraction of capital stock, the expression for capital stock (2.26) may be interpreted as a difference equation in capital stock. This equation has the solution:

$$K_n = (1-\delta)^n K_{t-n-1} + (1-\delta)^{n-1} I_{t-n} + (1-\delta)^{n-2} I_{t-n-1} + \ldots I_n,$$

where K_{t-n-1} and K_n are initial and terminal values of capital stock. Given estimates of initial and terminal values, an estimate of the parameter δ can be calculated from the solution given above. The resulting value of δ can be used to compute capital stock for all intervening periods. Initial and terminal values of capital stock for each of the four industrial groups were calculated for the beginning of years 1948 and 1960 by allocating data on capital stock, net of depreciation, for manufacturing and non-manufacturing sectors from the OBE study among the two subindustries in each case in proportion to the book values of net depreciable assets from *Statistics of Income* [60]. For the nonmanufacturing sector, data on net

---

[18]) Data on annual investment in plant and equipment were taken from *U. S. Income and Output* [58] and from unpublished data furnished by the Office of Business Economics. A report on the OBE Capital Goods Study is given by Jaszi, Wasson and Grose [26].

depreciable assets from the OBE study do not include the value of residential real estate (excluding land), net of depreciation, held by the nonfarm, nonmanufacturing sector; but these data are included in the balance sheet data on net depreciable assets from *Statistics of Income*; accordingly, data on residential real estate based on the estimates of Goldsmith were added to the estimates of net depreciable assets from the OBE study in the calculation of initial and terminal values of capital stock [19]).

Output in current prices is taken to be corporate plus noncorporate sales less changes in inventories. Data on corporate sales from the U.S. National Accounts were used as annual benchmarks for the nonmanufacturing sector. These data were revised upward to provide coverage of the noncorporate sector, using data on noncorporate receipts from *Statistics of Income* for 1947, 1953 and 1959. For the manufacturing sector and for trade sales and inventories, data on sales and inventories from the OBE Monthly Survey were employed [20]).

User cost is the implicit rental or "shadow price" of a unit of capital services. For direct taxation the amount of direct taxes is equal to the tax rate multiplied by profits before taxes. Where u_t is the tax rate in period t:

$$\text{direct taxes} = u_t[\text{profits before taxes}].$$

Profits before taxes are equal to revenue on current account less capital consumption allowances and net monetary interest. Capital consumption allowances are a certain proportion, say v_t in period t, of current replacement cost:

$$\text{capital consumption allowances} = v_t[\text{current replacement cost}].$$

Net monetary interest is a certain proportion, say w_t in period t, of cost of total capital:

$$\text{net monetary interest} = w_t[\text{cost of total capital}].$$

It would be possible to represent capital gains and losses as additions or subtractions from profits as measured in business accounting. All capital gains and losses are excluded from profits as measured in the U.S. national accounts [58, 59]. The capital gains taxes are not excluded from direct taxes as measured in the U.S. national accounts. Accordingly, the definition of

---

[19]) Data on assets in the form of residential real estate were obtained from Goldsmith [20, 21].

[20]) The OBE Monthly Survey is reported in the *Survey of Current Business* [59].

user cost may be written:

$$c_t = \frac{1-u_t v_t}{1-u_t} \delta + \frac{1-u_t w_t}{1-u_t} r_t - \frac{1}{1-u_t} \frac{\Delta q_t}{q_t},$$

where the functions u_t, v_t, and w_t are defined as above, r_t is the cost of capital, taken to be equal to the U.S. Government long-term bond rate, δ is the rate of replacement (a constant) and $\Delta q_t/q_t$ is the rate of growth of the investment deflator. In the actual calculations it was assumed that the rate of growth of the investment deflator is identically zero; this simplifying assumption has the economic interpretation that all capital gains from changes in the prices of capital equipment are regarded as transitory and do not affect the long-run demand for capital.

The measurement of the various quantities entering the definition of the functions describing the tax structure—u_t, v_t, w_t—cannot be described in detail for lack of space. The basic procedure was to obtain annual benchmarks for each of the quantities—profits before and after taxes, capital consumption allowances, current replacement cost, net monetary interest and cost of total capital—and to use various quarterly series to distribute these annual benchmarks. Current replacement cost is estimated as the rate of replacement, δ, multiplied by the net stock of depreciable assets at the beginning of the period, which is multiplied in turn by the deflator for investment goods. Cost of total capital is the cost of capital multiplied by the value of all capital, including the value of the net stock of depreciable assets in current prices, the book values of other fixed capital and working capital (assumed to be equal to the value of these assets in current prices)[21].

All data were seasonally adjusted by a regression method based on best, linear, unbiased estimation of the seasonal effects[22].

2.4. Tests of the theory

A general Pascal distributed lag function was fitted to relationships of the form (2.30) with two intermediate stages—anticipated investment expenditures one quarter hence and anticipated investment expenditures two quarters hence. Distributed lag functions were fitted to quarterly data for four industrial groups—total durables, total nondurables, total regulated

---

[21] For the purposes of this study, the cost of capital was taken to be equal to the U.S. Government long-term bond rate as reported in the *Survey of Current Business* [59].

[22] See [27] for a detailed description of the method of seasonal adjustment.

and all other. Distributed lag functions for total durables and total non-durables were fitted to data for the period 1952–1962, inclusive; anticipated investment expenditures are not available for these sectors prior to the third quarter of 1951. Distributed lag functions for total regulated and all other were fitted to data for the period 1949–1962. The results of the fitting are given in tables 2.1 and 2.2. To aid in the interpretation of these tables, we will provide a detailed description of the results for the total durables sector.

First letting I_t, IA_{t+2}, IAI_{t+1} represent actual investment expenditures, anticipated investment expenditures two quarters hence and anticipated investment expenditures one quarter hence, respectively, gross investment at each of these stages is a distributed lag function of changes in the demand for capital stock. We will consider the distributed lag function between changes in demand for capital stock and actual investment expenditures in detail. The general form of this function is the following:

$$I_t = v_2(\theta)v_1(\theta)v_0(\theta)[K_t^E - K_{t-1}^E] + \delta K_{t-1},$$

where $v_2(\theta)$ is the distributed lag function between anticipated investment expenditures one quarter hence and actual investment, $v_1(\theta)$ is the distributed lag function between anticipated investment two quarters hence and anticipated investment one quarter hence, and $v_0(\theta)$ is the distributed lag function between changes in demand for capital stock and anticipated investment expenditures two quarters hence. Representing the convolution of these three distributed lag functions as the ratio of two polynomials in the lag operator and substituting $\alpha p_t X_t / c_t$ for demand for capital, K_{t-1}^E, we obtain:

$$I_t = \frac{\alpha \gamma(\theta)}{\omega(\theta)} \left[\frac{p_t X_t}{c_t} - \frac{p_{t-1} X_{t-1}}{c_{t-1}} \right] + \delta K_{t-1}. \qquad (2.37)$$

As a particular form for the polynomials $\gamma(\theta)$ and $\omega(\theta)$, we select:

$$\gamma(\theta) = \gamma_3 \theta^3 + \gamma_4 \theta^4 + \gamma_5 \theta^5,$$
$$\omega(\theta) = 1 + \omega_1 \theta + \omega_2 \theta^2,$$

so that the distributed lag function (2.37) may be written:

$$I_t = \alpha \gamma_3 \left[\frac{p_{t-3} X_{t-3}}{c_{t-3}} - \frac{p_{t-4} X_{t-4}}{c_{t-4}} \right] + \alpha \gamma_4 \left[\frac{p_{t-4} X_{t-4}}{c_{t-4}} - \frac{p_{t-5} X_{t-5}}{c_{t-5}} \right]$$

$$+ \alpha \gamma_5 \left[\frac{p_{t-5} X_{t-5}}{c_{t-5}} - \frac{p_{t-6} X_{t-6}}{c_{t-6}} \right] - \omega_1 [I_{t-1} - \delta K_{t-2}]$$

$$- \omega_2 [I_{t-2} - \delta K_{t-3}] + \delta K_{t-1}.$$

TABLE 2.1

Unrestricted estimates of regression coefficients.

Regression	$\alpha\gamma_1$	$\alpha\gamma_2$	$\alpha\gamma_3$	$\alpha\gamma_4$	$\alpha\gamma_5$	ω_1	ω_2	δ
				Total durables				
$\nu_2\nu_1\nu_0$			0.00088 (0.00035)	0.00077 (0.00036)	0.00038 (0.00039)	−1.26794 (0.14017)	0.44979 (0.13324)	0.02266 (0.00281)
$\nu_1\nu_0$		0.00148 (0.00044)	0.00072 (0.00049)	0.00064 (0.00049)		−1.10844 (0.15188)	0.27190 (0.14608)	0.02685 (0.00363)
ν_0	0.00099 (0.00040)	0.00079 (0.00043)	0.00054 (0.00040)			−1.24220 (0.14205)	0.39380 (0.13868)	0.02561 (0.00309)
$\nu_2\nu_1$		0.80639 (0.04061)						0.01751 (0.00265)
ν_2	0.84615 (0.03286)							0.01921 (0.00211)
ν_1	0.95014 (0.03780)							0.02583 (0.00236)

Regression	$\alpha\gamma_1$	$\alpha\gamma_2$	$\alpha\gamma_4$	$\alpha\gamma_5$	$\alpha\gamma_6$	ω_1	ω_2	δ
				Total nondurables				
$\nu_1\nu_2\nu_0$					0.00017 (0.00032)	−1.13786 (0.14849)	0.35230 (0.14405)	0.01751 (0.00484)
$\nu_1\nu_0$				0.00048 (0.00031)		−1.13547 (0.14908)	0.32124 (0.14458)	0.02026 (0.00465)
ν_0			0.00058 (0.00029)			−1.21953 (0.13641)	0.41983 (0.13351)	0.01835 (0.00438)
$\nu_2\nu_1$		0.83027 (0.07108)						0.01791 (0.00466)
ν_2	0.87007 (0.05491)							0.01853 (0.00360)
ν_1	0.95166 (0.05376)							0.02542 (0.00347)

Turning now to table 2.1, we substitute for each of the unknown parameters —$\alpha\gamma_3$, $\alpha\gamma_4$, $\alpha\gamma_5$, ω_1, ω_2, δ—the corresponding fitted numerical value. These values are given in the first row of the table on the line denoted $\nu_2\nu_1\nu_0$, which is the distributed lag function fitted to the data. The distributed lag function (2.37) may be written:

$$I^{54}_{BUS_{MD}} = \frac{0.00088}{(0.00035)} \Delta \left[\frac{S^{54}_{MD}+\Delta INV^{54}_{MD}}{UKC_{MD}}\right]_{-3}$$

$$+ \frac{0.00077}{(0.00036)} \Delta \left[\frac{S^{54}_{MD}+\Delta INV^{54}_{MD}}{UKC_{MD}}\right]_{-4} + \frac{0.00038}{(0.00039)} \Delta \left[\frac{S^{54}_{MD}+\Delta INV^{54}_{MD}}{UKC_{MD}}\right]_{-5}$$

$$+ \frac{1.26794}{(0.14017)} \{[I^{54}_{BUS_{MD}}]_{-1} - \delta[K^{54}_{MD}]_{-2}\}$$

$$- \frac{0.44979}{(0.13324)} \{[I^{54}_{BUS_{MD}}]_{-2} - \delta[K^{54}_{MD}]_{-3}\} + \frac{0.02266}{(0.00281)}[K^{54}_{MD}]_{-1}.$$

The number in parentheses below each coefficient is the standard error of estimate for that coefficient.

In fitting the distributed lag function (2.37), the values of lagged net investment—$I_{t-1}-\delta K_{t-2}$, $I_{t-2}-\delta K_{t-3}$—were calculated by the method described in section 2.3 as part of the computation of capital stock. The computation of capital stock requires an initial estimate of the parameter δ; this initial estimate was used in the calculation of net investment. A fitted value of δ is obtained as the coefficient corresponding to capital stock in the distributed lag function (2.37). The fitted value provides a test of the theory of investment for replacement of previously acquired capital goods. Taking the initial value of δ, which is 0.02790 for total durables, as the null hypothesis, a conventional t-test applied to the fitted value of δ from the distributed lag function (2.37) results in acceptance of the null hypothesis at a level of significance of 0.05. Given acceptance of the null hypothesis that the parameter δ is equal to its initial value 0.02790 for total durables, this information may be used as a restriction to improve the efficiency of the estimators for the remaining unknown parameters. To make use of this restriction, the parameter δ as the coefficient for capital stock in the distributed lag function (2.37) is set equal to 0.02790. Subtracting δK_{t-1} (with $\delta = 0.02790$) from both sides of (2.37) we obtain:

$$I_t - \delta K_{t-1} = \frac{\alpha\gamma(\theta)}{\omega(\theta)}\left[\frac{p_t X_t}{c_t} - \frac{p_{t-1}X_{t-1}}{c_{t-1}}\right]. \tag{2.38}$$

We will refer to this form of the distributed lag function as the "restricted" form and the corresponding estimates of the parameters of the distributed lag function as "restricted" estimates.

TABLE 2.2

Restricted estimates of regression coefficients.

Regression	$\alpha\gamma_1$	$\alpha\gamma_2$	$\alpha\gamma_3$	$\alpha\gamma_4$	$\alpha\gamma_5$	ω_1	ω_2
			Total durables				
$w_2v_1v_0$			0.00096 (0.00036)	0.00080 (0.00037)	0.00034 (0.00040)	−1.29501 (0.14392)	0.42764 (0.13700)
w_1v_0		0.00151 (0.00042)	0.00073 (0.00048)	0.00065 (0.00048)		−1.10756 (0.14993)	0.26338 (0.14128)
v_0	0.00107 (0.00038)	0.00060 (0.00038)	0.00083 (0.00042)			−1.22784 (0.14001)	0.36394 (0.13200)
w_2v_1		0.87721 (0.04209)					
w_2	0.90892 (0.03419)						
w_1	0.96437 (0.03391)						

Regression	$\alpha\gamma_1$	$\alpha\gamma_2$	$\alpha\gamma_4$	$\alpha\gamma_5$	$\alpha\gamma_6$	ω_1	ω_2
			Total nondurables				
$w_2v_1v_0$					0.00009 (0.00033)	−1.19735 (0.14940)	0.33170 (0.14799)
w_1v_0				0.00046 (0.00031)		−1.17952 (0.14695)	0.31465 (0.14586)
w_0			0.00059 (0.00030)			−1.26339 (0.13848)	0.39227 (0.13656)
v_2v_1		0.90064 (0.06159)					
w_2	0.93389 (0.04883)						
v_1	0.96100 (0.04441)						

Restricted estimates of the distributed lag function (2.38) are given in table 2.2. Substituting the fitted numerical values in the first row of the table for the restricted form of the distributed lag function for each of the unknown parameters—$\alpha\gamma_3$, $\alpha\gamma_4$, $\alpha\gamma_5$, ω_1, ω_2—we obtain:

$$I^{54}_{\text{BUS}_{MD}} - \delta[K^{54}_{MD}]_{-1} = \frac{0.00096}{(0.00036)}\, \Delta \left[\frac{S^{54}_{MD}+\Delta INV^{54}_{MD}}{UKC_{MD}}\right]_{-3}$$

$$+ \frac{0.00080}{(0.00037)}\, \Delta \left[\frac{S^{54}_{MD}+\Delta INV^{54}_{MD}}{UKC_{MD}}\right]_{-4} + \frac{0.00034}{(0.00040)}\, \Delta \left[\frac{S^{54}_{MD}+\Delta INV^{54}_{MD}}{UKC_{MD}}\right]_{-5}$$

$$+ \frac{1.29501}{(0.14392)}\, \{[I^{54}_{\text{BUS}_{MD}}]_{-1} - \delta[K^{54}_{MD}]_{-2}\}$$

$$- \frac{0.42764}{(0.13700)}\, \{[I^{54}_{\text{BUS}_{MD}}]_{-2} - \delta[K^{54}_{MD}]_{-3}\}.$$

As before, the number in parentheses below each coefficient is the standard error of estimate for that cofficient.

Next we consider the distributed lag function between changes in demand for capital stock and anticipated investment expenditures one quarter hence. The general form of this function is the following:

$$IAI_{t+1} = v_1(\theta)v_0(\theta)[K^E_t - K^E_{t-1}] + \delta K_{t-1};$$

as before, $v_1(\theta)$ is the distributed lag function between anticipated investment expenditures two quarters hence and anticipated investment one quarter hence, while $v_0(\theta)$ is the distributed lag function between changes in demand for capital stock and anticipated investment two quarters hence. Representing the convolution of these two distributed lag functions as the ratio of two polynomials in the lag operator, we select as a particular form for these polynomials:

$$\gamma(\theta) = \gamma_2\theta^2 + \gamma_3\theta^3 + \gamma_4\theta^4,$$
$$\omega(\theta) = 1 + \omega_1\theta + \omega_2\theta^2.$$

Proceeding immediately to the fitted numerical form for the unrestricted distributed lag function, we obtain the numerical values of each of the unknown parameters from the second line of table 2.1, on the line denoted $v_1\,v_0$:

$$[IAI^{54}_{MD}]_{+1} = \frac{0.00148}{(0.00044)}\, \Delta \left[\frac{S^{54}_{MD}+\Delta INV^{54}_{MD}}{UKC_{MD}}\right]_{-2}$$

$$+ \frac{0.00072}{(0.00049)}\, \Delta \left[\frac{S^{54}_{MD}+\Delta INV^{54}_{MD}}{UKC_{MD}}\right]_{-3} + \frac{0.00064}{(0.00049)}\, \Delta \left[\frac{S^{54}_{MD}+\Delta INV^{54}_{MD}}{UKC_{MD}}\right]_{-4}$$

$$+ \frac{1.10844}{(0.15188)}\, \{IAI^{54}_{MD} - \delta[K^{54}_{MD}]_{-2}\} - \frac{0.44979}{(0.13324)}\, \{[IAI^{54}_{MD}]_{-1} - \delta[K^{54}_{MD}]_{-3}\}$$

$$+ \frac{0.02685}{(0.00363)}\, [K^{54}_{MD}]_{-1}.$$

The corresponding restricted form for this distributed lag function is given in table 2.2.

Finally, we consider the distributed lag function between changes in demand for capital stock and anticipated investment expenditures two quarters hence. The general form of this function is:

$$IA_{t+2} = v_0(\theta)[K_t^E - K_{t-1}^E] + \delta K_{t-1};$$

$v_0(\theta)$ is the distributed lag function between changes in demand for capital stock and anticipated investment two quarters hence. Representing this function as the ratio of two polynomials of the form:

$$\gamma(\theta) = \gamma_1 \theta + \gamma_2 \theta^2 + \gamma_3 \theta^3,$$
$$\omega(\theta) = 1 + \omega_1 \theta + \omega_2 \theta^2,$$

the fitted numerical form for the unrestricted distributed lag function is

$$[IA_{MD}^{54}]_{+2} = \frac{0.00099}{(0.00040)} \Delta \left[\frac{S_{MD}^{54} + \Delta INV_{MD}^{54}}{UKC_{MD}} \right]_{-1}$$

$$+ \frac{0.00079}{(0.00043)} \Delta \left[\frac{S_{MD}^{54} + \Delta INV_{MD}^{54}}{UKC_{MD}} \right]_{-2} + \frac{0.00054}{(0.00040)} \Delta \left[\frac{S_{MD}^{54} + \Delta INV_{MD}^{54}}{UKC_{MD}} \right]_{-3}$$

$$+ \frac{1.24220}{(0.14205)} \{[IA_{MD}^{54}]_{+1} - \delta[K_{MD}^{54}]_{-2}\} - \frac{0.39380}{(0.13868)} \{IA_{MD}^{54} - \delta[K_{MD}^{54}]_{-3}\}$$

$$+ \frac{0.02561}{(0.00309)} [K_{MD}^{54}]_{-1}.$$

The numerical value for each of the unknown parameters is obtained from the third row of table 2.1, on the line denoted $v_0(\theta)$. The corresponding restricted form is given in table 2.2.

Investment expenditures may be represented as a distributed lag function of anticipated investment one quarter hence and as a distributed lag function of anticipated investment two quarters hence. The general form for the distributed lag function between anticipated investment expenditures two quarters hence and actual investment expenditures is as follows:

$$I_t = v_2(\theta)v_1(\theta)[IA_{t+2} - \delta K_{t-1}] + \delta K_{t-1},$$

where $v_2(\theta)$ is the distributed lag function between anticipated investment one quarter hence and actual investment and $v_1(\theta)$ is the distributed lag function between anticipated investment two quarters hence and anticipated investment one quarter hence. Representing the convolution of these three distributed lag functions as the ratio of two polynomials in the lag operator, we obtain:

$$I_t = \frac{\gamma(\theta)}{\omega(\theta)}[IA_{t+2}-\delta K_{t-1}]+\delta K_{t-1}. \tag{2.39}$$

Given the particular forms for the distributed lag functions $v_2(\theta)v_1(\theta)v_0(\theta)$ and $v_0(\theta)$ as described above, the particular form for $v_2(\theta)v_1(\theta)$ must be:

$$\gamma(\theta) = \gamma_2\theta^2, \omega(\theta) = 1,$$

so that the distributed lag function (2.39) may be written:

$$I_t = \gamma_2[IA_t-\delta K_{t-3}]+\delta K_{t-1}.$$

The general form for the distributed lag function between anticipated investment expenditures one quarter hence and actual investment expenditures is:

$$I_t = v_2(\theta)[IA_{t+1}-\delta K_{t-1}]+\delta K_{t-1}.$$

Given the particular forms for the distributed lag functions $v_2(\theta)v_1(\theta)v_0(\theta)$ and $v_1(\theta)v_0(\theta)$ as described above, the particular form for $v_2(\theta)$ must be given by:

$$\gamma(\theta) = \gamma_1\theta, \omega(\theta) = 1,$$

so that the corresponding distributed lag function may be written:

$$I_t = \gamma_1[IA_t-\delta K_{t-2}]+\delta K_{t-1}.$$

Finally, anticipated investment expenditures one quarter hence may be represented as a distributed lag function of anticipated investment expenditures two quarters hence. The general form for this distributed lag function is:

$$IA_{t+1} = v_1(\theta)[IA_{t+2}-\delta K_{t-1}]+\delta K_{t-1}.$$

Given the particular forms for $v_2(\theta)v_1(\theta)$ and $v_2(\theta)$, the particular form for $v_1(\theta)$ must be given by:

$$\gamma(\theta) = \gamma_1\theta, \omega(\theta) = 1,$$

so that the corresponding distributed lag function may be written:

$$IA_{t+2} = \gamma_1[IA_t-\delta K_{t-2}]+\delta K_{t-1}.$$

The numerical values of each of the unknown parameters for the unrestricted distributed lag functions $v_2(\theta)v_1(\theta)$, $v_2(\theta)$ and $v_1(\theta)$ are presented in the

TABLE 2.3

Estimates of regression coefficients: total regulated.

Regression	$\alpha\gamma_1$	$\alpha\gamma_2$	$\alpha\gamma_3$	$\alpha\gamma_4$	$\alpha\gamma_5$	$\alpha\gamma_6$	$\alpha\gamma_7$	ω_1	ω_2	δ
					Unrestricted					
$v_2v_1v_0$					0.00298 (0.00144)	0.00212 (0.00142)	0.00235 (0.00147)	−0.94889 (0.13788)	0.24039 (0.13578)	0.00971 (0.00099)
v_1v_0				0.00406 (0.00170)	0.00208 (0.00170)	0.00376 (0.00172)		−0.79750 (0.13398)	0.14076 (0.13359)	0.01015 (0.00116)
v_0			0.00105 (0.00172)	0.00420 (0.00163)	0.00355 (0.00177)			−0.84056 (0.13833)	0.12278 (0.13791)	0.01029 (0.00112)
v_2v_1		0.77007 (0.05808)								0.01010 (0.00069)
v_2	0.86156 (0.05919)									0.00904 (0.00064)
v_1	0.81326 (0.05843)									0.01264 (0.00069)
					Restricted					
$v_2v_1v_0$					0.00197 (0.00135)	0.00111 (0.00133)	0.00118 (0.00134)	−1.00559 (0.13705)	0.27369 (0.13744)	
v_1v_0				0.00336 (0.00160)	0.00143 (0.00160)	0.00303 (0.00161)		−0.80923 (0.13406)	0.16287 (0.16287)	
v_0			0.00039 (0.00160)	0.00364 (0.00154)	0.00284 (0.00164)			−0.86350 (0.13681)	0.14602 (0.13633)	
v_2v_1		0.76935 (0.05969)								
v_2	0.83488 (0.06563)									
v_1	0.81282 (0.05946)									

fourth, fifth and sixth lines of table 2.1. The fitted numerical forms for these functions are:

$$I^{54}_{\text{BUS}_{MD}} = \frac{0.80639}{(0.04061)} \{IA^{54}_{MD} - \delta[K^{54}_{MD}]_{-2}\} + \frac{0.01751}{(0.00265)} [K^{54}_{MD}]_{-1}$$

$$I^{54}_{\text{BUS}_{MD}} = \frac{0.84615}{(0.03286)} \{IA1 - \delta[K^{54}_{MD}]_{-2}\} + \frac{0.01921}{(0.00211)} [K^{54}_{MD}]_{-1}$$

$$[IA1^{54}_{MD}]_{+1} = \frac{0.95014}{(0.03780)} \{[IA^{54}_{MD}]_{-1} - \delta[K^{54}_{MD}]_{-1}\}.$$

The corresponding restricted forms presented in fourth, fifth and sixth lines of table 2.2 are:

$$I^{54}_{\text{BUS}_{MD}} - \delta[K^{54}_{MD}]_{-1} = \frac{0.87721}{(0.04209)} \{IA^{54}_{MD} - \delta[K^{54}_{MD}]_{-3}\}$$

$$I^{54}_{\text{BUS}_{MD}} - \delta[K^{54}_{MD}]_{-1} = \frac{0.90892}{(0.03419)} \{IA1^{54}_{MD} - \delta[K^{54}_{MD}]_{-2}\}$$

$$[IA1^{54}_{MD}]_{+1} - \delta[K^{54}_{MD}]_{-1} = \frac{0.96437}{(0.03391)} \{[IA^{54}_{MD}]_{+1} - \delta[K^{54}_{MD}]_{-2}\}.$$

This completes the description of the results of fitting general Pascal distributed lag functions to relationships of form (2.30) to total durables. Results for the remaining three sectors may be interpreted by analogy with those for total durables. The particular forms selected for the distributed lag functions between anticipated investment one quarter hence and anticipated investment two quarters hence and between actual investment and anticipated investment one quarter hence are the same for each of the four sectors. The particular forms selected for the distributed lag function between anticipated investment two quarters hence and changes in demand for capital are different for each sector. These forms are the following:

total durables:
$$\gamma(\theta) = \gamma_3\theta^3 + \gamma_4\theta^4 + \gamma_5\theta^5,$$
$$\omega(\theta) = 1 + \omega_1\theta + \omega_2\theta^2;$$

total nondurables:
$$\gamma(\theta) = \gamma_6\theta^6,$$
$$\omega(\theta) = 1 + \omega_1\theta + \omega_2\theta^2;$$

total regulated:
$$\gamma(\theta) = \gamma_5\theta^5 + \gamma_6\theta^6 + \gamma_7\theta^7,$$
$$\omega(\theta) = 1 + \omega_1\theta + \omega_2\theta^2;$$

all other:
$$\gamma(\theta) = \gamma_3\theta^3 + \gamma_4\theta^4,$$
$$\omega(\theta) = 1 + \omega_1\theta.$$

Restricted and unrestricted estimates for each of the six distributed lag functions fitted for each sector are given in tables 2.1–2.4.

TABLE 2.4

Estimates of regression coefficients: all other.

Regression	$\alpha\gamma_1$	$\alpha\gamma_2$	$\alpha\gamma_3$	$\alpha\gamma_4$	ω_1	δ
			Unrestricted			
$v_2 v_1 v_0$			0.00039 (0.00014)	0.00030 (0.00014)	0.75236 (0.07780)	0.02119 (0.00190)
$v_1 v_0$		0.00032 (0.00015)	0.00015 (0.00016)		0.79460 (0.08130)	0.02220 (0.00201)
v_0	0.00033 (0.00016)	0.00024 (0.00016)			0.80276 (0.08095)	0.02216 (0.00217)
$v_2 v_1$		0.61425 (0.07858)				0.02135 (0.00214)
v_2	0.80068 (0.06283)					0.02269 (0.00154)
v_1	0.74536 (0.07270)					0.02309 (0.00195)
			Restricted			
$v_2 v_1 v_0$			0.00033 (0.00014)	0.00021 (0.00013)	0.84109 (0.06137)	
$v_1 v_0$		0.00009 (0.00015)	0.00031 (0.00015)		0.85596 (0.06748)	
v_0	0.00033 (0.00016)	0.00023 (0.00016)			0.85413 (0.06717)	
$v_2 v_1$		0.68239 (0.06539)				
v_2	0.84426 (0.05254)					
v_1	0.77698 (0.06003)					

We turn now to tests of the theory. First, we consider tests of the over-all goodness of fit of the distributed lag functions. As a basis for comparison, the fitted regressions are compared with a set of alternative models. As alternatives to the distributed lag models relating investment, anticipated

TABLE 2.5

Goodness of fit statistics, fitted, naive and forecasting models.

Regression	Fitted model, unrestricted estimates			Fitted model, restricted estimates			Naive and forecasting models		
	$\bar{R}^2$	s^2	VN	$\bar{R}^2$	s^2	VN	$\bar{R}^2$	s^2	VN
Total durables									
$v_2 v_1 v_0$	0.92073	0.00368	1.88422	0.94004 (0.91324)	0.00392	2.03829	0.78424	0.00842	0.79207
$v_1 v_0$	0.88385	0.00657	2.04502	0.90740 (0.88374)	0.00640	2.06095	0.75927	0.01145	1.46256
v_0	0.91678	0.00471	2.10132	0.93133 (0.91546)	0.00466	2.07754	0.79411	0.00979	0.80835
$v_2 v_1$	0.90718	0.00389	1.74878	0.91183 (0.87243)	0.00521	1.51790	0.23602	0.02981	0.34349
v_2	0.94261	0.00240	1.88439	0.94391 (0.91183)	0.00332	1.64228	0.37922	0.02422	0.23286
v_1	0.93905	0.00311	1.71484	0.95062 (0.93799)	0.00309	1.51000	0.78712	0.01012	0.62739
Total nondurables									
$v_2 v_1 v_0$	0.78593	0.00475	2.20343	0.83970 (0.76686)	0.00505	2.22230	0.71972	0.00552	1.48236
$v_1 v_0$	0.80073	0.00472	2.25410	0.84818 (0.79167)	0.00481	2.23447	0.73696	0.00552	1.46801
v_0	0.82060	0.00399	2.25403	0.86424 (0.80597)	0.00423	2.21971	0.73688	0.00522	1.28823
$v_2 v_1$	0.77933	0.00466	1.67614	0.83584 (0.76125)	0.00492	1.66458	0.38069	0.01219	0.52702
v_2	0.86593	0.00283	1.69944	0.89698 (0.85017)	0.00309	1.68629	0.16775	0.01638	0.33628
v_1	0.88688	0.00255	1.68976	0.91768 (0.88704)	0.00249	1.67710	0.73312	0.00561	0.45940

TABLE 2.5 (Continued)

Regression	Fitted model, unrestricted estimates			Fitted model, restricted estimates			Naive and forecasting models		
	$\bar{R}^2$	s^2	VN	$\bar{R}^2$	s^2	VN	$\bar{R}^2$	s^2	VN
Total regulated									
$v_2 v_1 v_0$	0.84922	0.00764	2.10057	0.69146 (0.83927)	0.00798	2.02793	0.78530	0.00952	1.58328
$v_1 v_0$	0.82783	0.01143	2.06014	0.59149 (0.82308)	0.01151	2.00217	0.75879	0.01401	1.77829
v_0	0.83210	0.01101	2.05193	0.66295 (0.82818)	0.01104	1.9919	0.76424	0.01352	1.81106
$v_2 v_1$	0.88124	0.00556	1.74979	0.75470 (0.87221)	0.00587	1.72970	0.39813	0.01953	0.72282
v_2	0.89742	0.00480	1.75897	0.74982 (0.86967)	0.00599	1.74220	0.22932	0.03415	0.35676
v_1	0.90799	0.00565	1.76168	0.77584 (0.90292)	0.00585	1.73736	0.76973	0.01337	0.87809
All other									
$v_2 v_1 v_0$	0.79380	0.00685	2.07851	0.79045 (0.78094)	0.00714	1.89495	0.72043	0.00846	1.56218
$v_1 v_0$	0.75628	0.00913	2.03345	0.75737 (0.74912)	0.00922	1.89142	0.69910	0.01026	1.92741
v_0	0.72731	0.01101	1.92577	0.75923 (0.92082)	0.01106	1.84890	0.66074	0.01248	1.64256
$v_2 v_1$	0.66770	0.01063	1.70939	0.66855 (0.65350)	0.01088	1.66517	0.59215	0.01235	0.79450
v_2	0.82397	0.00563	1.75847	0.82703 (0.81918)	0.00568	1.70611	0.84901	0.00457	1.40133
v_1	0.75050	0.00894	1.70070	0.75626 (0.74797)	0.00892	1.66049	0.83238	0.00572	0.92488

investment one quarter hence, and anticipated investment two quarters hence to changes in demand for capital, we take the "naive" models:

$$I_t = I_{t-1},$$
$$IA1_{t+1} = IA1_t,$$
$$IA_{t+2} = IA_{t+1};$$

in these models investment at each stage is set equal to its own value in the previous period. Although a naive model of this type is extremely simple, it provides quite stringent standards for judging the goodness of fit of a model estimated from seasonally adjusted quarterly data; this standard is much more stringent than that provided by the corresponding naive model for a regression model fitted to annual data. Statistics for comparison of each fitted model with the corresponding naive model are presented in table 2.5. For each fitted model and each naive model the principal standard for comparison is the variance around the regression, corrected for degrees of freedom; this standard is appropriate only if errors from the models are not autocorrelated. To test for the presence of autocorrelation, the Von Neumann ratio is computed from the residuals of each model.

Considering the results of the comparison between the distributed lag functions $v_2\,v_1\,v_0$, $v_1\,v_2$ and v_0 and the corresponding naive models for total durables, it can be seen that the variance around the regression is much less for the fitted models than for the naive models for both unrestricted and restricted estimates. For example, the variances around the regression for the restricted estimates are 0.00392, 0.00640 and 0.00466, which may be compared with the variances for the naive models of 0.00842, 0.01145, and 0.00979, respectively. The Von Neumann ratios for the fitted models are clearly within the region of acceptance for the null hypothesis of zero autocorrelation; for the naive models the Von Neumann ratios give very clear evidence of high positive autocorrelation. Despite the fact that tests for autocorrelation based on the Von Neumann ratio are biased toward randomness for distributed lag functions like those described above, this evidence strengthens the case for the superiority of fitted over naive models on the basis of comparison of variances around the regression. For completeness, $\bar{R}^2$ for each fitted model and for each corresponding naive model is presented. For the restricted estimates the dependent variable is not the same as for unrestricted estimates and for the naive model; R^2 for the dependent variable used in the fitting of the restricted distributed lag functions is presented for each model. In parentheses the value of $\bar{R}^2$ for the dependent variable used in the fitting of the unrestricted distributed lag function is presented for each of the restricted distributed lag functions.

A detailed comparison of fitted and naive models for total durables is given above. Similar comparisons between the distributed lag functions $v_2 v_1 v_0$, $v_1 v_0$, v_0 and the corresponding naive models for total nondurables, total regulated and all other reveal the clear superiority of the fitted models in every case. Variances around each regression are lower for the fitted models than for the corresponding naive models. In no case is it possible to reject the null hypothesis of zero autocorrelation for a fitted model; in almost every case the corresponding naive models are characterized by high positive autocorrelation of errors.

To test the goodness of fit of the distributed lag functions between actual investment expenditures and anticipated investment and between anticipated investment one quarter hence and anticipated investment two quarters hence, we take as the basis for comparison a set of "forecasting" models:

$$I_t = IA_t,$$
$$I_t = IA1_t,$$
$$IA1_t = IA_t;$$

in these models investment is set equal to anticipated investment two quarters hence lagged twice and to anticipated investment one quarter hence lagged once; anticipated investment one quarter hence is set equal to anticipated investment two quarters hence. These are the forecasts actually used by the Department of Commerce in presenting the results of the OBE-SEC survey, except that the data have been deflated and seasonally adjusted by a different method than that used by the Department; furthermore, no adjustment for "bias" is made in the forecasts.

The forecasting models for the subsectors total durables, total nondurables and total regulated give relatively poor results by comparison with the results for total manufacturing [23]) and the all other sector. For the first three sectors the fitted regressions are far superior to the "forecasting" models, both for variance around the regression and for absence of autocorrelation in the underlying errors. For the all other sector, the variance around the forecasting model is slightly below that for the fitted models in both restricted and unrestricted forms. However, there is clear evidence of high positive autocorrelation of the errors from the forecasting models, while the null hypothesis of zero autocorrelation cannot be rejected for the fitted models. Despite the simplicity of the distributed lag functions relating

---

[23]) See [28] for empirical results on total manufacturing.

actual investment expenditures to anticipated expenditures, a comparison of the resulting models with ordinary forecasts favors the fitted model by a wide margin.

Comparison of the fitted models relating investment to anticipated investment and anticipated investment one quarter hence to anticipated investment two quarters hence with fitted models relating investment and anticipated investment one quarter hence to changes in demand for capital shows that anticipated investment one quarter hence always provides a better fit to actual investment than changes in demand for capital; on the other hand, changes in demand for capital provide a better fit to actual investment than anticipated investment two quarters hence in two cases out of four—total durables and all other. Anticipated investment two quarters hence always provides a better fit to anticipated investment one quarter hence than changes in demand for capital.

Tests of the over-all goodness of fit of the distributed lag functions demonstrate the clear superiority of the resulting models to "naive" and "forecasting" models. The relatively high values of $\bar{R}^2$ obtained for each of the fitted models remain high even when the standard for comparison is taken to be a "naive" or a "forecasting" model. The Von Neumann ratios for the fitted models provide clear evidence that the high values of $\bar{R}^2$ are not due to autocorrelation of residuals.

We turn next to tests of the fine structure of the theory. These tests will be discussed under two headings: tests of the theory of investment for replacement and tests of the theory of investment for expansion.

The principal test of the theory of investment for replacement is agreement between estimates of the parameter δ and the initial value of this parameter obtained from the calculation of capital stock. The initial values of the parameter δ by sector are as follows:

SECTOR	δ
total durables	0.02790
total nondurables	0.02648
total regulated	0.01147
all other	0.02460

While recognizing that the ordinary t-tests of the null hypothesis that δ is equal to its initial value for each of the unrestricted distributed lag functions are not independent, it may be useful to tabulate the results of these tests. For total durables, the null hypothesis is rejected twice out of six tests; for total nondurables and total regulated, the null hypothesis is rejected

once out of six tests for each sector; for all other the null hypothesis is accepted in all six tests. These results suggest that the initial values of the parameter δ are very close to the true parameter values. At the same time
the fact that all but one of the twenty-four fitted values are below the corresponding initial value suggests that the initial values are somewhat too high.
A possible explanation for this fact lies in the well-known upward bias of
price indexes for investment goods. If initial and terminal values of capital
stock used in the calculation of an initial value for δ were revised to reflect
the bias in price indexes for investment goods and the data on investment
were revised accordingly, the value of δ obtained from the computation
would be reduced; whether the reduction would be large enough to result
in a better agreement between the initial values of δ and the fitted values
remains to be seen.

A second test of the theory of investment for replacement is the difference
between the fitted values of the parameter δ and zero; if replacement is not
proportional to capital stock, there is no reason for capital stock to appear
in the regression with a nonzero coefficient; applying ordinary t-tests
(which once again are not independent either of each other or of the tests
just discussed), we find that the fitted value of δ is between four and ten
times its standard error, with most of the t-values concentrated around ten;
this evidence is highly favorable to the theory of investment for replacement
and confirms the evidence against the so-called "echo effect" presented by
Meyer and Kuh [43, pp. 91–94].

The principal test of the theory of investment for expansion is the comparison of the distributed lag functions estimated from alternative bodies
of data—from actual expenditures and from anticipated investment both
one quarter hence and two quarters hence. A crude comparison can be made
by calculating the average lag implicit in each distributed lag function.
The results of this comparison are given in table 2.6. In this table the average
lag between changes in demand for capital and actual investment expenditure,
measured in quarters, is presented for each of the three distributed lag
functions relating actual investment and anticipated investment to changes in
demand for capital. Average lags are calculated from the restricted estimates
of the distributed lag functions; it is assumed that the average lag between
actual investment and anticipated investment one quarter hence is exactly
one quarter and that the average lag between actual investment and anticipated investment two quarters hence is exactly two quarters. For example,
the average lag between actual investment and changes in demand for capital
calculated from the restricted estimates of the distributed lag function

Dale W. Jorgenson

TABLE 2.6

Average lag between changes in demand for capital and actual investment expenditure.

Sector	Alternative Estimates		
	$v_2 v_1 v_0$	$v_1 v_0$	v_0
Total durables	7.02	7.43	7.58
Total nondurables	9.97	10.07	9.72
Total regulated	7.52	8.11	8.39
All other	8.68	9.72	9.27

$v_2 v_1 v_0$ for total durables is 7.02 quarters or less than two years; the average lag between anticipated investment one quarter hence and changes in demand for capital calculated from the restricted estimates of the distributed lag function $v_1 v_0$ is 6.43 quarters; adding one quarter to this estimate, we obtain 7.43 quarters as the estimate of the average lag between investment and changes in demand for capital from the distributed lag function $v_1 v_0$. Similarly, the average lag between anticipated investment two quarters hence and changes in demand for capital calculated from the distributed lag function v_0 is 5.58; this implies an average lag of 7.58 quarters between actual investment and changes in demand for capital.

In the absence of the sampling distributions of the average lags calculated from fitted distributed lag functions, it is impossible to carry out precise statistical tests of the equality of the average lags of the underlying "true" distributed lag functions. Nevertheless, there is remarkable similarity among the average lags estimated from the three different distributed lag functions for each sector. There is clearly a great deal more variability among sectors than within any given sector. Furthermore, there is only one case in which there is a difference of more than one quarter between any two estimates of the average lag for a given sector; this discrepancy occurs for the all other sector, where the average lag estimated from the distributed lag function $v_2 v_1 v_0$ is 8.68 quarters while the average lag estimated from the distributed lag function $v_1 v_0$ is 9.72 quarters.

In general, there is a fairly clear tendency for the average lag estimated directly from the distributed lag function between changes in demand for capital and actual investment expenditure to be lower than average lags estimated from anticipated investment (total nondurables is an exception to this generalization); this suggests that the lag between anticipated investment one quarter hence and actual investment may be less than one quarter and that the lag between anticipated investment two quarters hence and actual investment may be less than two quarters. This interpretation of the results is corroborated by similar findings of Theil [56, pp. 179–183]. In the absence of direct observations on investment expenditure at intervals of time shorter than one quarter, it is impossible to test this interpretation directly.

A more precise comparison among the distributed lag functions estimated from alternative bodies of data may be made by calculating the distributed lag function between changes in demand for capital and actual investment expenditures implied in the fitted distributed lag functions between changes in demand for capital and anticipated investment and between anticipated investment and actual investment expenditure. The direct estimate of this distributed lag function for total durables may be written:

$$\alpha v_2(\theta) v_1(\theta) v_0(\theta) = \frac{0.00096\,\theta^3 + 0.00080\,\theta^4 + 0.00034\,\theta^5}{1 - 1.29501\,\theta + 0.42764\,\theta^2}.$$

An indirect estimate obtained from distributed lag functions for anticipated investment one quarter hence is:

$$v_2(\theta) \cdot \alpha v_1(\theta) v_0(\theta) = \frac{0.00137\,\theta^3 + 0.00060\,\theta^4 + 0.00059\,\theta^5}{1 - 1.10756\,\theta + 0.26338\,\theta^2}.$$

An indirect estimate obtained from distributed lag functions for anticipated investment two quarters hence is:

$$v_2(\theta) v_1(\theta) \cdot \alpha v_0(\theta) = \frac{0.00094\,\theta^3 + 0.00053\,\theta^4 + 0.00073\,\theta^5}{1 - 1.22784\,\theta + 0.36394\,\theta^2}.$$

Differences among these alternative estimates of the distributed lag function between actual investment expenditures and changes in demand for capital stock appear to be well within the range of sampling variation. Similar calculations for the remaining sectors—total nondurables, total regulated, and all other—can be carried out from the estimates presented in tables 2.1–2.4; the results of these calculations are similar to those for total durables in that differences among alternative estimates of the distributed lag function $v_2\,v_1\,v_0$ appear to be well within the range of sampling variation.

We have presented two sets of tests of the fine structure of the theory of investment behavior: tests of the theory of replacement investment and tests of the theory of investment for expansion. The results of these tests are highly favorable to both parts of the theory. The hypothesis that replacement investment is proportional to capital stock is strongly supported by the tests; it appears that the initial estimates of the parameter δ obtained from the calculation of capital stock are somewhat too high but that these estimates are certainly very close to the true parameter values. Tests of the theory of replacement investment corroborate previous findings of the absence of an "echo effect" in replacement investment. The hypothesis that investment expenditures may be viewed as a distributed lag function of changes in demand for capital, where capital is determined in accord with maximization of net worth along standard neoclassical lines, is also strongly supported by the tests. In addition to the tests of goodness of fit described at the outset of the discussion of tests, tests of the fine structure of the theory reveal truly remarkable similarity among the alternative estimates of the distributed lag function between actual investment and changes in capital stock.

2.5. Structure of the investment process

Up to this point we have discussed only those implications of the theory of investment behavior relevant to testing the theory. We turn now to implications of the theory of investment for the response of investment expenditures to changes in conditions determining the demand for capital, especially changes in the tax structure. In tracing out the effects of changes in the conditions which determine the demand for capital, we consider each effect in isolation from the others; all of the changes we discuss are, of course, hypothetical in the sense that these changes would take place only if the hypotheses under which they are derived were realized.

For example, we study the effects of changes in the tax structure, holding constant such market conditions as the price of output, the price of investment goods and the rate of interest. Under another set of hypotheses, say that the price of output, the price of investment goods, and the rate of interest depend on the tax structure, the effects of changes in the tax structure on investment expenditure would undoubtedly be different. To study the effects of changes in the tax structure on investment expenditure under this more general set of hypotheses it would be necessary to combine the theory of investment behavior with relations determining the price and quantity of output, the price of investment goods and the rate of interest. Provided that the hypotheses underlying all of our conclusions about the structure of the investment process are kept clearly in mind, no confusion about the implications of these conclusions need arise.

We have emphasized repeatedly that the response of investment to changes in demand for capital services is distributed over time. Clearly, the response of investment to changes in the demand for capital services depends on the time elapsed after changes in demand have taken place. Accordingly, we begin by studying the time pattern of response of investment to changes in demand for capital in more detail than in the previous section.

From the complete theory of investment behavior (2.29) and the fundamental relationship between capital stock and investment expenditures (2.26) we can derive a different form of the complete theory of investment behavior, namely:

$$I_t = [1-(1-\delta)\theta]\mu(\theta)K_{t-1}^E,$$
$$= \eta(\theta)K_{t-1}^E \qquad (2.40)$$

where

$$\eta(\theta) = [1-(1-\delta)\theta]\mu(\theta).$$

The short-term response of investment to changes in the demand for capital depends on the time elapsed after changes in these conditions have taken place. To derive the response of investment for a change which persists τ periods, we suppose that:

$$K_t^E = K_{t-\varphi}^E \qquad (\varphi = 1, 2 \ldots \tau-1),$$

that is, that the demand for capital remains constant for τ periods, beginning $\tau-1$ periods before the current period. Then the theory of investment behavior (2.40) may be written:

$$I_t = \sum_{\varphi=1}^{\tau-1} \eta_\varphi K_{t-\varphi}^E + \sum_{\varphi=\tau+1}^{\infty} \eta_\varphi K_{t-\varphi}^E,$$
$$= \zeta_\tau K_t^E + \sum_{\varphi=\tau+1}^{\infty} \eta_\varphi K_{t-\varphi}^E,$$

where $\{\zeta_\tau\}$ is the sequence of cumulative sums of the coefficients of the power series $\eta(\theta)$. We will call this sequence of cumulative sums the *time pattern of response* of investment to a change in demand for capital; differentiating investment with respect to demand for capital which persists for τ periods, we obtain:

$$\frac{\partial I_t}{\partial K_t^E} = \zeta_\tau;$$

a change in demand for capital which persists for τ periods results in a change of ζ_τ times the change in demand for capital in the level of actual investment expenditures.

For the sequence $\{\zeta_\tau\}$, representing the time pattern of response of investment to a change in the demand for capital, each element may be represented in the form:

$$\zeta_\tau = \mu_\tau + \delta \sum_{\varphi=0}^{\tau-1} \mu_\varphi.$$

The limit of the sequence $\{\zeta_\tau\}$ is simply δ; that is, a change in demand for capital which persists indefinitely results in an increase in the level of investment expenditures equal to δ times the change in demand for capital. This change in the level of investment is, of course, simply the change in replacement investment which results from an increase of capital to its desired level. We will refer to this change in investment as the *long-term response* of investment to changes in the demand for capital. Since the sequence $\{\eta_\tau\}$ is not necessarily non-negative, the sequence $\{\zeta_\tau\}$ is not necessarily monotone. That is, the approach of the time pattern of response to its limit, the long-term response, may involve first an increase of investment expenditures to a level above the long-term level and then a decline to the long-term level. Any particular short-term response may exceed the long-term response. This characteristic of the time pattern of response has important implications for stabilization policy. These implications will be discussed below.

The time pattern of response of investment to a change in demand for capital is given in table 2.7 for each of the four sectors—total durables, total nondurables, total regulated and all other. The column labeled $\mu(\theta)$ gives the coefficients of the distributed lag function itself; each element of the sequence $\{\mu_\tau\}$ may be interpreted as the proportion of investment for expansion which results from a change in demand for capital τ periods previous to the current period. Taking total durables as an example, a change in demand for capital results in no change in investment for expansion until three periods later; at that point 0.05825 of the change in demand for capital results in actual investment expenditure for expansion. One period later 0.10418 of the change in demand for capital results in investment for expansion, and so on. The peak change in investment for expansion is reached five periods after the change in demand for capital, when 0.15190 of the change results in actual investment for expansion.

The full response of investment expenditures to a change in the demand for capital includes not only investment for expansion but also investment for replacement. The column labeled $\zeta(\theta)$ gives the coefficients of the time pattern of response; each element of the sequence $\{\zeta_\tau\}$ may be interpreted as the proportion of investment for both expansion and replacement which results from a change in demand for capital τ periods previous to the current period. Again taking total durables as an example, a change in demand for capital results in no change in investment until three periods later. In the third period after the change, 0.05825 of the change in demand for capital results in investment expenditure; all of this investment is for expansion of capital, and so the first nonzero element of the sequence $\{\zeta_\tau\}$ is equal to the first nonzero element of the sequence $\{\mu_\tau\}$. One period later, 0.10581 of the change in demand for capital results in actual investment; the actual investment is equal to investment for expansion plus a very small amount attributed to replacement of investment for expansion in the previous period. The peak change in investment expenditure for both expansion and replacement is reached six periods after the change in demand for capital, when 0.15738 of the change results in investment expenditure. This peak occurs one period after the peak in investment for expansion.

TABLE 2.7

Time form of lagged response.

Lag	$\mu(\theta)$	$\eta(\theta)$	$\zeta(\theta)$
	Total durables		
0	0	0	0
1	0	0	0
2	0	0	0
3	0.05825	0.05825	0.05825
4	0.10418	0.04756	0.10581
5	0.15190	0.05063	0.15644
6	0.14860	0.00094	0.15738
7	0.12718	—0.01727	0.14011
8	0.10208	—0.02155	0.11856
9	0.07905	—0.02018	0.09838
10	0.05991	—0.01693	0.08145
11	0.04479	—0.01345	0.06800
12	0.03319	—0.01035	0.05765
13	0.02445	—0.00781	0.04984
14	0.01794	—0.00583	0.04401
15	0.01313	—0.00431	0.03970
16	0.00959	—0.00317	0.03653
17	0.00700	—0.00232	0.03421
18	0.00510	—0.00170	0.03251
19	0.00371	—0.00125	0.03126
20	0.00270	—0.00091	0.03035
Remaining	0.00725	—0.00244	
Rate of decline	0.72864	0.72864	

Dale W. Jorgenson

TABLE 2.7 (Continued)

Lag	$\mu(\theta)$	$\eta(\theta)$	$\zeta(\theta)$
	Total nondurables		
0	0		
1	0		
2	0		
3	0		
4	0		
5	0		
6	0.12882	0.12882	0.12882
7	0.16275	0.03734	0.16616
8	0.15508	—0.00336	0.16280
9	0.13208	—0.01889	0.14391
10	0.10604	—0.02254	0.12137
11	0.08216	—0.02107	0.10030
12	0.06220	—0.01778	0.08252
13	0.04635	—0.01420	0.06832
14	0.03416	—0.01096	0.05736
15	0.02498	—0.00828	0.04908
16	0.01816	—0.00616	0.04292
17	0.01314	—0.00454	0.03838
18	0.00948	—0.00331	0.03507
19	0.00682	—0.00241	0.03266
20	0.00490	—0.00174	0.03092
Remaining	0.01288	—0.00444	
Rate of decline	0.72358	0.72358	
	Total regulated		
0	0		
1	0		
2	0		
3	0		
4	0		
5	0.01604	0.01604	0.01604
6	0.16352	0.14766	0.16370
7	0.25564	0.09400	0.25770
8	0.19687	—0.05584	0.20186
9	0.13267	—0.06194	0.13992
10	0.08581	—0.04534	0.09458
11	0.05472	—0.03011	0.06447
12	0.03472	—0.01937	0.04510
13	0.02199	—0.01233	0.03277
14	0.01392	—0.00782	0.02495
15	0.00881	—0.00495	0.02000

TABLE 2.7 (Continued)

Lag	$\mu(\theta)$	$\eta(\theta)$	$\zeta(\theta)$
Total regulated			
16	0.00557	—0.00314	0.01686
17	0.00352	—0.00199	0.01487
18	0.00223	—0.00125	0.01362
19	0.00141	—0.00079	0.01283
20	0.00089	—0.00050	0.01233
Remaining	0.00167	—0.00086	
Rate of decline	0.65234	0.65234	
All other			
0	0	0	0
1	0	0	0
2	0	0	0
3	0.08594	0.08594	0.08594
4	0.13330	0.04947	0.13541
5	0.11386	—0.01616	0.11925
6	0.09725	—0.01381	0.10544
7	0.08306	—0.01180	0.09364
8	0.07094	—0.01008	0.08356
9	0.06059	—0.00860	0.07496
10	0.05175	—0.00735	0.06761
11	0.04420	—0.00628	0.06133
12	0.03775	—0.00536	0.05597
13	0.03224	—0.00458	0.05139
14	0.02754	—0.00391	0.04748
15	0.02352	—0.00334	0.04414
16	0.02009	—0.00285	0.04129
17	0.01716	—0.00244	0.03885
18	0.01466	—0.00208	0.03677
19	0.01252	—0.00178	0.03499
20	0.01069	—0.00152	0.03347
Remaining	0.06294	—0.00887	
Rate of decline	0.85413	0.85413	

Returning to the column labeled $\mu(\theta)$, which gives the coefficients of the distributed lag function itself, we observe that this sequence of coefficients approaches zero as a limit; that is, investment for expansion as a proportion of the change in demand for capital eventually goes to zero. By contrast, the sequence of coefficients of the time pattern of response $\{\zeta_\tau\}$, given in the column labeled $\zeta(\theta)$ approaches the rate of replacement as a limit. For total durables the rate of replacement is 0.02790, and so the elements of the column $\zeta(\theta)$ approach 0.02790 as a limit. The third column in table 2.7, labeled $\eta(\theta)$, gives period-to-period changes in the sequence $\{\zeta_\tau\}$. The elements of this column are the coefficients of the power series $\eta(\theta)$ from the theory of investment behavior (2.40).

There has been much discussion of the relatively long lag between changes in demand for capital and changes in the level of investment expenditures. Most of this discussion appears to have centered on the distributed lag function $\mu(\theta)$ and, more specifically, on the average lag between changes in demand for capital and changes in the level of investment for expansion. As an empirical fact, the average lag for the four sectors considered in this study appears to be about two years; even so, the response of investment expenditure to changes in demand for capital over periods as short as four to six quarters is fairly substantial. For example, the response of investment for expansion to change in demand for capital in the total regulated sector is 0.25564 of the change in demand for capital after seven quarters have passed.

In much of the discussion of the lag between changes in demand for capital and actual investment expenditures, the time pattern of the response has been ignored. But for purposes of stabilization policy, the time pattern of the response is extremely important. Considering only investment for expansion, the time pattern of response is given in the columns of table 2.7 labeled $\zeta(\theta)$. For every industrial sector, investment expenditure for expansion rises quite rapidly to a fairly sharp peak; after the peak is attained the level of expenditure falls off toward its long-run level, which is zero for investment for expansion. The peak level of investment for expansion is reached at five quarters for total durables, seven quarters for the total nondurables and total regulated sectors and four quarters for the all other sector. After the peak has been reached, investment for expansion aggravates the problem of maintaining aggregate demand. In each subsequent period the level of investment expenditures for expansion declines, finally returning to its original level.

Concentration on the average lag between changes in demand for capital and investment for expansion at the expense of the time pattern of response has a further consequence which may have been unintended. This consequence is that the role of replacement investment has been almost wholly ignored. By comparing the corresponding elements in the columns $\mu(\theta)$, representing investment for expansion, and $\zeta(\theta)$, representing investment for replacement, it can be seen that investment for replacement comes to dominate the total effect of a change in the demand for capital by thirteen quarters for total durables, fifteen quarters for the total nondurables and total regulated sectors and sixteen quarters for the all other sector. Accordingly, even for a short-term stabilization policy, any approximation to the time pattern of response of investment to changes in demand for capital which neglects replacement investment is bound to be inadequate. The average lag between investment for expansion of capacity and changes in demand for capital by itself reveals almost nothing about the time pattern of response of total investment to changes in demand for capital.

Considering investment for both expansion and replacement, the time pattern of response is given in the columns of table 2.7 labeled $\zeta(\theta)$. For every industrial sector, total investment expenditure rises quite rapidly to a sharp peak, following closely the time pattern of response of investment for expansion. Even so, the effect of investment for replacement may change the timing of the peak as in total durables, where investment for expansion reaches a peak in five quarters but the peak in total investment is reached in six quarters. After the peak has been reached, total investment declines slowly to its long-term level. The most important feature of the time pattern of response of total investment is that it first rises and then falls so that total investment expenditures resulting from a change in demand for capital must eventually aggravate the problem of maintaining aggregate demand. A change in demand for capital has a positive effect on actual investment expenditures for periods between two and four quarters. The effects can be seen in the column of table 2.7 labeled $\eta(\theta)$; period-to-period changes in investment expenditures are positive for four quarters in total durables, two quarters in total nondurables and all other sectors and three quarters in the total regulated sector. Furthermore, these positive effects begin only three to six quarters after the change in demand for capital has taken place.

The time pattern of response of investment expenditures has important implications for the effectiveness of stabilization measures designed to stimulate aggregate demand by providing a once-over change in the demand for capital. Such measures would include reduction in the long-term interest rate, "liberalization" of depreciation allowances, reduction of the rate of taxation of business income, subsidizing investment expenditures through "investment allowances", and so on. We can conclude that any measures which result in a once-over change in demand for capital will result in a relatively short and sharp boom in investment demand followed by a lengthy period of steadily worsening stagnation induced by a decline in total investment expenditures relative to their peak levels. This feature of the empirical time pattern of response of total investment to change in the demand for capital seems to have been completely ignored in recent discussions of stabilization policy, perhaps because of a false analogy between the time pattern of response of investment and the monotonic approach of the demand for nondurable goods to long-run equilibrium in Marshallian partial equilibrium theory. This analogy simply does not hold for nondurable goods.

In discussing the time pattern of response of investment expenditures to changes in demand for capital, we have assumed throughout that any change in demand for capital persists for a fixed period of time, say τ periods up to the present. As we have already stated, in deriving the effects of changes in the conditions which determine the demand for capital, we consider each effect in isolation from the others. Both the changes we study and their time pattern, as described above, are derived on the hypothesis that all other conditions—that is, all elements of the tax structure and all market conditions except the one under consideration—are held constant. Whether the principal qualitative results derived under this set of hypotheses carry over to a more general set of hypotheses can be decided only by study of the complete econometric model of which this theory of investment behavior is only one part.

The short-term response of investment to changes in the conditions which determine demand for capital is the product of the short-term response of investment to changes in demand for capital and the change in demand for capital resulting from a change in the underlying conditions. For example, the τ-period response of investment to a change in the rate of interest is:

$$\frac{\partial I}{\partial r} = \frac{\partial I}{\partial K^{\mathrm{E}}} \cdot \frac{\partial K^{\mathrm{E}}}{\partial r} = \zeta_\tau \cdot \frac{\partial K^{\mathrm{E}}}{\partial r}.$$

A similar relationship holds for the response of investment to changes in any of the conditions determining demand for capital. We consider changes in demand for capital resulting from changes in each of the underlying conditions. To obtain the corresponding short-term changes in investment, it is necessary to multiply each change in demand for capital by the appropriate short-term response of investment to changes in the demand for capital as given by the sequence ζ_τ, tabulated for each sector in table 2.7.

Changes in demand for capital may be determined from the definition:

$$K^{\mathrm{E}} = \alpha \frac{pX}{c},$$

where pX is the value of output and c is the user cost of capital services:

$$c = q\left[\frac{1-uv}{1-u}\delta + \frac{1-uw}{1-u}r\right].$$

The response of demand for capital to a change in the rate of interest is:

$$\frac{\partial K^E}{\partial r} = -\alpha\frac{pX}{c^2}q\frac{1-uw}{1-u}.$$

Similarly, the response of demand for capital to changes in the price of output and price of investment goods is:

$$\frac{\partial K^E}{\partial q} = -\alpha\frac{pX}{c^2}\left[\frac{1-uv}{1-u}\delta + \frac{1-uw}{1-u}r\right],$$

$$\frac{\partial K^E}{\partial p} = \alpha\frac{X}{c}.$$

The response of demand for capital to changes in the tax structure works through changes in user cost. Where u is the rate of taxation of business income, the response of demand for capital to a change in the tax rate is:

$$\frac{\partial K^E}{\partial u} = -\alpha\frac{pX}{c^2}q\left[\frac{1-v}{(1-u)^2}\delta + \frac{1-w}{(1-u)^2}r\right].$$

Similarly, where v is the proportion of "true" depreciation allowed as a change against income for tax purposes, the response of demand for capital to a "liberalization" of depreciation allowances is:

$$\frac{\partial K^E}{\partial w} = \alpha\frac{pX}{c^2}q\frac{u}{1-u}\delta.$$

Where w is the proportion of capital cost allowed as a charge against income for tax purposes. The variation of K^E with respect to changes in this proportion is:

$$\frac{\partial K^E}{\partial w} = \alpha\frac{pX}{c^2}q\frac{u}{1-u}r.$$

The responses of demand for capital to changes in each of the market conditions and each of the elements of the tax structure are presented in table 2.8 for all four sectors. All variables are taken to be equal to their values at the fourth quarter of 1962.

To obtain the short-term response of investment to changes in the conditions which determine the demand for capital it is necessary first to specify the time which is allowed to elapse between the change in conditions and the change in investment expenditure. For example, if we consider the change in investment expenditures with respect to a change in the rate of interest after four quarters have elapsed, we multiply the element of table 2.8 for the corresponding sector by ζ_4 for that sector as given in table 2.7. For example, for total durables the fourth-period response of investment to a change in the rate of interest is:

$$\frac{\partial I}{\partial r} = \frac{\partial I}{\partial K^E} \cdot \frac{\partial K^E}{\partial r},$$

$$= \zeta_4 \cdot \frac{\partial K^E}{\partial r},$$

$$= 0.10581 \cdot -5.306,$$

$$= -0.56143.$$

The short-term response of investment to a change in the rate of interest for any time elapsed between the change and the response of investment may be derived by substituting the appropriate element of the sequence $\{\zeta_\tau\}$ for ζ_4 in the example given immediately above.

TABLE 2.8

Response of demand for capital to changes in market conditions and the tax structure.

Sector	Total durables	Total nondurables	Total regulated	All other
Market conditions				
$\dfrac{\partial K^E}{\partial r}$	—5.306	—1.399	—2.746	—3.139
$\dfrac{\partial K^E}{\partial q}$	—9.986	—2.558	—3.445	—5.510
$\dfrac{\partial K^E}{\partial p}$	11.877	3.132	6.147	7.025
Tax structure				
$\dfrac{\partial K^E}{\partial u}$	—5.531	—1.520	—4.253	—3.591
$\dfrac{\partial K^E}{\partial v}$	3.224	0.850	1.669	1.907
$\dfrac{\partial K^E}{\partial w}$	0.090	0.023	0.020	0.048

To derive the long-term response of investment to a change in the rate of interest, we simply substitute the limit of the sequence $\{\zeta_\tau\}$ for ζ_4 in the computation. The limit of this sequence is the rate of replacement, δ; for total durables, $\delta = 0.02790$, so that the long-term response of investment in this sector to a change in the rate of interest is:

$$
\frac{\partial I}{\partial r} = \frac{\partial I}{\partial K^E} \cdot \frac{\partial K^E}{\partial r}
$$

$$
= \delta \cdot \frac{\partial K^E}{\partial r}
$$

$$
= 0.02790 \cdot -5.306,
$$

$$
= -0.14804.
$$

The computation of short-term and long-term responses of investment to changes in market conditions other than the rate of interest or to changes in the tax structure is strictly analogous to that which we have given for changes in the rate of interest.

REFERENCES

1. ANDERSON, W. H. L. Forecasting Uses of Anticipatory Data: Comment, *Quarterly Journal of Economics* 73 (February, 1959) 169–170.
2. BAILEY, M. J. Formal Criteria for Investment Decisions, *Journal of Political Economy* 67 (October, 1959) 476–488.
3. CHENERY, H. B. Overcapacity and the Acceleration Principle, *Econometrica* 20 (January, 1952) 1–28.
4. CHIANG, C. L. On Regular Best Asymptotically Normal Estimates, *Annals of Mathematical Statistics* 27 (June, 1956) 336–351.
5. DOUGLAS, P. H. Are There Laws of Production? *American Economic Review* 38 (March, 1948) 1–42.
6. DURBIN, J. Estimation of Parameters in Time-Series Regression Models, *Journal of the Royal Statistical Society*, Series B, 22, No. 1 (1960) 139–153.
7. EISNER, R. Capital Expenditures, Profits and the Acceleration Principle, in *Models of Income Determination* (Conference on Research in Income and Wealth). Princeton: Princeton University Press, 1964, 137–176.
8. EISNER, R., and STROTZ, R. Determinants of Business Investment, in *Impacts of Monetary Policy*. Englewood Cliffs: Prentice-Hall, 1963, 60–333.
9. EISNER, R. A Distributed Lag Investment Function, *Econometrica* 30 (January, 1962), 1–29.
10. EISNER, R. Expectations, Plans, and Capital Expenditures: A Synthesis of *Ex Post* and *Ex Ante* Data, in *Expectations, Uncertainty, and Business Behavior*. Edited by M. J. Bowman. New York: Social Science Research Council, 1958, 165–188.
11. EISNER, R. Investment: Fact and Fancy, *American Economic Review* 53 (May, 1963) 237–246.

12. EISNER, R. Investment Plans and Realizations, *American Economic Review* 52 (May, 1962) 190–203.

13. EISNER, R. Realization of Investment Anticipations, in *The Brookings-SSRC Quarterly Econometric Model of the U.S.*, Chapter 3 of this volume.

14. FERGUSON, T. A Method of Generating Best Asymptotically Normal Estimates with Application to the Estimation of Bacterial Densities, *Annals of Mathematical Statistics* 29 (December, 1958) 1046–1062.

15. FISHER, I. *The Theory of Interest.* New York: Augustus M. Kelley, 1961 (1st ed., 1930).

16. FOSS, M. F., and NATRELLA, V. The Structure and Realization of Business Investment Anticipations, in *The Quality and Economic Significance of Anticipations Data* (Universities-National Bureau Committee for Economic Research). Princeton: Princeton University Press, 1960, 387–403.

17. FOSS, M. F., and NATRELLA, V. Ten Years' Experience with Business Investment Anticipations, *Survey of Current Business* 37 (January, 1957) 16–24.

18. FRIEND, I., and BRONFENBRENNER, J. Business Investment Programs and Their Realization, *Survey of Current Business* 30 (December, 1950) 11–22.

19. FRIEND, I., and BRONFENBRENNER, J. Plant and Equipment Programs and Their Realization, in *Short-Term Economic Forecasting* (Conference on Research in Income and Wealth). Princeton: Princeton University Press, 1955, 53–98.

20. GOLDSMITH, R. *The National Wealth of the United States in the Postwar Period.* Princeton: Princeton University Press, 1962.

21. GOLDSMITH, R. *A Study of Saving in the United States, 1897 to 1949.* Vols. I–II. Princeton: Princeton University Press, 1955.

22. GRILICHES, Z. The Demand for a Durable Input: Farm Tractors in the United States, 1921–1957, in *The Demand for Durable Goods.* Edited by A. C. Harberger. Chicago: University of Chicago Press, 1960, 181–207.

23. GRILICHES, Z. A Note on Serial Correlation Bias in Estimates of Distributed Lags, *Econometrica* 29 (January, 1961) 65–73.

24. HAAVELMO, T. *A Study in the Theory of Investment.* Chicago: University of Chicago Press, 1960.

25. HIRSHLEIFER, J. On the Theory of the Optimal Investment Decision, *Journal of Political Economy* 66 (August, 1958) 329–352; reprinted in *The Management of Corporate Capital.* Edited by E. Solomon. Glencoe: The Free Press, 1959, 205–228.

26. JASZI, G., WASSON, R., and GROSE, L. Expansion of Fixed Business Capital in the United States, *Survey of Current Business* 42 (November, 1962) 9–18.

27. JORGENSON, D. W. Minimum Variance Linear Unbiased Seasonal Adjustment of Economic Time Series, *Journal of the American Statistical Association* 59 (September, 1964) 681–724.

28. JORGENSON, D. W. Capital Theory and Investment Behavior, *American Economic Review* 53 (May, 1963) 247–259.

29. JORGENSON, D. W. Rational Distributed Lag Functions, *Econometrica*, to be published.

30. KEYNES, J. M. *The General Theory of Employment Interest and Money.* New York: Harcourt, Brace and Company, 1936.

31. KLEIN, L. R. *Economic Fluctuations in the United States 1921–1941.* New York: John Wiley and Sons, 1950.

32. KLEIN, L. R. The Estimation of Distributed Lags, *Econometrica* 26 (October, 1958) 553–565.

33. KOOPMANS, T. C., RUBIN, H., and LEIPNIK, R. B. Measuring the Equation Systems of Dynamic Economics, in *Statistical Inference in Dynamic Economic Models*. Edited by T. C. Koopmans. New York: John Wiley and Sons, 1950, 53–237.

34. KOYCK, L. M. *Distributed Lags and Investment Analysis*. Amsterdam: North-Holland Publishing Company, 1954.

35. KURTZ, E. B. *Life Expectancy of Physical Property Based on Mortality Laws*. New York: Ronald Press, 1930.

36. LERNER, A. P. User Cost and Prime User Cost, *American Economic Review* 33 (March, 1943) 131–132.

37. LEVINE, R. A. Capital Expenditures Forecasts by Individual Firms, in *The Quality and Economic Significance of Anticipations Data* (Universities-National Bureau Committee for Economic Research). Princeton: Princeton University Press, 1960, 387–403.

38. LEWIS, W. A. Depreciation and Obsolescence as Factors in Costing, in *Depreciation and Replacement Policy*. Edited by J. L. Meij. Amsterdam: North-Holland Publishing Company, 1961, 15–45.

39. LUTZ, F., and LUTZ, V. *The Theory of Investment of the Firm*. Princeton: Princeton University Press, 1951.

40. MALINVAUD, E. Estimation et Prévision dans les Models Economiques Autoregressifs, *Revue de l'Institut International de Statistique* 29 (1961) 1–32.

41. MANN, H. B., and WALD, A. On the Statistical Treatment of Linear Stochastic Difference Equations, *Econometrica* 11 (July–October, 1943) 173–220.

42. MARSTON, A., WINFREY, R., and HEMPSTEAD, J. C. *Engineering Evaluation and Depreciation*. 2d ed. revised. New York: McGraw-Hill, 1953.

43. MEYER, J., and KUH, E. *The Investment Decision*. Cambridge: Harvard University Press, 1957.

44. MODIGLIANI, F., and COHEN, K. J. *The Role of Anticipations and Plans in Economic Behavior and Their Use in Economic Analysis and Forecasting*. Urbana: University of Illinois, 1961.

45. MODIGLIANI, F., and WEINGARTNER, H. M. Forecasting Uses of Anticipatory Data on Investment and Sales, *Quarterly Journal of Economics* 72 (February, 1958) 23–54.

46. MODIGLIANI, F., and WEINGARTNER, H. M. Forecasting Uses of Anticipatory Data: Reply, *Quarterly Journal of Economics* 73 (February, 1959) 171–172.

47. NASSIMBENE, R., and TEETER, B. T. An Appraisal of OBE–SEC Estimates of Plant and Equipment Expenditures, 1947–1958, in *Statistical Evaluation Reports*. Office of Statistical Standards, Bureau of the Budget, Executive Office of the President (No. 1), October, 1959.

48. NATRELLA, V. Forecasting Plant and Equipment Expenditures from Businessmen's Expectations, *Proceedings, Business and Economic Statistics Section*, American Statistical Association, 1956.

49. NEYMAN, J. Contribution to the Theory of the χ^2 Test, in *Proceedings of the Berkeley Symposium on Mathematical Statistics and Probability*. Edited by J. Neyman. Berkeley: University of California Press, 1949, 239–273.

50. OKUN, A. M. The Predictive Value of Surveys of Business Intentions, *American Economic Review* 52 (May, 1962) 218–225.

51. ROOS, C. F., and VON SZELISKI, V. S. The Demand for Durable Goods, *Econometrica* 11 (April, 1943) 97–122.

52. Roos, C. F., and Von Szeliski, V. S. The Demand for Investment Goods, *American Economic Review* 38 (May, 1948) 311–320.

53. Scott, A. D. Notes on User Cost, *Economic Journal* 63 (June, 1953) 364–384.

54. Solow, R. M. On a Family of Lag Distributions, *Econometrica* 28 (April, 1960) 399–406.

55. Technical Committee on Industrial Classification, *Standard Industrial Classification Manual—1957*, Office of Statistical Standards, Bureau of the Budget, Executive Office of the President, 1957.

56. Theil, H. *Economic Forecasts and Policy.* 2d ed. Amsterdam: North-Holland Publishing Company, 1961.

57. Tinbergen, J. A Method and Its Application to Investment Activity, in Vol. I of *Statistical Testing of Business Cycle Theories.* Geneva: League of Nations, 1939.

58. U. S. Department of Commerce, Office of Business Economics. *U. S. Income and Output, A Supplement to the Survey of Current Business*, 1958.

59. U. S. Department of Commerce. *Survey of Current Business*, various monthly issues.

60. U. S. Department of Treasury, Internal Revenue Service. *Statistics of Income*, various annual issues.

61. Wicksell, K. A Mathematical Analysis of Dr. Åkerman's Problem, in Vol. I of *Lectures on Political Economy.* Translated by E. Classen. London: Routledge and Kegan Paul, 1934, 274–299 (first published in Swedish, 1923).

CHAPTER 3

REALIZATION OF INVESTMENT ANTICIPATIONS

Contents

3.1. Introduction. 95

3.2. The realizations function 96

3.3. The data 98

3.4. The specific model 100

3.5. Estimated relations 103

3.6. Accuracy of prediction 114

3.7. Summary and conclusions 127

REALIZATION OF INVESTMENT ANTICIPATIONS

ROBERT EISNER [1]

Northwestern University, Evanston, Illinois

3.1. Introduction

For econometric models restricted to the usual *ex post* variables, business investment has been difficult to predict. Yet investment anticipations data collected in surveys of business intentions have been widely accepted for forecasting purposes. Work in the investment realization sector aims at the utilization of anticipations data in a complete econometric model of the economy. For one may hope to improve the predictive and forecasting value of anticipations by applying estimated relations among anticipations, actual expenditures, and other relevant economic variables. These last may be exogenous or may, along with anticipations, be generated by the rest of the model. In this chapter, I should like to indicate the paths of inquiry taken thus far and to report on some preliminary single-equation estimates of a "realizations function" along with measures of its predictive and forecasting accuracy [2].

[1] As in previous work, the author has been aided immeasurably by his research assistant, Robert M. Coen. Financial support has come from the Social Science Research Council and the National Science Foundation. Earlier versions of various parts of this paper have appeared in several articles of the author: Investment Plans and Realizations, *American Economic Review* (May, 1962) 190–203; Realization of Investment Anticipations in a Quarterly Econometric Model of the United States Economy, presented to the 1963 CIRET Conference in Vienna, German translation published in *IFO Studien* 9. Jahrgang 1963 Heft 1/2, 1–37; and Forecasting Investment Spending, *The Economic Outlook for 1962* (Ann Arbor, Mich.: University of Michigan, 1963) 71–95.

[2] The concept of the realizations function has been developed by Franco Modigliani. See, most recently, Modigliani and Kalman J. Cohen, *The Role of Anticipations and Plans*

3.2. The realizations function

Underlying the work in the investment realization sector is the view that investment demand is jointly determined by the expected profitability of investment and the cost of capital. Investment anticipations at any point in time reflect essentially investment demand as then envisaged or investment demand as contemplated at some earlier point in time and embodied in current business documents or plans. Discrepancies between actual investment and previously expressed investment anticipations may therefore stem from supply factors or from changes in investment demand which have occurred subsequent to the date investment demand was reflected in expressed anticipations.

A prime determinant of the expected profitability of investment is the expected relation between existing capacity and future demand for output. This belief is supported by other studies. The cost of capital or other relative prices or production possibilities which may influence the desired ratio of capital stock to output may in principle of course also affect investment demand. It is doubtful, however, whether even in the reasonably long run such changes in capital-output ratios will prove important. Old Keynesian objections that the demand for capital is relatively inelastic with respect to the rate of interest or other measure of the cost of capital and that fluctuations in the relevant long-term rate of interest are relatively small may continue to have considerable force. But whatever the resolution of the long-run issue, short-run fluctuations in desired capital-output ratios, whether brought on by changes in technology or by changes in the cost of capital, are not likely to be large. This implies that errors in investment forecasts based on anticipations are likely to spring more from changes in expected demand for output than from changes in the desired capital-output ratio.

Expected demand for output is usually measured by the expressed expectation of future sales. Changes in expected demand for output which may affect the desired capital stock would therefore depend upon changes in expected sales. A measure of such changes in expected sales may be found

---

in *Economic Behavior and Their Use in Economic Analysis and Forecasting* (Urbana, Ill.: University of Illinois, Bureau of Economic and Business Research, 1961), especially Part II. For early empirical work with the concept see Robert Eisner, Expectations, Plans and Capital Expenditures: A Synthesis of *Ex-Post* and *Ex-Ante* Data, in *Expectations, Uncertainty and Business Behavior*, ed. Mary Jean Bowman (New York: Social Science Research Council, 1958) 165–188.

in the discrepancy between actual sales and the previously expressed expectations of those sales.

A realizations function can therefore be expressed as a relation involving "capital expenditure realizations", the difference between capital expenditures and capital expenditure anticipations, and "sales realizations", the difference between actual sales and sales expectations. Capital expenditures might be expected to exceed capital expenditure anticipations where actual sales exceed sales expectations. This would be true for the periods in which firms are in a position to correct capital expenditures in view of past or current discrepancies between actual and expected sales.

Capital expenditures are undertaken on the basis of expected demand in the future. The relevance of discrepancies between past or current actual sales and expected sales, to the extent that capital stock is not acquired for production in the current period, must depend upon the relevance of past and current sales to expected future sales or demand. This relevance is of course uncertain, and the relation between expected future sales and current sales is far from completely stable. Nevertheless, in conformity to old and respected notions that businessmen, for lack of better information, act as if "tomorrow" will be like "today", one may look for a positive relation between current sales and capital expenditure realizations.

Extending the assumption that businessmen expect the future to be like the present, a positive relation may also be found between capital expenditure realizations and actual sales changes. An increase in current sales would raise the level of expected future demand. Increases in sales that are greater than the increases on the basis of which entrepreneurs have formed their expectations will tend to increase the expected rate of growth of demand.

Another important measure of both actual and expected pressure of demand on capacity is unfilled orders. Changes in unfilled orders for machinery are likely to be a good measure of changes in the expected pressure of demand on capacity in industry generally.

The theory presented suggests little or no positive relation between past or current profits, per se, and capital expenditures. However, current profits may prove in part a proxy for expected profitability of investment, acting as something of a catchall for a number of the factors not encompassed in current sales. One may therefore wish to make use of information with regard to current profits, as well as current sales, in attempting to improve the usefulness of anticipatory capital expenditure data for forecasting purposes.

Finally, capital expenditures should be viewed as a dynamic phenomenon.

The adjustment of capital stock itself is a process which takes time. The development of the conviction that the capital stock needs adjustment takes time. Anticipations of different firms and their revision in the face of changing circumstances relate to different periods of time. All of these factors suggest that the realizations function must involve an intertemporal process of adjustment. Changes in variables which enter into the determination of capital expenditures, or discrepancies between their actual and previously anticipated values, will therefore generate differences between capital expenditures and their anticipations which will themselves endure for several periods.

3.3. The data

The data employed in this sector have been taken from a variety of sources and have been subjected to a number of manipulations aimed at making them reasonably appropriate to the task at hand. Basic information as to capital expenditures and anticipations came from the quarterly surveys conducted jointly by the Department of Commerce (Office of Business Economics) and the Securities and Exchange Commission of the U.S. Government. The capital expenditure anticipations utilized for this paper are the "first anticipations", expressed about two months before the beginning of the quarter to which they relate. Published anticipations in the *Survey of Current Business* in recent years have been corrected for bias as well as seasonally adjusted. Comparably corrected unpublished series for the earlier years were made available by Murray F. Foss, now editor of the *Survey of Current Business*, who was for some time responsible for the Department of Commerce reports on capital expenditures and capital expenditure anticipations. Expectations of annual sales change were made known in the first quarterly capital expenditures survey of each year.

We have worked thus far with capital expenditures and anticipations of four major industry groups—manufacturing durables, manufacturing nondurables, public utilities, and commercial and other (including communications)—which account currently for approximately 90 per cent of expenditures for new plant and equipment by U.S. business. We have endeavored to secure sales and profits data which relate as closely as possible to these industry-group expenditures and anticipations.

In the case of sales, for manufacturing durables and nondurables we used seasonally adjusted monthly figures reported by the Department of Commerce. For public utilities, we relied finally upon revenues from sales of electric power to ultimate customers, not seasonally adjusted, after finding the seasonal eccentricities of gas revenues too difficult to handle. For the heterogeneous "commercial and other" category, we used the figure for monthly retail sales, which is clearly crude, if only because of the major component of capital expenditures in communications.

Profits after taxes in manufacturing durables and nondurables were taken from the *Quarterly Financial Report for Manufacturing Corporations* of the Federal Trade Commission and Securities and Exchange Commission. Annual profits in public utilities were picked up from the national income accounts as reported by the Department of Commerce in *Income and Output* and the national income issues of the *Survey of Current Business*. Quarterly profits figures were then calculated by multiplying the annual profits for public utilities by the ratio of quarterly to annual profits in "electricity" published in *Business Statistics*. A similar procedure was applied to obtain estimates of quarterly profits for use in the "commercial and other" industry. The sums of annual profits figures for components of that broad group were multiplied by the ratios of quarterly to annual and, in this case, seasonally adjusted profits after taxes reported by the Department of Commerce for "all other industries" in a listing which included specifically manufacturing and transportation, communications and utilities. Thus in the commercial category, but in no other, profits were seasonally adjusted [3]).

Unfilled orders for machinery were taken from the unadjusted monthly series put together by the Department of Commerce. Arithmetic means of the monthly figures were used as the quarterly observations.

All of the data were reduced to constant, 1954 dollars. Capital expenditures and capital expenditure anticipations were deflated by averages of the GNP account implicit price deflators for "other (nonresidential) new construction" and "producers' durable equipment", weighted by actual expenditures in constant dollars. The capital expenditures deflator was also used for profits. Anticipations were deflated by the deflator of the quarter in which they were made known, on the assumption that businessmen expressed their anticipations in terms of current prices. Sales in durables and nondurables were generally deflated by the appropriate monthly wholesale price indices. For utilities the electric power wholesale price index

---

[3]) Exploratory analysis with other cyclically sensitive variables, such as average hours of employment, new orders and investment in inventories, has also been conducted. Further work along these lines will be attempted.

was used. For retail sales and the commercial category we took the consumer price index.

It should be clear even from the brief discussion above that many and substantial improvisations were undertaken in the selection and processing of the body of data utilized. A high priority in future work must be set for meticulous collection and preparation of relevant data. It is hoped that considerable progress will soon be made in this undertaking as a consequence of efforts of a number of those engaged in various sectors of the model currently being constructed.

3.4. The specific model

With no more than sixty usable quarterly observations from the period 1948 through 1962, it has not seemed desirable to attempt to estimate parameters of an unconstrained distributed lag function similar to those presented in the writer's cross section studies. Instead we have employed a modified Koyck-type distributed lag formulation for our analysis [4]). This involves two assumptions, the basis for the first of which we have suggested above: (1) Failure of anticipatory data to reflect fully current experience at the time they are reported, as well as the interval necessary to adjust capital expenditures to changed conditions, cause capital expenditure realizations to be affected by sales realizations and other factors over more than one quarter. (2) The adjustment over time of capital expenditure realizations to the variables which determine them may be expressed as a linear function in which, after a certain point, coefficients of successively lagged independent variables form a decaying geometric series.

To facilitate our exposition, let us introduce the following notation:

I_{BUS} = business gross investment in plant and equipment, billions of dollars

IA = current anticipated investment expenditures reported by business one quarter previously, billions of dollars

S = sales, billions of dollars

Z_{AU}^{NS} = corporate profits after tax but before inventory valuation adjustment, billions of dollars, not seasonally adjusted

$O_{U_{35+36}}$ = unfilled orders of machinery (electrical and nonelectrical), billions of dollars

---

[4]) L. M. Koyck, *Distributed Lags and Investment Analysis* (Amsterdam: North-Holland Publishing Company, 1954). However, Koyck used only one independent variable at a time.

SE = implicitly expected sales, billions of dollars

$\dfrac{I_{\text{BUS}} - IA}{IA}$ = capital expenditure realizations ratio

$SR = \dfrac{S - SE}{SE}$ = sales realizations ratio.

The general underlying equation assumed for the time series was:

$$\frac{I_{\text{BUS}}^{54} - IA^{54}}{IA^{54}} = a_0 + a_1 \left[\frac{(S^{54})_{-1} - (S^{54})_{-2}}{(S^{54})_{-2}} \right] + a_2 \left[\frac{(Z_{\text{AU}}^{\text{NS}54})_{-1} - (Z_{\text{AU}}^{\text{NS}54})_{-2}}{(Z_{\text{AU}}^{\text{NS}54})_{-2}} \right]$$

$$+ \sum_{i=0}^{\infty} \left[\gamma^i \left\{ a_3 \left[\frac{(S^{54})_{-2-i} - (S^{54})_{-3-i}}{(S^{54})_{-3-i}} \right] + a_4 \left[\frac{(Z_{\text{AU}}^{\text{NS}54})_{-2-i} - (Z_{\text{AU}}^{\text{NS}54})_{-3-i}}{(Z_{\text{AU}}^{\text{NS}54})_{-3-i}} \right] \right. \right.$$

$$\left. \left. + a_5 \left[\frac{(O_{\text{U}35+36}^{54})_{-1-i} - (O_{\text{U}35+36}^{54})_{-2-i}}{(IA^{54})_{-1-i}} \right] + a_6 \left[\frac{(I_{\text{BUS}}^{54})_{-1-i} - (IA^{54})_{-i}}{(I_{\text{BUS}}^{54})_{-1-i}} \right] \right\} \right] + u.$$

$$(3.1)$$

For manufacturing we constructed from annual sales expectations a crude synthetic quarterly sales realizations series [5]), the high serial correlation of which, however, made the inclusion of two sales realization terms undesirable. In using the sales realization series in manufacturing we assumed the parameter of the single-lagged sales realization variable, estimates of which had been relatively small, to be zero and did not include the unfilled orders variable. In this case we therefore worked from the underlying relation:

$$\frac{I_{\text{BUS}}^{54} - IA^{54}}{IA^{54}} = a_0 + a_2 \left[\frac{(Z_{\text{AU}}^{\text{NS}54})_{-1} - (Z_{\text{AU}}^{\text{NS}54})_{-2}}{(Z_{\text{AU}}^{\text{NS}54})_{-2}} \right]$$

$$+ \sum_{i=0}^{\infty} \left[\gamma^i \left\{ a_3 \left[\frac{(S^{54})_{-2-i} - (SE^{54})_{-2-i}}{(SE^{54})_{-2-i}} \right] \right. \right.$$

$$\left. \left. + a_4 \left[\frac{(Z_{\text{AU}}^{\text{NS}54})_{-2-i} - (Z_{\text{AU}}^{\text{NS}54})_{-3-i}}{(Z_{\text{AU}}^{\text{NS}54})_{-3-i}} \right] + a_6 \left[\frac{(I_{\text{BUS}}^{54})_{-1-i} - (IA^{54})_{-i}}{(I_{\text{BUS}}^{54})_{-1-i}} \right] \right\} \right] + u.$$

$$(3.2)$$

---

[5]) The Department of Commerce now furnishes a series of quarterly sales change expectations. As sufficient observations are accumulated for reasonable estimation, it would appear appropriate to substitute this truly quarterly series for the synthetic one described below.

As can be readily shown, we may obtain estimates of all of the parameters from a least squares regression of the transformed equation,

$$\Delta \left[\frac{I_{\text{BUS}}^{54} - IA^{54}}{IA^{54}} \right] = b_0 + b_1 \left[\frac{(S^{54})_{-1} - (S^{54})_{-2}}{(S^{54})_{-2}} \right]$$

$$+ b_2 \left[\frac{(S^{54})_{-2} - (S^{54})_{-3}}{(S^{54})_{-3}} \right] + b_3 \left[\frac{(Z_{\text{AU}}^{\text{NS54}})_{-1} - (Z_{\text{AU}}^{\text{NS54}})_{-2}}{(Z_{\text{AU}}^{\text{NS54}})_{-2}} \right]$$

$$+ b_4 \left[\frac{(Z_{\text{AU}}^{\text{NS54}})_{-2} - (Z_{\text{AU}}^{\text{NS54}})_{-3}}{(Z_{\text{AU}}^{\text{NS54}})_{-3}} \right] + b_5 \frac{(O_{\text{U}_{35+36}}^{54})_{-1} - (O_{\text{U}_{35+36}}^{54})_{-2}}{(IA^{54})_{-1}}$$

$$+ b_6 \left[\frac{(I_{\text{BUS}}^{54})_{-1} - IA^{54}}{(I_{\text{BUS}}^{54})_{-1}} \right] + b_7 \left[\frac{I_{\text{BUS}}^{54} - IA^{54}}{IA^{54}} \right]_{-1} + v \qquad (3.3)$$

where

$$\gamma = 1 + b_7, \quad a_0 = \frac{b_0}{1 - \gamma}, \quad a_1 = b_1, \quad a_2 = b_3, \quad a_3 = b_2 + \gamma b_1,$$

$$a_4 = b_4 + \gamma b_3, \quad a_5 = b_5, \quad a_6 = b_6, \quad \text{and} \quad v = u - \gamma u_{-1}.$$

In a number of instances, particularly where the estimated coefficients of change-in-profits variables differ little and not significantly from zero, some of the coefficients in (3.3) (particularly b_3 and b_4) are constrained to be zero, with readily evident implications for the structural coefficients in (3.1). (When we substitute $(SR)_{-2-i}$ for $[(S_{-2-i} - S_{-3-i})/S_{-3-i}]$ and delete $[(S_{-1} - S_{-2})/S_{-2}]$ we of course assume that $a_1 = b_1 = 0$, and we eliminate $[(S_{-1} - S_{-2})/S_{-2}]$ from the estimating equation.)

The synthetic quarterly expected sales series used in manufacturing was constructed by assuming, first, that expected annual sales could be written

$$SE^{\text{A}} = \left[1 + \frac{SE^{\text{A}} - S_{-1}^{\text{A}}}{S_{-1}^{\text{A}}} \right] S_{-1}^{\text{A}}.$$

The reported expected relative change in annual sales, $(SE^{\text{A}} - S_{-1}^{\text{A}})/S_{-1}^{\text{A}}$, is made known on the average in February. We assume further that the anticipated change in annual sales is expected to be realized by a constant linear [6]) change in monthly sales. Then, considering the sales of January of the current year as already known (S_1 in equation (3.4)) and extrapolating

---

[6]) This construction was in large part suggested by Peter Pashigian, but he assumed a constant per cent change in expected monthly sales in "The Accuracy and Determinants of Sales Anticipations", presented at the December, 1961 Econometric Society meetings.

the sales of the following January, we can derive

$$SE_m = S_1 + \left[\frac{m-1}{6}\right]\left[\frac{SE^A - S_1}{11} - S_1\right] \tag{3.4}$$

$$m = 2, 3, \ldots\ldots, 13$$

where m denotes the mth month of the year t and SE_{13} is expected sales in January of year $t+1$. Expected quarterly sales are the sum of the (synthetic) expected sales of each of the months of the quarter.

3.5. Estimated relations

Estimates of equation (3.3) derived from observations through the fourth quarter of 1960 without the change in unfilled orders of machinery are presented in tables 3.1 and 3.2. Table 3.1 shows sales realizations, changes in profits, and the lagged expenditures-minus-anticipations ratio, $([I_{BUS}^{54}]_{-1} - IA^{54})/[I_{BUS}^{54}]_{-1}$, all to be significant in the explanation of capital expenditure realizations. For all manufacturing and for manufacturing non-durables alone, the regressions including the lagged expenditures variable explain over 60 per cent of the variance in the dependent variable, the change in capital expenditure realizations. Comparison of the regressions for all manufacturing with and without $([I_{BUS}^{54}]_{-1} - IA^{54})/[I_{BUS}^{54}]_{-1}$ reveals that the presence of this lagged expenditures-minus-anticipations ratio increases the coefficients of other variables as well as the coefficient of deter-mination. It reduces the role of the lagged capital expenditure realizations term, however. (If the dependent variable were merely realizations, instead of its first difference, inclusion of $([I_{BUS}^{54}]_{-1} - IA^{54})/[I_{BUS}^{54}]_{-1}$ in the all-manu-facturing regression would reduce the coefficient of $[(I_{BUS}^{54} - IA^{54})/IA^{54}]_{-1}$ from 0.493 to 0.249.) Thus it apparently serves to pick up any systematic errors in anticipations, unrelated to sales or profits, which might be known before the quarter to which the anticipations relate, as well as to isolate more properly the coefficient of $[(I_{BUS}^{54} - IA^{54})/IA^{54}]_{-1}$, the parameter defining the lag distribution.

Table 3.2 offers estimates of parameters of the transformed equations for all industry groups, using the two sales change ratio variables instead of one. In manufacturing nondurables we see a relatively spectacular con-firmation of the role of changes in sales in determining capital expenditure realizations and, inferentially, in affecting actual capital expenditures. It may be noted that the total effect of the two sales change variables here is greater than that of the one sales realization variable included in the thirty-three-observation regression of nondurables realizations presented in table 3.1. This sales change effect seems to have replaced the (proxy?) role assumed by change in profits, for which neither of the coefficients is any longer significantly positive.

TABLE 3.1

Estimated equations with sales realizations and profits changes.

Variables [a]) or parameters	Regression coefficients and standard errors		
	Sector		
	Manufacturing (M)		Nondurable manufacturing (MN)
	Eq. (3.5)	Eq. (3.6)	Eq. (3.7)
Constant term	-0.011	-0.007	-0.004
$\dfrac{[S^{54}]_{-2}-[SE^{54}]_{-2}}{[SE^{54}]_{-2}}$	0.189 (0.121)	0.316 (0.094)	0.669 (0.214)
$\dfrac{[Z_{AU}^{NS54}]_{-1}-[Z_{AU}^{NS54}]_{-2}}{[Z_{AU}^{NS54}]_{-2}}$	0.182 (0.048)	0.190 (0.036)	0.166 (0.077)
$\dfrac{[Z_{AU}^{NS54}]_{-2}-[Z_{AU}^{NS54}]_{-3}}{[Z_{AU}^{NS54}]_{-3}}$	0.078 (0.048)	0.108 (0.037)	0.105 (0.079)
$\dfrac{[I_{BUS}^{54}]_{-1}-IA^{54}}{[I_{BUS}^{54}]_{-1}}$		0.435 (0.073)	0.720 (0.151)
$\left[\dfrac{I_{BUS}^{54}-IA^{54}}{IA^{54}}\right]_{-1}$	-0.507 (0.125)	-0.751 (0.102)	-1.063 (0.153)
n	50	50	33
$\bar{R}^2$	0.392	0.655	0.613
DW	1.953	1.943	

[a]) The dependent variable is $\varDelta\left[(I_{BUS}^{54}-IA^{54})/IA^{54}\right]$.

Independent variables are for the corresponding industry. Equations (3.5) and (3.6) are fitted from 1948 : 3 through 1960 : 4; equation (3.7), 1952 : 4 through 1960 : 4.

TABLE 3.2

Estimated equations with sales changes and profits changes.

Variables [a]	Regression coefficients and standard errors			
	Sector			
	Durable manufacturing (MD)	Nondurable manufacturing (MN)	Public utilities [b] (RP)	Commercial [c] (O*3)
	Eq. (3.8)	Eq. (3.9)	Eq. (3.10)	Eq. (3.11)
Constant term	−0.0004	−0.018	−0.013	0.002
$\dfrac{[S^{54}]_{-1}-[S^{54}]_{-2}}{[S^{54}]_{-2}}$	0.119 (0.224)	0.664 (0.316)	0.377 (0.288)	0.254 (0.229)
$\dfrac{[S^{54}]_{-2}-[S^{54}]_{-3}}{[S^{54}]_{-3}}$	0.222 (0.198)	0.797 (0.325)	0.165 (0.247)	−0.052 (0.219)
$\dfrac{[Z_{AU}^{NS54}]_{-1}-[Z_{AU}^{NS54}]_{-2}}{[Z_{AU}^{NS54}]_{-2}}$	0.079 (0.069)	0.012 (0.064)	−0.105 (0.062)	0.109 (0.058)
$\dfrac{[Z_{AU}^{NS54}]_{-2}-[Z_{AU}^{NS54}]_{-3}}{[Z_{AU}^{NS54}]_{-3}}$	0.005 (0.069)	0.014 (0.063)	0.008 (0.061)	0.064 (0.059)
$\dfrac{[I_{BUS}^{54}]_{-1}-IA^{54}}{[I_{BUS}^{54}]_{-1}}$	0.423 (0.108)	0.533 (0.088)	0.395 (0.090)	0.696 (0.090)
$\left[\dfrac{I_{BUS}^{54}-IA^{54}}{IA^{54}}\right]_{-1}$	−0.541 (0.108)	−0.825 (0.093)	−0.719 (0.112)	−0.953 (0.086)
n	52	52	52	52
$\bar{R}^2$	0.379	0.659	0.538	0.726
DW	1.742	1.857	2.176	1.237

[a] The dependent variable is $\Delta\left[(I_{BUS}^{54}-IA^{54})/IA^{54}\right]$. The equations were fitted to observations from 1948:1 through 1960:4.

[b] Sales are revenues from sales of electric power to ultimate customers, not seasonally adjusted.

[c] Retail sales only were used, and profits were seasonally adjusted, see p. 99.

TABLE 3.3

Structural equations with sales realizations and profits changes (transformations from table 3.1).

$$\frac{I_{\text{BUS}}^{54}-IA^{54}}{IA^{54}} = a_0+a_2\left[\frac{(Z_{\text{AU}}^{\text{NS54}})_{-1}-(Z_{\text{AU}}^{\text{NS54}})_{-2}}{(Z_{\text{AU}}^{\text{NS54}})_{-2}}\right]$$

$$+\sum_{i=0}^{\infty}\left[\gamma^i\left\{a_3\left[\frac{(S^{54})_{-2-i}-(SE^{54})_{-2-i}}{(SE^{54})_{-2-i}}\right]\right.\right.$$

$$\left.\left.+a_4\left[\frac{(Z_{\text{AU}}^{\text{NS54}})_{-2-i}-(Z_{\text{AU}}^{\text{NS54}})_{-3-i}}{(Z_{\text{AU}}^{\text{NS54}})_{-3-i}}\right]+a_6\left[\frac{(I_{\text{BUS}}^{54})_{-1-i}-(IA^{54})_{-i}}{(I_{\text{BUS}}^{54})_{-1-i}}\right]\right\}\right]$$

Variables or parameters	Structural coefficients		
	Sector		
	Manufacturing (M)		Nondurable manufacturing (MN)
	Eq. (3.5s)	Eq. (3.6s)	Eq. (3.7s)
Constant term	−0.022	−0.009	0.004
$\dfrac{[Z_{\text{AU}}^{\text{NS54}}]_{-1}-[Z_{\text{AU}}^{\text{NS54}}]_{-2}}{[Z_{\text{AU}}^{\text{NS54}}]_{-2}}$	0.182	0.190	0.166
γ	0.493	0.249	−0.063
$\dfrac{[S^{54}]_{-2-i}-[SE^{54}]_{-2-i}}{[SE^{54}]_{-2-i}}$	0.189	0.316	0.669
$\dfrac{[Z_{\text{AU}}^{\text{NS54}}]_{-2-i}-[Z_{\text{AU}}^{\text{NS54}}]_{-3-i}}{[Z_{\text{AU}}^{\text{NS54}}]_{-3-i}}$	0.168	0.155	0.095
$\dfrac{[I_{\text{BUS}}^{54}]_{-1-i}-[IA^{54}]_{-i}}{[I_{\text{BUS}}^{54}]_{-1-i}}$		0.435	0.720
$a_{s_r}^{\text{L}}$	0.373	0.421	0.629
a_p^{L}	0.513	0.396	0.255

Note $a_{s_r}^{\text{L}} = a_3/1-\gamma =$ long-run sales realization coefficient; $a_p^{\text{L}} = a_2+a_4/(1-\gamma) =$ long-run profits change coefficient.

TABLE 3.4

Structural equations with sales changes and profits changes (transformations from table 3.2).

$$\frac{I_{BUS}^{54} - IA^{54}}{IA^{54}} = a_0 + a_1\left[\frac{(S^{54})_{-1} - (S^{54})_{-2}}{(S^{54})_{-2}}\right] + a_2\left[\frac{(Z_{AU}^{NS54})_{-1} - (Z_{AU}^{NS54})_{-2}}{(Z_{AU}^{NS54})_{-2}}\right]$$

$$+ \sum_{i=0}^{\infty}\left[\gamma^i\left\{a_3\left[\frac{(S^{54})_{-2-i} - (S^{54})_{-3-i}}{(S^{54})_{-3-i}}\right] + a_4\left[\frac{(Z_{AU}^{NS54})_{-2-i} - (Z_{AU}^{NS54})_{-3-i}}{(Z_{AU}^{NS54})_{-3-i}}\right]\right.\right.$$

$$\left.\left. + a_6\left[\frac{(I_{BUS}^{54})_{-1-i} - (IA^{54})_{-i}}{(I_{BUS}^{54})_{-1-i}}\right]\right\}\right].$$

Variables or parameters	Structural coefficients			
	Sector			
	Durable manufacturing (*MD*)	Nondurable manufacturing (*MN*)	Public utilities (*RP*)	Commercial (*O*3*)
	Eq. (3.8s)	Eq. (3.9s)	Eq. (3.10s)	Eq. (3.11s)
Constant term	−0.001	−0.022	−0.018	0.002
$\dfrac{[S^{54}]_{-1} - [S^{54}]_{-2}}{[S^{54}]_{-2}}$	0.119	0.664	0.377	0.255
$\dfrac{[Z_{AU}^{NS54}]_{-1} - [Z_{AU}^{NS54}]_{-2}}{[Z_{AU}^{NS54}]_{-2}}$	0.079	0.012	−0.105	0.109
γ	0.459	0.175	0.281	0.047
$\dfrac{[S^{54}]_{-2-i} - [S^{54}]_{-3-i}}{[S^{54}]_{-3-i}}$	0.277	0.913	0.271	−0.040
$\dfrac{[Z_{AU}^{NS54}]_{-2-i} - [Z_{AU}^{NS54}]_{-3-i}}{[Z_{AU}^{NS54}]_{-3-i}}$	0.041	0.016	−0.021	0.069
$\dfrac{[I_{BUS}^{54}]_{-1-i} - [IA^{54}]_{-i}}{[I_{BUS}^{54}]_{-1-i}}$	0.423	0.533	0.395	0.696
a_s^L	0.632	1.771	0.754	0.212
a_p^L	0.155	0.032	−0.134	0.181

Note $a_s^L = a_1 + a_3/(1-\gamma)$ = long-run sales change coefficient; $a_p^L = a_2 + a_4/(1-\gamma)$ = long-run profits change coefficient.

Results are less sharp or somewhat ambiguous in the other industry groups but, in addition to difficulties which may stem from the particular crudeness of our measures of commercial and public utilities sales noted above, we offer the tentative hypothesis that in these other industries the character of capital expenditures may have been more predominantly longer run, and hence capital expenditure realizations would be less likely to be affected by the essentially short-run investment demand factors that we have been considering. One might, for example, even offer the fairly wild conjecture that the negative coefficient of once lagged profits changes for utilities captures inversely the role of short-run demand factors in other industries. By this reasoning, where investment demand elsewhere slackens, supply bottlenecks are eased in capital-goods-producing industries and deliveries to utilities are accelerated.

That the findings in none of the industry groups are clearly inconsistent, however, with the broad pattern we are developing, should be apparent from examination of tables 3.3 and 3.4, which set forth the estimates of parameters of the assumed structural equations, derived from the estimates presented in tables 3.1 and 3.2. The relative sales change coefficients are positive in all cases except one (where the value is virtually zero). In comparing the magnitude of impact of profits-change and sales-change variables, however, we should note that the standard deviation of the relative profits change was some three to five times as large as that of the relative sales-change variables. With smaller coefficients, profits changes might still have accounted, therefore, for more of the fluctuations in capital expenditure realizations. This conceded, we may point out that by usual statistical tests the profits change ratios did not seem clearly to play an independent role in equations including sales changes (but excluding changes in unfilled orders for machinery).

In further work with observations through the fourth quarter of 1962, we have dropped the change-in-profits variables and added lagged changes in unfilled orders of machinery, measured as ratios of lagged capital expenditure anticipations. This latter variable might be expected, in the main, to pick up more of the effect of changing pressure of demand on capacity. It might also, however, reflect in part the role of supply factors; an increase in unfilled orders of machinery might imply, for some purchasers of equipment, an inability to realize investment plans. Results shown in table 3.5 indicate a fairly clear positive role for both changes in unfilled orders of machinery and changes in sales for all industries except utilities.

The estimated relations presented in table 3.6 illuminate somewhat further

TABLE 3.5

Estimated equations with changes in sales and unfilled orders of machinery.

Variables or parameters a)	Regression coefficients and standard errors			
	Sector			
	Durable manufacturing (MD)	Nondurable manufacturing (MN)	Public utilities (RP) b)	Commercial c) (O*3)
	Eq. (3.12)	Eq. (3.13)	Eq. (3.14)	Eq. (3.15)
Constant term	0.000 (0.007)	−0.015 (0.005)	−0.007 (0.010)	0.000 (0.005)
$\dfrac{[S^{54}]_{-1}-[S^{54}]_{-2}}{[S^{54}]_{-2}}$	0.261 (0.129)	0.721 (0.236)	0.068 (0.179)	0.466 (0.180)
$\dfrac{[S^{54}]_{-2}-[S^{54}]_{-3}}{[S^{54}]_{-3}}$	0.180 (0.130)	0.597 (0.239)	0.013 (0.180)	0.081 (0.179)
$\dfrac{[O^{54}_{U_{35+36}}]_{-1}-[O^{54}_{U_{35+36}}]_{-2}}{[IA^{54}]_{-1}}$	0.084 (0.035)	0.056 (0.029)	−0.009 (0.021)	0.059 (0.030)
$\dfrac{[I^{54}_{BUS}]_{-1}-IA^{54}}{[I^{54}_{BUS}]_{-1}}$	0.575 (0.107)	0.644 (0.092)	0.378 (0.085)	0.661 (0.086)
$\left[\dfrac{I^{54}_{BUS}-IA^{54}}{IA^{54}}\right]_{-1}$	−0.736 (0.114)	−0.844 (0.082)	−0.726 (0.104)	−0.918 (0.079)
$\bar{R}^2$	0.447	0.681	0.509	0.713
n	60	60	60	60

a) The dependent variable is $\Delta\left[(I^{54}_{BUS}-IA^{54})/IA^{54}\right]$. The equations are fitted to observations from 1948 : 1 through 1962 : 4.

b) Sales are revenue from sale of electric power to ultimate customers, not seasonally adjusted.

c) Retail sales only were used.

the role of changes in profits in the divergence between capital expenditures and anticipations. Thus, in the case of durables, the coefficients of the immediately past and the more distant change-in-profits variables, when they were included in the regression but the change-in-unfilled-orders variable was excluded, were only 0.042 and 0.018, respectively. However, when

TABLE 3.6

Estimated equations with changes in sales, profits and unfilled orders of machinery.

Variables or parameters [a]	Regression coefficients and standard errors						
	Sector						
	Durable manufacturing (MD)			Public utilities (RP) [b]		Commercial [c] (O*3)	
	Eq. (3.16)	Eq. (3.17)	Eq. (3.18)	Eq. (3.19)	Eq. (3.20)	Eq. (3.21)	Eq. (3.22
Constant term	0.000	−0.001	0.000	−0.010	−0.014	0.004	0.005
	(0.007)	(0.007)	(0.006)	(0.010)	(0.011)	(0.005)	(0.004
$\dfrac{[S^{54}]_{-1}-[S^{54}]_{-2}}{[S^{54}]_{-2}}$	−0.040	0.181	—	0.327	0.424	0.253	—
	(0.205)	(0.204)		(0.250)	(0.269)	(0.205)	
$\dfrac{[S^{54}]_{-2}-[S^{54}]_{-3}}{[S^{54}]_{-3}}$	0.026	0.217	—	0.000	0.054	−0.066	—
	(0.179)	(0.178)		(0.214)	(0.221)	(0.201)	
$\dfrac{[Z^{NS54}_{AU}]_{-1}-[Z^{NS54}_{AU}]_{-2}}{[Z^{NS54}_{AU}]_{-2}}$	0.103	0.042	0.097	−0.068	−0.089	0.105	0.134
	(0.055)	(0.055)	(0.032)	(0.052)	(0.056)	(0.054)	(0.047
$\dfrac{[Z^{NS54}_{AU}]_{-2}-[Z^{NS54}_{AU}]_{-3}}{[Z^{NS54}_{AU}]_{-3}}$	0.071	0.018	0.072	0.047	0.046	0.062	0.061
	(0.054)	(0.054)	(0.033)	(0.051)	(0.051)	(0.056)	(0.049
$\dfrac{[O^{54}_{U_{35+36}}]_{-1}-[O^{54}_{U_{35+36}}]_{-2}}{[IA^{54}]_{-1}}$	0.111	—	0.111	—	−0.022	0.059	0.056
	(0.038)		(0.033)		(0.022)	(0.029)	(0.029
$\dfrac{[I^{54}_{BUS}]_{-1}-IA^{54}}{[I^{54}_{BUS}]_{-1}}$	0.576	0.438	0.580	0.396	0.388	0.657	0.646
	(0.106)	(0.101)	(0.103)	(0.084)	(0.084)	(0.084)	(0.082
$\left[\dfrac{I^{54}_{BUS}-IA^{54}}{IA^{54}}\right]_{-1}$	−0.746	−0.561	−0.747	−0.697	−0.723	−0.931	−0.926
	(0.113)	(0.100)	(0.111)	(0.101)	(0.105)	(0.079)	(0.079
$\bar{R}^2$	0.462	0.384	0.481	0.520	0.520	0.725	0.723
n	60	60	60	60	60	60	60

[a] The dependent variable is $\Delta\left[(I^{54}_{BUS}-IA^{54})/IA^{54}\right]$. The period of fit is 1948 : 1 through 1962 : 4.

[b] Sales are revenues from sales of electric power to ultimate customers, not seasonally adjusted.

[c] Retail sales only were used, and profits were seasonally adjusted. See p. 99.

changes in profits were included along with the previous change in unfilled orders of machinery, the coefficients of both change-in-sales variables proved close to zero, change-in-profits variables showed more definitely positive coefficients, and the change-in-unfilled-orders variable itself turned out to be quite significantly positive. This would appear to suggest that, in the case of durables, the component of changes in sales related to capital expenditure realizations (beyond that already measured by changes in unfilled orders of machinery) could be accounted for by changes in profit. The addition of the two profits variables actually did little to increase the adjusted coefficient of determination, raising this only from 0.447, in the regression involving sales-change and unfilled-order-change variables presented in table 3.5, to 0.462 in the current case. Where the sales-change variables were excluded, the profits-and-orders coefficients were significantly positive and the coefficient of determination was 0.481.

In regard to utilities, inclusion of profits variables results in somewhat higher coefficients for the sales-change variables, but the total effect of the profits variables themselves (as indicated by the structural coefficients) turns out to be slightly negative. The increase in the adjusted coefficient of determination is quite small as compared with the regression which relies only on sales, unfilled orders of machinery, the previous difference of anticipations and concurrent actual expenditures and previous realizations [7]).

We may also observe that their inclusion in the regressions for commercial capital expenditures results in positive coefficients for the change-in-profits variables but a reduction in the sales-change coefficients. Again the "fit" is only slightly improved. Inclusion of changes-in-profits variables proves of no value at all in the case of nondurables. Standard errors of estimate of sales-change variables without the profits-change variables were generally little or not at all higher than those from regressions involving both sales and profits. Because of this, as well as the difficulties introduced into

---

[7]) Utilities would appear to present a particular problem (perhaps aggravated by accounting peculiarities and data difficulties) which may relate to the relatively long-run character of utility investment. In any event, it will be noted that in this industry both the immediately previous change in profits and the immediately previous change in unfilled orders in machinery have small negative coefficients. To the extent that these should be taken seriously (they do not differ significantly from zero at usual probability levels), they may reflect supply factors. Thus, with high profits and great pressure on capacity in the economy generally, there may be some tendency for delivery to be delayed in relatively long-run utility investment projects, where competition among suppliers has been notoriously limited.

TABLE 3.7

Structural equations with changes in sales and unfilled orders of machinery (transformations from table 3.5).

$$\frac{I^{54}_{\text{BUS}}-IA^{54}}{IA^{54}} = a_0 + a_1 \left[\frac{(S^{54})_{-1}-(S^{54})_{-2}}{(S^{54})_{-2}}\right]$$

$$+ \sum_{i=0}^{\infty}\left[\gamma^i\left\{a_3\left[\frac{(S^{54})_{-2-i}-(S^{54})_{-3-i}}{(S^{54})_{-3-i}}\right]\right.\right.$$

$$+ a_5\left[\frac{[O^{54}_{U_{35+36}}]_{-1-i}-[O^{54}_{U_{35+36}}]_{-2-i}}{(IA^{54})_{-1-i}}\right]$$

$$\left.\left.+ a_6\left[\frac{(I^{54}_{\text{BUS}})_{-1-i}-(IA^{54})_{-i}}{(I^{54}_{\text{BUS}})_{-1-i}}\right]\right\}\right].$$

	Regression coefficients and standard errors			
	Sector			
Variables or parameters	Durable manufacturing (*MD*)	Nondurable manufacturing (*MN*)	Public utilities (*RP*)	Commercial (*O*3*)
	Eq. (3.12s)	Eq. (3.13s)	Eq. (3.14s)	Eq. (3.15s)
Constant term	0.000 (0.010)	−0.018 (0.006)	−0.010 (0.013)	0.000 (0.005)
$\dfrac{[S^{54}]_{-1}-[S^{54}]_{-2}}{[S^{54}]_{-2}}$	0.261 (0.129)	0.721 (0.236)	0.068 (0.179)	0.466 (0.180)
γ	0.264 (0.114)	0.156 (0.082)	0.274 (0.104)	0.082 (0.079)
$\dfrac{[S^{54}]_{-2-i}-[S^{54}]_{-3-i}}{[S^{54}]_{-3-i}}$	0.249 (0.130)	0.709 (0.238)	0.032 (0.206)	0.119 (0.184)
$\dfrac{[O^{54}_{U_{35+36}}]_{-1-i}-[O^{54}_{U_{35+36}}]_{-2-i}}{[IA^{54}]_{-1-i}}$	0.084 (0.035)	0.056 (0.029)	−0.009 (0.021)	0.059 (0.030)
$\dfrac{[I^{54}_{\text{BUS}}]_{-1-i}-[IA^{54}]_{-i}}{[I^{54}_{\text{BUS}}]_{-1-i}}$	0.575 (0.107)	0.644 (0.092)	0.378 (0.085)	0.661 (0.086)
a_s^L	0.599	1.561	0.111	0.584
a_m^L	0.114	0.066	−0.012	0.063
a_I^L	0.781	0.763	0.521	0.720

Note a^L terms are long-run adjustment coefficients. $a_s^L=a_1+a_3/(1-\gamma)$, $a_m^L=a_5/(1-\gamma)$, $a_I^L = a_6/(1-\gamma)$.

measurements of profits by recent changes in tax laws and subsequent decisions on accounting treatment of the investment tax credit and liberalized depreciation allowances, we have leaned more, for prediction purposes, to equations which excluded the profits variables.

Several points of interest may best be gleaned from examination of table 3.7, which presents estimates of parameters of the structural equations, as transformed from the estimated equations shown in table 3.5. First we may note that the low values of γ, ranging from 0.082 to 0.274, indicate that the bulk of the explained variance of capital expenditure realizations relates to variables lagged one and two quarters. Since the coefficient of each successively lagged term is only γ times the coefficient of the corresponding previous terms, the series decays rapidly.

Second, the relatively high coefficients of $[((I_{\text{BUS}}^{54})_{-1} - IA^{54})/(I_{\text{BUS}}^{54})_{-1}]_{-i}$ suggest that after adjusting for other variables, capital expenditures are more closely related to previous actual capital expenditures than to capital expenditure anticipations. In durables, for example, the coefficient 0.575 may be taken to signify that capital expenditures equal capital-expenditure anticipations plus effects due to sales changes and changes in unfilled orders plus 0.575 of the difference between previous capital expenditures and the concurrent anticipations of current expenditures. Thus, when adjusted for other factors, a point 0.575 of the way from anticipations to previous capital expenditures may be taken as the predictor of current capital expenditures.

Third, we may note the substantial effect of changes in demand as measured in the coefficients of changes in sales and changes in unfilled orders. These are most marked in the case of nondurables but are also quite clear in durables and commercial capital expenditures as well. Only in utilities do these variables offer little or nothing in the way of explanation of the divergence between capital expenditures and their anticipations. This, as conjectured above, may relate to the relatively long-run character of much utility investment. One might expect little divergence between capital expenditures and their anticipations on the basis of changes that occur in the one or two quarters previous to the expenditures.

Finally, we may wish to note some of the long-run adjustment coefficients. Each of these indicates the total eventual effect on investment realizations, that is, the divergence between actual and anticipated expenditures expressed as a ratio of capital-expenditure anticipations, of a unit change of an independent variable in any particular period. Thus, the coefficient 1.561 for a_s^L, in the case of nondurables, may be taken to mean that a permanent one per cent increase in sales would, over an infinity of time, generate a

TABLE 3.8

Structural equations with changes in sales, profits, and unfilled orders of machinery (transformations from table 3.6).

Variables or parameters	Regression coefficients and standard errors						
	Sector						
	Durable manufacturing (MD)			Public utilities (RP)		Commercial (O*3)	
	Eq. (3.16s)	(3.17s)	(3.18s)	(3.19s)	(3.20s)	(3.21s)	(3.22
Constant term	0.000	−0.001	0.000	−0.014	−0.019	0.004	0.00£
	(0.008)	(0.013)	(0.008)	(0.014)	(0.013)	(0.005)	(0.00£
$\dfrac{[S^{54}]_{-1}-[S^{54}]_{-2}}{[S^{54}]_{-2}}$	−0.040	0.181		0.327	0.424	0.253	
	(0.205)	(0.204)		(0.250)	(0.269)	(0.205)	
$\dfrac{[Z_{AU}^{NS54}]_{-1}-[Z_{AU}^{NS54}]_{-2}}{[Z_{AU}^{NS54}]_{-2}}$	0.103	0.042	0.097	−0.068	−0.089	0.105	0.134
	(0.055)	(0.055)	(0.032)	(0.052)	(0.056)	(0.054)	(0.047
γ	0.254	0.439	0.253	0.303	0.277	0.069	0.074
	(0.113)	(0.100)	(0.111)	(0.101)	(0.105)	(0.079)	(0.07£
$\dfrac{[S^{54}]_{-2-i}-[S^{54}]_{-3-i}}{[S^{54}]_{-3-i}}$	0.016	0.263		0.099	0.171	−0.049	
	(0.200)	(0.208)		(0.248)	(0.257)	(0.208)	
$\dfrac{[Z_{AU}^{NS54}]_{-2-i}-[Z_{AU}^{NS54}]_{-3-i}}{[Z_{AU}^{NS54}]_{-3-i}}$	0.097	0.029	0.097	0.026	0.021	0.069	0.071
	(0.064)	(0.072)	(0.036)	(0.052)	(0.052)	(0.056)	(0.048
$\dfrac{[O_{U_{35+36}}^{54}]_{-1-i}-[O_{U_{35+36}}^{54}]_{-2-i}}{[IA^{54}]_{-1-i}}$	0.111		0.111		−0.022	0.059	0.056
	(0.038)		(0.033)		(0.022)	(0.029)	(0.029
$\dfrac{[I_{BUS}^{54}]_{-1-i}-[IA^{54}]_{-i}}{[I_{BUS}^{54}]_{-1-i}}$	0.576	0.438	0.580	0.396	0.388	0.657	0.646
	(0.106)	(0.101)	(0.103)	(0.084)	(0.105)	(0.084)	(0.082
a_s^L	−0.019	0.640		0.469	0.661	0.200	
a_p^L	0.233	0.094	0.227	−0.031	−0.060	0.179	0.211
a_m^L	0.149		0.149		−0.030	0.063	0.060
a_I^L	0.772	0.781	0.776	0.568	0.537	0.706	0.698

Note a^L terms are long-run adjustment coefficients $a_s^L = a_1 + (a_3/(1-\gamma))$, $a_m^L = a_5/(1-\gamma)$, $a_p^L = a_2 + (a_4/(1-\gamma))$, $a_I^L = (a_6/(1-\gamma))$.

TABLE 3.9

rrors in anticipations versus errors in predictions from structural equations with sales realizations and profits
hanges: manufacturing, 1949 : 3 to 1960 : 4; nondurables, 1953 : 4 to 1960 : 4 (millions of 1954 dollars).

Teasure	Errors of prediction		Nondurable manufacturing (MN)
	Manufacturing (M)		
	Eq. (3.5s)	Eq. (3.6s)	Eq. (3.7s)
Mean error			
Anticipations: $(1/n) \sum (I_{BUS} - IA)$	-307	-307	-160
Predictions: $(1/n) \sum (I_{BUS} - \widehat{I_{BUS}})$	-115	-12	-52
Mean absolute error			
Anticipations: $(1/n) \sum |I_{BUS} - IA|$	519	519	291
Predictions: $(1/n) \sum |I_{BUS} - \widehat{I_{BUS}}|$	395	255	170
Root mean square of error			
Anticipations: $\sqrt{(1/n) \sum (I_{BUS} - IA)^2}$	670	670	374
Predictions: $\sqrt{(n^*/n^* - k) \cdot (\sum (I_{BUS} - \widehat{I_{BUS}})^2/n)}$	500	355	255
Number of observations, n	46	46	29
Number of independent parameters in estimating equation, k	5	6	6
Number of observations in estimating equation, n^*	50	50	33
erial correlation coefficient for errors of predictions	0.492	0.200	0.053
Durbin-Watson ratio for errors of predictions	1.015	1.584	1.734

1.561 per cent excess of capital expenditures over capital-expenditure anticipations.

3.6. Accuracy of prediction

We offer two kinds of measures of the possible usefulness of the realizations function for purposes of prediction and forecasting. One set of measures involves application of the estimated structural relations to the data from which they were estimated. Thus, for the period 1948 through 1960, we may compare the "errors of anticipations", that is, the differences between actual and anticipated quarterly, seasonally adjusted values of capital expenditures at annual rates, with the "errors of predictions", defined as the differences between actual capital expenditures and the values of capital expenditures predicted by the structural relations calculated from the transformed estimating equations.

Comparison of the mean errors of predictions and anticipations is hardly useful for the period from which the estimates were derived because of the well-known properties of least-squares estimates with reasonably normal

TABLE 3.10

Errors in anticipations versus errors in predictions from structural equations with sales changes and profi *changes: durables, nondurables, utilities and commercial, 1949 : 1 to 1960 : 4 (millions of 1954 dollars*

Measure	Errors of prediction				
	Durable manufac- turing (*MD*)	Nondurable manufactur- ing (*MN*)	Public utilities (*RP*)	Commer- cial (*O**3)	Tota
	Eq. (3.8s)	Eq. (3.9s)	Eq. (3.10s)	Eq. (3.11s)	
Mean error					
Anticipations: $(1/n) \sum (I_{\text{BUS}} - IA)$	−140	−156	−184	42	−43
Predictions: $(1/n) \sum (I_{\text{BUS}} - \widehat{I_{\text{BUS}}})$	−14	1	−34	25	−2
Mean absolute error					
Anticipations: $(1/n) \sum |I_{\text{BUS}} - IA|$	323	307	230	317	73
Predictions: $(1/n) \sum |I_{\text{BUS}} - \widehat{I_{\text{BUS}}}|$	219	172	134	185	40
Root mean square of error					
Anticipations: $\sqrt{(1/n) \sum (I_{\text{BUS}} - IA)^2}$	377	388	282	410	88
Predictions: $\sqrt{(n^*/n^*-k) \cdot (\sum(I_{\text{BUS}} - \widehat{I_{\text{BUS}}})^2/n)}$	297	233	184	258	56
Number of observations, *n*	48	48	48	48	4
Number of independent parameters in estimating equation, *k*	7	7	7	7	
Number of observations in estimating equation, *n**	52	52	52	52	5
Serial correlation coefficient for errors of prediction	0.533	0.183	0.036	0.330	0.29
Durbin-Watson ratio for errors of prediction	0.933	1.600	1.919	1.340	1.40

(or merely unskewed) residuals. (While estimates were made from variables in ratio form, this transformation was not such as to alter seriously the characteristics of the distribution of the residuals.) The mean error of predictions may be expected to approximate zero, and indeed it does, as indicated in tables 3.9 and 3.10, relating to 1948–1960 observations and the equations of tables 3.3 and 3.4, which did not utilize changes in unfilled orders of machinery.

A more meaningful measure is to be found in the mean of absolute values of errors in that while the least-squares properties would again virtually insure the greater accuracy of predictions, the relative magnitude of means of absolute errors offers some indication of the goodness of fit of the esti- mated structural relation. Further examination of tables 3.8 and 3.9 shows that the mean absolute error of predictions for equations excluding the orders variable (but including $([I_{\text{BUS}}^{54}]_{-1} - IA^{54})/I_{\text{BUS}}^{54}]_{-1})$ generally ran to less than 60 per cent of the mean absolute error of anticipations.

Perhaps the most useful tool for comparison of anticipations and predictions during the period from which the relations were estimated is the root mean square error. This is the mean of the squared differences between actual and anticipated values in the case of errors of anticipations and a similar mean adjusted for lost degrees of freedom in the case of errors of predictions. Examination of these root mean squares indicates that the error of predictions was substantially the smaller of the two. As seen, again, in tables 3.9 and 3.10, for equations with $([I_{BUS}^{54}]_{-1} - IA^{54})/[I_{BUS}^{54}]_{-1}$ but without changes in unfilled orders for machinery, it averaged about 60 per cent of the value of the error of anticipations.

TABLE 3.11

Forecasts of 1961: means of errors in anticipations and predictions (millions of 1954 dollars).

		Anticipations	Predictions
A.	Manufacturing, 1948 : 3 to 1960 : 4, equation (3.5s) a)		
	Mean error	−274	192
	Mean of absolute values of errors	274	363
B.	Manufacturing, 1948 : 3 to 1960 : 4, equation (3.6s) a)		
	Mean error	−274	136
	Mean of absolute values of errors	274	338
C.	Nondurable manufacturing, 1952 : 4 to 1960 : 4, equation (3.7s) a)		
	Mean error	−61	64
	Mean of absolute values of errors	98	210
D.	Durable manufacturing, equation (3.8s) b)		
	Mean error	−244	−143
	Mean of absolute values of errors	273	169
E.	Nondurable manufacturing, equation (3.9s) b)		
	Mean error	−61	42
	Mean of absolute values of errors	98	158
F.	Public utilities, equation (3.10s) b)		
	Mean error	−364	−124
	Mean of absolute values of errors	364	124
G.	Commercial, equation (3.11s) b)		
	Mean error	238	146
	Mean of absolute values of errors	424	313

a) Using sales realizations.   b) Using sales changes.

A second, more exacting test of the usefulness of our realizations function is provided by extrapolation of the relations to observations other than those used in estimating them. Such a test has been made initially with 1961 data, using equations estimated from observations ending in 1960. Further tests have then been carried out on forecasts of 1962 and the first two quarters of 1963, using equations estimated from observations through 1961. Again several possible measures of accuracy might be offered. We have concentrated attention on two: mean errors and means of absolute values of errors.

Tables 3.11 and 3.12 report these errors in 1961 forecasts on the basis of equations including changes in sales and profits but not unfilled orders for machinery. Mean errors of predictions in "all manufacturing", utilizing structural equations with sales realizations and changes in profits, shown in table 3.11, suggest that the realizations function performs nobly. While the superiority of predictions using the sales-realization variable does not apply to nondurables alone, even by the mean error test, it may be argued that in trying to improve on anticipations the target is usually small, and here it was impossibly small. The mean error of 1961 nondurables predictions of $ 64 million was little more than one per cent of actual capital expenditures, but this was not less (in absolute magnitude) than the mean error of anticipations of $-$ $ 61 million.

TABLE 3.12

Forecasts of 1961: Totals in manufacturing and all sectors; capital expenditures, anticipations and predictions using structural equations with sales changes (millions of 1954 dollars).

Quarter	Actual expenditures I_{BUS}	Anticipations IA	Predictions $\widehat{I_{BUS}}$	Errors of anticipations $[I_{BUS}-IA]$	Errors of predictions $[I_{BUS}-\widehat{I_{BUS}}]$
		A. Total manufacturing (durables plus nondurables)			
1961 : 1	11 203	11 710	11 296	-507	$-$ 93
1961 : 2	10 969	11 163	10 713	-194	256
1961 : 3	11 061	11 456	11 441	-395	-380
1961 : 4	11 384	11 506	11 571	-122	-187
Mean error				-304	-101
Mean of absolute values of errors				304	229
		B. Total: manufacturing, utilities and commercial			
1961 : 1	24 769	25 958	25 360	-1 189	-591
1961 : 2	24 416	24 607	24 173	$-$ 191	243
1961 : 3	25 241	25 228	25 145	13	96
1961 : 4	25 939	26 294	26 005	-355	-66
Mean error				-430	-80
Mean of absolute values of errors				437	249

It may be noted further that the implicit sales-realization variable which we have been able to synthesize reasonably well only in manufacturing is a quite imperfect measure of sales realizations. Until more quarterly data on sales expectations become available, it may be best to emphasize results with relations using simple sales changes rather than sales realizations.

Extrapolations of the sales-change relations to 1961 do well by the mean error test. Results are shown in table 3.12 in the form of totals for manufacturing durables and nondurables, and for these plus utilities and commercial. The total manufacturing mean error of predictions was only $- \$ 101$ million, compared with a mean error of anticipations of $- \$ 304$ million. For the total of all industries the mean error of predictions was only $- \$ 80$ million, which may be compared with a mean error of anticipations of $- \$ 430$ million, and total capital expenditures in the neighborhood of $\$ 25$ billion.

However, it may well be argued that mean errors present a misleadingly favorable picture of the success of predictions. With manufacturing structural equations using sales realizations, in particular, there were very large second-quarter errors in predictions which were partly compensated by errors in the opposite direction in subsequent quarters [8]). A more severe test of predictions might be the comparison with anticipations based upon means of absolute values of errors.

The predictions using structural equations with sales realizations do not turn out so well on such a test. For all manufacturing, as seen in table 3.11, the means of absolute values of errors of predictions were $\$ 363$ million and $\$ 338$ million, respectively, for equations with and without $([I^{54}_{BUS}]_{-1} - IA^{54})/[I^{54}_{BUS}]_{-1}$, as against a mean absolute error of anticipations of only $\$ 274$ million. For nondurables the error of predictions was $\$ 210$ million, compared to only $\$ 98$ million for anticipations.

Again the equations using sales changes, rather than the synthetic sales realization variable, do better. Table 3.11 reveals that for these equations the mean absolute error of predictions in manufacturing durables was $\$ 169$ million in 1961, as compared to $\$ 273$ million for raw anticipations. In nondurables, however, the mean absolute error of predictions was more than that for anticipations: $\$ 158$ million compared with $\$ 98$ million. In utilities, predictions carried the day decisively, with a mean absolute error

---

[8]) These errors in predictions for manufacturing using sales realizations can be accounted for by the major drop in our first-quarter profits figures reported by the Federal Trade Commission and Securities and Exchange Commission. As a consequence, for all manufacturing, the immediately previous change-in-profits variable was -0.179 in the second quarter of 1961 and $+0.363$ in the third quarter of 1961. The more distant change-in-profits variable was of course -0.179 in the third quarter of 1961. Except for these extreme fluctuations in reported profits, both the second- and third-quarter predictions would have been relatively accurate. Predictions based upon equations using sales changes, containing very small profits coefficients, are also more accurate.

TABLE 3.13

Forecasts of 1962 and 1963: durable manufacturing; based on equations (3.12) and (3.12s) containing changes in sales and unfilled orders of machinery and differences between anticipations and previous capital expenditures (millions of 1954 dollars).

Year and quarter	Expenditures				Errors			
	Actual	Antici-pated	Predicted		"Naive Model"	Antici-pations	Predictions	
			Structural	Direct			Structural	Direct
	I_{BUS}	IA	$\hat{I}_{BUS}$ from (3.12s)	$\hat{I}_{BUS}$ from (3.12)	$I_{BUS}-[I_{BUS}]_{-1}$	$[I_{BUS}-IA]$	$[I_{BUS}-\hat{I}_{BUS}]$	
1962 : 1	5 334	5 448	5 419	5 434	130	−114	−85	−100
1962 : 2	5 626	5 864	5 622	5 597	292	−238	4	29
1962 : 3	5 850	5 747	5 656	5 657	224	103	194	193
1962 : 4	5 917	5 850	5 854	5 907	67	67	63	10
1963 : 1	5 952	5 755	5 828	5 845	35	197	124	107
1963 : 2	6 177	5 911	5 981	6 015	225	266	196	162
1963 : 3		6 419	6 387	6 444				
Mean error, 1962 : 1 to 1963 : 2					162	47	83	67
Mean of absolute values of errors, 1962 : 1 to 1963:2					162	164	111	100

of only $ 124 million, compared to $ 364 million for anticipations. In the commercial sector, also, predictions turned out better than anticipations. Here the margin was $ 313 million to $ 424 million for anticipations.

Table 3.12, dealing with totals, shows predictions securing a greater advantage than anticipations from offsetting industry errors. Thus, the mean absolute error of predictions obtained for all manufacturing by summing predictions for durables and nondurables was $ 229 million, while the mean absolute error of anticipations was $ 304 million.

Perhaps the most interesting single test involves the comparison of combined anticipations and predictions for manufacturing, utilities and commercial. As noted earlier, these industries account for some 90 per cent of U. S. business capital expenditures. The results, displayed in section B of table 3.12, are a fairly clear victory for predictions. The mean absolute errors of anticipations, swelled by an overestimate of more than $ 1 billion in the first quarter, was $ 437 million. The mean absolute error of predictions was $ 249 million.

It may be noted that all predictions presented thus far have been based upon the structural equations, that is, our retransformations of the estimated equations. This may be justified on the assumption that the structural relations describe correctly the economic behavior with which we are concerned. A statistical implication of this assumption is that disturbances are not auto-correlated and, correspondingly, residuals from the structural equations are not serially correlated.

Now, actually, the residuals from the structural equations are serially correlated. Indeed, one merit of the transformation used for estimating purposes is that it transforms the disturbances in such a way as to introduce a negative autocorrelation, which would offset, for estimating purposes, any positive autocorrelation in the original structural disturbances. Durbin-Watson ratios reveal, however, that even with the transformation, residuals from the estimating equations were frequently positively serially correlated. Thus there is definite evidence of positive autocorrelation in the disturbances, evidence which has been sustained by tests of serial correlation in the errors of prediction from the structural equations.

Serial correlation in errors of predictions may be explained in terms of our earlier hypothesis that anticipations reflect essentially investment demand, while actual expenditures are also influenced by conditions of supply. But conditions of short supply, or acceleration of supply as backlogs are eased, are likely to persist for more than one quarter. For purposes of forecasting, therefore, we might do well to take into account the serial correlation of errors of anticipations, a serial correlation which will persist in errors of prediction if predictions are based exclusively on arguments of the investment *demand* function.

All this implies that we may do better in predictions from single equations if we use the originally estimated equations rather than the structural equations calculated from these estimates, for the original estimating equations, it will be recalled, include lagged capital expenditure realizations. That part of an error in anticipations due to a disturbance might therefore be picked up in our prediction of realizations.

We have extrapolated our originally estimated equations to 1961 data, and the results suggest that this has some merit. In all industries except durables, the errors in predictions are slightly less with the estimated equations than those we have shown using the structural equations. In view of this empirical confirmation of the suggestion that the originally estimated equations would prove more accurate in forecasting than the structural equations, balanced by our essential interest in the behavioral relations described by the structural equations, we shall report below results with both originally estimated and structural equations in our measures of accuracy of realizations function forecasts of 1962 and 1963 capital expenditures.

TABLE 3.14

Forecasts of 1962 and 1963: nondurable manufacturing; based on equations (3.13) and (3.13s) containing changes in sales and unfilled orders of machinery and differences between anticipations and previous capital expenditures (millions of 1954 dollars).

Year and quarter	Expenditures				Errors			
	Actual	Antici-pated	Predicted		"Naive Model"	Antici-pations	Predictions	
			Structural	Direct			Structural	Direct
	I_{BUS}	IA	$\widehat{I_{BUS}}$ from (3.13s)	$\widehat{I_{BUS}}$ from (3.13)	$I_{BUS}-[I_{BUS}]_{-1}$	$[I_{BUS}-IA]$	$[I_{BUS}-\widehat{I_{BUS}}]$	
1962 : 1	6 189	6 383	6 298	6 274	9	−194	−109	−85
1962 : 2	6 071	6 108	6 135	6 121	−118	−37	−64	−50
1962 : 3	6 294	6 233	6 147	6 139	223	61	147	155
1962 : 4	6 241	6 213	6 228	6 252	−53	28	13	−11
1963 : 1	6 073	6 363	6 212	6 216	−168	−290	−139	−143
1963 : 2	6 177	6 478	6 204	6 185	104	−301	−27	−8
1963 : 3		6 338	6 258	6 256				
Mean error, 1962 : 1 to 1963 : 2					−1	−122	−30	−24
Mean of absolute values of errors, 1962 : 1 to 1963 : 2					112	152	83	75

TABLE 3.15

Forecasts of 1962 and 1963: public utilities; based on equations (3.14) and (3.14s) containing changes in sales and unfilled orders of machinery and differences between anticipations and previous capital expenditures (millions of 1954 dollars).

Year and quarter	Expenditures				Errors			
	Actual	Antici-pated	Predicted		"Naive Model"	Antici-pations	Predictions	
			Structural	Direct			Structural	Direct
	I_{BUS}	IA	$\widehat{I_{BUS}}$ from (3.14s)	$\widehat{I_{BUS}}$ from (3.14)	$I_{BUS}-[I_{BUS}]_{-1}$	$[I_{BUS}-IA]$	$[I_{BUS}-\widehat{I_{BUS}}]$	
1962 : 1	4 194	4 472	4 398	4 362	−319	−278	−204	−168
1962 : 2	4 371	4 235	4 175	4 123	177	136	196	248
1962 : 3	4 640	4 614	4 464	4 520	269	26	176	120
1962 : 4	4 417	4 438	4 453	4 498	−223	−21	−36	−81
1963 : 1	4 211	4 296	4 319	4 309	−206	−85	−108	−98
1963 : 2	4 400	4 535	4 379	4 348	189	−135	21	52
1963 : 3		4 683	4 484	4 489				
Mean error, 1962 : 1 to 1963 : 2					−19	−60	8	12
Mean of absolute values of errors, 1962 : 1 to 1963 : 2					230	114	124	128

TABLE 3.16

Forecasts of 1962 and 1963: commercial; based on equations (3.15) and (3.15s) containing changes in sales and unfilled orders of machinery and differences between anticipations and previous capital expenditures (millions of 1954 dollars).

Year and quarter	Expenditures				Errors			
	Actual	Antici-pated	Predicted		"Naive Model"	Antici-pations	Predictions	
			Structural	Direct			Structural	Direct
	I_{BUS}	IA	$\hat{I}_{BUS}$	$\hat{I}_{BUS}$	$I_{BUS}-[I_{BUS}]_{-1}$	$[I_{BUS}-IA]$	$[I_{BUS}-\hat{I}_{BUS}]$	
			from (3.15s)	from (3.15)				
1962 : 1	10 139	10 490	10 390	10 419	97	−351	−251	−280
1962 : 2	10 402	10 587	10 379	10 357	263	−185	23	45
1962 : 3	10 853	10 928	10 621	10 623	451	−75	232	230
1962 : 4	11 185	11 055	10 950	10 971	332	130	235	214
1963 : 1	10 689	11 185	11 246	11 267	−496	−496	−557	−578
1963 : 2	10 738	11 094	10 916	10 867	49	−356	−178	−129
1963 : 3		11 505	10 971	10 954				
Mean error, 1962 : 1 to 1963 : 2					116	−222	−83	83
Mean of absolute value of errors 1962 : 1 to 1963 : 2					281	266	246	246

TABLE 3.17

Forecasts of 1962 and 1963: total—durables, nondurables, public utilities, and commercial; based on equations containing changes in sales and unfilled orders of machinery and differences between anticipations and previous capital expenditures (millions of 1954 dollars).

Year and quarter	Expenditures				Errors			
	Actual	Antici-pated	Predicted		"Naive Model"	Antici-pations	Predictions	
			Structural	Direct			Structural	Direct
	I_{BUS}	IA	$\hat{I}_{BUS}$		$I_{BUS}-[I_{BUS}]_{-1}$	$[I_{BUS}-IA]$	$[I_{BUS}-\hat{I}_{BUS}]$	
1962 : 1	25 856	26 793	26 505	26 489	550	−937	−649	−633
1962 : 2	26 470	26 794	26 311	26 198	614	−324	159	272
1962 : 3	27 637	27 522	26 888	26 939	1 167	115	749	698
1962 : 4	27 760	27 556	27 485	27 628	123	204	275	132
1963 : 1	26 925	27 599	27 605	27 637	−835	−674	−680	−712
1963 : 2	27 492	28 018	27 480	27 415	567	−526	12	77
1963 : 3		28 913	28 100	28 143				
Mean error, 1962 : 1 to 1963 : 2					364	−357	−22	−28
Mean of absolute values of errors 1962 : 1 to 1963 : 2					643	463	421	421

Forecasts of 1962 and 1963 capital expenditures have been made on the basis of equations analogous to those reported in tables 3.5 and 3.6 and tables 3.7 and 3.8 but estimated from observations ending with the fourth quarter of 1961[9]). Results for the relations using changes in unfilled orders of machinery and changes in sales are shown in tables 3.13 through 3.17, quarter-by-quarter and industry-by-industry, along with mean errors and means of absolute errors for each industry and for the total of all industries. The accuracy of forecasts based on predictions from the realizations function can now be compared both with the accuracy of anticipations alone and with "naive model" forecasts based on the assumption that capital expenditures in any quarter will be the same as in the previous quarter. Summary results for equations using change-in-profit variables are reported in table 3.18.

Predictions from the equations including changes in sales and unfilled orders but not changes in profits are not sensational in their accuracy as compared with the anticipatory data alone, but again suggest some merit to the realizations function approach. In durables, the mean error of anticipations was only $ 47 million, as shown in table 3.13. The corresponding mean errors of predictions were $ 83 million with the structural equation from table 3.7, and $ 67 million with the directly estimated equation from table 3.5. The difference between anticipations and predictions, however, was fairly well accounted for by a large offsetting anticipations error of − $ 238 million in the second quarter of 1962, when predictions were almost perfectly accurate (errors of $ 4 million or $ 29 million). The mean of absolute values of errors of durables anticipations was $ 164 million, while the mean of absolute values of errors in predictions was $ 111 million with the structural equation and $ 100 million with the estimated equation. The "naive model" mean of absolute errors, as well as mean error, was $ 162 million.

For nondurables, mean expenditures were $ 122 million less than anticipations but only $ 30 million less than structural predictions and $ 24 million less than predictions from the directly estimated equations, as seen in table 3.14. Predictions were more accurate than anticipations in four of the six quarters (and more accurate than "naive model" forecasts in five of six quarters) ending with remarkable (or lucky?) prediction errors of $ 27 million and $ 8 million in the second quarter of 1963, where antici-

---

[9]) The equations estimated from data through 1961 are in fact very similar to those utilizing all the data through 1962.

TABLE 3.18

Comparison of forecasts using change-in-profit variables.

Industry and quarters predicted	Means of absolute values of errors of predictions (millions of 1954 dollars)						
	From equations including $\dfrac{[I_{BUS}]_{-1} - IA}{[I_{BUS}]_{-1}}$ and						
	ΔS ΔO_U	ΔS ΔZ_{AU}	ΔS ΔZ^*_{AU} ΔO_U	ΔZ_{AU} ΔO_U ΔO_U	ΔZ^*_{AU} ΔO_U	ΔS ΔZ_{AU}	ΔS ΔZ^*_{AU}
A. Structural equations $[I_{BUS} - \widehat{I_{BUS}}]$							
Durable manufacturing 1962 : 1–1963 : 2	111	135	135	134	133	—	—
Public utilities 1962 : 1–1963 : 1	144	160	136	—	—	153	137
Commercial 1962 : 1–1963 : 1	260	371	324	371	313	—	—
B. Directly estimated equations $[I_{BUS} - \widehat{I_{BUS}}]$							
Durable manufacturing 1962 : 1–1963 : 2	100	120	110	117	109	—	—
Public utilities 1962 : 1–1963 : 1	143	136	124	—	—	133	126
Commercial 1962 : 1–1963 : 1	269	375	329	374	318	—	—

Note ΔZ^*_{AU} is change in after-tax profits adjusted to be consistent with previous profits figures but to include 1962 and 1963 effects of new depreciation guidelines and investment tax credit. The change-in-unfilled-orders variable (ΔO_U) is for total machinery (industries 35 plus 36).

pations were off \$ 301 million. Thus, the mean errors of predictions for nondurables were only $-$\$ 30 million and $-$\$ 24 million from structural and directly estimated equations, respectively, compared with a mean error of anticipations of $-$\$ 122 million (and a mean "naive model" error of only $-$\$ 1 million!). By the absolute value test, predictions were best. The means of absolute values in errors were \$ 152 million for anticipations, \$ 112 million for the "naive model", and \$ 83 million and \$ 75 million for structural and direct predictions, respectively.

For utilities the mean error of predictions was a trifling \$ 8 million, or \$ 12 million using the directly estimated equations, compared with $-$\$ 60 million for anticipations. Here though, the means of absolute errors of predictions were \$ 124 million and \$ 128 million, actually somewhat higher than the \$ 114 million for the mean of absolute values of anticipations but less than the $ 230 million for the "nai e model", as shown in table 3.15.

In commercial capital expenditures, the mean error of anticipations was − $ 222 million and the mean error of predictions (by either method) only − $ 83 million. In this case, however, it was predictions that benefited substantially from offsetting errors in different quarters. By the mean of absolute values test, predictions (by either method) were still more accurate but only by a very slight amount: $ 246 million as against $ 266 million for anticipations and $ 281 million for the "naive model". Details are offered in table 3.16.

Putting these results together we find that in three of the four industries (all except durables) predictions fared better than anticipations by the ordinary mean-of-errors test. Likewise, in three of the four industries (this time all except utilities) predictions fared better by the mean-of-absolute-errors test. And by this latter test, predictions were better than the "naive model" in all four industries. Comparing the sums of anticipations and predictions for all industries, we see in table 3.17 that the mean error of anticipations was − $ 357 million while the mean errors of predictions were only − $ 22 million and − $ 28 million for structural and directly estimated equations, respectively. The mean of absolute values of errors test here is decisive. The mean of absolute values of errors of anticipations was $ 463 million, while the mean of absolute values for both sets of predictions was only the moderately smaller $ 421 million. The mean of absolute errors of the "naive model", however, was the considerably higher figure of $ 643 million. Finally, one may compare the sum of the absolute values of errors in each industry. For the "naive model" which uses previous actual expenditures as the current forecast, this sum is $ 786 million; for anticipations the result is $ 696 million; while for predictions it is $ 564 million and $ 549 million for structural and direct estimates, respectively.

In preparing predictions from the additional equations including profits changes shown in tables 3.6 and 3.8, profits variables were adjusted from their reported values in an attempt to take into account the new ("guideline") liberalization of depreciation, assumed effective in the first quarter of 1962, and the investment tax credit, assumed effective in the third quarter of 1962. (Estimates of the magnitude of these two factors were derived from tables published by Lawrence Bridge in the *Survey of Current Business*, August 1963). Predictions utilizing the adjusted-profits variable proved generally somewhat more accurate than those using unadjusted profits, but in the case of durables and commercial capital expenditures the equations containing profits and sales proved less accurate by a mean-of-absolute-errors test (mean errors 9 per cent and 18 per cent greater, *at best*) than the equations excluding profits. In utilities, however, the best adjusted-profits equation was 13 per cent more accurate, in terms of means of absolute errors, than the equation without profits. A general comparison of the accuracy of forecasting equations using profits and sales variables is to be found in table 3.18 [10]).

3.7. *Summary and conclusions*

Despite a number of crude improvisations with underlying postwar data, we have been able to secure economically meaningful estimates of parameters of a distributed lag realizations function for quarterly capital expenditures. In all major industry groups a variable measuring the relative deviation of previous actual expenditures from the concurrently expressed anticipations of present expenditures proved significantly related to current errors of anticipations. Lagged sales changes were also positively associated with the error in anticipations in all industries. The association was most marked in the case of nondurables but barely different from zero in the case of utilities. A synthetic quarterly sales realization variable constructed in manufacturing, while also related positively to investment realizations, proved generally less useful than changes in actual sales. Previous changes in unfilled orders for machinery were positively related to the deviation of actual from anticipated expenditures in all industries except utilities. Profits changes generally added little to explained variance not already accounted for by other variables and were in some instances negatively related to the deviations between actual and anticipated expenditures.

The realizations function explained substantial portions of the error of anticipations for the observations from which it was estimated. Probably more important, the estimated equations and, to a slightly smaller degree, the structural equations calculated from them appeared somewhat superior to anticipations, and, a fortiori, to "naive model" forecasts in predicting in quarters after the periods of observations used for estimation. The record,

---

[10]) Other results, not presented in the tables, may be mentioned briefly. Equations estimated from observations to 1959 including sales and profits changes, but not unfilled inventories, were used earlier to predict 1960 utilities and commercial quarterly expenditures. The mean 1960 error of anticipations for the total expenditures of these industries was minus $ 285 million. The mean error of predictions was minus $ 13 million, out of expenditures of some $ 14 *billion!* The mean of absolute values of 1960 errors of anticipations for the utilities and commercial total was $ 400 million. The corresponding mean absolute error of predictions was $150 million.

however, is sufficiently mixed to call for careful attention to difficulties underlying the approach and to possible modifications in its application.

A number of improvements in the quality of the data are clearly in order. Some measure of seasonally adjusted sales or output changes should be introduced in utilities. In the commercial sector, measures of sales (and profits) corresponding reasonably precisely to the capital expenditure data should be utilized. One generally should be wary of errors in measurement. With changing tax laws and accounting treatment, reported profits are a particularly ill-defined and uncertainly measured variable. One may indeed even wonder whether actual capital expenditures are reported and measured precisely. Perhaps, in some instances, our predictions are a more accurate measure of actual expenditures than the figures for actual expenditures reported by the Department of Commerce! And a few of our predictions may prove more accurate when measured against revised figures for actual expenditures.

However, with all possible improvements in data and with all due allowances for errors in measurement and other "excuses", one should be under no illusions as to the potentialities of realizations functions limited to arguments of the kind used here. We must recognize that capital expenditures are based upon anticipations of their probable effects. These must relate largely to anticipations of the economic situation in prospect during the period from acquisition to likely disposal of the contemplated plant and equipment. Clearly, we can only expect to capture imperfectly, if at all, relevant changes in these anticipations. How, for example, can changes in past sales or unfilled orders be used to predict the capital expenditures stemming from developing anticipations of the effects of an $ 11 billion tax cut as the tax cut bill makes its tortuous progress through the houses of Congress and their committees? These various anticipations and the variables that determine them are conceptually measurable and useable in equations such as ours. But we are still a considerable way from getting all of the necessary measures and estimating the stable relations embodying these measures and from using the equations for accurate and fully reliable predictions.

On a positive note, while much work remains to be done, findings thus far do seem to suggest the potential usefulness of a realizations function, even as an isolated forecasting device. It may be hoped that such a function will also prove useful, both for forecasting and for predictions of the effects of parameter shifts and changes in exogenous variables, as part of a multi-equation econometric model encompassing the economy as a whole.

CHAPTER 4

FACTORS INFLUENCING INVESTMENT IN INVENTORIES

Contents

4.1. Introduction. 131

4.2. The manufacturing sector. 134

4.3. The trade sector 143

1. Limitations and qualifications affecting findings. 2. Some a priori considerations. 3. Regression findings 4. Suggestions for further research on trade inventory behavior.

4.4. Appendix. Supplementary tables. 157

References 160

FACTORS INFLUENCING INVESTMENT IN INVENTORIES

PAUL G. DARLING

Bowdoin College, Brunswick, Maine

and

MICHAEL C. LOVELL

Carnegie Institute of Technology, Pittsburgh, Pennsylvania [1])

4.1. Introduction

An econometric model of the U.S. economy, whether it be used to test cycle theories, to simulate the short-run impact of policy measures or to forecast short-term movements of the economy, must, if it is to be fruitful, contain sensitive functions determining investment in inventories. Mere inspection of national income and output statistics for the postwar period shows that the inventory investment component of aggregate demand fluctuates widely over the course of actual cycles in business activity. Using changes in deflated "goods output" (i.e. GNP less services and construction) during the intervals between peaks and troughs to measure the period's cycles [2]), one finds that shifts from investment to disinvestment in business inventories accounted for 60 per cent of the shrinkage in aggregate demand for goods output during the four recessions 1948–1949, 1953–1954, 1957–1958 and 1960–1961; during the first year of four periods of business expansion, on the other hand, shifts from disinvestment to investment in stocks accounted

---

[1]) Lovell's research on inventory behavior reported herein is supported by a National Science Foundation grant. His computations were performed at Yale University computation center by Seong Y. Park.

[2]) Cyclical fluctuations in output during the postwar years have manifested themselves almost entirely in the goods-producing sectors of the economy, while the service and construction components have exhibited predominantly smooth upward-sloping trends. For this reason "goods output" (GNP minus services and construction) is used for dating and measuring postwar cycles.

TABLE 4.1

Comparison of cyclical changes in business inventory investment and in goods output (GNP less services and construction) during the postwar period (based on seasonally adjusted quarterly data at annual rates in billions of constant 1954 dollars).

Period	Change in goods output	Change in inventory investment	Change in inventory investment as per cent of change in goods output
Four contractions			
1948 : 4 through 1949 : 4	−9.4	−10.1	107.4
1953 : 2 through 1954 : 2	−16.8	−6.1	36.3
1957 : 1 through 1958 : 1	−19.3	−7.1	36.8
1960 : 1 through 1961 : 1	−14.5	−12.6	86.9
Totals	−60.0	−35.9	59.8
First year of four expansions			
1949 : 4 through 1950 : 4	+26.9	+21.5	79.9
1954 : 2 through 1955 : 2	+19.5	+9.4	48.2
1958 : 1 through 1959 : 1	+17.6	+10.2	58.0
1961 : 1 through 1962 : 1	+22.9	+8.9	38.9
Totals	+96.9	+50.0	57.5

Source of underlying data: *U. S. Income and Output, 1958; Survey of Current Business*, July, 1962, and May, 1963.

for 58 per cent of the increase in total demand for goods [3]). Table 4.1 shows the detail underlying the calculations. These comparisons fall short of disclosing the full impact of the "inventory mechanism" on business cycles because they abstract from the feedback effects on other spending streams which are attributable to alterations in production and income. Evidence exists that both consumption and plant and equipment expenditures are affected by the income changes which stem from inventory-induced shifts in the level of production [4]). These considerations make it reasonably

[3]) For calculations relating inventory investment changes over cycles to total *GNP*, as contrasted with the above comparison with the goods components only, see Abramovitz [1, pp. 4–8] for the pre-World War II period and Stanback [17, Ch. 2] for both prewar and postwar comparisons.

[4]) See Darling [5, Ch. III], especially Tables 6 and 7. A comparison of actual *GNP* with a hypothetical *GNP* series corresponding to the path effective demand would have followed in the absence of inventory investment and the consumption it generates will be found in Lovell [12].

clear that the ability of an econometric model to conform in its movements to the actual short-run cyclical fluctuations of the U.S. economy
will hinge in large part on the precision of its inventory investment
equations.

The success achieved by the model in simulating the short-run impact of
policy measures will also depend to a considerable degree on the realism
of its inventory investment relationships. Changes in such policy variables
as tax rates, government purchases and transfer payments, and the cost and
availability of money, affect private and public spending streams and the
flow of new orders. These effects induce, in turn, changes in inventory
positions. Thus the economy's short-run response to a change in a policy
variable is likely to be an oscillatory, not a smooth, movement toward a
new equilibrium position. An accurate simulation of this short-run response
must rely on the "acceleration" forces inherent in the model's inventory
investment equations.

Where the model is used for long-run projections, however, the importance
of the inventory investment equations is much diminished. Over the long
haul, the net demand for output for the purpose of inventory accumulation
is a very small proportion of total output itself. To illustrate: from the
cyclical peak in deflated *GNP* in the fourth quarter of 1948 to the peak in the
second quarter of 1960, a period of eleven and one-half years, business
inventories grew by $ 34 billion. But this net investment in stocks amounted
to only 0.8 per cent of the $ 4 291 billion of gross goods and services produced
during the same period and to 1.46 per cent of gross goods output alone.
The contribution of investment demand to long-run growth rests almost
entirely on expenditure for plant and equipment rather than the secular
accumulation of inventories [5]).

This chapter presents the chief results of nonfarm inventory research
accomplished to date for the Brookings-SSRC econometric model project.
Section 4.2 describes research conducted by Michael C. Lovell with respect
to the manufacturing sector of the economy, and section 4.3 the results of
some preliminary investigations by Paul G. Darling concerning the trade
sector [6]). The formulation and testing of inventory functions for the farm
sector are reported elsewhere in this volume. The chapter concludes with an

---

[5]) On this point see also Chart 2 in Lovell [12, p. 248].

[6]) Section 4.2 of this chapter was prepared by Lovell and section 4.3 by Darling. Each
author gratefully acknowledges comments on his work by the other while retaining final
responsibility for his own section of the chapter.

appendix which defines the regression variables, lists data sources, and describes the data-adjustment procedures which were employed [7]).

4.2. The manufacturing sector

The flexible-accelerator concept provides the rationale underlying the inventory regressions to be reported here. This approach, which has been employed in most recent econometric studies of inventory behavior [8]), relies upon the assumption that the cost involved in changing the level of stocks leads to only a partial adjustment each quarter of inventories toward their long-run equilibrium level. The flexible-accelerator concept implies:

$$\Delta INV = d\{INV^E - [INV]_{-1}\}, \quad 0 < d < 1,$$

where ΔINV is inventory investment, INV^E is the equilibrium (i.e., desired) level of stocks suggested by such factors as current sales volume and $[INV]_{-1}$ denotes last period's stocks [9]).

Because equilibrium stocks are generally unobserved, the implementation of this approach requires some conjecture as to how equilibrium stocks are generated. As a simple example, it might be supposed that the equilibrium inventory sales ratio is some constant, b; then if S denotes sales volume we have:

$$INV^E = bS$$

and substituting into the equation for inventory investment yields:

$$\Delta INV = dbS - d[INV]_{-1}.$$

In implementing this approach, it is desirable to consider more complicated assumptions concerning the determinants of equilibrium inventories. In addition, complications arising as a result of errors made by firms in antici- pating sales volume must be considered. While it would also be desirable to consider the possible influence of various factors upon the speed of ad- justment, this complication is not considered here [10]).

---

[7]) For a bibliography of the literature on business inventories, see [2].

[8]) See, for example [4, 5, 8 and 13].

[9]) For a more detailed exposition of this model together with citations of relevant literature see Lovell [13].

[10]) A step in this direction through the use of a large number of dummy variables has been taken by Moriguchi Chikashi [4]. This approach has not been duplicated here; whatever its merits as a procedure for estimating structure, it requires the prior identifi- cation of cycle turning points and consequently is not easily applied in a study designed with prediction as a major objective.

The traditional assumption of profit maximization does not dictate the precise form of the equation generating equilibrium stocks[11]). Consequently, it has been necessary to resort to quite simple experimentation with regard to the effects of alternative assumptions concerning precisely what factors influence desired inventory position. In addition to sales volume, attention has been given to the possible influence of unfilled orders, a variable whose importance as a determinant of inventory investment was first stressed by Thomas Stanback, Jr. [12]). Consideration has also been given to the possible role of Department of Defense procurement activity as measured by the level of Department of Defense obligations and expenditures [13]). Examination of the regressions reported here suggests that procurement activities have a definite influence upon inventories. In addition, the possible influence of the rate of interest and the extent of capacity utilization were also examined. The investigation did not suggest that interest rates have any definite impact upon inventories; more promising results with regard to the possible influence of monetary variables upon inventory behavior are reported for the trade sector in section 4.3 of this paper.

A number of explanations have been presented as to why a supplier's backlog of unfilled orders should influence his inventory position. Because of lags in the production process, a stepping up of production in order to meet an increase in demand may first manifest itself in the form of enlarged stocks of goods in process. Of course, depending upon how rapidly suppliers of inputs to the firm can respond in turn to increased orders, the growth of goods in process may be partially offset by reductions in stocks of inputs. While it is true that one might expect a spurt in demand to lead to a reduction of finished goods inventory, it is also obvious that order backlogs will not accumulate when the increase in demand is accommodated in this way. These considerations provide one explanation as to why the change in the

---

[11]) That is not to say that there is difficulty in deriving an equation explaining inventory behavior with the aid of the assumption that firms maximize profits; the point is that a vast number of candidates are compatible with it and that the invocation of the assumption offers little help in narrowing down the range of possible equations. For a detailed derivation of a number of alternative behavior equations suitable for regression analysis, cf. [7]. Of course, a second potential source of a priori information is provided by a comparison of the dynamic implications of alternative assumptions concerning inventory behavior.

[12]) Stanback's preliminary statement appeared in 1955 [16].

[13]) For an interesting discussion of this problem see Murray L. Weidenbaum [18]. For a preliminary report of an attempt to actually estimate the magnitude of Department of Defense procurement upon inventory investment, cf. Michael C. Lovell [14].

backlog of unfilled orders may appear with a positive coefficient in an equation explaining inventory behavior.

Thomas Stanback, Jr. has provided an alternative explanation for the influence of orders upon inventory investment. He argues that the desired ratio of inventory to sales is tempered by the degree of market tightness. When supply conditions are tight and delivery subject to delays and uncertainties, firms find it advisable to carry larger inventories of purchased materials in order to forestall interruptions in the production process when difficulties arise in the procurement of key items [14]). In order to formalize this argument for purposes of regression analysis, it is necessary to observe that the ratio of unfilled orders to sales, which we may denote by O_U/S, constitutes a rough index of the average delivery lag. After all, if we typically have orders outstanding for fifteen items and five are delivered each period, the delivery lag must be three periods. For the equilibrium inventory sales ratio we have:

$$\frac{INV^E}{S} = b + c \left[\frac{O_U}{S} \right].$$

When the ratio of unfilled orders to sales is substituted into the adjustment equation we obtain:

$$\Delta INV = dbS + dc[O_U] - d[INV]_{-1}.$$

Equation (4.1) of table 4.2 provides estimates of the parameters of this last equation but with the change in unfilled orders included in an attempt to improve the approximation of the delivery lag provided by the ratio of orders to sales [15]). It must be noted that the coefficient of multiple determination (R^2) is not corrected for loss of degrees of freedom. Although the Durbin-Watson statistic is reported, it must be remembered that the customary test for autocorrelation is not precise when, as here, the regression equation includes a lagged endogenous variable. Care must be taken in interpreting the standard errors of the regression coefficients, for no correction has been made for the loss of degrees of freedom involved in adjusting time series for seasonal variation [16]).

---

[14]) This is the explanation presented in Stanback's book [17].

[15]) It should be noted that the Department of Commerce orders data are not entirely appropriate, for the respondents report the orders they have received from their customers rather than orders they themselves have placed with their suppliers. Since there are no alternative data sources, it is necessary to hope that the process of aggregation over industries helps to overcome the problem.

[16]) For a discussion of the difficulties created by the use of seasonally adjusted data cf. Lovell [14].

Nothing has as yet been said about the influence upon inventory investment of errors made by firms in anticipating sales volume. Of course, to the extent that goods are made for specific order rather than manufactured to stock, this complication can be neglected. Furthermore, if the sales anticipation error is distributed independently of the other explanatory variables it can be regarded as a stochastic disturbance without fear of biasing the parameter estimates. On the other hand, considerable improvement in predictive ability might be obtained if a convenient proxy for actual expectations were available. Equation (4.2) in table 4.2 incorporates the change in sales in an attempt to take into account the impact upon stocks of erroneous sales expectations; in contrast to some earlier work [17]), the regression coefficient of the change in sales is only a fraction of its standard error, suggesting that, at least in this application, this approach does not provide a fruitful procedure for taking expectational errors into account [18]). Pending the accumulation of sufficient observations on actual anticipations [19]) it proves necessary to regard the impact of errors made by firms in anticipating sales volume as stochastic in nature, a procedure first employed by Lawrence Klein [20]) and whose theoretical justification has been spelled out in detail by Edwin Mills [15].

Equation (4.3) in table 4.2 includes Frank de Leeuw's measure of capacity utilization KU_{FR_M} [6]. Since capacity utilization is a measure of market tightness, Thomas Stanback's argument concerning the role of unfilled orders implies that this variable should be related to desired stocks of purchased materials. The capacity concept enters the regression as the product of the proportion of capacity utilized times sales volume, an approach whose appropriateness is most clearly appreciated if we consider the following simple equation for the ratio of equilibrium inventory to sales:

$$\frac{INV^E}{S} = b + c \left[\frac{O_U}{S} \right] + g \, [KU_{FR_M}].$$

---

[17]) Lovell [13].

[18]) The four-quarter change in sales was also employed under the supposition that firms often utilized the same-date-last-year as a bench mark in forming their anticipations; this mode of behavior is motivated by the desire to correct for seasonal fluctuations. This variable was not significant, perhaps because seasonally corrected data had to be employed in this study.

[19]) For a provocative study of the behavior of individual firms employing data on anticipated sales volume see Whitaker [19].

[20]) Klein reports his regression in [8]. He regards the stochastic disturbance in his inventory regression as reflecting the undesired inventories generated as a result of errors of foresight.

TABLE 4.2

Durable manufacturing inventory regressions (quarterly data in billions of 1954 dollars).

$$\Delta INV^{54}_{MD} = -3.102 - \underset{(0.0355)}{0.0827} [INV^{54}_{MD}]_{-1} + \underset{(0.0464)}{0.2174} \left[\frac{S_{MD}}{WPI_{MD}}\right] + \underset{(0.0381)}{0.1095} \left\{\Delta \left[\frac{O_{U_{MD}}}{WPI_{MD}}\right]\right\} + \underset{(0.0089)}{0.0179} \left[\frac{O_{U_{MD}}}{WPI_{MD}}\right]$$

$$R^2 = 0.567, \quad S_e = 0.460, \quad DW = 1.38 \tag{4.1}$$

$$\Delta INV^{54}_{MD} = -3.148 - \underset{(0.0371)}{0.0841} [INV^{54}_{MD}]_{-1} + \underset{(0.0536)}{0.2211} \left[\frac{S_{MD}}{WPI_{MD}}\right] - \underset{(0.0722)}{0.0107} \left\{\Delta \left[\frac{S_{MD}}{WPI_{MD}}\right]\right\}$$

$$+ \underset{(0.0391)}{0.1104} \left\{\Delta \left[\frac{O_{U_{MD}}}{WPI_{MD}}\right]\right\} + \underset{(0.0091)}{0.0177} \left[\frac{O_{U_{MD}}}{WPI_{MD}}\right]$$

$$R^2 = 0.576, \quad S_e = 0.467, \quad DW = 1.38 \tag{4.2}$$

$$\Delta INV^{54}_{MD} = -3.035 - \underset{(0.0325)}{0.0509} [INV^{54}_{MD}]_{-1} + \underset{(0.0500)}{0.1132} \left[\frac{S_{MD}}{WPI_{MD}}\right] + \underset{(0.0336)}{0.1039} \left\{\Delta \left[\frac{O_{U_{MD}}}{WPI_{MD}}\right]\right\} + \underset{(0.0084)}{0.0073} \left[\frac{O_{U_{MD}}}{WPI_{MD}}\right]$$

$$+ \underset{(0.0247)}{0.0891} [KU_{FR_M}] \cdot \left[\frac{S_{MD}}{WPI_{MD}}\right]$$

$$R^2 = 0.679, \quad S_e = 0.406, \quad DW = 1.74 \tag{4.3}$$

$$\Delta INV^{54}_{MD} = -3.485 - \underset{(0.0313)}{0.1236} [INV^{54}_{MD}]_{-1} + \underset{(0.0462)}{0.3032} \left[\frac{S_{MD}}{WPI_{MD}}\right] - \underset{(0.1538)}{0.2034} \left[\frac{G_{MLDV_F}}{WPI_{MD}}\right] + \underset{(0.0520)}{0.2063} \left[\frac{DOD_{OBL}}{WPI_{MD}}\right]$$

$$+ \underset{(0.0212)}{0.0881} [KU_{FR_M}] \left[\frac{S_{MD}}{WPI_{MD}}\right]$$

$$R^2 = 0.623, \quad S_e = 0.436, \quad DW = 1.38 \tag{4.4}$$

$$\Delta INV^{54}_{MD} = -3.545 - \underset{(0.0290)}{0.0770} [INV^{54}_{MD}]_{-1} + \underset{(0.0493)}{0.1797} \left[\frac{S_{MD}}{WPI_{MD}}\right] - \underset{(0.1314)}{0.2391} \left[\frac{G_{MLDV_F}}{WPI_{MD}}\right] + \underset{(0.0452)}{0.1806} \left[\frac{DOD_{OBL}}{WPI_{MD}}\right]$$

$$R^2 = 0.733, \quad S_e = 0.370, \quad DW = 1.70 \tag{4.5}$$

$$\Delta INV^{54}_{MD} = -3.776 - \underset{(0.0453)}{0.0611} [INV^{54}_{MD}]_{-1} + \underset{(0.0613)}{0.1744} \left[\frac{S_{MD}}{WPI_{MD}}\right] + \underset{(0.0663)}{0.0545} \left\{\Delta \left[\frac{S_{MD}}{WPI_{MD}}\right]\right\}$$

$$- \underset{(0.0519)}{0.0168} \left\{\Delta \left[\frac{O_{U_{MD}}}{WPI}\right]\right\} + \underset{(0.0110)}{0.0032} \left[\frac{O_{U_{MD}}}{WPI}\right] - \underset{(0.205)}{0.3302} \left[\frac{G_{MLDV_F}}{WPI_{MD}}\right] + \underset{(0.0730)}{0.1917} \left[\frac{DOD_{OBL}}{...}\right.$$

$$\Delta INV_{MD}^{54} = -2.445 - \frac{0.1169}{(0.0465)} [INV_{MD}^{54}]_{-1} + \frac{0.1574}{(0.0532)} \left[\frac{S_{MD}}{WPI_{MD}}\right] - \frac{0.1482}{(0.1551)} \left[\frac{G_{MLDV_F}}{WPI_{MD}}\right] + \frac{0.1710}{(0.0459)} \left[\frac{DOD_{OBL}}{WPI_{MD}}\right]$$

$$+ \frac{\;}{(0.0236)} [KU_{FR_M}] \left[\frac{S_{MD}}{WPI_{MD}}\right] \qquad R^2 = 0.738, \quad S_e = 0.382, \quad DW = 1.71 \tag{4.6}$$

$$+ \frac{0.0930}{(0.0217)} [KU_{FR_M}] \left[\frac{S_{MD}}{WPI_{MD}}\right] + \frac{0.00032}{(0.00029)} TIME \qquad R^2 = 0.740, \quad S_e = 0.370, \quad DW = 1.78 \tag{4.7}$$

$$INV_{MD}^{54} = -1.075 - \frac{0.2377}{(0.0522)} [INV_{MD}^{54}]_{-1} + \frac{0.1069}{(0.0468)} \left[\frac{S_{MD}}{WPI_{MD}}\right] - \frac{0.4017}{(0.1493)} \left[\frac{G_{MLDV_F}}{WPI_{MD}}\right] + \frac{0.0134}{(0.0588)} \left[\frac{DOD_{OBL}}{WPI_{MD}}\right]$$

$$+ \frac{0.0745}{(0.0202)} \left\{ \Delta \left[\frac{O_{UMD}}{WPI_{MD}}\right] \right\} + \frac{0.0655}{(0.0160)} TIME + \frac{0.0638}{(0.0206)} [KU_{FR_M}] \left[\frac{S_{MD}}{WPI_{MD}}\right] \tag{4.8}$$

$$R^2 = 0.808, \quad S_e = 0.323, \quad DW = 1.68$$

Note Equations (4.1) through (4.4) are based on data from 1950 : 3 through 1962 : 1; equations (4.5) through (4.10), on data from 1950 : 3 through 1961 : 4.

The variables in order of appearance are:

INV_{MD} = inventory stock in durable manufacturing, billions of dollars

S_{MD} = shipments by manufacturers of durable goods, billions of dollars

WPI_{MD} = wholesale price index of manufacturers' durable goods, 1954 = 1.00

O_{UMD} = unfilled orders, durable goods industries, billions of dollars

KU_{FR_M} = manufacturing output as a percent of capacity (de Leeuw)

G_{MLDV_F} = Department of Defense net expenditures for development, procurement, research, test and evaluation, billions of dollars

DOD_{OBL} = Department of Defense obligations, billions of dollars

$TIME$ = time trend.

When this expression for the inventory sales ratio is multiplied by S and the customary complications added, sales times capacity utilizations appears as an explanatory variable in the inventory investment equation [21]). An additional argument for including the capacity variable is provided by the production smoothing concept. Firms typically build up stocks of finished goods in anticipation of periods of peak seasonal sales, even when their average level of output over the year does not constitute a high percentage of capacity. Indeed, one of the principal reasons for holding stocks is to enable firms to meet seasonal peaks in sales volume without excessive overtime, etc. In years in which the firm is experiencing a generally high level of capacity utilization, it will be necessary to start accumulating further in advance of the seasonal peak. Averaging at any point of time over a multitude of firms with diverse seasonal patterns of final demand, we will find that stocks must be higher than suggested solely by consideration of sales volume when firms generally are operating close to capacity. Of course, it must be conceded that an offsetting negative effect of capacity upon inventories may arise as a result of difficulty experienced in obtaining inputs when the economy is operating at a high level; but equation (4.3) reveals a highly significant positive relationship.

Two measures of Department of Defense procurement activities appear along with other explanatory variables in the remaining regressions reported in table 4.2. The Department of Defense expenditures variable, G_{MLDV_F}, denotes payments actually made for military hardware. Of course, expenditures appear twice in these equations, for they are also included by manufacturers in reporting their sales volume to the Department of Commerce. Consequently, the coefficient of G_{MLDV_F} represents the differential reaction of inventory investment to sales to the Department of Defense as opposed to sales to the civilian sector of the economy. Murray Weidenbaum has argued that actual expenditure will have a negative impact on stocks because payment coincides approximately in timing with the date of delivery of items to the military [18]. While the regression coefficient of expenditure is always negative, and indeed larger in magnitude than the coefficient of S, it is insignificant in most of the regressions. The second military variable DOD_{OBL} represents Department of Defense obligations; in essence, these are new orders placed by the military for defense items. The obligations variable

---

[21]) Since the capacity utilization rate is the ratio of actual to capacity output, this is approximately the same as having sales squared over the capacity stock in the inventory investment equation.

TABLE 4.3

Nondurable manufacturing inventory regressions (quarterly data in billions of 1954 dollars, 1950 : 3 through 1960 : 4).

$$\Delta INV_{MN}^{54} = -1.169 - \frac{0.0500}{(0.0487)} [INV_{MN}^{54}]_{-1} + \frac{0.0424}{(0.0203)} \left[\frac{S_{MN}}{WPI_{MN}}\right] - \frac{0.4174}{(0.0768)} \left\{\Delta\left[\frac{O_{U_{MN}}}{WPI_{MN}}\right]\right\} + \frac{0.3286}{(0.0742)} \left[\frac{O_{U_{MN}}}{WPI_{MN}}\right]$$
$$(4.9)$$

$$R^2 = 0.582 \qquad S_e = 0.176 \qquad DW = 1.87$$

$$\Delta INV_{MN}^{54} = 1.543 - \frac{0.1161}{(0.0624)} [INV_{MN}^{54}]_{-1} + \frac{0.0082}{(0.0781)} \left[\frac{S_{MN}}{WPI_{MN}}\right] - \frac{0.4314}{(0.0819)} \left\{\Delta\left[\frac{O_{U_{MN}}}{WPI_{MN}}\right]\right\} + \frac{0.3200}{(0.0941)} \left[\frac{O_{U_{MN}}}{WPI_{MN}}\right]$$

$$+ \frac{0.0039}{(0.0370)} [KU_{FR_M}] \left[\frac{S_{MN}}{WPI_{MN}}\right] + \frac{0.0005}{(0.0004)} [TIME] \left[\frac{S_{MN}}{WPI_{MN}}\right] \qquad R^2 = 0.626 \qquad S_e = 0.171 \qquad DW = 1.85 \qquad (4.10)$$

The variables are:

INV_{MN} = inventory stock in nondurable manufacturing, billions of dollars

S_{MN} = shipments by manufacturers of nondurable goods, billions of dollars

WPI_{MN} = wholesale price index of manufacturers' nondurable goods, 1954 = 1.00

$O_{U_{MN}}$ = unfilled orders, nondurable goods industries, billions of dollars

KU_{FR_M} = manufacturing output as a percent of capacity (de Leeuw)

$TIME$ = time trend.

remains significant when the Department of Commerce observations on orders are included in the regressions. Indeed, a comparison of equations (4.7) and (4.8) suggests that neither the level nor the change in unfilled orders adds much once the Department of Defense obligations variable is introduced.

A number of other candidates were also considered in the study of the behavior of durable inventory investment. A military prime contract awards variable was not found to have significant explanatory value. In regressions designed to determine whether durable manufacturing firms speculate successfully in inventories, the rate of price change was found to have a negative regression coefficient, contrary to hypothesis. The business loan rate was included in other regressions to test the conjecture that the higher the cost of credit the smaller the inventories that firms would want to carry, given the level of initial stocks and sales volume, etc; unfortunately, the interest rate variable appeared with a positive coefficient [22]). It has sometimes been argued that the combined effects of nonquantifiable factors such as automation, improved transportation and potential economizing on inventory as a result of the introduction of more advanced inventory control procedures, contribute to an economizing on inventory stocks. Since these factors cannot be quantified, time must be utilized as a proxy. In every regression in which the trend term is included, time enters with a positive coefficient, and in equation (4.8), the coefficient is significant. Such a positive coefficient might be attributed to shifts in the industry mix in manufacturing toward inventory using sectors; it is also conceivable that improved management control may actually involve larger inventories whose carrying costs are more than offset by reduced runouts and setup expense.

Let us now focus our attention upon inventories held by manufacturers of nondurable goods. Inspection of equation (4.9) in table 4.3 suggests that the orders variables have a marked role in influencing inventory behavior; while the regression coefficients are larger for the nondurable orders variables than they were in the durable regressions reported in table 4.2, it should be

---

[22]) This result, which may be due to the neglect of the simultaneous equation problem in fitting the equations by least squares, has usually been encountered with regressions designed to explain inventory behavior. One exception is a study utilizing undeflated data, by E. Cary Brown, Robert Solow, Albert Ando and John Kareken [3]. A second exception is Ta-Chung Liu's results with "An Exploratory Quarterly Model of Effective Demand in the Postwar U. S. Economy" [10]. Liu included nonfarm nonfinancial business holdings of money in his regression explaining nonfarm business inventories. Research by Paul Kuznets for his Yale Ph. D. dissertation suggests that internal and external sources of funds have an important influence upon equilibrium inventory.

remembered that in contrast to durable manufacturing most goods are made to stock and the orders variables themselves are small in magnitude. Difficulties were encountered in attempting to improve upon this regression. As proxies for errors in anticipating sales volume, the change in sales from the previous quarter and also the level of sales in the same quarter of the preceding year were added in two regressions without significant results. As with durables, the regression coefficients of the interest rate variable were always of perverse positive sign. When the capacity utilization variable was added, it was found to enter the regression equation with a negative slope. Equation (4.10) in table 4.3 shows the effect of including both capacity and a trend term; inspection of the t ratios reveals that neither variable individually is significant, and the improvement in R as a result of adding the two variables simultaneously also is not significant. While it seems best at the current stage of our work to retain equation (4.9) for nondurable manufacturing, it would be most interesting to determine whether the application of simultaneous equation-estimation techniques would yield a significant interest rate coefficient of acceptable sign.

4.3. The trade sector [23])

Although research on trade inventory investment undertaken to date for the Brookings-SSRC econometric model project has been much more limited in scope than is the case for manufacturers' inventories, a brief report on this work seems worthwhile on several grounds [24]). First, an interest rate variable has been found to possess a regression coefficient in some sectors of trade, which suggests that monetary policy may be influential in affecting

---

[23]) Computations for the regressions in this section were performed on the Federal Reserve System's computer in Washington, D.C. The author wishes to express his appreciation for this help to the Board of Governors and to Mr. M. H. Schwartz, Director of the Board's Division of Data Processing.

[24]) As noted earlier in the chapter, the research on trade inventory regressions and the preparation of this section of the report represent the work of Darling. He wishes to point out that during his tenure as inventory researcher for the project (from the project's inception to August, 1962) the major portion of his time was devoted to the behavior of inventory investment in the manufacturing sector, the results of which were reported to the two summer conferences at Dartmouth College in 1961 and 1962 and are reflected, in part, in his monograph for the Joint Economic Committee, "Inventory Fluctuations and Economic Instability" [5]. In view of the limited amount of time devoted to work on trade inventories, the results described should be considered tentative and suggestive in character rather than definitive or conclusive.

the holding of stocks. Price speculation, furthermore, may also be a factor determining inventory policies in trade if the results of the regressions reported below can be trusted. Both of these findings will be of interest to vineyard toilers, as most of the recent econometric work on inventory investment has failed to uncover a reliable connection between these two variables and the holdings of stocks. The investigation of trade inventory behavior suggests, as a third matter of special note, that for wholesalers, at least, the rate of capacity utilization by suppliers influences the holding of inventory by purchasing firms, a finding which parallels some conclusions reported by Lovell in section 4.2.

This report on inventory investment regressions for the trade sector is divided into four parts. In section 4.3.1 a number of important limitations affecting the research findings are made explicit. A brief discussion of inventory theory is presented in section 4.3.2, and the results of the regression analyses in section 4.3.3. In the final section, 4.4.4, some suggestions for further research are made.

4.3.1. *Limitations and qualifications affecting findings*

The regression findings reported below are circumscribed by a number of conditions the reader should note at the beginning. Perhaps the most limiting qualification is the fact that auto dealers' stocks were eliminated from the retail component of the trade data. This was done because a preliminary survey of the data suggested that the relationships among car deliveries to dealers, dealers' sales to customers and their own holdings of new cars awaiting sale departed substantially from analogous relationships for the balance of retail trade and would better be studied as a separate project. The findings reported below, then, are limited to trade inventories excluding the "automotive group" component of inventories.

In the second place, the sample period used in the regressions (which were run during the early summer of 1961) is a rather short one, quarterly from 1951 through 1960. This restriction to forty time series observations places bounds, of course, on the probable generality of the findings. Although data on trade stocks and sales for periods prior to 1951 have been published by the Department of Commerce, their reliability is considered to be far less than for the revised series which begins with 1951 [25].

---

[25]) A conclusion reached on the basis of discussions with officials of the Office of Business Economics. See also relevant footnotes to the published data in issues of *Business Statistics*.

Several other limitations and qualifications must be noted: (1) Only linear forms of regressions were employed. It should be kept in mind that further work, using nonlinear expressions suggested by theoretical considerations, might lead to significantly different results. (2) Most of the time series had to be adjusted to reduce them as nearly as possible to deflated physical-change-in-stock form, as described in section 4.4. Errors in these procedures may raise the "noise" level in the data and reduce the percentage of total variance which the regressions explain. (3) Additionally, the "noise" level in the data has been substantially increased by the Department of Commerce practice (at the time of this study) of releasing figures covering inventories and sales for trade only after they had been rounded to the nearest tenth of billion dollar units. (4) No reasonable solution to the problem of measuring anticipated values of the variables in inventory regressions has been found. This is troublesome and may result in biased estimates of parameters, since the a priori formulations of inventory functions are stated in terms of *planned* inventory change, based on expectations concerning sales and other variables, whereas these equations are regressed against data for *actual* inventory change. The limited nature of the single test conducted to determine whether errors of sales forecasting were systematically distributed (the same test reported above for manufacturing) leaves this matter not entirely settled. (5) Finally, as the reader will observe from the tabulations of simple correlation coefficients between the regression variables shown in table 4.8, multicollinearity is high among a number of the independent variables and the reliability of some of the regression coefficients is accordingly affected.

4.3.2. Some a priori considerations

In principle, the theory of inventory holdings and investment in the trade sector of the economy should be similar in general contour to the theory applicable to manufacturing. In both cases four sets of factors would appear on an a priori basis to be important determinants of desired inventory levels.

First, there exist important "transactions" motives for holding trade stocks. Several elements may be noted. Discounts commonly available for purchasing in large lots will dictate a policy of ordering supplies in discrete "lumps" so that, given the time pattern of the flow-out of stock, there will exist on average over time a balance of stocks on hand. Further, acts of production undertaken by the firm will themselves present a need for a balance of stocks on hand. Incoming materials must be programmed ahead of deliveries to customers in order to give the firm time to apply productive processes to them. The accounting systems of manufacturers explicitly segregate these materials as "goods-in-process" of production. Although trading firms do not normally make this accounting distinction, a set of basic productive acts requiring time is also necessarily undertaken: receiving and checking incoming merchandise, sorting, storing to provide quick delivery to customers, shelving for display, advertising, assembling and packaging shipments, etc. And finally, the influence of productive processes on the holding of inventory will reflect the extra costs attributable to shifting from one level of production to another. Efforts to smooth production over time in order to avoid these extra costs, for trade firms as well as manufacturers, will require larger stocks on an average than otherwise. For example, wholesalers and retailers will generally try to lay in stocks well ahead of predictable increases in sales in order to avoid overtime pay and extra employees in carrying out receiving, warehousing and selling functions.

"Precautionary" motives, in the second place, help explain the holding of stocks. Since the input stream of materials from suppliers, the sequence of productive acts applied to stocks on hand and the output flow of deliveries to customers are all three predictable only with some uncertainty, stocks held between stages of production within the firm must act partly as precautionary reserves, or buffers, to guard against the hazard of run-outs when errors of prediction are made.

A third factor which may at times influence inventory holdings is price speculation. Opportunities exist for the firm to speculate in inventory inasmuch as materials are purchased at one point in time and sold (as a component of delivered goods) at a later point in time. An expected rise in prices over the interval may, therefore, induce the firm to make larger purchases and keep larger stocks on hand than would otherwise be the case, and the converse.

Finally, major elements of cost directly attributable to the holding of inventory will, of course, limit their desired size. The opportunity (interest) cost of funds tied up in stocks, the overhead and direct costs of storage space and display shelves and the costs implied by spoilage and obsolescence (including changes in consumer tastes) are the chief charges which will restrict the size of desired inventories.

The foregoing generalized statements concerning the transactions, precautionary, speculative and cost elements of demand for trade inventories may be made somewhat more specific to the problem of formulating suitable inventory functions for regression analysis by drawing out some of their implications. If the above statements are correct, a given firm's desired level of inventory will be affected by changes in the following determinants, each considered separately:

(1) A change in (seasonally adjusted) sales [26]. A rise in sales which implies a larger scale of operation will require a larger holding of "transactions" and "precautionary" stocks, and the converse.

(2) Innovations by suppliers which are reflected in an upward shift in the discount pattern offered for large-lot ordering. These innovations will increase average stock levels.

(3) Innovations within the firm which alter the length of the production period. Shortening the period will, of course, reduce stock levels [27].

(4) Mergers of vertically oriented trading firms. These raise stocks per dollar of reported sales.

(5) Changes in competitive conditions in output markets which induce the firm to offer wider assortments of goods on display and larger stocks on hand to improve delivery performance as a means of maintaining market share.

(6) Changes in the incremental cost of a shift in the level of production. An increased need for specialized training of new personnel caused by new technology or an increase in overtime wage rates will serve as examples.

(7) Changes in supply conditions which affect the degree of uncertainty that purchased materials will be delivered when needed.

(8) Any change in the likelihood of work stoppages for the firm or its suppliers, including transporters of materials.

(9) Any of a host of possible changes in "exogenous" factors which affect the uncertainty of sales forecasting (e.g., introduction of legislation affecting taxes and expenditures of government, shifts in the international climate, etc.).

(10) Current price changes or other factors which generate expectations of future price movements related to the firm's holding of stocks.

---

[26] A purely seasonal increase in sales is likely, of course, to be accompanied by a reduction in inventory; such will be the case where economies can be secured by "smoothing" production, i.e., laying in stocks in advance of a seasonal peak in order to avoid sharp increases in the hiring of extra personnel or similar extra costs. Somewhat more generally, whenever there exists a reasonable basis for predicting sales changes, whether seasonal or other, production-smoothing considerations may affect the fluctuations over time in stocks and sales. Thus, what is involved in the statement in the text is the effect on stocks of a change in sales, abstracting from the influence of production smoothing.

[27] The production period may be affected not only by innovations in the product itself or in the overt processes of production directly applied thereto (e.g., the introduction in warehousing of powered fork-lift trucks) but also by improvements in accounting and inventory control such as might be made possible by electronic data-processing machines.

(11) Changes in the cost and availability of financing and in the costs of physically handling and storing inventory. Changes in interest rates and credit rationing would seem to be the most volatile element of these costs.

Not all of these inventory determinants are explicitly incorporated in the regressions equations used in the study. This investigation was more heavily committed to uncovering cyclical factors playing a role in the inventory mechanism than working explicitly with long-run structural or trend elements. For many of the latter, furthermore, readily available quantitative time-series measurements were lacking. In consequence, five explicit independent variables of a predominantly cyclical nature (and for which time-series data were available) were selected from the eleven sets of determinants with all other factors, most of which would seem to be influential only in a long-run sense, being taken into account (hopefully) by a linear trend variable added to the regressions. These five explicit variables, believed to be determinants of desired stocks on the a priori grounds explained above, are as follows:

S = trade sales, billions of dollars

$KU_{\mathrm{MH_M}}$ = per cent of capacity output utilized in manufacturing (McGraw-Hill)

$\Delta O_{U_{531}}$ = change in department stores' unfilled orders, billions of dollars

$\dfrac{[WPI]_{+1} - WPI}{WPI}$ = proportionate change in the wholesale price index during quarter $t+1$

RM_{BLS} = bank rate of interest on short-term business loans, average for 19 large cities, per cent.

The first variable, sales, measures the transactions demand for inventory stocks. Capacity utilization in manufacturing partially measures supply conditions faced by trade firms, and change in unfilled orders is used as an additional index of supply conditions. The hypothesis here was that during periods when unfilled orders are rising very fast and lead times are being rapidly extended firms will face greater uncertainty concerning supply conditions. As a proxy for price expectations held during the current quarter, the change in wholesale prices is used. Finally, the rate of interest charged by banks on business loans is used to measure an important element of the cost of holding stocks. All dollar data used in the regressions were deflated to constant dollar value form. Price definitions, sources of all figures, and descriptions of the adjustments made to the data are presented in Appendix tables 4.6 and 4.7.

Using linear expressions for the sake of simplicity during this first probing of the empirical record, desired stock levels were related to their determinants as follows:

$$INV^E = a_0 + a_1 S + a_2 [KU_{MH_M}] + a_3 \Delta O_{U_{531}}$$

$$+ a_4 \left\{ \frac{[WPI]_{+1} - WPI}{WPI} \right\} + a_5 RM_{BLS} + a_6 TIME$$

where INV^E is the level of stocks to be held at the end of quarter, $TIME$ is the trend variable mentioned above and a_0 is a constant introduced to take into account any difference between average and marginal relationships.

When actual holding of stocks, INV, departs from the desired level, INV^E, it is assumed that firms begin an adjustment process to eliminate the difference. During any single quarter, t, the adjustment will be only a partial one for two reasons: First, in view of the uncertainty underlying the expectations on which desired stock levels are based, it may be strategically best to make only a partial move toward the target; second, explicit cost and logistical factors may make a partial adjustment necessary [28]. Symbolically:

$$\widehat{\Delta INV} = d\{\widehat{INV^E} - [INV]_{-1}\}; \quad 0 < d < 1.$$

Here, $\widehat{\Delta INV}$ is the expected (planned) change in stocks during quarter t which is the result of a discrepancy recognized and acted upon in the previous quarter, $t-1$. Since the decision to adjust precedes the quarter of the change in stocks, the desired level of inventory for this coming period is based on expected values held at $t-1$ for INV^E and hence the use of the expectational symbol ($\wedge$) over the desired stock variable in the last equation. As noted in section 4.3.1 above, a difficulty in the regression analysis is the lack of a strong hypothesis concerning expectations. In the present instance the simplifying assumption is made that from one quarter to the next the firm's forecasts of sales, capacity usage and the other explanatory variables are made with randomly distributed errors. On this basis, actual values are employed in place of expected values, and our regression form becomes:

$$\Delta INV = b_0 + b_1 S + b_2 [KU_{MH_M}] + b_3 \Delta O_{U_{531}}$$

$$+ b_4 \left\{ \frac{[WPI]_{+1} - WPI}{WPI} \right\} + b_5 RM_{BLS} + b_6 TIME + b_7 [INV]_{-1} + u,$$

where u is the error term [29].

---

[28] For a succinct statement of this rationale see Ladd [9].

Before the regressions were run two other adjustments were made to the function. In order to test whether the direction and amount of change of sales is a factor inducing a systematic forecasting error, the independent variable $\Delta S = (S_t - S_{t-1})$ was added to the equation. Second, the equation above assumes that inventory investment of period t is a function solely of the same period's values of the independent variables; this seems unduly restrictive because good reasons can be found for believing that the values of the previous period, $t-1$, may cast some lingering, delayed, influence on ΔINV. Ideally, various distributed lag possibilities should be investigated, but in the present study the influence of the earlier period is arbitrarily measured by introducing inventory investment of the previous period, i.e. $[\Delta INV]_{-1}$ [30]).

The reader will note the methodological leap from hypothesizing inventory determination at the level of the individual firm to a regression equation destined to be fitted, in the following section, to data covering aggregates of wholesale and retail firms. Comments on some of the pitfalls of this sort of aggregation are made in section 4.3.4.

4.3.3. Regression findings

Five sets of least-squares regressions using quarterly price-deflated data were run: for combined wholesale and retail trade, for wholesale and retail trade separately and for retail durables and nondurables separately. As pointed out earlier, auto dealers' stocks were eliminated from the retail sector. The results for combined wholesale and retail trade, shown in table 4.4, are discussed first in some detail, followed by a summary tabulation of the findings for the components of trade.

Variables in addition to those defined in the preceding section are:

INV = business inventory stock, end of period, billions of dollars

CPI_{DEA} = durable commodities less automobiles component of consumer price index, 1954 = 1.00

CPI_N = nondurable commodities component of consumer price index, 1954 = 1.00

WPI_{CNEF} = wholesale price index for consumer nondurable goods except food, 1954 = 1.00.

---

[29]) And where $b_0 = da_0$; $b_1 = da_1$; $b_2 = da_2$; ... etc.; and $b_7 = -d$.

[30]) For an important contribution concerning distributed lags in inventory functions see Ladd [9].

TABLE 4.4

Inventory investment regressions; combined wholesale and retail trade (less autos), 1951 through 1960 (based on deflated quarterly data in billions of dollars).

$$\Delta INV_{T*}^{54} = \frac{0.0936}{(0.1001)} \left[\frac{S_{TW}}{WPI} + \frac{S_{TRD*}}{CPI_{DEA}} + \frac{S_{TRN}}{CPI_{N}} \right] - \frac{0.2258}{(0.0879)} \left[INV_{T*}^{54} \right]_{-1}$$

$$+ \frac{0.0156}{(0.0311)} \left[KU_{MH_M} \right] + \frac{11.64}{(8.78)} \left\{ \frac{[WPI]_{+1} - WPI}{WPI} \right\} + \frac{0.1428}{(0.1642)} \left[\Delta INV_{T*}^{54} \right]_{-1}$$

$$- \frac{0.2330}{(0.2960)} RM_{BLS} + \frac{0.0296}{(0.0971)} \left\{ \Delta \left[\frac{S_{TW}}{WPI} + \frac{S_{TRD*}}{CPI_{DEA}} + \frac{S_{TRN}}{CPI_{N}} \right] \right\}$$

$$- \frac{0.3700}{(1.300)} \Delta \left[\frac{O_{U_{531}}}{WPI_{CNEF}} \right] - \frac{0.0036}{(0.0593)} TIME - 0.0105$$

$$\qquad R^2 = 0.513 \qquad S_e = 0.261 \tag{4.11}$$

$$\Delta INV_{T*}^{54} = \frac{0.0963}{(0.0264)} \left[\frac{S_{TW}}{WPI} + \frac{S_{TRD*}}{CPI_{DEA}} + \frac{S_{TRN}}{CPI_{N}} \right] - \frac{0.2434}{(0.0648)} \left[INV_{T*}^{54} \right]_{-1}$$

$$+ \frac{0.0175}{(0.0103)} \left[KU_{MH_M} \right] + \frac{12.90}{(7.79)} \left\{ \frac{[WPI]_{+1} - WPI}{WPI} \right\}$$

$$+ \frac{0.1421}{(0.1464)} \left[\Delta INV_{T*}^{54} \right]_{-1} - \frac{0.2790}{(0.2020)} \left[RM_{BLS} \right] + 0.2679$$

$$\qquad R^2 = 0.510 \qquad S_e = 0.261 \tag{4.12}$$

$$\Delta INV_{T*}^{54} = \frac{0.0732}{(0.0165)} \left[\frac{S_{TW}}{WPI} + \frac{S_{TRD*}}{CPI_{DEA}} + \frac{S_{TRN}}{CPI_{N}} \right] - \frac{0.2408}{(0.0653)} \left[INV_{T*}^{54} \right]_{-1}$$

$$+ \frac{0.0253}{(0.0089)} \left[KU_{MH_M} \right] + \frac{15.44}{(7.62)} \left\{ \frac{[WPI]_{+1} - WPI}{WPI} \right\} - 0.1896$$

$$\qquad R^2 = 0.466 \qquad S_e = 0.273 \tag{4.13}$$

Sector subscripts used in equations (4.11) through (4.17) are:

M = manufacturing
MD = durable manufacturing
T^* = wholesale and retail trade excluding the retail automotive group
TR^* = retail trade excluding the retail automotive group
TRD^* = durable goods retail stores excluding the retail automotive group
TRN = nondurable goods retail stores
TW = wholesale trade.

The unadjusted coefficient of determination, R^2, and the unadjusted standard error of estimate, S_e, are given for each equation. Equation (4.11) shows the results of fitting the full equation discussed in the preceding section. Equations (4.12) and (4.13) show the results of successive steps of eliminating variables whose coefficients are small in comparison to their standard errors.

Inspection of equation (4.11) shows that the coefficients of the change-in-sales variable, ΔS, used as a test for systematic bias in sales forecasting, and of ΔO_U, a presumed index of supply conditions, are both probably not significant, and the latter has an unexpected negative sign. When these two variables together with the insignificant trend term are dropped, equation (4.12) is secured, with an R^2 of 0.510, not significantly below that for the full equation. Note that the coefficients for the price speculation variable and for the interest rate have the expected sign, although neither is very large relative to its standard error. Still, these two results are suggestive. Would further research of a more sophisticated and exhaustive kind add support to the hypothesis that trade firms are influenced in their inventory decisions by the possibility of price speculation and by changes in the interest rate? Certainly this cannot be ruled out at the present stage of the inquiry.

The four most important determinants of trade investment in stocks appear to be sales, last period's level of stocks, percentage of capacity utilized by suppliers and the percentage change in wholesale prices, if we are to judge by equation (4.13) of table 4.4, a refitting after dropping the $[\Delta INV]_{-1}$ and RM_{BLS} variables from the equation. Some caution is in order because of the presence of collinearity among some of the independent variables, a fact which may explain why the coefficient of KU_{MH_M} picks up weight (compare equations 4.12 and 4.13) when RM_{BLS} is dropped from the regression. As shown in table 4.8 the latter is inversely correlated with KU_{MH_M} in substantial degree.

The fact that the trend term, *TIME*, appears to be insignificant might be used to support a hypothesis that there has been little or no long-run structural change affecting trade inventory policy. This would, I believe, be a premature judgment. Unfortunately, some of the other independent variables, and especially the interest rate, which were included along with *TIME* in the regression exhibit strong trends too. The coefficient of simple correlation between the interest rate and the trend variable amounts to 0.928, as shown in the tabulation in table 4.8. Thus, one cannot rule out the possibility that some of the weight assigned to the interest rate variable is actually attributable to nonmonetary secular factors.

Turning to the breakdown of aggregate trade into components, wholesale and retail separately, and retail durables and nondurables separately, a summary of the regression findings is given in table 4.5. Only the independent variables which remained after eliminating those whose coefficients were substantially less than their standard errors are shown in the table. In brief, these are the chief findings:

(1) Current sales and last period's inventory level are probably significant determinants of inventory investment in all four subcategories of trade.

(2) The percentage of capacity utilized in manufacturing appears to be slightly more significant as a determinant of inventory investment for wholesale trade than for retail trade. For wholesale trade, the coefficient of this variable in equation (4.14) is slightly more than twice its standard error, while for retail trade [equation (4.15)] it is one and one-half times its error.

(3) The possibilities of price speculation in inventory, as measured by the coefficient of the variable for proportionate change in wholesale prices, seems to be influential mainly in retail durables (not surprisingly, since the more rapid turnover of nondurable stocks tends to reduce the opportunity to speculate) and in wholesale trade.

(4) What seems, at first glance at least, a somewhat surprising result is the fact that the interest rate variable remained as a (marginally) significant factor for retail trade but was found to be insignificant for wholesale trade. It may, of course, be that the interest rate variable operates as a proxy for variation in the severity of credit rationing which affects principally the smaller firms found in retail trade [31]).

---

[31]) I am not sure how to explain the fact that the interest rate coefficient for total retail trade, −0.2801, is so much greater than for retail nondurables, while at the same time it appears to be insignificant for retail durables. The fact of multicollinearity involving the interest rate variable, noted several paragraphs earlier in the text, may be a part of the explanation.

TABLE 4.5

Inventory investment regressions; selected components of trade, 1951 through 1960 (based on deflated quarterly data in billions of dollars).

$$\Delta INV_{TW}^{54} = \frac{0.0847}{(0.0159)} \left[\frac{S_{TW}}{WPI}\right] - \frac{0.2075}{(0.0555)} [INV_{TW}^{54}]_{-1} + \frac{0.0087}{(0.0040)} [KU_{MH_M}]$$

$$+ \frac{6.92}{(3.48)} \left\{\frac{[WPI]_{+1} - WPI}{WPI}\right\} - 1.116 \quad R^2 = 0.560 \quad S_e = 0.129 \quad (4.14)$$

$$\Delta INV_{TR*}^{54} = \frac{0.1024}{(0.0369)} \left[\frac{S_{TRD*}}{CPI_{DEA}} + \frac{S_{TRN}}{CPI_N}\right] - \frac{0.2468}{(0.0881)} [INV_{TR*}^{54}]_{-1}$$

$$+ \frac{0.0110}{(0.0072)} [KU_{MH_M}] + \frac{4.24}{(5.48)} \left\{\frac{[WPI]_{+1} - WPI}{WPI}\right\} + \frac{0.1945}{(0.1561)} [\Delta INV_{TR*}^{54}]_{-1}$$

$$- \frac{0.2801}{(0.1500)} [RM_{BLS}] + 1.026 \quad R^2 = 0.320 \quad S_e = 0.183 \quad (4.15)$$

$$\Delta INV_{TRD*}^{54} = \frac{0.0949}{(0.0497)} \left[\frac{S_{TRD*}}{CPI_{DEA}}\right] - \frac{0.3576}{(0.1063)} [INV_{TRD*}^{54}]_{-1} + \frac{0.0031}{(0.0036)} [KU_{MH_M}]$$

$$+ \frac{5.27}{(2.64)} \left\{\frac{[WPI_{MD}]_{+1} - WPI_{MD}}{WPI_{MD}}\right\} + \frac{0.1906}{(0.1551)} [\Delta INV_{TRD*}^{54}]_{-1} + 1.331$$

$$R^2 = 0.317 \quad S_e = 0.113 \quad (4.16)$$

$$\Delta INV_{TRN}^{54} = \frac{0.0666}{(0.0318)} \left[\frac{S_{TRN}}{CPI_N}\right] - \frac{0.1777}{(0.0763)} [INV_{TRN}^{54}]_{-1} + \frac{0.0062}{(0.0048)} [KU_{MH_M}]$$

$$+ \frac{0.2973}{(0.1485)} [\Delta INV_{TRN}^{54}]_{-1} - \frac{0.1404}{(0.1004)} [RM_{BLS}] + 0.2067$$

$$R^2 = 0.293 \quad S_e = 0.121 \quad (4.17)$$

A final comment on the inventory regressions presented may help the reader in assessing their significance. Inspection of the coefficients of determination, R^2, shows that the ability of these regressions to "explain" the total variance in inventory investment in trade is relatively much less than that of similar equations which have recently been fitted to aggregate manufacturing data [32]). As shown above, R^2 runs from 0.56 for wholesale trade to slightly under 0.3 for retail nondurables. In contrast, inventory investment regressions for manufacturing, which I have reported elsewhere [5, p. 37], yield coefficients of determination of 0.8 and over, and in one case, covering data for the short period from mid-1952 through 1958, an R^2 of 0.955. Why should there exist this very large difference in the explanatory power of inventory investment regressions for trade as compared with manufacturing? Undoubtedly, part of the answer is that inventory research on the trade sector has not been pushed as far, to date, as for manufacturing. Further study of trade inventory behavior may uncover new independent variables and more appropriate equation forms than the very simple linear expressions employed in the current investigation. Even so, the reader should note that the standard errors of estimates for the trade regressions of tables 4.4 and 4.5 above are not large when compared with those found in manufacturing investment regressions. To illustrate, for the best fitting equation used in investigating inventory investment in total manufacturing, the standard error of estimate covering the 52 quarters from 1948 through 1960 amounted to $ 0.373 billion [5, p. 37]. In comparison, the standard error of estimate for the total trade regression shown in equation (4.13) of table 4.4 is $ 0.273 billion. In short, even at the present stage of research on trade inventory investment, errors of forecast made on the basis of the kinds of equations reported above may turn out to be smaller in absolute size than for the manufacturing sector.

4.3.4. *Suggestions for further research on trade inventory behavior*

Several lines of research need to be pursued in order to improve inventory investment functions for the trade sector. Those which seem particularly important in view of the limited scope of the present study are as follows:

(1) Two aspects of the problem of aggregation need further investigation, one a "compositional" problem and the second a matter of causality, both of which pose some difficulties in securing good estimates of functional parameters. The problem of composition involves the fact that relationships at the level of the single firm, for example, the desired ratio of stocks to sales, will differ widely among different firms as well as *within* a single firm for different commodity groups. Functions fitted to an aggregate of these firms

---

[32]) When the equations for trade are put in the form of functions, explaining inventory level rather than inventory investment, the R^2's are, of course, raised to very much higher percentages.

may forecast accurately if the relative composition of firms and of commodity groups remains stable but probably not otherwise. The question that needs a better answer than we now have is how much disaggregation is needed to secure reliable estimates. In the present study, separate regressions for wholesale versus retail and for retail durables versus retail nondurables were run. However, further disaggregation may be necessary.

The causality aspect of the aggregative methods employed in the regressions for the trade sector also needs more attention. Because of such feedbacks as the influence of inventory investment by an aggregate of firms upon incomes external to the aggregate and thence back to their own sales, the application of simultaneous estimation techniques may be expected to influence substantially the parameter estimates for the inventory investment equations. Additionally, purchase-sales connections among firms *within* the aggregate can result in covariation among regression variables, the form of which may itself vary as a function of conditions not explicitly recognized by the regression equation [33]).

(2) Functional forms for the inventory investment equation can surely be improved over the very simple linear equations used in the present study. Some specific suggestions are these: (a) Independent variables expressed as ratios, such as the rate of capacity utilization and the interest rate, might more appropriately be related to the dependent variable expressed also as a ratio (e.g., the desired stock-sales ratio) rather than in the form of relationships shown above; (b) nonlinear relationships should certainly be tried, especially in view of the reasonableness of the proposition that firms will act more vigorously to correct a large imbalance in stocks than a small one; (c) because important structural changes may occur over the periods of 10 to 20 years commonly used to secure regression estimates, more work needs to be done in identifying and measuring the most important of these and explicitly introducing them into the regressions. The trend variable used in the present inquiry may be grossly overburdened!

(3) Some imaginative work is needed to cope with the multicollinearity problem which infests much of the data used in econometric research on inventory behavior during the postwar period. Part of this covariation is attributable to persistent economic growth which imparts sweeping upward trends to many of the time series used in the fittings. Another part is due to cyclical interdependencies, such as the tendency, at least during most of the

---

[33]) See Lovell's paper [11] dealing with aspects of the stability of these "internal" relationships among firms in the aggregate.

1950's, for the rate of interest, the rate of capacity utilization and the change in order backlogs to rise and fall together when measured by departures from a linear trend.

(4) Finally, the justification given above for regressing an equation defining *planned* inventory investment against empirical data measuring *actual* investment, the assumption that forecasting errors are randomly distributed with mean zero over the duration of the sample period, needs to be questioned and investigated. Further research, enabling one to introduce useful proxy variables to measure expected values of the most important factors influencing desired stocks, may be needed.

4.4. Appendix. Supplementary tables

TABLE 4.6

Manufacturing regression variables, data sources, and adjustments (period of measurement for all variables is quarterly).

INV^{54}	inventory stocks	End-of-period seasonally corrected data provided by the National Income Division, Department of Commerce
S	sales	Seasonally adjusted sales data from *Survey of Current Business* (in contrast to value-added data this is a gross concept)
O_U	unfilled orders	Seasonally adjusted end-of-period data published in *Survey of Current Business*
KU_{FR_M}	capacity utilization	Manufacturing output as a per cent of capacity, seasonally adjusted. Testimony by Frank de Leeuw, May 24, 1963, *Measures of Productive Capacity Hearings*, Joint Economic Committee, 1962
G_{MLDV_F}	*DOD* net expenditures	Department of Defense net expenditures for development, procurement and research, test and evaluation. Testimony of Charles J. Hitch, *Inventory Fluctuations and Economic Stabilization Hearings*, Joint Economic Committee, 1962, 153
DOD_{OBL}	*DOD* obligations	*Ibid*, p. 154
TIME	time	Quarterly linear trend using successive digits, 1, 2, 3, ...

Note The inventory data were provided in deflated 1954 dollar form by the National Income Division, Department of Commerce. The durable data on sales, orders and *DOD* net expenditures and obligations were deflated with the Bureau of Labor Statistics durable manufacturing index; the nondurable manufacturing index was used to deflate the nondurable data.

TABLE 4.7

Trade regression variables, data sources, and adjustments (period of measurement for all variables is quarterly).

INV^{54}	inventory stocks	End-of-period seasonally adjusted data. *For retail trade*: special tabulations provided by National Income Division of Department of Commerce, deflated to 1954 dollars, including "inventory valuation adjustment," by the Division; auto stocks eliminated from retail durables data by subtracting therefrom inventories of "motor vehicles and parts" from *Survey of Current Business* as deflated using "motor vehicles" component of BLS wholesale price incex. *For wholesale trade*: data from *Survey of Current Business*, deflated using BLS wholesale price index lagged one month.
S	sales	Gross trade sales seasonally adjusted from *Survey of Current Business*. *For retail durables*: sales of "motor vehicles and parts" were excluded and balance deflated using "durable commodities less cars" component of consumer price index. *For retail nondurables*: deflated using nondurables component of consumers price index. *For wholesale trade*: deflated using BLS wholesale price index.
$O_{U_{531}}$	unfilled orders	Outstanding purchase orders of department stores from *Federal Reserve Bulletin*, seasonally adjusted and deflated using BLS wholesale price index for consumer nondurables less food.
KU_{MH_M}	capacity utilization	Manufacturing output as percent of capacity: a seasonally adjusted series prepared on basis of McGraw-Hill surveys of growth of capacity in manufacturing.
RM_{BLS}	business loan rate	Bank rate of interest on short-term business loans in 19 large cities: quarterly series from *Federal Reserve Bulletin*.
$([WPI]_{+1} - WPI)/WPI$ proportionate change in prices		Proportionate change in wholesale price index. For regressions covering durables and nondurables components of retail trade, BLS indexes of durables and nondurables, respectively, were used.
$TIME$	time	Quarterly linear trend using successive digits, 1, 2, 3, ...

TABLE 4.8

Coefficients of simple correlation between pairs of variables used in regressions for combined wholesale and retail trade (see table 4.4).

	$\Delta INV_{T^*}^{54}$	S^{54}	ΔS^{54}	$\Delta O_{U_{531}}^{54}$	RM_{BLS}	$\% \Delta WPI_{+1}$	KU_{MH_M}	$[INV_{T^*}^{54}]_{-1}$	$[\Delta INV_{T^*}^{54}]_{-1}$	$TIME$
$\Delta INV_{T^*}^{54}$	1.000	0.106	0.428	−0.014	−0.038	0.213	0.271	−0.175	0.312	−0.039
S^{54}		1.000	0.000	−0.000	0.919	0.281	0.694	0.790	0.128	0.961
ΔS^{54}			1.000	0.345	−0.235	0.077	0.118	−0.285	−0.107	−0.093
$\Delta O_{U_{531}}^{54}$				1.000	−0.093	−0.269	−0.078	−0.126	−0.298	0.008
RM_{BLS}					1.000	−0.137	−0.727	0.713	0.065	0.928
$\% \Delta WPI_{+1}$						1.000	−0.022	0.446	0.162	0.201
KU_{MH_M}							1.000	−0.570	0.263	−0.854
$[INV_{T^*}^{54}]_{-1}$								1.000	0.134	0.776
$[\Delta INV_{T^*}^{54}]_{-1}$									1.000	0.005
$TIME$										1.000

Note   Deflators for sales and unfilled orders are given in table 4.7.

REFERENCES

1. ABRAMOVITZ, MOSES. *Inventories and Business Cycles with Special References to Manufacturers' Inventories.* New York: National Bureau of Economic Research, 1950.
2. ALLEN, JULIUS W., and GENTRY, RICHARD H. Inventories, Inventory Investment, and Inventory Control: A Selected Bibliography, in Part III, *Inventory Fluctuations and Economic Stabilization* (Joint Economic Committee). Washington, D. C.: U.S. Government Printing Office, 1961.
3. BROWN, E. C., SOLOW, R. M., ANDO, A., and KAREKEN, J. Lags in Fiscal and Monetary Policy, in *Stabilization Policies* (Commission on Money and Credit). Englewood Cliffs: Prentice-Hall, 1963.
4. CHIKASHI, MORIGUCHI. Manufacturers's Short-Term Decisions Under the Different Phases of Business Cycles as Shown by Selected Industries, 1949–1960. Unpublished Ph. D. Dissertation, University of Michigan, 1962.
5. DARLING, PAUL G. Inventory Fluctuations and Economic Instability: An Analysis Based on the Postwar Economy, in Part III of *Inventory Fluctuations and Economic Stabilization* (Joint Economic Committee). Washington, D. C.: U.S. Government Printing Office, 1961.
6. DE LEEUW, FRANK. Measures of Productive Capacity, *Hearings Before the Subcommittee on Economic Statistics*, Joint Economic Committee, Congress Of the United States, May, 1962, 129.
7. HOLT, CHARLES C., and MODIGLIANI, FRANCO. Firm Cost Structures and the Dynamic Response of Inventories, Production, Work Force, and Orders to Sales Fluctuations, in *Inventory Fluctuations and Economic Stabilization* (Joint Economic Committee). Washington, D. C.: U.S. Government Printing Office, 1961.
8. KLEIN, LAWRENCE. *Economic Fluctuations in the United States, 1921–1941*, Cowles Commission Monograph No. 11. New York: John Wiley and Sons, 1950.
9. LADD, GEORGE W. Distributed Lag Inventory Analyses, *Research Bulletin 515*, Agricultural and Home Economics Experiment Station, Iowa State University, April, 1963.
10. LIU, TA-CHUNG. An Exploratory Quarterly Model of Effective Demand in the Postwar U.S. Economy, *Econometrica* 31 (July, 1963).
11. LOVELL, MICHAEL C. Buffer Stocks, Sales Expectations and Stability: A Multi-Sector Analysis of the Inventory Cycle, *Econometrica* 29 (1962).
12. LOVELL, MICHAEL C. The Contribution of Inventory Investment to Cyclical Reversals in Economic Activity, in *Hearings on Inventory Fluctuations and Economic Stabilization.* Sub-committee on Economic Stabilization, Automation, and Energy Resources of The Joint Economic Committee. Washington, D. C.: U.S. Government Printing Office, 1962, 245–263.
13. LOVELL, MICHAEL C. Factors Determining Manufacturing Inventory Investment, in Part II, *Inventory Fluctuations and Economic Stabilization* (Joint Economic Committee). Washington, D. C.: U.S. Government Printing Office, 1961.
14. LOVELL, MICHAEL C. Seasonal Adjustment of Economic Time Series and Multiple Regression Analysis, *Journal of American Statistical Assoc.* 58 (December 1963) 993–1010.
15. MILLS, EDWIN. The Theory of Inventory Decisions, *Econometrica* 25 (April, 1957) 111–139.

16. STANBACK, THOMAS, Jr. Cyclical Behavior of Manufacturers' Inventories Since 1945, in *Proceedings, Business and Economic Statistics Section*, American Statistical Association. Washington, D. C.: 1957, 87–95.

17. STANBACK, THOMAS, Jr. *Postwar Cycles and Manufacturers' Inventories*. New York: National Bureau of Economic Research, 1962.

18. WEIDENBAUM, MURRAY L. The Timing of the Economic Inpact of Government Spending, *National Tax Journal* 12 (1959).

19. WHITAKER, GILBERT RILEY. The Short-Run Production Decision: An Empirical Study. Unpublished Ph. D. dissertation, University of Wisconsin, 1961.

CHAPTER 5

BUSINESS ANTICIPATORY DEMAND: AN ANALYSIS OF BUSINESS ORDERS, 1948–1962

Contents

5.1. The outline of the study 163

5.2. Statistical analysis: durable and nondurable new orders 164

5.3. Business new orders continued: subgroup of durable orders 168

5.4. Concluding comments 175

References 175

BUSINESS ANTICIPATORY DEMAND: AN ANALYSIS OF BUSINESS ORDERS, 1948–1962 [1])

MANORANJAN DUTTA

Rutgers, The State University, New Brunswick, New Jersey

5.1. The outline of the study

Economists' concern with the future needs no justification. An explanation of "ex ante" as against "ex post" demand has been considered useful, at least for short-run problems. This has been the motivation of many studies relating to expectations and intentions of economic variables.

Studies with respect to consumers' anticipatory demand have been undertaken by others. Not much has been done to analyze the anticipatory demand pattern of the business community, at least not within the framework of an over-all econometric model [2]). In this model, orders must be explained

---

[1]) I am indebted to Professor Lawrence R. Klein for his comments on a first draft of this paper and for his suggestions at various stages. Thanks are due to the Rutgers Bureau of Economic Research for aiding this study. I wish to thank the Department of Commerce for making available to me some special tabulations for the series on motor vehicles and equipment; stone, clay and glass; furniture and lumber; and iron and steel, and also the Department of Defense for the defense obligations series. The series on industrial output originating by sectors, and on the output of regulated industries, rail and nonrail, and also the price indices on manufacturers' durables and nondurables came to us through the courtesy of the Wharton School. My thanks are due also to Mr. Anthony S. Campagna for rendering helpful research assistance. The Rutgers University Computation Center did the statistical computation. I alone am responsible for any errors.

[2]) Zarnowitz [3] reports a recent study with respect to unfilled orders. While his results are interesting, he does not analyze new orders, which constitute the prime subject matter of this study. In another paper, Muth [2] concludes that "averages of expectations in an industry are more accurate than naive models, and as accurate as elaborate equation systems."

if, as is likely, they are to be used in inventory investment equations.

New orders constitute a reliable indicator of "ex ante" demand of the business sector. They are based on informed expectations of the related economic group and provide useful measures of business behavior patterns. In the Brookings-SSRC econometric model, the value added component of final sales and change in inventory holdings—two magnitudes which add up to the total national output—are analyzed separately. Inventories are explained in terms of final sales and unfilled orders. Unfilled orders constitute a residual category and may be obtained by the following identity, industry by industry:

$$O_U \equiv [O_U]_{-1} + O - S$$
$$O_U = \text{unfilled orders}$$
$$O = \text{new orders}$$
$$S = \text{gross sales.}$$

Thus, if new orders are related to recent sales, the inventory-order equations of the model together will give us output decision equations. In our order equations, the variations in order placement are explained by *GNP* components by type of product. These final sales constitute the demand for output. Thus variations in the final sales become correlated with variations in order placements by the producer sector of the economy.

The above identity is true in terms of observed data without seasonal adjustments and correction for price variations. However, the statistical analyses that follow are in terms of seasonally adjusted constant dollar sums. Accordingly, equations using known (a priori) seasonal and endogenous price adjustments close the system. Behavior equations are in real, adjusted terms. The accounting identities are in current, unadjusted terms. The conversion between these two terms is based on known or endogenous variables explained elsewhere in the model.

5.2. *Statistical analysis*: *durable and nondurable new orders*

In this section we report the findings of the statistical analysis relative to business new orders for the period 1948–1962. Behavior patterns for durable new orders are expected to be different from those for nondurable new orders. Hence the total new orders have been broken up into durable and nondurable new orders.

In what is at present the preferred form of the two equations relative to the two above-mentioned groups of business orders, quarterly new orders in 1954 dollars have been regressed on an activity variable representing a particular kind of demand, on a lagged value of the same variable, on a price-change variable, and on a dummy variable showing the impact of certain measurable exogenous disturbances. The activity variable in the equation for new orders received by manufacturers of nondurable goods is the final product of nondurable goods less the inventory change thereof, i.e., the final sales of nondurable goods. In the equations for new orders received by manufacturers of durable goods, the activity variable is final sales of durable goods, plus the new construction component of *GNP*. In the durable equation, the lagged value of the activity variable has been included as an independent regressor, but there appears to be no justification for including the lagged variable in the nondurable equation. That is what should be expected in the American economy, where the built-in capacity of business to augment the supply for nondurable final sales is highly elastic. A longer lag effect should be considered significant with respect to durables when we recognize the fact that the production of durables is more "roundabout". Indeed, we have reported two alternative formulations of the use of lagged values of the appropriate activity variable. The use of a two-quarter lag shows marginally better results. However, there is not much choice between the use of a one- and two-quarter lag. It might be satisfactory to take a simple average of the lagged values of the two preceding quarters.

A proxy variable has been introduced in the two equations in two different forms. In the durable equation, changes in government expenditure in 1954 dollars have been used as the appropriate proxy variable. It may be much more desirable to use government orders [3]) for defense purchases instead of actual expenditures. This would reflect the impact of multiple orders and the chain effect following the placement of government military orders. This variable based on changes in government defense expenditures has been christened a proxy variable; the usual impact of such government expenditures has already been taken care of when final sales are taken to be inclusive of government expenditures on durables. The inclusion of the variable in its present form is justified when we wish to isolate effects such as multiple ordering by business following abrupt changes in government activity, in military expenditures particularly. In the nondurable equation,

---

[3]) We did construct a subsample with a related series on government defense orders on the basis of data provided in the evidence of C. Hitch in Hearings of the Joint Economic Committee [1]. This series could not be extended over the entire sample period. The results obtained with the subsample were not, however, encouraging.

a dummy variable of the zero-one form was used. Only four quarters at the beginning of the Korean War period were assigned the value equal to one, while all other quarters were set equal to zero. This follows the pattern of the buying waves that occurred at the initial period of the Korean War but did not follow through the entire period of the war.

The preferred estimates are presented in table 5.1.

TABLE 5.1

New orders equations for durable and nondurable manufacturing.

$$O_{MD}^{54} = -48.058 + \frac{0.202}{(0.031)} \, [GNP_D^{54} - \Delta INV_D^{54} + GNP_{IC}^{54}]$$

$$- \frac{0.112}{(0.031)} \, [GNP_D^{54} - \Delta INV_D^{54} + GNP_{IC}^{54}]_{-1} + \frac{48.479}{(8.387)} \left\{ \frac{WPI_{MD}}{[WPI_{MD}]_{-1}} \right\}$$

$$+ \frac{0.424}{(0.054)} \left\{ \Delta \left[\frac{G_{MLF}}{P_{GF}} \right] \right\} \qquad S_e = 0.762 \qquad R^2 = 0.845 \qquad VN = 1.6050$$

(5.1a)

$$O_{MD}^{54} = -41.687 + \frac{0.184}{(0.021)} \, [GNP_D^{54} - \Delta INV_D^{54} + GNP_{IC}^{54}]$$

$$- \frac{0.096}{(0.021)} \, [GNP_D^{54} - \Delta INV_D^{54} + GNP_{IC}^{54}]_{-2} + \frac{42.482}{(8.154)} \left\{ \frac{WPI_{MD}}{[WPI_{MD}]_{-1}} \right\}$$

$$+ \frac{0.412}{(0.052)} \left\{ \Delta \left[\frac{G_{MLF}}{P_{GF}} \right] \right\} \qquad S_e = 0.727 \qquad R^2 = 0.855$$

(5.1b)

$$O_{MN}^{54} = -15.863 + \frac{0.136}{(0.004)} \, [GNP_N^{54} - \Delta INV_N^{54}] + \frac{11.224}{(4.620)} \left\{ \frac{WPI_{MN}}{[WPI_{MN}]_{-1}} \right\}$$

$$+ \frac{0.663}{(0.336)} \, DMYI \qquad S_e = 0.418 \qquad R^2 = 0.958 \qquad VN = 0.8231$$

(5.2)

The variables in order of appearance are:

O = manufacturers' net new orders, monthly rate, billions of dollars

GNP_D = durable goods component of gross national product, billions of dollars

INV = business inventory stock, billions of dollars

GNP_{IC} = construction component of gross national product, billions of dollars

WPI = wholesale price index, 1954 = 1.00

G_{ML_F} = federal government purchases of goods and services for national defense, billions of dollars

P_{GF} = implicit price deflator for federal government purchases of goods and services, 1954 = 1.00

GNP_N = nondurable goods component of gross national product, billions of dollars

$DMY1$ = 1, 1950 : 3 through 1951 : 2; 0, all other quarters.

Sector subscripts are:

MD = durable manufacturing

MN = nondurable manufacturing.

The estimates are encouraging. The value and signs of the coefficients estimated are plausible. The sampling errors of estimated parameters have been noted in parentheses. Following the common practice of assuming a zero critical value and a 95 per cent confidence level (5 per cent level of error), the t-test has been applied. The computed t-ratios of the coefficients substantiate the significance of the role of the variables in the estimated linear relationships. At a probability level of 5 per cent there is no evidence of serial correlation according to the von Neumann ratio in equation (5.1), while the computed ratio in equation (5.2) is indicative of the presence of autocorrelation. However, no attempt has been made to obtain estimates free of such correlation bias with respect to equation (5.2).

The sign of the price variable is, as expected, positive. The variable is based on price ratio, and as this ratio moves up, the business community appears to increase its orders to beat further rises in prices. The coefficients of the activity variable and its lagged value carry opposite signs and merit some explanation. The results appear as follows:

$$O = \alpha GNP_k - \beta [GNP_k]_{-1}.$$

This can be written as $O = [\alpha - \beta]GNP_k + \beta[\Delta GNP_k]$. Putting in the estimated values of α and β from the first equation, we have $[0.202 - 0.112]GNP_k + 0.112[\Delta GNP_k] = 0.090[GNP_k] + 0.112[\Delta GNP_k]$. In other words, the durable new orders appear to be positively correlated with both level and change in the level of final sales of durable goods plus new construction activity. Such findings appear acceptable.

Following the foregoing statistical analysis, we can rewrite the identities and accounting relationships (as referred to in section 5.1). We can set two separate identities relating to durables and nondurables. These are

$$O_{U_{MD}}^{NS} = [O_{U_{MD}}^{NS}]_{-1} - S_{MD}^{NS} + O_{MD}^{NS}$$

and

$$O_{U_{MN}}^{NS} = [O_{U_{MN}}^{NS}]_{-1} - S_{MN}^{NS} + O_{MN}^{NS}.$$

Then we have the following accounting relationships

$$S_{MD}^{NS} = g_s S_{MD}; \qquad O_{MD}^{NS} = g_0 O_{MD}; \qquad O_{U_{MD}}^{NS} = g_u O_{U_{MD}}$$
$$S_{MN}^{NS} = g_s' S_{MN}; \qquad O_{MN}^{NS} = g_0' S_{MN}; \qquad O_{U_{MN}}^{NS} = g_u' O_{MN},$$

where g_s, g_0, etc. are known seasonal adjustment coefficients. We may use last year's seasonal adjustments for the current year. To close our subsystem, we must somehow reconcile final sales used in the estimated equations and gross sales used in the identities. We have approximated this by choosing components of gross national product which are seemingly closely related to each sector's activity.

5.3. *Business new orders continued*: *subgroup of durable orders*

It is natural to extend the analysis relating to business new orders to disaggregated subgroups thereof, especially since an ultimate model contemplated will have individual sectors as fine as those reporting separate orders data. Following the contemplated pattern of disaggregation of the Brookings-SSRC econometric model, durable orders have been broken down into eight major subgroups: (1) primary metals; (2) fabricated metals; (3) nonelectrical machinery; (4) electrical machinery; (5) transportation equipment; (6) furniture and lumber; (7) stone, clay and glass; (8) other durables. Estimates have also been obtained for motor vehicles and equipment orders, the major individual component in the transportation equipment subgroup. The eight major breakdowns add up approximately to total durable orders.

This extended study relates to quarterly observations of the time period from 1948 through 1960. However, for some of these subgroups the available series did not cover the entire time period. The quarterly real dollar order sums of each category have been regressed on one activity variable, on a price change variable, and on a variable for government activity. The lagged value of the appropriate activity variable and a time-trend variable have been found significant in some equations. The activity variable in the equations should be appropriate demands, which feed back to stimulate orders. But to construct appropriate demand series requires knowledge of the end use of each category of goods ordered. Ignorance on this score forced us to take two short cuts. In some equations, orders were regressed on sectoral output. This approach has its limitations because inventory changes by sector are not accounted for. Orders, even when correctly matched with sectoral outputs, might be the result of unexplained stockholding. For other subgroups and in some alternate equations demand is approximated by *GNP* components. A priori, in a quarterly model, the current level of new orders should be related to demand of the recent past. However, statistical estimates with lagged values of the final demand variable alone, in multiple regressions with price and other related variables, did not show encouraging results. Rather, the use of demand of both period t and period $t-1$ appeared to give improved estimates. As in the case of total durable orders, results obtained in subgroup estimates indicate that the level of new orders is positively correlated with the current level and changes in the level of demand.

The price change variable, based on price ratios between successive time points, appears to give significant results in equations for most subgroups. In equations for electrical machinery and transportation equipment, this price variable has been found, as expected, to be highly insignificant. A major share of new orders in these subgroups comes from government, and, as such, the normal price mechanism may not be expected to work. The government variable used is the change in the federal military expenditure, i.e., (military expenditure$_t$ − military expenditure$_{t-1}$). This also serves as a proxy variable for disturbed order situations as in the Korean war period.

Estimated equations for subgroup orders, in their preferred forms, are presented in table 5.2.

Table 5.2

New order equations for two-digit manufacturing industries.

Primary metal industries

$$O_{33}^{54} = -10.695 + \frac{0.036}{(0.017)} \left[\frac{C_D}{P_{CD}} + \frac{I_{BUS_{EAF}}}{P_{IPDE}} \right] - \frac{0.039}{(0.017)} \left[\frac{C_D}{P_{CD}} + \frac{I_{BUS_{EAF}}}{P_{IPDE}} \right]_{-1}$$

$$+ \frac{12.645}{(1.973)} \left\{ \frac{WPI_{33}}{[WPI_{33}]_{-1}} \right\}$$

$$n = 51 \qquad S_e = 0.285 \qquad R^2 = 0.429 \qquad VN = 1.170 \qquad (5.3)$$

Fabricated metal products

$$O_{34}^{54} = -3.221 + \frac{0.027}{(0.007)} \left[\frac{C_D}{P_{CD}} + \frac{I_{BUS_{EAF}}}{P_{IPDE}} \right] - \frac{0.021}{(0.007)} \left[\frac{C_D}{P_{CD}} + \frac{I_{BUS_{EAF}}}{P_{IPDE}} \right]_{-1}$$

$$+ \frac{3.802}{(0.862)} \left\{ \frac{WPI_{34}}{[WPI_{34}]_{-1}} \right\} + \frac{0.047}{(0.010)} \left\{ \Delta \left[\frac{G_{ML_F}}{P_{GF}} \right] \right\} + \frac{0.007}{(0.003)} TIME$$

$$n = 51 \qquad S_e = 0.112 \qquad R^2 = 0.705 \qquad VN = 2.1470 \qquad (5.4)$$

Machinery except electrical

$$O_{35}^{54} = -3.918 + \frac{0.084}{(0.023)} \left[\frac{I_{PDE}}{P_{IPDE}} \right] - \frac{0.054}{(0.023)} \left[\frac{I_{PDE}}{P_{IPDE}} \right]_{-1}$$

$$+ \frac{4.640}{(1.346)} \left\{ \frac{WPI_{35}}{[WPI_{35}]_{-1}} \right\} + \frac{0.117}{(0.016)} \left\{ \Delta \left[\frac{G_{ML_F}}{P_{GF}} \right] \right\} + \frac{0.017}{(0.002)} TIME$$

$$n = 48 \qquad S_e = 0.167 \qquad R^2 = 0.790 \qquad VN = 1.9380 \qquad (5.5)$$

Electrical machinery, equipment and supplies

$$O_{36}^{54} = 0.025 + \frac{0.019}{(0.008)} \left[\frac{C_D}{P_{CD}} + \frac{I_{PDE}}{P_{IPDE}} \right] + \frac{0.065}{(0.018)} \left\{ \Delta \left[\frac{G_{ML_F}}{P_{GF}} \right] \right\}$$

$$+ \frac{0.006}{(0.004)} TIME$$

$$n = 51 \qquad S_e = 0.207 \qquad R^2 = 0.513 \qquad VN = 1.5760 \qquad (5.6a)$$

$$O_{36}^{54} = 0.363 + \frac{0.356}{(0.073)} X_{36}^{54} - \frac{0.229}{(0.073)} [X_{36}^{54}]_{-1} + \frac{0.064}{(0.015)} \left\{ \Delta \left[\frac{G_{ML_F}}{P_{GF}} \right] \right\}$$

$$n = 51 \qquad S_e = 0.177 \qquad R^2 = 0.645 \qquad VN = 1.9597 \qquad (5.6b)$$

TABLE 5.2 (Continued)

Transportation equipment

$$O_{37}^{54} = -0.628 + \frac{0.160}{(0.034)} X_{RT}^{54} + \frac{0.162}{(0.031)} \left\{ \Delta \left[\frac{G_{ML_F}}{P_{GF}} \right] \right\}$$

$$n = 47 \qquad S_e = 0.383 \qquad R^2 = 0.546 \qquad VN = 1.1707 \qquad (5.7a)$$

$$O_{37}^{54} = 0.650 + \frac{0.148}{(0.033)} X_{37}^{54} + \frac{0.223}{(0.033)} \left\{ \Delta \left[\frac{G_{ML_F}}{P_{GF}} \right] \right\} - \frac{0.014}{(0.008)} TIME$$

$$n = 47 \qquad S_e = 0.361 \qquad R^2 = 0.606 \qquad VN = 1.3441 \qquad (5.7b)$$

Motor vehicles and motor vehicle equipment

$$O_{371}^{54} = -7.636 + \frac{0.176}{(0.016)} X_{371}^{54} + \frac{7.733}{(2.140)} \left\{ \frac{WPI_{3711}}{[WPI_{3711}]_{-1}} \right\}$$

$$+ \frac{0.146}{(0.054)} \left\{ \Delta \left[\frac{G_{ML_F}}{P_{GF}} \right] \right\} - \frac{0.009}{(0.002)} TIME$$

$$n = 32 \qquad S_e = 0.125 \qquad R^2 = 0.850 \qquad VN = 2.6575 \qquad (5.8)$$

Lumber and wood products and furniture and fixtures

$$O_{24+25}^{54} = 0.278 + \frac{0.015}{(0.002)} \left[\frac{C_D}{P_{CD}} + \frac{I_{CNFR}}{P_{ICNFR}} \right] + \frac{0.061}{(0.018)} \left\{ \Delta \left[\frac{G_{ML_F}}{P_{GF}} \right] \right\}$$

$$- \frac{0.012}{(0.001)} TIME$$

$$n = 32 \qquad S_e = 0.043 \qquad R^2 = 0.801 \qquad VN = 1.7899 \qquad (5.9a)$$

$$O_{24+25}^{54} = 0.281 + \frac{0.016}{(0.003)} \left[\frac{C_D}{P_{CD}} + \frac{I_{CNFR}}{P_{ICNFR}} \right] - \frac{0.013}{(0.001)} TIME$$

$$n = 32 \qquad S_e = 0.050 \qquad R^2 = 0.722 \qquad VN = 1.2249 \qquad (5.9b)$$

$$O_{24+25}^{54} = 0.096 + \frac{0.140}{(0.022)} X_{24+25}^{54} - \frac{0.011}{(0.001)} TIME$$

$$n = 32 \qquad S_e = 0.048 \qquad R^2 = 0.742 \qquad VN = 1.1560 \qquad (5.9c)$$

TABLE 5.2 (Continued)

Stone, clay and glass products

$$O_{32}^{54} = -0.795 + \frac{0.024}{(0.005)} I_C^{54} + \frac{0.741}{(0.660)} \left\{ \frac{WPI_{325}}{[WPI_{325}]_{-1}} \right\} - \frac{0.006}{(0.001)} TIME$$

$$n = 32 \quad S_e = 0.043 \quad R^2 = 0.561 \quad VN = 1.7949 \qquad (5.10)$$

Other durable manufacturing industries

$$O_{38+39*}^{54} = 4.322 + \frac{0.007}{(0.003)} \left[\frac{C_D}{P_{CD}} + \frac{I_{PDE}}{P_{IPDE}} \right] - \frac{0.003}{(0.001)} \left[\frac{C_D}{P_{CD}} + \frac{I_{PDE}}{P_{IPDE}} \right]_{-1}$$

$$+ \frac{4.964}{(1.614)} \left\{ \frac{WPI_{MD}}{[WPI_{MD}]_{-1}} \right\}$$

$$n = 32 \quad S_e = 0.063 \quad R^2 = 0.458 \quad VN = 1.6139 \qquad (5.11)$$

The variables in order of appearance are:

O = manufacturers' net new orders, monthly rate, billions of dollars

C_D = personal consumption expenditures on durable goods, billions of dollars

P_{CD} = implicit price deflator for personal consumption expenditures on durable goods, 1954 = 1.00.

I_{BUS} = business gross investment in plant and equipment, billions of dollars

P_{IPDE} = implicit price deflator for investment in producers' durable equipment, 1954 = 1.00

WPI = wholesale price index, 1954 = 1.00

G_{ML_F} = federal government purchases of goods and services for national defense, billions of dollars

P_{GF} = implicit price deflator for federal government purchases of goods and services, 1954 = 1.00

I_{PDE} = gross private domestic investment in producers' durable equipment, billions of dollars

$TIME$ = time trend

X = gross product originating [by industry], billions of dollars.

I_{CNFR} = GNP expenditures for nonfarm residential construction, billions of dollars

P_{ICNFR} = implicit price deflator for *GNP* expenditures on nonfarm residential construction, $1954 = 1.00$

I_C = new construction component of gross private domestic investment, billions of dollars.

Sector subscripts:

EAF   = nonfarm
MD   = durable manufacturing
RT   = transportation industry
33   = primary metal industries
34   = fabricated metal products, except ordnance, machinery, and transportation equipment
35   = machinery, except electrical
36   = electrical machinery, equipment, and supplies
37   = transportation equipment
371   = motor vehicles and motor vehicle equipment
3711   = motor vehicles
24+25 = lumber and wood products, and furniture and fixtures
32   = stone, clay, and glass products
325   = structural clay products
38+39* = instruments and miscellaneous manufacturing industries (including ordnance from 1953 through 1956).

The calculated test statistics substantiate the significance of the role of the variables used in the estimated relationships, except in the case of the time-trend variables in equations (5.6a) and (5.7b) and the price-change variable in equation (5.10), where the appropriate *t*-table values are found to be much larger than the corresponding computed *t*-ratios. At a 5 per cent probability level, there is no evidence of the presence of serial correlation in equations (5.4), (5.5), (5.6a), (5.6b), (5.9a), (5.10) and (5.11), according to the von Neumann ratio; there is no evidence of such correlation in equation (5.8). But the computed ratios with respect to equations (5.3), (5.7a), (5.7b), (5.9b) and (5.9c) are indicative of the presence of serial correlation.

The lagged value of the related activity variable has been found significant in equations (5.3), (5.4), (5.5), (5.6b) and (5.11). Together they compose the major share of the new orders. The coefficient of the lagged variable in the above-mentioned equations carries a negative sign uniformly. Interestingly enough, this was so even in the aggregate durable goods order equation. The results so obtained can be worked in most cases to show a positive coefficient with respect to current level of activity and also to changes in the level of activity between the current and past time periods, except for equation (5.3).

Government military expenditures have been found to be an important variable in all equations except the ones for primary metals; stone, clay and glass; and other durables. The variable was expected to be important with respect to primary metals, and further investigation is called for before a conclusion can be reached. On the other hand, contrary to expectation, the variable appears highly important in the equation for furniture and lumber. Actually, this is one reason why an alternative formulation (5.9b), excluding the government activity variable, has been reported. In general, it may be concluded that government military expenditures significantly affect the levels of business new orders. This emphasizes the need for constructing a series of government military orders which would be a more appropriate variable in this respect.

The variable based on price ratios has been found insignificant only in equations for transportation equipment, electrical machinery and furniture and lumber. Such results were not unexpected for equations pertaining to transportation equipment and electrical machinery. The estimated coefficient of the price variable in (5.10) appears to be statistically insignificant, but the inclusion of the variable in the preferred estimate was considered necessary. To isolate the disturbing influence of government interference in transportation equipment in general, an independent equation with respect to the motor vehicles and equipment component alone has been estimated. The variable based on price ratios appears to be highly significant (5.8). The role of price with respect to furniture and lumber should be further examined. The price ratios between successive quarters are, in general, ratios of the prices of the goods ordered. However, prices of the goods ordered were not available in all cases and, therefore, prices of closely related goods were used.

The use of the time-trend variable was found important in most of these equations. The trend was found to be positive with respect to fabricated metals, nonelectrical machinery, and electrical machinery, while negative in the case of transportation equipment; furniture and lumber; stone, clay and glass; and motor vehicles and equipment. However, further investigation is called for before we can make any conclusion with respect to this variable.

5.4. Concluding comments

Taking an aggregative view of the production sectors of the economy, orders received and orders placed reduce to the same economic magnitude. This generalization has been a maintained hypothesis of this study.

The present study falls short of its objective from some important points of consideration. Orders for durables as well as for nondurables should be investigated in more detail on the basis of finer sector disaggregation. Furthermore, it has been suggested that multiple ordering is a characteristic phenomenon in the business world. The use of a proxy variable based on changes in government defense purchases, as has been done in this study, may be considered too arbitrary. Supply restrictions also have a bearing on the ordering pattern of the business community. The ratio of labor force participation or unemployment might be considered a representative index of the relevant economic situation in subsequent work.

REFERENCES

1. U. S. CONGRESS, Joint Economic Committee. *Hearings on Joint Economic Report, 1961* (cf. pp. 653–654, 659, 661, 667–668). *Hearings on Inventory Fluctuations and Economic Stabilization, 1962* (cf. pp. 148, 152, 154, 157).
2. MUTH, JOHN F. Rational Expectations and the Theory of Price Movements, *Econometrica* 29 (July, 1961) 316.
3. ZARNOWITZ, VICTOR. Unfilled Orders, Price Changes and Business Fluctuations, *The Review of Economics and Statistics* (November, 1962). Reprinted as National Bureau of Economic Research Occasional Paper No. 84.

PART III

Consumer expenditure decisions

CHAPTER 6

NONBUSINESS CONSTRUCTION

Contents

6.1. Introduction 179

6.2. Market structure 185
   1. New dwellings. 2. Other residential construction. 3. Social and recreational construction.

6.3. Data 189

6.4. The estimating equations 194
   1. New dwellings. 2. Other residential construction. 3. Social and recreational construction.

6.5. Evaluation and future estimates 199

NONBUSINESS CONSTRUCTION

SHERMAN J. MAISEL [1]

Federal Reserve Board, Washington, D.C.

6.1. Introduction

Nonbusiness construction includes three final demand sections—new dwellings; additions, alterations and nonhousekeeping; social and other nonresidential—of the *GNP* accounts. These, together with their values and an indication of their variability, are shown in table 6.1. These construction estimates exclude building for farms, business and government. Business construction expenditures are contained in the estimates of plant and equipment, while government construction is part of the purchases of goods and

TABLE 6.1

GNP expenditures for nonbusiness construction.

Type	1961 (billions of dollars)		Coefficient of variation
	Current	1954	
New dwellings	17.0	13.1	42.3
Residential, additions and other	6.1	5.1	25.0
Social and other nonresidential	3.4	2.8	16.2
Total	26.5	21.0	

Source   U. S. Department of Commerce

[1] The research for this project was undertaken while the author was a member of the faculty of the University of California, Berkeley; it was aided by funds from the Center for Real Estate and Urban Economics, University of California, Berkeley, and the Capital Markets Research Project, Harvard University.

services made at each level of government. Nonbusiness construction makes up slightly less than 5 per cent of final demand but has a variability that is among the largest for all sectors.

TABLE 6.2

Nonbusiness construction equations.

$$I^{54}_{\text{CNFRD*}} = \left\{ 0.41 \left\{ \left[\frac{PM_{\text{ICRD}}}{P_{\text{ICNFR}}} \right] [HU_{\text{STS}}] \right\} + 0.49 \left\{ \left[\frac{PM_{\text{ICRD}}}{P_{\text{ICNFR}}} \right] [HU_{\text{STS}}] \right\}_{-1} \right.$$

$$\left. + 0.10 \left\{ \left[\frac{PM_{\text{ICRD}}}{P_{\text{ICNFR}}} \right] [HU_{\text{STS}}] \right\}_{-2} \right\} 10^{-6}. \tag{6.1}$$

$$I^{54}_{\text{CNFRO*}} = \left\{ -383.65 + \frac{0.05244}{(0.00167)} [HU_{\text{AVL}}] - \frac{1217.69}{(416.58)} \left[\frac{P_{\text{ICNFR}}}{P_{\text{GNP}}} \right]_{-2} \right\} 10^{-3}.$$
$$R^2 = 0.98 \tag{6.2}$$

$$I^{54}_{\text{CO}} = -164.33 + \frac{0.47796}{(0.06247)} \left[\sum_{i=-4}^{0} w_i IP^{54}_{\text{CO}_i} + \frac{1.9233}{(0.1290)} \left\{ \tfrac{1}{3} \sum_{i=-4}^{-2} \left[\frac{Y_D}{P_{\text{GNP}}} \right]_i \right\} \right].$$
$$R^2 = 0.95. \tag{6.3}$$

$$HU_{\text{STS}} = -172.9 + \frac{0.5908}{(0.333)} [\Delta HH] + \frac{2.546}{(1.50)} HU_{\text{REM}} - \frac{0.1441}{(0.0367)} [HU_{\text{VAC*}}]_{-1}$$

$$+ \frac{2.673}{(0.905)} \left[\frac{CPI_{\text{SR}}}{P_{\text{ICNFR}}} \right]_{-1} - \frac{20.25}{(6.73)} \left\{ \tfrac{1}{3} \sum_{i=-4}^{-2} [RM_{\text{GBS3}}]_i \right\}$$

$$+ \frac{0.3177}{(0.1420)} [HU_{\text{STS}}]_{-1} - \frac{0.2357}{(0.0780)} [HU_{\text{STS}}]_{-3}.$$
$$R^2 = 0.85. \tag{6.4}$$

$$\frac{PM_{\text{ICRD}}}{P_{\text{ICNFR}}} = -5555.31 + \frac{2.935}{(0.328)} \left\{ \tfrac{1}{3} \sum_{i=-4}^{-2} \left[\frac{Y_D}{P_{\text{GNP}} \cdot HH} \right]_i \right\} 10^6$$

$$- \frac{296.4}{(119.4)} \left\{ \tfrac{1}{3} \sum_{i=-4}^{-2} [RM_{\text{GBS3}}]_i \right\}.$$
$$R^2 = 0.76. \tag{6.5}$$

TABLE 6.2 (Continued)

$$\left[\sum_{i=-4}^{0} w_i IP_{CO_i}^{54} \right] = 0.129 J_{BLDG} + 0.294 [IP_{CO}^{54}]_{-1} + 0.281 [IP_{CO}^{54}]_{-2}$$
$$+ 0.181 [J_{BLDG}]_{-3} + 0.115 [J_{BLDG}]_{-4} . \tag{6.6a}$$

$$IP_{CO}^{54} = -52.53 + \frac{0.7873}{(0.0866)} [IP_{CO}^{54}]_{-1} + \frac{0.5294}{(0.247)} \left\{ \frac{1}{3} \sum_{i=-4}^{-2} \left[\frac{Y_D}{P_{GNP}} \right]_i \right\} .$$
$$R^2 = 0.85 \tag{6.6b}$$

$$\Delta HH = \left[\frac{MAR}{MARE} \right] [\Delta HHE] \tag{6.7a}$$

$$\Delta \left[\frac{MAR}{MARE} \right] = 0.4303 - \frac{0.17}{(0.11)} [\Delta RU_{M1824}] - \frac{0.4299}{(0.0710)} \left\{ \frac{1}{3} \sum_{i=-4}^{-2} \left[\frac{MAR}{MARE} \right]_i \right\} .$$
$$R^2 = 0.47 \tag{6.7b}$$

$$HU_{REM} = 21.4 + 0.001 \, HU_{AVL} . \tag{6.8}$$

$$CPI_{SR} = 0.7441 + \frac{0.00226}{(0.00008)} \left[\frac{Y_D}{P_{GNP}} \right]_{-1} - \frac{0.00005}{(0.00002)} [HU_{VAC*}]_{-1} .$$
$$R^2 = 0.97 \tag{6.9}$$

$$I_{CNFR}^{54} = [I_{CNFR*}^{54}][DMY15] . \tag{6.10a}$$

$$I_{CNFR*}^{54} = I_{CNFRD*}^{54} + I_{CNFRO*}^{54} . \tag{6.10b}$$

$$HU_{FIN} = [HU_{STS}^{S}]_{-2} + [HU_{STS}^{M}]_{-4} . \tag{6.11a}$$

$$HU_{FIN} = \Delta HH + HU_{REM} + \Delta HU_{VAC} . \tag{6.11b}$$

$$HU_{AVL} = [HU_{AVL}]_{-1} + [HU_{FIN}] - [HU_{REM}] . \tag{6.12}$$

$$HU_{VAC} = [HU_{VAC}]_{-1} + \Delta HU_{AVL} - \Delta HH . \tag{6.13a}$$

$$HU_{VAC*} = HU_{VAC} - 26.73 \, TIME . \tag{6.13b}$$

$$\Delta HU_{UC} = HU_{STS} - HU_{FIN} . \tag{6.14}$$

The variables in order of appearance are:

I_{CNFRD*} = current level expenditures on new, nonfarm dwelling units, quarterly rate, billions of dollars

PM_{ICRD} = average cost per unit of private housing starts, dollars

P_{ICNFR} = implicit price deflator for *GNP* expenditures on nonfarm residential construction, $1954 = 1.00$

HU_{STS} = number of private housing units started, thousands

I_{CNFRO*} = current level expenditures on residential, nonfarm construction other than new dwelling units, quarterly rate, billions of dollars

HU_{AVL} = total available housing units, thousands

P_{GNP} = implicit price deflator for *GNP*, $1954 = 1.00$

I_{CO} = private nonresidential, nonbusiness construction, quarterly rate, billions of dollars

IP_{CO}^{54} = value of building permits for private, nonresidential, nonbusiness construction, quarterly rate, deflated by price of private, nonbusiness construction other than residential nonfarm, billions of 1954 dollars

Y_D = disposable personal income, billions of dollars

HH = number of households, thousands

HU_{REM} = net removals of housing units, thousands

HU_{VAC*} = adjusted vacant available housing units, thousands

CPI_{SR} = rent component of consumer price index, $1947-1949 = 100$

RM_{GBS3} = average market yield of three-month U.S. Treasury bills, per cent

MAR = number of marriages, thousands

$MARE$ = number of expected marriages, thousands

HHE = expected households based on population cohorts, thousands

RU_{M1824} = rate of unemployment among males aged 18 through 24, fraction

I_{CNFR} = *GNP* expenditures on nonfarm residential construction, billions of dollars

$DMY15$ = converter from quarterly rate current level expenditures on residential construction to *GNP* expenditures on residential construction at annual rate

I_{CNFR*} = current level expenditures on nonfarm residential construction, quarterly rate, billions of dollars

HU_{FIN} = housing units completed, thousands

HU_{STS}^{S} = number of single-family private housing units started, thousands

HU_{STS}^{M} = number of multifamily private housing units started, thousands

HU_{VAC} = vacant available housing units, thousands

$TIME$ = time trend

HU_{UC} = stock of housing units under construction, thousands.

Table 6.2 shows the list of relationships used in this sector. The numbering of relationships in the remainder of this chapter follows that found in this table. Fourteen equations are used to derive (a) the total of nonbusiness construction, (b) an estimate of household formation, and (c) a rent index. As inputs in these relationships, this sector requires five variables from the rest of the model: short-term interest rates, disposable income, young males unemployed, construction costs and the general price level. It also uses three predetermined variables: potential households based on population, potential net marriage rates and a *GNP* converter. It constructs internally 13 variables which do not leave this sector.

A fairly lengthy process of planning and contracting occurs before construction activity actually takes place. The model constructed for this sector takes advantage of this fact. Equations (6.1), (6.2) and (6.3) estimate actual expenditures. We note that (6.1) and (6.3) are relationships based upon previous contract awards. Equations (6.4), (6.5) and (6.6b) are estimates for the amount of contracts to be awarded in any quarter.

This dual set of relationships allows the model to follow the real world more closely and logically than do those systems which attempt to compress both demands and production, covering a rather long time period in a single equation. Another advantage is that for short-run forecasts—up to a year—whenever they become available actual awards (roughly contracts) can be substituted for awards normally estimated within the model. The equations for contracts contain sizable lags in order to account for the period required for planning, architectural drawings and award of bids.

The flow chart shows in abbreviated form the relationships among the variables. The first series of boxes shows the initial variables found in the sector. New total dwelling units is equal to previous stock plus completions less removals. Changes in the marriage rate are a function of recent marriages and young male unemployment. The new level of vacancies is the previous level plus or minus the difference between new households and net additions to the stock. Rents are a function of vacancies and disposable income. The inventory under construction or lagged starts depends upon previous and current starts.

The third block shows basic demand or net household formation plus the level of removals. This demand is compared with newly completed units which are a function of previous starts. The difference between demand and completions is the change in vacancies (shown in the second block).

The fourth section shows the total number of dwellings started and their average value. The number started depends on basic demand, vacancies,

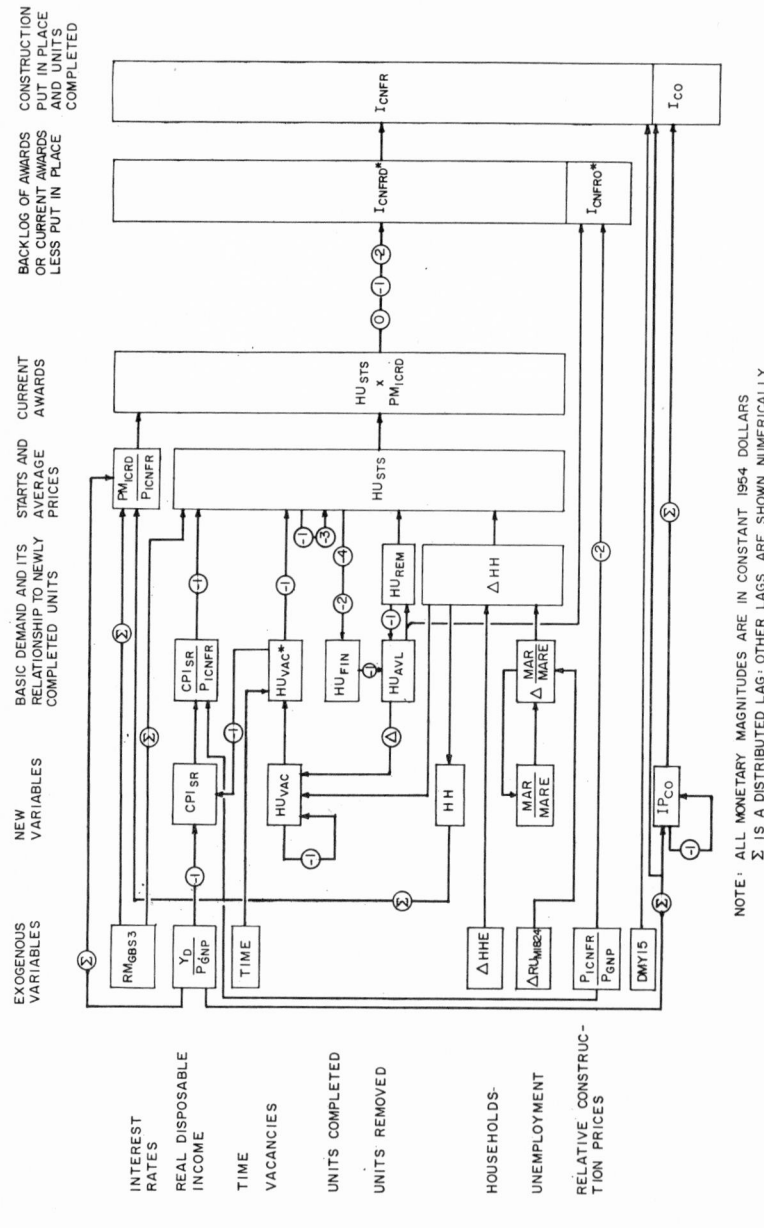

NOTE: ALL MONETARY MAGNITUDES ARE IN CONSTANT 1954 DOLLARS
Σ IS A DISTRIBUTED LAG; OTHER LAGS ARE SHOWN NUMERICALLY
Δ IS A FIRST DIFFERENCE.

Figure 6.1. Flow diagram for non-business construction.

rents relative to prices, interests rates and the level of inventories or previous starts. The average value depends on a moving average of lagged and current real income per household and the interest rate.

The number of starts times the average value of each gives the current awards for dwelling units. Current awards for alterations, additions and other residential expenditures are a function of the size of the existing stock and relative prices. The new awards are added to the existing backlog. The amount of construction put in place and the number of dwellings completed in any period are a physical function of the backlog of awards.

6.2. Market structure

6.2.1. New dwellings

The market for new dwellings accounts for over 60 per cent of the expenditures on nonbusiness construction and for still more of the variability. We examine it first and with greater detail than the remaining sectors [2]). Orders for residential construction require decisions along two separate paths: (a) What should be the number of housing units (family accommodations) built; and (b) what should be the average size, quality and value of each unit? The total amount of awards depends upon both dimensions. New housing construction is the product of the number of units times their average value.

Three basic groups enter orders for new housing. Individuals who contract for or build a house for their own use, builders or developers who start rental units and builders who start houses that they expect to sell to new owner-occupiers. While the percentages in these various groups have varied widely in different periods, for the first three years of the 1960's they roughly appear to have divided the market one-quarter, one-quarter and one-half, respectively.

What determines the number of dwelling units the entrepreneurs will order? (We will not consider separately those who build or order for their own use. Their impact on the market is the same as the other groups, even

---

[2]) I have published two articles which review in great detail the previous literature and theory in this sphere. The reader interested in bibliography or evaluation of previous work is referred to S. J. Maisel and L. Grebler, Determinants of Residential Construction, in *Impacts of Monetary Policy* (New York: Commission on Money and Credit, Research Study 4, 1963), and S. J. Maisel, A Theory of Fluctuations in Residential Construction Starts, *American Economic Review* (June, 1963).

though it may be somewhat more erratic because of noneconomic considerations.) Builders plan on being able to sell or rent their new units to newly formed households or to those whom they may attract from existing units. Emptied dwellings in turn either attract new households, are filled with families from other older units or perhaps are removed from the market. Any housing unit which fails to attract customers will remain vacant. One cannot assume that all new houses are filled by new families. In fact, the opposite is true. New sale units primarily attract already existing households. Movements within the stock of new and used units are extremely complex. For this reason it is simplest to deal with certain basic relationships which must exist within the total housing market, while recognizing that for some purposes a division into separate components might improve the model.

At any time the stock of dwellings, HU_{AVL}, divides into those containing a household, HH, or those vacant and available for occupancy, HU_{VAC}. (For convenience we consider houses reported as not available for use as removed from the stock.)

In each time period the stock of housing is increased by the number of completed new units, HU_{FIN}, plus or minus the number of net removals, HU_{REM}. A net increase in households, ΔHH, may also occur. Certain identities must hold among these various components.

The stock in period one plus completions minus removals equals the stock in period two. The change in the stock in period one minus the change in households must equal the change in vacancies, or:

$$HU_{\text{FIN}} - HU_{\text{REM}} - \Delta HH = \Delta HU_{\text{VAC}} = HU_{\text{VAC}} - [HU_{\text{VAC}}]_{-1}$$

where

$$[HU_{\text{AVL}}]_{-1} - [HH]_{-1} = [HU_{\text{VAC}}]_{-1}$$
$$[HU_{\text{AVL}}]_{-1} + HU_{\text{FIN}} - HU_{\text{REM}} = HU_{\text{AVL}}$$
$$[HH]_{-1} + \Delta HH = HH$$
$$HU_{\text{AVL}} - HH = HU_{\text{VAC}}.$$

Thus we note the obvious but critical fact that if completions outrun the rate at which final demand ($\Delta HH + HU_{\text{REM}}$) increases, vacancies will build up and vice versa. We can utilize this fact to describe the market's functioning. The equilibrium number of new dwellings required in any period is equal to changes in final demand (i.e., household formation and removals). The actual number of new dwelling units coming into the market—completions, HU_{FIN}—will be a lagged function of previous housing contracts or starts, HU_{STS}. A disequilibrium reflects itself in changed vacancies.

If available vacancies expand (contract) faster than normal, builders' profits will decline (rise) because there is a cost in holding vacancies or because their selling price or rents, CPI_{SR}, will be subject to price pressures from the excess vacancies. As a result builders will lower their estimates of market demand and cut back on future starts. Builders may also alter their starts in response to changing profit expectations resulting from movements of wages and materials, P_{ICNFR}, or credits, $RM_{GBS\,3}$.

Thus housing starts should fluctuate in response to movements in final demand, because of inventory changes in vacant units or because of inventory fluctuations in the stock of units under construction. The inventory movements in turn are influenced by costs, rents, the price of credit and the average period units remain vacant.

In addition to fluctuating with the number of units started, the amount of awards for new housing varies with the average value, PM_{ICRD}, for each unit. The average value of units started depends in turn upon both the annual amounts households will spend for rent or imputed rents and the rates at which these rents are capitalized to give current values.

Normal demand theory tells us that the amount spent for housing should depend positively on average family income, Y_D/HH, and negatively on the relative price of residential construction, P_{ICNFR}/P_{GNP}. For owner occupiers, credit terms will determine how much housing capital can be bought with a given level of annual housing payments. Credit terms have three dimensions: the interest rate, payments to capital (amortization) and the required downpayment. All would be expected to influence the value of houses purchased, and all appear to do so. These same credit variables determine the profitability of any given rent payments to a landlord. The more he can borrow and the less he must pay for mortgage money, the more an investor can afford to put into apartments.

6.2.2. *Other residential construction*

While considerable time and analysis have been given to movements in new dwelling awards, this is not true for expenditures on "other residential construction", even though this category includes nearly a quarter of the purchases of nonbusiness construction. This series consists primarily of additions, alterations or other improvements made to our housing capital stock. In recent years, however, nonhousekeeping units—primarily motels, with a few hotels—have added significantly to this total.

We would expect expenditures on capital stock to be related in some form to the existing amount of stock, HU_{AVL}. We could also list income, prices and many other variables which might influence spending in this category. Unfortunately, the data are poor and our knowledge of the decision process in this sphere is slight. It therefore seems worthwhile to adopt the simplest possible theory to explain this construction. We utilize a model based on changes in stock and in prices rather than attempting to fit a more elaborate one. Since for this category the individual building jobs tend to be small, we assume no significant lag between awards and actual construction.

6.2.3. Social and recreational construction

Most of the final category of nonbusiness construction is made up of social and recreational expenditures. This group accounts for slightly over 10 per cent of the total. It consists primarily of churches, private schools, hospitals, universities and recreational buildings, together with a small scattering of miscellaneous engineering and building work. This category does not include the bulk of social and recreational construction, which in recent years has been paid for by public funds and which as a result appears in the governmental sector.

These buildings tend to be somewhat larger than the average house. Therefore, they have a longer construction period. As a result it again appears more useful to follow the housing procedure and to use one equation to estimate awards or contracts and another distribution or realization function to estimate GNP expenditures. Unfortunately, data on actual awards are not published. Therefore, we have had to construct a series of awards from building permit data. It is this series which is then related to expenditures through a realization function.

In periods of strong population and suburban growth, needs for social construction are great. The factor limiting their production appears to be the ability of what are primarily nonprofit groups to raise money. As a result, it is not surprising that expenditures appear related to previous income levels. Differing types of growth in area and population could also influence this construction. However, since during recent periods almost all growth was strong and interrelated, the likelihood appears small of being able to distinguish among their effects on purely statistical grounds.

6.3. Data

The previous section indicated that to estimate the number of housing units started we need data on the housing stock, HU_{AVL}; plus the factors changing it, i.e., housing starts, completions and removals. We also need measures of its existing utilization by occupying households and vacancies plus their quarterly changes. Finally, data on costs, income and profits appear necessary to reflect pressures on builders. We also need data on the average value of starts and on the awards for and actual work done on other types of construction.

Housing data are notoriously bad. While they have been improving rapidly, they remain quite poor. The best sources for the most basic series are available in the decennial censuses of population and housing. It is difficult, however, to find adequate information for their movements on a quarterly or even annual basis. While some needed data are issued for shorter periods, such series appear to have sizable errors; they do not agree with each other, and in almost every case the decade totals of the current measures fail to agree with the basic decennial census totals. For other series, no short-period data exist at all.

In trying to fill these gaps, we assumed that the stocks and changes in the stocks reported by the decennial census are correct. In order to obtain estimates of movements on a quarterly basis, we interpolated the data with whatever current series seemed appropriate. The basic control totals are listed in table 6.3. This shows the stock in existence and its utilization on April 1, 1960 plus the changes which occurred in it from the previous census on April 1, 1950.

The data used in the regression models consists of quarterly interpolations of the changes shown in the bottom part of table 6.3 or moving totals for the following series: private housing starts, completions, net removals, dwelling stock, household formation, total households and available vacant units. A discussion of these data follows.

6.3.1. Private housing starts in the U. S. (HU_{STS}), including Alaska and Hawaii (seasonally adjusted). Source for 1959–1962, New Series, Total Private Housing Starts, U. S. Bureau of the Census, *Construction Reports-Housing Starts*, Series C-20. For the period 1950–1958, the government agencies report serious errors in published series. We have assumed that the reported movements of the data were correct in ratios but that they had been applied to an incorrect base. We selected as a base the total housing starts shown in table 6.3. To achieve this total we inflated the estimates for 1950–1958, found in U. S. Housing and Home Finance Agency, *Housing Statistics* (Historical Supplement, October, 1961, p. 3.). The data for 1950–1956 were inflated by 1.20. For 1957–1958, the multiplier decreased evenly per quarter from 1.20 to 1.15 to reflect reported inflations of the basic series during this period by the Bureau of Labor Statistics.

TABLE 6.3

The housing stock and its utilization in the U. S. on April 1, 1960.

Total available dwelling units April 1, 1960		54 966 000
Total occupied = total households by definition		53 021 000
Available vacancies		1 975 000
Nonavailable vacancies		3 328 000

Changes in the components since April 1, 1950

Net additions to households		9 645 000
Net removals		
Losses from available stock		
Mergers from existing units	900 000	
Demolitions	2 050 000	
Other losses	1 947 000	
Vacancies held off market	692 000	
Subtotal		5 589 000
Increase in seasonal units		337 000
Offsetting gains (negative removals)		
Public housing completions	425 000	
Trailers, institutional, group quarters, etc.	962 000	
From conversions of other structures, splits, etc.	1 700 000	
Decrease in dilapidated vacancies	6 000	
Subtotal		−3 093 000
Total net removals		2 833 000
Increase in available vacant units		1 245 000
Change in inventory under construction		−37 000
Total private housing starts:		13 686 000

Source   Adapted from U. S. Census of Housing 1960 Components of Inventory Change, HD (4), Part 1A–1, table C: U. S. Census of Housing 1950, Vol. 1, Part I; and 1960 Advance Reports, HC(A2)–1. Adaptation necessary because of change in definitions and sampling variability compared to decennial census.

6.3.2. Private dwellings completed (HU_{FIN}). No available data exist for this series. Studies of local markets indicated that an average lag from start to completion of two quarters for single family dwellings and four quarters for multifamily units appeared logical. This series was therefore estimated from starts (divided into single family and multifamily units) by an unvarying lag.

$$HU_{\text{FIN}} = [HU^{\text{S}}_{\text{STS}}]_{-2} + [HU^{\text{M}}_{\text{STS}}]_{-4}. \qquad (6.11a)$$

6.3.3. Changes in inventory under construction $(HU_{\text{FIN}} - HU_{\text{STS}})$. The changes in inventory under construction are by definition equal to completions minus starts.

6.3.4. Net removals from existing stock (HU_{REM}). Table 6.3 lists 9 separate types of action which may raise or lower the rate of net removals from the housing stock. Data for most of these items are only available for the decade. We have no knowledge of how they or the total varied on a quarterly basis. We used different methods of interpolating the total based on series such as income, log and linear growth functions and a constant removal rate. The final system of equations was rather insensitive to the particular form used in these estimates. We finally adopted a function which assumed a constant number plus a slowly increasing rate of other removals that depended on the changing number of dwelling units in existence. While this function has a basic logic, it appears no sounder than any of the other forms. Until more interim data are available, we will not know whether either the level (in 1963 about 320 000 units per year) or the shape of this function is logical.

$$HU_{\text{REM}} = 21.4 + 0.001 HU_{\text{AVL}}. \qquad (6.8)$$

6.3.5. Total stock of dwelling units (HU_{AVL}). Changes in the total stock depend directly on the previous data.

$$HU_{\text{AVL}} = [HU_{\text{AVL}}]_{-1} + [HU_{\text{FIN}}] - [HU_{\text{REM}}] \qquad (6.12)$$

or

$$\Delta HU_{\text{AVL}} = HU_{\text{FIN}} - HU_{\text{REM}}.$$

6.3.6. Net household formation (ΔHH). There are two basic sources for measures of household formation. One utilizes the annual estimates of number of households reported by the Census in the current population reports, corrected to agree with the decennial census. The adjusted annual movements can be distributed through a formula to the quarterly periods. We constructed such a series but felt that for econometric work it was inferior to the following procedure.

The second method distributes the decade change in households by quarters based on the growth and aging of the age-sex cohorts of the population. Adjustments among quarters for potential household formation are then based on movements reported by the National Office of Vital Statistics in current marriages and divorces.

6.3.7. Total Households (*HH*) depend completely on previous households and household formation.

$$HH = [HH]_{-1} + [\Delta HH].$$

6.3.8. Available vacant units (HU_{VAC}). There are also two sources for available vacancies. One is the series on Housing vacancies reported in U.S. Census *Current Housing Reports*, Series H-111. This series appears to have a sizable sampling error. In addition it is rounded approximately to the nearest 60 000. It appears probable that quarterly movements resulting from sampling and rounding errors exceed in magnitude the basic movements in the true variables.

We preferred to derive our vacancy data from the identity:

$$HU_{\text{VAC}} = HU_{\text{AVL}} - HH.$$

On the assumption that some increase in available vacancies is normal as the stock grows and therefore should not influence the number of starts, we corrected the estimated vacancies by a linear trend.

$$HU_{\text{VAC}*} = HU_{\text{VAC}} - 26.73 \, TIME. \tag{6.13b}$$

6.3.9. Average cost per unit of private housing starts in 1954 dollars, seasonally adjusted (PM_{ICRD}). This series published initially by the BLS and more recently by the census would be expected to have errors for the same reasons as the related starts data. It therefore should require revisions. However, there is no independent estimate available for such errors. As a result, we corrected the pre-1959 series only slightly to agree with the changed estimates of type of structure started.

6.3.10. Other residential construction in 1954 dollars, seasonally adjusted (I_{CNFRO}^{54}). This series contains estimates for new construction put in place for "additions and alterations" and "nonhousekeeping". The former series has been revised several times, but currently data prior to 1959 have not been inflated in the official series to agree with the present level of estimates. We multiplied the earlier series by 1.115 to agree with the new level.

6.3.11. Other nonresidential building in 1954 dollars seasonally adjusted (I_{CO}^{54}). This series contains the totals for "other private nonresidential building" and "all other private" as reported by the BLS and more recently, the Census.

6.3.12. Other nonresidential construction authorized by building permits (IP_{CO}^{54}). No published data exist for contract awards in this sphere. The closest available series is for building permits for social and recreational buildings. The form of these reports changed several times during the decade. We utilized the current series to set the proper level and revised previous series so that they would link at equivalent points.

All of the other required series, including prices, rents, interest and incomes employed in the regressions were the standard series found in the *Survey of Current Business.*

6.3.13. Rent index (CPI_{SR}). To close the model, it is necessary that this standard series be estimated. Prices, interest and income are received from other parts of the model. This sector, however, has to generate the rent index. It appears that the level of rents depends upon previous levels of income and vacancies.

$$CPI_{SR} = 0.7441 + \frac{0.00226}{(0.00008)} \left[\frac{Y_D}{P_{GNP}} \right]_{-1} - \frac{0.00005}{(0.00002)} [HU_{VAC*}]_{-1}$$

$$R^2 = 0.97. \quad (6.9)$$

Clearly, the lack of exactitude in the available series remains a major problem. However, the series utilized do appear somewhat better and more logical than those employed in previous studies. In addition, in several cases alternative estimates were used in the fitting of equations. Use of separate measures caused movements in the parameters and in the size of the errors, but in no case did they change the basic relationship or require a revision of our underlying theory of how the nonbusiness construction market operates.

6.4. The estimating equations

6.4.1. New dwellings

To obtain expenditures on new dwellings, we first estimate the value of awards in each period. These are then distributed to the following quarters through the procedure followed by the Department of Commerce which utilizes a distributed lag function that is changed rarely and then only after new field surveys. The value of awards is the product of separate estimates of the number of units started in a period and their average value.

The equations follow the structure of the market explained in section 6.2. Estimates of final demand for households and removals are made separately. They are then placed in a single equation with variables that influence the willingness of builders to accumulate inventories of units under construction and unoccupied vacancies.

Number of households   (*HH*)—Household movements are estimated from (a) long-run trends in the rate of marriages and other types of household formation applied to the changing size and structure of the population plus (b) short-run changes which result from cyclical pressures.

$$\Delta HH = \left[\frac{MAR}{MARE} \right] [\Delta HHE]. \qquad (6.7a)$$

ΔHHE is a predetermined variable based on the actual changes in household formation rates and population over the decade of the 1950's as reported by the Census together with projected changes for the next decade based on the 1960 structure of the population and trend in household formation.

Short-run changes in household formation have been found to depend on the current income or job situation plus the backlog or shortfall in potential formation. It must be recognized that there are two quite different types of household formation. The first is the change in the number of married couples resulting from marriages and divorces. The second is a movement toward greater privacy by nonmarried adults who decide to maintain separate households rather than living with relatives or in boarding houses or other institutions. Both of these trends are contained in the variable. However, on a current basis only changes in the marriage and divorce rates are available. The ratio of actual to expected net marriages is taken as the dependent variable in equation (6.7b) and its changes are applied to the entire population variable.

$$\Delta \left[\frac{MAR}{MARE} \right] = 0.4303 - \frac{0.17}{(0.11)} [\Delta RU_{M1824}] - \frac{0.4299}{(0.0710)} \left\{ \frac{1}{3} \sum_{-4}^{-2} \left[\frac{MAR}{MARE} \right]_i \right\}$$

$$R^2 = 0.49 \qquad S_e = 0.0099 \qquad DW = 1.55. \qquad (6.7b)$$

The unemployment variable is the rate of unemployment among males from 18 to 24. This group is particularly sensitive to income movements. It also is the group within which most marriages occur. The model assumes marriages will be postponed as unemployment increases. At the same time, if the rate of actual marriages remains below the potential ones for a considerable period this will tend to raise current marriage rates.

Net removals from existing stock (HU_{REM})—The equation (6.8) for this estimate and its derivation were described in the previous section.

Private housing units started (HU_{STS})—At one point in our estimating process, we attempted to obtain quarterly starts by adding the separate results obtained from each of the equations measuring the four basic forces causing alterations in starts, i.e., household formation, net removals, vacancies under construction and final vacancies. It appeared clear, however, that this was pushing the data too far because of missing information, the necessary relations between certain series and the way in which the remaining ones were derived. Therefore, in place of the sum of four separate estimates, we decided to use a single reduced form that included the movements of final demand $(\Delta HH + HU_{REM})$ together with changes in the inventory under construction, $[HU_{STS}]_{-1} - [HU_{STS}]_{-3}$, final nonnormal vacancies, HU_{VAC*}, plus factors influencing the willingness to increase starts or hold vacancies as expressed through short-term credit or interest rates, rents and costs. The results are:

$$HU_{STS} = -172.9 + \frac{0.5908}{(0.333)} [\Delta HH]$$

$$+ \frac{2.546}{(1.50)} HU_{REM} - \frac{0.1411}{(0.0367)} [HU_{VAC*}]_{-1}$$

$$+ \frac{2.673}{(0.905)} \left[\frac{CPI_{SR}}{P_{ICNFR}} \right]_{-1} - \frac{20.25}{(6.73)} \left\{ \frac{1}{3} \sum_{i=-4}^{-2} [RM_{GBS3}]_i \right\}$$

$$+ \frac{0.3177}{(0.1420)} [HU_{STS}]_{-1} - \frac{0.2357}{(0.0780)} [HU_{STS}]_{-3}$$

$$R^2 = 0.85 \qquad S_e = 17.01 \qquad DW = 2.09. \qquad (6.4)$$

Figure 6.2 contrasts the actual deviations of housing starts from their means with the deviations estimated by this equation.

It also shows the contributions of the individual variables to the estimates. The results appear in complete agreement with the basic theory. We note the relatively minor impact, only about 15 per cent of final demand on the fluctuations from the mean, compared with that of changes in inventories.

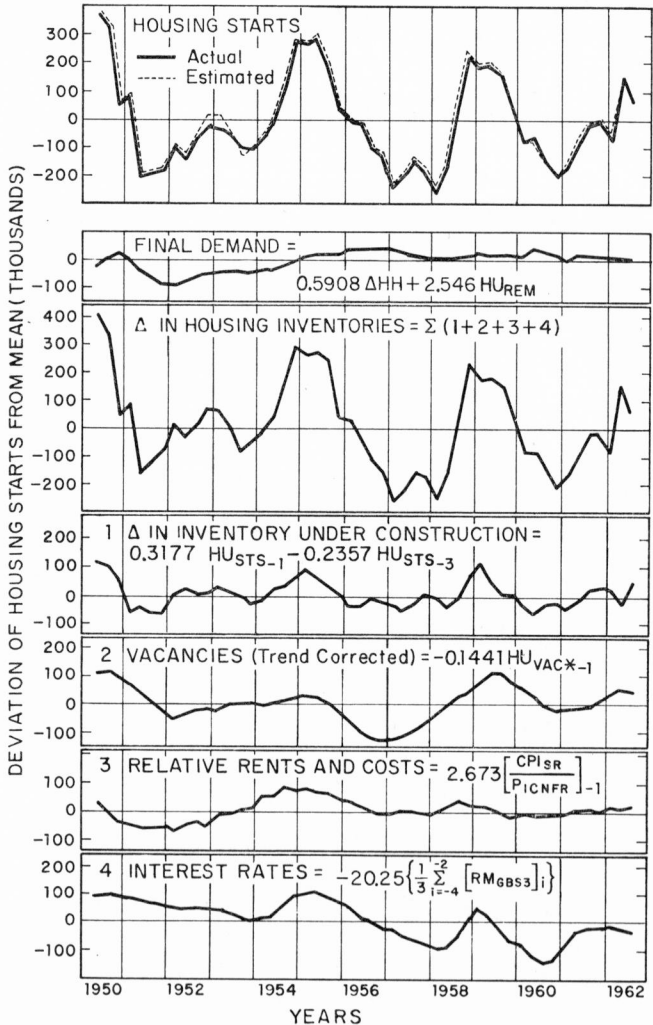

Figure 6.2. Relationships between housing starts and the independent variables (Thousands of starts—seasonally adjusted annual rates).

On the other hand, the final demand furnishes over 90 per cent of the equilibrium (mean level) of starts for the period.

Among the variables influencing the resulting inventory changes, the reaction time of inventories under construction, changes in interest rates and movements in final vacancies seem to be about equally important. Relative rents and costs appear to have less weight, but it is possible that this reflects some built-in bias toward stability in their underlying indexes.

Average value per housing start   In estimating average values per start, we found separate series for down payments, amortization and interest payments available on a cross-sectional basis. Their variations showed a statistically significant impact in the regressions. However, equivalent data were not available in time series. In our final equation, therefore, these different types of credit series are represented by the single credit measurement of short-term interest rates. We chose short-term rates in preference to an available series for long-term mortgage rates on the assumption that all dimensions of credit move in close agreement with the short-term availability, as reflected by its rate. Relative prices and household income have already been noted as obvious variables which should influence average expenditures. However, only household income had a significant coefficient. The resulting equation is:

$$
\frac{PM_{\text{ICRD}}}{P_{\text{ICNFR}}} = -5555.31 + \frac{2.935}{(0.328)} \left\{ \frac{1}{3} \sum_{i=-4}^{-2} \left[\frac{Y_D}{P_{\text{GNP}} \cdot HH} \right]_i \right\} 10^6
$$

$$
- \frac{296.4}{(119.4)} \left\{ \frac{1}{3} \sum_{i=-4}^{-2} [RM_{\text{GBS3}}]_i \right\}
$$

$$
R^2 = 0.76 \qquad DW = 0.46. \tag{6.5}
$$

In this equation, the time lags are primarily empirical. Because of the considerable planning period before contracts are let, it appears logical for a sizable time lag to exist. We note the low Durbin-Watson coefficient and the obviously high autocorrelation in this case.

Value of new dwelling unit construction   ($I_{\text{CNFRD*}}$)—The number of units started and their average value give us a total for contracts awarded in each quarter. The amount of actual construction in each period is in turn a quarterly distributed lag function derived from the monthly formula used for this purpose by the Department of Commerce.

$$I^{54}_{\text{CNFRD*}} = \left\{0.41 \left\{\left[\frac{PM_{\text{ICRD}}}{P_{\text{ICNFR}}}\right] \cdot [HU_{\text{STS}}]\right\} + 0.49 \left\{\left[\frac{PM_{\text{ICRD}}}{P_{\text{ICNFR}}}\right] \cdot [HU_{\text{STS}}]\right\}_{-1}\right.$$

$$\left. + 0.10 \left\{\left[\frac{PM_{\text{ICRD}}}{P_{\text{ICNFR}}}\right] \cdot [HU_{\text{STS}}]\right\}_{-2}\right\} 10^{-6}. \tag{6.1}$$

6.4.2. Other residential construction

The equation for estimating the amount of other residential construction follows directly from the theory. While many potential variables can be considered, a comparatively good explanation is obtained by utilizing only the size of the existing dwelling unit stock and relative prices. In this case, the lag from awards to time of construction is insufficient to require an additional equation.

$$I^{54}_{\text{CNFRO*}} = \left\{-383.65 + \frac{0.05244}{(0.00167)} [HU_{\text{AVL}}] - \frac{1217.69}{(416.58)} \left[\frac{P_{\text{ICNFR}}}{P_{\text{GNP}}}\right]_{-2}\right\} 10^{-3}.$$

$$R^2 = 0.87 \qquad S_e = 99.71 \qquad DW = 0.53. \tag{6.2}$$

Again we note the high degree of autocorrelation. By adding together expenditures on new and used dwellings, we should have the total *GNP* expenditure on residential construction.

$$I^{54}_{\text{CNFR*}} = I^{54}_{\text{CNFRD*}} + I^{54}_{\text{CNFRO*}}. \tag{6.10b}$$

Unfortunately, however, our estimates utilized the new Commerce series on housing and the revisions in the pre-1959 data required to bring them up to current levels. The national accounts use the opposite system. They have not yet revised the earlier period and so they adjust the current data back to the levels of the pre-1959 period. As a result, we require a predetermined converter to shift the current level generated by our model back to that of the pre-1959 estimates used in the national accounts.

$$I^{54}_{\text{CNFR}} = [I^{54}_{\text{CNFR*}}][DMY15] \tag{6.10a}$$

6.4.3. Social and recreational construction

The amount of expenditures on social and recreational construction depends upon a realization function of previous awards. However, we do not have an exact measure of these awards. Instead we have only an index for building permits issued in any period. The level of the permits is assumed to depend upon a considerable planning period during which population pressures alter and income levels change. The planning period is reflected through a form of distributed lag of previous permits.

$$IP_{CO}^{54} = -52.53 + \frac{0.7873}{(0.0866)}[IP_{CO}^{54}]_{-1} + \frac{0.5294}{(0.2470)}\left\{\frac{1}{3}\sum_{i=-4}^{-2}\left[\frac{Y_D}{P_{GNP}}\right]_i\right\}$$

$$R^2 = 0.85. \tag{6.6b}$$

If these permits were of the exact level of construction, they could be distributed over future periods as was done for the value of dwelling units. However, the building permits are an index; they vary from the level of construction depending on income and other forces. Our procedure is to measure the influence of previous permits on expected construction in any period, through a distributed lag function. This function is similar to the actual phasing of construction awards into construction put in place for social and recreational buildings.

$$[\sum_{i=-4}^{0} w_i IP_{CO_i}^{54}] = 0.129 IP_{CO}^{54} + 0.294[IP_{CO}^{54}]_{-1} + 0.281[IP_{CO}^{54}]_{-2}$$

$$+ 0.181[IP_{CO}^{54}]_{-3} + 0.115[IP_{CO}^{54}]_{-4}. \tag{6.6a}$$

This index of the expected level of construction in each period is then used as a major variable in a realization function from which we obtain the actual estimates of other nonresidential construction put in place.

$$I_{CO}^{54} = -164.33 + \frac{0.47796}{(0.06247)}[\sum_{i=-4}^{0} w_i IP_{CO_i}^{54}] + \frac{1.9233}{(0.1290)}\left\{\frac{1}{3}\sum_{i=-4}^{-2}\left[\frac{Y_D}{P_{GNP}}\right]_i\right\}$$

$$R^2 = 0.95. \tag{6.3}$$

6.5. *Evaluation and future estimates*

We have tested equation (6.4) (that for housing starts) through forecasts for annual periods by recomputations for periods outside of those used in the initial fitting, as well as by the data shown in figure 6.2. No tests contradict the underlying theory expressed previously. There appears to be a general equilibrium level of required new dwelling units (equivalent to household formation and units lost to the stock) around which the actual number of starts may fluctuate widely as a result of forces influencing inventory accumulation. For these tests, recomputations which added the years 1960, 1961 and part of 1962 showed the same parameters to be still statistically significant. The changes in the size of the regression coefficients were less than 10 per cent for 3 parameters and less than a third for the remainder. The forecasts from the original equations called each of the turning points but were about 5 per cent too low.

It is difficult to say whether or not these tests indicate satisfactory results. The forecasts were better than any other published forecasts that have come to our attention. On the other hand, they clearly are not satisfactory for many uses. It is likely that one cannot expect much better estimates unless the underlying data are greatly improved. Both more exact estimates of the existing quarterly series and data for new series not yet in existence are needed to improve the results.

Paramount among the new measurements required would be current series for removals and completions. If some data were available for these important measurements, it would then be possible to utilize the Census estimates on household formation and vacancies as independent checks on what is happening. Since identities exist among all of the series, it would be possible to use different combinations of the identities to obtain two or three separate estimates for each series. These could then be used in different combinations to see whether or not they altered the existing estimates of the parameters.

Another area for future work would be to examine the credit variables more carefully. We tested Federal National Mortgage Association purchases plus other types of interest rates in our previous regressions. While none gave as good results in the equations as did short-term rates, there are logical reasons for feeling that the best credit variables may differ in the future. As an example, the Federal Reserve has been attempting to change the interrelationships among the various credit markets in order to influence the balance of payments. This may be a structural shift which should be included in the model. We would also like to have better measures of the more direct qualitative policy variables, such as changes in the rates on FHA-VA insured loans and in sums voted for FNMA. It is hard to say whether the inability to separate credit variables in the past data occurs because of a lack of a true relationship, poor data, or highly collinear series.

Another useful approach would be an attempt to have separate equations for the markets for single-family and multifamily housing. One would expect significant differences in causation and particularly in the lags for each of these markets. If they have unique reactions this would not have been important during much of the period covered in the previous tests because the ratios between the two markets changed only slowly. Since

1960, however, the growth of the percentage of the market formed by starts of multifamily units has been rapid. One would expect that this shift would increase the lag between vacancies and their depressing effect on new starts. The shift to multifamily units would also be expected to lower the average value of starts. It might be possible to shift the parameters of the present model in an *ad hoc* way to correct for these movements, but to build a statistical model containing separate equations for single-family and multifamily units is difficult because more complete data would be required than are now available.

Another important fact should be noted about the nonbusiness construction sector. In the past decade most of its variance has come from shifts in the number of starts. With more data and a better theory, we were able to construct a much more satisfactory set of equations for starts than for the other factors influencing construction expenditures. The other estimates, which together with starts give the final expenditure estimates, depend primarily on the slow-moving forces of income and existing stock. The amount of autocorrelation in their derivation is high. This means we cannot be certain that we have any really adequate concept of the true structure of these other markets. If they continue to move slowly, as in the past, our forecasts should be adequate. On the other hand, we have no way of testing the impact of potentially important policy variables. While we may be able to estimate the results of changes in income and relative prices, we cannot have much confidence in the accuracy of our parameter estimates.

No simple methods exist to solve these problems. Better results probably await better data. It would be helpful if series became available for local areas. Some attempts to fit equivalent models, either to time series in local areas or on a cross-sectional basis, appear promising. The greatest difficulty remains that which is found nationally—insufficient data.

Until more time passes and more tests can be performed we will lack the ability to push much beyond our existing model. New theories could be developed, and we could probably get equivalently good results based on the use of the existing data. It is clear, however, that until more detailed information is available the selection of other theories will remain primarily a matter of individual choice.

CHAPTER 7

CONSUMPTION REGRESSIONS WITH QUARTERLY DATA

Contents

7.1. Introduction 203

7.2. Liquid assets 204

7.3. Stocks of durables 205

7.4. Lagged dependent variable. 205

7.5. Consumer attitudes 206

7.6. Data 206

7.7. Results 207

7.8. Automobile demand. 207

7.9. Other durables 214

7.10. Food demand 215

7.11. Other nondurables 215

7.12. Services 216

7.13. Income and total consumption. 216

7.14. Limitations. 217

7.15. Appendix. Supplementary tables 218

References 223

CONSUMPTION REGRESSIONS WITH QUARTERLY DATA

DANIEL B. SUITS and GORDON R. SPARKS

The University of Michigan

7.1. Introduction

In this chapter we present consumption regressions describing the behavior of consumer expenditures disaggregated into five categories: automobiles, other durables, food, other nondurables and services. Not only is such disaggregation of interest in its own right, but a model is more useful when the behavior of its subsectors can be related to different sets of factors. Moreover, the ability to trace impacts on individual sectors is often essential to effective policy analysis.

The fivefold disaggregation used here follows the major expenditure categories of the national accounts, which represent widely differing degrees of homogeneity. Automobile expenditure, while hardly a homogeneous category, is an effective unit in the sense that it cannot be further disaggregated without a great increase in the complexity of the analysis. The step from the market for automobiles as a whole to that for any individual make or model involves a great elaboration of the equations and a large increase in the number of variables that must be taken into account. The heterogeneity of the service category is so great, on the other hand, that any number of subdivisions might be made of it without more complexity than is implied by the mere increase in the number of equations. By the same token, however, there is relatively little gain from such further disaggregation.

The formulation of each equation incorporates disposable income and a number of other variables whose role in consumer behavior has been emphasized in modern theory. Since the publication of Keynes' *General Theory*, a vast body of literature has been written on the consumption function [1]). The developments have resulted from both a dissatisfaction with Keynes' armchair formulation of the consumption-income relationship and the inconsistencies in the empirical data which indicated long-run constancy of the average propensity to consume but a short-run marginal propensity to consume less than the average. Research on consumption beyond simple regression of annual aggregate expenditures on income has revealed that the explanation of short-run consumer behavior requires many variables besides income.

7.2. Liquid assets

One important variable used in these equations is the stock of liquid assets owned by households. This variable enters significantly into the equations for other durables, nondurables and services, but its true role in the analysis is by no means certain. Ackley [1] has pointed out that the influence of asset holdings could account for the divergence between the short- and long-run marginal propensities to consume. If, in the long run, asset holdings increase in proportion to income, a proportional consumption-income relationship may be observed. In the short run, however, when income declines, assets do not decline proportionately and so consumption declines less than in proportion to income [2]). The influence of wealth in the form of liquid assets has been suggested as the cause of the upward shift in the consumption function from the prewar to the postwar period. Suits [16] fitted disaggregated consumption functions and found the influence of liquid asset holdings to be much greater in the postwar period. He suggested that the upward shift might be explained by an interaction between income and liquid assets.

Liquid asset holdings are also correlates of the longer run economic status of households, as distinguished from their current income. Several recent modifications of consumption theory have emphasized the inadequacy of current income as a determinant of consumption. The permanent income hypothesis of Friedman and its life-cycle variant developed by Modigliani, Brumberg and Ando relates the individual's consumption, defined as expenditures on nondurable goods and services plus depreciation of durable goods, to his total stock of wealth defined as net worth plus the present value

---

[1]) We shall attempt here only a brief summary of the literature on the aggregate consumption function. For a more complete discussion, the reader is referred to [6] and [16].

[2]) A similar explanation has been discussed recently by Ando and Modigliani in the context of the life-cycle hypothesis [2].

of expected future nonproperty income. Over time, measured income deviates from permanent income derived from the stock of wealth because of the timing of receipts, fluctuations in economic conditions, windfall gains or lossses, etc. Similarly, permanent or planned consumption differs from expenditures because of the timing of outlays for durable goods, impact of emergencies, etc.

7.3. Stocks of durables

The equations for automobile demand and for other durables contain the existing stock of the commodity. Relationships formulated in this way can be interpreted as a stock-adjustment mechanism. For example, we may postulate that the level of expenditures over and above replacement demand depends on the gap between the desired stock and the existing stock. Thus we have the relationship:

Expenditures $= \alpha$ (desired stock $-$ actual stock) $+$ depreciation. If the desired stock is proportional to income and the depreciation rate on the existing stock is constant, expenditures will be a linear function of income and stock. It should be recognized, however, that the stock-adjustment mechanism does not always operate on the level of the individual household. For example, the logic of the stock-adjustment mechanism would appear to mean that, income given, a household without a car or with an old used car would be more likely to buy a new car than a household with a relatively new car. As any car salesman knows, the reverse is true. New cars are generally purchased by habitual new-car buyers and the ownership of new cars is thus positively correlated with new-car purchases. This cross-sectional relationship does not contradict the negative role of stock in the determination of total demand. Since the new car buyer must still sell his old car in competition with the existing stock, the latter exerts a back pressure on new sales.

7.4. Lagged dependent variable

The attempt was made to introduce lagged values of the dependent variable in all the nondurables equations. The theoretical role of these lags is to represent the dynamic impact of past consumption on present habits. The first formulation of this theory by Duesenberry [5] and Modigliani [14] related present consumption expenditure to past peak income. This permits the marginal propensity to consume at below peak income to be lower than that exhibited when income rises to new peaks. The disadvantage of the mechanism is that it does not permit a corresponding dynamic readjustment of consumption standards when income falls.

The lagged value of the dependent variable provides dynamic adjustments with both rising and falling income. Any change in income generates a smaller change in expenditure at first, and expenditure approaches asymptotically a new equilibrium level.

There are serious statistical problems associated with the use of the lagged dependent variable, especially when levels, rather than first differences, are used in the regressions. When a growing economy is observed over a long time period, there is relatively little difference between any variable and its own value lagged one quarter. Regardless of the actual underlying demand mechanism the variable is significantly correlated with the lagged value, a fact that may yield not only spuriously high correlations but serious bias in the estimates of the other coefficients. The formulations to be discussed below, using a weighted mean of past incomes, were employed partly for this reason.

7.5. Consumer attitudes

Mueller and Katona [11, 12], have shown that in an economy of high incomes and high-asset holdings, consumers' attitudes and expectations affect their discretionary purchases, particularly of durables which involve commitments to future consumption. The Survey Research Center at the University of Michigan provides an index of consumer attitudes based on data obtained by sample surveys. Tests in the form of time series regressions have indicated that this index is a highly significant factor in predicting subsequent purchases of durable goods, and we have incorporated it in our demand equations.

The consumer attitudes index makes a significant contribution to the automobile demand equation, but its role in the model raises serious problems of interpretation that will be discussed later.

7.6. Data

Except as noted, all variables used are seasonally adjusted at annual rates, expressed in billions of 1954 dollars. Except for the food and the service series, data for all dependent variables are taken directly from the National Accounts. The food data are those prepared by Karl Fox for use in the agricultural submodel. Department of Commerce service expenditures have been modified by removing all imputed services.

7.7. Results

The regression equations are presented in table 7.1. Two formulations are given for each of the three nondurable categories. The first of these is a straightforward regression fitted to the levels. The second involves the general level of past income, represented by a weighted mean, and the deviation of current income from that past average. The two results are entirely consistent, but their comparison serves to show some important facts about the role of current income and of lagged variables in the analysis. In addition the second form is on a per capita basis.

The equations of table 7.1 are the result of a number of experiments in which various formulations and combinations were tried. Some of the alternative results are shown in table 7.3. The final form was selected on the basis of the goodness of fit shown by $\bar{R}^2$, and by the significance of individual regression coefficients.

7.8. Automobile demand

C_{DA}, consumer expenditure for new and net used automobiles, depends on disposable income net of all transfer payments except servicemen's insurance dividends. These transfer payments are deducted on the grounds that, since they consist of unemployment benefits, retirement pensions and relief payments, they are unlikely to find their way into the automobile market. In addition, demand depends on the stock of new cars and new car equivalents of used cars on the road at the end of the preceding period.

The data series for stock of cars was derived from the formula

$$CARS = [1 - RDPN_{DA}][CARS]_{-1} + REGS - [1 - RPDN_{DA}]^n [REMS]$$
$$\text{where } n = AGE_{CDA}.$$

TABLE 7.1

Consumer expenditure equations [a]).

Automobiles

$$C_{DA}^{54} = \overset{0.0790}{\underset{((0.275))}{(0.0221)}} [Y_D^{54} - V^{54} + V_{INS_{GF}}^{54}] - \overset{0.5124}{\underset{((0.092))}{(0.2512)}} [CARS]_{-1}$$

$$+ \overset{0.2329}{\underset{((0.646))}{(0.0307)}} [ATT]_{-1} - 19.6860 \qquad \bar{R}^2 = 0.686. \tag{7.1}$$

Other durables

$$C_{DEA}^{54} = \overset{0.1615}{\underset{((0.366))}{(0.0299)}} Y_D^{54} - \overset{0.1780}{\underset{((0.174))}{(0.0528)}} [K_{CDEA}^{54}]_{-1} + \overset{0.0485}{\underset{((0.149))}{(0.0157)}} \left[\frac{ALQD_{HH}}{P_C}\right]_{-1}$$

$$- 26.2094 \qquad \qquad \bar{R}^2 = 0.942. \tag{7.2}$$

Food

$$C_{NF}^{54} = + \overset{0.0656}{\underset{((0.232))}{(0.0165)}} Y_D^{54} - \overset{10.93}{\underset{((0.271))}{(2.49)}} \left[\frac{P_{CNF}}{P_C}\right] + \overset{0.1889}{\underset{((0.198))}{(0.0522)}} [N + N_{ML}]_{-1}$$

$$+ 21.0928 \qquad \qquad \bar{R}^2 = 0.991. \tag{7.3a}$$

$$\frac{C_{NF}^{54}}{[N + N_{ML}]_{-1}} = \overset{0.0549}{\underset{((0.173))}{(0.0170)}} \left\{\frac{Y_D^{54}}{[N + N_{ML}]_{-1}} - \sum_{i=1}^{12} b_i \frac{[Y_D^{54}]_{-i}}{[N + N_{ML}]_{-i-1}}\right\}$$

$$+ \overset{0.0278}{\underset{((0.259))}{(0.0068)}} \left\{\sum_{i=1}^{12} b_i \frac{[Y_D^{54}]_{-i}}{[N + N_{ML}]_{-i-1}}\right\} - \overset{0.0821}{\underset{((0.356))}{(0.0162)}} \left[\frac{P_{CNF}}{P_C}\right] + 0.3938$$

$$\bar{R}^2 = 0.837. \tag{7.3b}$$

Other nondurables

$$C_{NEF}^{54} = \overset{0.1691}{\underset{((0.779))}{(0.0127)}} Y_D^{54} + \overset{0.0743}{\underset{((0.182))}{(0.0213)}} \left[\frac{ALQD_{HH}}{P_C}\right]_{-1} + 4.2712$$

$$\bar{R}^2 = 0.979. \tag{7.4a}$$

[a]) Figures in parentheses ( ) are standard errors; figures in double parentheses (( ))
are coefficients of partial determination.

TABLE 7.1 (Continued)

$$\frac{C_{\text{NEF}}^{54}}{[N+N_{\text{ML}}]_{-1}} = \begin{matrix}0.1525\\(0.0386)\\((0.245))\end{matrix} \left\{ \frac{Y_{\text{D}}^{54}}{[N+N_{\text{ML}}]_{-1}} - \sum_{i=1}^{12} b_i \frac{[Y_{\text{D}}^{54}]_{-i}}{[N+N_{\text{ML}}]_{-i-1}} \right\}$$

$$+ \begin{matrix}0.1697\\(0.0134)\\((0.780))\end{matrix} \left\{ \sum_{i=1}^{12} b_i \frac{[Y_{\text{D}}^{54}]_{-i}}{[N+N_{\text{ML}}]_{-i-1}} \right\} + \begin{matrix}0.0496\\(0.0242)\\((0.066))\end{matrix} \left\{ \frac{ALQD_{\text{HH}}}{[P_{\text{C}}][N+N_{\text{ML}}]} \right\}_{-1}$$

$$+0.0563 \qquad \bar{R}^2 = 0.895. \qquad (7.4b)$$

Services

$$C_{\text{S}}^{54} - C_{\text{IS}}^{54} = \begin{matrix}0.0555\\(0.0144)\\((0.239))\end{matrix} Y_{\text{D}}^{54} - \begin{matrix}13.65\\(6.60)\\((0.069))\end{matrix} \left[\frac{P_{\text{CS}}}{P_{\text{C}}}\right] + \begin{matrix}0.8099\\(0.0500)\\((0.856))\end{matrix} \{\tfrac{1}{4}\sum_{i=1}^{4}[C_{\text{S}}^{54}-C_{\text{IS}}^{54}]_{-i}\}$$

$$+ \begin{matrix}0.0572\\(0.0148)\\((0.240))\end{matrix} \left[\frac{ALQD_{\text{HH}}}{P_{\text{C}}}\right]_{-1} +2.6820 \qquad \bar{R}^2 = 0.9985. \qquad (7.5a)$$

$$\frac{C_{\text{S}}^{54} - C_{\text{IS}}^{54}}{[N+N_{\text{ML}}]_{-1}} = \begin{matrix}0.0808\\(0.0342)\\((0.094))\end{matrix} \left\{ \frac{Y_{\text{D}}^{54}}{[N+N_{\text{ML}}]_{-1}} - \sum_{i=1}^{12} b_i \frac{[Y_{\text{D}}^{54}]_{-i}}{[N+N_{\text{ML}}]_{-i-1}} \right\}$$

$$+ \begin{matrix}0.3873\\(0.0233)\\((0.862))\end{matrix} \left\{ \sum_{i=1}^{12} b_i \frac{[Y_{\text{D}}^{54}]_{-i}}{[N+N_{\text{ML}}]_{-i-1}} \right\} + \begin{matrix}0.1993\\(0.0255)\\((0.577))\end{matrix} \left\{ \frac{ALQD_{\text{HH}}}{[P_{\text{C}}][N+N_{\text{ML}}]} \right\}_{-1}$$

$$- \begin{matrix}0.3441\\(0.0767)\\((0.303))\end{matrix} \left[\frac{P_{\text{CS}}}{P_{\text{C}}}\right] -0.0739 \qquad \bar{R}^2 = 0.972. \qquad (7.5b)$$

The variables in order of appearance are:

C_{DA} = personal consumption expenditures for new and net used automobiles and parts, billions of dollars

Y_{D} = disposable personal income, billions of dollars

V = transfer payments to persons, billions of dollars

$V_{\text{INS}_{GF}}$ = servicemen's insurance dividend component of transfer payments to persons, billions of dollars

$CARS$ = end-of-quarter stock of new cars and new car equivalents of used cars, millions

ATT = index of consumers' attitudes and inclinations to buy, 1954 = 100

C_{DEA} = personal consumption expenditures for durable goods other than new and used automobiles and parts, billions of dollars

K_{CDEA} = stock of consumer durable goods excluding automobiles and parts, billions of dollars

$ALQD_{HH}$ = end-of-quarter stock of liquid assets held by households: currency, demand deposits and fixed-value redeemable claims, billions of dollars

P_C = implicit price deflator for personal consumption expenditures, 1954 = 1.00

C_{NF} = personal consumption expenditures for food, including imputations, billions of dollars

P_{CNF} = implicit price deflator for personal consumption expenditures on food, 1954 = 1.00

N = civilian population including Alaska and Hawaii, end-of-quarter, millions of persons

N_{ML} = military population including armed forces overseas, end-of-quarter, millions of persons

C_{NEF} = personal consumption expenditures for nondurables other than food, including imputations, billions of dollars

C_S = personal consumption expenditures for services, including imputations, billions of dollars

C_{IS} = personal consumption expenditures for services, imputed, billions of dollars

P_{CS} = implicit price deflator for personal consumption expenditures on services, 1954 = 1.00

$RDPN_{DA}$ = rate of depreciation of automobiles, per cent

$REGS$ = registrations of new passenger cars, quarterly rate, millions

AGE_{CDA} = average age of cars scrapped, quarters of years

$REMS$ = removals of automobiles, quarterly rate, millions.

In applying the formula a depreciation rate of 6.325 per cent per quarter was used, based on estimates by Gregory Chow [4, p. 150]. The basic data used and the series derived are given in table 7.4.

Finally, expenditure on new cars depends on $[ATT]_{-1}$, the level of the index of consumer attitudes (1954 = 100) during the preceding quarter.

In fitting the equation, data for the period 1953 : 3–1961 : 4 were used. The immediate post-World War II period and the Korean war were omitted because of shortages and production controls and because of the great disequilibrium between stock and income. Results of including the earlier period are shown in table 7.3. The difference in behavior between the earlier years and the period since 1953 : 3 can clearly be seen in figure 7.1.

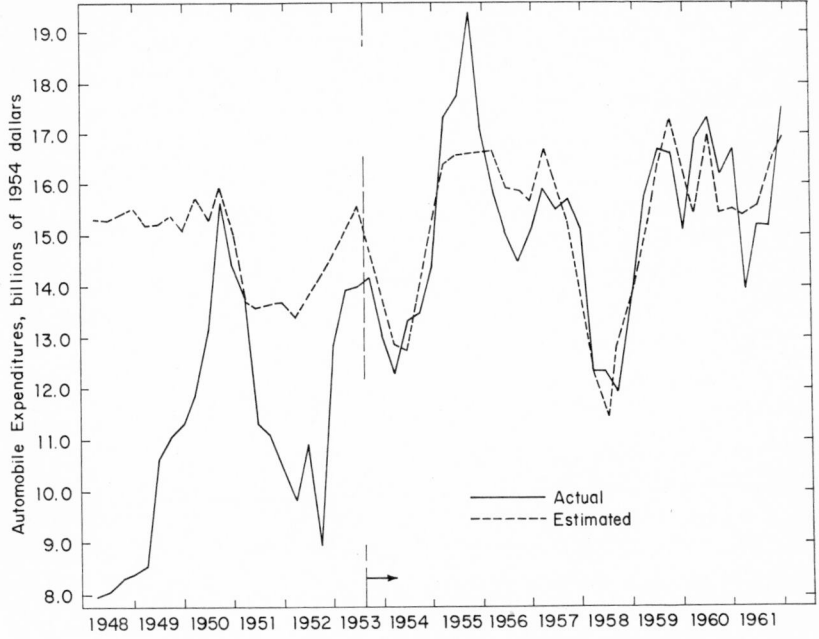

Figure 7.1. Actual and calculated automobile demand.

The most powerful factor in the equation is consumer attitudes (partial $R^2 = 0.646$), indicating that much of the observed behavior in the automobile market is traced to consumer psychology rather than endogenous economic factors. On the other hand, it is clear that consumer attitudes are themselves, to some extent, determined by economic events. Any change in income will necessarily be accompanied by some change in attitudes—the extent and direction doubtless depending on the source of the change in income. For this reason, the income coefficient, 0.079, cannot be interpreted as a "marginal propensity to consume automobiles". Any policy action designed to raise income will also change attitudes, and the full effect of the policy on the automobile market can only be estimated if we know the relationship between attitudes and policy. This means that while the equation is optimal purely for *forecasting* automobile demand from information on income and attitudes, it will not serve well for policy analysis until the reaction of attitudes to policy is also incorporated in the model.

This matter is worth further analysis: the simple correlation coefficient between income and attitudes is only -0.087, and, in keeping with this, the coefficient measuring the effect of income on automobile sales is virtually unaffected by whether attitudes are taken into account in the equation. This does *not* mean that income and attitudes are really independent. The fact is that while income has a strong upward trend over the period, the index of attitudes does not. (Indeed, by the nature of its measurement it cannot.) The low correlation between these variables is no more than a low correlation between their trends. When the index of attitudes is compared with the deviations of income from its own trend, as in figure 7.2, a substantial positive correlation appears. It follows that the apparent impact of attitudes as a variable in the demand for automobiles is to some (undetermined) extent due to its association with short-term income movements.

Income proper makes the second largest contribution to the behavior of automobile expenditure (partial $\bar{R}^2 = 0.275$). The magnitude of the income coefficient is quite consistent with the observation that about 5 per cent of income, at the margin, is spent on new cars. Of course, to whatever extent this coefficient represents an income "effect", it greatly overstates the long-run relationship of income to automobile demand; for a rise in income is accompanied by an increase in the stock of cars, which tends to reduce new purchases below the rate initially attained. This is shown by the significant negative coefficient on the stock of cars.

The dynamics of the adjustment process can be explored as follows. Ignoring attitudes and the constant term, we can write

$$C_{DA}^{54} = 0.079[Y_D^{54} - V^{54} + V_{INS_{GF}}^{54}] - 0.5124[CARS]_{-1}.$$

Moreover, approximately,

$$CARS \approx [CARS]_{-1} + REGS - RDPN_{DA}[CARS]_{-1};$$

where *REGS* is the number of new registrations (at quarterly rates) in millions. Taking \$2 000 as a typical car price, we have

$$REGS = \tfrac{1}{4} \cdot \frac{C_{DA}^{54}}{2},$$

and we know that $RDPN_{DA} = 0.0633$. From these we get

$$CARS = [CARS]_{-1} + 0.0099[Y^{54} - V^{54} + V_{INS_{GF}}^{54}] - 0.0641[CARS]_{-1}$$
$$- 0.0633[CARS]_{-1}$$

or

$$CARS = 0.8726[CARS]_{-1} + 0.0099[Y_D^{54} - V^{54} + V_{INS_{GF}}^{54}].$$

The equilibrium solution of this process is

$$CARS^E = 0.0777[Y_D^{54} - V^{54} + V_{INS_{GF}}^{54}].$$

When this value is substituted in the demand equation, we have

$$C_{DA}^{54} = 0.0790[Y_D^{54} - V^{54} + V_{INS_{GF}}^{54}] - 0.5124\{0.0777[Y_D^{54} - V^{54} + V_{INS_{GF}}^{54}]\}$$
$$= 0.039[Y_D^{54} - V^{54} + V_{INS_{GF}}^{54}].$$

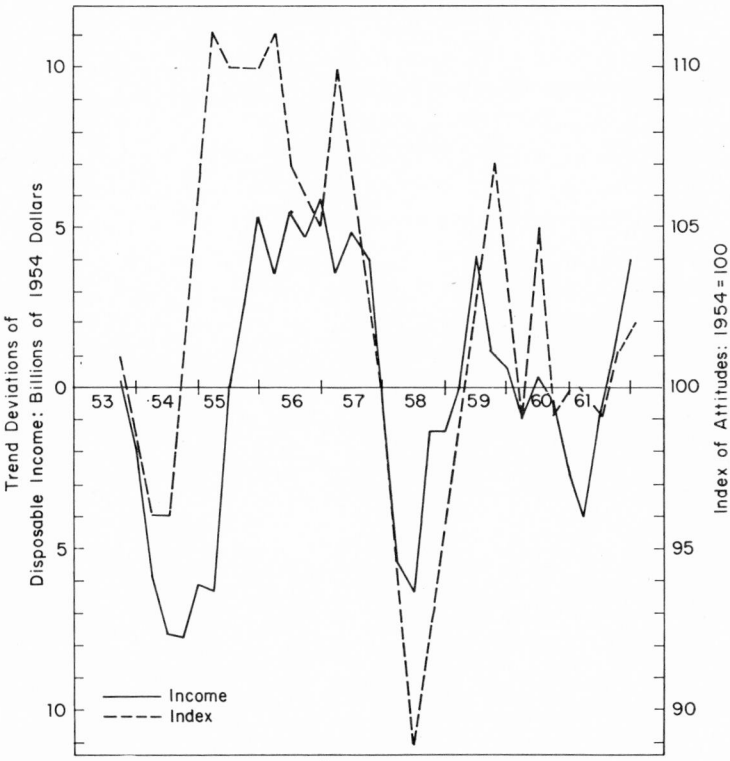

Figure 7.2. Index of consumer attitudes and deviation of disposable income from trend (1953–1961).

In other words, an increase of income by $1 billion to a new level raises automobile demand by $0.079 billion initially, but as the stock grows, demand declines to an equilibrium position only about $0.04 billion above its old level.

Incidentally, the equilibrium stock position lends itself directly to interpretation in terms of a stock-adjustment process.

The true equilibrium stock of cars was given by

$$CARS^E = 0.0777[Y_D^{54} - V^{54} + V_{INS_{GF}}^{54}].$$

This represents 0.0777 cars per \$1 000 of net disposable income, or one car per \$12 900 of income. Bearing in mind that these are new cars and new car equivalents of used cars, this is a reasonable figure.

7.9. Other durables

C_{DEA}, the demand for durables other than automobiles, is similar to the above, depending on disposable income (but with all transfers included) and on $[K_{CDEA}]_{-1}$, the existing stock at the end of the preceding quarter. The stock figures are those derived by Lawrence Klein by applying a 12-year life in straight-line depreciation of past purchases.

In addition, demand for other durables depends on $ALQD_{HH}$, the stock of liquid assets held by households at the end of the preceding quarter. These consist of currency, demand deposits and fixed-value redeemable claims as estimated in the Federal Reserve Board flow of funds. The data are given in table 7.5.

The several variables are highly intercorrelated, as is shown by the low partial $\bar{R}^2$'s in comparison with the coefficient of total determination.

As in the case of automobile demand, the ultimate impact of rising income on purchases of durables is smaller than the initial impact. Since straight-line depreciation was used in computing the stock of durables, we have

$$K_{CDEA}^{54} = \tfrac{1}{4} \sum_{i=0}^{47} \left[1 - \frac{i}{48}\right] [C_{DEA}^{54}]_{-i}.$$

In equilibrium, $[C_{DEA}^{54}]_{-i} = C_{DEA}^{54}$ and

$$K_{CDEA}^{54} = 6.125[C_{DEA}^{54}].$$

Substituting in the regression equation, we obtain an equilibrium relationship of durable expenditure to income of

$$C_{DEA}^{54} = 0.077[Y_D^{54}]$$

in contrast to the initial effect of 0.162. This implies an equilibrium stock of

$$K_{CDEA}^{E54} = 0.472[Y_D^{54}].$$

This means that the value of the stock of consumer durables, aside from automobiles, is at equilibrium a little less than one-half of annual income.

7.10. Food demand

Two formulations are given of food demand. In the first, expenditure on food depends on disposable income, on the relative price of food and on population. Measured at the means, the price coefficient corresponds to a food demand elasticity of -0.192. The contribution of price to demand behavior is surprisingly large (partial $\bar{R}^2 = 0.271$).

The second formulation is used here and in the following categories to determine whether information about the *current* level of income—as distinguished from its general average level over the past several years—contributes to the understanding of current demand. It also serves, as we shall see, to explore the nature of certain lags. In this formulation, demand is made a function of a weighted mean of past incomes defined by

$$\sum_{i=1}^{12} b_i \frac{[Y_D^{54}]_{-i}}{[N+N_{\mathrm{ML}}]_{-i-1}} \quad \text{where } b_i = \left[\frac{1}{\displaystyle\sum_{i=1}^{12} w^i}\right] w^i.$$

Several values of w were experimented with, and the value $w = 0.8$ was chosen on the basis of the contribution made by the weighted average to the explanation of the dependent variables.

The alternative formulation shows that the deviation of current per capita income from its past weighted mean accounts for 17 per cent of the variance in food expenditure after the weighted mean is taken into account. In fact, by combining the first two terms in the equation, we see that, the current level of per capita income given, little significant information [3]) is contained in the past mean. This finding is quite consistent with the results shown in table 7.3. If population is incorporated in the food-consumption equation, the lagged value of food consumption does not enter the relationship significantly. In the second formulation, use of per capita data takes sufficient account of population to eliminate the effect of the lagged term. Note again the large contribution of food prices. Measured at the means the coefficient represents a price elasticity of -0.233.

7.11. Other nondurables

The analysis of other nondurables is similar to that for food. Consumer expenditure for other nondurable commodities depends on disposable

---

[3]) The coefficient on the past mean is -0.0271, with a standard error of 0.0157.

income and liquid assets, although, as can be seen from table 7.3, replacing liquid assets by lagged consumption gives almost as good an over-all result.

The second formulation, as in the case of food demand, shows that knowledge about current, as distinct from average past, income makes a significant contribution to the estimate of demand. Moreover, if the first two terms are combined we see that the average itself is of no significance if liquid assets are taken into account, a result consistent with the first formulation.

7.12. Services

The demand for services shows that consumer expenditure for service items (net of imputations) depends on disposable income, price, lagged expenditure and liquid assets. Although the contribution of price is small ($\bar{R}^2 = 0.069$), it is statistically significant. Measured at the means the price elasticity is -0.180. The largest contribution to the observed behavior of services demand is that of the lagged demand itself ($\bar{R}^2 = 0.856$). This is further tested by the second formulation. Note that in this case not only is it important to know current income, given the past average, but given current income it is even more important to know the past, which shows a coefficient of partial determination of $+0.862$. It is also interesting to note the increased values of the coefficients of partial determination for both price and liquid assets in the second formulation. Price elasticity measured at the mean is -0.748.

Since the lagged terms are important in service demand there is again a difference between the initial impact to be expected from a rise in income and its long-run equilibrium. Since, essentially,

$$C_S^{54} - C_{IS}^{54} = 0.0555 Y_D^{54} + 0.8099[C_S^{54} - C_{IS}^{54}]_{-1}$$

the equilibrium is given by

$$C_S^{E54} - C_{IS}^{E54} = 0.292 Y_D^{54}.$$

Thus a rise in income of \$1 billion would raise demand for services only \$0.056 billion the first quarter but would ultimately generate a rise to \$0.292 billion above the initial level.

7.13. Income and total consumption

The impact of income on total demand, subject to the remarks made about consumer attitudes above, can be seen from the sum of the income coefficients. Using the first forms only, we see that an increase of $1 billion in income tends to be associated with a short-run rise in expenditure of $0.531 billion. Taking account of the dynamics, however, this figure becomes $0.643 billion in the long run. The biggest difference between the two figures lies in the dynamic behavior of service demand. Both figures agree well with the other results obtained from annual data.

7.14. Limitations

The equations presented here are subject to a number of very serious limitations which must be taken into account in their evaluation. The most serious question is whether the equations given are, in fact, *quarterly* equations. Presumably by a *quarterly model* we mean something more than a model obtained from quarterly data; we want the result to tell us something about quarter-to-quarter movements. The proper criterion for evaluating a quarterly model is how well it predicts quarterly first differences. Regardless of how the equations are fitted, unless the result can successfully distinguish levels in one quarter from those in nearby quarters, it is not a quarterly model. The comparison of correlations between actual and calculated first differences with those between the corresponding levels is given in table 7.2. Two R^2 are shown for the first differences, the first involving the calculated level for the current period minus the actual level for the previous period (i.e., $\hat{C}_t - C_{t-1}$ vs. $C_t - C_{t-1}$) and the second involving the first difference in the calculated levels (i.e., $\hat{C}_t - \hat{C}_{t-1}$ vs. $C_t - C_{t-1}$). It is clear that most of the power of the equations lies in describing the long-run levels.

TABLE 7.2

Squared multiple correlation coefficients for first differences and levels.

Expenditure	Unadjusted R^2		
	Levels	First differences	
		(1)	(2)
Automobiles	0.714	0.552	0.280
Other durables	0.946	0.517	0.021
Food	0.991	0.419	0.162
Other nondurables	0.980	0.504	0.00006
Services	0.9986	0.224	0.205

Source   See text.

The coefficients in our equations are quite consistent with those found by using annual data. This is hardly an accident, for aside from the fact that the data consist of individual points in the one case and of points averaged together in groups of four in the other, there is virtually no difference between the technique used here and that used with annual models. In other words, the only "quarterly" aspect of these equations is the slight shift in timing of the lag terms. Obtaining effective consumption functions requires the use of a statistical technique that has sufficient "resolving power" to distinguish the events of one quarter from those of the next.

The second serious question is perhaps even more fundamental. The equations given here follow the usual theoretical pattern in which income is taken as "cause" and consumption expenditure as "result". There is ample evidence that many American households can, within limits, select their own incomes. Thus to some extent consumption standards determine income rather than the other way around. To this extent income and consumption are mutually determined variables and the interpretation of the regression coefficient is quite different from a "marginal propensity" in any real sense.

Argument with respect to these questions has been pursued elsewhere [16] and need not be elaborated here, but the reader will do well to remember that the title of this chapter was deliberately chosen.

7.15. Appendix. Supplementary tables

TABLE 7.3

Summary of regression equations (1948 : 1–1960 : 4).

$Y_D^{54} - V^{54} + V_{INS_{GF}}^{54}$	$[ATT]_{-1}$	Automobiles C_{DA}^{54}			Constant term	R^2
		$\dfrac{P_{CDA}}{P_C}$	$\left[\dfrac{ALQD_{HH}}{P_C}\right]_{-1}$	$[CARS]_{-1}$		
0.0655	0.2715				−30.2454	0.7732
(0.0063)	(0.0401)					(DF = 49)
0.0643	0.2753	−9.22			−20.8353	0.7742
(0.0064)	(0.0401)	(8.32)				(DF = 48)
−0.0053	0.2709		0.0392	0.0773	−25.8633	0.7768
(0.0436)	(0.0398)		(0.0308)	(0.0468)		(DF = 47)

TABLE 7.3 (Continued)

Other durables C_{DEA}^{54}

Y_D^{54}	$[K_{CDEA}^{54}]_{-1}$	$\left[\dfrac{ALQD_{HH}}{P_C}\right]_{-1}$	$[ATT]_{-1}$	Constant term	$\bar{R}^2$
0.1781	−0.0397			−21.2837	0.9322
(0.0318)	(0.0142)				(DF = 49)
0.1615	−0.0445	0.0485		−26.2094	0.9423
(0.0299)	(0.0132)	(0.0157)			(DF = 48)
0.1418	−0.0355	0.0470	0.0304	−24.9967	0.9427
(0.0344)	(0.0153)	(0.0157)	(0.0266)		(DF = 47)

Food C_{NF}^{54}

Y_D^{54}	$\dfrac{P_{CNF}}{P_C}$	$[N+N_{ML}]_{-1}$	$\frac{1}{4}\sum_{i=1}^{4}[C_{NF}^{54}]_{-i}$	Constant term	$\bar{R}^2$
0.0656	−10.93	0.1889		21.0928	0.9907
(0.0165)	(2.49)	(0.0522)			(DF = 48)
0.0799	−9.73		0.3446	27.0645	0.9889
(0.0159)	(2.93)		(0.1212)		(DF = 44)
0.0560	−13.64	0.2124	0.0119	21.8217	0.9905
(0.0170)	(3.05)	(0.0745)	(0.1620)		(DF = 43)

Other nondurables C_{NEF}^{54}

Y_D^{54}	$\frac{1}{4}\sum_{i=1}^{4}[C_{NEF}^{54}]_{-i}$	$\dfrac{P_{CNEF}}{P_C}$	$\left[\dfrac{ALQD_{HH}}{P_C}\right]_{-1}$	Constant term	$\bar{R}^2$
0.1688	0.2275			5.1393	0.9783
(0.0301)	(0.1412)				(DF = 45)
0.1688	0.2275	0		5.1445	0.9778
(0.0312)	(0.1469)	(11.65)			(DF = 44)
0.1691			0.0743	4.2712	0.9794
(0.0127)			(0.0213)		(DF = 49)

Services $C_S^{54} - C_{IS}^{54}$

Y_D^{54}	$\frac{1}{4}\sum_{i=1}^{4}[C_S^{54}-C_{IS}^{54}]_{-i}$	$\dfrac{P_{CS}}{P_C}$	$\left[\dfrac{ALQD_{HH}}{P_C}\right]_{-1}$	Constant term	$\bar{R}^2$
0.0338	0.9469			−3.3125	0.9980
(0.0117)	(0.0380)				(DF = 45)
0.0285	0.9517	+3.55		−5.7809	0.9981
(0.0144)	(0.0390)	(5.60)			(DF = 44)
0.0555	0.8099	−13.65	0.0572	2.6820	0.9985
(0.0144)	(0.0500)	(6.60)	(0.0148)		(DF = 43)

TABLE 7.4

Stock of cars.

Year and quarter		New registrations seasonally adjusted (millions)	Scrappage (millions)	Stock beginning of quarter (millions)
1948	1	0.920	0.407	6 462
	2	0.750	0.432	6 963
	3	0.892	0.471	7 261 [a])
	4	0.955	0.523	7 682
1949	1	0.981	0.576	8 137
	2	1.143	0.628	8 589
	3	1.367	0.653	9 172
	4	1.345	0.652	9 943
1950	1	1.415	0.651	10 642
	2	1.390	0.650	11 367
	3	1.892	0.666	12 016
	4	1.644	0.699	13 136
1951	1	1.558	0.731	13 931
	2	1.253	0.764	14 589
	3	1.219	0.782	14 900
	4	1.058	0.784	15 156
1952	1	1.012	0.787	15 235
	2	1.098	0.789	15 263
	3	0.862	0.800	15 376
	4	1.193	0.819	15 245
1953	1	1.396	0.838	15 452
	2	1.450	0.857	15 849
	3	1.468	0.878	16 274
	4	1.428	0.902	16 687
1954	1	1.310	0.925	17 033
	2	1.463	0.948	17 236
	3	1.302	0.958	17 577
	4	1.495	0.954	17 734
1955	1	1.708	0.950	18 072
	2	1.796	0.945	18 600
	3	1.932	0.961	19 180
	4	1.789	0.995	19 857

TABLE 7.4 (Continued)

Year and quarter		New registrations seasonally adjusted (millions)	Scrappage (millions)	Stock beginning of quarter (millions)
1956	1	1.567	1.030	20 345
	2	1.498	1.064	20 575
	3	1.501	1.062	20 718
	4	1.399	1.023	20 852
1957	1	1.594	0.984	20 874
	2	1.460	0.945	21 092
	3	1.507	0.924	21 165
	4	1.443	0.920	21 281
1958	1	1.228	0.916	21 326
	2	1.127	0.912	21 153
	3	1.087	0.937	20 891
	4	1.231	0.993	20 604
1959	1	1.477	1.048	20 475
	2	1.570	1.104	20 598
	3	1.536	1.125	20 803
	4	1.454	1.113	20 959
1960	1	1.673	1.101	21 025
	2	1.701	1.088	21 306
	3	1.508	1.084	21 598
	4	1.705	1.080	21 679
1961	1	1.396	1.08 [b])	21 951
	2	1.451	1.08 [b])	21 898
	3	1.322	1.08 [b])	21 903
	4	1.703	1.08 [b])	21 778

[a]) Initial figure determined from age composition of the stock as of July 1.

[b]) Estimated.

Sources

New registrations: *Business Statistics and Survey of Current Business.*
Scrappage: Interpolated from annual figures in *Automobile Facts and Figures,*
1962 edition, p. 9.

TABLE 7.5

Liquid asset holdings, beginning of quarter, seasonally adjusted (billions of 1954 dollars).

1948	1	186.3	1955	1	207.5
	2	183.3		2	210.3
	3	182.0		3	211.6
	4	183.3		4	212.7
1949	1	185.0	1956	1	214.1
	2	186.2		2	215.5
	3	188.8		3	216.3
	4	189.1		4	216.0
1950	1	189.6	1957	1	216.9
	2	190.2		2	217.7
	3	187.6		3	218.9
	4	184.1		4	218.3
1951	1	179.7	1958	1	219.6
	2	178.4		2	222.4
	3	179.4		3	226.3
	4	179.9		4	228.7
1952	1	182.5	1951	1	232.7
	2	182.9		2	235.2
	2	184.4		3	237.6
	4	185.5		4	237.5
1953	1	189.8	1960	1	238.6
	2	192.6		2	239.2
	3	193.4		3	241.6
	4	194.4		4	243.5
1954	1	195.8			
	2	197.8			
	3	201.2			
	4	203.8			

Sources

> *Federal Reserve Bulletin*, various issues and Flow of Funds Supplement.

> Quarterly changes for 1948–1951 were estimated by using as benchmarks savings by individuals in the U. S. as reported in *U. S. S.E.C. Statistical Bulletin*, 1949–1953.

REFERENCES

1. ACKLEY, GARDNER. The Wealth-Saving Relationship, *Journal of Political Economy* 59 (April, 1951) 596–598.
2. ANDO, ALBERT, and MODIGLIANI, FRANCO. The "Life Cycle" Hypothesis of Saving, *American Economic Review* 53 (March, 1953) 55–84.
3. CHOW, GREGORY. *Demand for Automobiles in the United States*. Amsterdam: North-Holland Publishing Company, 1957.
4. CHOW, GREGORY. Statistical Demand Functions for Automobile and Their Use for Forecasting, in *The Demand for Durable Goods*. Edited by Arnold C. Harberger. Chicago: University of Chicago, 1960.
5. DUESENBERRY, JAMES. *Income, Saving and the Theory of Consumer Behavior*. Cambridge, Mass.: Harvard University Press, 1949.
6. FERBER, ROBERT. Research on Household Behavior, *American Economic Review* 52 (March, 1962) 19–63.
7. FRIEDMAN, MILTON. *A Theory of the Consumption Function*. Princeton: National Bureau of Economic Research, 1957.
8. KATONA, GEORGE. *The Powerful Consumer*. New York: McGraw-Hill, 1960.
9. KATONA, GEORGE. *Psychological Analysis of Economic Behavior*. New York: McGraw-Hill, 1951.
10. KEYNES. JOHN MAYNARD. *The General Theory of Employment, Interest and Money*. New York: Harcourt, Brace, and Co., 1936.
11. MUELLER, EVA, and KATONA, GEORGE. *Consumer Attitudes and Demand, 1950–1952*. Ann Arbor, Mich.: Institute for Social Research, University of Michigan, 1953.
12. MUELLER, EVA, and KATONA, GEORGE. *Consumer Expectations, 1953–1956*. Ann Arbor, Mich.: Institute for Social Research, University of Michigan, 1957.
13. MUELLER, EVA, and KATONA, GEORGE. The Function of Expectational and Motivational Data, *1960 Survey of Consumer Finances*. Ann Arbor, Mich.: Survey Research Center, 1961, 171–185.
14. MODIGLIANI, FRANCO. Fluctuations in the Saving-Income Ratio: A Problem in Economic Forecasting, in *Studies in Income and Wealth* (Vol. 11). New York: National Bureau of Economic Research, 1949, 371–443.
15. MODIGLIANI, FRANCO, and ANDO, ALBERT. The "Permanent Income" and the "Life Cycle" Hypotheses of Saving Behavior: Comparison and Tests, in *Proceedings of the Conference on Consumption and Saving* (Vol. 2). Edited by Irwin Friend and Robert Jones. Philadelphia: 1960.
16. SUITS, DANIEL B. "The Determinants of Consumer Expenditure: A Review of Present Knowledge", in Commission on Money and Credit, *Impacts of Monetary Policy*, New York: Prentice-Hall, 1963.
17. SUITS, DANIEL B. The Demand for Automobiles in the United States, 1929–1956, *Review of Economics and Statistics* 40 (August, 1958) 273–280.
18. ZELLNER, ARNOLD. The Short Run Consumption Function, *Econometrica* 25 (October, 1957) 552–567.

PART IV

Income distribution, price and wage determination and labor force

CHAPTER 8

INCOME DISTRIBUTION AND EMPLOYMENT OVER THE BUSINESS CYCLE

Contents

8.1. Introduction. 227

8.2. The analytical structure 234
    1. General. 2. Cyclical production functions.

8.3. Employment equations 241
    1. Production workers: manufacturing. 2. Nonproduction workers: manufacturing. 3. Employment functions: all industries.

8.4. Production worker hour demand equations. 254

8.5. Estimation summary 258
    1. Final equations. 2. Error structure of man-hour estimates.

8.6. The complete distribution 265
    1. Entrepreneurial income. 2. Interest income 3. Inventory valuation adjustment. 4. Dividends.

8.7. Conclusions 277

INCOME DISTRIBUTION AND EMPLOYMENT OVER THE BUSINESS CYCLE

EDWIN KUH [1]

Massachusetts Institute of Technology, Cambridge, Massachusetts

8.1. Introduction

Much controversy, some of it quite interesting, has been generated over the question of what determines the functional distribution of income. Most of that controversy has been about the long-run determinants, while my objective is to explain income distribution in the context of a quarterly econometric model [2]). A proposition established earlier, that cyclical varia-

[1]) The debt owed to a skilled group of research assistants is great. James Howe handled the exploratory phases with competence and energy. Subsequent efforts by Bill Mihaltse, Steve Rosenthal and Mike Copeland, as well as the considerable secretarial abilities of Mrs. Kathleen Wolf, are equally appreciated. The London School of Economics Statistical Research Unit was kind enough to undertake some of the early calculations. Most of the calculations in this paper were made on the MIT Sloan School of Management IBM 1620. Financial support provided by the National Science Foundation is gratefully acknowledged. William Phillips assisted in the interpretation of lags as well as in discussing some of the main results of the employment equations. Lawrence R. Klein and James S. Duesenberry made helpful comments, and other members of this project had earlier offered valuable criticism. I proffer the usual disclaimers.

[2]) An initial descriptive account of global share fluctuations will be followed by analytical treatment of cyclical production functions. Both aspects of this paper owe much to the excellent paper by Charles L. Schultze, "Short Run Movements of Income Shares," Conference on Research in Income and Wealth, April 28–29, 1961, National Bureau of Economic Research, New York (mimeographed). My emphasis on the strategic importance of cyclical productivity variations seems fully consistent with Schultze's approach relating profits shares to deviations from capacity output. Irving B. Kravis, Relative Income Shares in Fact and Theory, *American Economic Review* (December, 1959) 917–949,

tions in the share of profits originate primarily from cyclical variations in labor productivity, will be given a firmer foundation in the dynamics of business employment decisions.

Four major differences arise between this task and the one upon which most previous discussion has centered. First, there are substantial short-run dynamic effects which are irrelevant for the long-run steady-state solution. Second, discussion has been carried on the simplified context of two-factor incomes, wages and profits. A more detailed income distribution must be explained here namely, that which appears in the national income accounts, including wages and salaries plus supplements, income of unincorporated business, net interest and rental income, as well as corporate profit and its constituents, retained earnings and dividends. Third, this model is fundamentally structured around industry production and income-generating behavior rather than just the aggregates. Fourth, the distribution of income when unemployment prevails has been neglected in much of the long-run discussion of factor shares.

By way of general factual background, table 8.1 presents gross private nonfarm income distribution during the postwar period. Indirect business taxes have been excluded. In order to describe more recent secular changes in factor shares, comment on tables 8.1 and 8.2 will initially be restricted to periods of relatively high activity. At cyclical peaks the private wage and salary share increased moderately from 60.4 per cent in the fourth quarter of 1948 to 62.2 per cent in the second quarter of 1960. There have been offsetting changes within the property income category, primarily the doubling of the net interest share, mostly at the expense of the noncorporate business share and partly from the corporate profits share. A reminder is given here: business and professional income is a mixture of wages, salaries and profits, and so the use of the term "nonwage" or "property income" is somewhat misleading.

Table 8.2, recording net private nonfarm income shares, shows the wage and salary share rising sharply from 64.8 to 69.1 per cent from 1948 to 1960. Much of that increase had taken place by the 1953 cyclical peak. The larger share of net interest now appears to be achieved mostly at the expense of corporate profits, whose share fell from 16.8 to 12.9 per cent, and also the

---

presents a useful appraisal of the treatment of long-run factor shares. R. R. Nield, *Pricing and Employment in the Trade Cycle* (Cambridge, England, 1963), has studied the behavior of English labor productivity and profits, arriving at conclusions similar to my own in many respects.

TABLE 8.1

Distribution of gross private nonfarm national income shares [a]) (*per cent*).

	1948:4	1949:2	1953:2	1954:2	1957:3	1958:1	1960:2	1961:1	1962:4
	P_1	T_1	P_2	T_2	P_3	T_3	P_4	T_4	
Private wages and salaries plus supplements	60.4	60.8	61.8	61.9	61.5	62.8	62.2	62.1	
Gross business and professional income	14.2	14.8	12.8	13.3	12.7	13.0	12.1	12.0	
Rental income of persons	03.7	04.1	03.7	03.9	03.4	03.6	03.0	03.1	
Gross corp. profits and IVAC	19.5	18.0	18.9	17.6	18.7	16.4	18.2	17.0	
Net interest	02.0	02.3	02.8	03.2	03.8	04.2	04.5	04.9	

[a]) Explanatory footnotes are appended to table 8.5.

TABLE 8.2

Distribution of net private nonfarm national income shares [a]) (*per cent*).

	1948:4	1949:2	1953:2	1954:2	1957:3	1958:1	1960:2	1961:1
	P	T	P	T	P	T	P	T
Private wages and salaries plus supplements	64.8	65.6	67.2	68.1	68.2	69.9	69.1	69.9
Business and professional	12.0	12.5	10.5	10.9	10.3	10.4	09.7	09.7
Rental income of persons	03.9	04.4	04.0	04.3	03.8	04.0	03.3	03.4
Corp. profits and IVAC	16.8	15.0	15.2	13.2	13.7	10.8	12.9	11.5
Net interest	02.2	02.5	03.1	03.5	04.3	04.7	05.0	05.0

[a]) Explanatory footnotes are appended to table 8.5.

decline in business and professional income from 12 to 9.7 per cent. Evidently the "profit squeeze" mostly originated in the rapid depreciation increase from the early postwar years. This point is brought out particularly clearly by table 8.3, which shows the proportional distribution of charges against gross corporate product [3]). Employee compensation is almost the same proportion of gross corporate product in each recorded year of high cyclical activity—1929, 1939, 1948 and 1962. However, the distribution of nonwage income has undergone various changes over this period. From 1929 to 1962

---

[3]) This table is based upon one contained in a most interesting article by Robert E. Graham, Jr. and Jacqueline Bauman, Corporate Profits and National Output, *The Survey of Current Business* (November, 1962) 27.

the share of indirect business taxes nearly doubled, rising from 6.2 to 10.5 per cent. Over the same thirty-three year span, the share of profits and interest declined from 22 to 16 per cent.

The main contrast noted between net national income and gross national income, the rising share of capital consumption allowances (mostly depreciation allowances), reappears in these data. During the postwar benchmark years, capital consumption allowances rose from 5.5 to 9.5 per cent, while indirect business taxes increased slightly, from 8.9 to 10.5 per cent. Thus net profits during the postwar period declined about 5.5 percentage points, while gross corporate profits dropped by less than half that amount, from 27 to 25.2 per cent. Furthermore, depreciation in 1948 was abnormally low by any prior year comparison. In the early postwar years depreciation based upon original asset cost was seriously understated relative to the price of assets currently purchased. This deficiency had been largely corrected by 1962, as most of the assets in the depreciable capital base were now valued in postwar prices. In addition, various legislative changes had made it possible to accelerate depreciation, and so in 1962 its share of gross corporate product was larger by a modest amount than it had been in either 1929 or 1939.

TABLE 8.3

Distribution of charges against corporate gross product (per cent).

	1929	1939	1948	1962 [a]
Corporate gross product	100.0	100.0	100.0	100.0
Capital consumption allowances	8.3	8.5	5.5	9.5
Indirect business taxes	6.2	11.6	8.9	10.5
Employee compensation	63.3	64.2	64.0	64.0
Net interest	3.0	3.1	0.2	0.3
Profits before tax, including *IVAC*	19.0	12.5	21.3	15.7
Addendum: profits and interest	22.0	15.6	21.5	16.0

Source   *Survey of Current Business* (November, 1962) p. 27.

[a]) Data for first 6 months.

Cyclical factor share patterns can be observed from the preceding tables. The peaks and troughs noted in tables 8.1 and 8.2 were picked according to constant dollar *GNP* peaks and troughs. Some moderate cyclical variations in the shares are clearly visible. The private wage and salary share was larger in every cyclical trough relative to the cyclical peak. The sharpest postwar recession, which occurred in 1957–1958, showed the largest rise in

TABLE 8.4

Change in shares of gross private nonfarm national income: annual rates [a][b]) (*per cent*).

	1948 : 4	1949 : 2	1953 : 2	1954 : 2	1957 : 3	1958 : 1	1960 : 2
	P	T	P	T	P	T	P
Gross income							
Private wages and salaries plus supplements	1.2	0.4	0.2	0.0	4.1	−0.4	−0.2
Gross business and professional	8.3	−3.6	3.8	1.4	4.6	−3.2	−1.1
Rental income of persons	20.5	−2.5	5.2	−4.1	11.4	−8.0	4.4
Gross corp. profits and *IVAC*	−16.0	1.2	−7.1	1.8	−26.2	4.6	−9.0
Net interest [c])	28.7	5.0	13.3	4.1	20.0	3.0	11.3
Net income							
Business and professional	0.8	−4.3	3.7	−1.7	1.9	−3.1	0.0
Corp. profits and *IVAC*	−22.6	03.3	−13.6	1.1	(47.2)	7.9	−15.7

[a]) Changes in each column are based on forward first differences.

[b]) Explanatory footnotes are appended to table 8.5.

[c]) The calculations in this row are highly unreliable because of the low number of significant digits.

the wage and salary share. Gross business and professional income, rental income and the net interest component (which is subject to a much greater trend than any of the other series) also increase their income share in a recession. Hence, all of the cyclical change in the wage and salary share as well as the other remaining (nonprofit) components must by definition have been a consequence of a smaller corporate profit share.

This point stands out in the top section of table 8.4, which reports cyclical per cent changes in the gross factor shares. All the per cent changes have been reduced to an annual rate of change. The private wages and salary share rose at a 9 per cent annual rate during the 1948–1949 recession, at a 6.5 per cent rate in the 1954 recession and by similar rates in 1958 and 1961. The relative decline in gross corporate profits, fluctuating between 9 and 26 per cent, is reflected in moderate increases in other nonwage shares and private wages and salaries; the severer the recession, the greater the shift toward wages and salaries as well as the remaining property incomes. Thus, in the most severe postwar recession of 1957–1958 there was a 4 per cent shift in wages and salaries, while in the more moderate recessions the

TABLE 8.5

Cyclical changes in gross factor income: annual rates [a] *(per cent).*

	1948 : 4	1949 : 2	1953 : 2	1954 : 2	1957 : 3	1958 : 1	1960:
	P	T	P	T	P	T	P
Compensation of employees	−04.8	09.8	−01.5	06.8	−04.4	06.8	−00.3
Private wages and salaries	−07.2	09.0	−02.2	06.6	−06.8	06.5	−02.1
Government (+ military) wages	−03.0	12.6	00.9	05.3	05.4	05.8	06.9
Net nonfarm proprietors income	−23.6	03.1	−02.7	04.1	03.0	01.0	−01.2
Gross business and professional	−01.8	05.7	01.5	05.6	−05.0	03.6	−01.3
Rental income of persons	12.8	06.4	03.7	02.9	01.6	−01.1	01.1
Gross corporate profits before tax	−39.4	12.6	−12.2	09.2	−36.8	12.3	−11.7
Net interest	−17.8	13.3	10.5	12.8	07.2	09.8	10.1
Gross property income = (gross national income − compensation of employees)	−15.6	07.3	−03.1	06.8	−11.6	06.5	−03.3
Real *GNP* ($1954)	−4.7	6.2	−3.7	4.3	−9.0	5.2	−2.6
Current $ *GNP*	−7.3	9.0	−2.7	6.8	−7.0	6.8	−0.6

[a]) Changes in each column are based on forward first differences.

Notes to tables 8.1, 8.2, 8.4 and 8.5:

1) The tables are based upon peaks and troughs in constant dollar *GNP* for the dates indicated in the table headings. The next to the last row of table 8.5 shows the per cent changes in real *GNP*.

2) *Sources* National income by type of income. 1948–1955, *U. S. Income and Output*, table I–9 (p. 128); 1957–1961, *Survey of Current Business* (July, 1962) table 2 (p. 6); 1962, *Economic Report of the President*, 1963.

3) Definitions and data adjustment:

   a) Government wages and military wages were added together to give "government (plus military) wages".

   b) "Proprietors' income" is as listed in the tables. It includes a farm component but no capital consumption allowance.

   c) Capital consumption allowance (*CCA*) figures were obtained as follows: 1948–1955, *U. S. Income and Output*, table I–18 (pp. 1–10); 1957–1961, *Survey of Current Business*, table 3 (p. 6); 1962, *Economic Report of the President*, 1963.

   The *CCA* for each peak and trough was split into two components in the same proportion as the corporate depreciation was with respect to the noncorporate depreciation changes for each period in question. (The depreciation data were found in *U. S. Income and Output*, tables VI–19 and VI–18 (p. 217) and in *Survey of Current Business* (July, 1962) tables 47 and 48 (p. 27).

   Thus the results for "corporate profits before tax (plus *CCA* component)" include the appropriate portion of the period's capital consumption allowance. The remaining portion of the *CCA* is included in "business and professional (plus *CCA* component)."

   d) The "gross property income" listing was determined by adding total *CCA* to national income and subtracting compensation of employees.

4) Procedure:

   After the appropriate data were tabulated for each peak and trough listed above, the following calcula-

shift varied from none at all to 1.2 per cent. The other income components, subject to a variety of secular trends, need not be described here. Quite obviously the most volatile income element is corporate profits, while the other constituents of the income distribution are relatively much more stable. The bottom of table 8.4 shows analogous changes for net property income. Since the base is smaller and has been declining secularly, the per cent change in the share of corporate profits (and to a much smaller extent business and professional income) substantially exceeds comparable gross income changes recorded in the top part of table 8.4.

Table 8.5 shows the per cent change in gross factor incomes rather than in their income share. Real *GNP* and current dollar *GNP* annual rate per cent changes appear at the bottom of the table. Private wages and salaries move almost exactly in proportion to current dollar *GNP*. Business and professional incomes fluctuate in the same manner. Rental income of persons declined only once, during the 1958 recession.

Gross property income, i.e., gross national income less compensation of employees, is evidently considerably less volatile than its most volatile constituent, corporate profits. At an annual rate corporate profits declined 39.4 per cent in the 1949 recession, 36.8 per cent in the somewhat severer 1957–1958 recession and only about 12 per cent in the milder 1954 and 1960 recessions.

A marked cyclical pattern is apparent in the behavior of corporate profits which seems closely geared to the severity of the cycle swings, a fact which can be shown to be closely related to cyclical variations in labor productivity. Furthermore, variations in private compensation appear to move in proportion to the value of output during the cycle. Finally, other sources of income are for the most part subject to either trend increases or only diminution in rates of growth during cyclical declines of aggregate output.

---

tions were made for each adjacent peak and trough: (a) an algebraic change in magnitude; (b) an average (mean) level between this peak and trough.

The ratio of (a) to (b) was calculated and was divided by the time span in years (i.e., quarters times four) between the peak and trough under consideration.

The resulting annual relative changes between successive peaks and troughs are shown in the tables.

Sample calculation: 1948 : 4 and 1949 : 2

	Peak	*Trough*	*Change*	*Mean*	*Time span* (years)
Compensation of employees	144.5	141.1	−3.4	142.8	0.5

$$(\text{change}/\text{mean}) \times (\text{time span}) = -0.048$$

8.2. *The analytical structure*

8.2.1. *General*

From the preceding brief factual summary several propositions emerge that bear on the analytical structure adopted for this econometric model. In particular, the secular distribution of income differs systematically from the cyclical distribution of income. More specifically, the considerations which affect corporate profits (and other components too, but to a smaller extent) display a specific cyclical pattern which stands in clear contrast to the altogether slow-moving trends or relative stability in the peak output factor shares. While elegance and completeness will require that cyclical and secular determinants be welded into one consistent theory at some future time, the approach initially taken here is that research can proceed efficiently without becoming involved with the thorny theoretical conflicts of secular income distribution.

In this paper, production functions will be developed in the guise of man-hour demand equations, with considerable attention given to the processes of dynamic adjustment. My earlier study, as well as research by others, developed the proposition that the basic determinants of cyclical variations in corporate profits arise from cyclical variations in labor productivity. These cyclical variations in labor productivity are properties of a moderately complicated adjustment process whose characteristics will be established later on.

In the study referred to, the variance of the change in profits was partitioned in ways that made it possible to derive the following description of the variance of changes affecting profits:

(1) changes in receipts are heavily dominated by changes in output (rather than changes in price), (2) changes in the wage bill arise mostly from man-hour changes although changes in the wage rate are influential too, (3) man-hours are relatively much more important than the wage rate change while the wage rate change in turn is more important than the price change with associated profit variations, (4) the output change is relatively more important than the man-hour change in profit fluctuations and finally (5) quantity effects (output and man-hour input) were substantially larger than price-wage effects associated with profit change [4]).

The key point in the preceding analysis is that cyclical input-output relations of the sort pictured in figures 8.1 and 8.2, dominate short-run profit-share changes rather than price-wage changes. The importance of price and wage behavior for a variety of important problems needs no

---

[4]) E. Kuh, *Profits, Profit Markups, and Productivity—An Examination of Corporate Behavior Since 1947*, Joint Economic Committee, U. S. Congress, January, 1960, 74–75.

reiteration here. Prices in this model, according to the analysis of Charles L. Schultze and Joseph Tryon in chapter 9, are treated primarily as mark-up on normal (i.e., long run) unit cost subject to some adjustment from cyclical demand changes. Nevertheless, while the dramatic peak-trough-early-recovery shifts in the profit share originate in cyclical labor productivity variations, the usual late cyclical recovery period decline in the corporate profit share depends to some extent on (a) a slackening in the rate of increase in productivity, (b) the steady cumulative effect of wage increases greater than price increases, and (c) the smaller national income share originating in the corporate sector toward the end of a typical postwar cyclical recovery. In substance, price determination is most closely akin to Kalecki's markup hypothesis, although the demand component has been excluded in the Kalecki formulation. However, the complete theoretical constructs are not the same, since explicit production functions are an integral part of this distribution theory. Kalecki's theory involves a rather straightforward markup approach, with no variations in the markup permitted due to demand changes; nor are costs affected by productivity changes [5]). Finally, money wages, according to the structure of this model, are determined by the level of unemployment, the rate of change of the cost of living index and, to a smaller extent, the rate of change in profits.

A word should be said about the investment function because the gross stock of capital and output (as well as lagged values of these and employment) are the main arguments of the cyclical production function. The investment function, according to Jorgenson, chapter 2, is based upon present value maximization of net worth subject to a Cobb-Douglas production function constraint. The principal investment demand determinants are the relative cost of physical capital and labor and the financial cost of capital. Alternative investment functions using similar economic variables are operationally equivalent to a large degree. Thus, labor scarcity, final product prices and the cost of capital do affect the demand for labor via these effects on the rate of capital accumulation, even though these neo-

---

[5]) Reder makes the debatable assertion that Kalecki's theory is not a distribution theory. It is not a general equilibrium theory, which is an entirely different matter. Melvin Reder, Alternate Theories of Labor's Share, in Abramovitz and others, *The Allocation of Resources* (Stanford, 1959) 182–184. The Schultze-Tryon price markup formulation has several more refined aspects than a price formation equation which explains a corporate price index by labor productivity and wage rate (in a manner that is essentially equivalent to unit labor costs) and a demand ratchet. E. Kuh, *Profits, Profit Markups and Productivity, op. cit.*, 82–84.

classical variables do not explicitly appear in the production-employment function.

The demand for labor input is divided into the demand for production workers and the demand for overhead workers, as well as into the demand for hours to be worked by production workers. Overhead workers are assumed to work a standard 40-hour week. These combined man-hour inputs (subject to labor supply restrictions only at full employment), together with wage rates, determine the wage bill. Output is determined by final sector demand fed back to the relevant industrial sectors, and this, together with the prices of industry product, determines value added receipts. The difference between value added receipts and the wage bill is gross property income, which in turn, through additional equations, is allocated among income of unincorporated enterprises, rental income, indirect business taxes, interest payments and depreciation. Net corporate profits are finally obtained from the standard income accounting identity. Retained earnings and dividends are derived from a dividend equation which basically follows the pattern originally developed by John Lintner [6]).

This summarizes the main theoretical structure. The price equations reflect the view that markup pricing is an appropriate way to describe most business behavior outside of the farm sector. It is compatible with some qualitative implications of long-run neoclassical price theory, since relative factor scarcity will show up in unit cost differences among different industries, and this in turn will be reflected in relative price changes over the long run. Cost-oriented long-run price behavior, furthermore, is compatible with the studies by John Kendrick and W. E. G. Salter on American and British data, which indicate that reductions in relative unit labor costs lead to approximately equiproportional reduction in relative prices [7]).

Explanation will be undertaken at several levels. It is hoped that reasonably valid structural estimates can be obtained for the cyclical production functions or employment demand equations. In a number of other instances, rough empirical approximations with relatively shallow structural justification will have to suffice when relations are needed to complete the model but theoretical or data inadequacies prevent doing more. The interest

[6]) John Lintner, Distribution of Incomes of Corporations Among Dividends, Retained Earnings, and Taxes, *Proceedings of the American Economic Review* 46 No. 2 (May, 1956) 97–113.

[7]) John W. Kendrick, *Productivity Trends in the United States* (Princeton, New Jersey: Princeton University Press, 1961). W. E. G. Salter, *Productivity and Technical Change* (Cambridge, England: Cambridge University Press, 1960).

income equations and corporate-noncorporate income split definitely fall in this latter category.

8.2.2. *Cyclical production functions*

Ordinary production functions express output as some function of inputs: various labor inputs and a fascinating substance called "technical change". The classical production function would, if well behaved, be convex,

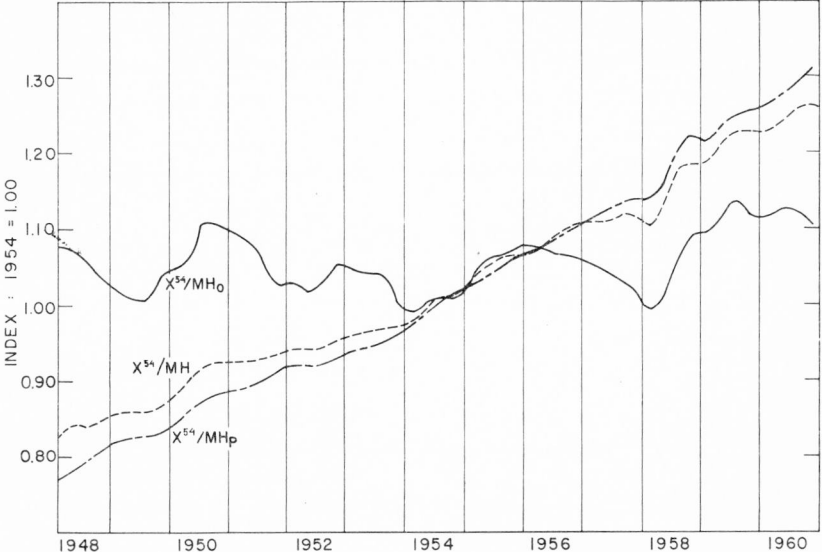

Figure 8.1. Labor productivity in nondurable manufacturing.

displaying diminishing returns over relevant ranges of production. While such constructs provide much interesting intellectual fare and are the foundation of neoclassical income distribution theory, they exclude considerations which are critical for a short-term quarterly econometric model. The neglected features include lags in adjustment processes and, at an aggregate level, the failure to distinguish between overhead and production workers, a proposition which will be established in due course [8]). It is a

---

[8]) As a matter of literary convenience nonproduction workers will usually be referred to as overhead workers, a designation which covers a wide range of activities including supervisory workers, office personnel, sales personnel, technicians, the professions, etc. Walter Oi, in Labor as a Quasi-Fixed Factor, *Journal of Political Economy* (December, 1962) 538–555, explores in some detail the economic reasons (with supporting factual evidence) for treating overhead workers differently from production workers.

matter of analytic indifference whether the production function is an implicit function, expresses output as a function of the inputs previously enumerated or, finally as we shall do here, expresses employment demand as a function of output and the remaining input eq. variables. However, it does make a difference for this model, since we seek to explain explicitly the hiring decision, in principle at the firm or industry level. Estimation using maximum likelihood methods will likewise be unaffected, although the arbitrary

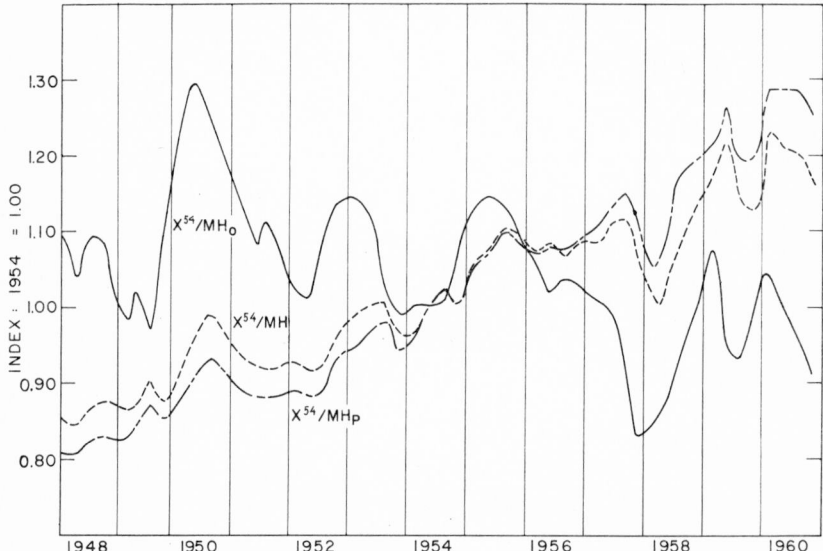

Figure 8.2. Labor productivity in durable manufacturing.

normalization in two-stage least squares would influence the statistical estimates.

Therefore, the demand for man-hours will be expressed as a function of output, capital stock, the level of hours and the lagged value of hours worked and, finally, lagged values of employment and output. This expanded dynamic version is justified by general considerations bearing on dynamic systems and explicit cost considerations exemplified by the dynamic programming approach of Holt, Modigliani, Muth and Simon in their study, *Planning Production, Inventories, and Work Force* [9]). For two different reasons, the adjustment of inputs and outputs is unlikely to be contemporaneous. First, expected output is a random variable, and so changes in

[9]) C. C. Holt, F. Modigliani, J. F. Muth, and H. A. Simon, *Planning Production, Inventories and Work Force* (Englewood Cliffs, N. J.: Prentice-Hall, 1960).

output must persist for some time before belief in their continuation is firmly established; second, different types of adjustments cost money. While such adjustments might be characterized by a quadratic cost function, that particular hypothesis is not essential for our purposes. Rapid labor turnover, which ordinarily leads to substantial inefficiencies, would disturb a going organization. In addition, one would expect the work force to be adjusted to expected production, which would certainly not be done on a short-run basis according to erratic fluctuations in recent sales but instead would depend on some smoothed average process. These dynamic considerations, perhaps quite irrelevant to a steady state, full-employment production function, are essential to the understanding of short-term variations in employment and man-hour inputs. Furthermore, the distinction between hours and employment is vital. Given a sharp change in output, it pays managers to adjust hours rapidly, i.e., to place the initial brunt of the adjustment on hours rather than employment until it becomes reasonably certain that the change in output is not a random departure from the previous level. Therefore, one would expect hours and their rate of change to influence and be influenced by the rate of change of output and employment [10]).

The demand for hours depends in part on the considerations described above and in part on the fact that at any one time there is an institutionally established standard work week from which moderate to large deviations can be quite expensive. Overtime typically costs one and one-half to two times straight-time pay, and so substantial overtime can seriously increase costs. When there is short-time work, the normal overhead costs associated with arriving at work, as well as a tendency for work spreading, lead to inefficient use of the work force and hence higher costs. It therefore seems reasonable to suppose that the standard work week will be about 40 hours for manufacturing. Deviations from this norm will be determined primarily by the need for adjustments of total inputs into the production process. Thus hours are viewed as providing the principal short-run adjustment to output variations, whereas employment changes in the long run provide most of the adjustments to variations in the level of output, given the level of capital stock and the rate of technical progress.

In addition to these ingredients, the relative scarcity of labor could be instrumental in determining the demand for hours. The level of unemploy-

---

[10]) Length of work week is considered one of the important leading indicators. See G. Bry, *The Average Workweek as an Economic Indicator*, National Bureau of Economic Research Occasional Paper No. 69, 1959.

ment is an additional argument of the hours equation as well as the rate of change in unemployment, which is entered as an expectational variable in the context of this equation on the grounds that tight labor markets generate a demand for additional hours. The burden of overtime costs in these circumstances is increasingly offset by deterioration in the quality of the marginal work force. Therefore the complete demand-for-hours equation in principle should include lagged hours, output and lagged output (indicated by the rate of change of output), the level of unemployment and, finally, the rate of change of unemployment. Since the last two variables received uncertain statistical validation, no subsequent attention will be devoted to them.

Because it is not possible to obtain accurate measures of hours worked by nonproduction workers, these workers have been arbitrarily treated as working a constant 40 hours per week in this study. There are times when this assumption would do serious violence to the description of the production process, but it seems more likely that inputs and outputs are more directly related in production activities than in most overhead activities. Lack of available data and the rather different nature of the production process for nonproduction workers determine the advisability of this course of action.

A basic transformation of the postwar labor market in the U.S. has been reflected in dramatic increases in the proportion of the labor force in nonproduction capacities. The Index of Industrial Production rose about 60 per cent from 1950 to 1962, while total employment increased only slightly. However, the number of nonproduction workers grew by approximately 60 per cent from about 2.7 million to 4.3 million, while production worker employment dropped to about 12.5 million in 1962 from a 1953 peak of 14 million.

A Department of Labor study reports the proportion of nonproduction workers in goods-producing industries in table 8.6. A strong trend toward nonproduction workers exists in the service industries, in which most rapid output growth has been occurring in recent years [11]).

It would not be surprising to find altogether different cyclical behavior in hiring and layoffs for production workers and overhead workers. Separate employment functions were initially estimated, and these could be combined if the equation properties turned out to be similar. As will become evident shortly, the underlying behavior patterns, as surmised, were sufficiently different that pooling seemed quite unthinkable. Anticipating the later

---

[11]) Carol A. Barry, White-Collar Employment: I.—Trends and Structure, *Monthly Labor Review* (February, 1961) table 4, pp. 16–17.

empirical results, distributed lags in employment, particularly in overhead labor, provide the main explanation for cyclical variations in labor productivity and in the profit share of income.

8.3. *Employment equations*

8.3.1. *Production workers: manufacturing*

The choice of functional form requires comment. Since this study is exploratory, the possibility of using various functional forms with different statistical and theoretical properties remains open in principle. Linear arithmetic equations are the most expedient, since it is always possible to reinterpret the elasticities associated with this function as if they were the parameters of a log-linear Cobb-Douglas relation. An unsatisfactory implication of the linear formulation is that the marginal productivities of the various factors are theoretically independent of the quantity of associated inputs. This makes it especially desirable to restrict most economic interpretation to the Cobb-Douglas alternative described above, which overcomes this particular deficiency. In addition, these simplified "value added" production functions omit intermediate inputs which in principle belong in a correctly specified production function.

TABLE 8.6

Proportion of nonproduction workers in total employment (per cent).

	1947	1952	1959
All goods-producing industries	15.4	18.2	22.8
Mining	10.4	12.8	21.3
Contract construction	11.0	11.5	14.3
Manufacturing	16.3	19.5	24.3

Sources   Carol A. Barry, White-Collar Employment: I-Trends and Structure, *Monthly Labor Review* (February, 1961) table 4, p. 17.

The capital stock variable requires further explanation. It is obvious that the stock of capital enters as merely another productive agent in a static production function, but in a dynamic context technical change should be explicitly measured, if possible. Given the objectives of the econometric model, it seemed most efficient at this time to confound the results of technical change with the effects of capital and concentrate on short-run adjustment processes. In a longer-run growth-oriented context, such a failure to distinguish technical change from quantity of capital would lead to seriously distorted interpretation. For cyclical purposes, however, where the range of behavior to be explained will not extend much beyond six years, this confluence should not seriously affect economic interpretation. It should be clearly understood that the capital stock coefficient will pick up the influence of technical change, which occurs approximately as a smooth monotonic function of time; there will therefore be a much stronger correlation with the stock of capital than with output. Embodied technical change will appear quite directly in the form of capital.

The output variable is deflated gross value added by industry of origin according to standard national income accounting procedures. This variable, along with the employment series, was constructed by Charles L. Schultze and Joseph Tryon. Capital stock variables finally used are composed of cumulated quarterly constant dollar investment estimates by Dale Jorgenson (for which annual depreciation was interpolated linearly between years), prepared according to procedures described in chapter 2. Many estimates reported used closely related procedures. For several industries no capital stock data were available, and so time trends were used instead. The hours and employment variables are based on regularly published monthly series collected on an establishment basis by the Bureau of Labor Statistics. Overhead workers are assumed to work a 40-hour week, barring availability of any superior data as well as conceptual problems of defining input in terms of hours for this general category. For manufacturing industries employees are split into production and nonproduction (overhead) categories. In nonmanufacturing industries the split-up is not available and all employees who have variable hours are treated as production workers. Employees in the nonrail transport, services and finance and insurance industries had constant hours. They are all considered overhead workers.

Taking into account the various elements of the employment decision, there are two classes of variables that enter into the determination of employment. The first set includes variables associated with standard production functions—current output and capital stock. The second set of variables includes lagged variables which depict the nature of the adjustment process—lagged employment, lagged output and the single-quarter lagged change in hours. The first result, and in some ways the most unusual, concerns production workers in nondurable manufacturing. Equation (8.1) presents the original estimated equation.

$$E_{P_{MN^*}} = -\frac{0.2719}{(0.2305)} + \frac{0.0408}{(0.0055)} X_{MN^*}^{54} - \frac{0.0360}{(0.0054)} [X_{MN^*}^{54}]_{-1}$$

$$-\frac{0.005028}{(0.002067)} K_{MN-1}^{54} + \frac{0.1018}{(0.0162)} [\Delta H_{P_{MN^*}}]_{-1} + \frac{1.0425}{(0.0344)} [E_{P_{MN^*}}]_{-1}$$

$$\bar{R}^2 = 0.9738 \qquad S_{\mathrm{e}} = 0.0309. \tag{8.1}$$

The variables are:

E_P = employment of production workers, millions
X = gross product originating (by industry), billions of dollars
K = stock of business capital, billions of dollars
H_P = average work week of production workers, hours.

Sector subscripts are:

MN = nondurable manufacturing
MN^* = nondurable manufacturing plus mining of crude petroleum and natural gas.

Several characteristics of the estimated parameters stand out. First, the coefficient of lagged output is approximately equal to, but opposite in sign from, that of current output. Both coefficients clearly have independent influence, as indicated by the ratio of each output coefficient to its standard error. When lagged output was added to another estimating equation which already included current output, capital stock and lagged employment variable, the standard error of estimate fell from 0.064 to 0.042 and the usual F test on the significance of multiple correlation doubled. Hence, output and lagged output bear equal weight but with opposite effect. Second, the hours change variable makes a considerable statistical contribution, since the standard error of estimate falls from 0.042 to 0.031 when it is included with the remaining explanatory variables [12]). Similarly, the F statistic on the significance of multiple correlation increased from 215 to 328 when it was included. Third, a curious and at first puzzlingly high value is recorded for the weight of the lagged dependent variable, 1.0425, a parameter value which implies a negative reaction coefficient and an unstable first-order difference equation in production worker employment. As we now proceed to show, this is closely related to the apparently curious

---

[12]) It is lagged one additional period beyond that of the hour per cent change whose results are reported in table 8.9. These calculations present the stated hypothesis more accurately than the more contemporaneous hours change, but the estimated parameters cannot be compared because of the different lags.

behavior of output. We can closely approximate equation (8.1) in the following way:

$$\Delta E_{P_{MN^*}} \cong 0.0408 \Delta X_{MN^*}^{54} + 0.1018 [\Delta H_{P_{MN^*}}]_{-1}$$
$$- 0.005028 K_{MN_{-1}}^{54} - 0.2719. \quad (8.2)$$

This somewhat surprising result would appear to have sufficient validity and so a sensible interpretation of it need not be strained. When hours and output remain unchanged, production worker employment will decline with a constant stock of capital whose composition is constantly changing to embody new technology. Hence, output must increase at a rather healthy clip in order to maintain the level of production worker employment in the nondurable industries, let alone increase it.

Viewed from a slightly different aspect, this result indicates that the complete production worker employment response to output change occurs with no lag, whereas an "indefinitely" long lag occurs on the capital stock term. Suppose capital grew linearly with time, so that $K_t = \lambda t + K_0$ is a "reasonable" approximation for this trend-dominated variable. Then the solution of (8.2) (with $\Delta H_P = 0$ and $X_0 = K_0 = 0$) can be written as:

$$E_{P_{MN^*_t}} = \alpha X_{MN^*_t}^{54} - \frac{\lambda t^2}{2} - ct = 0.0408 X_{MN^*_t}^{54} - 0.005 \frac{\lambda t^2}{2} - 0.272t. \quad (8.3)$$

Production worker employment responses in the durable goods industries (indicated by sector subscript MD) are qualitatively more familiar, since they do not imply that the employment response is contemporaneous—yet results are analogous. The estimating equation is shown below.

$$E_{P_{MD}} = \frac{0.5065}{(0.2762)} + \frac{0.0519}{(0.0050)} X_{MD}^{54} - \frac{0.0352}{(0.0057)} [X_{MD}^{54}]_{-1}$$

$$- \frac{0.026145}{(0.00710)} K_{MD-1}^{54} + \frac{0.1526}{(0.0488)} [\Delta H_{P_{MD}}]_{-1}$$

$$+ \frac{0.9149}{(0.0444)} [E_{P_{MD}}]_{-1}$$

$$\bar{R}^2 = 0.9730 \qquad S_e = 0.1023. \quad (8.4)$$

The statistical properties of the estimating equation are qualitatively much like those in nondurable manufacturing but with two differences. First, the weight placed on current output is considerably greater though opposite in sign from that placed on lagged output. Second, the weight on the lagged dependent variable, 0.9149, is compatible with a stable difference equation, although, as will be shown momentarily, the behavior still closely resembles that of nondurable production workers.

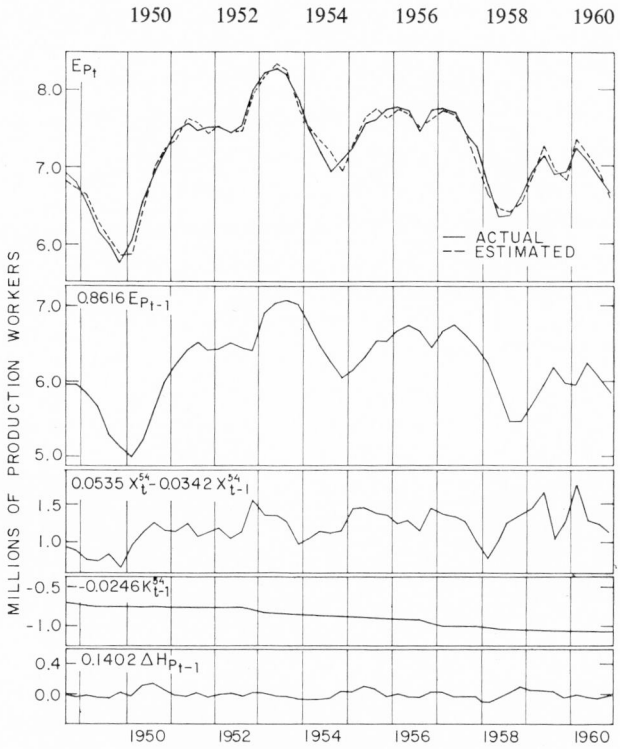

Figure 8.3. Durable manufacturing production worker employment equation. Based on final equation (8.10), pag. 259.

While the equation characteristics already described indicate the nature of appropriate employment and hour relations, additional insight can be gained through an explicit treatment of the lag distributions of the dependent variables expressed in terms of weighting functions of the explanatory variables. To do so, write equation (8.4) in lagged form as follows, using the lag operator z.

$$[1-0.9149z]E_{P_{MD}} = 0.0519[1-0.773z]X_{MD}^{54}-0.026145 K_{MD-1}^{54}$$
$$+0.1526[z-z^2]H_{P_{MD}}+0.506. \quad (8.5)$$

Thus output is seen to affect employment with a big weight in the initial period but with much smaller weights subsequently. While not so striking as the complete intraperiod response in nondurables, the output response is nevertheless extremely rapid and there is a long distributed lag on the capital stock and intercept.

8.3.2. Nonproduction workers: manufacturing

Turning now to employment of overhead workers (E_O), a standard production function with a simple distributed lag characterizes this process quite well. Similar linear estimates with lagged output as well as the change in hours were made, but the statistical effects were minor. The estimating equations selected are shown below.

Nondurable manufacturing

$$E_{O_{MN^*}} = \frac{0.0533}{(0.0137)} + \frac{0.0025}{(0.0005)} X_{MN^*}^{54} + \frac{0.001735}{(0.001223)} K_{MN-1}^{54} + \frac{0.8244}{(0.0538)} [E_{O_{MN}}]_{-1}$$

$$\bar{R}^2 = 0.9976 \qquad S_e = 0.0080. \qquad\qquad (8.6)$$

Durable manufacturing

$$E_{O_{MD}} = -\frac{0.0709}{(0.0374)} + \frac{0.0042}{(0.0007)} X_{MD}^{54} + \frac{0.00266}{(0.00364)} K_{MD-1}^{54} + \frac{0.8573}{(0.0587)} [E_{O_{MD}}]_{-1}$$

$$\bar{R}^2 = 0.9946 \qquad S_e = 0.02737. \qquad\qquad (8.7)$$

Except for intercept values the two equations are much the same. Table 8.7 presents the lag weights for each of the first four quarters following a unit step increase in the relevant independent variable.

It is possible for durable goods manufacturing to compare the different responses of overhead and production workers. First, the lag in output is rather gradual for overhead workers, diminishing slowly, as shown. The first-year effect of a unit change in output is one-half the total effect. For production workers the normalized response to a unit change in output is unity, but then the response drops off sharply to 0.24, thereafter trailing off slowly [13]). A comparison of the relative speeds of reaction of overhead and production workers requires examination of the normalizing coefficients

---

[13]) To the extent that the response trails off very slowly, as shown, one would suspect that a somewhat more completely estimated lag distribution would have enabled the output variable to converge rapidly to zero instead of at the same relative rate as the capital stock variable, a mode of behavior which is forced on this estimating equation because only one lag appears in the lagged dependent variable.

TABLE 8.7

Lag weights for employment equations (per cent).

	Production workers [a]			Overhead workers			
	Durables			Durables		Nondurables	
Normalized coefficients for lag	X^{54}	$[\Delta H_p]_{-1}$	K^{54}_{-1}	X^{54}	K^{54}_{-1}	X^{54}	K^{54}_{-1}
0	1.00	0.00	1.00	1.00	1.00	1.00	1.00
1	0.24	1.00	0.92	0.86	0.86	0.82	0.82
2	0.22	−0.09	0.84	0.74	0.74	0.67	0.67
3	0.20	−0.08	0.77	0.64	0.64	0.55	0.55
4	0.18	−0.07	0.61	0.55	0.55	0.35	0.35
First-year effect	1.85	0.77	4.13	3.79	3.79	3.39	3.39
Total effect	3.85	0	11.76	7.14	7.14	5.68	5.68
First-year fraction of total effect	0.48	[c]	0.35	0.53	0.53	0.60	0.60
Normalizing coefficient [b]	0.052	0.152	−0.02614	0.0042	0.00266	0.0025	0.00173

[a] This procedure does not apply to nondurable production workers because the difference equation in E_p is not damped.

[b] To obtain proper scaling, all coefficients in the table above would have to be multiplied by the coefficient of the relevant unlagged independent variable whose value is recorded in this row.

[c] Not applicable.

recorded at the bottom of table 8.7. While there are one-quarter to one-fifth as many overhead workers as there are production workers, the output coefficient for overhead workers is one-tenth that for production workers, and so the relative impact of an output change is twice as great for production as it is for nonproduction workers. On the nondurables equations, the comparison is even more clear-cut, since the total production worker response occurs simultaneously.

8.3.3. Employment functions: all industries

Long-run production-function attributes can be most readily observed from an examination of the steady-state output and capital stock elasticities. The steady-state implications of the influence of capital stock and output shown by the long-run elasticities in table 8.8 are obtained by setting the rate of output change and rate of change in hours to zero. It is interesting to observe that equiproportional changes in capital stock and output barely change the demand for production workers in manufacturing. Manufacturing overhead worker impact elasticities are about the same as those for production workers, while the long-run elasticities are substantially less. It should also be noted that capital is complementary with nondurable

overhead, although the coefficient is very small relative to its standard
error. For overhead workers in both durables and nondurable goods, a
1 per cent increase in capital and output would eventually result in an
increase in overhead employment of 1.5 and 0.9 per cent, respectively.
Regression results for the major industries which underlie these elasticities
are reported in table 8.9.

TABLE 8.8

Elasticities and reaction coefficients [a]) (*manufacturing aggregates*).

Industry	Reaction coefficient	Short run		Long run	
		Output	Capital stock	Output	Capital stock
Manufacturing, production workers					
Total	0.019	0.163	−0.160	8.578	−8.421
Durables	0.099	0.210	−0.165	2.121	−1.666
Nondurables	−0.080	0.066	−0.049	0.825	−0.613
Manufacturing, overhead workers					
Total	0.149	0.168	0.007	1.127	0.046
Durables	0.100	0.160	−0.011	1.600	−0.110
Nondurables	0.209	0.106	0.076	0.507	0.363

a) Explanatory variables: output, capital stock, lagged employment, per cent output
change, per cent hours change. Dependent variable: employees (millions).

The preference accorded the forms adopted depends on both theoretical
and statistical considerations. While in principle the overhead employment
equations might also contain lagged output, the statistical impact of lagged
output—given the inclusion of lagged employment, capital stock and current
output—left unaffected all regression coefficients, standard errors of parameters and equations and Von Neumann ratios. Hence the first-order
lag in employment unambiguously conformed with both theoretical and
statistical criteria.

Production-worker employment equations require more detailed justification. As an experimental proposition, standard production functions were
estimated explaining employment by output and capital stock. Multiple
correlations for manufacturing are disappointingly low. While durable
goods manufacturing has a moderately "respectable" multiple correlation
of 0.794, the nondurable goods manufacturing industry component has a
multiple correlation of only 0.598. Total manufacturing records a multiple
correlation of 0.615. It is evident that the standard error of estimate for total

TABLE 8.9

Employment functions [a] *(all industries).*

Industry	Estimated equation measures			Regression coefficients [b]					
	R^2	Standard error of estimate	Von Neumann ratio	Output ($bill./yr)$(t)$	Cap. stock ($bill.)$(t-1)$	Empl. $(t-1)$	Per cent output change/quart.	Per cent change in hr./wk.	Intercept
Manufacturing production workers									
Total	0.968	0.1259	1.888	0.018 (0.004)	−0.0238 (0.0047)	0.981 (0.034)	0.0342 (0.0113)	0.1211 (0.0507)	0.1390 (0.4559)
Durables	0.972	0.1007	1.948	0.024 (0.005)	−0.0360 (0.0067)	0.901 (0.042)	0.0167 (0.0058)	0.0643 (0.0318)	0.5242 (0.2672)
Nondurables	0.958	0.0358	1.918	0.007 (0.002)	−0.0056 (0.0025)	1.080 (0.042)	0.0212 (0.0042)	−0.0060 (0.0109)	−0.5923 (0.2859)
Manufacturing overhead workers									
Total	0.996	0.0288	1.996	0.005 (0.001)	0.0003 (0.0023)	0.851 (0.056)	−0.0022 (0.0026)	0.0079 (0.0116)	−0.0350 (0.0396)
Durables	0.994	0.0282	2.112	0.005 (0.001)	−0.0006 (0.0044)	0.900 (0.070)	−0.0016 (0.0016)	0.0099 (0.0094)	−0.0443 (0.0414)
Nondurables	0.998	0.0082	1.277	0.003 (0.001)	0.0023 (0.0015)	0.791 (0.071)	−0.0004 (0.0011)	−0.0008 (0.0024)	0.0617 (0.0165)

[a] Explanatory variables: output, capital stock, lagged employment, per cent output change, per cent hours change. Dependent variable: Employees (millions).

[b] Standard errors of regression coefficients are reported in parentheses.

TABLE 8.9 (Continued)

Industry	Estimated equation measures			Regression coefficients [a]					
	R^2	Standard error of estimate	Von Neumann ratio	Output ($bill./yr)($t$)	Cap. stock ($bill.)($t-1$)	Empl. ($t-1$)	Per cent output change/quart.	Per cent change in hr./wk.	Intercept
Nonmanufacturing									
Mining	0.968	0.0195	1.902	0.000 (0.000)	−0.0029 (0.0009)	0.633 (0.110)	0.0014 (0.0007)	−0.0018 (0.0009)	0.0926 (0.0649)
Construction	0.980	0.0318	1.922	0.066 (0.012)	−0.0017 (0.0004)	0.582 (0.079)	−0.0008 (0.0027)	0.2000 (0.0037)	0.4072 (0.0828)
Wholesale trade	0.996	0.0120	1.378	0.019 (0.002)	0.0000 (0.0005)	0.835 (0.042)	0.0001 (0.0007)	−0.1004 (0.0071)	0.0920 (0.0961)
Retail trade	0.994	0.0399	1.155	0.027 (0.005)	−0.0051 (0.0025)	0.862 (0.061)	−0.0006 (0.0026)	−0.0009 (0.0082)	−0.0246 (0.3918)
Finance and insurance	1.000	0.0062	0.857	0.005 (0.004)	0.0025 (0.0015)	0.812 (0.075)	0.0008 (0.0010)	0.3472 (6.1848)	0.1958 (0.0918)
R.R. transportation	0.986	0.0226	2.431	0.019 (0.006)	−0.0068 (0.0084)	0.983 (0.022)	0.0044 (0.0009)	−0.0024 (0.0027)	0.1365 (0.3451)
Nonrail transportation	0.863	0.0378	2.034	0.055 (0.011)	0.0929 (0.0480)	0.152 (0.141)	−0.0041 (0.0034)	78.6931 (35.8777)	−0.3686 (0.5444)
Public utilities	0.986	0.0030	1.718	−0.002 (0.002)	0.0014 (0.0009)	0.755 (0.123)	−0.0005 (0.0004)	0.0010 (0.0016)	0.1094 (0.0514)
Services	0.996	0.0216	0.848	0.015 (0.009)	0.0019 (0.0013)	0.815 (0.079)	0.0073 (0.0045)	−12.4966 (72.9704)	0.2352 (0.1330)

[a]) See footnote on page 249.

manufacturing of 565 000 workers is exceedingly large. This is hardly enough accuracy to contemplate successful predictions from quarter to quarter. However, the error covariances among the individual two-digit industries are substantial, as the calculations in table 8.10 reveal.

TABLE. 8.10

Covariance components of error variances: employment explained by output and capital stock.

Industry	Production workers		Overhead workers	
	Standard error of estimate (1)	Covariant error variance fraction (2)	Standard error of estimate (3)	Covariant error variance fraction (4)
Manufacturing	0.5647	0.9228	0.0831	0.8199
Durables	0.3628	0.8610	0.0037	−75.9532
Nondurables	0.1422	0.6868	0.0198	0.5144

The sum of two-digit industry error variances has been subtracted from the total error variance, which leaves a number equal to twice the sum of the individual error variances. That number, termed the covariant error variance component, has been divided by the total error variance and recorded in columns (2) and (4). Improved specification tends to reduce this undesirable interdependence. Disaggregation clearly "pays off" for industry prediction purposes, since the aggregate error variance is so much greater than the sum of the individual variances. Nevertheless, at any one point of time, errors will tend to be in the same direction, a fact that could only be established through this sort of disaggregation.

Overhead workers in manufacturing are explained, statistically speaking, to a substantially greater extent than are production workers. The multiple correlations are in the neighborhood of 0.98 or 0.99, and the standard errors of estimates are trivially small by comparison with those for production workers. There is patently much less unexplained variance remaining for overhead workers, and much of the explanation is provided by the level of output and the stock of capital, in strong contrast to the demand for production workers in manufacturing.

When lagged employment is introduced, multiple correlations rise sharply for the production worker equations, as one would normally expect, mounting from 0.794 to 0.967 for durable manufacturing and to 0.934 from 0.958 for nondurables manufacturing. At the same time, for this set of explanatory variables the serial correlation characteristics were disturbingly

large: 0.950 for durable manufacturing and only 0.748 for nondurables [14]).
It is frequently argued that introducing the lagged dependent variable
provides an undue amount of confidence in large multiple correlations. To
the extent that predicting the change in the dependent variable is the principal
objective, there is substance to this view. However, when the dependent
variable has its origins in some dynamic process, it is essential to represent
that dynamic process through the introduction of lags in the dependent
variable and/or lags of relatively high order in the explanatory variables.
In present circumstances, there is every reason to expect, according to the
analytic structure described in section 8.2, that there will be lags in the adjustment process, and so it is appropriate to include the lagged dependent
variable here.

Finally, when lagged output is included (which in the inital phases of this
work was introduced as current per cent change in output), several important
statistical improvements result. The most striking effect of output rate of
change is on the degree of serial correlation. The Von Neumann statistic
for manufacturing mounted to 1.707 from 0.706, the statistic for durables
rose to 1.776 and the one for nondurables to 1.707. Standard errors of estimate have also been sharply reduced. Much of the added variables influence
was to increase the independence of the errors and thereby reduce the aggregate error variance. This is illustrated by comparing tables 8.10 and 8.11.

TABLE 8.11

Covariance components of error variances: employment explained by output, capital stock, lagged employment, per cent change in output.

Industry	Production workers		Overhead workers	
	Standard error of estimate (1)	Covariant error variance fraction (2)	Standard error of estimate (3)	Covariant error variance fraction (4)
Manufacturing	0.1325	0.6802	0.0287	0.5569
Durables	0.1042	0.5230	0.0282	0.5565
Nondurables	0.0377	0.6947	0.0081	0.5369

[14]) The statistic actually calculated by the available computer program was the Von
Neumann ratio, although the Durbin-Watson test statistics are reported. With almost
fifty observations the calculated statistics differ by only about 2 per cent. At this stage
accuracy of this order provides all the required refinements. The Theil-Nagar modification
cannot be used with confidence, since production workers and hours time series did not
have strong trends in most instances, which is a sufficient condition for the Theil-Nagar
approximation to be valid. The doubtful validity of these tests in the presence of the
lagged dependent variable should be recognized.

The influence of output rate of change on the covariant component was most marked in the production worker equation, as the covariant fraction for durables, nondurables and manufacturing fell sharply. Overhead worker equations, already well specified, showed little change in any other significant statistical attribute, nor do they in this instance. There seems to be a close relation between accuracy of specification and the relative importance of the covariance. The more adequate the specification, the less the contemporaneous error covariances will be. Remaining covariant elements are still too large to warrant complacency.

Finally, hours are the most rapidly adjustable component of labor input, but at the same time, when deviations from the standard number of hours are large, hours become more costly than adjustment in employment. On prior grounds we would expect that the per cent change in hours variable would have a positive sign: the larger the rate of change in hours in the previous period, the greater will be employment in this period as a substitute, in order to reduce hours toward normal and thus minimize overtime production.

This variable has negligible effects on standard errors of estimate for production workers, causing only very small proportional reductions for durables, nondurables and manufacturing. One noticeable effect, however, is a reduction in serial correlation of the errors, the Von Neumann ratio for nondurable goods moving from 1.707 to 1.918, that for durable goods moving from 1.776 to 1.948 and that for manufacturing going from 1.707 to 1.888. The overhead worker standard errors of estimate and serial correlation are unaffected.

8.4. Production worker hour demand equations

The basic model for hours can be readily outlined. The main determinant of hours to be worked is a convention established through bargaining and a variety of social and institutional forces. There is a lagged adjustment to the desired constant level of hours (more accurately, a gently declining trend) and a strong transient response to the rate of change in output. The equation below sets out the description verbally presented.

$$\Delta H_P = \alpha[\gamma - (H_P)_{-1}] + \beta \left[\frac{\Delta X^{54}}{X^{54}} \right] + \varepsilon.$$

The nonmanufacturing sector shows a wide variety of over-all results in table 8.12 for the basic hour demand model. Communications has a correlation of only 0.527 and a standard error as large as 1.302 hours per week. At the other extreme, wholesale trade has a substantial correlation of 0.899

$$H_{P_{MD}} = 5.0918 + 0.8731 \, H_{P_{MD-1}} + 5.61 \, [\varDelta X^{54}_{MD}/X^{54}_{MD-1}]_t$$

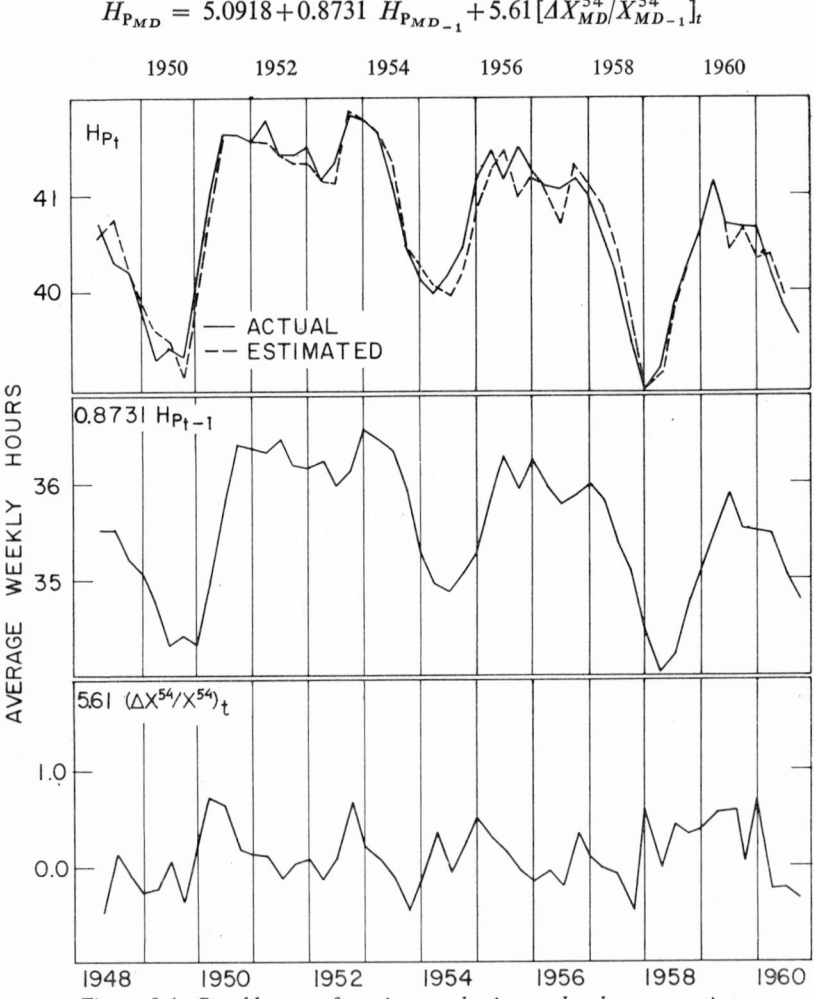

Figure 8.4. *Durable manufacturing production worker hours equation.*

and a standard error of estimate of only 0.099 hours per week. Volatile industries in this category, particularly construction, mining, railroads and communications have rather large standard errors, running from about half an hour to an hour per week. On rather subjective grounds, we cannot consider these results highly satisfactory, although it is not obvious how

TABLE 8.12

Production worker hour demand functions [a]) (*manufacturing and nonmanufacturing sectors*).

Industry	Estimated equation measures		Regression coefficients [b])		Intercept
	$\bar{R}^2$	Standard error of estimate	Hr./wk. $(t-1)$	Per cent output change /quarter	
Manufacturing	0.937	0.161	0.859 (0.037)	0.0735 (0.0060)	5.565 (1.503)
Durables	0.935	0.207	0.869 (0.038)	0.0558 (0.0050)	5.282 (1.535)
Nondurables	0.830	0.190	0.794 (0.061)	0.1173 0.0141)	8.009 (2.414)
Nonmanufacturing					
Mining	0.745	1.081	0.806 (0.073)	0.1175 (0.0216)	7.468 (2.829)
Construction	0.619	0.457	0.820 (0.092)	−0.0073 (0.0266)	6.637 (3.428)
Wholesale trade	0.808	0.099	0.874 (0.063)	0.0120 (0.0043)	5.081 (2.534)
Retail trade	0.914	0.288	0.971 (0.043)	0.0004 (0.0152)	1.071 (1.701)
R.R. transportation	0.806	0.057	0.888 (0.064)	0.0768 (0.0194)	4.589 (2.648)
Communications	0.278	1.302	0.408 (0.099)	−0.2334 (0.1564)	23.503 (3.933)
Public utilities	0.863	0.117	0.899 (0.053)	0.0296 (0.0133)	4.077 (2.184)

Explanatory variables: hours $(t-1)$ and output per cent change. Dependent variable: production worker hours/week.

Standard errors of regression coefficients are reported in parentheses.

one could do a great deal better. Serial correlation is so slight that reducing the unexplained variance through respecification does not appear to offer much hope.

Durable goods manufacturing presents a more satisfactory statistical picture than the nonmanufacturing sector, according to table 8.12. Since a correlation of 0.967 and a standard error of estimate of 0.207 hours per week are recorded, the basic purposes of the model should be adequately served. It is not obvious that a great deal of improvement is possible, since the two-digit industry results have much smaller standard errors of estimate.

Generally speaking, the nondurable manufacturing hour equations have substantially smaller individual error variances. The largest four error variances in the durable goods sector exceed the largest error variance in the nondurables sector. The aggregate standard error of estimate is the same for nondurables and durables, although the correlation for nondurables is noticeably smaller than that for durables.

The main impression that emerges from table 8.12 which records the parameters for nonmanufacturing industries, is that most explanatory power for the nonmanufacturing industries lies in the autoregression of hours on lagged hours. Nevertheless, statistically significant independent explantory ability exists for the output rate of change in mining, wholesale trade, railroads and public utilities.

In manufacturing, while the autoregressive component is definitely relevant, genuine weight attaches to rate of the change in output, since for the aggregates of manufacturing, durable goods and nondurable goods the rate of change in output regression coefficient is at least ten times its standard error.

The output rate of change variable is statistically significant at usual levels of significance (particularly on a one-tail basis) in seven of the eleven durable goods industries and all ten nondurable industries. Its importance in the nondurable sector seems, on the whole, greater, a fact indicated by the higher coefficient, double the weight placed by durable goods on per cent change in output.

A further set of calculations lends support to this hypothesis. The calculated long-run "desired" or target level of hours (defined as the intercept divided by the reaction coefficient) ought to be in the vicinity of the standard forty-hour week if the estimating equation is a valid one. In fact, the results presented in table 8.13 vary between 39 and 41 hours for durable manufacturing two-digit industries and, except for a slightly low value of 35.6 and six-tenths hours for the apparel industry, also fall within a narrow appropriate range. The same close correspondence also exists for the nonmanufacturing sectors.

The production worker hour equations had included the rate of change of output in per cent form along with the level of unemployment and the per cent change in unemployment. When output entered linearly with unrestricted coefficients on current and lagged output, the restriction that output enter only as a rate of change was validated, since the coefficient of lagged output was nearly equal in magnitude and opposite in sign to that

TABLE 8.13

Reaction coefficients and target hours/week from production worker hour equations.

Industry	Reaction coefficient	Target hours per week	$\bar{R}^2$	Standard error of estimate
ggregates				
Mining	0.194	38.49	0.745	1.081
Construction	0.180	36.87	0.619	0.457
Wholesale trade	0.126	40.32	0.808	0.099
Retail trade	0.029	36.93	0.914	0.288
R.R. transportation	0.112	40.97	0.806	0.565
Communications	0.592	39.70	0.278	1.302
Public utilities	0.101	40.36	0.863	0.117
urables two-digit				
Primary metals	0.155	39.55	0.674	0.767
Fabricated metal products	0.138	40.65	0.812	0.331
Nonelectrical machinery	0.080	41.20	0.830	0.514
Electrical machinery	0.143	40.55	0.738	0.353
Motor vehicles and parts	0.414	40.47	0.359	0.999
Other transportation	0.562	40.37	0.558	0.635
Instruments	0.181	40.07	0.924	0.236
Lumber and wood products	0.095	40.38	0.815	0.268
Furniture and fixtures	0.164	40.24	0.712	0.342
Stone, clay and glass	0.096	39.74	0.841	0.330
Miscellaneous mfg.	0.084	39.25	0.880	0.208
Nondurables two-digit				
Food and beverages	0.076	40.26	0.832	0.187
Tobacco	0.331	38.11	0.666	0.373
Textile mill products	0.169	38.92	0.852	0.408
Apparel	0.210	35.58	0.623	0.364
Paper and allied	0.118	41.59	0.906	0.191
Printing and publishing	0.071	37.65	0.826	0.149
Chemicals	0.211	40.90	0.733	0.126
Integrated petroleum	0.573	40.73	0.203	0.316
Rubber products	0.191	39.81	0.859	0.407
Leather and products	0.208	37.17	0.762	0.346

of the current value of the output variable. As a final selection, therefore, the level of errors will be explained by lagged hours for production workers and the per cent change in output [15]). The lag distributions are shown for these regressions in table 8.14.

[15]) Equations (8.8) and (8.9) are in linear form to facilitate the computation of lags. Equations in table 8.12 represent output and lagged output in percentage change form in order to avoid improper scaling.

Table 8.14

Lag weights for production worker hour equations.

Normalized coefficient for lag	Output	
	Durables (Eq. 8.8)	Nondurables (eq. 8.9)
0	1.000	1.000
1	−0.187	−0.215
2	−0.167	−0.173
3	−0.149	−0.139
4	−0.133	−0.112
First year effect	0.364	0.361
Total effect [a]	0.000	0.000
Normalizing coefficient	0.815×10^{-4}	0.220×10^{-3}

[a]) The difference between the two output coefficients is negligible, and so, in accordance with the theory, the long-run effect has been set equal to zero.

Durable manufacturing

$$H_{P_{MD}} = \frac{0.892}{(0.0442)} [H_{P_{MD}}]_{-1} + \frac{0.8150 \times 10^{-4}}{(0.0910 \times 10^{-4})} [X_{MD}^{54}]$$

$$- \frac{0.8792 \times 10^{-4}}{(0.0881 \times 10^{-4})} [X_{MD}^{54}]_{-1} + \frac{4.716}{(1.726)}$$

$$\bar{R}^2 = 0.927 \qquad S_e = 0.274 \qquad VN = 1.82. \tag{8.8}$$

Nondurable manufacturing

$$H_{P_{MN^*}} = \frac{0.804}{(0.063)} [H_{P_{MN^*}}]_{-1} + \frac{0.2195 \times 10^{-3}}{(0.0274 \times 10^{-3})} [X_{MN^*}^{54}]$$

$$- \frac{0.2236 \times 10^{-3}}{(0.0274 \times 10^{-3})} [X_{MN^*}^{54}]_{-1} + \frac{7.817}{(2.467)}$$

$$\bar{R}^2 = 0.835 \qquad S_e = 0.193 \qquad VN = 2.06. \tag{8.9}$$

8.5. Estimation summary

8.5.1. Final equations

A final set of parameters, using revised data, were estimated, and at the same time the sectors were made compatible with the aggregation levels

TABLE 8.15

Final least squares estimates for hours and employment functions.

Part A: Production worker and total employment equations.

$$E_{P_{MD}} = \frac{0.6886}{(0.3189)} + \frac{0.0535}{(0.0052)} X_{MD}^{54} - \frac{0.0342}{(0.0064)} [X_{MD}^{54}]_{-1} - \frac{0.0246}{(0.0065)} K_{MD-1}^{54}$$

$$+ \frac{0.1402}{(0.0496)} [\Delta H_{P_{MD}}]_{-1} + \frac{0.8616}{(0.0554)} [E_{P_{MD}}]_{-1}$$

$$\bar{R}^2 = 0.974 \qquad S_e = 0.1012 \tag{8.10}$$

$$E_{P_{MN^*}} = \frac{0.2261}{(0.2975)} + \frac{0.0378}{(0.0049)} X_{MN^*}^{54} - \frac{0.0326}{(0.0051)} [X_{MN^*}^{54}]_{-1} - \frac{0.0097}{(0.0037)} K_{MN-1}^{54}$$

$$+ \frac{0.0961}{(0.0169)} [\Delta H_{P_{MN^*}}]_{-1} + \frac{0.9866}{(0.0394)} [E_{P_{MN^*}}]_{-1}$$

$$\bar{R}^2 = 0.974 \qquad S_e = 0.0309 \tag{8.11}$$

$$E_C = \frac{0.1425}{(0.1197)} + \frac{0.0503}{(0.0107)} X_C^{54} - \frac{0.0016}{(0.0019)} TIME + \frac{0.6370}{(0.0818)} [E_{P_C}]_{-1}$$

$$\bar{R}^2 = 0.9641 \qquad S_e = 0.0446 \tag{8.12}$$

$$E_T = -\frac{0.2174}{(0.3981)} + \frac{0.0219}{(0.0038)} X_T^{54} + \frac{0.0053}{(0.0041)} [X_T^{54}]_{-1} - \frac{0.0065}{(0.0023)} TIME$$

$$+ \frac{0.8599}{(0.0457)} [E_{P_T}]_{-1} \qquad \bar{R}^2 = 0.996 \qquad S_e = 0.0419 \tag{8.13}$$

Part B: Overhead worker employment equations.

$$E_{O_{MD}} = \frac{0.1646}{(0.0530)} + \frac{0.0052}{(0.0008)} X_{MD}^{54} + \frac{0.0076}{(0.0040)} K_{MD-1}^{54} + \frac{0.7910}{(0.0686)} [E_{O_{MD}}]_{-1}$$

$$\bar{R}^2 = 0.996 \qquad S_e = 0.0261 \tag{8.14}$$

$$E_{O_{MN^*}} = \frac{0.0680}{(0.0232)} + \frac{0.0023}{(0.0005)} X_{MN^*}^{54} - \frac{0.0038}{(0.0019)} K_{MN-1}^{54} + \frac{0.9972}{(0.0534)} [E_{O_{MN^*}}]_{-1}$$

$$\bar{R}^2 = 0.998 \qquad S_e = 0.0078 \tag{8.15}$$

TABLE 8.15 (Continued)

Part C: Direct man-hour demand equations.

$$MH_R = -\frac{0.3529}{(0.7161)} + \frac{0.1465}{(0.0365)} X_R^{54} - \frac{0.0814}{(0.0416)} [X_R^{54}]_{-1} - \frac{0.0278}{(0.0077)} TIME$$

$$+ \frac{0.8548}{(0.0933)} [MH_R]_{-1} \qquad \bar{R}^2 = 0.824 \qquad S_e = 0.1314 \tag{8.16}$$

$$MH_{O^*} = -\frac{0.0687}{(0.4601)} + \frac{0.2101}{(0.0319)} X_{O^{*1}}^{54} - \frac{0.1612}{(0.0421)} [X_{O^{*1}}^{54}]_{-1}$$

$$-\frac{0.0056}{(0.0038)} TIME + \frac{0.8476}{(0.0891)} [MH_{O^{*1}}]_{-1}$$

$$\bar{R}^2 = 0.996 \qquad S_e = 0.0691 \tag{8.17}$$

Part D: Production worker hour equations.

$$H_{P_{MD}} = \frac{5.0918}{(1.6113)} + \frac{5.61}{(0.53)} \left\{\frac{\Delta X_{MD}^{54}}{[X_{MD}^{54}]_{-1}}\right\} + \frac{0.8731}{(0.0396)} [H_{P_{MD}}]_{-1}$$

$$\bar{R}^2 = 0.927 \qquad S_e = 0.2168 \tag{8.18}$$

$$H_{P_{MN^*}} = \frac{11.1846}{(2.4602)} + \frac{11.20}{(1.50)} \left\{\frac{\Delta X_{MN^*}^{54}}{[X_{MN^*}^{54}]_{-1}}\right\} + \frac{0.7135}{(0.0623)} [H_{P_{MN^*}}]_{-1}$$

$$\bar{R}^2 = 0.56 \qquad S_e = 0.3146 \tag{8.19}$$

$$H_{P_C} = \frac{4.7027}{(2.8250)} + \frac{2.62}{(0.71)} \left\{\frac{\Delta X_C^{54}}{[X_C^{54}]_{-1}}\right\} + \frac{0.8719}{(0.0756)} [H_{P_C}]_{-1}$$

$$\bar{R}^2 = 0.74 \qquad S_e = 0.4598 \tag{8.20}$$

Note   An equation for H_{P_T} appears in chapter 18.

chosen for the model at this stage of research. These estimates are presented in table 8.15. The estimates were calculated with a double-precision program. Where estimates comparable with the earlier data are available, changes in the estimated parameter values are small except for overhead workers in nondurable manufacturing. Instead of the positive effect of capital with overhead employment, a statistically significant negative coefficient and a much larger coefficient on lagged employment are recorded. I believe this is largely an aggregation fluke, since the substantial majority of two-digit industry results have positive or zero coefficients on capital stock and smaller weights on the lagged dependent variable. The possibility remains open, however, that estimates on revised two-digit output and capital stock data would change these results, although I doubt it.

Changes in equation form should be noted. For the regulated sector (public utilities, nonrail transportation and railroads) and the residual sector (services, finance and insurance, and mining) at least one component industry did not have production worker hours available. In these instances, therefore, direct estimates of man-hours as a function of output, capital stock and lagged man-hours were obtained.

The variables in order of appearance are:

E_P = employment of production workers, millions
X = gross product originating (by industry), billions of dollars
K = stock of industry fixed capital, billions of dollars
H_P = average work week of production workers, hours
E = employment, millions of persons
$TIME$ = time trend
E_O = employment of overhead workers, millions
MH = man-hours, billions per year.

Sector subscripts are:

C = contract construction
MD = durable manufacturing
MN = nondurable manufacturing
MN^* = nondurable manufacturing plus mining of crude petroleum and natural gas
O^*1 = residual industries: mining except crude petroleum and natural gas; finance and insurance; services except household and institutional
R = regulated industries: transportation, communications and public utilities
T = wholesale and retail trade.

8.5.2. *Error structure of man-hour estimates*

An error analysis of the employment-hours relations is contained in table 8.16. The proximate objective of this segment of the model is not the prediction of employment alone or hours per week alone but their product, man-hours.

The following symbols will be used:

E_O or E_P = actual overhead or production worker employment
$\hat{E}_O$ or $\hat{E}_P$ = predicted overhead or production worker employment
ε_O or ε_P = error of predicting overhead or production worker employment
H_P = actual production worker hours
$\hat{H}_P$ = predicted production worker hours
ε_H = error in predicting production worker hours
ε_O or ε_{PH} = error in predicting overhead or production worker man-hours
ε_E = error in predicting total employment man-hours = $\varepsilon_O + \varepsilon_{PH}$.

$$E_P = \hat{E}_P + \varepsilon_P$$

$$H_P = \hat{H}_P + \varepsilon_H$$

$$MH_P = \hat{E}_P \hat{H}_P + \varepsilon_{PH}$$

$$\varepsilon_{PH} = \varepsilon_P \varepsilon_H - \varepsilon_P H_P - \varepsilon_H E_P$$

$$\sigma_{PH}^2 = \sum \varepsilon_{PH}^2 / d.f.$$

$$R_{PH}^2 = 1 - \frac{\sigma_{\varepsilon PH}^2}{\sigma_{PH}^2}$$

$$\varepsilon_E = \varepsilon_P \varepsilon_H - \varepsilon_P H_P - \varepsilon_H E_P + \varepsilon_O$$

$$R_E^2 = 1 - \frac{\sigma_{\varepsilon E}^2}{\sigma_E^2}$$

The above definitions and relations provide the relevant framework for evaluating the errors in production man-hours. By adding the error in the overhead worker man-hour equation (which arises only from the employment element, since hours are assumed fixed), the aggregate man-hour employment error, ε_E, with associated statistics, is obtained. Degrees of freedom are calculated by subtracting from the total number of observations a number equal to the total parameters fitted in the two or three equations used in obtaining the errors. This error analysis presupposes that all the errors originate in the employment and hours series and that output is known with certainty. Unless output can actually be predicted with extreme accuracy, the true error variances will exceed those reported in table 8.16. As a method of evaluating the statistical attributes of these equations conditional on output, however, these calculations are valid.

TABLE 8.16

Error variance analysis: manufacturing.

Equation	Variables appearing in regressions								Error variance (million man-hours/year)	
	Production worker employment			Overhead worker employment	Production worker hour demand					
	$X^{54} K_{-1}^{54} [E_P]_{-1}$	$\frac{\Delta X^{54}}{X_{-1}^{54}}$	$\frac{\Delta H_P}{H_{p-1}}$	$X^{54} K_{-1}^{54} [E_O]_{-1}$	$\frac{\Delta X^{54}}{X_{-1}^{54}}$	$[H_P]_{-1}$	U	$\frac{\Delta U}{U}$	σ_{PH}^2	σ_E^2
(1 M)	×			×	×	×	×	×	279 206	303 789
(2 M)	×	×		×	×	×	×	×	125 983	135 545
(3 M)	×	×	×	×	×	×	×	×	97 296	106 037
(4 M)	×	×	×	×	×	×	×		93 397	101 371
(5 M)	×	×		×	×	×	×		121 605	130 345
(6 M)	×			×	×	×	×		272 123	295 210
(1 MD)	×			×	×	×	×	×	130 049	143 024
(2 MD)	×	×		×	×	×	×	×	72 738	78 312
(3 MD)	×	×	×	×	×	×	×	×	60 180	65 932
(4 MD)	×	×	×	×	×	×	×		58 883	64 291
(5 MD)	×	×		×	×	×	×		71 160	76 374
(6 MD)	×			×	×	×	×		126 915	139 171
(1 MN)	×			×	×	×	×	×	23 326	24 792
(2 MN)	×	×		×	×	×	×	×	10 892	11 845
(3 MN)	×	×	×	×	×	×	×	×	7 722	8 532
(4 MN)	×	×	×	×	×	×	×		11 342	12 865
(5 MN)	×	×		×	×	×	×		15 017	16 715
(6 MN)	×			×	×	×	×		26 543	28 624

Notes   1) The first-order serial correlations are derived from the Durbin-Watson Statistic according to $\rho - 1 = -\frac{1}{2} DW$.

           2) The mean of the product errors were used in all calculations of variances but were approximately zero in all instances.

TABLE 8.16 (Continued)

Multiple correlations		Durbin-Watson Statistics		First-order serial correlations		Correlations	
R^2_{PH}	R^2_E	DW_{PH}	DW_E	$\rho_{PH,(t-1)}$	$\rho_{E,(t-1)}$	$r_{\varepsilon P, \varepsilon H}$	$r_{\varepsilon PH, \varepsilon O}$
0.915	0.933	0.691	0.729	0.654	0.635	0.273	−0.173
0.961	0.970	1.691	1.772	0.154	0.113	0.471	−0.222
0.970	0.976	1.707	1.787	0.146	0.106	0.130	−0.199
0.971	0.977	1.700	1.781	0.149	0.109	0.101	−0.199
0.963	0.971	1.688	1.770	0.155	0.114	0.441	−0.222
0.917	0.935	0.686	0.724	0.656	0.637	0.265	−0.172
0.939	0.954	0.928	1.009	0.535	0.495	0.223	−0.136
0.966	0.974	1.695	1.832	0.152	0.083	0.372	−0.226
0.972	0.978	1.766	1.921	0.116	0.039	0.094	−0.203
0.972	0.979	1.768	1.924	0.115	0.037	0.101	−0.201
0.967	0.975	1.697	1.834	0.151	0.082	0.375	−0.223
0.941	0.955	0.930	1.011	0.534	0.494	0.221	−0.135
0.883	0.855	0.629	0.659	0.685	0.670	0.134	−0.288
0.945	0.931	1.541	1.638	0.229	0.180	0.195	−0.187
0.961	0.950	1.440	1.565	0.279	0.217	−0.149	−0.160
0.943	0.925	1.591	1.694	0.204	0.152	0.229	−0.038
0.925	0.902	1.637	1.721	0.181	0.139	0.575	−0.078
0.867	0.833	0.715	0.761	0.642	0.619	0.312	−0.207

These are the main impressions which emerge from table 8.16. First, the prediction error is heavily concentrated in the durable goods sector. Second, the preponderant error source lies in the prediction of production worker man-hours, which constitute roughly 70 per cent of the total error variance. Third, for the preferred equation form (3), the percentage of variance explained measured by $\bar{R}^2$ is the high value of 97 per cent. It must be realized, however, that the error variance in a difference equation model is an increasing function of time, and so even if output were given exactly, the reported error variances are unbiased estimates for one quarter away but downward biased for subsequent periods [16]).

Fourth, the serial correlation properties of the preferred estimates are quite good for both production workers and the total. In general, the individual error characteristics of the various equations carried over into the product form under examination here. Fifth, in the "worst" specified equations (1), (2), (5) and (6), fairly large positive correlations exist between the production worker hour equation and employment equation. This undesirable attribute is absent in the better specified equations (3) and (4). Sixth, in both manufacturing and durables there is a persistent, small negative correlation between production worker man-hours and nonproduction worker man-hours (about -0.20) which helps moderately to reduce the aggregate man-hour error variance. In nondurables the unemployment rate of change appears to increase negative correlation.

Seventh, the principal source of error variance in ε_E is from the term $\varepsilon_p H$, as can be seen from table 8.17. Since this term is the variance of a product, the most significant gains in prediction accuracy must come from making this series small term by term (since plus and minus covariance terms do not cancel) through reducing the error variance of the production worker employment equation, ε_p. Improved specification of the hour equation, while clearly desirable, is less urgent at the present time. It is also evident that the covariances among the errors make a negligible contribution to the aggregate variance.

8.6. The complete distribution

The previous emphasis on the employment-wage bill element in the income

---

[16]) For an illustration of this see Edwin Kuh, A Note on Prediction from Keynesian Models, *Review of Economics and Statistics* (August, 1956) 295–297. Duesenberry, Eckstein and Fromm derived Monte Carlo estimates for a larger system in "A Simulation of the United States Economy in Recession", *Econometrica* (October, 1960) 749–809, with comparable results.

TABLE 8.17

Normalized covariance matrix of total employment error ε_E.

Eq.	Manufacturing				Durables				Nondurables			
	$\varepsilon_P \varepsilon_H$	$\varepsilon_P H_P$	$\varepsilon_H E_P$	ε_O	$\varepsilon_P \varepsilon_H$	$\varepsilon_P H_P$	$\varepsilon_H E_P$	ε_O	$\varepsilon_P \varepsilon_{HP}$	$\varepsilon_P H_P$	$\varepsilon_H E_P$	ε_O
1	0.0000				0.0000				0.0000			
	−0.0002	0.8770			−0.0010	0.8830			−0.0001	0.8459		
	−0.0001	0.0978	0.0458		−0.0003	0.0789	0.0468		0.0000	0.0764	0.1228	
	0.0000	0.0239	0.0116	0.0144	−0.0001	0.0224	0.0224	0.0294	0.0001	0.0372	0.0225	0.0142
2	0.0000				0.0000				0.0000			
	−0.0007	0.7016			−0.0025	0.7713			−0.0007	0.6274		
	−0.0005	0.2267	0.1058		−0.0010	0.1719	0.0880		0.0000	0.1319	0.2644	
	0.0000	0.0419	0.0268	0.0332	−0.0002	0.0577	0.0322	0.0553	0.0000	0.0066	0.0485	0.0306
3	0.0000				0.0000				0.0000			
	−0.0003	0.8119			−0.0014	0.8603			−0.0002	0.7891		
	−0.0004	0.0735	0.1392		−0.0008	0.0498	0.1077		−0.0001	−0.1558	0.3778	
	0.0000	0.0338	0.0352	0.0436	−0.0002	0.0481	0.0398	0.0476	−0.0002	−0.0144	0.0694	0.0437
4	0.0000				0.0000				0.0000			
	−0.0003	0.8250			−0.0014	0.8570			−0.0005	0.5084		
	−0.0004	0.0589	0.1417		−0.0008	0.0537	0.1074		−0.0002	0.1548	0.3183	
	0.0004	0.0344	0.0365	0.0433	−0.0002	0.0479	0.0397	0.0673	−0.0003	−0.0092	0.0194	0.0282
5	0.0000				0.0000				0.0000			
	−0.0008	0.7094			−0.0025	0.7689			−0.0007	0.4323		
	−0.0006	0.2184	0.1072		−0.0009	0.1748	0.0879		−0.0005	0.3264	0.2381	
	0.0000	0.0428	0.0276	0.0335	−0.0002	0.0576	0.0325	0.0551	−0.0001	0.0045	0.0145	0.0211
6	0.0000				0.0000				0.0000			
	−0.0001	0.8781			−0.0011	0.8829			−0.0004	0.7128		
	−0.0001	0.0969	0.0460		−0.0003	0.0791	0.0469		−0.0004	0.1784	0.1353	
	0.0000	0.0240	0.0118	0.0144	−0.0001	0.0224	0.0173	0.0294	−0.0001	0.0313	0.0082	0.0119

Notes 1) The covariance elements of $\varepsilon_E = \varepsilon_P \varepsilon_H - \varepsilon_P H_P - \varepsilon_H E_P - \varepsilon_O$ have been normalized by dividing through by the error variance of total employment.

2) The off-diagonal terms are actually twice the normalized covariance and neglect the sign implied by the equation for ε_E.

3) Equation numbers correspond to table 8.16.

distribution was dictated by the relative neglect of this subject and its significance for corporate profits. In addition, the volatility of corporate profits, which will be obtained as a residual, is largely attributable to cyclical variations in labor productivity in the most volatile sectors. It is now time to complete the picture and consider the more stable items. Suppose for the moment that gross product (or gross value added) and the wage-plus-salary component have been determined. The next step will be to allocate this remainder to a variety of nonwage and salary incomes, entrepreneurial income, depreciation and capital consumption allowances, indirect business taxes, interest, rent, corporate profits before and after inventory valuation, corporate taxes, retained earnings and dividends.

The allocation process provisionally selected is indicated by the following set of relations:

(Gross value added)$_j$ − (wages plus salaries plus supplements)$_j$ = ("gross gross" residual)$_j$

The "gross gross" residual accounting relation for each industry has a ratio estimate of entrepreneurial income, denoted below by λ_j, deducted from it.
("Gross gross" residual)$_j$ − λ_j (gross value added)$_j$ = ("gross" residual)$_j$

These individual "gross" residuals are then summed to provide an "aggregate gross" residual, which is allocated to various sources at the aggregate level.

$\sum_j$ ("gross" residual)$_j$ = aggregate gross residual
= statistical discrepancy
− subsidies less current surplus of government enterprises
+ business transfers
+ interest income originating
+ indirect business taxes
+ capital consumption allowances
+ inventory valuation adjustment
+ corporate taxes
+ corporate retentions
+ dividends

The first three items are exogenous. Rental income will be explained by the stock of housing and the average rental index. The last five items con-

TABLE 8.18

Ratio of gross entrepreneurial income to gross product originating (National income basis).

Industry	1947	1948	1949	1950	1951	1952	1953	1954	1955	1956	1957	1958	1959	1960
Nonagricultural total	0.121	0.117	0.112	0.115	0.108	0.104	0.102	0.105	0.103	0.105	0.102	0.102	0.101	0.095
Contract construction	0.254	0.258	0.259	0.269	0.240	0.238	0.235	0.232	0.242	0.241	0.238	0.229	0.234	0.222
Manufacturing	0.028	0.023	0.021	0.024	0.022	0.020	0.019	0.018	0.017	0.017	0.016	0.016	0.014	0.013
Wholesale and retail trade	0.241	0.222	0.209	0.216	0.209	0.201	0.196	0.193	0.185	0.188	0.179	0.171	0.166	0.159
Regulated	0.038	0.037	0.037	0.037	0.034	0.034	0.033	0.034	0.032	0.032	0.033	0.033	0.031	0.030
Residual	N.A.	0.214	0.222	0.209	0.203	0.201	0.201	0.205	0.207	0.206	0.204	0.207	0.209	0.199

Notes

1) Data for the years 1947–1955 are from *U. S. Income and Output* (1958): the income of unincorporated enterprises by industry division, 1947–1955, are from table VI-4 (p. 202). Noncorporate depreciation charges for 1947–1955 are from table VI-19 (p. 217); these are added together to give gross enterpreneurial income.

Data for the years 1956–1960 are from the *Survey of Current Business*, July, 1962: for unincorporated enterprises, income is from table 44 (p. 26) and depreciation charges are from table 47 (p. 27).

Gross product originating 1947–1960 is taken from table 6 (p. 14) of the *Survey of Current Business*, October, 1962.

2) All data are used as listed in the designated table except the category Nonagricultural total, which is always "all industries, total" minus "agriculture, forestry and fisheries."

Sample calculation for 1947 (billions of dollars):

	Income	Depr.	GPO	Ratio
All industrial total	37.0	5.8	234.3	$(21.3 + 4.4)/213.0 = 0.12$
Agriculture, etc.	15.7	1.4	21.3	
Nonagricultural total	21.3	4.4	213.0	

stitute the final residual, which is by definition gross corporate profits before inventory valuation adjustment. Finally, the tax and capital consumption items will be analyzed in other chapters, and the remaining ones will now be described [17]).

8.6.1. Entrepreneurial income

Ratio estimates of gross noncorporate or entrepreneurial income originating to gross income originating are used to estimate entrepreneurial income. It can be seen from table 8.18 that the share of entrepreneurial income has a steady trend and very little cyclical movement. For nonagricultural income, the postwar high of 12 per cent dropped to 10 per cent in 1960. It can be seen from the other industry sectors for which these data are reported that the ratios have been gently declining for most industries over the postwar period.

8.6.2. Interest income

Interest income in the model eventually will be determined primarily through financial and real sector interactions which generate interest rates and changes in the stock of debt. At the present time this has been only partly executed, and so some patching is required to help close the income side of the model. Because interest income involves rather complicated and sometimes curious accounting conventions in the treatment of financial intermediaries in private interest payments, what follows should be taken as roughly indicative at best. This need be of small technical concern, since this variable has been, and under most conceivable circumstances will continue to be, subject to an extremely steady trend.

Personal interest consists of transfer payments on government debt and interest income originating in the private sector. Both were treated in general according to the treatment described below, although there are important differences in detail. By definition, $INT = \sum_r RM_r B_r$, where INT represents interest income, RM interest rate, B face value of dollar amount of bonds outstanding and the subscript r all rates at which bonds have been issued. This expression can be simplified by expressing $B = \sum B_r$ and $RM = \sum RM_r$

---

[17]) Capital consumption allowances are a function of the stock of capital (as well as its composition) and legislative action, while corporate profits taxes are best treated as a policy parameter which in recent years has been a stable 0.47 of net corporate profits before inventory valuation adjustment. Indirect business taxes depend on a variety of individual industry demand characteristics and tax rates.

as properly weighted averages.

$$INT = RM \cdot B.$$

Then ignoring second-order terms, the change in interest income will be:

$$\Delta INT = RM[\Delta B] + B[\Delta RM]. \tag{8.21}$$

The first term represents increments to the stock of debt financed at the ruling (average) interest rate, while the second term stands for refinancing of the existing asset stock. If the total stock is not refinanced, but only a part of it, one would anticipate a smaller regression coefficient on the latter series than on the former. Observation errors will be introduced if refinancing is done at rates different from the average rate. For the period 1948 : 3–1956 : 1, two-thirds of the values of ΔINT are zero and the remainder one-tenth of a billion. When ΔINT was subject to greater variation from 1956 : 2 onward, the proportion of variance explained, after correcting for degrees of freedom, was about one-third and serial correlation effectively zero.

$$\Delta INT_G = \frac{0.5880}{(0.4813)} [RM_{GBS3}][\Delta BF] + \frac{0.0661}{(0.0231)} [BF][\Delta RM_{GBS3}] + \frac{0.1167}{(0.0267)}$$

$$\bar{R}^2 = 0.355 \qquad S_e = 0.1152 \qquad VN = 1.962. \tag{8.22}$$

Period of fit: 1956 : 2–1960 : 4.

The variables used in equations (8.22) and (8.23) are:

INT_G = personal interest income paid by government, billions of dollars
RM_{GBS3} = average market yield on three-month U.S. Treasury bills, per cent
BF = total federal government debt, billions of dollars
INT_{BUS} = personal interest income paid by business, billions of dollars
RM_{GBL} = average yield during quarter on U.S. securities maturing or callable in ten years or more, per cent
I_{CNFR} = *GNP* expenditures on nonfarm residential construction, billions of dollars
K_{CD} = stock of consumer durable goods measured at original cost, billions of dollars.

A related approach was used for interest income originating in the private sector, which is based on debt financing of consumer durables and residential housing. Therefore the approximate identity of equation (8.21) will not hold when these stocks are used in place of the dollar values of the financial instruments. The identity was further fractured by using the current dollar sum of construction plus consumer durables times the interest rate as a measure of interest times the stock change and the change in interest times the stock of consumer durables (measured at original cost). While it would have been conceptually desirable to use the total stock of construction plus consumer durables, reliable housing stock figures were not readily available. Furthermore, consumer durables are short lived relative to housing, which suggests that the "refinancing" term's short-run movements would be dominated by the consumer durable segment. The estimated equation is then:

$$\Delta INT_{\text{BUS}} = \frac{1.19}{(0.25)} RM_{\text{GBL}}[I^{54}_{\text{CNFR}} + \Delta K^{54}_{\text{CD}}] + \frac{0.17}{(0.08)} [K^{54}_{\text{CD}}][\Delta RM_{\text{GBL}}]$$

$$+ \frac{0.0427}{(0.0530)} \qquad R^2 = 0.388 \qquad S_e = 0.116 \qquad (8.23)$$

Period of fit: 1948 : 2–1960 : 4.

These results indicate that the interest rate times construction plus consumer durables carries most of the explanatory weight, while the refinancing term is of much less significance. In general, the statistical attributes of the estimates appear to be qualitatively acceptable.

8.6.3. Inventory valuation adjustment

Some calculation must be made of the inventory valuation adjustment in order to close out the national income accounts. This adjustment is significant only when prices are changing rapidly. While it has been negligible in recent years, immediately postwar, during the Korean War and in 1956–1957 it reached the magnitude of several billion dollars per year. Since the inventory valuation adjustment procedures of the Department of Commerce are extremely intricate, we are obliged to devise a simple artifact to be used in a quarterly econometric model.

The variables used in this section are:

$PIVA$ = price index used to estimate inventory valuation adjustment, 1954 = 1.00
INV = business inventory stock, billions of dollars
INV_{EAF} = nonfarm business inventory stock, billions of dollars
X_{M*} = gross product originating in manufacturing plus mining of crude petroleum and natural gas, billions of dollars

WPI_{EAF} = wholesale price index of commodities other than farm products and food, 1954 = 1.00.

$$\Delta\{[PIVA][INV^{54}]\} = PIVA[\Delta INV^{54}]+[INV^{54}][\Delta PIVA]$$
$$+[\Delta PIVA][\Delta INV^{54}]. \quad (8.24)$$

By ordinary definitions of national income accounting, the elements of (8.24) are ΔINV^{54} = constant dollar inventory investment,

$[PIVA][\Delta INV^{54}] \cong$ current dollar inventory investment,

$[INV^{54}][\Delta PIVA] \cong$ inventory valuation gain.

Dividing through the estimated current value of inventory accumulation by an estimate of the constant dollar value of the inventory change will yield an estimate of a weighted average price index for the stock of inventory.

$$\widehat{PIVA} \cong \frac{PIVA\,[\Delta INV^{54}]}{\Delta INV^{54}}. \quad [8.25]$$

We can therefore conceive of an inventory valuation adjustment procedure as follows. First, estimate the level of this price index for one quarter into the future and then calculate the change. Second, multiply this change by the estimated constant dollar inventory stock figure in order to arrive at the estimate of the inventory valuation adjustment.

$$-\widehat{IVA} = [\Delta\widehat{PIVA}][INV^{54}]. \quad (8.26)$$

Series of the estimated price index are recorded in table 8.19 and next to them an "interpolated" series. The smoother interpolated series was employed because there were some discontinuous jumps in the calculated price index which seem to have arisen from rounding errors. The large jumps occurred almost exclusively when the estimated constant dollar inventory investment used as a divisor in (8.25) was very small, and so rounding errors could be substantial. The interpolated series is the one to be explained statistically.

Two considerations enter the explanation of the weighted average index. First, the wholesale price index with various lags should be a major determinant. Second, the rate of inventory accumulation and decumulation could strongly influence the implicit price index. During periods of rapid inventory accumulation, the average price realized on production would be low because goods are charged to inventory at direct cost. Conversely, when inventory is being decumulated, profits will be realized on previously accumulated inventory, and so the average realized price will go up on

TABLE 8.19
Price indexes related to inventory valuation.

Year and quarter	$\widehat{PIVA}$	$\widehat{PIVA}$ interpolated $= PIVA$	Nonfarm wholesale price index $1954 = 100$
1948 : 1	1.21	0.93	94.6
2	0.94	0.94	95.6
3	0.95	0.95	98.4
4	0.93	0.93	95.3
1949 : 1	1.50	0.91	92.1
2	0.89	0.89	89.8
3	0.75	0.88	89.1
4	0.87	0.87	88.7
1950 : 1	0.92	0.87	89.1
2	0.88	0.88	90.1
3	0.93	0.93	95.3
4	0.95	0.95	99.5
1951 : 1	1.01	1.01	105.2
2	0.99	0.99	105.0
3	0.99	0.99	103.2
4	0.97	0.97	103.0
1952 : 1	1.00	1.00	102.1
2	1.00	1.00	101.1
3	1.03	1.00	101.5
4	1.00	1.00	100.2
1953 : 1	0.94	0.98	99.5
2	0.98	0.99	99.4
3	1.00	1.00	100.5
4	1.00	1.00	99.7
1954 : 1	1.08	1.02	100.3
2	0.94	1.00	100.3
3	1.04	0.99	100.0
4	2.00	0.98	99.5
1955 : 1	0.97	0.97	99.9
2	0.98	0.98	99.9
3	1.02	1.02	100.6
4	1.02	1.02	101.0
1956 : 1	1.06	1.06	101.9
2	1.07	1.07	103.4
3	1.04	1.08	104.0
4	1.10	1.10	105.1

TABLE 8.19 (Continued)

Year and quarter	$\widehat{PIVA}$	$\widehat{PIVA}$ interpolated $= PIVA$	Nonfarm wholesale price index 1954 = 100
1957 : 1	1.20	1.10	106.0
2	1.11	1.11	106.3
3	1.62	1.14	107.2
4	1.15	1.15	107.1
1958 : 1	1.18	1.18	108.1
2	1.16	1.16	108.2
3	1.19	1.19	108.0
4	1.08	1.14	108.0
1959 : 1	1.13	1.13	108.3
2	1.13	1.13	108.7
3	0.79	1.12	108.3
4	1.06	1.12	107.9

Note   Interpolation was done by visual inspection without reference to the wholesale price index.

this account. To take account of this effect, the ratio of total nonfarm constant dollar inventory accumulation to constant dollar manufacturing production was used as an index of the proportion of production going into or leaving inventory. To scale this ratio properly, it was subtracted from one, and so this new variable $\{1-(\Delta INV_{EAF}^{54}/X_{M*}^{54})\}$, fluctuates in the vicinity of unity. The final estimating equation selected was:

$$PIVA = \alpha + \beta_1 \left\{ \left[1 - \frac{\Delta INV_{EAF}^{54}}{X_{M*}^{54}} \right] [WPI_{EAF}] \right\}$$

$$+ \beta_2 \left\{ \left[1 - \frac{\Delta INV_{EAF}^{54}}{X_{M*}^{54}} \right] [WPI_{EAF}]_{-1} \right\} + \beta_3 [PIVA]_{-1}. \qquad (8.27)$$

The expected sign of $\partial PIVA/\partial \{1-(\Delta INV_{EAF}^{54}/X_{M*}^{54})\}$ is positive if the price behavior discussed above is in fact operative. The distributed lag in *PIVA* cleared up considerable error in serial correlation and, furthermore, makes a great deal of sense when the lag distribution properties are fully spelled out.

The estimated parameters of (8.27) are:

$$PIVA = -\frac{1.5350}{(3.8088)} + \frac{1.0090}{(0.1753)} \left[1 - \frac{\Delta INV_{EAF}^{54}}{X_{M*}^{54}} \right] [WPI_{EAF}]$$

$$-\frac{0.9100}{(0.1545)} \left[1 - \frac{INV_{EAF}^{54}}{X_{M*}^{54}} \right] [WPI_{EAF}]_{-1} + \frac{0.9204}{(0.0559)} [PIVA]_{-1}$$

$$\bar{R}^2 = 0.9639 \quad S_e = 1.647 \text{ index points} \quad VN = 2.4128. \tag{8.28}$$

Using the lag operator z we can rewrite (8.28) as:

$$\{1 - \alpha[z]\} PIVA = \{1 - \beta[z]\} WPI_{EAF} + \gamma + \varepsilon. \tag{8.29}$$

The numerical representation of (8.29) can be written:

$$[1 - 0.9024z] PIVA = [1 - 0.9100z] WPI_{EAF} - 1.5350. \tag{8.30}$$

The solution for this particular lag structure can then be obtained.

$$PIVA = \left[\frac{1 - 0.912z}{1 - 0.922z} \right] WPI_{EAF} - \frac{1.535}{[1 - 0.922]} \cong 1.0 WPI_{EAF} - 19.2. \tag{8.31}$$

The main result is that a one-point rise in the weighted wholesale price index is fully reflected in a one-point increase in the implicit price deflator. The single lag in $PIVA$ clears up positive serial correlation, since $PIVA$ regressed only against WPI_{EAF} and $[WPI_{EAF}]_{-1}$ had a Von Neumann statistic of 1.1622. These are not consistent estimates, however. The lags in $PIVA$ and WPI_{EAF} largely cancel, leaving estimated results that have theoretically acceptable steady-state values. The intercept, at one-half its standard error, can be viewed as essentially zero, serving only to adjust between the mean levels of the two price indexes.

8.6.4. Dividends

The rationale of the dividend equation is John Lintner's, with a modification to include depreciation proposed by Paul Darling [18]). The Lintner formulation asserts that the dividend change is proportional to the difference between desired dividends at the end of the period and dividends at the beginning of the period. Desired dividends are assumed to be proportional to the current after-tax profit level. This is the usual first-order adjustment

---

[18]) John Lintner, Distribution of Incomes of Corporations Among Dividends, Retained Earnings and Taxes, *op. cit.*; Paul G. Darling, The Influence of Expectations and Liquidity on Dividend Policy, *Journal of Political Economy* 65, No. 3 (June, 1957) 209–224.

model. Least squares estimates using profits adjusted and unadjusted for inventory valuation showed little difference on that score. On the grounds that most entrepreneurs would be less likely to pay dividends out of capital gains than from inventory valuation gain, it was decided to use profits adjusted for inventory valuation.

Because the equations fit nearly perfectly in original unit form when after-tax profits are net of depreciation on the one hand or gross on the other (and it is the depreciation element which has been stressed by Paul Darling), it was decided to predict the dividend change rather than the dividend level as a function of lagged dividends and either net profit after tax or gross profit after tax as explanatory variables [19]).

$$\Delta DIV = \frac{0.1069}{(0.0333)} Z_A - \frac{0.1028}{(0.0380)} [DIV]_{-1} - \frac{0.8834}{(0.5001)}$$

$$\bar{R}^2 = 0.1832 \quad S_e = 0.4713 \qquad\qquad VN = 2.1570. \qquad\qquad (8.32)$$

Period of fit: 1948–1 : 1960–4

$$\Delta DIV = \frac{0.09935}{(0.02166)} [Z_A + CCAC] - \frac{0.3545}{(0.0767)} [DIV]_{-1} + \frac{0.2601}{(0.2846)}$$

$$\bar{R}^2 = 0.2662 \quad S_e = 0.4336 \qquad\qquad VN = 1.9585. \qquad\qquad (8.33)$$

Period of fit: 1948–1 : 1960–4.

The symbols are:

DIV = dividends, billions of dollars
Z_A = corporate profits after taxes and after inventory valuation adjustment, billions of dollars
$CCAC$ = corporate capital consumption allowances, billions of dollars.

The net profit equation has a lower multiple correlation and, as an obvious implication, a higher standard error of estimate. Furthermore, the implied long-run dividend payout from net profit (found here by dividing the profit coefficient by the lagged dividend coefficient and changing the sign of the quotient) has the somewhat implausible value of unity, which is well above

---

[19]) Using postwar quarterly data and functions which treated net profits after tax and depreciation as separate series (as Darling previously treated annual data for a longer time period) generated the intuitively unacceptable result that about thirty cents out of every increase in depreciation is paid out in dividends in the next quarter, a much higher rate than out of an increase in net profits. In estimates presented here a single coefficient is estimated for the sum of net profits after tax plus depreciation.

values found for manufacturing during the interwar period by John Lintner. The long-run dividend payout of one-third using gross corporate profit has greater stability over time [20]).

8.7. Conclusions

In this study, I have sought to expand the structural basis for income determination in the presence of cyclical variations in output and employment. The main empirical regularity that must be encompassed by theory and structural equations is the much greater amplitude of fluctuations in the level and national income share of corporate profits than appears in other factor shares. The close relation of profit variations to output has been found to originate in the lagged adjustment of employment to output, particularly in the case of nonproduction workers. Other short-run fixed or slowly adjusting costs serve to reinforce the squeeze on profits during a cyclical decline and during their rapid expansion in the early recovery phase.

The demand for labor inputs distinguishes four kinds: production worker employment, nonproduction worker employment, hours worked by production workers, and hours worked by overhead workers (the last assumed to work a constant number of hours per week). Each category displayed substantially different behavior, thus justifying the division for the purposes of studying a cyclical process.

Other aspects of the income distribution process were treated less intensively. As for the remaining items, primary reliance was placed on Lintner's formulation of the dividend process and simple ratio estimates appear adequate to portray unincorporated business income. An equation for determining the inventory valuation adjustment should not require revision in the immediate future. The explanations of interest income appear in need of further investigation, however.

---

[20]) As a final modification, it appears desirable to exclude the last two quarters of 1950 and the first quarter of 1951 when a dividend of unprecedented generosity by General Motors created a correspondingly large error. The censored data yielded the following estimates:

$$\Delta DIV = \frac{0.09485}{(0.02274)} [Z_A + CCAC] - \frac{0.3309}{(0.0785)} [DIV]_{-1} + \frac{0.1737}{(0.2138)}$$

$$\bar{R}^2 = 0.2334 \qquad S_e = 0.3183 \qquad VN = 2.5467 \qquad\qquad (8.34)$$

Slope coefficients and multiple correlation were little affected while the intercept dropped. The standard error of estimate decreased sharply, but inverse serial correlation in the error term also appeared.

Most of the components which enter income distribution have been investigated. Three of the separate components—employment of production and nonproduction workers and production worker hours—have been scrutinized in combination. Nevertheless, the next important step in evaluating the validity of these hypotheses, the simulation of the entire income distribution process under a variety of economic circumstances, has a high priority on the agenda of work yet to be undertaken.

CHAPTER 9

PRICES AND WAGES

Contents

9.1. Prices 281
    1. The definition of price. 2. Price behavior hypotheses. 3. Formulation
    of the model. 4. Results: specific industry groups.

9.2. Wages 311
    1. Choice of the "wage" variable. 2. Explanatory variables. 3. Lag
    structure. 4. Lagged wage changes. 5. Other variables. 6. Regression
    results. 7. Implications of the lagged wage change variable. 8. The
    magnitude of wage inflation. 9. Other aspects of the regression results.

9.3. Some further results 331

9.4. Appendix 332

PRICES AND WAGES

CHARLES L. SCHULTZE,

U.S. Bureau of the Budget, Washington, D.C.*)

and

JOSEPH L. TRYON

National Planning Association, Washington, D.C.

and

Georgetown University, Washington, D.C.

This chapter presents the background analysis and preliminary results of the price-wage sectors of the Brookings-SSRC econometric model. The price and wage equations were developed separately through standard single equation least-squares techniques. The direct and indirect mutual interaction of prices and wages, of course, requires the use of simultaneous equation techniques. These will be employed in constructing later versions of the Brookings-SSRC econometric model. Our results at this preliminary stage suffer from the inadequacies associated with fitting the two sectors separately. However, as explained in the section on wages, the lag structure in our wage equations is such as to reduce (although not eliminate) the problem.

9.1. Prices

9.1.1. The definition of price

Our hypothesis about price determination is based on a modified markup model. Before examining this hypothesis in detail, however, it is necessary to consider what sort of price measurements are relevant for the purpose at hand. Two different types of prices show up in the model, and a particular hypothesis may take different forms, depending on which variety of price is used. The first type is the usual market price. This is the price at which goods

---

*) The author is currently on leave from the University of Maryland and the Brookings Institution.

or services are exchanged and covers all costs and profits. For an industry, an index of prices of this type would be constructed in the usual manner, using market prices and some appropriate weights.

The second type is the price of production originating within an industry. This type of price covers only those costs and profits which originate *within a given industry* [1]). It may be called the "price of gross product originating" or the "value-added price". It excludes the cost of raw materials or other inputs purchased from outside the industry.

The phrase "value-added price" suggests the nature of our second type of price. Value added within an industry consists of gross factor returns plus indirect taxes. Value-added price, therefore, is simply the total value added divided by production, i.e., it is value added per unit of output. As the sum of component factor costs per unit rises, the value-added price will also rise. In this study, four components of value added or gross product originating are recognized. These four are labor, net property income, capital consumption allowances and indirect business taxes. A finer break-down which separates industry net property income into rent, interest, corporate profits and entrepreneurial income is one potentially desirable elaboration that has been postponed for lack of data.

The basic method of calculating value-added prices can be given briefly, as follows: Let X be the current dollar value of gross product originating in a given industry. Let X^{54} be the constant dollar value of gross output less the constant dollar value of purchases from other industries. X^{54}, in other words, is gross product originating, or value added, in constant dollars. X/X^{54}, the "price of value added", can be viewed in two ways: (1) it is the price of industry output less the unit cost of purchases from other industries, and (2) it is the sum of gross factor costs per unit of net output. The appropriately weighted sum of value-added prices at each stage in the production of any final good is equal to the final market price of that good.

In a general econometric model, the question arises of whether industry value-added prices or market prices by final demand category ought to be used as the independent variables in the price equation. On the one hand, the aspects of the model relating to the demand for goods on the part of consumers, investors and governments are stated in terms of the various categories of final goods. Decisions of buyers and sellers are influenced by the market prices of those goods. Market prices are the observed variables;

---

[1]) For a fuller exposition of this kind of price and some examples of how it may be used, see Charles L. Schultze, *Prices, Costs and Output for the Postwar Decade: 1947–1957*, a supplementary paper of the Committee for Economic Development, December, 1959.

value-added prices are not. The relevant *GNP* deflators are based upon market prices of various categories of goods. On the other hand, the basic data and decision-making framework in the area of costs, factor prices and demands for factors relate primarily to an industry structure. Employment, wage, depreciation and profit data are classified by industry. Quarterly time series on unit labor and other costs may be calculated on an industrial classification breakdown and not by final commodity sector.

If, in the model, it is decided to explain the market prices of final goods directly, some mechanism must be found to translate data on *industry* costs and factor demand into *commodity* categories which match the market prices of final goods in order to relate the dependent and independent variables. Conversely, if value-added prices are the dependent variables of the price equations, it will ultimately be necessary to translate those prices into the market prices of final goods, since most industry output is intermediate in the flow of goods to final users.

Initially, a decision was made to use value-added prices, by industry, as the independent variables of the price equations and to construct a conversion technique for relating industry prices to the price of final output [2]). Value-added prices were constructed for 21 manufacturing and 11 nonmanufacturing industries. These were to be aggregated into the more summary industry classification used in the final Brookings-SSRC econometric model. An examination of the quarterly time series of value-added prices, however, revealed serious flaws in their quality. The value-added prices were constructed by dividing quarterly estimates of current dollar gross product originating by quarterly estimates of constant dollar gross product originating. The basic national income accounts do not directly furnish the data necessary for either the numerator or the denominator of the value-added price ratio. As a consequence, substantial further estimation was required to provide the necessary time series, relying upon raw data from other sources and, unfortunately, upon various techniques of interpolating annual data with less satisfactory quarterly series. Consequently, the quarterly series on the price of value added picked up all of the imperfections in both of the basic series. Moreover, the value-added prices in some industries appeared to have systematic cyclical errors, *rising* sharply during recessions and *falling* during recoveries. Such systematic error could occur for two reasons: (1) the basic gross income series (the numerator) understated the actual cyclical fluctuations in income; or (2) the output series

---

[2]) The construction of these price-conversion devices is explained in chapter 17.

(the denominator) overstated those fluctuations. Since we had no means of correcting either for the apparent random imperfections of the series or for the systematic cyclical bias, we were forced, as a general rule, to abandon the value-added series.

We have no evidence as to whether or not the production indexes systematically exaggerate the fluctuations in output. Therefore this factor remains a possible explanation, though we suspect it is not the real culprit. We also have no direct evidence as to whether or not fluctuations in gross income originating are systematically understated. However, examination of the behavior of profits, an important component of X, strongly suggests that this may be where the trouble lies. In several industries unit net business income, which is mostly profits, fails to rise as much as expected in booms, and vice versa. In at least one instance, net business income per unit of output showed a *rise* during a strike period! In part, the apparent failure of statistically reported profits to reflect fully the "true" quarterly changes in income may arise simply from the fact that quarterly corporate statements do not incorporate all the adjustments necessary to depict the true course of profits. These adjustments are often likely to be made in year-end statements but ignored in the intervening quarterly data.

Because cost and factor input data are available only by industry classifications, we retained the concept of using industry prices as the independent variables in the price equations, converting the industry results to final demand categories. However, in view of the flaws in the constructed value-added prices, we switched to an industry *market price* concept. By *industry market prices* we mean a weighted average of wholesale prices of goods produced in each industry. In a few industries, suitable indexes of market prices could not be obtained or constructed and value-added price indexes were used instead. In some of those industries—e.g., finance and insurance—value-added prices and market prices are conceptually quite close, since purchases from other industries are quite small. In the case of retail and wholesale trade, a value-added price is very appropriate, since it was constructed to represent an index of the gross margin per unit of commodities distributed.

9.1.2. Price behavior hypotheses

Our hypothesis about price determination has three basic parts: (1) prices are set by a markup on standard costs, i.e., costs at "normal" levels of operation; (2) temporary changes in costs (i.e., deviations of actual costs from standard costs) also affect prices but less than permanent changes; and (3) the markup will be influenced by excess or insufficient demand relative to available supply [3]). As a subsidiary hypothesis we wish to test whether the influence on price of excess and insufficient demand is asymmetrical.

Clearly, in an aggregative econometric model, we are interested in explaining the *movement* of prices, not their *level*. Given the first hypothesis, this implies that our interest is in the factors which cause standard costs to change. Whether the standard generally used in a given industry is equal to the minimum point on the cost curve is irrelevant for our purposes. Moreover, whether in a given industry the *conscious* mechanism of price setting incorporates the addition of a markup to standard, or normal, costs is also irrelevant. Applied to changes in costs, the chief feature of the "markup on standard cost" hypothesis is that the variations in costs which enter into the pricing decision are not primarily the very short-run cost changes which occur from month to month or quarter to quarter as output fluctuates. Rather, it is hypothesized that, other things being equal, prices are related to changes in costs which are expected to be more lasting in nature. This carries over into the field of pricing decisions a concept which has proven very fruitful elsewhere. Friedman's consumption theory related consumer outlays to long-run income expectations. Inventory theory is based, in part, on the concept of an adaptation of output to longer-run changes in sales expectations. Recent investment theory similarly relates investment to long-run sales expectations. In all of these models the essential phenomenon is that the dependent variable is not fully adjusted to short-run or erratic changes in the independent variable but rather to some form of a smoothed movement of the latter.

To make the concept of normal costs operational, the following corollaries to the standard cost hypothesis were adopted:

a) Changes in wage rates are considered by producers to be permanent changes in costs.

b) Short-run fluctuations in productivity do not enter fully into the calculation of normal unit labor costs. Rather, it is only "permanent" changes in productivity which are relevant. After some examination of the basic time series, we chose as a measure of "permanent" productivity a moving average of productivity based on the current quarter and the previous 11 quarters. Since productivity has an upward trend, a moving average will

---

[3]) To the best of our knowledge, the first use of the "normal cost" and markup concepts in an aggregate econometric price model was made by Gary Fromm in an unpublished paper delivered at the December, 1960 meetings of the Econometric Society.

understate the level of productivity which enters the normal cost calculation. To approximate the "true" level of normal unit labor costs, the moving average of productivity should be adjusted upward to take into account this trend. However, this correction merely adds a constant percentage adjustment to the moving average of unit labor costs. Consequently, we ignored the correction in our calculations [4]). Our normal unit labor cost variable, therefore, was estimated as:

$$ULC_t^N = \frac{RWSS_t}{\bar{X}},$$

where

ULC^N = normal unit labor costs

$RWSS$ = compensation per man-hour

$\bar{X}$ = 12-term moving average of output per man-hour.

c) In the regulated industries, where depreciation is a major factor, the normal unit labor cost variable was supplemented by an estimate of the trend value of depreciation per unit of output, with a break in the trend in 1951. The major reason for not including such an estimate in the equation for all industries stems from the fact that substantial accounting changes have occurred in the treatment of depreciation over the postwar period. In many industries the five-year accelerated amortization of the Korean war substantially increased depreciation allowances in the 1951 to 1958 period and substantially reduced depreciation in the subsequent five years. Changes in the tax code in 1954, permitting double-rate declining balance and sum-of-the-years-digits depreciation accounting, further complicated the interpretation of the reported data. On balance it was felt that the use

---

[4]) Assume the following price equation:

$P = a_0 + a_1[RWSS/\bar{X}] + a_z Z \ldots$ (Z represents all other variables).

A "true" estimate of normal unit labor costs, taking account of the trend in productivity, would be:

$ULC^N = [RWSS/\bar{X}(1+b)^{5.5}]$ where "b" equals the trend rate of increase in productivity per quarter. The price equation therefore should have been fitted as follows:

$$P = c_0 + c_1 \left[\frac{RWSS}{\bar{X}(1+b)^{5.5}}\right] + c_z Z.$$

However, since $(1+b)^{5.5}$ is a constant over the entire period, a_1 in the first equation can be corrected to equal c_1, the "true" markup value:

$$a_1 = \frac{c_1}{(1+b)^{5.5}}.$$

of normal depreciation per unit would introduce more distortions than information. In the regulated industries, however, depreciation is such a large share of total cost and, thus, an integral part of price setting, that we did include an estimate of normal depreciation per unit of output.

d) In manufacturing industries, a third cost, raw materials, was introduced as a separate variable. "Normal" raw materials cost was represented by a four-quarter moving average of a raw materials price index.

In general, further experimentation is needed in the construction of "normal" unit cost indexes. In particular, various different periods for normalizing raw materials prices ought to be explored. Other elements of cost, notably, indirect taxes, were not included in the analysis. These other cost elements were left out because (1) they were small relative to other costs and would therefore have little effect on unit costs, or (2) they were little more than linear trends. If the omitted ones that may have made up a substantial part of costs had been included as part of normal costs, it would only have changed the "tilt" of normal unit costs over time because such costs have been little more than trends. It would not affect the shorter-run variation of the series. The size of the regression coefficient for normal unit costs would change, but the importance of normal costs as a variable would be about the same. This point is discussed with a specific example in the analysis of the regressions for regulated industries below.

Our second hypothesis concerns the effect of deviations of actual unit costs from normal. For this variable we used the difference between actual unit labor costs and normal unit labor costs. With the exception of manufacturing, where raw materials costs often vary considerably in the short run, labor costs are by far the major determinant of short-run cost variation. Other costs are not important in determining the difference between actual and normal costs. In manufacturing, a quarterly raw materials price index was included to represent separately the influence of short-run raw materials cost variation.

The third hypothesis concerns the effect on markups of demand conditions relative to supply. To investigate these problems several variables were used. In industries where capacity has some meaning, a capacity utilization variable was used. It soon became painfully evident that the capacity and capacity utilization series were extremely weak. The measurement of capacity by large industry groups for purposes of deriving short-run changes in capacity utilization still leaves much to be desired. The series used here are no exception. This problem is made more difficult by the fact that in the years after 1957 the economy never returned to full-capacity utilization.

It has been suggested that with respect to the impact of capacity utilization price behavior is asymmetrical. Under this hypothesis, increases in demand relative to capacity have a larger upward effect on prices than decreases in demand. To test this, capacity utilization was split into two variables – positive and negative deviations from a "normal" utilization ratio. If the ratchet hypothesis is correct, the positive deviations should have a larger (positive) regression coefficient than the negative deviations.

In some industries the trend deviations in capacity utilization of supplying industries were used as variables. If we assume a situation of excess demand by industry A for the products of industry B and that the price of industry B's product does not fully adjust to wipe out the excess demand, a shortage of capacity in industry B might operate, with respect to A's price markups, just as would a shortage of capacity in A itself. We experimented, therefore, with the use of a capacity utilization variable for major supplying industries in place of the capacity utilization rate of the consuming industry itself.

Finally, as another indication of demand relative to supply, deviations from a straight-line trend of the ratio of inventories to output was used [5]). The ratio has a trend in some industries which reflects long-run changes in inventory holding patterns. Since this variable is to reflect short-run changes in supply relative to demand, deviations from the trend were used. The ratio used for a given quarter was the ratio of inventories at the end of the previous quarter to output in the previous quarter. Two versions of this variable were used, one with inventories and output in current prices and the other with inventories and output in constant (1954) prices. Output in this ratio is measured on a value-added basis; hence the ratio is really inventories to value added. Conceptually it might be better to work with an inventory-sales ratio. This was not done because sales is not a variable which is explained elsewhere in the over-all model. At the level of aggregation for which this variable was used—durable and nondurable manufacturing and wholesale and retail trade—the inventory-output ratio is probably satisfactory. At lower levels of aggregation, say at the two-digit manufacturing level, an inventory-sales ratio might be superior.

9.1.3. *Formulation of the model*

The following symbols are used. All variables refer to the industry to which the price variable belongs except the raw materials prices and supplier capacity utilization rates.

---

[5]) Some regressions were tried using the ratio of unfilled orders to inventories. The results were inconclusive and are not presented here.

WPI = wholesale price index
PV = value-added price
ULC = unit labor cost
ULC^N = normal unit labor cost
PR = raw materials price
PR^N = normal raw materials price.

$(+)\left\{\dfrac{X}{X_K} - \left[\dfrac{X}{X_K}\right]^{N}\right\}^{54} =$ positive deviation of actual from normal capacity utilization rates

$(-)\left\{\dfrac{X}{X_K} - \left[\dfrac{X}{X_K}\right]^{N}\right\}^{54} =$ negative deviation of actual from normal capacity utilization rates

$(+)\left\{\dfrac{X_S}{X_{KS}} - \left[\dfrac{X_S}{X_{KS}}\right]^{N}\right\}^{54} =$ positive deviation of actual from normal capacity utilization rates for principal supplying industry

$(-)\left\{\dfrac{X_S}{X_{KS}} - \left[\dfrac{X_S}{X_{KS}}\right]^{N}\right\}^{54} =$ negative deviation of actual from normal capacity utilization rates for principal supplying industry

$\left\{\dfrac{INV}{X} - \left[\dfrac{INV}{X}\right]^{T}\right\} =$ deviations from trend of ratio of inventories to output, both in current prices

$\left\{\dfrac{INV^{54}}{X^{54}} - \left[\dfrac{INV^{54}}{X^{54}}\right]^{T}\right\} =$ deviations from trend of ratio of inventories to output, both in 1954 prices.

The following formulation serves to present our expectations about the regression coefficients:

$$WPI \text{ or } PV = \beta_0 + \beta_1 ULC^N + \beta_2[ULC - ULC^N]$$

$$+ \beta_3 PR + \beta_4 PR^N + \beta_5(+)\left\{\frac{X}{X_K} - \left[\frac{X}{X_K}\right]^{N}\right\}^{54}$$

$$+ \beta_6(-)\left\{\frac{X}{X_K} - \left[\frac{X}{X_K}\right]^{N}\right\}^{54} + \beta_7(+)\left\{\frac{X_S}{X_{KS}} - \left[\frac{X_S}{X_{KS}}\right]^{N}\right\}^{54}$$

$$+ \beta_8(-)\left\{\frac{X_S}{X_{KS}} - \left[\frac{X_S}{X_{KS}}\right]^{N}\right\}^{54} + \beta_9\left\{\frac{INV}{X} - \left[\frac{INV}{X}\right]^{T}\right\}.$$

If our hypotheses are correct, we should find β_1 and β_2 positive, but β_1 greater than β_2. β_3 through β_8 should be positive. However, β_5 should be greater than β_6 and β_7 greater than β_8 if the "ratchet effect" exists. β_9 should be negative, since high inventories relative to output should have a depressing effect on prices and vice versa. The sign for the inventory variable in constant prices, if it is used, should of course be negative.

At the time the first plans were made for the model, it was hoped and expected that the hypotheses discussed above could be tested for several levels of aggregation. The finest division was to be a breakdown of manufacturing into two-digit SIC industries. The regressions were to be run on both the original quarterly time series and on first differences between quarters a year apart. Alas, this beautiful picture has not been painted. Instead we can only offer a preliminary sketch. The sketch, to be sure, is a most interesting one, with much of the picture filled in. But it is painfully blank in places and rather rough in others. Unfortunately the usual data gaps, computational difficulties and time shortages prevented completion of the finished product. We hope that subsequent work on the model will round out the picture. With this warning about the gaps to be expected, let us turn to the regression results.

Broadly speaking, the hypotheses outlined above were borne out, with the exception of the asymmetrical relationship of capacity utilization to price. We suspect, however, that our capacity data are not sufficiently accurate to warrant any firm conclusions from our failure to verify the hypothesis. In other cases, details must be modified, and several conclusions do not have strong evidence to support them. Some general conclusions may, however, be drawn, and they are given immediately below. These general conclusions are followed by a more detailed analysis of the individual regressions.

a) "Normal" costs, measured by normal unit labor costs, or in a few industries by the sum of normal unit labor and normal depreciation costs, are the dominant influences on prices.

b) Temporary cost changes, measured by deviations of actual from normal unit labor costs, in some industries have an effect on prices, but this influence, where it exists, is much less than changes in normal costs.

c) Raw materials prices, where raw materials are an important element of cost, exercise a significant influence on prices. As would be expected, the less aggregated levels of industry show raw materials as a stronger influence than the more highly aggregated levels. Surprisingly, however, in the durable and nondurable manufacturing aggregates it is raw materials prices of the current quarter rather than "normal" raw materials prices which generally yield the better fit, have higher regression coefficients and have lower standard errors. Thus short-run variations in raw materials prices appear to be passed on more consistently than short-run labor cost variations.

d) In many industries, but not all, markups over normal costs are modified by excess or deficient demand relative to supply. In far too many cases the capacity utilization variable proved disappointing. Among the aggregative industry groups, only in nondurable manufacturing did this variable show significant results, and even here the inventories/output measure of relative supply pressure yielded a better fit. Interestingly enough, the positive deviations of the capacity utilization ratio in the nondurable group have a significant regression coefficient; the negative deviation did not. In the case of some two-digit manufacturing industries, the capacity variable did prove important. In those industries where the capacity utilization ratio appeared to be significant, the positive deviations of the utilization ratio were generally more important. Coefficients for negative deviations either were smaller or insignificant or had the wrong sign. The major exception was the petroleum industry, where the coefficient of the negative capacity utilization deviation was substantially larger than the coefficient of the positive deviation.

The ratio of inventories to output was also used as a measure of demand conditions for some industries and proved to have a somewhat stronger influence than capacity utilization. The influences of capacity utilization and inventories relative to output are, however, hard to separate. In theory, the magnitude of the inventories/output ratio might be said to represent very short-run supply-demand disequilibria. The capacity utilization variable should represent longer-run disequilibria. In practice, however, our measures are not precise enough to separate out the two factors. We further suspect that the measures of capacity utilization are not good enough to warrant any firm inference from the failure of the capacity utilization ratio to be significant in many industries.

9.1.4. *Results*: *specific industry groups*

The regressions on which the conclusions summarized above depend, are given in tables 9.1 to 9.5. Results are presented for several levels of aggregation, for different definitions of the same variables and for first differences between quarters a year apart. The discussion which follows is in terms of these individual results. It includes some of the caveats which bear on the conclusions presented in section 9.1.3.

A note on aggregation is in order here. Tables 9.1 and 9.2 present the regression results for the six nonagricultural sectors of the present

TABLE 9.1

Price regressions for nonagricultural production sectors, [a]) *1948 : 2–1960 : 4* [b]).

Industry	Equation number	Dependent variable	Constant term	ULC^N	$ULC^N + UCCA^N$	$ULC - ULC^N$	PR [c])	PR^N	$(+)\left\{\dfrac{X}{X_K}-\left[\dfrac{X}{X_K}\right]^N\right\}^{54}$	$(-)\left\{\dfrac{X}{X_K}-\left[\dfrac{X}{X_K}\right]^N\right\}^{54}$	$\left\{\dfrac{INV}{X}-\left[\dfrac{INV}{X}\right]^T\right\}_{-1}$	$\left\{\dfrac{INV^{54}}{X^{54}}-\left[\dfrac{INV^{54}}{X^{54}}\right]^T\right\}_{-1}$	$\bar{R}^2$
Durable manufacturing	9.1	WPI_{MD}	−0.0226	1.845 (0.042)		0.371 (0.151)						−0.059 (0.012)	0.974
	9.1a	WPI_{MD}	−0.0076	1.839 (0.055)		0.086 (0.185)			−0.174 (0.111)	0.106 (0.086)			0.963
	9.1b	WPI_{MD}	−0.0292	1.855 (0.043)		0.341 (0.153)					−0.062 (0.013)		0.974
	9.1c	WPI_{MD}	0.0064	1.883 (0.066)		0.076 (0.170)		−0.058 (0.053)					0.962
	9.1d	WPI_{MD}	−0.0113	1.889 (0.055)		0.360 (0.150)		−0.044 (0.045)			−0.062 (0.013)		0.974
	9.1e	WPI_{MD}	−0.0219	1.864 (0.050)		0.348 (0.156)	−0.015 (0.041)		−0.333 (0.091)	−0.097 (0.080)	−0.064 (0.014)		0.973
	9.1f	WPI_{MD}	−0.0254	1.734 (0.061)		0.181 (0.154)	0.090 (0.049)				−0.077 (0.013)		0.979

TABLE 9.1 (Continued)

Industry	Equation number	Dependent variable	Constant term	ULC^N	$ULC^N + UCCA^N$	$ULC - ULC^N$	$PR^{c})$	PR^N	$(+)\left\{\frac{X}{X_K} - \left[\frac{X}{X_K}\right]^N\right\}^{54}$	$(-)\left\{\frac{X}{X_K} - \left[\frac{X}{X_K}\right]^N\right\}^{54}$	$\left\{\frac{INV}{X} - \left[\frac{INV}{X}\right]^T\right\}_{-1}$	$\left\{\frac{INV^{54}}{X^{54}} - \left[\frac{INV^{54}}{X^{54}}\right]^T\right\}_{-1}$	$\bar{R}^2$
Nondurable manufacturing plus mining of crude petroleum and natural gas	9.2	WPI_{MN}^*	-0.0627	1.490 (0.072)			0.279 (0.018)					-0.098 (0.013)	0.900
	9.2a	WPI_{MN}^*	0.3841	1.182 (0.182)		0.079 (0.924)			0.757 (0.185)	-0.059 (0.284)			0.520
	9.2b	WPI_{MN}^*	0.5621	0.894 (0.146)		-0.442 (0.896)						-0.077 (0.036)	0.417
	9.2c	WPI_{MN}^*	-0.6383	0.765 (0.140)		-2.301 (0.865)							0.455
	9.2d	WPI_{MN}^*	0.1853	1.232 (0.017)		-1.456 (0.742)		0.181 (0.046)			0.092 (0.032)		0.516
	9.2e	WPI_{MN}^*	0.2445	1.169 (0.211)		-1.669 (0.086)		0.159 (0.064)			0.021 (0.042)		0.508
	9.2f	WPI_{MN}^*	-0.1115	1.510 (0.107)		-0.473 (0.518)	0.316 (0.031)				-0.056 (0.023)		0.828
	9.2g	WPI_{MN}^*	-0.0836	1.561 (0.011)		-0.201 (0.529)	0.254 (0.035)		0.395 (0.129)	-0.031 (0.162)	-0.013 (0.026)		0.852

TABLE 9.1 (Continued)

Industry	Equation number	Dependent variable	Constant term	ULC^N	$ULC^N + UCCA^N$	$ULC - ULC^N$	PR c)	PR^N	$(+)\left\{\frac{X}{X_K} - \left[\frac{X}{X_K}\right]^N\right\}^{54}$	$(-)\left\{\frac{X}{X_K} - \left[\frac{X}{X_K}\right]^K\right\}^{54}$	$\left\{\frac{INV}{X} - \left[\frac{INV}{X}\right]^T\right\}_{-1}$	$\left\{\frac{INV^{54}}{X^{54}} - \left[\frac{INV^{54}}{X^{54}}\right]^T\right\}_{-1}$	$\bar{R}^2$
Wholesale and retail trade	9.3	PV_T	0.3461	1.159		1.423					−0.028		0.952
				(0.037)		(0.164)					(0.009)		
	9.3a	PV_T	0.3484	1.158		0.957						0.054	0.952
				(0.037)		(0.020)						(0.017)	
Regulated industries	9.4	PV_R	−0.0605		1.556	0.956							0.967
					(0.041)	(0.155)							
	9.4a	PV_R	−0.9566	3.480		0.677							0.809
				(0.236)		(0.385)							
Contract construction	9.5	P_{IC}	0.0603	0.858		0.349	0.036						0.988
				(0.052)		(0.095)	(0.006)						
	9.5a	P_{IC}	0.0424	0.767		0.311		0.441					0.984
				(0.093)		(0.116)		(0.104)					
Residual industries	9.6	PV_{O*1}	0.1070	1.701		1.748							0.987
				(0.027)		(0.395)							

a) Unit labor and depreciation costs and value-added prices for these sectors were estimated by aggregating the estimates for several individual industries.

b) Standard errors are shown in parentheses beneath the respective regression coefficients.

c) PR for durable manufacturing = P_M = implicit price deflator for imports of goods and services, 1954 = 1.00.
PR for nondurable manufacturing = P_{AF} = implicit price deflator for farm gross product, 1954 = 1.00.
PR for contract construction = $WPIS_{CM}$ = special wholesale price index for construction materials, 1954 = 1.00.

TABLE 9.2

Price regressions for nonagricultural production sectors using first differences between quarters one year apart: 1949 : 1–1960 : 4 a).

Industry	Equation number	Dependent variable b)	Constant term	ULC^N	$ULC^N + UCCA^N$	$ULC - ULC^N$	PR c)	PR^N	$\left\{\dfrac{X}{X_K} - \left[\dfrac{X}{X_K}\right]^N\right\}^{54}$	$\left\{\dfrac{INV}{X} - \left[\dfrac{NV}{X}\right]^T\right\}_{-1}$	$\left\{\dfrac{INV^{54}}{X^{54}} - \left[\dfrac{INV^{54}}{X^{54}}\right]^T\right\}_{-1}$	$\bar{R}^2$
Durable manufacturing	9.1bD	WPI_{MD}	0.0090	1.367 (0.214)		0.376 (0.105)				−0.055 (0.010)		0.531
	9.1dD	WPI_{MD}	0.0150	1.031 (0.244)		0.318 (0.102)		0.086 (0.053)			−0.049 (0.007)	0.606
	9.1eD	WPI_{MD}	0.0158	0.935 (0.234)		0.258 (0.102)	0.144 (0.044)			−0.036 (0.011)		0.619
	9.1gD	WPI_{MD}	0.0173	0.920 (0.210)		0.280 (0.090)	0.130 (0.041)				−0.035 (0.008)	0.660
	9.1hD	WPI_{MD}	0.0173	0.898 (0.217)		0.301 (0.104)	0.127 (0.042)		0.025 (0.051)		−0.032 (0.011)	0.657
Nondurable manufacturing plus mining of crude petroleum and natural gas	9.2cD	$WPI_{MN}*$	−0.0205	3.440 (0.632)		−1.657 (0.799)				−0.033 (0.037)		0.425
	9.2fD	$WPI_{MN}*$	0.0027	1.360 (0.420)		−0.526 (0.469)	0.371 (0.039)			−0.073 (0.021)		0.815
	9.2hD	$WPI_{MN}*$	−0.0102	2.812 (0.046)		−0.282 (0.561)		0.180 (0.059)			−0.146 (0.022)	0.712
	9.2iD	$WPI_{MN}*$	0.0004	1.496 (0.032)		−0.056 (0.037)	0.292 (0.030)		−0.064 (0.089)		−0.098 (0.018)	0.893

Table 9.2 (Continued)

Industry	Equation number	Dependent variable [b]	Constant term	ULC^N	$ULC^N + UCCA^N$	$ULC - ULC^N$	PR [c]	PR^N	$\left\{\dfrac{X}{X_K} - \left[\dfrac{X}{X_K}\right]^N\right\}^{54}$	$\left\{\dfrac{INV}{X} - \left[\dfrac{INV}{X}\right]^T\right\}_{-1}$	$\left\{\dfrac{INV^{54}}{X^{54}} - \left[\dfrac{INV^{54}}{X^{54}}\right]^T\right\}_{-1}$	$\bar{R}^2$
Wholesale and retail trade	9.3D	PV_T	−0.0029	1.213 (0.324)		1.244 (0.161)				0.002 (0.014)		0.655
	9.3aD	PV_T	−0.0041	1.264 (0.304)		0.961 (0.176)					0.039 (0.016)	0.696
Regulated industries	9.4D	PV_R	0.42		1.222 (0.205)	1.017 (0.132)						0.684
	9.4aD	PV_R	1.18	1.229 (0.202)		1.020 (0.131)						0.689
Contract construction	9.5D	P_{IC}	0.0031	0.710 (0.106)		0.314 (0.069)	0.038 (0.052)					0.777
	9.5aD	P_{IC}	0.0085	0.488 (0.175)		0.333 (0.101)		0.370 (0.109)				0.606
Residual industries	9.6D	PV_{O*I}	1.46	0.793 (0.177)		1.991 (0.277)						0.630

a) Standard errors are shown in parentheses beneath the respective regression coefficients.

b) First differences between quarters one year apart.

c) PR for durable manufacturing = P_M = implicit price deflator for imports of goods and services, 1954 = 1.00
PR for non-durable manufacturing = P_{AF} = implicit price deflator for farm gross product, 1954 = 1.00.
PR for contract construction = $WPIS_{CM}$ = special wholesale price index for construction materials, 1954 = 1.00.

TABLE 9.3

Price regressions for global aggregates: [a] *1948 : 1—1960 : 2* [b].

Industry	Equation number	Dependent variable	Constant term	ULC^N	$ULC^N + UCCA^N$	$ULC - ULC^N$	PR [c]	$(+)\left\{\dfrac{X}{X_K} - \left[\dfrac{X}{X_K}\right]^N\right\}54$	$(-)\left\{\dfrac{X}{X_K} - \left[\dfrac{X}{X_K}\right]^N\right\}54$	$(+)\left\{\dfrac{X_S}{X_{KS}} - \left[\dfrac{X_S}{X_{KS}}\right]^N\right\}54$	$(-)\left\{\dfrac{X_S}{X_{KS}} - \left[\dfrac{X_S}{X_{KS}}\right]^N\right\}54$	$\bar{R}^2$
Durable manufacturing	9.1i	WPI_{MD}	−0.203		1.821 (0.553)	2.17 (0.182)	0.112 (0.030)					0.965
Nondurable manufacturing	9.2j	$WPI_{MN}*$	−0.138		1.409 (0.088)		0.282 (0.025)	0.454 (0.106)	[d]			0.854
Nondurable manufacturing [e]	9.2k	$WPI_{MN}*$	−0.094		1.378 (0.059)	0.368 (0.271)	0.263 (0.021)			0.591 (0.087)	0.153 (0.056)	0.931
Private nonfarm nonmanufacturing	9.0	Value-added price	−0.014	2.020 (0.045)		0.718 (0.212)						0.990

[a] Data for this set of equations were directly estimated at the aggregate level rather than being aggregated from estimates for individual industries.

[b] Standard errors are shown in parentheses beneath their respective coefficients.

[c] PR for durable manufacturing = P_M = implicit price deflator for imports of goods and services, 1954 = 1.00. PR for nondurable manufacturing = P_{AF} = implicit price deflator for farm gross product, 1954 = 1.00.

[d] Practically zero.

[e] Includes mining of crude petroleum and natural gas.

TABLE 9.4

Price regressions for individual industries, 1948 : 2—1960 : 4 [a].

Industry	Dependent variable	Constant term	ULC^N	$ULC^N + UCCA^N$	$ULC - ULC^N$	PR	$(+)\left\{\dfrac{X}{X_K} - \left[\dfrac{X}{X_K}\right]^N\right\}^{54}$	$(-)\left\{\dfrac{X}{X_K} - \left[\dfrac{X}{X_K}\right]^N\right\}^{54}$	$(+)\left\{\dfrac{X_S}{X_{KS}} - \left[\dfrac{X_S}{X_{KS}}\right]^N\right\}^{54}$	$(-)\left\{\dfrac{X_S}{X_{KS}} - \left[\dfrac{X_S}{X_{KS}}\right]^N\right\}^{54}$	$\bar{R}^2$
Primary metals	WPI_{33}	0.180		1.152 (0.035)	0.424 (0.121)		0.275 (0.177)	0.275 (0.064)			0.959
	WPI_{33}	−0.059		1.042 (0.070)	0.318 (0.132)	0.302 (0.169)	0.346 (0.177)	0.214 (0.071)			0.961
Fabricated metals	WPI_{34}	0.346		0.827 (0.031)	0.122 (0.104)		−0.071 (0.079)	0.175 (0.057)			0.945
	WPI_{34}	0.282		0.076 (0.070)	0.101 (0.055)	0.660 (0.060)	0.016 (0.042)	0.043 (0.032)			0.985
	WPI_{34}	0.343		0.823 (0.030)	0.120 (0.102)		−0.044 (0.078)	0.108 (0.069)	0.189 (0.132)	0.039 (0.044)	0.949
Non-electrical machinery	WPI_{35}	−0.051		1.440 (0.033)	0.396 (0.148)		−0.039 (0.086)	0.110 (0.046)			0.979
	WPI_{35}	−0.114		0.392 (0.110)	−0.174 (0.103)	0.827 (0.085)	0.074 (0.051)	−0.111 (0.035)			0.993
	WPI_{35}	−0.060		1.435 (0.027)	0.628 (0.132)		0.050 (0.074)	−0.020 (0.051)			0.985

[a] Standard errors of regression coefficients are shown in parentheses beneath the coefficients.

TABLE 9.4 (Continued)

Industry	Dependent variable	Constant term	ULC^N	$ULC^N + UCCA^N$	$ULC - ULC^N$	PR	$(+)\left\{\dfrac{X}{X_K} - \left[\dfrac{X}{X_K}\right]^N\right\}^{54}$	$(-)\left\{\dfrac{X}{X_K} - \left[\dfrac{X}{X_K}\right]^N\right\}^{54}$	$(+)\left\{\dfrac{X_S}{X_{KS}} - \left[\dfrac{X_S}{X_{KS}}\right]^N\right\}^{54}$	$(-)\left\{\dfrac{X_S}{X_{KS}} - \left[\dfrac{X_S}{X_{KS}}\right]^N\right\}^{54}$	$\bar{R}^2$
Electrical machinery	WPI_{36}	-0.038		1.368 (0.079)	0.384 (0.257)		-0.067 (0.113)	0.239 (0.103)			0.879
	WPI_{36}	0.166		0.080 (0.058)	0.234 (0.071)	0.778 (0.033)	0.117 (0.032)	0.021 (0.030)			0.991
	WPI_{36}	-0.026		1.340 (0.076)	0.339 (0.248)		-0.023 (0.112)	0.003 (0.146)	0.259 (0.203)	0.119 (0.079)	0.888
Motor vehicles and parts	WPI_{371}	0.278		-0.121 (0.087)	-0.088 (0.081)	0.791 (0.045)	-0.099 (0.043)	-0.151 (0.038)			0.964
	WPI_{371}	0.426		1.108 (0.140)	-0.328 (0.218)		-0.143 (0.119)	0.283 (0.102)			0.731
	WPI_{371}	0.434		1.083 (0.140)	-0.386 (0.233)		-0.252 (0.132)	-0.329 (0.123)	0.473 (0.333)	0.040 (0.098)	0.739
Other trans- portation equipment	WPI_{37-371}	0.299		0.924 (0.162)	2.430 (0.264)		0.077 (0.039)	0.456 (0.063)			0.696
	WPI_{37-371}	1.226		1.778 (0.187)	2.984 (0.219)	0.614 (0.102)	0.751 (0.116)	0.311 (0.053)			0.828
	WPI_{37-371}	0.350		0.911 (0.138)	2.330 (0.226)		0.085 (0.033)	0.459 (0.060)	-0.722 (0.179)	0.146 (0.160)	0.780

TABLE 9.4 (Continued)

Industry	Dependent variable	Constant term	ULC^N	$ULC^N + UCCA^N$	$ULC - ULC^N$	PR	$(+)\left\{\dfrac{X}{X_K} - \left[\dfrac{X}{X_K}\right]^N\right\}54$	$(-)\left\{\dfrac{X}{X_K} - \left[\dfrac{X}{X_K}\right]^N\right\}54$	$(+)\left\{\dfrac{X_S}{X_{KS}} - \left[\dfrac{X_S}{X_{KS}}\right]^N\right\}54$	$(-)\left\{\dfrac{X_S}{X_{KS}} - \left[\dfrac{X_S}{X_{KS}}\right]^K\right\}54$	$\bar{R}^2$
Instruments	WPI_{38}	0.064		1.258 (0.055)	1.081 (0.153)		-0.317 (0.128)	0.100 (0.061)			0.923
	WPI_{38}	0.024		1.560 (0.271)	1.142 (0.162)	-0.183 (0.161)	-0.419 (0.155)	0.136 (0.068)			0.924
	WPI_{38}	0.052		1.259 (0.050)	1.048 (0.142)		-0.173 (0.129)	-0.013 (0.068)	0.284 (0.136)	0.051 (0.040)	0.936
Furniture and fixtures	WPI_{25}	-0.303		1.532 (0.151)	0.661 (0.202)		0.692 (0.293)	0.304 (0.181)			0.665
	WPI_{25}	-0.473		0.309 (0.183)	-0.195 (0.171)	1.193 (0.151)	0.019 (0.210)	-0.337 (0.143)			0.857
	WPI_{25}	-0.335		1.560 (0.142)	0.807 (0.197)		0.697 (0.281)	0.701 (0.208)	-0.078 (0.391)	0.472 (0.162)	0.716
Tobacco	WPI_{21}	0.374	4.536 (0.273)		0.997 (1.006)		0.552 (0.115)	0.562 (0.316)			0.904
	WPI_{21}	0.500	4.267 (0.364)		1.341 (1.049)	-0.085 (0.077)	0.567 (0.115)	-0.261 (0.145)			0.904

TABLE 9.4 (Continued)

Industry	Dependent variable	Constant term	ULC^N	$ULC^N + UCCA^N$	$ULC - ULC^N$	PR	$(+)\left\{\dfrac{X}{X_K} - \left[\dfrac{X}{X_K}\right]^N\right\}^{54}$	$(-)\left\{\dfrac{X}{X_K} - \left[\dfrac{X}{X^K}\right]^N\right\}^{54}$	$(+)\left\{\dfrac{X_S}{X_{KS}} - \left[\dfrac{X_S}{X_{KS}}\right]^N\right\}^{54}$	$(-)\left\{\dfrac{X_S}{X_{KS}} - \left[\dfrac{X_S}{X_{KS}}\right]^N\right\}^{54}$	$\bar{R}^2$
Paper	WPI_{26}	-0.110	1.774 (0.086)		1.478 (0.377)		0.845 (0.192)	-0.087 (0.140)			0.905
	WPI_{26}	-0.723	-0.054 (0.174)		0.135 (0.235)	1.754 (0.161)	-0.015 (0.129)	-0.204 (0.075)			0.973
Printing and publishing	WPI_{27}	0.042	1.244 (0.024)		1.233 (0.161)	-0.023 (0.063)	0.268 (0.214)	0.232 (0.145)			0.990
	WPI_{27}	0.045	1.271 (0.076)		1.288 (0.212)		0.294 (0.227)	0.251 (0.156)			0.990
Chemicals	WPI_{28}	0.295	1.329 (0.180)		0.795 (0.211)		0.127 (0.048)	0.437 (0.114)			0.668
	WPI_{28}	-0.315	1.240 (0.127)		-0.076 (0.193)	0.643 (0.092)	-0.036 (0.041)	-0.004 (0.102)			0.838
Integrated petroleum	WPI_{29+13}	0.660	1.186 (0.231)		-0.648 (0.755)						0.347
	WPI_{29+13}	0.775	0.895 (0.177)		3.441 (0.882)		0.464 (0.349)	1.340 (0.216)			0.644
	WPI_{29+13}	0.932	0.925 (0.179)		3.751 (0.931)		0.579 (0.366)	1.436 (0.235)			0.644

TABLE 9.4 (Continued)

Industry	Dependent variable	Constant term	ULC^N	$ULC^N + UCCA^N$	$ULC - ULC^N$	PR	$(+)\left\{\frac{X}{X_K} - \left[\frac{X}{X_K}\right]^K\right\}^{54}$	$(-)\left\{\frac{X}{X_K} - \left[\frac{X}{X^K}\right]^N\right\}^{54}$	$(+)\left\{\frac{X_S}{X_{KS}} - \left[\frac{X_S}{X_{KS}}\right]^N\right\}^{54}$	$(-)\left\{\frac{X_S}{X_{KS}} - \left[\frac{X_S}{X_{KS}}\right]^N\right\}^{54}$	$\bar{R}^2$
Rubber	WPI_{30}	0.035	1.324 (0.092)		0.588 (0.294)						0.805
	WPI_{30}	0.009	1.361 (0.081)		1.237 (0.304)		0.505 (0.347)	0.221 (0.158)			0.850
	WPI_{30}	−0.612	1.275 (0.074)		0.762 (0.292)	0.679 (0.174)	0.214 (0.207)	0.173 (0.145)			0.886
Leather and leather products	WPI_{31}	−0.041	1.294 (0.149)		0.991 (0.446)						0.597
	WPI_{31}	−0.122	1.372 (0.147)		1.390 (0.515)		1.071 (0.439)	−0.129 (0.251)			0.630
	WPI_{31}	0.512	−0.652 (0.515)		0.566 (0.490)	1.040 (0.257)	0.835 (0.384)	−0.237 (0.218)			0.723

TABLE 9.5

Price regressions for individual industries using value-added price as dependent variable: 1949 : 2-1960 : 4 [a].

Industry	Dependent variable	Constant term	ULC^N	$ULC^N + UCCA^N$	$ULC - ULC^N$	PR	$(+)\left\{\dfrac{X}{X_K} - \left[\dfrac{X}{X_K}\right]^N\right\}54$	$(-)\left\{\dfrac{X}{X_K} - \left[\dfrac{X}{X_K}\right]^N\right\}54$	$[ULC-ULC^N]_{-1}$	R^2
Mining	PV_{OM-13}	0.515		0.622 (0.161)	0.229 (0.256)		0.462 (0.274)	−0.046 (0.104)		0.199
Mining	PV_{OM-13}	0.502		0.562 (0.196)	0.192 (0.266)	0.056 (0.105)	0.497 (0.284)	−0.063 (0.110)		0.187
Wholesale trade	PV_{TW}	0.199	1.201 (0.046)		0.786 (0.191)		0.197 (0.242)	−0.049 (0.117)		0.962
Retail trade	PV_{TR}	0.516	0.913 (0.076)		1.464 (0.275)		−0.002 (0.200)	−0.320 (0.138)		0.917
Retail trade	PV_{TR}	0.497	0.954 (0.061)		1.177 (0.226)		−0.043 (0.160)	−0.140 (0.116)	0.825 (0.159)	0.947
Finance and insurance	PV_{OFO}	0.188	1.204 (0.092)		2.436 (0.302)		1.492 (0.345)	−0.403 (0.167)		0.881
Finance and insurance	PV_{OFO}	0.136	1.279 (0.099)		1.362 (0.668)		2.066 (0.465)	−3.98 (0.163)	1.481 (0.828)	0.887
Nonrail transportation	PV_{RTN}	0.336	1.050 (0.059)		1.103 (0.161)		0.092 (0.154)	−0.030 (0.118)		0.906
Services	PV_{OSO}		2.035 (0.030)		2.262 (0.225)		−0.307 (0.108)	0.375 (0.200)		0.995

[a] Standard errors of regression coefficients are shown in parentheses beneath the coefficients.

Brookings-SSRC aggregative model. In this group, unit labor and unit depreciation costs and, when applicable, value-added prices, were estimated by aggregating the estimates for several individual industries. In table 9.3, regression results are presented for durable and nondurable manufacturing and for a total nonmanufacturing industries group, based upon a different set of data. The data for this latter set of equations were directly estimated at the aggregate level, with data from various published sources, rather than being aggregated from quarterly time series estimates of individual industries. These have been dubbed "global" aggregates. In industries which are the same for the Brookings-SSRC aggregate sectors and the global aggregates, and where the same variables were used, slightly differing results were obtained.

Tables 9.4 and 9.5 present the results for selected industries, mostly at lower levels of aggregation than in the first three tables. Several of these are for two-digit manufacturing industries. The series used for this group of industries are the ones which were aggregated to get the series for the Brookings-SSRC aggregate sectors.

The price regressions for six of the seven sectors [6]) are given in table 9.1. Corresponding regressions using first differences between quarters a year apart are given in table 9.2. [7]) These overlapping first differences gave substantially the same results as the original data and will not be discussed separately.

In durable manufacturing, normal unit labor costs dominate, with the inventory/output ratio also showing consistent strength. As noted earlier,

---

[6]) The seventh sector, agriculture, was not included here, since it was analyzed separately by Karl Fox.

[7]) The first-difference regressions were used as a check on the regressions obtained with the original series. In general, the two sets of regressions are quite consistent with each other. However, the type of differences used here, between quarters a year apart, are biased statistically to a better fit than the ordinary first differences between successive quarters. Adjacent values of differences between quarters a year apart have an overlap of three quarters in their time period and hence are not independent of each other. This mechanically introduces some autocorrelation into the series, which in turn is likely to improve the fit and reduce the standard error of the regression coefficients in comparison with corresponding estimates based on quarter-to-quarter differences. It was felt that because of the "noise" inherent in the quarterly series the differences between quarters a year apart would give a better indication of the movement of the series than differences between successive quarters. One method of avoiding the overlap problem would be to throw out all overlapping observations. This would reduce the number of observations from forty-eight to twelve, a rather alarming loss. We preferred to use all forty-eight observations and to keep the effects of the overlap in mind when interpreting the results.

the capacity utilization variable was generally insignificant and usually appeared with the wrong sign. The deviation of actual from normal unit labor costs, $[ULC-ULC^N]$, has a positive coefficient but has less influence and is usually only on the border of being statistically significant. The importance of raw materials prices is also unclear; this last result is probably because the series used is not satisfactory. The major input into the durable manufacturing group as a whole is from the mining industry, chiefly metal ores of various kinds. In general, however, production of ore is carried on by firms which also refine and process the ores. Quoted prices have little meaning, and the first market price is usually at the refined stage. (Steel, copper, lead, zinc and aluminum are the chief constituents of this group.) As a consequence, it is impossible to derive a meaningful price series. As a very poor substitute we used the price index of imported crude materials. The composition of this index is probably not suitable for the use to which we put it. Moreover, it tends to be extremely sensitive to short-run variations in world supply conditions which may often be unrepresentative of the U.S. mineral supply situation.

In nondurable manufacturing, normal unit labor costs are again statistically dominant. $[ULC-ULC^N]$ is generally insignificant and usually showed up with a negative sign. The capacity utilization variables give poor results, although there is some indication that high utilization rates exert some upward pressure on prices. Deflated inventories relative to output appear to be an important explanatory variable, much superior to the capacity utilization variables. Raw materials prices also exert an important influence, and, in fact, explain a substantial part of the variance in prices not accounted for by normal unit labor costs. In general, the current-quarter raw materials index outperforms the same variable in its smoother form. Superior results with raw materials prices in this industry, as compared to durable manufacturing, undoubtedly stem from the fact that we were able to use a more appropriate series. A price index of agricultural output was used for this purpose in nondurable manufacturing, and this index undoubtedly matches raw materials inputs to nondurables better than the import index matches durables. This suggests that a more suitable raw materials index for durables would give better results.

In trade, the price series used was a value-added price. This is equivalent to the gross margin per unit of real output distributed by the trade sector. As a consequence of our definition of price, purchases by retailers and wholesalers are not a cost, and consequently no "materials" price was calculated. In the trade regressions, only unit labor costs appear to be significant explanatory variables. And, in this industry, ULC^N is not uniformly larger than $[ULC-ULC^N]$. Yet it is difficult to believe that short-run variations in unit labor costs in retail and wholesale trade are promptly reflected in gross margins. Our results probably stem from the nature of the data.

Our value-added prices are equal to total income originating per unit of output. Statistically they were derived by dividing a gross income estimate by an output estimate. Since labor income accounts for a very large fraction —some 60 per cent—of total income in this industry, the sum of ULC^N and $[ULC-ULC^N]$ automatically equals a large fraction of the value-added price. This, in and of itself, would not be important if our income and output measures were perfect. If, as we suspect, short-run variations in trade sector unit costs are not fully reflected in changes in the trade sector price, profits per unit of output would fluctuate in the opposite direction and the coefficient of $[ULC-ULC^N]$ would be substantially less than the coefficient of ULC^N. If, however, our income data, and particularly the profits data, understate the true cyclical fluctuations in income, or if the output data overstate the cyclical movements of output, our estimated value-added prices will be higher than "true" value-added prices at low points in the cycle and lower than the true prices at the high point. As we indicated earlier in this paper, we believe that the data are subject to one or the other form of this bias [8]). In either case the deviations in our price from the true price will be positively associated with the variations in $[ULC-ULC^N]$, since $[ULC-ULC^N]$ is itself a cyclical variable which tends to rise in recession and fall in recoveries. This hypothesis is confirmed in a rather peculiar way. Deflated inventories relative to output is a variable even more closely associated with the cycle than is $[ULC-ULC^N]$. When this variable is used, it takes on a positive sign (compared to the expected negative sign) and the coefficient of $[ULC-ULC^N]$ declines and is slightly below the coefficient of ULC^N. (This shows up more strongly in the overlapping first-difference equations than in the price-level equations.) In other words, the probable systematic bias in our price indexes is partially picked up by the cyclical inventory-sales variable rather than carried solely by $[ULC-ULC^N]$.

One other feature of the equations in the trade sector warrants comment, namely, the high value of the constant. This stems, we believe, from the fact that in the early postwar period, 1947 and 1948 and again in 1950 and

---

[8]) This basic point was discussed earlier in connection with the explanations of why we chose market prices rather than value-added prices in the manufacturing industries.

1951, profit margins in trade were abnormally high. In the immediate post-war period of goods shortages, many manufacturers held their prices below the levels which demand conditions would have warranted. Retail prices, however, tended to adjust more rapidly to demand conditions. As a consequence, trade profits rose to an abnormal and unsustainable level. A similar bulge in trade profits occurred during the upsurge of consumer scare buying in the critical stages of the Korean war. Thereafter, trade profit margins declined. Increases in unit labor costs were partially absorbed in profit margins. In fitting the over-all Brookings-SSRC econometric model, we believe it would be appropriate to include a dummy variable for this early period in order to allow for this phenomenon. Otherwise the unit labor cost coefficient will be understated.

In the regulated industries, as in trade, value-added prices were used. Although the coefficient for $[ULC - ULC^N]$ is larger than we believe to be warranted, it is still significantly below that for ULC^N. In this one industry it was felt that depreciation is too large an element of cost to be omitted, particularly in light of the regulatory process which explicitly recognizes these costs in rate determination. The industry includes transportation, public utilities and communications, and the capital costs in these industries are higher than in most others. The use of the sum of normal unit labor and normal unit depreciation for normal cost works as expected. The coefficient falls by comparison to ULC^N alone—the markup is smaller on the larger base of the two costs combined—and the fit improves. Capacity utilization data were not available, and raw materials prices and inventories were not considered to be important enough to investigate.

The simple markup hypothesis works well for the construction industry, using normal unit labor costs, ULC^N, the deviation of actual from normal unit labor costs, $[ULC - ULC^N]$, and the current price of raw materials. Capacity and inventory data were not available.

Residual industries is the catchall. It contains some services, most of mining and finance and insurance. The price for this industry is value-added price. Again, normal and actual minus normal unit labor costs show up with about equal importance. The prior comments about this result in the trade sector apply equally well here.

The regressions presented above were also tried with variables lagged one quarter and with combinations of lagged and unlagged variables. The regressions obtained had poorer fits than the unlagged versions, and, almost without exception, the standard errors of the regression coefficients were larger. In view, however, of the feedback from prices to cost-of-living to wages, these results do not necessarily indicate that unlagged variables provide the best structural solutions. In this kind of situation, where relatively short lags are undoubtedly involved, the choice among possible lag structures cannot be made by an examination of measures of goodness of fit or the magnitude of error terms. To the extent that time series analysis can be used at all in this problem, the use of simulation techniques in the context of a more complete economic model would appear more appropriate.

The regressions chosen for the model for the six industries are as follows:

TABLE 9.6

Final price equations.

$$WPI_{MD} = -0.0226 + \frac{1.845}{(0.042)} ULC^N_{MD} + \frac{0.371}{(0.151)} [ULC_{MD} - ULC^N_{MD}]$$

$$- \frac{0.059}{(0.012)} \left\{ \left[\frac{INV^{54}_{MD}}{X^{54}_{MD}} \right] - \left[\frac{INV^{54}_{MD}}{X^{54}_{MD}} \right]^T \right\}_{-1} \qquad \bar{R}^2 = 0.974. \quad (9.7)$$

$$WPI_{MN*} = -0.0627 + \frac{1.490}{(0.072)} ULC^N_{MN*} + \frac{0.279}{(0.018)} P_{AF}$$

$$- \frac{0.098}{(0.013)} \left\{ \left[\frac{INV^{54}_{MN*}}{X^{54}_{MN*}} \right] - \left[\frac{INV^{54}_{MN*}}{X^{54}_{MN*}} \right]^T \right\}_{-1} \qquad \bar{R}^2 = 0.900. \quad (9.8)$$

$$PV_T = 0.3461 + \frac{1.159}{(0.037)} ULC^N_T + \frac{1.423}{(0.164)} [ULC_T - ULC^N_T]$$

$$- \frac{0.028}{(0.009)} \left\{ \left[\frac{INV_T}{X_T} \right] - \left[\frac{INV_T}{X_T} \right]^T \right\}_{-1} \qquad \bar{R}^2 = 0.952. \quad (9.9)$$

$$PV_R = -0.0605 + \frac{1.556}{(0.041)} [ULC^N_R + UCCA^N_R]$$

$$+ \frac{0.956}{(0.155)} \{ [ULC_R + UCCA_R] - [ULC^N_R + UCCA^N_R] \quad \bar{R}^2 = 0.967. \quad (9.10)$$

$$P_{IC} = 0.0603 + \frac{0.858}{(0.052)} ULC^N_C + \frac{0.349}{(0.095)} [ULC_C - ULC^N_C]$$

$$+ \frac{0.036}{(0.006)} WPIS_{CM} \qquad \bar{R}^2 = 0.988. \quad (9.11)$$

$$PV_{O*1} = 0.1070 + \frac{1.701}{(0.027)} ULC^N_{O*1}$$

$$+ \frac{1.748}{(0.395)} [ULC_{O*1} - ULC^N_{O*1}] \qquad \bar{R}^2 = 0.987. \quad (9.12)$$

The variables in order of appearance are:

WPI = wholesale price index, 1954 = 1.00
ULC^N = normal unit labor costs, dollars per dollar of gross product
originating $= \dfrac{WSS}{MH} \div \frac{1}{12} \sum_{i=-11}^{0} \left[\dfrac{X}{MH}\right]_i$
ULC = unit labor cost (compensation of employees per unit of gross product originating), dollars per dollar
INV = business inventory stock, billions of dollars
X = gross product originating (by industry), billions of dollars
$\left[\dfrac{INV}{X}\right]^T =$ trend of ratio of inventory stock to gross product originating, fraction
P_{AF} = implicit price deflator for farm gross product, 1954 = 1.00
PV = implicit price deflator for gross product originating (by industry), 1954 = 1.00
CCA = capital consumption allowances, billions of dollars
$UCCA$ = unit capital consumption allowances (capital consumption allowance per unit of gross product originating), dollars per dollar
$UCCA^N$ = normal unit capital consumption allowances (smoothed ratio of CCA to capacity output), dollars per dollar
P_{IC} = implicit price deflator for construction component of GNP, 1954 = 1.00
$WPIS_{CM}$ = special wholesale price index for construction materials, 1954 = 1.00.

Sector subscripts are:

MD = durable manufacturing.
MN^* = nondurable manufacturing plus mining of crude petroleum and natural gas.
T = wholesale and retail trade.
R = regulated industries: transportation, communications, public utilities.
C = contract construction.
O^*1 = residual industries: mining excluding crude petroleum and natural gas, finance and insurance, services except household and institutional.

These regressions were chosen on the basis of fit, agreement of regression coefficients with expected signs, and statistical significance of the regression coefficients. With improved data, some of these should be modified. Certainly raw materials prices belong in durable manufacturing, and probably $[ULC - ULC^N]$ belongs in nondurable manufacturing. The capacity utilization influence is such an attractive hypothesis that one hates to abandon it. Perhaps improved data will eventually bear it out, although the inventory/output ratio reflects the short-run influence of capacity utilization to a substantial degree.

Table 9.3 contains some price regressions for durable and nondurable manufacturing and private nonfarm nonmanufacturing. The normal and actual minus normal cost series were directly estimated, as contrasted with the same variables for the aggregate sectors, which were estimated by aggregating estimates for several industries. The regressions for both sets of data seem to be consistent with each other.

Tables 9.4 and 9.5 contain regressions for a large number of individual industries. Most of the SIC two-digit manufacturing industries are included, as well as some others at lower levels of aggregation than the aggregate sectors. The data for costs for these industries were used to calculate the corresponding aggregated series in the aggregate sectors.

Unfortunately these tables are incomplete. A number of industries are missing, and only a few of the possible combinations of variables were tried. The available results are presented to show some of the effects of working with lower levels of aggregation than the aggregate sectors. They are not conclusive, but they do suggest directions for further work.

In the individual industries, normal unit labor cost or the sum of normal unit labor cost and normal unit depreciation is again usually the dominant influence on price. In quite a few industries, normal costs are apt to be collinear with raw materials costs, and the normal cost coefficients estimates become unreliable when the two variables are included in the same regression.

The coefficients for short-run variations in unit labor costs, i.e., the actual minus normal unit labor costs, are generally positive but usually smaller than that for normal unit costs. In a good many industries this coefficient is not significantly different from zero. Our capacity utilization and supplier variables again proved disappointing.

The results for the lower levels of aggregation suggest that the basic price hypotheses will hold in much the same way for these industries as they do for the more aggregative levels. The principal difference is that raw materials prices become very important for some industries. A difficulty with raw materials prices, at least in the period studied here, is that they have been collinear with other costs, particularly normal unit labor costs. This condition, of course, makes for poor estimates of the coefficients.

9.2. Wages

The wage equations of the Brookings-SSRC econometric model basically derive from a disequilibrium model. The model makes no attempt to explain the level of wages but only their rate of change. The disequilibrium aspect arises, of course, not from the fact that we have chosen to estimate rates of change of the dependent variable but from the fact that these rates of change are driven by variables which, with one exception, are themselves *level* variables.

In summary, the equations finally selected state that the rate of change in compensation per man-hour in a given industry depends upon the level of general unemployment, the ratio of profits to income originating and the rate of change in consumer prices.

In addition the model displays a second-order lagged adjustment process [9])—the actual rate of change in wages adjusts in an oscillating manner to the rate specified by the independent variables. A given set of values of the independent variables calls for a specified annual rate of wage increase. But the actual wage adjustment in the first year tends to overshoot this long-term rate, then in the next year to underadjust and so on in a damped oscillation around the equilibrium rate of increase.

9.2.1. Choice of the "wage" variable

At first it would seem desirable to separate wages, salaries and supplements and within wages to take separate account of straight-time wages and overtime. A number of considerations forced us to abandon this route. From a theoretical standpoint the distinction between wages and fringe benefits is questionable. During the postwar period many union wage bargains have involved a trade-off of wage increases for improved fringe benefits, e.g., supplementary unemployment benefits, pension plans, longer vacations, etc. As a consequence, the combinations of wages plus supplements and salaries plus supplements are probably more relevant variables

---

[9]) The term "second-order" adjustment process is used to describe a situation in which there is a lagged adjustment not to an equilibrium *level* of a variable but to an "equilibrium" rate of increase in a variable.

than their separate components. Statistical considerations also forced us to use a more aggregated variable. We did construct a quarterly series on wages, salaries and supplements for two-digit manufacturing industries. Their quality, however, left much to be desired, since they required quarterly interpolation of annual data on salaries and supplements per employee, which itself appeared to be an erratic series. An attempt to construct equations which would explain the year-to-year rate of change in salaries per employee came to naught, in part at least because of the quality of the data [10]). Finally, it turned out that equations using compensation per employee man-hour were as good or better, in terms of closeness of fit, as equations based on straight-time wage rates. In view of these considerations we decided to use "compensation per man-hour" as the basic independent variable. To avoid this awkward term, however, we shall use "wage rate" in its place throughout the remainder of this paper.

9.2.2. *Explanatory variables*

Unemployment   Clearly the rate of change in wages will be affected by the magnitude of the excess demand for labor. We have chosen the reciprocal of the over-all unemployment rate as a measure of excess demand. Unemployment, however, is by no means a perfect index of the state of aggregate excess demand in the labor market. *Aggregate* supply-demand balance exists when the level of unfilled job vacancies matches the level of unemployment. Clearly, therefore, the level of unemployment consistent with aggregate supply-demand balance can vary over time as the level of structural unemployment changes. The kind of relationship involved is shown in figure 9.1.

In a situation in which labor mobility—inter-regional and interoccupational—is high and in which the schedule of job requirements closely matches the available skills in the labor force, the vacancy-unemployment relationship will be depicted by curve I. At point A job vacancies and unemployment are equal; aggregate labor demand and supply are in balance at a very low level of unemployment, U_1. There is little mismatching between job requirements and available labor supply. A sharp change in the geographical or skill mix of labor demand, however, would shift the vacancy-

---

[10]) The apparently erratic behavior of the salary-per-employee figures is, of course, partly reflected in the data we have used for compensation per man-hour. However, the error is largely swamped by the basic wage data, and the problem involved in making the split between wages and salaries is avoided.

unemployment relationship up to curve II. The same unemployment level, U_1, now represents a large aggregate excess demand for labor. As the composition of the demand and supply of labor changes, the level of unemployment consistent with aggregate supply-demand balance changes.

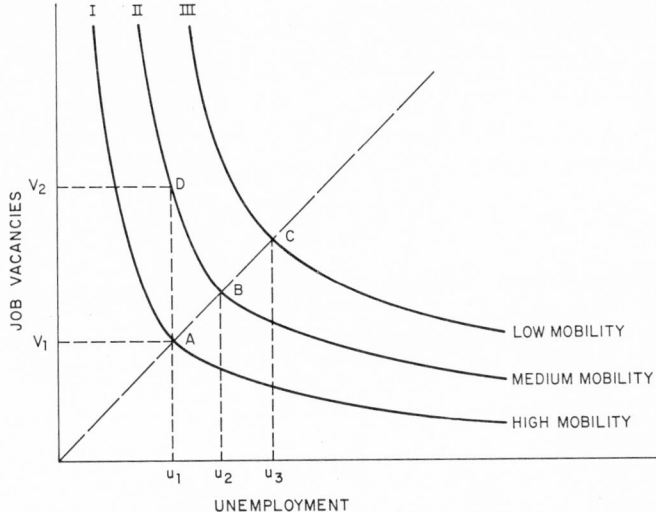

Figure 9.1. Unemployment and aggregate excess demand for labor.

The voluntary quit rate provides an alternative, and possibly superior, measure of the aggregate excess demand for labor. It should reflect the magnitude of unfilled demand for labor relative to the pool of qualified unemployed. We tried such a measure in an equation explaining changes in the wage rate for manufacturing as a whole, and it gave slightly better results than the unemployment rate. However, its use in an over-all econometric model was ruled out by the simple fact that an equation or set of equations explaining the quit rate itself would have had to be developed. This, in turn, threatened to pose rather serious difficulties. As a consequence we chose to use unemployment as an index of excess demand in the labor market.

Some experimentation with various alternatives suggested the aggregate unemployment rate to be a more relevant variable than industry-specific unemployment rates. This, in general, coincides with a priori reasoning. The labor market is not, in general, industry oriented. Geographic and occupational rigidities are, of course, important, and a very detailed model which built up wage rates by occupation and by geographic region would clearly have to use such specific unemployment indexes[11]). In an industry model, however, the general unemployment rate appears to be the most appropriate measure.

The unemployment variable was transformed into its reciprocal for familiar reasons. The literature on the Phillips curve, and related empirical work, seems to show that the impact on the wage rate of a given change in unemployment is much greater when unemployment is low than when it is high. When unemployment is very high and widespread, large pools of unutilized labor exist in most communities and in most occupations. Underemployment, reflected in reduced hours of work and cyclically low productivity, is also widespread. A substantial increase in employment can therefore occur which does not result in excess demand for labor in any particular skill or occupation. On the other hand, the lower the level of aggregate unemployment the larger the number of occupations and localities in which a given increased demand for labor will lead to excess labor demand. This is one reason for the fact that the response of wage rate changes to a given change in unemployment is larger when aggregate unemployment is low than when it is high. Another reason relates to the fact that wage rates tend to respond sluggishly to sharp decreases in labor demand. During periods of substantial unemployment, wage rates have not fully adjusted to the depressed economic conditions. Conversely, however, when the magnitude of excess labor supply diminishes, wage rates do not readjust sharply upward, since they already, to some extent, reflect economic circumstances of an earlier, more prosperous period.

Profits   Many theories of wage rate behavior give a significant role to profits as an explanatory variable. The empirical studies of Klein and Bhatia[12]), Eckstein and Wilson[13]) and Lipsey and Steuer[14]) confirm this, as do our own findings, at least in part.

There is of course some collinearity between profits and unemployment.

---

[11]) Theoretical considerations would suggest that a model which specified wage rates of a particular occupation in a particular locality should use an unemployment index in which the geographical, occupational and aggregate unemployment rate each received some weight.

[12]) L. R. Klein and R. J. Bhatia, Profits and the Rate of Change in Money Earnings in the United States: 1953–59, *Economica* 29 (August, 1962) 255–263.

[13]) Otto Eckstein and T. A. Wilson, The Determination of Money Wages in American Industry, *Quarterly Journal of Economics* 76, No. 3 (August, 1962) 379–414.

[14]) R. G. Lipsey and M. D. Steuer, Relation Between Profits and Wage Rates, *Economica* 28 (May, 1961) 137–155.

Nevertheless, profits play an independent role. The basic theoretical framework for their role is particularly well articulated by Alfred Kuhn [15]) and has been summarized by C. Schultze [16]). In a world of relatively large, more or less oligopolistic firms, an increase in profits above some long-run "normal" for the industry is quite likely to find its way into increased wages. Workers do not tend to move from firm to firm on the basis of relatively small wage differentials. At the same time there is, at any given time, a significant number of workers who voluntarily leave their jobs in order to seek permanently better employment. It will normally pay a firm to establish a reputation as a high-wage firm in order to have access to this pool of workers. Other advantages to the firm from a high-wage policy flow from the productivity implications of low worker morale—within relatively modest bounds, a high wage policy is not inconsistent with low unit labor costs. The firm has, therefore, some positive advantages to gain from sharing part of any increase in profits with its employees in the form of a wage increase.

The advantages of such a policy are strengthened by the fact that other uses to which abnormally high profits may be put carry with them certain dangers. In oligopolistic industries the continuation of very high profit margins invites entry by new firms. Price reductions are difficult to make for well-known reasons. In the typical oligopolistic setting, enlarged profit margins, such as those resulting from sharp increases in productivity, are less likely to be reduced to "normal" by price decreases than purely competitive equilibrium theories would suggest. A large share of increased profits, of course, goes toward financing investment outlays and toward increasing the research and development budget to the end of securing new products or processes. The techniques of nonprice competition can suggest many uses for internal sources of funds. Nevertheless, for any given level of other factors influencing the wage rate, from the firm's viewpoint, the higher the level of its profits relative to the size of its operations, the higher the optimum rate of increase in wages.

These factors are strengthened by considerations relating to bargaining power between union and management. Given any reasonable degree of control by the union over the supply of labor, high profit margins increase the cost of resisting labor's demands. The contract curve is shifted to labor's advantage as profits increase. And, in the postwar situations where govern-

---

[15]) Alfred Kuhn, Market Structure and Wage-Push Inflation, *Industrial and Labor Relations Review* 12 (January, 1959) 243–251.

[16]) *Recent Inflation in the United States*, Study Paper No. 1, Joint Economic Committee, *Study of Employment Growth and Price Levels*, U. S. Congress, 1959.

ment has tended to play a role, however indirect and diffuse, in influencing the terms of settlement in major labor disputes, the existence of large profit margins strengthens the hand of labor in making its case before the public.

Consumer price index   The third major explanatory variable in our model is the change in the consumer price index. Essentially a rise in consumer prices increases the supply price of labor. To the extent that a money illusion is absent, real wages should be the target of wage demands. To the extent that public opinion and governmental pressure influences the size of wage settlements, a rise in consumer prices strengthens the likelihood of a higher settlement. And finally, of course, to the extent that cost-of-living escalation is built into labor contracts, a rise in the consumer price index automatically results in wage increases.

9.2.3. Lag structure

We chose to fit wage changes four quarters apart. In other words, our basic independent variable is $[(RWSS - RWSS_{-4})/RWSS_{-4}]$.

The basic rationale for this was developed by Dow and Dicks-Mireaux [17] and applied to data on the British economy by Klein and Ball [18]. Wage determinations are not made quarterly. The average wage increases for a group of industries from one quarter to the next usually reflect a much larger increase for a fraction of the firms involved. As a matter of fact, the tendency for multiyear wage contracts in a large number of industries calls the concept of our annual wage change into question. Even in multiyear contracts, of course, annual increments—whether they are called "improvement factors" or something else—are quite common. Nevertheless, in such multiyear contracts, the basic wage increments are set for several years in advance, and the annual wage increase in a given period will have been determined by events of several years earlier. Eckstein and Wilson obtained very good results by isolating a small number of discrete "wage rounds" in the postwar period, calculating wage increases from one round to the next and fitting these increases to profit and unemployment rates. We rejected this approach for two reasons. First, for a comprehensive predictive economic model the wage-round technique tends to be very cumbersome,

---

[17] J. C. R. Dow and L. A. Dicks-Mireaux, The Excess Demand for Labor: A Study of Conditions in Great Britain, 1946–1956, *Oxford Economic Papers*, New Series, 10 (1958), 1–33.

[18] L. R. Klein and R. J. Ball, Some Econometrics of the Determination of Absolute Prices and Wages, *Economic Journal* 69 (September, 1959) 465–482.

since it requires predictions of when the next round will occur. Second, and more important, there is substantial wage "drift" between rounds. Even though a number of key and reinforcing wage bargains do tend to cluster together, setting the wage pattern for some time to come, the behavior of wages for broad industry aggregates is quite diffuse with respect to timing. As a consequence, the annual rate of wage increase in years between major "rounds" is, of course, still substantial and tends to vary with economic circumstances. In short, even though multiyear contracts do tend to lead to discrete wage rounds at substantial intervals, there remains sufficient variability in the annual size of the wage increment in years between rounds to justify a model fitted to annual wage changes.

The wage increase between one quarter and the same quarter a year later is actually made up of a number of different wage changes. In any given quarter, for a broad industry aggregate, a fraction of the workers in the industry will be getting a wage increase. Consequently the average increase in wages between $t-4$ and t for the industry as a whole is a weighted average of the annual increase received by different groups of workers in t, $t-1$, $t-2$, and $t-3$. In turn, therefore, the independent variables of the wage equations must be expressed in terms of their influence not merely on the annual wage bargain struck in period t but also those struck in the preceding three quarters. As a consequence our variables are defined as follows:

Wage change $= [(RWSS-RWSS_{-4})/RWSS_{-4}]$.

Profit rate (corporate profits before taxes including inventory valuation adjustment as proportion of gross product originating) =

$$\frac{1}{4}\sum_{i=-3}^{0}\left[\frac{Z_B}{X}\right]_i.$$

Unemployment rate (reciprocal of five-quarter average centered on $t-2$) $= 1/RU^*$ where $RU^* = \frac{1}{8}RU_{-4}+\frac{1}{4}RU_{-3}+\frac{1}{4}RU_{-2}+\frac{1}{4}RU_{-1}+\frac{1}{8}RU$, and $RU = $ rate of unemployment, fraction.

Change in consumer price index =

$$\frac{1}{4}\sum_{i=-3}^{0}\left[\frac{CPI-CPI_{-4}}{CPI_{-4}}\right]_i.$$

9.2.4. Lagged wage changes

In each major industry group the introduction of the dependent variable, lagged four quarters, i.e., the wage change one year earlier, substantially

Wage regressions for nonagricu

Industry	Equation number	Constant term	$\frac{1}{4}\sum\limits_{i=-3}^{0}\left[\frac{CPI-CPI_{-4}}{CPI_{-4}}\right]_i$	$\frac{1}{4}\sum\limits_{i=-3}^{0}\left[\frac{Z_{Bj}}{X_j}\right]_i$	$\frac{MH_j-MH_{j,-4}}{MH_{j,-4}}$	$\frac{1}{RU^*}$
Contract construction	9.13	−0.041	0.146 (0.209)	2.33 (0.75)		0.00192 (0.00056
	9.13a	−0.061	0.018 (0.222)	2.61 (0.81)		0.00176 (0.00060
	9.13b	−0.056	0.223 (0.195)	3.27 (0.71)	−0.130 (0.040)	0.00155 (0.00053
	9.13c	−0.042	0.245 (0.202)	2.64 (0.73)	−0.100 (0.043)	0.00153 (0.00055
	9.13d	0.025	0.374 (0.215)			0.00194 (0.00061
	9.13e	−0.058	0.074 (0.209)	2.86 (0.77)		0.00201 (0.00057
	9.13f	−0.036	0.359 (0.215)	3.19 (0.88)	−0.153 (0.049)	
Durable manufacturing	9.14	0.0187	0.883 (0.109)	0.132 (0.049)		0.00106 (0.00034
	9.14a	0.0072	0.806 (0.128)	0.147 (0.059)		0.00042 (0.00037
	9.14b	0.0090	0.897 (0.108)	0.199 (0.069)	−0.035 (0.026)	0.00116 (0.00035
	9.14c	0.0046	1.084 (0.142)	0.187 (0.066)	−0.117 (0.049)	0.00149 (0.00038
	9.14d	0.0127	0.982 (0.138)	0.133 (0.055)		0.00093 (0.00040
	9.14e	0.0053	1.185 (0.172)	0.154 (0.076)	−0.105 (0.056)	0.00132 (0.00044
	9.14f	0.0047	1.097 (0.134)	0.199 (0.065)	−0.112 (0.041)	0.00131 (0.00033
	9.14g	0.0057	1.071 (0.140)	0.187 (0.067)	−0.112 (0.048)	0.00145 (0.00037
	9.14h	0.0176	0.873 (0.118)	0.140 (0.068)		0.00105 (0.00035

a) Dependent variable is proportionate change in compensation of employees per man-hour be quarters one year apart.

duction sectors [a]), *1950 : 1–1960 : 4* [b]).

$\dfrac{\cdot}{E_j} - \left[\dfrac{\cdot}{E_j}\right]_{-4}$ $\left[\dfrac{E_{P_j}}{E_j}\right]_{-4} - 0.035$	$\dfrac{MH_{P_j}}{MH_j} - \left[\dfrac{MH_{P_j}}{MH_j}\right]_{-4}$	$\dfrac{MH_{P_j}}{MH_j} - \left[\dfrac{MH_{P_j}}{MH_j}\right]_{-4}$ $\left[\dfrac{MH_{P_j}}{MH_j}\right]_{-4} - 0.035$	$RWSS_{j,-2} - RWSS_{j,-6}$ $RWSS_{j,-6}$	$RWSS_{j,-3} - RWSS_{j,-7}$ $RWSS_{j,-7}$	$RWSS_{j,-4} - RWSS_{j,-8}$ $RWSS_{j,-8}$	$\bar{R}^2$
					−0.337 (0.117)	0.439
						0.337
				−0.359 (0.113)		0.522
					−0.310 (0.111)	0.498
					−0.382 (0.127)	0.319
				−0.312 (0.124)		0.414
			−0.092 (0.145)			0.341
					−0.430 (0.101)	0.708
						0.582
					−0.497 (0.111)	0.715
		−18.3 (9.4)			−0.468 (0.108)	0.734
				−0.352 (0.136)		0.635
		−19.6 (10.9)		−0.346 (0.150)		0.650
23.1 (10.0)					0.417 (0.111)	0.744
	5.10 (2.72)				−0.473 (0.108)	0.733
		1.18 (5.05)			−0.442 (0.114)	0.701

Standard errors are shown in parentheses beneath their respective regression coefficients.

TABLE 9.7

Industry	Equation number	Constant term	$\frac{1}{4}\sum_{i=-3}^{0}\left[\dfrac{CPI-CPI_{-4}}{CPI_{-4}}\right]_i$	$\frac{1}{4}\sum_{i=-3}^{0}\left[\dfrac{Z_{B_j}}{X_j}\right]_i$	$\dfrac{MH_j-MH_{j,-4}}{MH_{j,-4}}$	$\dfrac{1}{RU^*}$
Nondurable manufacturing plus mining of crude petroleum and natural gas	9.15	0.0390	0.763 (0.108)	0.036 (0.079)		0.00070 (0.00029)
	9.15a	0.0042	0.570 (0.147)	0.140 (0.108)		0.00034 (0.00040)
	9.15b	0.0053	0.599 (0.108)	0.249 (0.095)	−0.170 (0.051)	0.00066 (0.00026)
	9.15c	0.0283	0.843 (0.173)	0.062 (0.106)		0.00048 (0.00038)
	9.15d	0.0145	0.501 (0.107)	0.187 (0.073)		0.00004 (0.00002)
	9.15e	0.0346	0.451 (0.108)	0.056 (0.105)	0.230 (0.135)	0.00016 (0.00028)
Wholesale and retail trade	9.16	0.0445	0.068 (0.099)			0.00113 (0.00027)
	9.16a	0.0282	−0.097 (0.113)			0.00090 (0.00033)
	9.16b	0.0336	0.088 (0.116)	−0.073 (0.144)		0.00088 (0.00033)
	9.16c	0.0693	0.138 (0.096)	−0.294 (0.116)		0.00106 (0.00026)
	9.16d	0.0947	0.328 (0.118)	−0.281 (0.141)	−0.145 (0.094)	
	9.16e	0.0449	0.004 (0.142)	−0.157 (0.162)		0.00096 (0.00034)
	9.16f	0.0416	−0.069 (0.158)	−0.195 (0.165)	0.109 (0.102)	0.00099 (0.00034)
	9.16g	0.0284	−0.200 (0.136)	−0.006 (0.177)	−0.109 (0.089)	

321

(Continued)

$\dfrac{E_{P_j}}{E_j} - \left[\dfrac{E_{P_j}}{E_j}\right]_{-4}$	$\left[\dfrac{E_{P_j}}{E_j}\right]_{-4} - 0.035$	$\dfrac{MH_{P_j}}{MH_j} - \left[\dfrac{MH_{P_j}}{MH_j}\right]_{-4}$	$\left[\dfrac{MH_{P_j}}{MH_j}\right]_{-4}$	$\dfrac{MH_{P_j}}{MH_j} - \left[\dfrac{MH_{P_j}}{MH_j}\right]_{-4}$	$\left[\dfrac{MH_{P_j}}{MH_j}\right]_{-4} - 0.035$	$\dfrac{RWSS_{j,-2} - RWSS_{j,-6}}{RWSS_{j,-6}}$	$\dfrac{RWSS_{j,-3} - RWSS_{j,-7}}{RWSS_{j,-7}}$	$\dfrac{RWSS_{j,-4} - RWSS_{j,-8}}{RWSS_{j,-8}}$	R^2
								−0.559 (0.088)	0.689
									0.381
								−0.580 (0.078)	0.753
							−0.369 (0.142)		0.458
46.9 (10.6)								−0.582 (0.072)	0.790
95.2 (30.3)								−0.577 (0.071)	0.800
								−0.556 (0.119)	0.415
									0.117
									0.101
								−0.661 (0.119)	0.485
								−0.741 (0.166)	0.301
							−0.209 (0.187)		0.106
							−0.097 (0.214)		0.110
						0.468 (0.181)			0.097

Industry	Equation number	Constant term	$\frac{1}{4}\sum\limits_{i=-3}^{0}\left[\frac{CPI-CPI_{-4}}{CPI_{-4}}\right]_i$	$\frac{1}{4}\sum\limits_{i=-3}^{0}\left[\frac{Z_{Bj}}{X_j}\right]_i$	$\frac{MH_j-MH_{j,-4}}{MH_{j,-4}}$	$\frac{1}{RU^*}$
Regulated industries	9.17	−0.0440	0.359 (0.157)	0.534 (0.308)		0.000095 (0.000045)
	9.17a	−0.0403	0.327 (0.150)	0.489 (0.299)		0.000046 (0.000044)
	9.17b	−0.0386	0.370 (0.146)	0.513 (0.289)		
	9.17c	−0.0704	0.410 (0.152)	0.693 (0.340)	−0.069 (0.069)	
	9.17d	−0.0246	0.248 (0.142)	0.313 (0.286)		−0.000110 (0.000416)
	9.17e	−0.0416	0.258 (0.146)	0.405 (0.361)	−0.029 (0.070)	−0.000051 (0.000443)
	9.17f	−0.0530	0.392 (0.160)			−0.000150 (0.000438)
Residual industries	9.18	−0.0220	0.521 (0.118)	0.592 (0.328)		0.000513 (0.000413)
	9.18a	−0.0305	0.473 (0.149)			0.000264 (0.000430)
	9.18b	−0.0443	0.488 (0.145)	0.724 (0.404)		0.000153 (0.000479)
	9.18c	−0.0219	0.524 (0.122)	0.597 (0.334)	−0.012 (0.086)	0.000507 (0.000420)
	9.18d	−0.0402	0.472 (0.135)	0.662 (0.349)		
	9.18e	−0.0361	0.566 (0.113)	0.789 (0.289)		
	9.18f	−0.0603	0.394 (0.147)	0.841 (0.392)		−0.000540 (0.000496)
	9.18g	−0.0378	0.531 (0.166)	0.647 (0.350)	0.118 (0.099)	
	9.18h	−0.0395	0.510 (0.104)			0.000873 (0.000371)

(ntinued)

$\dfrac{E_j'}{E_j} - \left[\dfrac{E_j'}{E_j}\right]_{-4}$	$\left[\dfrac{E_{P_j}}{E_j}\right]_{-4} - 0.035$	$\dfrac{MH_{P_j}}{MH_j} - \left[\dfrac{MH_{P_j}}{MH_j}\right]_{-4}$	$\left[\dfrac{MH_{P_j}}{MH_j}\right]_{-4}$	$\dfrac{MH_{P_j}}{MH_j} - \left[\dfrac{MH_{P_j}}{MH_j}\right]_{-4}$	$\left[\dfrac{MH_{P_j}}{MH_j}\right]_{-4} - 0.035$	$\dfrac{RWSS_{j,-2} - RWSS_{j,-6}}{RWSS_{j,-6}}$	$\dfrac{RWSS_{j,-3} - RWSS_{j,-7}}{RWSS_{j,-7}}$	$\dfrac{RWSS_{j,-4} - RWSS_{j,-8}}{RWSS_{j,-8}}$	R^2
								−0.109 (0.151)	0.120
									0.130
								−0.104 (0.147)	0.141
								−0.120 (0.148)	0.141
							0.363 (0.135)		0.247
							0.349 (0.141)		0.231
								−0.055 (0.151)	0.076
								−0.498 (0.106)	0.511
									0.214
									0.255
								−0.502 (0.113)	0.498
									0.271
								−0.452 (0.100)	0.504
							0.291 (0.139)		0.313
						−0.114 (0.150)			0.267
								−0.514 (0.109)	0.483

improves the regression results. In all cases the sign of the coefficient associated with the lagged dependent variable was negative and, with one exception (the regulated industry group), significant. The implications of this result are discussed later.

9.2.5. Other variables

In addition to the three major independent variables discussed above, several other variables were listed and eventually discarded. (The results of all the alternative regressions are shown in table 9.7.)

We are using a "wage" series which is actually compensation per man-hour. Both wages and salaries are included in the numerator and both production and nonproduction workers in the denominator. However, when the proportion of production to nonproduction workers changes, compensation per man-hour for the industry group will also change, since salaries per hour are generally higher than wages per hour. There are sizeable cyclical swings in the ratio of production to nonproduction worker, since nonproduction worker employment is much more stable cyclically than production worker employment. Clearly it would be desirable to account for this element of variation, even though it is not an influence which related directly to bargaining practices.

In an effort to account for the influence of labor force mix changes, five variables were tried. Let:

E_P = number of production workers employed

E_O = number of nonproduction workers employed

MH_P = production worker manhours

MH_O = nonproduction worker manhours

$E_P + E_O = E$, and $MH_P + MH_O = M$.

Using these symbols, we define the following variables for use in the discussion:

$$\frac{\frac{E_O}{E_P} - \left[\frac{E_O}{E_P}\right]_{-4}}{\left[\frac{E_O}{E_P}\right]_{-4}} \qquad VAR\ 1$$

$$\frac{\dfrac{E_P}{E} - \left[\dfrac{E_P}{E}\right]_{-4}}{\left[\dfrac{E_P}{E}\right]_{-4}} \qquad\qquad VAR\ 2$$

$$\frac{\dfrac{E_P}{E} - \left[\dfrac{E_P}{E}\right]_{-4}}{\left[\dfrac{E_P}{E}\right]_{-4} - 0.035} \qquad\qquad VAR\ 3$$

$$\frac{\dfrac{MH_P}{MH} - \left[\dfrac{MH_P}{MH}\right]_{-4}}{\left[\dfrac{MH_P}{MH}\right]_{-4}} \qquad\qquad VAR\ 4$$

$$\frac{\dfrac{MH_P}{MH} - \left[\dfrac{MH_P}{MH}\right]_{-4}}{\left[\dfrac{MH_P}{MH}\right]_{-4} - 0.035} \qquad\qquad VAR\ 5$$

VAR 1, *VAR* 2 and *VAR* 4 are simply proportionate changes in three ratios which will reflect the change in production worker-nonproduction worker mix in an industry. They were tried to see whether a simple ratio variable could be used to capture the mix change influence on wages. *VAR* 3 and *VAR* 5 were efforts to get an approximation to the actual effect or proportionate change from a mix change. They are approximately equal to the contribution to proportionate change in wages coming from the mix change [19]).

As can be seen from table 9.7, these variables were not very successful in explaining changes in average compensation per man-hour. In particular, the sign of the coefficients in the nondurable industry group were positive when they should have been negative. An increase in the proportion of total employment of man-hours accounted for by production workers should reduce the change in average compensation per man-hour rather than raise it as shown by the regression. We suspect that this results from the fact that the "mix" variable generally tends to move with the over-all demand for labor—when total employment is expanding rapidly, in a recovery

---

[19]) For the derivation of the *VAR* 3 and *VAR* 5 approximations, see section 9.4.

from recession, the production worker proportion of the total also expands. The converse is true of periods in which total employment is decreasing. Hence the "mix" variable to some extent acts as a proxy for changes in the demand for labor, and so its presumed influence on compensation per man-hour through the mix phenomenon is veiled by its other role. Why its strength as a proxy for labor demand should come through strongly in the nondurable goods industry group and not in the durable we have been unable to explain. We have not included it in our recommended list of explanatory variables for the over-all Brookings-SSRC econometric model.

As an alternative to the unemployment rate we tried changes in man-hours of employment as a measure of the strength of labor demand. (This assumes that in the short run, shifts in the labor supply curve are relatively unimportant.) In general, this variable gave less satisfactory results than the unemployment variable. When both variables were used in the same regression, the man-hour change variable was generally insignificant and almost always had a negative rather than the expected positive sign (table 9.7)[20]).

9.2.6. *Regression results*

The equations finally chosen are shown in table 9.8.

Before discussing the regression results, one warning is in order. The proportionate changes in the variables are one year apart between quarters. Successive observations have a three-quarter overlap. This overlap undoubtedly introduces some autocorrelation with each of the series. The variables which are moving averages possess this characteristic even more. Since all the variables have some autocorrelation, such intercorrelation as otherwise exists among the explanatory variables is strengthened. Moreover, the loss of independence between successive observations biases both the standard error of estimate and the standard error of the coefficients downward.

Another technical point should be made here, relating to the inclusion of change in consumer prices as an explanatory variable. To the extent that the wage change itself leads to a price change in the same period the direction of causality is reversed from that which we are trying to determine. The error term in the wage change equation is itself positively correlated with the

---

[20]) The man-hour change variable is itself a proxy for a "mix" variable (discussed above), since the two move together. Ironically, in each case the proxy variable more often had the expected sign than the true variable!

TABLE 9.8

Wage equations.

Industry	Equation number	Constant term	$\frac{1}{4}\sum\limits_{i=-3}^{0}\left[\dfrac{CPI-CPI_{-4}}{CPI_{-4}}\right]_i$	$\frac{1}{4}\sum\limits_{i=-3}^{0}\left[\dfrac{Z_{B_j}}{X_j}\right]_i$	$\dfrac{1}{RU^*}$	$\dfrac{RWSS_{j,-4}-RWSS_{j,-8}}{RWSS_{j,-8}}$	$\bar{R}^2$
Contract construction	(9.13)	−0.041	0.15 (0.21)	2.33 (0.75)	0.00192 (0.00056)	−0.34 (0.12)	0.44
Durable manufacturing	(9.14)	0.0187	0.88 (0.11)	0.13 (0.05)	0.00106 (0.00034)	−0.43 (0.10)	0.71
Nondurable manufacturing	(9.15)	0.0390	0.76 (0.11)	0.04 (0.08)	0.00070 (0.00029)	−0.56 (0.09)	0.69
Wholesale and retail trade	(9.16)	0.0445	0.07 (0.10)	−	0.00113 (0.00027)	−0.56 (0.12)	0.42
Regulated industries	(9.17)	−0.044	0.36 (0.16)	0.53 (0.31)	0.00095 (0.00045)	−0.11 (0.15)	0.12
Residual industries	(9.18)	−0.022	0.52 (0.12)	0.59 (0.33)	0.00051 (0.00041)	−0.50 (0.11)	0.51

price variable in our estimating equation. As a consequence the coefficient of the price variable is biased upward. However, the wage change variable is defined as the proportionate change from $t-4$ to t. The price change, as noted earlier, is a moving average of annual changes in prices for the four periods:

$$\tfrac{1}{4}\sum_{i=-3}^{0}\left[\frac{CPI-CPI_{-4}}{CPI_{-4}}\right]_i.$$

Hence, even if wage changes in the present period affect prices of the same period, price changes over three quarters of the period involved in the price change variable are predetermined. The simultaneity problem is substantially reduced, even if not totally absent [21]). In fitting the complete

---

[21]) This statement must be qualified to the extent that the price-change variable is itself highly intercorrelated. In this case the bias creeps back into the least-squares estimating equation.

Brookings-SSRC econometric model, of course, simultaneous-equation techniques will be used, further reducing the problem of bias which the wage-price-wage interaction introduces into simple least squares estimates.

9.2.7. *Implications of the lagged wage change variable*

Let q_t represent all the independent variables in the wage-determining equations and treat q, for the moment, as a constant. Also, since we are dealing with wage changes at discrete intervals of one year, we shall collapse the time notation to annual intervals, and so our 4-quarter lagged wage-change variable is expressed as a one-period lag. Then,

$$\Delta w_t = a_1 q - \lambda \Delta w_{t-1}.$$

This first-order difference equation has the solution:

$$\Delta w_t = (-\lambda)^t \Delta w_0 + \frac{a_1 q}{1+\lambda}\left(1-(-\lambda)^t\right),$$

where Δw_0 is the rate of change of wages in an initial period when time (t) equals zero. So long as $\lambda < 1$, all terms except $a_1 q/(1+\lambda)$ eventually vanish, given sufficient time. In other words, there is an equilibrium rate of change which will result from a given set of values of the independent variables. If the value of q changes, a new equilibrium of Δw is set up. But Δw approaches this in a damped oscillatory manner. Large wage changes are followed by smaller ones and then in turn by larger ones—though not so large as the initial change. The larger λ is, the larger the oscillations will be and the longer the time period before Δw settles down to its new "equilibrium" rate of advance.

Assume, for example, that the independent variables change, resulting in an increase in the "equilibrium" rate of wage advance from 5 to 7 per cent per year. So long as the values of the independent variables remained at their new level, the pattern of annual wage changes which would occcur (given specified levels of λ) is shown in table 9.9.

Our wage variable is actually compensation per man-hour. In turn, the quarterly values of the variable for each industry group are the result of extensive estimation procedures, some of which involved interpolation of annual benchmarks with quarterly data of lower quality. It might be thought that the negative value of λ results from the influence of the annual benchmarks steadily "pulling" quarterly errors back to corrected levels. However, we also fitted data on straight-time production worker wages in the same equations and also obtained highly significant negative values for λ. While these data, as published by the Bureau of Labor Statistics, may themselves by influenced by the effect of annual correction to benchmarks, this effect is probably not strong enough to give the consistent results we found. Barring further evidence to the contrary, we believe that there is some tendency for larger than equilibrium wage gains to be followed by less than equilibrium gains and vice versa.

TABLE 9.9

Wage rate increases for
alternative adjustment parameters.

Period	% Δw	
	$\lambda = 0.25$	$\lambda = 0.5$
$t-1$	5.0	5.0
t	8.0	7.50
$t+1$	6.5	6.88
$t+2$	7.25	7.03
$t+3$	6.88	6.99
$t+4$	7.06	7.00 [a]
$t+5$	6.97	7.00
$t+6$	7.01	7.00

[a]) Approximately.

Clearly, of course, the fact that our single-equation estimates of the wage adjustment process show it to be a damped oscillation process does not of itself imply that the entire wage-price mechanism itself has this damped character. The solution of our first-order difference equation assumed constant values of the independent variables. But, to take only the most obvious case, prices will eventually respond to wage advances, and so the complete solution is less likely to be damped as much as our results indicate. Only an investigation of the dynamics of the entire Brookings-SSRC econometric model can determine the ultimate degree of damping involved.

9.2.8. *The magnitude of wage inflation*

From the equations listed above we can answer the following question: Assume an economy with 4 per cent unemployment, a normal profit margin in each industry and no change in the consumer price index. Under these conditions how fast would wages advance, if 1948–1960 relationships continue to prevail? Defining the "normal" profit ratio as the average prevailing in 1948–1960 plus $\frac{1}{2}\sigma$, setting the change in the consumer price index equal to zero and letting RU^* equal 0.04 (that is, $1/RU^* = 25$), we get the following equilibrium wage increases (table 9.10) [22]:

TABLE 9.10

Equilibrium wage change for given unemployment levels, profit share and price level.

Industry	Equilibrium change in wages under stated assumptions [a]
Contract construction	5.8
Durable manufacturing	5.0
Nondurable manufacturing	4.1
Wholesale and retail trade	4.7
Regulated industries	5.0
Residual industries	4.1

[a]) For assumptions, see text.

Since the rates of increase refer to average compensation per man-hour, they are slightly higher than the separate rates of advance of wages and salaries. There has been a steady secular rise during the postwar period in the ratio of salaried to wage employees. As we noted earlier, this "mix" change above will tend to raise average compensation per man-hour, since average salaries per hour are higher than average wages per hour.

Given a 3 per cent annual rate of increase in labor productivity, our results imply an "ex ante" wage push lifting unit labor costs by 1.5 to 2 per cent per year under conditions of full employment, without excess demand for labor. This estimate, of course, represents only a partial solution. The ultimate price creep would, of course, be somewhat larger as the influence of wages on prices led to a rise in the consumer price index and a further wage gain. To some extent this feedback might be offset if some part of the rise in unit labor costs was absorbed in profit margins. A full simultaneous solution will be necessary to take into account all of the indirect repercussions and to estimate the price "creep" associated with full employment.

9.2.9. *Other aspects of the regression results*

In all industries except the regulated group (which gives generally poor results), the unemployment rate is an important influence on the rate of change in wages. With our reciprocal formulation, the wage impact of a

[22]) The equilibrium wage increase is that which would prevail after the oscillations had disappeared so that $\varDelta w_t = \varDelta w_{t-4}$. The equilibrium therefore equals $a_1 q/(1+\lambda)$ where $a_1 q$ takes on values dictated by our assumptions listed above.

given change in unemployment is larger the lower the level of unemployment. On the basis of an unemployment coefficient obtained by averaging the durable and nondurable manufacturing coefficients, a decrease in unemployment from 4 to 2 per cent raises the annual rate of wage increase by 2.25 per cent, while an increase in unemployment from 4 to 6 per cent reduces this annual rate of wage gain by 0.75 per cent. In contract construction the general level of unemployment appears to have a larger influence on the rate of wage gain than in other industries, while, as noted before, it has little effect on the rate of wage advance in the regulated industries.

The coefficients for changes in the consumer price index vary substantially. In both durable and nondurable manufacturing the coefficients are large and significant. This is also true to a smaller extent in the residual industry group. In contract construction and trade, however, the consumer price index coefficients are small and insignificant. These results probably reflect differences in union and industry structure. Manufacturing industries tend to be characterized by relatively strong unions with industrywide wage bargains. Unions are also strong in construction, but wage bargains are geographically discrete. As a consequence, wage determinations are more likely to be influenced by local conditions, with less attention being paid to changes in the consumer price index. In the trade industries, unionism is weak and the consumer price index is much less likely to be taken explicitly into account. On the other hand, in both contract construction and trade the state of excess demand for labor (represented by the unemployment rate) is more important than in manufacturing.

The magnitude of the profit coefficient varies widely from industry to industry. In part this stems from the fact that the ratio of corporate profits to income originating is so different from one industry to another. In the case of contract construction, which is heavily represented by unincorporated firms, corporate profits are only a small percentage of total profits. Since quarterly estimates of unincorporated profits in this and other industries are of notoriously poor quality, we choose to use corporate profits as the best available proxy for total profits. While this leaves much to be desired, it appeared to be the most suitable alternative available.

9.3. Some further results

Gary Fromm recently refitted a number of the price and wage equations presented in this paper. The quarterly interpolations of output and income were re-estimated, using additional data; advantage was also taken of new and revised industry output, income, employment, and manhour series. In addition, the equations were fitted to time series starting after the Korean period (eliminating observations from 1949 through 1953:2) and running through 1962.

The results of the newly-fitted regressions differ from those presented here in several ways:

Price equations.   The deviations of actual from normal unit labor costs $(ULC - ULC^N)$ turned up with more "reasonable" coefficients in several industries. In the nondurable goods industries, this term now has a low coefficient of positive sign (compared to the negative coefficient in our results). In trade, our results showed the deviation coefficient larger than the normal unit labor cost coefficient; the revised fit for 1953–1962 shows the deviation coefficient in trade to be lower than the normal unit labor cost coefficient.

Wage equations.   When the equations were fitted to improved data for 1953–1962, the coefficients for changes in the CPI in the various industries tended to cluster more closely together than is true of our results. (Excluding the "residual" industry, the range is from 0.50 to 0.85.) The coefficient of the lagged wage change variable in durable and nondurable goods was much lower than in our results and not significantly different from zero. On the other hand, its importance in the regulated industries was much greater. The profits coefficient in durable goods loses significance and that for non-durable goods gains in significance when data from the later period are fitted.

The changes in coefficients which occurred when the period of fit was altered perhaps signal that further work needs to be done in isolating the proper structural relationships in the price and wage models. While we believe that the basic elements of our structural formulation are appropriate, it is clear that substantial further work needs to be done, particularly in experimenting with variations in lag structure and in the detailed specifications of variables.

9.4. *Appendix: Derivation of variables reflecting the effect on wage rates of a mix change in the labor force*

Let: MH_P = production worker man-hours
$\quad MH_O$ = nonproduction worker man-hours
$\quad W_P$ = production worker wages
$\quad W_O$ = nonproduction worker wages
$\quad W$ = average wage in the industry
$\quad MH$ = $MH_P + MH_O$.

Then:

$$W = W_P \left[\frac{MH_P}{MH}\right] + W_O \left[\frac{MH_O}{MH}\right] = W_P \left[\frac{MH_P}{MH}\right] + W_O \left[1 - \frac{MH_P}{MH}\right]$$

$$= \frac{MH_P}{MH}[W_P - W_O] + W_O. \tag{9.19}$$

Holding constant all variables except MH_P/MH, the proportionate change in W would be:

$$\frac{dW}{W} = \left[[W_P - W_O]d\frac{MH_P}{MH}\right] \bigg/ \left[\frac{MH_P}{MH}[W_P - W_O] + W_O\right].$$

Over a finite time span this expression would be approximated by:

$$\varDelta\left[\frac{MH_P}{MH}\right] \bigg/ \left[\frac{MH_P}{MH} + \frac{W_O}{[W_P - W_O]}\right].$$

In the case where the proportionate wage change was taken between quarters a year apart this would be:

$$\left(\frac{MH_P}{MH} - \left[\frac{MH_P}{MH}\right]_{-4}\right) \bigg/ \left(\left[\frac{MH_P}{MH}\right]_{-4} + \frac{W_O}{[W_P - W_O]}\right).$$

Assuming that $W_O/[W_P - W_O]$ is constant over the period in question, the expression depends only on MH_P/MH, the proportion of production worker man-hours to total man-hours. The value of $W_O/[W_P - W_O]$ for all manufacturing was $3.55/(2.52 - 3.55) = -0.0345$ in 1960. This was rounded to -0.035 and assumed to be constant over the period 1948 to 1960, giving the variable

$$\left(\frac{MH_P}{MH} - \left[\frac{MH_P}{MH}\right]_{-4}\right) \bigg/ \left(\left[\frac{MH_P}{MH_O}\right]_{-4} - 0.035\right) \qquad VAR\ 5$$

VAR 3 was found in a similar manner, with employment times average hours being put in place of man-hours in equation (9.19).

These two variables are clearly only rough approximations of the actual contribution of labor force mix change to wage rate changes. They are derived from expressions based on infinitesimal changes, and they assume the constancy of the ratio $W_O/(W_P - W_O)$. Since the changes are finite and the ratio changes over time, VAR 3 and VAR 5 would only be rough approximations. The hope was that the constant adjustment factor in the denominator would produce a variable which was linearly related to per cent wage change, which the simple per cent change in the proportion of production worker man-hours to total man-hours is not. Judging by the regression results, this aim was not accomplished.

CHAPTER 10

THE LABOR FORCE AND MARRIAGES AS ENDOGENOUS FACTORS

Contents

10.1. The labor force. 335

1. Introduction. 2. Unemployment. 3. Armed forces. 4. Hours. 5. Unpaid family workers. 6. Credit. 7. Wage rates.

10.2. Marriages 359

1. Introduction. 2. Armed forces. 3. Sex ratio. 4. The labor market. 5. Personnel procurement. 6. Population ratios. 7. Final results: marriages.

THE LABOR FORCE AND MARRIAGES AS ENDOGENOUS FACTORS [1])

STANLEY LEBERGOTT

Wesleyan University, Middletown, Connecticut

10.1. The labor force

10.1.1. Introduction

What makes the labor supply go round? Received theory tends to assume that hours fluctuate, that efficiency fluctuates—but that labor force participation rates respond hardly at all to economic forces. One of the most balanced reviews of recent thinking on cycle changes finds that "labor-force participation rates are largely determined by social attitudes, by techniques of production, and by economic factors which are only indirectly related to the balance of supply and demand in the labor market, e.g., the effect of the level of real income on the school leaving and retirement ages" [2]). In seeking to explain the rate of accumulation, Joan Robinson recently referred to Von Neumann's system, in which the labor force grows at the same rate as the stock of capital, being evoked by the necessary wage. She concludes that this will not do: "No doubt there is a connection between the rate of growth of population and the standard of life but it is unreliable and

[1]) For a very considerable amount of machine computation generously given the Brookings-SSRC econometric project, thanks are due to the Federal Reserve Board and Robert Steinberg, as well as to the Wesleyan University Computing Center and Thomas Buxton, and to the Dartmouth Computing Center and Thomas Kurtz. Seasonally adjusted labor force data, plus unpublished detail, were kindly prepared by Harold Goldstein and Robert Stein, of the Bureau of Labor Statistics. Lively and helpful comments were provided by faculty seminars at Stanford and Dartmouth.

[2]) James Duesenberry, *Business Cycles and Economic Growth* (New York: McGraw-Hill, 1958), p. 310. On pp. 313ff. Duesenberry shrewdly qualifies the conclusion, albeit apparently forced on him by the findings of labor economics.

apt to go in the contrary direction. We must allow the growth of the labor force to follow its own rate" [3]. Various models of growth produce extreme oscillations because the labor supply is defined as indifferent to economic forces, not being reliably available as a complement to capital in growth and responding so sluggishly to incentives as to make it no close substitute for any other input. There are, it is true, some compensations for the presence of this indifferent "bull in the china shop" of economics; by presuming a much weaker supply elasticity of labor than capital over recent decades, Kravis has explained apparent paradoxes in relative share trends [4]. But are these sufferings necessary for this small advantage? Since 1940 there has been an enormous rise in real *GNP*, accompanied by a substantial increase in labor supply. We know that the aggregate decline in hours has been small despite widespread concern about shorter hours. The best indication of this fact is that in 1960 hours worked by production workers in manufacturing averaged 39.7—within one point of the 1946 end-of-war figure, or indeed any year since then. If we look to hours for the entire labor force, the average fell markedly from 1946 to 1949 but has changed little since then [5].

It is possible that the other components of labor supply rose significantly. But with all due allowance for the zeal generated by the coffee break, or the growing effectiveness of reallocation among industries and occupations, we must do more if we are to explain how the huge rise in output was accommodated.

Let us begin with one initial point. The proportion in the labor force in this country *does* appear to be what Klein and Kosobud have happily termed one of the "great ratios" in economics. Indeed, estimates of my own suggest that the proportion of the population of 14 years and over in the labor force was 55.5 per cent under McKinley, was much the same under Harding and even by Mr. Eisenhower's time had risen only 3 percentage points. Does such apparent stability mean, as has been inferred, that the labor force is insensitive to economic pressures? [6] No more so than

[3] Joan Robinson, The Basic Theory of Normal Prices, *Quarterly Journal of Economics* (February, 1962) p. 13.

[4] Irving Kravis, Relative Income Shares in Fact and Theory, *American Economic Review* (December, 1959) p. 942.

[5] U. S. Bureau of the Census, Current Population Reports, Series P–50, No. 13, *Annual Report on the Labor Force, 1948*, p. 28, and Bureau of Labor Statistics, *Labor Force and Employment in 1961*, Special Report No. 23, p. A–27.

[6] The classic discussion is, of course, to be found in Clarence Long's *The Labor Force Under Changing Income and Employment* (Princeton, N. J.: Princeton University Press, 1958).

if a ratio of aggregate inputs maintained a near constant proportion to output. Certainly, to understand the process at work or merely to venture out on the high wire where economic predictors operate, we must first discern what basic forces were at work under this pleasant stability. Only then can we begin to consider the question, with any hope of solution, of whether such net stability (a) arises from mere chance or (b) reflects some massive compensating mechanism at work.

Suppose there were no connection between economic events in the intermediate term and the path taken by participation rates? Then we would have to attach a finite probability to the possibility that the course of labor supply would at times grossly exacerbate the course of the cycle. In depression years we would see an enormous flood of workers entering the labor market; in prosperity years we would find a sudden calm and an overwhelming shortage of workers in all occupations. Yet our experience shows no such apparent lack of contact. A comparison of unemployment rates since 1900 with the National Bureau of Economic Research cycle measures shows a fair consistency.

In labor force analysis this problem was posed most acutely during the later years of the great depression. The problem then was: Had unemployment been inflated by additional entrants, pressed into the labor market by need? If so, the increase in final demand required to abolish mass unemployment could be significantly milder than if no such labor market multiplier were at work. Put the husbands back to work and the women and children who had entered the labor force and joined the unemployed would voluntarily withdraw—so said one school. Another group found that no extra workers had entered the labor force. Despite extensive debate between Woytinsky, Don Humphrey and others, the issue remained unresolved when the war began, largely because the relevant empirical data were not close enough to the point. By referring to some data collected as part of the 1940 Census but never published we may, however, come to a somewhat firmer conclusion on this point (table 10.1).

Three aspects of table 10.1 are to be noted: (1) The participation rates for wives with husbands who were seeking work in all cases were above those for wives with employed husbands. In nearly all cases the excess was significant and sizable. Since some number of the employed husbands had surely been unemployed for a lengthy period, with a presumably similar direction of response, the difference between rates for women with husbands who had never been unemployed and those with unemployed husbands must have been still greater. (2) The excess in rates for those with husbands

TABLE 10.1

Participation rates for married women: April 1940 [a]).

Labor force	Age of wife				
	18–24	25–29	30–34	35–44	45–64
I. U.S. total					
Without children under 10					
a. Husband employed	27.87	35.86	30.94	13.78	8.53
b. Husband seeking work	30.08	46.04	42.86	33.16	15.29
c. Ratio: $b \div a$	1.08	1.28	1.39	1.77	1.79
With children under 10					
d. Husband employed	6.55	8.69	8.61	7.25	5.26
e. Husband seeking work	7.79	13.37	14.90	12.71	18.60
f. Ratio: $e \div d$	1.19	1.54	1.73	1.75	3.54
II. Metropolitan districts of 100 000 or more					
Without children under 10					
a. Husband employed	35.02	41.24	35.04	20.76	9.48
b. Husband seeking work	39.99	51.65	48.10	36.25	16.13
c. Ratio $b \div a$	1.14	1.25	1.37	1.75	1.70
With children under 10					
d. Husband employed	6.78	9.05	8.91	7.63	5.40
e. Husband seeking work	9.37	15.08	15.88	13.50	8.46
f. Ratio: $e \div d$	1.38	1.67	1.76	1.77	1.57

Source   Unpublished data from the 1940 Census.
[a]) With husband present.

seeking work increased steadily and markedly by age. We take this to be a reflection of duration. Those who had been exposed to unemployment as a family unit for only a relatively short period—e.g., wives 18 to 24—showed the least response. As the exposure of the family unit to unemployment lengthened, this response increased, and so the 7.9 per cent excess for the youngest age group became 79.2 per cent for the oldest. (3) Data by type of region show similar contrasts, of which we show only the figures for the major metropolitan districts. The excess rates, in other words, are not a reflection of any composition difference; data for urban or rural exposure to unemployment, when exposure was for more than a brief period, showed an increased volume of women in the labor force. The data for married women are particularly significant because they have been the central group in the rise in participation rates since 1940. Yet it is not unreasonable to assume that women generally, and the younger males as well, tended to enter the labor market under the stimulus of depression unemployment [7]).

How is it, then, that the major study on this point gives us a dusty answer, suggesting that, while there was some such response (for nonwhites in certain areas), for the central white groups (and thereby for the U.S. totals) this is by no means true and concluding that there appears to have been little response to this long span of unemployment? [8]) The answer is essentially this: While there was a positive response to unemployment there was a negative response to emergency work—and the published Census data combine the two groups. The employment of the husband on emergency work provided income sufficient to attenuate the labor force response of the wife to a total lack of family income. Moreover, the legal conditions for receipt of such income tended to outlaw work by the wife [9]).

Referring now to data for more recent periods we can make two types of comparison. For the first we may refer to figures given by the Monthly Report on the Labor Force for the years since 1950 [10]):

Participation Rates for Wives	All ages		Ages 25–44
	1950	1957	1957
Husbands employed—total	23.2	32.3	28.8
Husbands unemployed	33.1	40.4	43.5

So far we have been making comparisons on cross section data. The variety of cohorts that can be singled out in the 1940 Census data are such as to give us reasonable confidence. The more recent figures permit only two-way

---

[7]) This, of course, was evident in the 1937 Census of Partial Employment, Unemployment and Occupations, although the magnitude of the increase in actual participation rates seems to have been exaggerated by some respondents. Cf. Calvert Dedrick and Morris Hansen, *The Enumerative Check Census*, Vol. 4 (Washington D.C.: U. S. Government Printing Office, 1938).

[8]) Long, *op. cit.*

[9]) In addition, it is possible that the very low rates for those with wives doing emergency work were understated to the census enumerators for fear of discovery. If so, the true figures would show an even greater excess of participation rates for wives with unemployed husbands. However, analysis of the data by rural-urban categories suggests this not to have been so.

[10]) U. S. Bureau of the Census, Current Population Reports, Series P–50.

comparisons, and while the differences are statistically significant it is possible that other contributory variables are at work.

As one guide we can turn to the actual experience in the months since April 1940, for which we have continuing reports of the Monthly Report on the Labor Force. These record worker rates for each age-sex group, though unfortunately not by family status. However a special tabulation by Arnold Katz (then of the Bureau of Labor Statistics) for a Yale thesis reveals the contrast between the experience of women with husbands unemployed in 1958 and those with husbands not unemployed in that year [11]). Of 100 in each group, some 22 in the unemployed-husband group increased their own rates from 1958 to 1959, as against 11 in the other.

Husband's employment status in 1958	Wife's labor force status 1958 to 1959		
	Increased rate	No change	Decreased rate
Unemployed 100	21.6	61.6	16.8
Employed 100	11.1	72.3	16.6

Our review of the above data suggests, in sum, that participation rates do not go their way grandly indifferent to the state of the labor market.

After this introductory review, let us turn to our immediate concern—to explain quarterly variations in the participation rates as reported by the Current Population Reports data.

10.1.2. Unemployment

Variations in labor force rates must somehow link with the over-all state of the labor market as evidenced by unemployment. But what must that link be? (a) It is clear that heavy unemployment, pervasive and debilitating to the economy, will cut job opportunities and thereby keep some women from entering the market. Moreover, it will block wages from rising at their accustomed rate and may even depress them. Such consequences would then become a further force to keep women from entering the labor market and actually drive some out of it. (b) On the other hand, more than price effects will be at work. One obvious result of the rise in unemploy-

---

[11]) In an unpublished paper presented at the 1960 Annual Meeting of the Econometric Society.

ment will be a decline in the number of husbands at work. The consequent drop in family income will induce some wives (and secondary earners in general) to enter the labor force.

We need not take a polar position in favor of only one of the above forces being at work, for they all were. Our question then becomes an empirical one: On balance are there net exits or entrances?

TABLE 10.2

Correlations of female labor force participation rates and unemployment [a]).

A. Based on data for 1948:4–1960:3

      0.12   unemployment rate
   −0.40   reciprocal of unemployment rate

B. Based on data for 1949:3–1960:4 and data for 1948:4–1960:3

Unemployment period	1949:3–1960:4	1948:4–1960:3
−5 weeks	0.28	0.42
5–14 weeks	0.24	0.36
15+ weeks	0.40	0.45
27+ weeks		0.49

C. Based on data for 1949:1–1960:4

      Number unemployed 27+ weeks as a ratio to:

        0.49   Total unemployment [b])
        0.45   Total labor force
        0.48   Male total labor force
        0.45   Male total labor force: prior quarter

      Number unemployed 19+ weeks as a ratio to:
        0.44   Male civilian labor force

[a]) Column headings indicate period of fit.
[b]) 1949:3–1960:4.

In table 10.2 we present data relevant to an answer for 1949–1960 [12]). The relationship with the unemployment rate per se as shown in that table is surely a trivial one. If we take the reciprocal of the rate, however, as some have urged, a very substantial rise in the correlation coefficient occurs. Despite the attractiveness of this high coefficient we reject the use of the

[12]) Because a variety of runs were made on different computers, involving different analyses, the time periods used were not always uniform.

reciprocal. We do so largely because the basis for choosing it is simply a
hunch that it will work: Its amplitude *is* greater than that of the rate for an
equal change in the labor market. But the reason for choosing it should lie
in the economic forces at work rather than the arithmetic of relationship.
And these cannot be discerned by contemplating our reciprocal, however
extended such contemplation may be.

   If we emphasize income effects, then surely an analysis by duration is
more meaningful. Temporary interruptions of family income are common-
place for many million American families. In 1961, for example, over 15
million American workers went through a period of unemployment [13]).
If we turn to the war-production high-employment year of 1951, when priori-
ties, labor incentives and a tight labor market were all present, we still
find that a third of all full-time workers (both total and male) worked less
than 50 weeks [14]). In large measure this means that they were unemployed
for part of the year. The response of families to such a regular level of work
interruptions must affect their general level of participation. It could perhaps
explain why the female participation rates are about 30 per cent rather
than, for example, 15 or 20 per cent (if we lived in a persistently full-employment economy) or 40 or 50 per cent (if men were employed even less regularly
but jobs could always be found for women because of their lower wage rates
—or greater charm). But we are dealing with a single decade out of our
total experience. Figures from the monthly Report on the Labor Force
became available only in 1940. The 1940–1941 end-of-depression results
are surely not relevant for making current estimates of labor force functions,
while the 1942–1947 rates are so affected by the war, demobilization and
postwar restocking that they too are not closely relevant. Let us take as
given that substratum of knowledge and customary reactions which goes to
fix the general level of labor force rates. Doing so, we find it reasonable for
there to be a clear-cut, if mild, response to short-term unemployment.
The numbers unemployed "less than 5 weeks" correlate 0.28 with female
labor force rates—about the same correlation as for the "5 to 14 week"
group but substantially below the 0.40 for the "15 week and over" unemployment group. It is not unemployment but harsh experience of prolonged
unemployment and loss of income that eventually induces a set of family
adjustments. The most significant of these are probably those apparent to

[13]) *Manpower Report of the President*, 1963, p. 162.
[14]) U. S. Bureau of the Census, Current Population Reports, *Work Experience of the
Population in 1951*, Series P–50, No. 43, p. 7.

the social agency and the marriage counselor. The effects that appear in the labor market include a rising tide of wives and children who enter the market. Some of the children come in a while before they normally would —perhaps taking a part-time job while still in school. Some of the wives return to work somewhat before their children are at the age when they planned to return. But a goodly number of wives and children enter who would not otherwise enter.

By extending our span of experience to include an additional three quarters (1948 : 4 through 1949 : 2), we improve the correlation coefficients significantly for the short-duration groups. However, that for the long-duration group changes only mildly. This difference in sensitivity to about a 10 per cent increase in observations suggests that in addition to our analytic preference for the long-duration group the empirical results are stabler for that group too—hence, to be preferred if we are seeking basic structural relationships.

For measuring the hard-core unemployment group a variety of alternatives are available. The absolute number in this group is no sufficient measure; under a given set of productivity advances it could rise slowly over time. It could certainly gain with the mere rise in the size of the labor force, although this does *not* seem to have taken place between 1949 and 1960. Alternatively we may use the hard core as a proportion of total unemployment. Although this ratio does give the highest correlation, it is undesirable for predictive use for it requires us to forecast unemployment, despite the fact that we typically want to forecast the labor force in the first place largely to help forecast unemployment (as a residual). This constitutes no problem for the use of these equations in the context of a complete model but does when utilized in partial systems. Alternatively we may choose the ratio to the total labor force or to the male total labor force. Both are satisfactory. Both give much the same correlations. Projections of the male labor force, however, can be made with a smaller percentage of error than those of the total. But should we use the ratio to the male total labor force in the given or in the prior quarter? We prefer the latter. Time is required for the family to recognize the bleak record of the general labor market and to admit that the dismal experience of the family head has been a persistent and not a transient state. A further response lag occurs before the wife adjusts her horizons to entering the labor market, makes arrangements for the children and actually begins either to look for work or (if she enters the labor force only when she becomes employed) actually finds a job.

10.1.3. Armed forces

It is quite clear, as wartime experience boldly revealed, that participation rates are far higher for women with husbands in the armed forces than those otherwise employed. Current Population Reports data for three years permit us to underscore this generalization: [15])

Participation rate for wives	1944	1951	1953
Husband employed	22	25	31
Husband in armed forces	52	40	42

But these cross section data, without further detail, do not result in much progress. It is obvious that women with husbands in the armed forces are typically younger and more likely, therefore, to be at work regardless of the status of their husbands.

A straightforward correlation of the participation rate for women aged 14 and older with the size of the armed forces is a positive 0.20. However, the size of the armed forces will show a scale effect, and the relationship might be that produced by any rising series. To remove such a trend we compute armed forces as a ratio to male population, thus marking more precisely the shift in relative importance of husbands and fathers in the armed forces to all husbands and fathers. The correlation drops to 0.04, about as close to zero as is practicable in correlation analysis. Hence, the apparent relation to armed forces proves to be much more one with a rising trend and in significant measure reflects rising defense output, rising employment opportunities, wage rates, etc.

We turn, therefore, to an alternative measure of this factor. For this purpose we use figures on personnel procurement by the Defense Department, including inductions, first enlistments, reenlistments and militia call-ups [16]).

Correlations with components of this total and various combinations of components were made, but the best results were those for the combined group. In part this may reflect variations in the accuracy of coding, changing differences in the advantage of entering the armed forces in one category

---

[15]) U. S. Bureau of the Census, Current Population Reports, Series P-50.

[16]) Data from Office of the Secretary of Defense, Directorate for Statistical Services, *Selected Manpower Statistics* (February 1, 1953) and corresponding tables for earlier years kindly provided by Harold Wool, Office of the Secretary of Defense.

as against another, etc.—but in any event factors apparently unrelated to participation rates of females. The overall correlation is 0.32, but a negative 0.32, a point we shall discuss shortly. For the period 1949 : 3–1960 : 4 the correlation is −0.39, and when we divide personnel procurement by the male population, that variable correlates −0.45 with the total participation rate for females.

Analysis by age helps explain the negative coefficient.

Age of females	Correlation coefficients of female participation rates and Defense Department personnel ratio
20+	−0.45
14–19	0.43
20–24	0.22
25–34	−0.11
35–44	−0.43
45–54	−0.53

For the age group from which husbands were inducted in large numbers, ages 14 to 19, the correlation is positive and high. For the other age group with heavy inductions, ages 20 to 24, the correlation is likewise positive, though not as high. We presume the lower correlation coefficient here is reporting the effect of young children on participation rates—for those 20 to 24 had more young childeren than those 14 to 19, thus partially offsetting the impulse to work related to husbands' entrance into the armed forces. But while loneliness, economic need and other factors in differing combination were incentives for younger women to work when their husbands or boy friends entered the armed forces, such incentives could not apply with equal effect to the entire category of women in any of the older age groups. In fact the coefficients are negative, very significantly so for the older age groups. Here we take the results to mean simply that personnel procurement is operating as a proxy for income effects—increases in the armed forces tend to be concurrent with increases in hardware procurement, inflationary pressures, rises in wage rates and upward occupational mobility. These factors generate higher incomes for husbands of older women, thereby reducing their incentive to work. In our final equation for the participation rate of women 20 and over as a single group, these influences are adequately allowed for by the inclusion of other variables, and the partial correlation coefficient for the personnel procurement ratio becomes +0.452, in contrast with the simple coefficient of −0.45.

10.1.4. Hours

After reviewing a considerable number of other measures of cycle conditions, we have ended by utilizing average hours worked in durable manufacturing. Some of the other variables—such as orders-sales ratios, orders, production and employment—treated with various transformations, yielded slightly better correlation coefficients. However, for simplicity in continued operation of the model, the hours estimate is preferable. It functions here as a measure of labor market opportunities, but in a special way. It will be noted that the simple correlation coefficient is -0.39, while the partial in the final equation is -0.554. Does this mean that the fewer the job opportunities the more women enter the labor market, remembering that we allow for unemployment per se in the multiple correlation that produces this -0.554 partial? By no means. It is rather that the hours figure is reporting on the course of recovery and decline. At the weaker points in the cycle, associated with lower average hours, women stand a better chance of finding work than men. The process of breaking down barriers to the employment of women in particular jobs takes place at a greater rate then, advantage then being taken of the lower wage rates they typically accept. At peak stages in the cycle it is more advantageous in many instances to have the existing labor force—dominantly a male labor force—work additional hours. No hiring costs are incurred for breaking-in time, less delay is incurred in getting out orders and additional incomes are paid to the existing labor force without actually changing the wage structure. The correlation with average hours reflects this process of changing advantage.

10.1.5. Unpaid family workers

The number of unpaid family workers as reported in the Current Population Reports constitutes a special category in the total. They are beneath the level of notice if they work 14 hours or less but are immediately welcomed into the count at 15 hours. The distinction is, of course, one of those necessary if arbitrary ones required in practical survey work. It is an attempt to rule out those engaged only incidentally in the process of production on farms (and the small group in other family enterprises). But it is this measurement distinction that is at the root of the positive coefficient we find for this variable. At first sight one would surely expect a negative sign: the rise in farm incomes would attract unpaid family workers away—to school or to repose. And so it must. But, on balance, there is evidently a prior, and a more substantial, effect at work. It transforms the hidden remnant of family workers, once ignored by the enumerating process because they worked a handful of hours, into persons working a much fuller work week. But once they cross the magic 15-hour line they become visible in our count of unpaid family workers. Hence, rising off-farm job opportunities, which tend to increase farm wage rates and costs, induce farmers to employ family workers more fully and thereby increase the reported female labor force. (The additional movement off farms does not apparently affect the labor force totals, merely shifting workers from one industry to another.)

10.1.6. Credit

We turn now to a variable that reflects a combined set of family decisions, one result of which is the entrance of the wife into the labor force. That variable is the volume of consumer credit extensions (deflated by the GNP consumer durable implicit price index) in the prior quarter. Some years ago, the Federal Reserve Board sponsored a special supplement to the Current Population Reports, providing information on both debts and labor force activity of identical families [17]). We have elsewhere taken these data to show that families with working wives are more likely to have debts than families that do not—debts for consumer durables in particular [18]). From this fact we have inferred that a linked set of family decisions involves the decision to acquire a consumer durable, the wife's entering the labor force, the use of credit to permit immediate acquisition of the durable and, finally, the wife's income providing the marginal income required to pay off the debt thus incurred. Certainly some wives entered the labor force to help pay for the durable. The need to keep payments up on a previously acquired car forced some other wives to enter the labor force. But for many families the sequence of decisions is unclear and the formal facts on purchases, beginning of new jobs, etc., do not testify clearly to the causal ordering. Most importantly, it is the combined interrelated set of forces and decisions that is of keenest interest. We take the figures on credit extensions as indicators of the forces in that sequence which induce women to enter the

---

[17]) Federal Reserve Board, *Consumer Installment Credit*, Vol. I, Part 2, *Growth and Import* (1957); cf. in particular the section by Murray Wernick, pp. 191ff.

[18]) Cf. S. Lebergott, Population Change and the Supply of Labor, in *Demographic and Economic Change in Developed Countries*, Universities-National Bureau of Economic Research (Princeton, N. J.: Princeton University Press, 1960), pp. 400ff.

labor force in our particular era. Since the automobile and television set constitute the quintessence of family achievement, we assume that the era is one that will persist for some time, with these variables being of continuing relevance.

10.1.7. Wage rates

It will be noted that no wage rate series is used in the final equations, although perhaps the highest correlations are with wage rates—whether the Bureau of Labor Statistics retail hourly earnings, the special hourly wage and salary earnings series that Charles Schultze has developed for the Brookings-SSRC econometric model from Bureau of Labor Statistics and Office of Business Economics data, the factory earnings series, etc. One basic reason is that all the wage series are obviously highly collinear. By using the retail earnings series to reflect wage trends for females, it is not certain how much of the trend is a general one for all wage rates and prices—hence, not particularly relevant to the female labor force. Let us attempt to allow for this, for instance, by taking the retail wage rate as a percentage of the manufacturing—to indicate the advantage offered in an industry primarily employing women as against the general wage trend. The correlation coefficient, as table 10.3 shows, becomes negative—significantly negative. What has happened, it is clear, is that a single equation system is incapable of handling such a relationship. For the negative coefficient suggests we are then contemplating a demand relationship rather than a supply one. It is not that the retail wage rate induces women to leave the labor force but that a substantial flow of women into the labor force tends to depress (relatively) wages in those industries into which they enter in disproportionately great numbers.

Multiple regressions in table 10.4 combine the various influences on female participation rates that had previously been treated separately. These equation forms, or variants of them, are to be used in the Brookings-SSRC model.

Two alternative measures of the participation for females 20 years and older were developed. The first series, $[L_{F20+}] - [L_{F20+}]^{PRO}$ measures the excess over trend. It has been suggested that instead of direct use of participation we consider deviations from trend. The problem here, of course, is how one is to establish the trend. One procedure, originating with the work by Loring Wood and John Durand, is to select dates of "normal" participation, fitting a curve to these figures and extrapolating.

TABLE 10.3

Table 10.3

Correlation coefficients of specified variables and labor force participation rates for females aged 20 and over [a]).

Cycle Measure	
Average weekly hours, manufacturing	−0.35
Average weekly hours, durable manufacturing	−0.40
Orders-sales ratio	−0.35
Orders-sales ratio, prior quarter	−0.28
Employment of production workers, manufacturing	−0.15
Unemployment	
Number unemployed for 27 or more weeks	0.51
Number unemployed 27 or more weeks as proportion of total unemployment	0.48
Number unemployed 27 or more weeks as proportion of total male labor force	0.48
Number unemployed 27 or more weeks as proportion of total male labor force, prior quarter	0.45
Number unemployed for 15 or more weeks, prior quarter less four quarters previously	−0.10
Number unemployed for 15 or more weeks as proportion of total unemployment, lagged change (see last variable in equation 10.4)	0.05
Credit	
Deflated consumer credit extensions, prior quarter	0.87
Deflated consumer credit extensions, ratio of change from prior quarter to the difference of extensions in the prior quarter and three quarters previously	0.18
Defense Personnel Procurement	
U.S. armed forces military personnel procurement	−0.39
Procurement as proportion of male population aged 14 and over	−0.45
Earnings	
Average hourly wages and salaries in retail trade	0.95
Average hourly wages in retail trade	0.95
Average hourly earnings of production workers in manufacturing	0.95
Average hourly earnings, retail trade as proportion of manufacturing	−0.40
Marginal Participation	
Unpaid females employed 15 or more hours per week in agriculture	−0.29

[a]) 1949 : 3–1960 : 4.

TABLE 10.4

Labor force participation rate equations for females aged 20 and over [a].

$$\frac{L_{F20+}}{N_{F20+}} = 0.5595 + \underset{(0.265)}{0.840}\left[\frac{DRFT}{N_{M14+}}\right] + \underset{(0.01496)}{0.03713} E_{F15AF} - \underset{(0.001831)}{0.007624} H_{MD} + \underset{(0.2891)}{0.7928}\left[\frac{U27+}{L_{M14+}}\right]_{-1}$$

$$+ \underset{(0.00015)}{0.00169}\left[\frac{CDTE_P}{P_{CD}}\right]$$

$$\bar{R}^2 = 0.818 \qquad S_e = 0.00661 \tag{10.1}$$

$$\frac{L_{F20+}}{N_{F20+}} = 0.5457 + \underset{(0.053)}{0.121} DRFT + \underset{(0.01532)}{0.02436} E_{F15AF} - \underset{(0.00193)}{0.00687} H_{MD} + \underset{(0.00015)}{0.00169}\left[\frac{CDTE_P}{P_{CD}}\right]$$

$$\bar{R}^2 = 0.808 \qquad S_e = 0.00713 \tag{10.2}$$

$$\frac{L_{F20+}}{N_{F20+}} = 0.2919 + \underset{(0.048)}{0.039} DRFT + \underset{(0.321)}{0.591}\left[\frac{U27+}{L_{M14+}}\right]_{-1} + \underset{(0.00016)}{0.00154}\left[\frac{CDTE_P}{P_{CD}}\right] \qquad \bar{R}^2 = 0.766 \qquad S_e = 0.00777 \tag{10.3}$$

$$\frac{L_{F20+}}{N_{F20+}} = 0.2679 + \underset{(0.336)}{1.062}\left[\frac{U27+}{L_{M14+}}\right] + \underset{(0.049)}{0.036} DRFT + \underset{(0.01591)}{0.02632} E_{F15AF} + \underset{(0.00015)}{0.00159}\left[\frac{CDTE_P}{P_{CD}}\right]$$

$$- \underset{(0.0025)}{0.0042}\frac{\left[\frac{U15+}{U}\right]_{-1} - \left[\frac{U15+}{U}\right]_{-2}}{\frac{1}{2}\left\{\left[\frac{U15+}{U}\right]_{-2} - \left[\frac{U15+}{U}\right]_{-4}\right\}}$$

$$\bar{R}^2 = 0.806 \qquad S_e = 0.00725 \tag{10.4}$$

$$\frac{L_{F20+}}{N_{F20+}} = 0.2719 + \underset{(0.047)}{0.064} DRFT + \underset{(0.00702)}{0.02154}[U27+] + \underset{(0.01556)}{0.01978} E_{F15AF} + \underset{(0.00016)}{0.00156}\left[\frac{CDTE_P}{P_{CD}}\right] \tag{10.5}$$

$$\bar{R}^2 = 0.795 \qquad S_e = 0.00726$$

$$\frac{L_{F20+}}{N_{F20+}} = 0.2721 + (0.247) \ldots + (0.345)\left[\frac{}{N_{M14+}}\right]\ldots_{-1} + (0.01565) E_{F15AF} + (0.00016)\left[\frac{CDTE_P}{P_{CD}}\right] \tag{10.6}$$

$$\bar{R}^2 = 0.771 \qquad S_e = 0.00742$$

$$\frac{L_{F20+}}{N_{F20+}} = 0.2957 + \frac{0.732}{(0.288)}\left[\frac{U27+}{L_{M14+}}\right] - \frac{0.0038}{(0.0023)}\left\{\left[\frac{U15+}{U}\right]_{-1} - \left[\frac{U15+}{U}\right]_{-2} - \frac{1}{2}\left\{\left[\frac{U15+}{U}\right]_{-2} - \left[\frac{U15+}{U}\right]_{-4}\right\}\right\} + \frac{0.00150}{(0.00014)}\left[\frac{CDTE_P}{P_{CD}}\right] \tag{10.7}$$

$$\bar{R}^2 = 0.773 \qquad S_e = 0.00738$$

$$\frac{L_{F20+}}{N_{F20+}} = 0.2043 + \frac{1.82}{(1.66)}\left[\frac{U27+}{L_{M14+}}\right]_{-1} + \frac{0.04308}{(0.00813)} E_{F15AF} + \frac{0.08663}{(0.00381)} RWS_{TR} \qquad \bar{R}^2 = 0.937 \qquad S_e = 0.00386 \tag{10.8}$$

$$\frac{L_{F20+}}{N_{F20+}} = 0.2719 + \frac{0.988}{(0.318)}\left[\frac{U27+}{L_{M14+}}\right] + \frac{0.0272}{(0.0158)} E_{F15AF} - \frac{0.0048}{(0.0023)}\left\{\left[\frac{U15+}{U}\right]_{-1} - \left[\frac{U15+}{U}\right]_{-2} - \frac{1}{2}\left\{\left[\frac{U15+}{U}\right]_{-2} - \left[\frac{U15+}{U}\right]_{-4}\right\}\right\}$$

$$+ \frac{0.00155}{(0.00014)}\left[\frac{CDTE_P}{P_{CD}}\right]$$

$$\bar{R}^2 = 0.784 \qquad S_e = 0.00721 \tag{10.9}$$

$$\frac{L_{F20+}}{N_{F20+}} = 0.4970 + \frac{0.0177}{(0.0065)}[U27+] + \frac{0.783}{(0.258)}\left[\frac{DRFT}{N_{M14+}}\right] + \frac{0.0369}{(0.0149)} E_{F15AF} + \frac{0.00607}{(0.00185)} H_{MD} + \frac{0.00168}{(0.00015)}\left[\frac{CDTE_P}{P_{CD}}\right] \tag{10.10}$$

$$\bar{R}^2 = 0.818 \qquad S_e = 0.00660$$

$$\frac{L_{F20+}}{N_{F20+}} = 0.2959 + \frac{0.56}{(0.30)}\left[\frac{U27+}{L_{M14+}}\right]_{-1} - \frac{0.0036}{(0.0024)}\left\{\left[\frac{U15+}{U}\right]_{-1} - \left[\frac{U15+}{U}\right]_{-2} - \frac{1}{2}\left\{\left[\frac{U15+}{U}\right]_{-2} - \left[\frac{U15+}{U}\right]_{-4}\right\}\right\} + \frac{0.00152}{(0.00015)}\left[\frac{CDTE_P}{P_{CD}}\right] \tag{10.11}$$

$$\bar{R}^2 = 0.757 \qquad S_e = 0.00764$$

TABLE 10.4 (Continued)

	$\dfrac{L_{F20+}}{N_{F20+}}$	$CDTE_P$	$DRFT$	$\dfrac{DRFT}{N_{M14+}}$	H_{MD}	$\dfrac{U27+}{L_{M14+}}$	$\left[\dfrac{U27+}{L_{M14+}}\right]_{-1}$	$\dfrac{\left[\frac{U15+}{U}\right]_{-1} - \left[\frac{U15+}{U}\right]_{-2}}{\frac{1}{2}\left\{\left[\frac{U15+}{U}\right]_{-2} - \left[\frac{U15+}{U}\right]_{-4}\right\}}$	E_{F15AF}		$U27+\ RWS_{TR}$
$\overline{X}$	0.3533	34.97	0.8525	0.01518	40.73	0.00659	0.00653	−0.7418	0.7355	0.3176	1.340
σ	0.0153	8.30	0.2865	0.00581	0.79	0.00412	0.00407	4.8831	0.0833	0.0131	0.184
Correlations											
Zero order	0.86	−0.39	−0.45	−0.40	0.48	0.45	0.05	−0.29	0.51	0.95	
Partial in eq.											
(10.1)		0.88		0.45	−0.55		0.40		0.37		
(10.2)		0.87	0.35		−0.49				0.24		
(10.3)		0.83	0.13				0.28				
(10.4)		0.86	0.11			0.45		−0.26	0.26		
(10.5)		0.85	0.21						0.20	0.44	
(10.6)		0.84		0.20		0.42			0.18		
(10.7)		0.85				0.37		−0.24			
(10.8)							0.17		0.64	0.96	
(10.9)		0.86				0.44		−0.31	0.26		
(10.10)		0.88		0.43	−0.47				0.37	0.40	

a) See pp. 357–358 for definition of variables.

TABLE 10.5

Labor force participation rate equations for females aged 20 and over.

A. Deviation from projection

$$[L_{F20+}] - [L_{F20+}]^{\text{PRO}} = 9.709 + \underset{(0.454)}{1.159}\,[U27+] + \underset{(18.3)}{55.3}\left[\frac{DRFT}{N_{M14+}}\right] + \underset{(1.050)}{4.028}\,E_{F15_{AF}} - \underset{(0.1301)}{0.3608}\,H_{MD}$$

$$+ \underset{(0.001)}{0.084}\left[\frac{CDTE_P}{P_{CD}}\right] \tag{10.12}$$

$$\bar{R}^2 = 0.666 \qquad S_e = 0.4650$$

$$[L_{F20+}] - [L_{F20+}]^{\text{PRO}} = -3.677 + \underset{(23.5)}{65.9}\left[\frac{U27+}{L_{M14+}}\right] + \underset{(16.8)}{28.4}\left[\frac{DRFT}{N_{M14+}}\right] + \underset{(1.064)}{2.952}\,E_{F15_{AF}} + \underset{(0.001)}{0.079}\left[\frac{CDTE_P}{P_{CD}}\right] \tag{10.13}$$

$$\bar{R}^2 = 0.607 \qquad S_e = 0.5049 \qquad \bar{X} = 2.12 \qquad \sigma = 0.796$$

$[L_{F20+}] - [L_{F20+}]^{\text{PRO}}$:

Correlations	$CDTE_P$	$\dfrac{DRFT}{N_{M14+}}$	H_{MD}	$U27+$	$\dfrac{U27+}{L_{M14+}}$	$E_{F15_{AF}}$
Zero order	0.73	−0.31	−0.29	0.41	0.38	−0.08
Partial in eq. (10.12)	0.79	0.44	−0.41	0.38		0.52
(10.13)	0.75	0.26			0.41	0.40

354

TABLE 10.5 (Continued)

B. As proportion of trend

$$\frac{L_{F20+}}{[L_{F20+}]^T} = 1.231 + \frac{0.0325}{(0.0152)}[U27+] + \frac{1.63}{(0.61)}\left[\frac{DRFT}{N_{M14+}}\right] + \frac{0.1339}{(0.0351)}E_{F15AF} - \frac{0.009855}{(0.004316)}H_{MD} + \frac{0.00237}{(0.00035)}\left[\frac{CDTE_P}{P_{CD}}\right] \quad (10.14)$$

$\bar{R}^2 = 0.573$ $S_e = 0.01553$

$$\frac{L_{F20+}}{[L_{F20+}]^T} = 0.865 + \frac{1.84}{(0.76)}\left[\frac{U27+}{L_{M14+}}\right] + \frac{0.892}{(0.550)}\left[\frac{DRFT}{N_{M14+}}\right] + \frac{0.1044}{(0.0345)}E_{F15AF} + \frac{0.00223}{(0.00036)}\left[\frac{CDTE_P}{P_{CD}}\right] \quad (10.15)$$

$\bar{R}^2 = 0.526$ $S_e = 0.01637$

$\dfrac{L_{F20+}}{[L_{F20+}]^T}$: $\bar{X} = 1.046$ $\sigma = 0.0235$

Correlations	$\frac{CDTE_P}{P_{CD}}$	$\frac{DRFT}{N_{M14+}}$	H_{MD}	$U27+$	$\frac{U27+}{L_{M14+}}$	E_{F15AF}
Zero order	0.661	−0.252	−0.219	0.334	0.311	0.012
Partial in eq. (10.14)	0.736	0.392	−0.341	0.324		0.521
(10.15)	0.702	0.251			0.356	0.432

TABLE 10.6

Labor force participation rate equations for females aged 14 to 19 and 14 and over.

A. Females aged 14 to 19

$$\frac{L_{F1419}}{N_{F1419}} = 0.2573 + \frac{0.07612}{(0.02038)}\, E_{F15_{AF}} - \frac{1.134}{(0.412)} \left[\frac{U27+}{L_{M14+}}\right] \qquad \bar{R}^2 = 0.503 \qquad S_e = 0.00985 \qquad (10.16)$$

$$\frac{L_{F1419}}{N_{F1419}} = 0.2524 + \frac{0.0743}{(0.0204)}\, E_{F15_{AF}} - \frac{0.92}{(0.46)} \left[\frac{U27+}{L_{M14+}}\right] + \frac{0.317}{(0.300)} \left[\frac{DRFT}{N_{M14+}}\right] \qquad \bar{R}^2 = 0.481 \qquad S_e = 0.00984 \quad (10.17)$$

$\dfrac{L_{F1419}}{N_{F1419}}$: $\quad \bar{X} = 0.3058 \qquad \sigma = 0.01351$

B. Females aged 14 and over

$$\frac{L_{F14+}}{N_{F14+}} = 0.4769 + \frac{0.01342}{(0.00617)}\,[U27+] + \frac{0.738}{(0.241)} \left[\frac{DRFT}{N_{M14+}}\right] + \frac{0.0445}{(0.0143)}\, E_{F15_{AF}} - \frac{0.00562}{(0.00177)}\, H_{MD} + \frac{0.00147}{(0.00014)} \left[\frac{CDTE_P}{P_{CD}}\right] \qquad (10.18)$$

$\bar{R}^2 = 0.773 \qquad S_e = 0.006318$

$\dfrac{L_{F14+}}{N_{F14+}}$: $\quad \bar{X} = 0.3479 \qquad \sigma = 0.01312$

	$\dfrac{CDTE_P}{P_{CD}}$	$\dfrac{DRFT}{N_{M14+}}$	H_{MD}	$E_{F15_{AF}}$	$\dfrac{U27+}{L_{M14+}}$	$U27+$
Partial correlation in eq. (10.16)				0.50	-0.39	
(10.17)		0.16		0.49	-0.30	
(10.18)	0.86	0.43	-0.45	0.45		0.33

TABLE 10.7

Labor force participation rate equations for males aged 20 and over and 14 to 19.

A. Males aged 20 and over

$$\frac{L_{M20+}}{N_{M20+}} = 0.9634 - \frac{0.48}{(0.10)}\left[\frac{U27+}{L_{M14+}}\right]_{-1} + \frac{0.001512}{(0.000500)}H_{MD} - \frac{0.4188}{(0.0271)}\left[\frac{L_{F20+}}{N_{F20+}}\right]_{-1} \quad \bar{R}^2 = 0.920 \quad S_e = 0.0024 \quad (10.19)$$

$$\frac{L_{M20+}}{N_{M20+}} = 1.0352 + \frac{0.0039}{(0.0020)}OBM_M - \frac{0.0335}{(0.0188)}\left[\frac{U27+}{U}\right] - \frac{0.4542}{(0.0358)}\left[\frac{L_{F20+}}{N_{F20+}}\right]_{-1} \quad \bar{R}^2 = 0.862 \quad S_e = 0.0032 \quad (10.20)$$

$$\frac{L_{M20+}}{N_{M20+}}: \quad \bar{X} = 0.8745 \quad \sigma = 0.0088$$

Correlations	$DRFT$	H_{MD}	$\left[\frac{L_{F20+}}{N_{F20+}}\right]_{-1}$	OBM_M	$\frac{U27+}{U}$	$\frac{U27+}{L_{M14+}}$
Zero order	0.553	0.427	-0.899	0.368	-0.615	-0.609
Partial in eq. (10.19)			-0.923			
(10.20)			-0.890	0.292	-0.265	

B. Males aged 14 through 19

$$\frac{L_{M1419}}{N_{M1419}} = 0.2405 - \frac{0.76}{(0.64)}\left[\frac{U27+}{L_{M14+}}\right] - \frac{0.292}{(0.533)}\left[\frac{DRFT}{N_{M14+}}\right] + \frac{0.1235}{(0.0303)}E_{F15_{AF}} + \frac{0.0017}{(0.0003)}\left[\frac{CDTE_P}{P_{CD}}\right] + \frac{0.0050}{(0.0036)}H_{MD} \quad (10.21)$$

$$\bar{R}^2 = 0.743 \quad S_e = 0.0134$$

$$\frac{L_{M1419}}{N_{M1419}}: \quad \bar{X} = 0.4660 \quad \sigma = 0.02626$$

To preclude any biasing of results in the light of posteriori information, we take the 1950–1960 projections made by John Durand in his classic, *The Labor Force in the United States, 1890–1960* [19]). The deviation of actual participation of females 20 years and over from the interpolated trend was computed to give series $[L_{F20+}] - [L_{F20+}]^{PRO}$.

An alternative trend measure was also computed. For this measure, we took series for employment in full employment years by the major sectors employing large and increasing numbers of women—trade, finance, and services—weighting each by the proportion of females to total employment in the category in the full employment year 1940 [20]). The ratio of actual to trend is $L_{F20+}/[L_{F20+}]^{T}$.

As the results in table 10.5 indicate, the use of neither trend measure produces differing results of any interest except with respect to the number of unpaid family workers in agriculture. The significantly higher partial correlation that these trend measures have with this number is a fact, but it is not a fact particularly helpful in understanding the determinants of the rates. The downward trend in agriculture and shift from unpaid to paid employment does not become a more vital force merely because we relate it to a synthetic series with a strong trend computed and deducted. It does, however, confirm the wisdom of using the $E_{F15_{AF}}$ variable.

Because of space limits we have not discussed the functions developed for the individual age groups or those for the male participation rates. These, of course, involve variables beyond those discussed here.

The variables in the labor force equations are:

L_{F20+} = female civilian labor force aged 20 and over, millions of persons

N_{F20+} = civilian noninstitutional female population aged 20 and over, millions of persons

$DRFT$ = U.S. armed forces military personnel procurement, millions of persons

N_{M14+} = civilian noninstitutional male population aged 14 and over, millions of persons

---

[19]) John D. Durand, *The Labor Force in the United States, 1890–1960* (New York: Social Science Research Council, 1948).

[20]) The employment series were from S. Lebergott's *Manpower in Economic Growth; the American Record since 1800* (New York: McGraw-Hill, 1964), Table A–5.

$E_{F15_{AF}}$ = unpaid females employed 15 or more hours per week in agriculture, millions

H_{MD} = average work week in durable manufacturing, hours

$U27+$ = number unemployed for 27 or more weeks, millions of persons

L_{M14+} = total male labor force aged 14 and over, millions of persons

$CDTE_p$ = consumer credit extensions, billions of dollars

P_{CD} = implicit price deflator for personal consumption expenditures on durable goods, 1954 = 1.00

$U15+$ = number unemployed for 15 or more weeks, millions of persons

U = unemployed civilian labor force, millions of persons

RWS_{TR} = wages and salaries per man-hour in retail trade, dollars per hour

$[L_{F20+}]^{PRO}$ = John Durand's projection of female labor force aged 20 and over, millions of persons

$[L_{F20+}]^{T}$ = trend of female labor force aged 20 and over, millions of persons

L_{F1419} = female civilian labor force aged 14 through 19, millions of persons

N_{F1419} = civilian noninstitutional female population aged 14 through 19, millions of persons

L_{F14+} = female civilian labor force aged 14 and over, millions of persons

N_{F14+} = civilian noninstitutional female population aged 14 and over, millions of persons

L_{M20+} = male civilian labor force aged 20 and over, millions of persons

N_{M20+} = civilian noninstitutional male population aged 20 and over, millions of persons

OBM_M = months of orders backlog in manufacturing

L_{M1419} = male civilian labor force aged 14 through 19, millions of persons

N_{M1419} = civilian noninstitutional male population aged 14 through 19, millions of persons.

10.2. Marriages

10.2.1. Introduction

For more than a century male economists have considered what relationships link changes in the economy with changes in the marriage rate. In
that time they have added their mite to the immortal opening of *Pride
and Prejudice*: "It is a truth universally acknowledged that a single man in
possession of a good fortune must be in want of a wife." The thread of
discussion runs without break from Malthus through Mill, to Marshall and
Keynes. Since our view is not Malthus' long-range one, we may begin with
McCullough, better than a century ago, who quoted approvingly from
Milne: "Any material reduction in the price of wheat is almost always
accompanied by an increase of both the marriages and births ..." [21])
More systematic discussion appeared in a succession of dull and distinguished reports by William Farr. Farr concluded that marriages tend to increase alike "when provisions are cheap", when employment is increasing,
and when peace follows upon war [22]).

The flurry of marriages and births after World War I was investigated
by William Ogburn and Dorothy Thomas [23]), while the equally noteworthy
rise after World War II led to Dudley Kirk's perceptive study [24]). Both
studies observed that marriages and measures of aggregate activity were
significantly linked. Kirk related nuptiality and personal income for the
years from 1920 through 1941 (both series measured in deviations from

[21]) J. R. McCullough, *A Treatise on the Circumstances Which Determine the Rate of
Wages and the Condition of the Labouring Classes* (London: G. Routledge and Co.,
1854), p. 30.

[22]) Cf. his eighth and subsequent reports in *Vital Statistics: a Memorial Volume of Selec-
tions from the Reports and Writings of William Farr*, ed. by Noel A. Humphreys (London:
The Sanitary Institute, 1885), pp. 68ff. For a related set of comments cf. Alfred Marshall,
Principles of Economics, eight edition (New York: Macmillan, 1948), pp. 173–192 and
Sidney Webb, *Industrial Democracy*, II (London and New York: Longmans, Green,
1897), p. 874.

[23]) William Ogburn and Dorothy Thomas, The Influence of the Business Cycle on
Certain Social Conditions, *Journal of the American Statistical Association* (September,
1922); Maurice Hexter, *Social Consequences of Business Cycles* (Boston and New York:
Houghton Mifflin Company, 1925), pp. 75, 152, finds marriages and unemployment
correlating −0.41 with marriages lagged 6 months, and 0.47 with wholesale prices,
marriages lagged 1 month.

[24]) Dudley Kirk, The Influence of Business Cycles on Marriage and Birth Rates, in
Demographic and Economic Change in Developed Countries (Universities-National Bureau
of Economic Research) (Princeton, N. J.: Princeton University Press, 1960).

trend) to get a correlation of 0.80. The nuptiality correlation with unemployment came to −0.73. His results for the quarters between 1947 : 1 and 1958 : 1 are most relevant to our present concern. They report a correlation of 0.61 between deviations from the trend in nuptiality and that in industrial production.

In the present analysis (of the period 1949 : 3–1960 : 4) our focus was primarily on factors that affect potential income of marital aspirants. Let us assume sex—visible, provocative and effective. Let us further assume the life force. We have then no need to explain *whether* marriages take place but only *when* they do. For example, social and economic changes that separated 1940 from 1954 were massive, and, in retrospect, incredible. Yet they were associated with a surprisingly small change in the proportion of women that were married. That proportion rose only from 60 to 66 per cent [25]). The enormous fluctuations in the number of marriages taking place in the 1940's, therefore, were largely linked to factors that determined when marriages took place. (For a different society, or for our own during a period of underemployment equilibrium, of course, any such inference would probably be nonsensical.)

If our focus is on when marriages take place, we are less interested in measures of aggregate economic activity than in ones reflecting cyclical variation per se. We first attempt to measure the pressures of prospective demand as it bears on the existing supply by using variables reflecting unfilled orders: production workers, man-hours and average hours in manufacturing. The latter correlates 0.56 with marriages, but its partial is trivial when used with the defense personnel series that serves us well later on. As an alternative for spotting the influence of the business cycle, we therefore turn to various measures of unemployment. The correlation results (for different duration periods) are as follows [26]):

> −0.44 number unemployed 5 weeks or less
> −0.41 number unemployed 5–14 weeks
> −0.43 number unemployed 5 weeks and over
> −0.43 number unemployed 15 weeks and over.

---

[25]) U. S. Bureau of the Census, Current Population Reports, Series P–20, No. 56, p. 1; we use age-adjusted data.

[26]) These figures apply to the period from the third quarter of 1949 on. For the period from May, 1948 on we can contrast individual duration intervals with the employment rate per se. For the number unemployed 15 weeks and over the correlation is −0.40, much the same as for the shorter period, while the figure for the unemployment rate per se is a weaker −0.34.

Before adopting a general unemployment measure of this sort (encompassing the experience of teenagers, the elderly and the dissipated), we should test a rate more specific to the group involved: the nubile. Hence, we turn to the unemployment rate for males ages 20 to 24, a series which by great good fortune is not only most relevant analytically but (at -0.52) yields the highest correlation.

10.2.2. Armed forces

Slumps and peaks in the series for marriages should in some way be related to variations in the armed forces. We might hypothesize that the larger the complement of young men in the armed forces the *smaller* the number of marriages—fewer men being available for marriage. On the other hand, we might surmise that the recruiting officer makes work for the parson. We might choose for our variable the total number in the armed services, or the number entering it, or the number leaving or some happy combination of all three. Picking from this richness of speculative possibility we have selected some measures of entrance into the armed forces [27]).

Correlating the number of marriages with the number of inductions into the armed forces since 1950 : 1 gives us the following correlation coefficients: 0.40 with inductions in the prior quarter and 0.59 with inductions in the current quarter. Both stimulus and response apparently take place within the current period. The relationship—for which one could rationalize a priori either a positive or negative sign (albeit not with equal agility)— proves to be positive. The brassy brilliant call of country leads young people to marry not only "until" but *before* "death do them part". Perhaps in more halcyon times, or climes, the rate of time discount would not be so formidable. Marriages would then be deferred. But in the U.S. in this period they were speeded up.

Before leaving this factor, however, we should look not merely to inductions but to somewhat wider categories of entrance to the armed forces. The correlations are as follows [28]): 0.59 for inductions, 0.72 for inductions plus first enlistments and 0.78 for total Defense Department personnel procurement. The superiority of the coefficient for the total entrance figure

---

[27]) All data on Defense Department personnel procurement used in this section were kindly provided by the Office of the Secretary of Defense, *Selected Manpower Statistics*, February 1, 1963, and corresponding lithoprinted sheets entitled "Enlisted Personnel Recruiting Summary" for the years 1949 through fiscal year 1962.

[28]) Correlations for the *prior* quarter run: 0.40, 0.40, 0.45.

may derive merely from statistical reasons: a hundred harassed army clerks will vary in the precision with which they distinguish a first enlistment from a reenlistment or an induction from an enlistment. Therefore, the broader series may move with a more majestic truth, being unaffected by such petty errors. But it is surely possible that superiority flows from other factors as well. For one, the degree of advantage in voluntary enlistment (e.g., for choosing one's branch of service) may vary through time as compared with the alternatives of being an involuntary inductee. Such changing relative advantage could change the share of each component but not affect the total and hence be quite without relevance to those factors that sway marriage rates [29]). Finally, one component of the total—national guard call-ups—is not in the induction plus enlistment group. Variations in call-ups may telegraph more prompt urgent information relevant to the marriage choice than do variations even in the total [30]).

We have reported on correlations using data since 1950, believing them most appropriate to a society in which peacetime conscription has become a normal element in its way of life—and death, but it may not be without interest to survey a longer period. Fitting from 1949 : 3 cuts the coefficient significantly from 0.78 to 0.63. The effect of entrances into the armed forces on the marriage rate was therefore much different in the earlier period. We assume a basic structural change beginning in June, 1950, from a period of comparative innocence and hope, and one without conscription as an integral part of the political structure. Hence we fit data for 1950 and later as most relevant for understanding the present structure of our economy.

Because we are working with figures for total marriages there is obvious possibility of collinearity between marriages and the personnel procurement total. Even were this consideration unimportant empirically, the use of any such variable for projection runs into difficulty over time as the size of the army changes. Hence we correlate with the change in personnel procurement from prior to given quarter. The correlation proves to be virtually identical with that for the level. An alternative procedure for the same purpose uses Defense personnel procurement as a ratio to the male total labor force. This correlation also proves to be much the same.

---

[29]) From 1952 : 1 to 1952 : 2 the number of inductions rose while the number of marriages fell significantly—but total personnel procurement changed little because enlistments rose.

[30]) We do not use the guard series as a variable because it is susceptible to decisive short-term changes for reasons irrelevant to our present purposes, as history from Debs to Meredith has indicated.

10.2.3. Sex ratio

All societies develop characteristic modes of existence that affect the rate of marriages. In some, the absolute control of choice by the family means that variations in that rate will reflect the familial sense of urgency as to the year by which the shy maiden or lusty youth should be married. Others reflect a different set of forces. Many cultures seek to improve the market by using professional matchmakers (not, until recently, encompassing electronic ones), while all swarm with amateur matchmakers ("What shall we do about John?"). In our society the summation of these efforts is rather bluntly referred to in terms of "the marriage contract".

Behind any contract curve lies a sequence of intersecting supply and demand curves. If between two periods the supply curve shifts so that, for example, there is an excess supply of unmarried females, one would expect some tendency toward a price change—with an increasing number of young women seeking out disconsolate bachelors of 50, or poets predestined to poverty or venturing out across traditional lines of class, color or nationality. Typically such a shift occurs during wartime when young males of traditional qualifications become less available for marriage. And, unlike markets in which money returns are being maximized, the market need not clear. One would then find that an increased number of marriageable women become spinsters, enter nunneries or emigrate to another region or country [31].

Variations in the number of marriages, therefore, will be affected by the proportion of "eligible" men to eligible women [32]. Although eligibility is a function of an intense and immense variety of considerations, we use age and draft status as an available summary indicator. Most marriages in the U.S. take place between persons both of whom are in the 14 to 24 age category, even though a scattering of December-May marriages do occur. Hence, those in this central age group are more eligible than those outside it. In addition, we know that men in the armed forces are less available then those in civilian life. True, men in the peacetime army marry, and World War II newspapers inevitably carried a report of the man in the

---

[31] True, even these reactions are not totally without parallel in labor markets (emigration) or even commodity markets (painters retaining their own paintings, etc.).

[32] It has been suggested that we use the inventory of unmarried females as a variable. But that inventory can be high in a numerical sense without increasing the marriage rate—as World War II indicated. What is relevant is the size of the inventory relative to a relevant measure, which we here take as the number of men in the appropriate age interval.

Solomons marrying his childhood sweetheart from Dubuque, by proxy. But the civilian–armed force distinction is usually a dominant one, as the enormous decline in marriages during World War II suggests.

We consider various measures of eligibility as reflected by the ratio of male to female population. Four possibilities are [33]):

$$\frac{N_{M1419}}{N_{F1419}}, \quad \frac{L_{M1419}}{N_{F1419}}, \quad \frac{N_{M2024}}{N_{F1419}}, \quad \left[\frac{N_{M2024}}{N_{F1419}}\right]_{-1}.$$

In all calculations we use Census data for the population [34]). The first possibility reflects the sex ratio for the youngest age group at which marriages begin in our society—a group that may be most responsive to changes in the ratio. The second possibility relates to the same age group but excludes males in the armed forces or not in the labor force. Both excluded groups may be considered as less available for marriage than those in the civilian labor force. The third possibility is similar to the first except that we use the next older age group for males in recognition of the pattern in our society for men to marry women who are about two and one-half years younger than they are [35]). The fourth possibility is the third lagged, a measure that seeks to reflect a lag in response to changes in the relevant ratio.

The variables used in the final marriage equations and in preliminary computations reported in tables 10.8 and 10.9 are:

MAR = number of marriages, thousands
$DRFT$ = U.S. armed forces military personnel procurement, millions of persons
N_{M14+} = civilian noninstitutional male population aged 14 and over, millions of persons
RU_{M2024} = rate of unemployment among males aged 20 through 24, fraction
N_{M2024} = civilian noninstitutional male population aged 20 through 24, millions of persons

---

[33]) Definitions are shown in the symbol list below.

[34]) By summing the numbers in the labor force and those not in the labor force as reported in Current Population Reports, Series P–50. These data relate only to the civilian noninstitutional population. No current data are available giving the age distribution of the armed forces.

[35]) For first marriages in 1959 the difference was 2.6 years, while for remarriages it was almost 5 years. Cf. National Office of Vital Statistics, *Vital Statistics of the United States*: (1959). *Marriage and Divorce Statistics*, section 2, pp. 2–19.

N_{F1419} = civilian noninstitutional female population aged 14 through 19, millions of persons

N_{FS14+} = unmarried civilian females aged 14 and over, millions of persons

L_{M2024} = male civilian labor force aged 20 through 24, millions of persons

L_{M1419} = male civilian labor force aged 14 through 19, millions of persons

N_{M1419} = civilian noninstitutional male population aged 14 through 19, millions of persons

$U27+$ = number unemployed for 27 or more weeks, millions of persons

L_{M14+} = total male labor force aged 14 and over, millions of persons

N_{F2024} = civilian noninstitutional female population aged 20 through 24, millions of persons

N_{M2534} = civilian noninstitutional male population aged 25 through 34, millions of persons

L_{M2534} = male civilian labor force aged 25 through 34, millions of persons

N_{F2534} = civilian noninstitutional female population aged 25 through 34, millions of persons.

10.2.4. The labor market

Of the variables shown in table 10.8, perhaps the oddest result is the negative coefficient for L_{M2024}/N_{M2024}. If we reckon in the armed force variable $\Delta[DRFT/N_{M14+}]$ however, the partial for L_{M2024}/N_{M2024} becomes -0.027, indistinguishable from zero. And if we further add in N_{M2024}/N_{F1419}, the partial becomes 0.397, a significant positive value. The coefficient for the younger age group, L_{M1419}/N_{M1419} is high to start with; the partials when similar variables are added become 0.392 and then 0.282.

In both instances, the labor force participation of young males is significantly related to variations in marriages. However, that participation is itself affected by market forces. Hence, it is desirable to deal more directly with the market forces. Table 10.8 shows substantial effects for long-duration unemployment. But both variables relate to the over-all market—which impinges differentially on young and old, men and women. We therefore prefer a measure that reports directly on the experience of the young, as does RU_{M2024}. A further advantage of a measure for this group is that it reflects the net result of all those entrances or exits that affect the civilian labor force. School leavings flood the market in which young men seek jobs. Army inductions reduce the number in that market, taking a disproportionate number of the less skilled, less economically successful and, hence, more unemployed. The net of all these influences appears in the unemployment rate for this age group, which shows a zero order correlation of -0.47, considerable weight for one variable [36]). (For the record, when combined with the preferred $\Delta[DRFT/N_{M14+}]$ and $[N_{M2024}/N_{F1419}]_{-1}$ variables discussed below, the R when using $[U27+/L_{M14+}]_{-1}$ is 0.762, when using $U27+/L_{M14+}$ 0.0810, but when using RU_{M2024}, 0.873. The analytic argument for using the latter is therefore stronger than an argument from marked advantage in improving the correlation.)

TABLE 10.8

Marriages and key variables: zero order correlations.

Variables	1949 : 2–1960 : 4	1950 : 3–1960 : 4
Defense personnel procurement		
$DRFT$	0.53	0.71
$\Delta DRFT$	0.51	0.55
$\dfrac{DRFT}{N_{M14+}}$	0.55	0.70
$\Delta\left[\dfrac{DRFT}{N_{M14+}}\right]$	0.57	0.57
Labor market		
$\dfrac{L_{M2024}}{N_{M2024}}$	-0.19	-0.05
$\dfrac{L_{M1419}}{N_{M1419}}$	0.21	0.19
RU_{M2024}	-0.47	-0.56
$\dfrac{U27+}{L_{M14+}}$	-0.38	-0.39
$\left[\dfrac{U27+}{L_{M14+}}\right]_{-1}$	-0.23	-0.20

---

[36]) The fact that we combine this with an armed force measure below gives rise to no collinearity problem. The correlation between the two measures is 0.07.

TABLE 10.8 (Continued)

Variables	1949 : 2–1960 : 4	1950 : 3–1960 : 4
Population ratios		
$\dfrac{N_{M1419}}{N_{F1419}}$	−0.02	−0.04
$\left[\dfrac{N_{M1419}}{N_{F1419}}\right]_{-1}$	0.24	0.22
$\varDelta\left[\dfrac{N_{M1419}}{N_{F1419}}\right]$	−0.56	−0.62
$\varDelta\left[\dfrac{N_{M1419}}{N_{F1419}}\right]_{-1}$	−0.23	−0.23
$\dfrac{L_{M1419}}{N_{F1419}}$	0.66	0.70
$\left[\dfrac{L_{M1419}}{N_{F1419}}\right]_{-1}$	0.73	0.76
$\varDelta\left[\dfrac{L_{M1419}}{N_{F1419}}\right]$	−0.20	−0.17
$\varDelta\left[\dfrac{L_{M1419}}{N_{F1419}}\right]_{-1}$	−0.21	−0.20
$\dfrac{N_{M2024}}{N_{F2024}}$	0.30	0.24
$\left[\dfrac{N_{M2024}}{N_{F2024}}\right]_{-1}$	0.36	0.32
$\varDelta\left[\dfrac{N_{M2024}}{N_{F2024}}\right]$	−0.40	−0.45
$\varDelta\left[\dfrac{N_{M2024}}{N_{F2024}}\right]_{-1}$	−0.29	−0.31
$\dfrac{L_{M2024}}{N_{F2024}}$	0.31	0.25

TABLE 10.8 (Continued)

Variables	1949 : 2–1960 : 4	1950 : 3–1960 : 4
$\left[\dfrac{L_{M2024}}{N_{F2024}}\right]_{-1}$	0.38	0.35
$\varDelta\left[\dfrac{L_{M2024}}{N_{F2024}}\right]$	−0.40	−0.47
$\dfrac{N_{M2534}}{N_{F2534}}$	−0.31	−0.36
$\left[\dfrac{N_{M2534}}{N_{F2534}}\right]_{-1}$	−0.14	−0.18
$\varDelta\left[\dfrac{N_{M2534}}{N_{F2534}}\right]$	−0.45	−0.49
$\dfrac{L_{M2534}}{N_{M2534}}$	−0.46	−0.44
$\left[\dfrac{L_{M2534}}{N_{M2534}}\right]_{-1}$	−0.36	−0.33
$\varDelta\left[\dfrac{L_{M2534}}{N_{M2534}}\right]$	−0.29	−0.32
$\dfrac{N_{M2024}}{N_{F1419}}$	0.57	0.72
$\left[\dfrac{N_{M2024}}{N_{F1419}}\right]_{-1}$	0.59	0.71
$\varDelta\left[\dfrac{N_{M2024}}{N_{F1419}}\right]$	−0.40	−0.45

10.2.5. Personnel procurement

Of the four variables shown in table 10.8, there is a clear advantage for the first two: For the period 1950 and later, they give distinctly higher correlations. We nonetheless reject them in favor of the latter two because *DRFT*, in particular, is substantially affected by longer term changes in the size of the armed forces. The level of intake, for example, with a 10 million-man armed service will necessarily be greater than that with a

3 million or 1 million level. Yet the proportionate relationship to marriages may well be different at the greater level. To deal with such potential non-linearities, we utilize (1) first differences as first preference and (2) the number as a ratio to male population as second best. As it turns out, the first differences behave better when combined with other variables—not so much increasing over-all results but showing the more significant partial correlations.

10.2.6. Population ratios

Of the three population ratios that simply relate male to female population in the same age group, that for the 14 to 19 group is virtually zero, that for the 25 to 34 group is -0.31—presumably reflecting some third variable or variables—and that for the 20 to 24 group is 0.30. But the highest population ratio proves to be that for N_{M2024}/N_{F1419} in which recognition of the differential age at marriage yields 0.57. Although the ratios of male civilian labor force to female population yield as good or better results, they necessarily reflect not merely the labor market link which we would desire to have reported here, but also the impact of armed forces inductions in varying the number in the civilian labor force. It is clearly desirable to deal with the armed forces effect explicitly, and no more than once. Hence, the population ratios per se are to be preferred.

We have a choice of time period here. It is clearly possible that the number of marriages reflects some disproportion not in the current quarter but in an earlier one. Since all the relevant partial correlation coefficients are virtually identical—largely because N_{M2024}/N_{F1419} and itself lagged correlate 0.99—and the regression coefficients lead to almost precisely similar results, our only guide must be from a judgment about the mechanism at work. We assume that some allowance for a delay function is required. (Operationally, of course, it is distinctly more convenient for forecasting to use data from an earlier period.)

10.2.7. Final results: marriages

The foregoing choices and alternatives, reported in table 10.9 lead to the final equation for estimating marriages, which is as follows:

$$MAR = 1450.8 + \frac{9580.}{(1560.)} \Delta \left[\frac{DRFT}{N_{M14+}} \right]$$

$$- \frac{1336.8}{(201.6)} RU_{M2024} + \frac{306.12}{(54.48)} \left[\frac{N_{M2024}}{N_{F1419}} \right]_{-1} \tag{10.22}$$

One final note may be added as to why we have sought to explain the number of marriages rather than the marriage rate. The answer is twofold. First, the rate—typically one relating marriages to the unmarried female population ages 15 to 14, or sometimes to the female population—is a computation that implies a relationship between the number of females in a particular population group and the number of marriages. Instead of implying any such relationship, we have sought to deal directly with measures of the number of unmarried females, and, as outlined above, have concluded that the relevant variable is in fact reflected by a ratio of males 20 to 24

TABLE 10.9

Marriage and marriage rate equations.

$$MAR = 1450.8 + \frac{9580.}{(1560.)} \Delta \left[\frac{DRFT}{N_{M14+}}\right] - \frac{1336.8}{(201.6)} RU_{M2024} + \frac{306.12}{(54.48)} \left[\frac{N_{M2024}}{N_{F1419}}\right]_{-1}$$

$$\bar{X} = 1546.5 \qquad \bar{R}^2 = 0.746 \qquad S_e = 39.650 \tag{10.22}$$

$$MAR = 1401.6 + \frac{10300.}{(1600.)} \Delta \left[\frac{DRFT}{N_{M14+}}\right] - \frac{1260}{(216)} RU_{M2024} + \frac{379.7}{(83.2)} \left[\frac{N_{M2024}}{N_{F1419}}\right]_{-1}$$

$$\bar{X} = 1540.56 \qquad \bar{R}^2 = 0.797 \qquad S_e = 35.84 \tag{10.23}$$

$$\frac{MAR}{N_{FS14+}} = 189.6 + \frac{1500.}{(400.)} \Delta \left[\frac{DRFT}{N_{M14+}}\right] - \frac{360}{(48)} RU_{M2024} + \frac{106.2}{(13.6)} \left[\frac{N_{M2024}}{N_{F1419}}\right]_{-1}$$

$$\bar{X} = 228 \qquad \bar{R}^2 = 0.753 \qquad S_e = 9.84 \tag{10.24}$$

$$\Delta MAR = 684.0 - \frac{0.4792}{(0.0976)} [MAR]_{-1} + \frac{9600.}{(1700.)} \Delta \left[\frac{DRFT}{N_{M14+}}\right] + \frac{82.68}{(75.60)} \left[\frac{N_{M2024}}{N_{F1419}}\right]_{-1}$$

$$\bar{R}^2 = 0.552 \qquad S_e = 0.4320 \tag{10.25}$$

$$\Delta MAR = 595.8 - \frac{0.4518}{(0.1092)} [MAR]_{-1} + \frac{10500.}{(1700.)} \Delta \left[\frac{DRFT}{N_{M14+}}\right] + \frac{1.68}{(117.24)} \left[\frac{N_{M2024}}{N_{F1419}}\right]_{-1}$$

$$\bar{R}^2 = 0.634 \qquad S_e = 0.3828 \tag{10.26}$$

$$\Delta MAR = 521.5 - \frac{0.3397}{(0.0747)} [MAR]_{-1} + \frac{11500}{(1600)} \Delta \left[\frac{DRFT}{N_{M14+}}\right]$$

$$\bar{R}^2 = 0.634 \qquad S_e = 0.3876 \tag{10.27}$$

TABLE 10.9 (Continued)

Correlations		$\Delta \left[\dfrac{DRFT}{N_{M14+}}\right]$	$[MAR]_{-1}$	RU_{M2024}	$\left[\dfrac{N_{M2024}}{N_{F2024}}\right]_{-1}$
Zero order in eq.	(10.22)	0.57	0.67	0.47	0.59
	(10.23)	0.57	0.68	−0.56	0.71
	(10.25)	0.54	−0.45	0.03	−0.05
	(10.26)	0.68	−0.41	0.08	0.00
	(10.27)	0.68	−0.41	0.08	0.00
Partials in eq.	(10.22)	0.678		−0.706	0.645
	(10.23)	0.725		−0.687	0.595
	(10.24)	0.489		−0.729	0.763
	(10.25)	0.641	−0.595		0.162
	(10.26)	0.706	−0.557		0.220
	(10.27)	0.761	−0.588		

Note Equations (10.22) and (10.25) are fitted from 1949 : 1 or 1949 : 2 through 1960 : 4. Other equations are fitted 1950 : 3 through 1960 : 4.

to females 14 to 19. A second consideration is that no current data are available on the number of females in the various marital status categories—not even any very recent annual data. Some attention was given to a count of females in each marital status category, since divorcees are more likely to remarry than widows or single women 19 and over. But the existing data are too weak to permit any analysis that actually adds information rather than merely interprets findings tacitly put there by the interpolation procedure.

PART V

Subsectors: foreign trade and agriculture

CHAPTER 11

THE FOREIGN SECTOR

Contents

11.1. Introduction 375

11.2. Scope of a foreign sector submodel 376
    1. Relation to the rest of the model. 2. Policy questions to be answered.
    3. Closing the model.

11.3. Import and export equations for the aggregative version of the model . 380
    1. Comparison of subperiods. 2. Explanatory power and forecasting
    efficiency of the equations. 3. Customs duties.

11.4. Import functions for individual commodity groups 395
    1. Forecasts from commodity group equations. 2. Annual equations
    for special commodities. 3. Concluding remark.

THE FOREIGN SECTOR

RUDOLF R. RHOMBERG and LORETTE BOISSONNEAULT [1])

International Monetary Fund, Washington, D.C.

11.1. Introduction

Until a few years ago, it was possible to discuss countercyclical policy in the U. S. without taking account of the effects of domestic policy measures on the balance of payments. In models of the U. S. economy published to date the foreign sector has, therefore, not been very elaborate. It was usually thought sufficient to allow in some fashion for the contribution of foreign trade to aggregate demand. For instance, in a model of the interwar period by Lawrence R. Klein [2]), net exports of goods and services are combined with government expenditure to form an exogenous variable. More recently, an import equation was included in the Klein-Goldberger model [3]), and separate export and import functions were provided in the Wharton School model [4]).

In its treatment of the foreign sector, the present version of the model described in this volume advances beyond the Wharton School model only to the extent that the effect of prices on foreign trade is explicitly taken into account. Moreover, imports are separated into two classes, namely, imports of unfinished goods (raw materials and semimanufactures) and imports

---

[1]) The views expressed by the authors are personal and not necessarily those of the International Monetary Fund.

[2]) L. R. Klein, *Economic Fluctuations in the United States, 1921–1941*, Cowles Commission Monograph No. 11 (New York: John Wiley and Sons, 1950).

[3]) L. R. Klein and A. S. Goldberger, *An Econometric Model of the United States, 1929–1952* (Amsterdam: North-Holland Publishing Co., 1955).

[4]) A quarterly model of the U.S. economy prepared by the economics department of the Wharton School of Finance and Commerce, University of Pennsylvania (unpublished).

of finished goods (foodstuffs and finished manufactures) and services. Preliminary estimates of these import and export functions will be presented in section 11.3. Section 11.4 reports on some experiments with a finer classification of imports by commodity group, which may be useful in a subsequent expanded version of the model.

Recent discussion of U. S. economic policy and of the constraint which balance of payments considerations may place upon certain policy measures indicates that the usefulness of a model of the U. S. economy may be considerably enhanced if, in comparison with earlier models, greater scope is given to the foreign sector. Some suggestions for further elaboration of the model along these lines are offered in section 11.2.

11.2. Scope of a foreign sector submodel

The scope and construction of a submodel of the foreign sector of the U. S. economy depend on the answers to three questions: First, which of the variables occurring in the main model are to be explained in the foreign sector submodel? Second, what are the policy problems to whose solution the model is expected to contribute? Third, how can the model be closed short of constructing a full world economic model; that is to say, which of the "foreign" variables entering into the submodel can be safely taken as exogenous?

11.2.1. Relation to the rest of the model

A complete submodel of the foreign sector of the U. S. economy would be linked to the domestic part of the model in four ways:

(a) The balance of exports and imports of goods and services (in real terms) appears in the *GNP* identity.

(b) Export prices depend on domestic price developments, which are in turn affected by import prices.

(c) Changes in exports and variations in output of import-competing industries due to import substitution enter as demand shifts into the input-output sector of the model. Exports of agricultural commodities also play a major role in the agricultural submodel.

(d) International capital flows and changes in gold reserves are affected by developments in the financial sector, or submodel, and in turn influence these developments.

The complete submodel would, therefore, have to explain all of the balance of payments categories, some of them in a breakdown showing considerable detail.

11.2.2. Policy questions to be answered

The foreign sector submodel should be so constructed that it is possible to assess the direct and indirect effects of a variety of economic policies on the external accounts. The types of question which the model should be able to answer may be illustrated as follows:

(a) What will be the effect on the balance of payments of a policy of tax reduction or increased government expenditure designed to raise income and employment? In the case of this and similar questions we should allow the model to account for (i) the effect of the change in income or production on imports and perhaps on the supply price of exports, (ii) the effect of induced changes in domestic prices and wage rates on imports and on export supply prices and (iii) the effect of the induced increases in foreign incomes and exchange earnings on U. S. exports. This is, of course, not a complete list of the induced effects of a change in budget policy on the foreign accounts. In particular, we have left out some of the influences that would make themselves felt through changes in the monetary and financial sector; these relations are discussed in connection with the following question.

(b) What will be the effect on the foreign balance of a change in monetary policy? Certain variables in the financial sector of the model will be designated instruments of monetary policy in the sense that they are under the direct control of the monetary authorities and affect, in the first instance, mainly the quantity of money or the yields on financial assets, or both. Changes in these instruments of monetary policy will affect income and production and will, therefore, have similar effects on the balance of payments as the fiscal policy changes discussed above. In addition, changes in interest rates and in the equilibrium distribution of asset holdings will also directly affect the capital account of the balance of payments.

(c) What will be the effect of tariff reductions on the balance of payments and on domestic employment? The answer to this question requires, among other things, that the model show the price elasticities of the U. S. import demand and of the foreign supply of imported goods.

(d) What would be the ultimate effect on the balance of payments, and on domestic income and employment, of a change in development aid expenditures on the part of the U. S. or other industrial countries? In order to be helpful in connection with this question the model must allow for the repercussions on U. S. exports of changes in foreign exchange receipts on the part of the underdeveloped countries.

Although one could easily add to this list of policy questions, enough has been said under this heading and under the previous one of the linkage between the main model and the foreign sector submodel to indicate the principal structural features which the submodel should, ideally, possess. To summarize these desiderata: (a) The quantities of imported and exported commodities should be explained by functions showing their dependence not only on income or some other economic activity variable but also on prices; (b) the model should explain export and import supply prices; (c) capital movements should be explained with reference to economic activity and financial variables and, where applicable, with reference to interest differentials; (d) the "foreign repercussions" of changes in economic activity or in economic policies in the U. S. should find adequate expression in the model; finally, (e) these relations should be formulated on an accounting basis and at a level of disaggregation prescribed by the structure of the main model.

11.2.3. Closing the model

We turn now to the last of the three questions which must be considered before the general structure of the model can be laid out: How far is it advisable to go in the direction of making the foreign sector submodel a model of the world economy? Considering first only the current account of the balance of payments, one could, at one extreme, take exports as exogenously determined. This possibility has already been discarded above on the grounds that such a procedure would preclude the use of the model in connection with some important policy problems. Moreover, such a limited scope of the submodel—while perhaps appropriate for a small aggregative model of the type which takes investment expenditure as an exogenous variable—would hardly be in keeping with the character of the Brookings-SSRC econometric model. But the compelling reason against such a limited approach lies in the importance of the foreign trade of the U. S. for developments in the world economy. It cannot safely be assumed that U. S. exports are independent of the outflow of private and public capital from the U. S. and of U. S. imports. Similar considerations preclude the assumption that the volume of U. S. imports does not affect the prices paid for these imports, especially in the case of primary products.

It is obviously impractical to contemplate the approach at the opposite extreme, which would consist in constructing a large and detailed econometric model for every country and in linking all these country models together. For a compromise solution, it will initially be convenient to fall back on one of the existing world trade models, such as the models by Polak [5]) and by Neisser and Modigliani [6]) for the interwar years or the more recent attempt by Rhomberg and Boissonneault [7]) for the postwar period. This model is based on a division of the trading world into three regions (U. S., Western Europe and the rest of the world). Exports from the U. S. to Western Europe are determined by income and the change in inventories in the recipient region and by relative prices. U. S. exports to the rest of the world are taken to be a constant marginal fraction of that region's total imports, which in turn tend to equal its foreign exchange receipts from exports to the U. S. and Western Europe (explained by the respective import functions) and from the inflow of capital and foreign aid. The model thus takes account of the major feedback effects of changes in U. S. imports and capital flows on U. S. exports, though further regional or commodity disaggregation may be desirable.

Such an approach, which requires the estimation of a fairly large number of equations for trade and service flows among the non-U.S. regions, has the disadvantage of considerably increasing the size of the foreign sector submodel. In order not to burden the main model unduly, it may be possible to process this submodel as a separate entity which generates certain variables used by the main model. It may even be necessary, or desirable, to keep the full submodel on a basis of annual data and to use it as a checking and correction device in conjunction with a much less ambitious set of foreign sector equations that form a permanent part of the main model.

From what has been said about the policy questions which should be capable of being analyzed within the framework of the model, and also in

---

[5]) J. J. Polak, *An International Economic System* (Chicago: University of Chicago Press, 1953).

[6]) H. Neisser and F. Modigliani, *National Incomes and International Trade* (Urbana, Ill.: University of Illinois Press, 1953).

[7]) R. R. Rhomberg and L. Boissonneault, "Effects of Income and Price Changes on the U.S. Balance of Payments", *International Monetary Fund Staff Papers* (March, 1964). See also J. J. Polak and R. R. Rhomberg, Economic Instability in an International Setting, *American Economic Review* (May, 1962), and R. R. Rhomberg, "A Three-Region World Trade and Income Model, 1948–1960", a paper presented to the Summer Meeting of the Econometric Society at Ann Arbor, September, 1962 (mimeographed).

view of the interaction between trade and financial flows, it is clear that the foreign sector submodel should deal not only with the current account of the balance of payments but also with capital movements. In this latter area, however, not much econometric work has been reported so far [8]). The extent to which it will be possible to "close" the submodel in this respect cannot be gauged until further exploratory work is undertaken.

11.3. *Import and export equations for the aggregative version of the model*

As has been indicated elsewhere in this volume, the Brookings-SSRC econometric model is at present still cast in a relatively aggregative form. This is also reflected in the treatment of the foreign sector at this stage. For purposes of the present version of the model the foreign sector consists of three demand equations: one for U. S. exports of goods and services, one for U. S. imports of finished goods (food and finished manufactures) and services, and one for U. S. imports of unfinished goods (raw materials and semimanufactures). The supply of imports is taken to be infinitely elastic at the exogenous import price levels of the two classes of imports, a simplification which ought to be abandoned, at least with respect to unfinished goods, in later versions of the model. The supply of exports is also taken to be infinitely elastic at the export price level, which is determined elsewhere in the model.

The export variable and the sum of the two import variables, expressed in 1954 prices and seasonally adjusted, correspond to the national income accounts entries and are, therefore, consistent with the equation defining real gross national product. This feature is mentioned here because of the increasing difficulties on this score which will have to be faced when the submodel is cast into a less aggregative form.

---

[8]) The two principal econometric studies of U.S. capital movements are: Philip W. Bell, "Private Capital Movements and the U.S. Balance-of-Payments Position", in U.S. Congress, Joint Economic Committee, *Factors Affecting the United States Balance of Payments*, Part VI (Washington, D.C.: Government Printing Office, 1962), pp. 395–481; and Peter B. Kenen, "Short-Term Capital Movements and the U.S. Balance of Payments", U.S. Congress, Joint Economic Committee, *Hearings on the United States Balance of Payments*, Part I (Washington, D.C.: Government Printing Office, 1963), pp. 153–191. For a critique of these two studies see Benjamin I. Cohen, "A Survey of Capital Movements and Findings Regarding Their Interest Sensitivity", *ibid.*, pp. 192–212. Some findings on U.S.-Canadian capital movements are reported in Rudolf R. Rhomberg, A Model of the Canadian Economy Under Fixed and Fluctuating Exchange Rates, *Journal of Political Economy* (February, 1964).

The three equations are shown below. Quarterly real imports and exports (1948–1961, fifty-six observations) have been regressed on a deflated price variable, on one or two variables expressing changes in economic activity, and on their own lagged values, implying an exponentially decaying lag of the effect of changes in the other variables. Real disposable income is the activity variable in the equation for imported finished goods and services, while total manufacturing production and changes in nonfarm business inventories fill this role in the equation for imports of unfinished goods. The "activity" variable in the export equation is world exports excluding U. S. exports, i.e., U. S. exports are estimated to be a certain marginal fraction of the rest of the world's exports, modified by the effect of changes in the ratio of the U. S.'s to the rest of the world's export prices.

The equations are:

$$M_{\text{FIN*}}^{54} = \frac{0.547}{(0.108)}[M_{\text{FIN*}}^{54}]_{-1} + \frac{0.0383}{(0.0095)}\left[\frac{Y_D}{P_C}\right] - \frac{2.64}{(1.67)}\left[\frac{PM_{\text{MFIN*}}}{P_{\text{GOOD}}}\right] - \frac{1.93}{(1.75)}$$
$$\bar{R}^2 = 0.977 \tag{11.1}$$

$$M_{\text{EFIN*}}^{54} = \frac{0.474}{(0.105)}[M_{\text{EFIN*}}^{54}]_{-1} + \frac{0.0183}{(0.0044)}X_{M*}^{54} + \frac{0.0304}{(0.0084)}\Delta INV_{EAF}^{54}$$
$$- \frac{1.61}{(0.41)}\left[\frac{PM_{\text{MEFIN*}}}{P_{\text{GOOD}}}\right] + \frac{2.16}{(0.50)}$$
$$\bar{R}^2 = 0.879 \tag{11.2}$$

$$EX^{54} = \frac{0.711}{(0.065)}[EX^{54}]_{-1} + \frac{0.0945}{(0.0174)}EX_W^{54} - \frac{10.9}{(3.7)}\left[\frac{P_{\text{EX}}}{PM_{\text{EXW}}}\right] + \frac{10.1}{(3.2)}$$
$$\bar{R}^2 = 0.957. \tag{11.3}$$

The variables, in order of appearance, are:

$M_{\text{FIN*}}$ = imports of finished goods and services and crude foodstuffs, billions of dollars

Y_D = disposable personal income, billions of dollars

P_C = implicit price deflator for personal consumption expenditures, 1954 = 1.00

$PM_{\text{MFIN*}}$ = unit value index of imports of finished goods and services and crude foodstuffs, 1954 = 1.00

P_{GOOD} = implicit price deflator for *GNP* goods, 1954 = 1.00

$M_{\text{EFIN*}}$ = imports of crude materials and semimanufactures, billions of dollars

X_{M*} = gross product originating in manufacturing, plus mining of crude petroleum and natural gas, billions of dollars

INV_{EAF} = nonfarm business inventory stocks, billions of dollars

PM_{MEFIN*} = unit value index of imports of semimanufactures and crude materials, 1954 = 1.00

EX = U. S. exports of goods and services, billions of dollars

EX_W = world exports excluding U. S. exports, billions of dollars

P_{EX} = implicit price deflator for exports of goods and services, 1954 = 1.00

PM_{EXW} = unit value index of world exports excluding U. S. component, 1954 = 1.00.

TABLE 11.1

Imports of finished goods and services, including food [a, b]).

Independent variables	Fitting period		
	1948–1961	1948–1953	1954–1961
Imports lagged one quarter	0.547	0.390 [c])	0.454
	(0.108)	(0.196)	(0.141)
Real disposable income [b])	0.0389	0.0540 [d])	0.0181 [c])
	(0.0095)	(0.0191)	(0.0125)
Deflated import price (1954 = 1) [e])	−2.64 [c])	−2.63 [c])	−17.26 [d])
	(1.67)	(3.69)	(6.31)
Constant term	−1.93 [c])	−3.94 [c])	19.18 [d])
	(1.75)	(2.62)	(8.59)
$\bar{R}^2$	0.977	0.859	0.953
ρ^2	0.324	0.421	0.503
Standard error of estimate as per cent of mean	3.9	5.2	3.1
Durbin-Watson test	2.06	2.22	2.05
Elasticities (*at 1948–1961 means*)			
Disposable income	0.80	1.11	0.37
Price	−0.19	−0.21	−1.2

Note Standard errors are shown parenthetically below their coefficients. The definition of ρ^2 is given on p. 390.

[a] Imports of goods and services less imports of unfinished goods (crude materials and semimanufactures); mean for 1948–1961: $ 13.1 billion.

[b]) Seasonally adjusted at annual rates in billions of 1954 dollars. Mean of real disposable income for 1948–1961: $ 268 billion.

[c]) Not significant at the 5 per cent level.

[d]) Not significant at the 1 per cent level.

[e]) Implicit price deflator of imports of finished goods and services divided by *GNP* goods price deflator.

TABLE 11.2

Imports of unfinished goods [a, b].

Independent variables	Fitting period		
	1948–1961	1948–1953	1954–1961
Imports lagged one quarter	0.474	0.380[c]	0.456
	(0.105)	(0.206)	(0.122)
Manufacturing production [b]	0.0183	0.0290[d]	0.0118[c]
	(0.0044)	(0.0103)	(0.0073)
Change in nonfarm business inventories [b]	0.0304	0.0437[d]	0.0355[d]
	(0.0084)	(0.0166)	(0.0136)
Deflated import price (1954 = 1) [e]	−1.61	−2.44	−1.72[d]
	(0.41)	(0.75)	(0.74)
Constant term	2.16	2.31	3.17[d]
	(0.50)	(0.71)	(1.27)
$\bar{R}^2$	0.879	0.795	0.809
ρ^2	0.446	0.466	0.557
Standard error of estimate as per cent of mean	4.5	6.0	3.6
Durbin-Watson test	1.65[f]	1.63[f]	2.00
Elasticities (*at* 1948–1961 *means*)			
Manufacturing production	0.41	0.66	0.27
Price	−0.32	−0.49	−0.34

[a] Sum of imports of crude materials and semimanufactures; mean for 1948–1961: $ 5.11 billion.

[b] Seasonally adjusted at annual rates, in billions of 1954 dollars. Mean of manufacturing production for 1948–1961: $ 116 billion.

[c] Not significant at the 5 per cent level.

[d] Not significant at the 1 per cent level.

[e] Unit value of imports of unfinished goods divided by *GNP* goods price deflator.

[f] Durbin-Watson test falls in the "inconclusive" range.

The results for these regression equations are more fully presented in tables 11.1 through 11.3. In addition to the equations listed above, separate demand functions have been fitted for finished imports, excluding food, for imports of food and for exports of goods; these results are given in tables 11.4 through 11.6.

The estimated coefficients reported above must be interpreted in terms of the units in which the variables are expressed. It is somewhat more convenient to discuss these estimates after transforming them into elasticities evaluated at the sample means of the respective variables, as shown in table 11.7. Since the estimated equations assume a distributed lag of the effect of the explanatory on the explained variables, the values given in table

TABLE 11.3

Exports of goods and services [a]).

Independent variables	Fitting period		
	1948–1961	1948–1953	1954–1961
Exports lagged one quarter	0.711	0.511	0.747
	(0.065)	(0.106)	(0.098)
World exports excluding U.S. [b])	0.0945	0.0837	0.114
	(0.0174)	(0.0188)	(0.038)
Deflated export price (1954 = 1) [c])	−10.9	−12.2	−22.8 [d])
	(3.7)	(3.6)	(10.4)
Constant term	10.1	15.0	20.3 [d])
	(3.2)	(4.0)	(8.5)
$\bar{R}^2$	0.957	0.784	0.901
ρ^2	0.320	0.497	0.387
Standard error of estimate as per cent of mean	4.2	4.1	4.0
Durbin-Watson test	2.01	1.92	2.56 [e])
Elasticities (at 1948–1961 means)			
World trade	0.33	0.30	0.40
Price	−0.57	−0.64	−1.20

[a]) Seasonally adjusted at annual rates, in billions of 1954 dollars; mean for 1948–1961: $ 19.4 billion.

[b]) Seasonally adjusted at annual rates, in billions of 1954 dollars; mean for 1948–1961: $ 68.6 billion.

[c]) Implicit price deflator of exports of goods and services, divided by world export unit value excluding U.S. component (1954 = 1).

[d]) Not significant at the 1 per cent level.

[e]) Durbin-Watson test falls in the "inconclusive" range.

11.7 are "impact elasticities", that is, they show the effects of changes in the explanatory variables in the quarter during which these changes occur. Long-run (or equilibrium) elasticities can, in principle, be derived from the impact elasticities by multiplying them by the reciprocal of unity minus the coefficient of the lagged dependent variable in the corresponding equation. The long-run elasticities would accordingly be about twice to three times the values of the respective impact elasticities shown in table 11.7. Such a calculation rests on the hypotheses that (a) the form of the equation correctly specifies the lag pattern and (b) the lag patterns of all explanatory variables included in the equation are identical. Since these hypotheses have not been tested, it would be unwise to place much reliance on the results of such further processing of figures which are themselves subject

TABLE 11.4

Imports of finished goods and services, excluding food [a, b].

Independent variables	Fitting period		
	1948–1961	1948–1953	1954–1961
Imports lagged one quarter	0.697	0.697	0.568
	(0.088)	(0.148)	(0.136)
Real disposable income [b]	0.0218	0.0226 [c]	0.0196 [d]
	(0.0069)	(0.0103)	(0.0096)
Deflated import price (1954 = 1) [e]	−3.12 [d]	−2.32 [d]	−11.61 [e]
	(1.76)	(2.08)	(4.78)
Constant term	0.189 [d]	−0.833 [d]	10.49 [d]
	(2.100)	(2.680)	(5.55)
$\bar{R}^2$	0.985	0.911	0.959
ρ^2	0.324	0.449	0.503
Standard error of estimate as per cent of mean	3.9	5.4	3.2
Durbin-Watson test	1.51 [f]	1.43 [f]	1.45 [f]
Elasticities (at 1948–1961 means)			
Disposable income	0.62	0.64	0.56
Price	−0.32	−0.24	−1.20

[a]) Imports of finished manufactures and services; mean for 1948–1961: $ 9.43 billion.

[b]) Seasonally adjusted at annual rates, in billions of 1954 dollars. Mean of real disposable income for 1948–1961: $ 268 billion.

[c]) Not significant at the 1 per cent level.

[d]) Not significant at the 5 per cent level.

[e]) Implicit price deflator of imports of finished goods divided by *GNP* goods price deflator (1954 = 1).

[f]) Durbin-Watson test falls in the "inconclusive" range.

to a considerable margin of error. For this reason the long-run elasticities implied in the estimated equations have not been tabulated.

The first column of table 11.7 refers to the equations fitted for the period 1948–1961. The estimated (short-run) income elasticity of demand for imported finished goods and services is quite high (about $\frac{3}{5}$ or $\frac{4}{5}$, depending on whether food imports are excluded from or included in this category), with the implication of a long-run elasticity considerably in excess of 1 and perhaps close to 2. As has been argued elsewhere [9]), it is likely that the appearance of high income elasticity of demand for U. S. imports of manufactured products (including automobiles) during the postwar period was

[9]) R. R. Rhomberg and Lorette Boissonneault, "Effects of Income and Price Changes on the U.S. Balance of Payments", *op. cit.*

TABLE 11.5

Imports of food [a,b].

Independent variables	Fitting period		
	1948–1961	1948–1953	1954–1961
Real disposable income [b]	0.00950	0.0167 [c]	−0.00038 [c]
	(0.00106)	(0.0084)	(0.00540)
Deflated import price [d]	−1.13	−0.784 [c]	−4.24
(1954 = 1)	(0.40)	(1.460)	(1.38)
Constant term	2.04	0.164 [c]	7.60
	(0.39)	(1.010)	(2.74)
$\bar{R}^2$	0.591	0.351	0.664
ρ^2	0.478	0.622	0.560
Standard error of estimate as per cent of mean	7.8	7.6	6.7
Durbin-Watson test	1.78	2.59 [e]	2.17
Elasticity (at 1948–1961) means			
Disposable income	0.70	1.22	−0.03
Price	−0.25	−0.18	−0.96

[a]) Imports of crude and manufactured food. Mean for 1948–1961: $ 3.66 billion.

[b]) Seasonally adjusted at annual rates, in billions of 1954 dollars. Mean of real disposable income for 1948–1961: $ 268 billion.

[c]) Not significant at the 5 per cent level.

[d]) Implicit price deflator of imports of food divided by index of domestic food prices (U.S. wholesale prices: consumer foods; 1954 = 1).

[e]) Durbin-Watson test falls in the "inconclusive" range.

due to certain trends which may or may not continue in the future. (The lower income elasticities found for the subperiod 1954–1961 seem to corroborate this.) The elasticity of demand for imports of unfinished goods with respect to manufacturing production and the elasticity of U. S. exports with respect to world exports (both about $\frac{1}{3}$ in the impact period) may be accepted as of a plausible order of magnitude, the former implying a long-run elasticity of somewhat less than unity, the latter perhaps one that is slightly in excess of unity.

As expected, the price elasticity of U. S. demand for imported unfinished goods is fairly low; the impact elasticity of $-\frac{1}{3}$ implies a long-run elasticity of about $-\frac{2}{3}$. U. S. exports show a somewhat greater degree of price elasticity [10]. It was not possible to get reliable estimates of the price elasticity

[10]) These findings concerning price elasticities of demand for U.S. imports and exports are on the whole consistent with estimates for the same period, though computed from annual data and on a regional basis, in Rhomberg and Boissonneault, *op. cit.*

TABLE 11.6

Exports of goods [a]).

Independent variables	Fitting period		
	1948–1961	1948–1953	1954–1961
Exports of goods lagged one quarter	0.700	0.521	0.752
	(0.069)	(0.103)	(0.095)
World exports excluding U.S. [b])	0.0703	0.0646	0.0929
	(0.0132)	(0.0150)	(0.0305)
Deflated export price [c])	−10.2	−10.0	−23.2 [d])
(1954 = 1)	(3.2)	(3.0)	(9.0)
Constant term	9.61	11.7	20.5
	(2.75)	(3.3)	(7.4)
$\bar{R}^2$	0.928	0.766	0.846
ρ^2	0.308	0.515	0.377
Standard error of estimate as per cent of mean	5.0	4.6	4.8
Durbin-Watson test	1.96	2.06	2.54 [e])
Elasticities (at 1948–1961 means)			
World trade	0.35	0.32	0.46
Price	−0.74	−0.73	−1.7

[a]) Seasonally adjusted at annual rates, in billions of 1954 dollars; mean for 1948–1961: $ 13.9 billion.

[b]) Seasonally adjusted at annual rates, in billions of 1954 dollars; mean for 1948–1961: $ 68.6 billion.

[c]) Implicit price deflator of exports of goods and services, divided by world export unit value excluding U.S. component (1954 = 1).

[d]) Not significant at the 1 per cent level.

[e]) Durbin-Watson test falls in the "inconclusive" range.

of demand for imports of finished goods and services, either inclusive or exclusive of foodstuffs.

In a set of alternative computations the explanatory variables in the import demand functions have been lagged by one quarter [11]). The resulting equations were, by the criterion of $\bar{R}^2$ and the standard errors of the regression coefficients, uniformly inferior to those reported above. Changes in

[11]) Except for the import prices in the numerators of the price ratios. These unit value indices reflect the prices at the time of the conclusion of the contracts rather than at the time of importation; they are, therefore, in a sense automatically lagged by the appropriate time interval. In the alternative calculations mentioned in the text, only the domestic price deflators in the denominators of the price ratios have been lagged and not the ratios themselves.

TABLE 11.7

Foreign trade elasticities [a]): aggregate import and export equations.

Equation	Fitting period		
	1948–1961	1948–1953	1954–1961
Imports of finished goods and services (including food)			
Disposable income	0.80	1.11 [b])	0.37 [c])
Deflated price	−0.19 [c])	−0.21 [c])	−1.20 [b])
Imports of finished goods and services (excluding food)			
Disposable income	0.62	0.64 [b])	0.56 [c])
Deflated price	−0.32 [c])	−0.24 [c])	−1.20 [b])
Imports of food			
Disposable income	0.70	1.22 [c])	(−0.03) [c])
Deflated price	−0.25	−0.18 [c])	−0.96
Imports of unfinished goods			
Manufacturing production	0.41	0.66 [b])	0.27 [c])
Deflated price	−0.32	−0.49	−0.34 [b])
Exports of goods and services			
World trade excluding U.S.	0.33	0.30	0.40
Deflated price	−0.57	−0.64	−1.20 [b])
Exports of goods			
World trade excluding U.S.	0.35	0.32	0.46
Deflated price	−0.74	−0.73	−1.70 [b])

[a]) Evaluated at the sample means (1948–1961) of the respective variables.

[b]) Not significant at the 1 per cent level.

[c]) Not significant at the 5 per cent level.

income and in the prices of substitutes might have been thought of as preceding the import changes they induce. But to the extent that these changes are anticipated by the importers, the induced import changes may be roughly simultaneous with the changes in the causal variables. It would appear that there is no a priori presumption in favor of lag relations. In this connection, it is interesting that earlier work of the International Monetary Fund [12]) on quarterly U. S. imports showed a close relation between certain import categories and the new orders series published by the U. S.

---

[12]) Timothy D. Sweeney, "Short-Range Forecasting of U.S. Imports", *IMF Staff Papers* (September, 1954) pp. 1–21.

Department of Commerce; new orders themselves tend to "lead" the major indicators of economic activity, and so a simultaneous relationship between these indicators and imports does not appear implausible.

11.3.1. Comparison of subperiods

The main model is fitted to data for the period from 1948 to 1961. In connection with the foreign trade equations the question arises, however, whether certain structural features of world trade have remained invariant as between the earlier and the later part of this period. In particular, the early postwar period was characterized by supply shortages, especially in the European countries, and by exchange restrictions imposed by many countries in order to preserve their scanty foreign exchange reserves. A further disturbance during the early years of the sample period, which finds particularly pronounced expression in the data on foreign trade quantities and prices, was the Korean War. In order to test whether these factors seriously impair the usefulness of equations fitted over the whole fourteen-year period, the equations selected by theoretical and statistical criteria have also been computed for two subperiods. The first of these, from the first quarter of 1948 to the fourth quarter of 1953 (24 observations), includes the experience of the early postwar years as well as of the Korean War. The second subperiod is slightly longer, covering 32 quarters, from the first quarter of 1954 to the fourth quarter of 1961.

The last two columns of table 11.7 show computed elasticities, evaluated at the means (1948–1961) of the respective variables, for the two subperiods. Comparison of the two subperiods is made difficult by the fact that some of the elasticities are not significantly different from zero at acceptable levels of confidence. It appears, nevertheless, that—excepting imports of unfinished goods—the price elasticities tended to be somewhat higher in the second subperiod. The computed elasticities of import demand with respect to disposable income or manufacturing production, respectively, are slightly lower for the second subperiod than for the first. On the other hand, the elasticity of U. S. exports with respect to the rest of the world's exports seems to have risen somewhat from the earlier to the later of the two periods.

On the evidence presented in table 11.7 one may be inclined to favor the use, for forecasting and policy simulation purposes, of foreign trade equations fitted to data of a more recent period, which would more closely reflect the present behavior of imports and exports in response to changes in prices and in economic activity. One's decision in this respect should, however, also take into account the degree of success achieved with equations based on alternative sample periods in "forecasting" beyond the end of the sample period. Such a comparison is discussed in the following paragraphs.

11.3.2. *Explanatory power and forecasting efficiency of the equations*

The equations reported in this chapter generally show high correlation coefficients. The question arises whether $\bar{R}^2$ is not too lenient a test of the explanatory power of an equation fitted to quarterly time series which show a considerable degree of autocorrelation[13]). In a sense, $\bar{R}^2$ shows the performance of an equation compared with the naive hypothesis that the dependent variable always takes its mean value. In view of the question raised above, a second coefficient on goodness of fit has been computed. It measures the explanatory power of an equation compared with the (somewhat less) naive hypothesis that the value of the dependent variable in period t will be the same as its value in period $t-1$. In view of its similarity to $\bar{R}^2$ this statistic has been labeled ρ^2. It is computed as follows:

$$\rho^2 = 1 - \frac{\sum_{2}^{n}(y_t - \hat{y}_t)^2}{\sum_{2}^{n}(y_t - y_{t-1})^2}$$

where y and $\hat{y}$ are, respectively, the actual and computed values of the dependent variable in question. The denominator in the fraction above represents the sum of the squared errors from the equation

$$\hat{y}_t = y_{t-1}$$

where $\hat{y}_t$ is the naive estimate of y_t. It should be noted that ρ^2 is not the same as $\bar{R}^2$ for the equivalent equation fitted to first differences of the variables but is a somewhat less exacting test of the quarter-to-quarter explanatory power of a regression equation[14]).

The tables show ρ^2 in addition to $\bar{R}^2$. As expected, ρ^2 is in most cases considerably lower than $\bar{R}^2$, in many cases about half the value of the latter. Although significance tests have not been computed for this statistic, it

---

[13]) See also the comments on this topic by Suits and Sparks in Chapter 7 on consumption expenditure in this volume.

[14]) The statistic ρ^2 is related to both $\bar{R}^2$ and the serial correlation coefficient, $[\text{cov}(y_t, y_{t-1})]/\sigma_y^2$, of the dependent variable; approximately, ρ^2 exceeds, or falls short of, $\bar{R}^2$ according as the serial correlation coefficient falls short of, or exceeds, the value of 0.5.

appears that most of the equations perform fairly satisfactorily under this criterion.

As a final test of the suitability of the proposed equations for the purpose at hand, a comparison has been made of the forecasting efficiency of the equations computed from the entire sample (1948–1961) and those computed from the sample of the second subperiod (1954–1961). Table 11.8 shows the

TABLE 11.8

Test of forecasting efficiency of aggregate import and export equations, four quarters of 1962.

Equation	Standard percentage error of forecast for four quarters of 1962 from equation fitted to period [a])		ρ^2 of forecast for four quarters of 1962 from equation fitted to period [b])	
	1948–1961	1954–1961	1948–1961	1954–1961
Imports of finished goods and services (including food)	2.1	2.1	−0.29	−0.27
Imports of finished goods and services (excluding food)	3.9	2.1	−0.10	0.69
Imports of food	6.8	8.9	0.31	−0.21
Imports of unfinished goods	2.8	2.7	0.33	0.35
Exports of goods and services	3.2	3.5	0.33	0.22
Exports of goods	5.6	5.7	−0.09	−0.13

[a]) Square root of the mean of the squared percentage residuals for four quarters of 1962.

[b]) ρ^2, as explained in the text, measures the explanatory performance of the equation relative to the naive hypothesis that the dependent variable will in every period assume its own value of the preceding period. A value of 1 would indicate perfect performance, that is, the computed values during the "forecast" period are equal to the actual values; a value of zero would indicate that the forecasts from the equation are no better than forecasts with the help of the naive hypothesis; negative values indicate that forecasts from the naive hypothesis would have been superior to those from the equation.

results of forecasts from the two sets of equations for the four quarters of 1962, that is to say, for the first four quarters following the end of the sample period. Two measures are shown in this table: first, the standard percentage error of forecast for the four quarters, and second, the value of ρ^2 as applied to the forecast period [15]). The latter again evaluates the quarter-by-quarter forecasting power of the equation compared to the naive hypothesis of an unchanged value of the dependent variable.

Somewhat surprisingly, it is found that equations fitted to the shorter, and more recent, subperiod are not clearly superior to the regressions computed for the whole period. For exports, and for imports of food, the standard percentage errors of forecast are lower, and the values of ρ^2 are algebraically higher (i.e., better) for the equations fitted to the total period than for those fitted to the shorter period. For imports of finished goods and services excluding food the opposite is true. For imports of unfinished goods, and for imports of finished goods and services including food, equations from the entire period and from the shorter period seem to perform about equally well under the criteria reported in table 11.8. This table also shows that one should not expect great accuracy of forecasts outside of the sample period from these equations. In this connection it must be noted, however, that 1962 may have been a particularly difficult year to forecast, since both exports and imports of goods and services rose considerably during this year (exports by 6 per cent and imports by 11 per cent) in comparison with 1961. The respective activity variables rose much more slowly during 1962, and prices did not change significantly.

These comparisons of equations computed from alternative sample periods would seem to lead to the following conclusions: Some of the structural changes in the foreign sector of the U. S. economy occurring between the early part of the postwar period and more recent years are sufficiently pronounced to be detectable even in the aggregative import and export functions presented in this section. In particular, there seems to be some evidence that the import and export price elasticities have increased somewhat since the early postwar years. In principle, one would wish to use equations reflecting the structural features of the most recent period for which reliable computations can be made. The figures on which these judgments about structural changes are based are, however, subject to considerable margins of error. The case for using equations computed from a shorter and more recent sample period for purposes of the Brookings-SSRC econometric

---

[15]) In this case ρ^2 is computed by the formula given in the text with the summations running from the first to the fourth quarter of 1962. A value of unity would show perfect forecasting; a value of zero would indicate that the forecasts are on the whole neither better nor worse than the forecast of "no change from the preceding quarter"; negative values show that, taking all four quarters together, the naive hypothesis is superior to the tested equation.

model is further weakened by the fact that the equations for the entire period (1948–1961) were on the whole no less successful than those based on the shorter period (1954–1961) in forecasting the values of the dependent variables for the four quarters of 1962. Unless further study of this question produces evidence on one side or the other, there do not seem to be compelling reasons for shortening the SSRC sample period for purposes of the foreign sector equations.

11.3.3. Customs duties

In order to complete the government sector of the model, it is necessary to have an equation explaining the amount of customs duties collected. Experiments with quarterly data were initially not very successful in the sense that the estimated coefficients did not correspond closely enough to what is known about duty rates and the proportions of dutiable to total imports in various commodity classes. For this reason we report at this time only an equation fitted to annual data (1948–1962):

$$TX_{CU_{GF}}^A = \frac{0.159}{(0.025)} M_{FINM}^A + \frac{0.0293}{(0.0153)} [M_{EFIN*}^A] + \frac{0.148}{(0.132)} M_{FINF}^A$$

$$- \frac{0.0150}{(0.0090)} TIME + \frac{0.0172}{(0.0898)} \quad \bar{R}^2 = 0.987 \quad DW = 1.38. \quad (11.4)$$

In this equation $TX_{CU_{GF}}^A$ stands for U.S. customs receipts in billions of dollars as published by the U. S. Treasury Department [16]).

The other variables are:

M_{FINM} = imports of finished manufactures, billions of dollars
M_{EFIN} = imports of crude materials and semimanufactures, billions of dollars
M_{FINF} = imports of manufactured foodstuffs and beverages, billions of dollars
$TIME$ = time trend.

Raw foodstuffs are almost entirely duty free and are not included in the equation. The regression coefficients of the first three variables to the right of the equality sign are thus estimated marginal duty rates on all imports, dutiable and free, in the corresponding commodity classes. Allowing for the ratio of dutiable to total imports in these classes, the estimated duty

---

[16]) U.S. Treasury Department, *Treasury Bulletin.*

TABLE 11.9

Imports of crude materials (adjusted) [a,b].

Independent variables	Fitting Period					
	1948–1961		1948–1953		1954–1961	
	(1)	(2)	(1)	(2)	(1)	(2)
Imports of crude materials lagged one quarter	0.359 (0.118)	—	0.176 [c] (0.263)	—	0.552 (0.145)	—
Manufacturing production [b]	0.00867 (0.00324)	0.0106 (0.0034)	0.00731 [c] (0.00857)	0.00929 [c] (0.00793)	0.0114 [c] (0.0057)	0.00614 [c] (0.00675)
Change in nonfarm business inventories [b]	0.0104 [d] (0.0048)	0.0146 (0.0049)	0.0167 [c] (0.0111)	0.0201 [c] (0.0098)	0.00726 [c] (0.00769)	0.0149 [e] (0.0091)
Deflated import price (1954 = 1) [e]	−0.447 [d] (0.178)	−0.398 [d] (0.191)	−0.564 [c] (0.326)	−0.612 [c] (0.313)	−0.697 [c] (0.378)	0.040 [c] (0.399)
Trend ($t = 1, 2, \ldots$)	−0.00704 [d] (0.00289)	−0.00999 (0.00293)	−0.00240 [c] (0.01480)	−0.00435 [c] (0.01430)	−0.00796 [d] (0.00374)	−0.00843 [c] (0.00459)
Constant term	0.91 (0.32)	1.42 (0.29)	1.46 [c] (0.81)	1.68 [d] (0.73)	0.33 [c] (0.59)	1.23 [c] (0.66)
$\bar{R}^2$	0.546	0.473	0.325	0.344	0.632	0.447
ρ^2	0.438	0.333	0.395	0.378	0.583	0.339
Standard error of estimate as per cent of mean	5.5	6.0	7.2	7.1	4.3	5.3
Durbin-Watson test	1.86	1.40 [f]	1.88	1.73	2.03	1.23 [f]
Elasticities (at 1948–1961 means)						
Manufacturing production	0.51	0.62	0.43	0.54	0.67	0.36
Price	−0.24	−0.21	−0.30	−0.32	−0.37	+0.02

a) Imports of crude materials (Dept. of Commerce) less crude petroleum, mean for 1948–1961: $ 1.98 billion.

b) Seasonally adjusted at annual rates, in billions of 1954 dollars. Mean of manufacturing production for 1948–1961: $ 116 billion.

c) Not significant at the 5 per cent level.

d) Not significant at the 1 per cent level.

e) Unit value of adjusted crude material imports deflated by crude materials component of U.S. wholesale price index (1954 = 1).

f) Durbin-Watson test falls in the "inconclusive" range.

rates are not implausible in the light of the scanty information on average
duty rates by commodity group [17]).

11.4. Import functions for individual commodity groups

In order to prepare for a later, more disaggregated, version of the foreign
sector of the Brookings-SSRC econometric model, a number of import
functions have been computed for various commodity groups. For this
purpose the commodity groups published by the Department of Commerce
have been adjusted in an effort to make the resulting subgroups less heterogeneous. The resulting groups are as follows:
   (1) crude materials excluding crude petroleum
   (2) crude foodstuffs excluding coffee
   (3) manufactured foodstuffs excluding sugar
   (4) semimanufactures plus newsprint and jute burlaps
   (5) finished manufactures excluding automobiles (except trucks), news-
       print and jute burlaps
   (6) coffee
   (7) sugar
   (8) automobiles
   (9) crude petroleum.
The reasons for the exclusions are obvious. Crude petroleum has for some
time been imported in accordance with import quotas; for purposes of the
model it would be best to estimate crude oil imports from the formula applied by the authorities administering the import quotas. The reasons for
excluding sugar are similar, though the forecasting of sugar imports may be
somewhat more difficult than that of crude oil. Finally, coffee and automobiles are excluded from their respective categories, since the behavior
of these imports deviates considerably from the behavior of the remainder
of the respective commodity groups.
   Tables 11.9 through 11.13 show the results of regression equations computed for the five adjusted commodity groups. The import variables have
been seasonally adjusted and expressed at annual rates in billions of dollars
of 1954 purchasing power. The unit values of imports in these categories
have been derived by dividing the seasonally adjusted values in current

---

[17]) In an alternative approach, data for dutiable, rather than total, imports in the two
commodity classes were used and the ratios of dutiable to total imports were explained
by separate trend equations. The results obtained with this more complex scheme were,
however, not clearly superior to those reported in the text.

TABLE 11.10

Per capita imports of crude foodstuffs (adjusted) [a, b]

Independent variables	Fitting period					
	1948–1961		1948–1953		1954–1961	
	(1)	(2)	(1)	(2)	(1)	(2)
Per capita imports of crude foodstuffs lagged one quarter	0.286 (0.071)	—	0.139 [c] (0.120)	—	0.350 [d] (0.132)	—
Per capita real disposable income [b]	0.00127 (0.00046)	0.00154 (0.00052)	0.00236 [c] (0.00169)	0.00351 [d] (0.00138)	0.00103 [c] (0.00109)	−0.00018 [c] (0.00109)
Deflated import price (1954 = 1) [e]	−3.66 (0.41)	−4.42 (0.42)	−4.42 (0.73)	−4.67 (0.71)	−2.97 (0.64)	−2.77 (0.70)
Constant term	4.60 (0.73)	6.11 (0.71)	4.28 [c] (2.59)	3.38 [c] (2.50)	4.01 [c] (1.96)	7.22 (1.69)
$\bar{R}^2$	0.757	0.688	0.812	0.809	0.472	0.362
ρ^2	0.705	0.615	0.784	0.767	0.647	0.552
Standard error of estimate as per cent of mean	8.0	9.1	7.6	7.6	8.4	9.3
Durbin-Watson test	1.53 [f]	0.76 [g]	1.27 [f]	1.04 [f]	1.66	0.92 [g]
Elasticities (at 1948–1961 means)						
Disposable income	0.50	0.60	0.92	1.37	0.40	(−0.07)
Price	−0.88	−1.10	−1.10	−1.10	−0.72	−0.68

[a] Imports of crude foodstuffs (Dept. of Commerce) less coffee; per capita mean for 1948–1961: $ 4.14.

[b] Seasonally adjusted at annual rates, in 1954 dollars. Mean of per capita real disposable income for 1948–1961: $ 1.616.

[c] Not significant at the 5 per cent level.

[d] Not significant at the 1 per cent level.

[e] Unit value of adjusted imports of crude foodstuffs deflated by farm products component of U.S. wholesale price index (1954 = 1).

[f] Durbin-Watson test falls in the "inconclusive" range.

[g] Serial correlation present (5 per cent level of significance).

TABLE 11.11

Per capita imports of manufactured foodstuffs (adjusted) [a], [b].

Independent variables	Fitting period					
	1948–1961		1948–1953		1954–1961	
	(1)	(2)	(1)	(2)	(1)	(2)
Per capita imports of manufactured food, lagged one quarter	0.548	—	0.344 [c]	—	0.535	—
	(0.076)		(0.136)		(0.109)	
Per capita real disposable income [b]	0.00370	0.00839	0.00519	0.00919	0.00419	0.00863
	(0.00070)	(0.00038)	(0.00173)	(0.00079)	(0.00112)	(0.00089)
Deflated import price (1954 = 1) [d]	−6.61	−10.3	−5.45	−5.58	−9.17	−16.2
	(1.06)	(1.3)	(1.10)	(1.23)	(2.07)	(2.0)
Constant term	2.75 [c]	1.30 [e]	0.02 [e]	−4.69 [c]	4.59 [c]	6.86 [c]
	(1.08)	(1.49)	(0.03)	(2.02)	(2.04)	(2.66)
$\bar{R}^2$	0.955	0.911	0.926	0.907	0.917	0.852
ρ^2	0.534	0.017	0.720	0.616	0.485	0.043
Standard error of estimate as per cent of mean	5.3	7.4	5.5	6.2	4.7	6.3
Durbin-Watson test	1.86	1.01 [f]	2.47 [g]	2.12	2.00	1.33 [g]
Elasticities (at 1948–1961 means)						
Disposable income	1.4	3.0	1.9	3.4	1.5	3.2
Price	−1.5	−2.3	−1.2	−1.3	−2.1	−3.7

[a] Imports of manufactured foodstuffs (Dept. of Commerce) less sugar; per capita mean for 1948–1961: $ 4.42.

[b] Seasonally adjusted at annual rates, in 1954 dollars. Mean of per capita real disposable income for 1948–1961: $ 1,616.

[c] Not significant at the 1 per cent level.

[d] Unit value of imports of manufactured foodstuffs deflated by processed foods component of U.S. wholesale price index (1954 = 1).

[e] Not significant at the 5 per cent level.

[f] Serial correlation present (5 per cent level of significance).

[g] Durbin-Watson test falls in the "inconclusive" range.

TABLE 11.12

Imports of semimanufactures (adjusted) [a, b].

Independent variables	Fitting period					
	1948–1961		1948–1953		1954–1961	
	(1)	(2)	(1)	(2)	(1)	(2)
Imports of semimanufactures lagged one quarter	0.313 (0.111)	—	0.0370 [c] (0.2040)	—	0.159 [c] (0.128)	—
Manufacturing production [b]	0.0169 (0.0033)	0.0255 (0.0013)	0.0341 (0.0082)	0.0355 (0.0029)	0.0146 (0.0042)	0.0189 (0.0024)
Change in nonfarm business inventories [b]	0.0142 (0.0043)	0.0182 (0.0043)	0.0105 [c] (0.0071)	0.0110 [c] (0.0066)	0.0241 (0.0054)	0.0243 (0.0054)
Deflated import price (1954 = 1) [d]	−1.94 (0.37)	−2.33 (0.37)	−3.50 (0.77)	−3.59 (0.58)	−2.27 (0.40)	−2.40 (0.39)
1959 steel strike dummy variable [e]	0.204 [c] (0.103)	0.311 (0.102)	—	—	0.281 (0.080)	0.346 (0.061)
Constant term	2.13 (0.40)	2.50 (0.41)	2.74 (0.62)	2.79 (0.54)	3.23 (0.59)	3.36 (0.58)
$\bar{R}^2$	0.930	0.920	0.891	0.897	0.941	0.940
ρ^2	0.519	0.464	0.623	0.625	0.783	0.770
Standard error of estimate as per cent of mean	4.0	4.3	5.3	5.1	2.3	2.3
Durbin-Watson test	0.99 [f]	0.83 [f]	1.16 [g]	1.17 [g]	1.52 [g]	1.49 [g]
Elasticities (at 1948–1961 means)						
Manufacturing production	0.62	0.93	1.24	1.29	0.53	0.69
Price	−0.61	−0.73	−1.10	−1.13	−0.72	−0.76

[a] Imports of semimanufactures (Department of Commerce) plus newsprint and jute burlaps; mean for 1948–1961: $ 3.17 billion.

[b] Seasonally adjusted at annual rates, in billions of 1954 dollars. Mean of manufacturing production for 1948–1961: $ 116 billion.

[c] Not significant at the 5 per cent level.

[d] Unit value of adjusted imports of semimanufactures deflated by intermediate materials component of U.S. wholesale price index.

[e] Unity in third and fourth quarters of 1959, otherwise zero.

[f] Serial correlation present (5 per cent level of significance).

[g] Durbin-Watson test falls in the "inconclusive" range.

TABLE 11.4

Imports of finished manufactures (adjusted) a, b).

Independent variables	Fitting period					
	1948–1961		1948–1953		1954–1961	
	(1)	(2)	(1)	(2)	(1)	(2)
Imports of finished manufactures lagged one quarter	0.638 (0.079)	—	0.363 c) (0.165)	—	0.708 (0.099)	—
Real disposable income b)	0.00102 d) (0.00153)	0.00442 d) (0.00224)	0.00133 d) (0.00359)	0.00185 d) (0.00393)	0.00148 d) (0.00417)	0.0194 (0.0057)
Change in nonfarm inventories	0.0163 (0.0035)	0.0266 (0.0048)	0.0127 (0.0043)	0.0180 (0.0040)	0.0250 (0.0062)	0.0288 (0.0106)
Deflated import price (1954 = 1) e)	−1.34 c) (0.53)	−0.973 d) (0.795)	−0.966 c) (0.342)	−1.04 c) (0.37)	−4.55 c) (1.83)	−1.88 d) (3.04)
r^2 ($t = 1, 2, \ldots$)	0.00033 (0.00009)	0.00091 (0.00008)	0.00078 d) (0.00039)	0.00130 (0.00034)	0.00037 d) (0.00023)	0.00115 (0.00034)
Constant term	1.43 d) (0.73)	0.769 d) (1.086)	1.19 d) (0.94)	1.39 d) (1.03)	4.63 d) (2.52)	−1.64 d) (4.01)
$\bar{R}^2$	0.992	0.981	0.963	0.955	0.983	0.951
ρ^2	0.561	−0.034	0.643	0.531	0.634	0.137
Standard error of estimate as per cent of mean	4.9	7.3	5.3	5.8	4.2	7.1
Durbin-Watson test	1.62 f)	0.76 g)	1.31 f)	1.65 f)	1.86	0.58 g)
Elasticities (at 1948–1961 means)						
Disposable income	0.14	0.58	0.18	0.24	0.20	2.60
Price	−0.65	−0.48	−0.47	−0.51	−2.20	−0.92

a) Imports of finished manufactures less automobiles (except trucks), newsprint and jute burlaps; mean for 1948–1961: $ 2.03 billion.

b) Seasonally adjusted at annual rates, in billions of 1954 dollars. Mean of real disposable income for 1948–1961: $ 268 billion.

c) Not significant at the 1 per cent level.

d) Not significant at the 5 per cent level.

e) Unit value of adjusted imports of finished manufactures, current quarter, deflated by finished goods component of U.S. wholesale price index, lagged one quarter, (1954 = 1).

f) Durbin-Watson test falls in the "inconclusive" range.

g) Serial correlation present (5 per cent level of significance).

dollars by the corresponding values in 1954 dollars. In order to test whether significant distortion has resulted from this method of deriving the unit values, all regressions shown have also been computed with seasonally unadjusted import data and with unit values derived from seasonally unadjusted current dollar and constant dollar values for imports; in these cases seasonal dummy variables were included in the equations. These tests, which are not separately shown in this chapter, led to the conclusion that no serious distortion has resulted from seasonal adjustment of the import value and quantum variables.

The results are summarized in table 11.14 in terms of the computed elasticities, evaluated at the sample means (1948–1961) of the respective variables.

TABLE 11.14

Foreign trade elasticities a)*: commodity group import equations.*

	Fitting period					
Equation	1948–1961		1948–1953		1954–1961	
	(1)	(2)	(1)	(2)	(1)	(2)
Crude materials						
Manufacturing pro-						
duction	0.51	0.62	0.43 c)	0.54 c)	0.67 c)	0.36 c)
Deflated price	−0.24 b)	−0.21 b)	−0.30 c)	−0.32 c)	−0.37 c)	(0 c)
Crude foodstuffs						
Disposable income	0.50	0.60	0.92 c)	1.37 b)	0.40	(0 c)
Deflated price	−0.88	−1.10	−1.10	−1.10	−0.72	−0.68
Manufactured food-						
stuffs						
Disposable income	1.4	3.0	1.9	3.4	1.5	3.2
Deflated price	−1.5	−2.3	−1.2	−1.3	−2.1	−3.7
Semimanufactures						
Manufacturing pro-						
duction	0.62	0.93	1.24	1.29	0.53	0.69
Deflated price	−0.61	−0.73	−1.10	−1.13	−0.72	−0.76
Finished manufactures						
Disposable income	0.14 c)	0.58 c)	0.18 c)	0.24 c)	0.20 c)	2.60
Deflated price	−0.65 b)	−0.48 c)	−0.47 b)	−0.51 b)	−2.20 b)	−0.92 c)

Note   Equations labeled (1) include the lagged dependent variable on the right-hand side of the equation, while those labeled (2) do not.

a) Evaluated at the sample means (1948–1961) of the respective variables.

b) Not significant at the 1 per cent level.

c) Not significant at the 5 per cent level.

The elasticities tabulated are on the whole in accordance with a priori expectations and also with results recently reported by Ball and Marwah [18]. Price elasticities are fairly low for crude materials (-0.2 to -0.4) but are surprisingly high (in absolute value), as well as statistically reliable, for crude foodstuffs (around -1) and for manufactured foodstuffs (-1.5 or somewhat higher). The price elasticities of semimanufactures and of finished manufactures are somewhat lower, although they are, at least in the case of semimanufactures, statistically fairly reliable.

A general comment should be made in connection with the computed price elasticities. From a number of trade studies of the postwar period, and particularly of the more recent years, one feels encouraged to venture the opinion that the well-known failure of earlier econometric foreign trade studies [19] to arrive at reasonably reliable estimates of price elasticities with the theoretically expected sign (and of plausible magnitude) is not necessarily inherent in the methods used nor an accurate reflection of economic reality in general[20]; it may at least to some extent have been a result of the peculiarities of the late interwar period and of the first four or five years following World War II. Moreover, improved results may be expected when commodity categories are chosen which are sufficiently homogeneous to permit the selection of a suitable price deflator.

11.4.1. Forecasts from commodity group equations

The results of forecasting imports of the five adjusted commodity groups are summarized in table 11.15. As in the case of the more aggregative equations discussed in the preceding section, there is no clear indication that the

---

[18] R. J. Ball and K. Marwah, The U.S. Demand for Imports, 1948–1958, *Review of Economics and Statistics* (November, 1962). Ball and Marwah use unadjusted commodity group data, a fact which may explain some of the differences in the results presented here from theirs.

[19] For a survey of these results see H. S. Cheng, Statistical Estimates of Elasticities and Propensities in International Trade: A Survey of Published Studies, *IMF Staff Papers* (April, 1959).

[20] See S. J. Prais, Econometric Research in International Trade: A Review, *Kyklos* 15 (1962) Fasc. 3., 560–579. Nothing said in the text is intended to deny the existence, in the case of most price elasticity estimates, of "aggregation bias" as described by G. H. Orcutt in Measurement of Price Elasticities in International Trade, *Review of Economics and Statistics*, 32 (1950) 117ff.; or the possibility that in some cases measured elasticities may be biased downward for a number of other reasons given in Orcutt's pioneering article.

equations fitted over the more recent subperiod yield better forecasts than the corresponding equations for the entire period. Indeed, for crude materials and semimanufactures, the forecasting errors are clearly lower, and the ρ^2 values for the forecast period are algebraically considerably higher for the 1948–1961 equations than for those fitted to the period 1954–1961.

TABLE 11.15

Test of forecasting efficiency of commodity group import equations, four quarters of 1962.

Equation	Standard percentage error of forecast for the four quarters of 1962 from equation fitted to period [a])		ρ^2 of forecast for the four quarters of 1962 from equation fitted to period [b])	
	1948–1961	1954–1961	1948–1961	1954–1961
Crude materials (1)	2.7	5.5	−0.35	−4.60
(2)	1.2	3.4	0.73	−1.07
Crude foodstuffs (1)	5.3	3.4	0.86	0.95
(2)	8.2	5.4	0.67	0.86
Manufactured (1)	7.0	6.7	0.23	0.28
foodstuffs (2)	7.6	6.4	0.09	0.35
Semimanufactures (1)	1.7	4.3	0.68	−1.03
(2)	1.7	4.8	0.70	−1.47
Finished (1)	2.3	1.9	0.77	0.83
manufactures (2)	2.7	2.7	0.67	0.67

Note   Equations labeled (1) include the lagged dependent variable on the right-hand side of the equation, while those labeled (2) do not.

[a]) Square root of the mean of the squared percentage residuals for four quarters of 1962.

[b]) ρ^2, as explained in the text, measures the explanatory performance of the equation relative to the naive hypothesis that the dependent variable will in every period assume its own value of the preceding period. A value of 1 would indicate perfect performance, that is, the computed values during the "forecast" period are equal to the actual values; a value of zero would indicate that the forecasts from the equation are no better than forecasts with the help of the naive hypothesis; negative values indicate that forecasts from the naive hypothesis would have been superior to those from the equation.

The forecasting performance of these equations is on the whole disappointing, especially in the case of crude and manufactured foodstuffs. What has been said in the preceding section about the apparently unusual increase in imports during 1962 applies also to the individual commodity groups. It is apparent that we are faced here with effects which are not adequately encompassed by the income and price variables which appear in these equations.

11.4.2. Annual equations for special commodities

Experiments with equations fitted to quarterly data for imports of coffee, sugar and automobiles revealed a number of problems which suggested that exploratory work might best begin with annual data.

Coffee The following equation for the annual volume of coffee imports per head was computed from data for the 15-year period 1948–1962:

$$\frac{M_{COF}^{A54}}{N_{14+}^{A}} = \frac{0.00460}{(0.00232)} \left[\frac{Y_D^A}{P_C^A \cdot N_{14+}^A} \right] - \frac{12.9}{(2.3)} \left[\frac{PM_{COF}^A}{P_{CN}^A} \right] + \frac{14.5}{(6.0)} \qquad \bar{R}^2 = 0.767.$$

(11.5)

The variables are:

M_{COF} = imports of coffee, billions of dollars
N_{14+} = noninstitutional population aged 14 and over, end of quarter, billions of persons
Y_D = disposable personal income, billions of dollars
P_C = implicit price deflator for personal consumption expenditures, 1954 = 1.00
PM_{MCOF} = unit value index of coffee imports, 1954 = 1.00
P_{CN} = implicit price deflator for personal consumption expenditures on nondurable goods, 1954 = 1.00.

The price elasticity at the means of the variables is -0.5, while the elasticity with respect to real disposable income per head is about 0.6. Both of these elasticities are somewhat higher than corresponding values reported for U. S. real coffee consumption per head [21]. Since coffee importers allow their stocks to vary in accordance with current and expected coffee prices, a higher price elasticity should be expected for imports than for consumption.

Sugar Imports of sugar correspond very closely to the "final adjusted quota" for sugar imports set by the Secretary of Agriculture during the

---

[21] In a recent study published by the U.S. Department of Commerce (*Coffee Consumption in the United States, 1920–1965*, Washington, D.C., 1961) price and income elasticities of real coffee consumption per head are estimated as -0.16 and 0.22, respectively. These computations are based on a prewar and postwar sample period (1920–1940 and 1950–1959).

year to which the quota applies, though much less closely to the "final basic quota" announced in December of the preceding year. An attempt was therefore made to relate sugar imports directly to the principal factors taken into consideration by the Department of Agriculture in arriving at these quotas [22]). The estimated relation (1948–1962) does not, however, give a very satisfactory explanation of sugar imports:

$$Q^A_{MSUG} = \frac{0.585}{(0.159)} Q^A_{CASUG} - \frac{0.286}{(0.257)} Q^A_{XASUG} + \frac{0.304}{(0.860)} \qquad \bar{R}^2 = 0.613. \quad (11.6)$$

The variables are [23]):

Q^A_{MSUG} = imports of sugar, millions of short tons per year.
Q^A_{CASUG} = anticipated consumption of sugar (consumption during the preceding year inflated by the rate of population growth from the preceding to the current year), millions of short tons per year.
Q^A_{XASUG} = available supply of sugar (domestic, including offshore, production of the preceding crop year plus the deviation of sugar stocks from linear trend, 1948–1962, thereof), millions of short tons per year.

It is interesting to note that the relation between the "final basic import quota" and these explanatory variables was much less close ($\bar{R}^2 = 0.28$) than that shown in the equation above.

Automobiles   Between 1954 and 1959 imports of automobiles into the U. S. (in 1954 prices) rose twentyfold, but from 1959 to 1962 they declined by two-thirds. The sharp increase to 1959 is the result of a shift in tastes toward the smaller European cars, as well as of increased supply capabilities and a considerable sales effort in the U. S. market on the part of European automobile producers. The subsequent precipitous decline in automobile imports must be ascribed in good part to the increased production of U. S. compact cars; from 1959 to 1961 the proportion of "compacts" to total domestic output of automobiles rose from 11 to 35 per cent. Any regression equation explaining the behavior of automobile imports would have to take account both of the initial change in taste [24]) and of the response of

[22]) These considerations are listed in U.S. Department of Agriculture, *Sugar Reports* (October, 1963) p. 10.
[23]) The data are taken from *Sugar Reports*.
[24]) Part, though undoubtedly not a major part, of the sharp increase in car imports in the late 1950's may be explained by the rise in prices of domestic automobiles relative to those of imported cars.

U. S. manufacturers to this shift. So far it has not been possible to find an acceptable "taste variable" [25]). The equations shown below must therefore be regarded as exploratory exercises.

A logarithmic equation was fitted to annual data (1948–1962) without the "ratio of compacts" variable:

$$\log M_{DA}^{A54} = \frac{5.91}{(1.03)} \log \left[\frac{Y_D^A}{P_C^A}\right] - \frac{3.34}{(1.04)} \log \left[\frac{PM_{MDA}^A}{WPI_{3711}^A}\right] - \frac{15.5}{(2.5)}$$

$$\bar{R}^2 = 0.892. \tag{11.7a}$$

The variables are [26]):

M_{DA} = imports of automobiles, billions of dollars
Y_D = disposable personal income, billions of dollars
P_C = implicit price deflator for personal consumption expenditures, 1954 = 1.00
PM_{MDA} = unit value index of imported automobiles, 1954 = 1.00
WPI_{3711} = wholesale price index of motor vehicles, 1954 = 1.00.

The corresponding equation fitted to seasonally adjusted quarterly data is:

$$\log M_{DA}^{54} = \frac{7.64}{(0.58)} \log \left[\frac{Y_D}{P_C}\right] - \frac{2.68}{(0.53)} \log \left[\frac{PM_{MDA}}{WPI_{3711}}\right] - \frac{19.7}{(1.4)}$$

$$\bar{R}^2 = 0.861. \tag{11.7b}$$

The quarterly equation has an extremely low Durbin-Watson ratio (0.38), partly reflecting the fact that the 1954–1961 "hump" is not explained by the included variables. This hump exaggerates the income elasticity computed in these equations; nevertheless, automobile imports would appear to be highly income elastic even if the hump were adequately explained by additional variables.

$REGS_{COM}/REGS_{DOM}$, the ratio of compact to all domestically produced cars [27]), was found significant in quarterly equations fitted to the original

---

[25]) In another study by the authors, the "hump" of automobile imports between 1955 and 1961 was removed from the total of U.S. imports from Western Europe by freehand methods. (Rhomberg and Boissonneault, *op. cit.*, chart 2.)

[26]) Automobile import volume and unit values are taken from U.S. Department of Commerce, *World Trade Information Service*, and the U.S. wholesale price index of motor vehicles from the *Survey of Current Business*.

[27]) The variable represents the ratio of new compact cars to total new domestic cars registered in the United States. The data are from *Automobile News*.

data (rather than to their logarithms), one of which is shown below:

$$M_{DA}^{54} = \frac{0.925}{(0.044)} [M_{DA}^{54}]_{-1} + \frac{0.000823}{(0.000350)} \left[\frac{Y_D}{P_C}\right] - \frac{0.149}{(0.062)} \left[\frac{PM_{MDA}}{WPI_{3711}}\right]$$

$$- \frac{0.286}{(0.092)} \left[\frac{REGS_{COM}}{REGS_{DOM}}\right] - \frac{0.0443}{(0.1080)} \qquad \bar{R}^2 = 0.960. \qquad (11.7c)$$

In this equation, too, serial correlation of the residuals is indicated by a Durbin-Watson ratio of 1.00. The "longer run" coefficient of $REGS_{COM}/REGS_{DOM}$ for an adjustment over 8 quarters would be around 3, a value which would indicate that a rise by 0.24 in the fraction of compacts produced in the U. S., such as has occurred from 1959 to 1961, would tend to lower automobile imports by about $ 0.7 billion. The actual reduction in imports (in 1954 prices) from 1959 to 1961 was $ 0.5 billion, a figure which, after allowance for additional imports induced by the rise in disposable income, is reasonably close to the computed value of $ 0.7 billion.

Crude petroleum   As has been indicated earlier in this section, imports of crude petroleum should be treated for forecasting purposes by applying the formula used by the Bureau of Mines for determining the import quota. In principle, this formula relates the import quota to past domestic production, but there are additional complications with respect to imports from Canada and imports into California which cannot be described in this chapter.

11.4.3. Concluding remark

The exploratory work reported in this section has been presented as background material for further research on a more disaggregated foreign sector of the Brookings-SSRC econometric model. It should, however, be emphasized that the most appropriate manner of refining the model has not yet been determined. It may be that a different classification of imports will later appear more promising and better adapted to the requirements of the rest of the model.

CHAPTER 12

A SUBMODEL OF THE AGRICULTURAL SECTOR

Contents

12.1. Outline of the agricultural submodel as a whole 410

12.2. Determining prices of farm products 411
    1. Causal ordering and matrix structure. 2. Comments on the individual equations.

12.3. Determining net income of farm operators 437
    1. Causal ordering and matrix structure in the farm income subset. 2. Comments on the individual equations.

12.4. Causal ordering and estimation in the farm price and income blocks combined 448

12.5. Ancillary equations: gross farm investment, agricultural employment and net acquisitions of farm products for price support purposes . . . 449
    1. Gross farm investment. 2. Agricultural employment. 3. Commodity credit corporation net outlays for price support purposes. 4. Total consumption of food livestock products as a function of the volume of farm marketings of livestock and livestock products.

12.6. Conclusion 459

References 459

A SUBMODEL OF THE AGRICULTURAL SECTOR [1])

KARL A. FOX

Iowa State University, Ames, Iowa

This chapter focuses upon the determination of agricultural sector equations to be incorporated into the Brookings-SSRC econometric model. The agricultural sector will be discussed in more detail than is customary in econometric work. In the past, builders of econometric models have failed to establish living contact with either research economists or policy makers

[1]) I must first of all acknowledge my indebtedness to M. V. R. Sastry, my research assistant during 1962–1963, for effective interpretation of some very complicated instructions to an IBM 7074. Mary Clem, Rosemary Boles, and Howard Jespersen, of the Iowa State University Computing Center, also helped with data processing, and my daughter, Karen Fox, assisted with basic tabulations and data adjustments during the summer of 1962.

Several economists and former colleagues in the Economic Research Service, United States Department of Agriculture, provided me with basic data, special tabulations and advice. I wish particularly to thank C. Kyle Randall, Richard D. Butler, Donald D. Durost, Helen Eklund, Reuben Hecht, Robert Masucci, Rex F. Daly and Robert Olson. A dozen other persons in USDA responded to more limited requests for data.

Also, several colleagues at Iowa State University gave me valuable comments on an earlier draft, including Wilbur R. Maki, James R. Prescott, J. K. Sengupta, Bob R. Holdren, and Robert W. Thomas. I have profited from many discussions with Wilbur Maki on area delineation (geographic disaggregation in the present context), and from his analyses of inventory fluctuations and other phenomena in the livestock economy.

I wish to congratulate George E. Brandow, of Pennsylvania State University, on his outstanding 1961 achievement in creating a disaggregated model of the demand side of food and agriculture and to thank him for permitting me to use the consumer demand matrix which appears as table 12.3. I am also indebted to Earl O. Heady for many demonstrations of the feasibility of disaggregating the production side of agriculture by commodities and regions and of building bridges between micro- and macroanalysis—normative as well as positive—in the agricultural sector.

concerned with the agricultural sector. I shall therefore try to indicate how the present submodel can be related to major lines of research being pursued by agricultural economists. Also, I hope to indicate ways in which agricultural economists and policy makers may be encouraged to supply information and pose questions at what is for them a practical level of disaggregation and ways in which the proprietors of the Brookings-SSRC econometric model can help them to obtain consistent answers at this same level.

12.1. Outline of the agricultural submodel as a whole

The submodel consists of 15 equations. It may be divided into one block of eight equations focusing on the determination of farm product prices and a second block of seven equations directed toward the estimation of net farm income.

The price block contains two equations expressing domestic consumer demand for foods of livestock and crop origin, respectively. Next, it includes two supply functions for food marketing services relating, respectively, to livestock and crop foods. Equations (12.8 and 12.9) are identities, specifying that the retail price of each food group must equal the sum of the supply price for marketing services and the equivalent price received by farmers.

Equation (12.10) is another identity, combining equivalent farm prices for food crops and food livestock into a price index for all farm food products. Equation (12.11) expresses the official index of prices received by farmers for *all* commodities, food and nonfood, as a function of the farm price of food products and prices of two of the most important nonfood commodities and groups—cotton and feed grains.

The price block presented serious problems of multicollinearity, and a priori information was used in novel ways, particularly in specifying certain coefficients in the consumption functions.

Equations (12.12) through (12.18) express the determination of gross farm income from commodity production, the imputed rental value of farm operators' dwellings, current farm operating expenditures, depreciation, the net change in farmer-owned inventories located on farms (both in deflated and in current prices) and, finally, through an identity relationship, the net income of farm operators.

Thus, equations (12.2), (12.3), and (12.6) through (12.11) are needed to determine prices of farm products. Farm prices and other variables are then employed to determine net farm income.

In addition, some equations were calculated which lead out of the agricultural sector. These equations are designed to estimate gross investment in farm buildings and machinery and the number of workers engaged in agricultural production. Another equation is designed to estimate net Commodity Credit Corporation (CCC) loans and purchases for price support. A final equation expresses the total quantity of food livestock products available for domestic consumption as a function of the volumes of farm livestock products marketed in the current and preceding quarters, plus a time trend. The standard error of estimate of the dependent variable, approximately 1 per cent of its basic level, gives some idea of the "tightness" with which livestock production and consumption relationships might be fitted together in a recursive supply and demand model.

Some special interest attaches to the manner in which the consumption functions for foods of livestock and crop origin were grafted into the set of consumption functions for major components of personal consumption expenditures. Also, the domestic demand for nonfood products of farm origin is not explicitly taken into account in the agricultural submodel. In later versions of the Brookings-SSRC econometric model, this deficiency could be partly remedied by input-output links. And we have already noted the lack of explicit linkage between the agricultural submodel and the foreign trade sector.

Some of the relationships leading out of agriculture may have been clarified elsewhere in this volume by the persons responsible for integrating the various sectors into a complete model. Others may be improved or resolved in descendants of the basic Brookings-SSRC econometric model.

12.2. Determining prices of farm products

We shall first discuss the price-determining set of eight equations from the standpoint of causal ordering and statistical estimation and then turn to a discussion of the individual equations.

12.2.1. Causal ordering and matrix structure

The concept of causal ordering [27] will be useful in the following exposition. We shall consider only the following variables: (1) weather, (2) disposable personal income, (3) charge for marketing services, (4) production, (5) consumption, (6) retail price, and (7) farm price. Three of these seven variables may be regarded as strictly exogenous or predetermined, namely, weather, disposable personal income and the charge for marketing services.

We assume that the charge made for marketing services is determined by competitive conditions in the food marketing system and is not influenced by fluctuations in either the retail or the farm price of the commodity.

With respect to this model, weather, consumer income, and the charge for marketing services are of causal order 0. The four endogenous variables—production, consumption, retail price, and farm price—are activated or "driven" from one period to the next by the three exogenous variables. Each endogenous variable may also contain a random error or disturbance component which is statistically independent of the exogenous variables.

If we ignore the error terms, changes in the three exogenous variables lead to changes in the endogenous variables in the following sequence: Production is dependent upon weather and nothing else; production, therefore, is determined at causal order 1. Consumption depends only on production, so consumption is determined at causal order 2. Retail price is a function of disposable consumer income (which is of causal order 0) and also of consumption, which is of causal order 2. Retail price, then, is determined at causal order 3, as it cannot be estimated appropriately until consumption has been determined. The farm price depends upon the retail price (causal order 3) and on marketing charges (causal order 0); therefore, farm price is determined at causal order 4.

This schema can be expressed in terms of the following diagram:

Causal Order

0	X_1			X_2	X_3
1		X_4			
2			X_5		
3				X_6	
4					X_7

X_1 = weather
X_2 = disposable personal income
X_3 = charge for marketing services
X_4 = production
X_5 = consumption (quantity offered for sale by retailers)
X_6 = retail price
X_7 = farm price.

Figure 12.1. Illustration of causal ordering of farm price determination.

We can express the information in our arrow diagram in the following matrix form; including the error terms (u's) as well as the "exact part" of the model:

$$
\begin{bmatrix}
1 & 0 & 0 & 0 & 0 & 0 & 0 \\
0 & 1 & 0 & 0 & 0 & 0 & 0 \\
0 & 0 & 1 & 0 & 0 & 0 & 0 \\
\cdots & \cdots & \cdots & \cdots & \cdots & \cdots & \cdots \\
b_{41} & 0 & 0 & 1 & 0 & 0 & 0 \\
0 & 0 & 0 & b_{54} & 1 & 0 & 0 \\
0 & b_{62} & 0 & 0 & b_{65} & 1 & 0 \\
0 & 0 & b_{73} & 0 & 0 & b_{76} & 1
\end{bmatrix}
\begin{bmatrix}
X_{1(t)} \\
X_{2(t)} \\
X_{3(t)} \\
\cdots \\
X_{4(t)} \\
X_{5(t)} \\
X_{6(t)} \\
X_{7(t)}
\end{bmatrix}
=
\begin{bmatrix}
k_{1(t)} \\
k_{2(t)} \\
k_{3(t)} \\
\cdots \\
a_4 \\
a_5 \\
a_6 \\
a_7
\end{bmatrix}
+
\begin{bmatrix}
0 \\
0 \\
0 \\
\cdots \\
u_{4(t)} \\
u_{5(t)} \\
u_{6(t)} \\
u_{7(t)}
\end{bmatrix}
$$

$$(12.1.1)$$

If the error terms in the lower four equations are statistically independent of one another, each of the six arrows in the diagram can be replaced by a simple or partial least-squares regression coefficient in the matrix. For any time unit t each of the variables X_1, X_2 and X_3 is a given number indicated, respectively, by $k_{1(t)}$, $k_{2(t)}$ and $k_{3(t)}$. Thus the first three rows of the matrix equation are definitions or identities and do not require statistical estimation.

The four lower rows in the matrix equation represent four regression equations. In matrix notation, the first three and the other four equations can be separated or "partitioned" as follows:

$$
\begin{bmatrix} I & 0 \\ B_{10} & B_{11} \end{bmatrix}
\begin{bmatrix} x_0 \\ x_1 \end{bmatrix}
=
\begin{bmatrix} k \\ a \end{bmatrix}
+
\begin{bmatrix} 0 \\ u \end{bmatrix}; \quad \text{or} \qquad (12.1.2)
$$

$$Ix_0 = k \qquad (12.1.3)$$

$$B_{10}x_0 + B_{11}x_1 = a + u. \qquad (12.1.4)$$

Here x_0 indicates the vector of exogenous variables and x_1 the vector of endogenous variables. Matrix equation (12.1.4) indicates that each of the endogenous variables is to be regressed upon either exogenous variables, other endogenous variables or both.

It will be noted that the matrix B_{11} is triangular—that is, all entries above and to the right of the main diagonal are zero. This triangularity is characteristic of fully recursive models. If the error terms in the four equations are independent of (uncorrelated with) one another, each equation can be estimated optimally by least squares, although this result might have to be modified when the agricultural sector is embedded in the complete model.

If the error terms are not independent of one another, triangularity would justify the following procedure: Regress X_4 on X_1; then, regress X_5 on X_4, where X_4 is estimated from the first regression equation; next, regress X_6 upon X_2 and upon X_5 as estimated from the second sequential regression; finally, regress X_7 upon X_3 and upon $\hat{X}_6$ as estimated from the third sequential regression.

As $\hat{X}_4$, $\hat{X}_5$ and $\hat{X}_6$ are exact functions of the exogenous variables, they are independent of the error terms and are suitable regressors for the successive least-squares equations. This sequential procedure based on causal ordering is logically very close to two-stage least squares.

If some nonzero coefficients appeared above the main diagonal of B_{11} the model would not be fully recursive, and two or more endogenous variables would have to be determined simultaneously. Logically, this situation calls for estimating techniques such as two-stage least squares or limited information maximum likelihood.

Table 12.1 shows the structure of the coefficient matrix for the determination of farm prices in the agricultural submodel. The array of coefficients corresponds to the matrices B_{10} and B_{11} of the preceding example.

It will be noted that the matrix B_{11} is strictly triangular. There are 19 variables of causal order 0 which—from the standpoint of the farm price submodel—are regarded as exogenous or predetermined. (Some of these variables, such as disposable personal income, are endogenous from the standpoint of the Brookings-SSRC econometric model as a whole, but in exploratory work on the agricultural submodel it is necessary to regard variables determined in the nonfarm sector as exogenous. A qualification with respect to disposable income, which includes the income of farm proprietors, will be noted below.) Each of the five statistical equations (12.6, 12.7, 12.2, 12.3 and 12.11) was estimated by least squares.

It will be noted that the matrix B_{10} is very nearly block diagonal. This reflects the fact that (for example) the cluster of variables directly determining charges for marketing services is quite distinct from the cluster of exogenous variables in the consumer demand functions. On a common-sense basis, this appears highly favorable to identification and separate estimation of the two pairs of equations, which have no common variable other than a time trend. The equation explaining prices received by farmers for all commodities has no variable in common with either the consumption or the marketing services equations.

The different sets of "exogenous" variables just mentioned are related indirectly through the Brookings-SSRC econometric model as a whole.

TABLE 12.1

Determination of farm prices [a]).

Causal order	Equation number	Exogenous or predetermined variables (causal order 0)																			Endogenous variables (Causal orders 1–6)							
		19	23	27	24	25	26	28	16	17	18	20	21	22	29	29a	30	30a	7a	8a	3	4	6	1	2	5	7	8
1	12.6	X	X		X	X	X														1							
1	12.7	X	X	X	X	X																1						
2	12.9							X														X	1					
3	12.2	X							X	X	X	X	X										X	1				
3	12.3	X							X	X	X	X	X	X									X		1			
4	12.8							X													X			X		1		
5	12.10																							X		X	1	
6	12.11														X	X	X	X	X	X				X			X	1

[a]) For compactness, variables are identified by numbers (X_1 through X_{30}) used to identify them in the regression program of the Iowa State University Computing Center. The equations and endogenous variables are numbered in the same sequence as in the text, and the exogenous variables are included only to show their near approach to independence or block diagonality.

Intuitively, however, the structure of B_{10} suggests that policy instruments appropriate for influencing consumer demand for food will have only minor effects upon the supply functions for marketing services. Conversely, policy instruments appropriate for shifting the supply function for marketing services are not likely to have significant *direct* effects on the positions of the consumer demand functions for food.

12.2.2. Comments on the individual equations

(A) *Consumer demand functions*   Least-squares estimates of the two consumer demand functions for food are as follows:

Food livestock products

$$PM_{FAN_{TR}} = \frac{634.3751}{(121.9413)} - \frac{0.2083}{(0.1869)} TIME + \frac{24.3988}{(5.9470)} DMY16$$

$$+ \frac{0.4504}{(0.1033)} [PM^*_{FAN_{TR}}]_{-1} + \left\{ -11.3177 J_{FAN/N} + 0.1222 PM_{FCR_{TR}} \right.$$

$$\left. + 0.012718 P_{CEF} + 0.2360 \frac{Y_D}{[P_C][N + N_{ML}]} \right\} \qquad (12.2)$$

$R^2 = 0.7226$; $S_e = \$15.3026$; $DW = 1.9788$ (these refer to $PM^*_{FAN_{TR}}$ in 12.2.3). Standard deviations of dependent variable:
   Original $[PM_{FAN_{TR}}]$: \$31.0537.
   Adjusted $[PM^*_{FAN_{TR}}]$: \$28.2530.
   Per cent of variance of $PM_{FAN_{TR}}$ explained by equation 12.2:
$R^2 = 1 - (15.3026)^2/(31.0537)^2 = 0.7572$.

Food crop products

$$J_{FCR/N} = \frac{27.3305}{(10.1136)} + \frac{0.016163}{(0.010021)} TIME + \frac{0.3533}{(0.3519)} DMY16$$

$$+ \frac{0.7600}{(0.0878)} [J^*_{FCR/N}]_{-1} + \left\{ -0.15952 J_{FAN/N} - 0.06776 PM_{FCR_{TR}} \right.$$

$$\left. + 0.0007527 P_{CEF} + 0.01397 \frac{Y_D}{[P_C][N + N_{ML}]} \right\} \qquad (12.3)$$

$R^2 = 0.6340$; $S_e = 0.9161$; $DW = 1.8627$ (these refer to $J^*_{FCR/N}$ in 12.3.3). Standard deviation of dependent variable:
   Original $[J_{FCR/N}]$: 0.9862 index points.
   Adjusted $[J^*_{FCR/N}]$: 1.4726 index points.

Per cent of variance of $J_{\text{FCR}/\text{N}}$ explained by equation 12.3:
$R^2 = 1 - (0.9161)^2/(0.9862)^2 = 0.1371$.

The variables in equations (12.2) and (12.3) in order of their appearance, are:

$PM_{\text{FAN}_{TR}}$ = retail value of livestock component of the food market basket, dollars

$TIME$ = time trend

$DMY16$ = 1, 1947 : 1 through 1948 : 3
                1950 : 3 through 1952 : 4
      = 0, all other quarters

$PM^*_{\text{FAN}_{TR}}$ = adjusted retail value of livestock component of the food market basket, dollars

$J_{\text{FAN}/\text{N}}$ = index of per capita consumption of food livestock products, 1947–1949 = 100

$PM_{\text{FCR}_{TR}}$ = retail value of crop component of the food market basket, dollars

P_{CEF} = implicit price deflator for personal consumption expenditures, on goods and services except food, 1954 = 1.00

Y_{D} = disposable personal income, billions of dollars

P_{C} = implicit price deflator for personal consumption expenditures, 1954 = 1.00

N = civilian population including Alaska and Hawaii, millions of persons

N_{ML} = military population including armed forces overseas, millions of persons

$J_{\text{FCR}/\text{N}}$ = index of per capita consumption of food crop products, 1947–1949 = 100

$J^*_{\text{FCR}/\text{N}}$ = adjusted index of per capita consumption of food crop products, 1947–1949 = 100.

During most of the 1947–1960 period, the Department of Agriculture has made little direct effort to support prices of livestock products. Therefore, it is appropriate to regard the retail price of food livestock products as a dependent variable and the supply of food livestock products purchased by consumers (hence, offered for sale by retailers) in a given quarter as a predetermined variable. Time lags and inertia in the production of livestock products justify this treatment in quarterly data [2]).

---

[2]) The causal ordering for livestock products corresponds to the diagram on p. 412.

In contrast, equation (12.3) takes per capita consumption of foods of crop origin as the dependent variable and the corresponding retail price as a predetermined variable. The rationalization for this is that prices of many crops have been supported at the farm level. Some perishable crops, such as vegetables, have been in abundant supply, and harvesting costs have provided a floor under farm prices of many of these crops in many time intervals during 1947–1960 [3]). In other respects equation (12.3) is identical in form with equation (12.2). In each equation, the four coefficients in square brackets are based on a priori information.

The coefficients connecting prices of the two food groups with their respective per capita consumptions reflect a complex use of a priori information. There is a long tradition of statistical demand analysis for farm products and foods in the U. S., going back as far as the early work of H. L. Moore [24, 25]. In 1951, I published statistical demand analyses for a large number of foods and farm products based on 1922–1941 data [6, 7, and 10]. Several other economists have published analyses for particular commodities or commodity groups for the interwar period; more recently, some analyses have been based directly on post-World War II data.

There have also been a number of major studies of food purchases by households at particular points in time, made by the U. S. Department of Agriculture, the U. S. Bureau of Labor Statistics and other groups. In the 1951 article cited, I included a table of income elasticities of demand for 11 food groups, for various subtotals and for all food based on a 1948 U. S. Department of Agriculture (USDA) survey (table 12.2). More recent and more extensive analyses have been published by Rockwell [26] and Burk [2], based on a USDA survey of household food consumption made in 1955.

In a 1961 publication, George E. Brandow reviewed all of the better-known demand analyses for food in the U. S. and, following a suggestion by Frisch [14], synthesized from them a complete matrix of elasticities and

---

[3]) In terms of the diagram, farm price (X_7) is determined by harvesting costs or by government action; retail price (X_6) is equal to the sum of X_7 and X_3 (marketing charges); and consumption (X_5) is determined by X_6 and X_2 (disposable personal income). To the extent that government price supports are involved, the free market causal ordering is reversed by the deliberate use of a policy instrument. When some quantities of a perishable crop are left unharvested because price has fallen to the level of harvesting cost, an inequality needed for maintenance of the normal causal ordering (p. 412) is replaced by an equality—a "boundary condition" becomes effective—and the effect on causal ordering is the same as in the government price support case.

TABLE 12.2

Food expenditures and quantities purchased: logarithmic regressions upon familty income, urban families, United States, Spring 1948.

Item	Effect of 1 per cent change in income upon:			
	(1) Relative importance [a]	(2) Expenditure	(3) Quantity purchased	(4) Col. (2) minus col. (3)
	Percent [b]			
Per family				
All food expenditures		0.51		
At home		0.40		
Away from home		1.12		
Per family members [c]				
All food expenditures		0.42		
At home		0.29		
Away from home		1.14		
Per 21 meals at home [c]				
All food (excluding accessories)	100.0	0.28	0.14 [d]	0.14
All livestock products	50.8	0.33	0.23 [d]	0.10
Meat, poultry and fish	29.2	0.36	0.23	0.13
Dairy products (excluding butter)	16.9	0.32	0.23	0.09
Eggs	4.7	0.22	0.20	0.02
Fruits and vegetables	19.0	0.42	0.33 [d]	0.09
Leafy, green and yellow vegetables	4.9	0.37	0.21	0.16
Citrus fruit and tomatoes	5.2	0.41	0.42	−0.01
Other vegetables and fruits	8.9	0.45	0.35	0.10
Other foods	30.2	0.08	−0.12 [d]	0.20
Grain products	11.4	0.02	−0.21	0.23
Fats and oils	9.8	0.13	−0.04	0.17
Sugars and sweets	5.2	0.20	−0.07	0.27
Dry beans, peas and nuts	1.5	−0.07	−0.33	0.26
Potatoes and sweet potatoes	2.3	0.05	−0.05	0.10

Note   Basic data from United States Bureau of Human Nutrition and Home Economics, *1948 Food Consumption Surveys*, Preliminary Report No. 5 (May 30, 1949), tables 1 and 3.

Source   Karl A. Fox, *Econometric Analysis for Public Policy* (Ames, Ia.: Iowa State University Press, 1958), p. 127.

[a] Per cent of total expenditures for food used at home, excluding condiments, coffee and alcoholic beverages.

[b] Regression coefficients based upon logarithms of food expenditures or quantities purchased per 21 meals at home and logarithms of estimated spring 1948 disposable incomes per family member, weighted by proportion of total families falling in each family income group. The object was to obtain coefficients reasonably comparable with those derived from time series.

[c] Per capita regression coefficients are lower than per family coefficients in this study whenever the latter are less than 1.0. This happens because average family size was positively correlated with family income among the survey group.

[d] Weighted averages of quantity-income coefficients for subgroups.

cross-elasticities of consumer demand for twenty-four foods and food groups. Constraints implied in the pure theory of consumer demand were used in forcing a consistent set of demand elasticities (price and income) for the twenty-four foods.

Table 12.3 reproduces Brandow's consumer demand matrix in its entirety. Most of the own-price elasticities (the elements in the major diagonal) are based on time series analyses; so are some of the larger cross-elasticities, particularly within the meat, poultry and fish group. The smaller cross-elasticities have been supplied by Brandow on a reproducible but inevitably somewhat arbitrary basis.

The nature of the conditions imposed from consumption theory may be illustrated in terms of row 1 (beef). Column 1 indicates that a 1 per cent increase in the retail price of beef would reduce beef consumption by 0.95000 per cent. One per cent increases in the prices of the other twenty-three foods would tend to increase beef consumption; the sum of these twenty-three cross-elasticities is 0.32490. Column 25 indicates that a 1 per cent increase in the prices of all foods, including beef, would reduce beef consumption by 0.62150 per cent (the algebraic sum of the own-elasticity of −0.95000 and the twenty-three cross-elasticities). Column 26 implies that an increase of 1 per cent in prices of all consumer goods and services other than foods would increase food consumption by 0.15510 per cent. Column 27 indicates an elasticity of 0.47000 for beef consumption with respect to income [4]. The algebraic sum of columns 25, 26 and 27 is zero, implying that a 1 per cent increase in the prices of all commodities (a by-product of which would be a 1 per cent increase in money income) would leave the consumption of beef unchanged.

The figure at the intersection of row 25 and column 25 implies that a 1 per cent increase in the prices of all foods would decrease the consumption of all foods by 0.34137 per cent. This figure, −0.34137, is a weighted average of the first twenty-four figures in column 25, using percentages of total food expenditures as weights. For a fuller statement, see Brandow [1, pp. 15–18] and Frisch [14].

As Brandow's results seemed reasonable to me and were in close accord with my own analyses, I aggregated his matrix into three commodity groups —food livestock products, food crops and nonfoods. In concept, these

[4] Empirical evidence on cross-elasticities of demand for individual foods with respect to nonfood prices is limited. Brandow sets each of these cross-elasticities equal to 0.33 times the corresponding income elasticity.

exhaust personal consumption expenditures or (if we lump personal savings with nonfoods) disposable personal income. The coefficients are elasticities, so the three aggregates can be expressed as equations in the logarithms of all variables:

$$
\begin{bmatrix} \log J_{\text{FAN/N}} \\ \log J_{\text{FCR/N}} \\ \log J_{\text{CEF}} \end{bmatrix} = \begin{bmatrix} -0.479227 & 0.046226 & 0.107438 \\ 0.078203 & -0.304264 & 0.056090 \\ -0.098000 & -0.100700 & -1.025560 \end{bmatrix}
$$

$$
\begin{bmatrix} \log PM_{\text{FAN}_{TR}} \\ \log PM_{\text{FCR}_{TR}} \\ \log P_{\text{CEF}} \end{bmatrix} + \begin{bmatrix} 0.325568 \\ 0.169971 \\ 1.224260 \end{bmatrix} \log \left\{ \frac{Y_{\text{D}}^{54}}{[N+N_{\text{ML}}]} \right\}. \tag{12.4}
$$

Each row satisfies the homogeneity condition except for rounding errors.

For reasons already noted, it was necessary to choose retail price rather than consumption as the dependent variable in the food livestock products equation. This was done by transposing $\log PM_{\text{FAN}_{TR}}$ to the dependent position in the first row (equation) and substituting the resulting right-hand member into the second- and third-row (equations), respectively:

$$
\begin{bmatrix} \log PM_{\text{FAN}_{TR}} \\ \log J_{\text{FCR/N}} \\ \log J_{\text{CEF}} \end{bmatrix} = \begin{bmatrix} -2.086694 & 0.096460 & 0.224190 \\ -0.163186 & -0.296721 & 0.073622 \\ 0.204496 & -0.110153 & -1.047531 \end{bmatrix}
$$

$$
\begin{bmatrix} \log J_{\text{FAN/N}} \\ \log PM_{\text{FCR}_{TR}} \\ \log P_{\text{CEF}} \end{bmatrix} + \begin{bmatrix} 0.679361 \\ 0.223099 \\ 1.157683 \end{bmatrix} \log \left\{ \frac{Y_{\text{D}}^{54}}{[N+N_{\text{ML}}]} \right\}. \tag{12.5}
$$

The elasticity coefficients in rows 1 and 2 were then multiplied by ratios of the 1947–1960 mean values of the appropriate variables to convert the equations into arithmetic form. Row 3 was discarded at this point, as the variable J_{CEF} is deeply imbedded in the nonagricultural sectors of the Brookings-SSRC econometric model and it would not have been useful to the total project to add an equation explaining J_{CEF} to the agricultural submodel. The arithmetic forms of the first and second rows (equations) are as follows:

$$
PM_{\text{FAN}_{TR}} = -11.317682\, J_{\text{FAN/N}} + 0.122229\, PM_{\text{FCR}_{TR}} + 0.0127178\, P_{\text{CEF}}
$$

$$
+ 0.236049 \left[\frac{Y_{\text{D}}}{[P_{\text{C}}][N+N_{\text{ML}}]} \right] \tag{12.2.1}
$$

$$J_{\text{FCR/N}} = -0.159516 \, J_{\text{FAN/N}} - 0.067764 \, PM_{\text{FCR}_{TR}} + 0.00075271 \, P_{\text{CEF}}$$

$$+ 0.013971 \, \frac{Y_{\text{D}}}{[P_{\text{C}}][N + N_{\text{ML}}]}. \tag{12.3.1}$$

Per capita income in real terms is assumed to be an exogenous variable with respect to the agricultural submodel; there is no need to allow for interactions between it and the other predetermined variables in equations (12.2.1) and (12.3.1).

In one version of the livestock consumption equation, the coefficients of equation (12.2.1) were imposed in the following fashion:

$$PM^*_{\text{FAN}_{TR}} = PM_{\text{FAN}_{TR}} - \left\{ -11.3177 \, J_{\text{FAN/N}} + 0.1222 \, PM_{\text{FCR}_{TR}} \right.$$

$$\left. + 0.012718 \, P_{\text{CEF}} + 0.2360 \, \frac{Y_{\text{D}}}{[P_{\text{C}}][N + N_{\text{ML}}]} \right\}. \tag{12.2.2}$$

The adjusted variable was regressed on its own value for the previous quarter, on time, and on the dummy "inflationary period" variable, yielding the following equation:

$$PM^*_{\text{FAN}_{TR}} = \frac{634.3751}{(121.9413)} - \frac{0.2083}{(0.1869)} \, TIME + \frac{24.3988}{(5.9470)} \, DMY16$$

$$+ \frac{0.4504}{(0.1033)} \, [PM^*_{\text{FAN}_{TR}}]_{-1} \tag{12.2.3}$$

$$R^2 = 0.7226; \qquad S_e = 15.3026; \qquad DW = 1.9788.$$

The expression in brackets (containing the four a priori coefficients) was then added to each side of the last equation to obtain the form presented in equation (12.2).

The crop food consumption equation was handled in the same way, using an adjusted variable

$$J^*_{\text{FCR/N}} = J_{\text{FCR/N}} - \left\{ -0.15952 \, J_{\text{FAN/N}} - 0.06776 \, PM_{\text{FCR}_{TR}} \right.$$

$$\left. + 0.0007527 \, P_{\text{CEF}} + 0.01397 \, \frac{Y_{\text{D}}}{[P_{\text{C}}][N + N_{\text{ML}}]} \right\}. \tag{12.3.2}$$

The adjusted variable was regressed on its own value for the preceding quarter, on time, and on the dummy variable, yielding:

$$J^*_{FCR/N} = \frac{27.3305}{(10.1136)} + \frac{0.016163}{(0.010021)} TIME + \frac{0.3533}{(0.3519)} DMY16$$

$$+ \frac{0.7600}{(0.0878)} [J^*_{FCR/N}]_{-1} \tag{12.3.3}$$

$$R^2 = 0.6340: \qquad S_e = 0.9161; \qquad DW = 1.8627.$$

The expression in brackets was then added to each side of the above equation to obtain equation (12.3).

Brandow felt that the income elasticities in table 12.3 were too high when used for time series simulation. The difficulties in interpretation of the coefficients in table 12.2 and of other coefficients and data presented by Rockwell [26] and Burk [2] are such that point estimates cannot be stated with certainty. Hence, alternative versions of the two consumption functions were calculated assuming income elasticities of 0.2 for livestock and 0.1 for crops, compared with those of 0.325568 and 0.169971, respectively, derived from table 12.3 [5]). The results were as follows:

Food livestock products

$$PM_{FAN_{TR}} = \frac{722.7575}{(134.3316)} + \frac{0.1579}{(0.1613)} TIME + \frac{25.0754}{(5.8635)} DMY16$$

$$+ \frac{0.4359}{(0.1029)} [PM^*_{FAN_{TR}}]_{-1} + \left\{ -11.3177 \, J_{FAN/N} + 0.1222 \, PM_{FCR_{TR}} \right.$$

$$+ 0.012718 \, P_{CEF} + 0.1450 \frac{Y_D}{[P_C][N + N_{ML}]} \right\}. \tag{12.2a}$$

$R^2 = 0.5665$; $S_e = \$ 15.0301$; $DW = 2.0266$ (these refer to $PM^*_{FAN_{TR}}$ in 12.2.3a—not shown).
Standard deviation of adjusted variable $[PM^*_{FAN_{TR}}]$: $\$ 22.1974$.
Per cent of variance of $PM_{FAN_{TR}}$ explained by equation 12.2a:
$= 1 - (15.0301)^2/(31.0537)^2 = 0.7657$.

Food crop products

$$J_{FCR/N} = \frac{30.2599}{(10.7526)} + \frac{0.026836}{(0.011162)} TIME + \frac{0.3781}{(0.3406)} DMY16$$

---

[5]) For time series simulation, Brandow reduced each income elasticity by 0.1, implying elasticities of 0.23 and 0.07, respectively, for livestock and crop food products and 0.157 for all foods. The weighted average of income elasticities of 0.2 for livestock and 0.1 for crops is almost identical, namely, 0.156.

$$+ \frac{0.7518}{(0.0874)} [J^*_{FCR/N}]_{-1} + \left\{ -0.15952\, J_{FAN/N} - 0.06776\, PM_{FCR_{TR}} \right.$$

$$\left. + 0.0007527\, P_{CEF} + 0.008306\, \frac{Y_D}{[P_C][N + N_{ML}]} \right\}. \qquad (12.3a)$$

$R^2 = 0.7434$; $S_e = 0.8832$ index points; $DW = 1.8650$ (these refer to $J^*_{FCR/N}$ in 12.3.3a—not shown).

Standard deviation of adjusted variable $J^*_{FCR/N}$: 1.6954 index points.

Per cent of variance of $J_{FCR/N}$ explained by equation 12.3a:

$R^2 = 1 - (0.8832)^2/(0.9862)^2 = 0.1931$.

It will be noted that in each function a lower estimate of the income elasticity leads to a higher estimate of the trend effect:

	Income elasticity imposed	Trend effect	
		Coefficient	Standard error
Food livestock products	0.325568	−0.2083	0.1869
	0.200000	0.1579	0.1613
Food crops	0.169971	0.016163	0.010021
	0.100000	0.026836	0.011162

This occurs because of a high positive intercorrelation ($r = 0.9785$) between income and time.

The high degree of multicollinearity among the explanatory variables in both consumption functions makes it impossible to estimate certain coefficients from time series. The correlation matrix of the four most highly intercorrelated variables is:

	$TIME$	P_{CEF}	$\dfrac{Y_D}{[P_C][N+N_{ML}]}$	$PM_{FCR_{TR}}$
$TIME$	1.0000	0.9926	0.9785	0.9330
P_{CEF}	0.9926	1.0000	0.9749	0.9406
$\dfrac{Y_D}{[P_C][N+N_{ML}]}$	0.9785	0.9749	1.0000	0.9003
$PM_{FCR_{TR}}$	0.9330	0.9406	0.9003	1.0000

The value of the determinant is approximately 0.00009, a very near approach to singularity! (Recall that the determinant of a matrix with zero intercorrelation would have a value of 1.) If we assign a priori coefficients to three of these variables we can estimate the coefficient of the fourth variable by statistical means. The intercorrelations of the other three explanatory variables among themselves and with the trend-dominated four are not unduly high.

Brandow's matrix provides us with a priori coefficients for three of the four trend-dominated variables and for one other $J_{FAN/N}$. Hence, the combination of a priori and statistical information is sufficient to give us useful estimates of the net effects of all seven explanatory variables upon retail prices of food livestock products and per capita consumption of food crops.

The elasticity coefficients in matrix equation (12.4) look reasonable in relation to some earlier results of my own. The own-price elasticity of -0.48 for food livestock products may be compared with my estimates of -0.52 to -0.56 during 1922–1941 [6]). The own-price elasticity of -0.34 for all food compares with my 1922–1941 estimates of -0.34 to -0.37 [7]). Note, however, that my aggregation of Brandow's matrix implies equal percentage changes of all individual prices within each aggregate. It can be shown that the time series regression coefficient of a price index upon a per capita consumption index also depends on the relative variances and covariances of the consumption series for all commodities included [8]).

It might appear that my use of Brandow's consumer demand matrix is

---

[6]) See [10, p. 116].

[7]) See [9, p. 65].

[8]) This can be shown as follows: Assume that all explanatory variables other than the amounts of different commodities available for consumption (q_1) remain constant. Our problem is to interpret the time series regression coefficient of an index of retail prices of all food upon an index of per capita consumption of all food. For two commodities we may write

$$\begin{bmatrix} p_1 \\ p_2 \end{bmatrix} = \begin{bmatrix} b_{11} & b_{12} \\ b_{21} & b_{22} \end{bmatrix} \begin{bmatrix} q_1 \\ q_2 \end{bmatrix}$$

or, in compact matrix notation,

$$p = Bq.$$

Now, assume the p_i and q_i are price and quantity relatives and are combined into Laspeyres indexes, P and Q, using the same set of expenditure weights, $w_1 + w_2 = 1$. Thus, $P = (w_1 p_1 + w_2 p_2)$. and $Q = (w_1 q_1 + w_1 q_2)$, or

$$P = w \cdot p$$

and

$$Q = w \cdot q.$$

We propose to take time series observations on P and Q and estimate a least-squares regression coefficient, β.

much too elaborate in relation to the limited objectives and high level of aggregation of the initial Brookings-SSRC econometric model. I have already commented on the importance of establishing a continuing relationship between the basic model and submodels of various sectors expressed at levels of detail which would be useful to economists and decision makers concerned with sector policies [9]).

The formula for β is

$$\beta = \frac{\sum\limits_{t=1}^{n} PQ}{\sum\limits_{t=1}^{n} Q^2}.$$

For each time t the appropriate elements in the numerator and denominator of the above equation are:

$$P_{(t)} Q_{(t)} = w \cdot Bqq \cdot w, \text{ and}$$
$$Q^2_{(t)} = q \cdot ww \cdot q.$$

If we sum these elements over the n time units, the denominator becomes a matrix of variances and covariances of the q_i, with the variances weighted by w_i^2 and the covariances weighted by $w_i w_j$. In the numerator, each structural coefficient b_{ii} and b_{ij} is complexly weighted by combinations of variances and covariances of the q_i with terms in w_i^2 and $w_i w_j$.

If the covariances were all zero and the cross-flexibilities of price were zero or small, it is clear that the regression coefficient, β, in different time periods would depend upon the relative variances of the different q_i.

[9]) The explanatory value of the consumption functions for food crops is distinctly unimpressive in terms of the per cent of original variance explained. Still other a priori specifications of the coefficients in brackets have reduced the standard error of estimate to as low as 0.65 index points, "explaining" over 40 per cent of the original variance. However, these specifications are not derived from Brandow's matrix and offer no clear path to future disaggregation. Note also the following:
(A) The original standard deviation of $J_{FCR/N}$ is only 0.9862 index points. The mean value of $J_{FCR/N}$ is 99.96, so we are trying to reduce a coefficient of variation of only 1 per cent!
(B) The original standard deviation of $J_{FAN/N}$ is 2.5492 index points and the mean is 102.26, resulting in a coefficient of variation of 2.5 per cent, and the coefficient of variation of $PM_{FAN_{TR}}$ is \$ 31.0537/\$ 554.62, or about 5.6 per cent. The variation in $PM_{FAN_{TR}}$ unexplained by equation (12.2a) has a coefficient of variation of \$ 15.0301/\$ 554.62, or 2.7 per cent.
Given the own-price flexibility of -2.09 for livestock products, the unexplained variation in $PM_{FAN_{TR}}$ would be consistent with a coefficient of unexplained variation in $J_{FAN/N}$ of about 1.3 per cent. Consumption of food crops could evidently be predicted about as accurately as consumption of food livestock products during 1957–1960; see also equation (12.26) on p. 457.

An important reason for relating my consumer demand equations to Brandow's work is that Brandow also specifies functions for passing from retail farm prices for each of the 24 commodities or groups and works out derived demand matrices for farm products (cattle, hogs, eggs, wheat, etc.) at the level of aggregation and in the units of measure with which legislators and practical administrators of farm price policies must work. Brandow has used his complete model to estimate the consequences of alternative price support programs, and economists in the USDA are also attempting to use and improve upon Brandow's model. Hence, it offers a very promising bridge between the Brookings-SSRC econometric model and the kinds of data flows and technical advice that USDA economists are in a position to provide.

Some specific comments on variables appearing in the food consumption equations are as follows:

The retail food values, $PM_{FAN_{TR}}$ and $PM_{FCR_{TR}}$, are components of a USDA series called "retail value of the food market basket". This is a Laspeyres value index, with fixed-quantity weights representing quantities of food products originating on U. S. farms and consumed by representative wage-earner and clerical-worker families in the course of a year (1952). The level of the series for all food as of 1960 was a little over $ 1 000. During 1947–1960, the food livestock component averaged about $ 550 and the food crop component about $ 450. Official estimates of the retail value of the food market basket are published on a quarterly basis with considerable subgroup and commodity detail.

The series $J_{FAN/N}$ and $J_{FCR/N}$ are official USDA indexes of per capita food consumption. They are Laspeyres indexes on the base 1947–1949 = 100. They are slightly more inclusive than the corresponding price series, as the consumption indexes include fish and imported food products such as tea, coffee, cocoa and bananas in addition to foods originating on U. S. farms.

The official per capita consumption indexes are published only on an annual basis. Available data on food livestock production, cold-storage holdings, farm inventories, imports and exports are (in my judgment) sufficiently complete and accurate to permit construction of a quarterly index of per capita consumption of food livestock products. At my request, such an index was constructed on a preliminary basis by a USDA economist; however, we did not feel that the series should be used in any published form until more thorough data work had been completed. Plans for further development of the Brookings-SSRC econometric model could lend appropriate impetus to the construction of an official quarterly index of per capita consumption of food livestock products.

The outlook for a quarterly index of per capita consumption of food crops is less favorable. However, something could no doubt be done; also, since the majority of the total variance in the index of per capita consumption of all foods during 1957–1960 was contributed by the livestock component, it might be feasible and useful to publish a quarterly index of per capita consumption of all food.

The variable P_{CEF} is associated with the process of "grafting" equations (12.2) and (12.3) of the agricultural submodel into the consumption functions reported in Chapter 7 by Suits and Sparks. The weighted sum of $PM_{FAN_{TR}}$ and $PM_{FCR_{TR}}$ is an index of retail value of all foods. Similarly, the weighted sum of $J_{FAN/N}$ and $J_{FCR/N}$ is an index of per capita consumption of all foods. The product of these two series may be used as an index of the per capita value of consumer expenditures for foods measured at retail store prices. This value series multiplied by total U. S. population yields an index of total consumer expenditures for food.

I constructed such an index of total food expenditures on the base 1954 = 100 and used it to "move" 1954 personal consumption expenditures for food (excluding alcoholic beverages). These expenditures amounted to $ 57.7 billion in 1954. The resulting series on personal consumption expenditures for food (which differs somewhat, though not markedly, from the official Department of Commerce series) was subtracted from total personal consumption expenditures to give a residual which may be regarded as current dollar expenditures for nonfoods.

The index of per capita food consumption multiplied by U. S. population was also used to move 1954 consumption expenditures for food. This series was subtracted from total personal consumption expenditures in 1954 dollars to yield a residual which may be regarded as "consumer expenditures for nonfood goods and services at 1954 prices". The ratio of the residual series in current value terms and the residual series in 1954 dollars yields an implicit price deflator which was treated as an index of consumer prices of nonfood goods and services, P_{CEF} [10]).

---

[10] The unofficial and preliminary quarterly index of per capita consumption of food livestock products, combined with the food crop component on an annual basis, was used in the grafting process just noted and in the derivation of P_{CEF}. However, the per capita consumption series used in equations (12.2) and (12.3) are the annual published series; the annual figure is used in each of the four quarters of a given calendar year. This introduces some spurious inertia into these quarterly series, and the lagged values of the same series are used to help insulate the other coefficients from this effect.

Some improvements could be made upon this grafting procedure at a later date if the Brookings-SSRC econometric model were disaggregated to recognize such elements as value added in restaurant meals over and above the equivalent retail store prices of foods served.

(B) *Supply functions for marketing services*   The least-squares supply functions for marketing services with respect to food livestock and food crop products are as follows:

Food livestock

$$PM_{FAN_{TR}} - PM_{FAN_{AF}}$$

$$= \frac{16.4395}{(3.3136)} + \frac{0.3421}{(0.0911)} TIME + \frac{0.3470}{(0.1279)} [PM_{FAN_{TR}} - PM_{FAN_{AF}}]^*_{-1}$$

$$- \frac{5.7034}{(3.7931)} DMY17 + \{1.5\ ULC_{FM} + 50\ PM_{PDFS}\}. \tag{12.6}$$

$R^2 = 0.7131$; $S_e = \$ 6.1707$; $DW = 1.9999$ (these refer to $[PM_{FAN_{TR}} - PM_{FAN_{AF}}]^*$ in equation 12.6.1—not shown).
Standard deviations of dependent variable:
     Original $[PM_{FAN_{TR}} - PM_{FAN_{AF}}]$: \$ 28.7045.
     Adjusted $[PM_{FAN_{TR}} - PM_{FAN_{AF}}]^*$: \$ 11.2017.
     Per cent of variance of $[PM_{FAN_{TR}} - PM_{FAN_{AF}}]$ explained by equation
(12.6):

$$R^2 = 1 - \frac{(6.1707)^2}{(28.7045)^2} = 0.9538.$$

Food crops

$$PM_{FCR_{TR}} - PM_{FCR_{AF}}$$

$$= \frac{49.8815}{(11.2195)} + \frac{0.4419}{(0.1219)} TIME + \frac{0.4917}{(0.1182)} [PM_{FCR_{TR}} - PM_{FCR_{AF}}]^*_{-1}$$

$$- \frac{7.1672}{(3.6806)} DMY17 + \{1.5\ ULC_{FM} + 50\ PM_{PDFS}\}. \tag{12.7}$$

$R^2 = 0.8757$; $S_e = \$ 6.0093$; $DW = 1.8094$ (these refer to $[PM_{FCR_{TR}} - PM_{FCR_{AF}}]^*$ in equation 12.7.1—not shown).
Standard deviations of dependent variable:
     Original $[PM_{FCR_{TR}} - PM_{FCR_{AF}}]$: \$ 34.2764.
     Adjusted $[PM_{FCR_{TR}} - PM_{FCR_{AF}}]^*$: \$ 16.5704.

Per cent of variance of $[PM_{FCR_{TR}} - PM_{FCR_{AF}}]$ explained by equation (12.7):

$$R^2 = 1 - \frac{(6.0093)^2}{(34.2764)^2} = 0.9694.$$

The dependent variables are part of USDA's set of estimates relating to the food market basket previously described. The two value series combined total about $ 600 a year per family of three average U. S. consumers. In 1960, for example, $PM_{FAN_{TR}} - PM_{FAN_{AF}}$ was about $ 280 and $PM_{FCR_{TR}} - PM_{FCR_{AF}}$ about $ 360.

The coefficients in braces { } are specified on an a priori basis. The variable ULC_{FM} is an index of unit labor costs in food marketing operations (including processing, transportation and distribution) which intervene between farm and retail price levels. The official USDA series on unit labor costs is available only on an annual basis. I used an index of retail prices of nonfoods to give the official series some quarterly movement within each calendar year but without changing the official calendar year average.

USDA studies indicate that the direct labor costs of employees in food processing, transportation and distribution firms are equivalent to somewhat more than half of the total charge for food marketing services. The mean value of food marketing charges during 1947–1960 was about $ 550; direct labor costs for the food market basket unit would have averaged about $ 300. Hence, a 1 per cent increase in the index of unit labor costs in food marketing should tend to raise the marketing margin for all foods by about $ 3; I have divided this equally between food livestock and food crop products.

The second variable in brackets, PM_{PDFS}, is based on an annual index of prices of purchased materials and services—packaging materials, electricity and the like—used in food marketing. The costs of these services are equivalent to about 20 per cent of total food marketing charges. The coefficient assumes that a 1 per cent increase in PM_{PDFS} (representing a basic value of about $ 110 on the average during 1947–1960) would raise total marketing costs (and charges) by about $ 1, divided equally between food livestock products and food crops.

For each quarter, the term in brackets in equation (12.6) was subtracted from the dependent variable, as in equation (12.2). The adjusted variable, $[PM_{FAN_{TR}} - PM_{FAN_{AF}}]^*$, was then regressed upon its own value for the preceding quarter, upon time and upon the dummy variable. Equation (12.7) was derived in the same way. In each case, the term in brackets was added to both sides of the statistical equation, giving equations (12.6) and (12.7) as shown.

The rationale for *DMY17* is as follows: World War II induced major shifts in population from rural areas to cities; the impacts on different cities were of very different magnitudes. There was also a continued natural increase in population during World War II and very little construction of new houses.

From 1945 through 1949, there was a rapid expansion of new housing to accommodate the wartime population increases and shifts. This was accompanied by the building of many new shopping centers and food supermarkets. Virtually all of the new food stores were supermarkets, while many of those which benefited from population congestion in established residential and business districts during World War II were small groceries with (in most cases) considerably higher unit costs than are attained with the supermarket scale and pattern of operation.

There is evidence that the capacity and location of retail food stores caught up with population and housing shifts sometime during 1949–1950, and there was a rapid readjustment of food marketing charges to the new situation. Marketing charges decreased significantly in each of three successive quarters during 1949–1950; this phenomenon does not reappear in subsequent years.

In (12.6) and (12.7) as well as (12.2) and (12.3) the need to impose some of the coefficients a priori (that is, on the basis of information external to the particular set of time series observations) arises from an otherwise hopeless degree of intercorrelation among the explanatory variables. An ordinary multiple regression of $PM_{FAN_{TR}} - PM_{FAN_{AF}}$ upon the five explanatory variables would yield a high R^2, but the individual coefficients would have large standard errors and would make very little economic sense. The coefficients would be useless for policy purposes.

The standard deviation of the adjusted variable is only \$ 11.2017, compared with \$ 28.7045 for the original variable. In effect, nearly 85 per cent of the original *variance* is explained by the term in braces. The coefficient of determination, $R^2 = 0.7131$, implies that 71 per cent of the remaining variance is associated with *TIME*, *DMY17*, and $[PM_{FAN_{TR}} - PM_{FAN_{AF}}]^*_{-1}$.

Thus, R^2 is misleadingly small. A "pseudo-R^2" coefficient, $R^2_{ps} = 1 - (6.1707)^2/(28.7045)^2 = 0.9538$, indicates that 95 per cent of the original variance is explained by the combination of a priori and statistically estimated coefficients in equation (12.6). Over 96 per cent of the original variance in $PM_{FCR_{TR}} - PM_{FCR_{AF}}$ is explained by equation (12.7).

The coefficients of *TIME* in equations (12.6) and (12.7) need further study and rationalization. The two coefficients in braces { } imply that 1 per cent increases in both unit labor costs and prices of materials and services used in marketing would increase the charge for food marketing services about 0.7 per cent. This follows from the fact that these two components are equivalent to roughly 70 per cent of total food marketing charges and from our assumption that any increases in unit marketing costs will force offsetting adjustments in retail price, farm price or both. The other 30 per cent of marketing charges should go largely for depreciation and for factor payments other than direct wages and salaries. As price levels rise generally in the economy, it is reasonable to expect that these other costs and payments per physical unit of food marketed will also rise. At some point, it would be desirable to identify other "real" explanatory factors which will reduce the apparent contributions of the time trends.

(C) *The determination of farm prices for* (1) *food products and* (2) *all products*
Equations (12.8) through (12.11) are as follows:

$$PM_{FAN_{AF}} = PM_{FAN_{TR}} - [PM_{FAN_{TR}} - PM_{FAN_{AF}}] \tag{12.8}$$

$$PM_{FCR_{TR}} = PM_{FCR_{AF}} + [PM_{FCR_{TR}} - PM_{FCR_{AF}}] \tag{12.9}$$

$$PM_{F_{AF}} = PM_{FCR_{AF}} + PM_{FAN_{TR}} - [PM_{FAN_{TR}} - PM_{FAN_{AF}}]. \tag{12.10}$$

Prices received by farmers, all commodities

$$\Delta PM_{AF} = \frac{0.003568}{(0.000372)} \Delta PM_{F_{AF}} + \frac{0.1015}{(0.0348)} \Delta PM_{HAY_{AF}}$$

$$+ \frac{0.008032}{(0.002594)} \Delta PM_{COT_{AF}} \tag{12.11}$$

$$R^2 = 0.7783; \ S_e = 0.04248 \text{ index points}; \ DW = 1.7923.$$

Standard deviations of dependent variables:

Original [PM_{AF}]:   0.23707 index points
Adjusted [ΔPM_{AF}]: 0.08846 index points

Per cent of original variance of PM_{AF} explained by equation (12.11):

$$R^2_{ps} = 1 - \frac{(0.04248)^2}{(0.23707)^2} = 0.9680.$$

New variables used in equations (12.6) through (12.11) are:

$PM_{FAN_{TR}}$ = retail value of livestock component of the food market basket, dollars

$DMY17$ = 1, 1949 : 3 through 1950 : 1;
0, all other quarters

ULC_{FM} = index of unit labor costs in food marketing operations, 1957–1959 = 100

PM_{PDFS} = price index of purchased materials and services used in food marketing, 1947–1949 = 1.00

$PM_{FCR_{AF}}$ = current value at farm level of crop component of the food market basket, dollars

$PM_{F_{AF}}$ = current value at farm level of the food market basket, livestock and crop components combined, dollars

PM_{AF} = index of prices received by farmers for all commodities, food and nonfood, 1910–1914 = 1.00

$PM_{HAY_{AF}}$ = index of prices of feed grains and hay at the farm level, 1910–1914 = 1.00

$PM_{COT_{AF}}$ = U. S. average price of cotton at the farm level, cents per pound.

Equation (12.8) is an identity stating that the estimated value of livestock food products at the farm level is equal to the estimated retail value minus the estimated charge for marketing services.

Equation (12.9) treats the farm value of crop food products, $PM_{FCR_{AF}}$, as predetermined. An estimate of the retail price of crop food products would be obtained by adding $PM_{FCR_{AF}}$ to the estimated marketing charge for crop food products.

Equation (12.10) simply adds equations (12.8 and 12.9) to give an estimate of the equivalent net farm value of the food market basket for crop and livestock food products combined. In 1960 the equivalent net farm values were approximately $ 280 and $ 120 for food livestock and food crops, respectively, or a total of $ 400 for all items included in the food market basket. The corresponding retail value was over $ 1 000. Hence, in 1960 slightly less than 40 per cent of the consumers' food dollar went to farmers and slightly more than 60 per cent to processing, transportation and distribution agencies.

Equations (12.2) through (12.10) have all dealt with food products and have neglected nonfood products of farm origin. Equation (12.11) establishes a bridge from the equivalent farm value of food products to the official index of prices received by farmers for all commodities. The latter variable, PM_{AF} is regressed upon farm food values, the farm price of feed grains and hay and the farm price of cotton. The latter two variables are regarded as predetermined; they account for a considerable proportion of farm cash receipts from marketings of nonfood products and hence for a large proportion of the nonfood component of PM_{AF}. All variables are expressed as first differences—changes from the preceding quarter.

During 1947–1960, government price supports were important and perennial determinants of the farm prices of cotton and feed grains. In most years, prices of these crops have rested heavily on the supports. Nevertheless, the decision to treat current farm prices of cotton, feed grains and food crops as predetermined variables is only an approximation of the truth and would need careful attention in disaggregated models directed toward the analysis of real commodity policies.

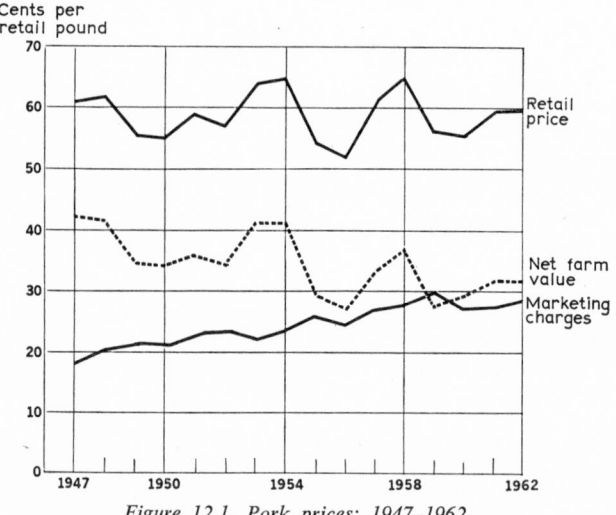

Figure 12.1. Pork prices: 1947–1962.

Before leaving the price-determining equations as a block, one comment and exhibit should be noted in connection with the treatment of charges for food marketing services.

Figure 12.2 shows on an annual basis retail prices, equivalent net farm values and marketing charges for pork [11]). On a year-to-year basis, retail

---

[11]) The "equivalent net farm value" concept allows for weight reduction in processing and retailing and for the value of byproducts. Thus the net farm value in 1960 is the value of 2.13 pounds of live hog *minus* an allowance of 4.5 cents for the value of lard and other byproducts. The marketing charges are those allocated to pork and not to the byproducts.

pork prices and equivalent net farm values have changed by nearly the same absolute amounts. The marketing margin has shown very moderate year-to-year changes; its most conspicuous attribute was an upward trend during most of the 1947–1960 period. The movement of the marketing margin series for pork is consistent with the view that charges for food marketing services are largely determined by competitive factors and costs within the food processing and distribution system. Wages of food marketing employees are determined in a labor market which cuts across all industries; prices of materials and services used in food marketing are also influenced by price policies and cost conditions in the industries from which these materials and services are procured. There is a strong presumption, therefore, that equations explaining marketing margins for foods may be fitted independently of consumer demand functions.

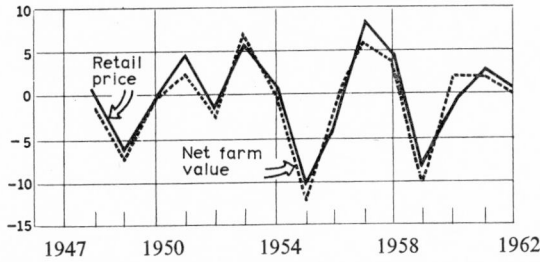

Figure 12.3. Year to year changes in pork prices.

Retail food prices are collected from retail stores. Gross farm value series are based on direct reports and estimates of farm prices; most byproduct allowances are based on market news reports. Equivalent net farm value is obtained by subtracting byproduct allowances from gross farm value. All of the basic series (retail price, gross farm value and byproduct allowance) are intended to be direct observations of real phenomena.

The marketing margin series is obtained by subtracting equivalent net farm value from retail price. As the collecting procedures (and agencies) for the retail price and farm value series are independent, we should expect to find a larger error of measurement in the marketing margin series than in either of the other two. If we know the measurement-error variances in retail price and equivalent net farm value, we could estimate the error variance in the series on marketing margins as the sum of the error variances in the other two series.

TABLE 12.4

Determination of farm income and expenditures [a].

Causal order [b]	Equation number	Exogenous or predetermined variables (causal order 0)																Endogenous variables (causal orders 1 to 4)					
		34	19	33	35	36	37	38	39	40	41	42	29	5 [c]	8a=32a	31	8 [c]	10	11	12	13	14	15
1	12.13	X																1					
1	12.14		X	X	X	X													1				
1	12.15						X	X	X											1			
1	12.16									X	X	X									1		
2	12.17												X	X								1	
3	12.12			X											X	X	X					X	1
4	12.18														X	X	X			X	X	X	1

[a] For convenience variables are given the identifying numbers used on my work sheets for the Iowa State University Computing Center. The equations are numbered as in the text, and the dependent endogenous variable in each equation is assigned the equation number. The exogenous variables are included to show the nearly diagonal arrangement (virtual independence) of the equations in the farm income block.

[b] Assuming that X_5 and X_8 are treated as exogenous variables.

[c] It is recognized that X_5 and X_8 are endogenous variables in the farm price subset (table 12.1) and hence in the agricultural submodel as a whole. The complete submodel will be discussed in connection with table 12.5.

12.3. Determining net income of farm operators

As in the preceding section, we shall first consider the causal ordering and matrix structure of the seven equations used in estimating net farm income and related variables. We shall then discuss the individual equations.

12.3.1. Causal ordering and matrix structure in the farm income subset

Table 12.4 is directly analogous to table 12.1. If we class as exogenous *all variables whose values are not determined within the farm income subset,* the subset consists of 16 exogenous or predetermined variables (causal order 0) and 7 endogenous variables. Four of the endogenous variables depend only on exogenous or predetermined variables and are determined at causal order 1. The three remaining variables are determined in successive causal orders—causal orders 2, 3 and 4 *from the standpoint of the farm income subset.*

The matrix of endogenous variables is triangular; in fact, except for equation (12.17) and the identity equation (12.18), it is diagonal. The matrix involving regression coefficients of endogenous variables upon exogenous or predetermined variables is also nearly diagonal, suggesting that the clusters of factors explaining the various components of farm income and expenditures are quite distinctive [12]). Only one exogenous variable, namely, the proportionate change in the physical volume of farm product marketings from the preceding quarter, appears in two equations. It is a factor in the determination of gross farm income from commodity production and also in the explanation of current farm production expenditures.

---

[12]) The extent of independence among the six statistically estimated equations may be illustrated by the following linear transformation:

$$J_{10} = X_{34} \tag{12.13}$$

$$J_{11} = (\lambda_{19} X_{19} + \lambda_{33,11} X_{33} + \lambda_{35} X_{35} + \lambda_{36} X_{36}) \tag{12.14}$$

$$J_{12} = (\lambda_{37} X_{37} + \lambda_{38} X_{38} + \lambda_{39} X_{39}) \tag{12.15}$$

$$J_{13} = (\lambda_{40} X_{40} + \lambda_{41} X_{41} + \lambda_{42} X_{42}) \tag{12.16}$$

$$J_{14} = (\lambda_{29} X_{29} + \lambda_5 X_5) \tag{12.17}$$

$$J_9 = (\lambda_{33,9} X_{33} + \lambda_{32_a} X_{32_a} + \lambda_{31} X_{31} + \lambda_8 X_8) \tag{12.12}$$

where the λ_i's may be either statistical regression coefficients or coefficients assigned

If table 12.4 reflects the true structure of the farm income and expenditure subset, and if the error terms in the various equations are statistically independent, five of the equations can clearly be estimated by least squares; only one, equation (12.17), *might* benefit from two-stage least squares or some other "simultaneous" estimation procedure. The final equation is an identity.

At this point we will simply note that two of the variables which are taken as predetermined or exogenous in table 12.4 were treated as endogenous variables in the farm price subset (table 12.1). We will consider the implications of combining the farm price and farm income subsets after we discuss the individual equations of the latter.

12.3.2. *Comments on the individual equations*

The seven equations may be divided into four subsets determining, respectively, gross farm income, production expenditures, inventory change and net farm income.

The seven equations are based on official USDA series. Estimates of gross farm income, total farm production expenditures, inventory change and net

---

a priori. In matrix form we may write the transformed equation as:

$$
\begin{bmatrix}
X_{10} & & & & & \\
& X_{11} & & & & \\
& & X_{12} & & & \\
& & & X_{13} & & \\
& & c_{13} & X_{13} & X_{14} & \\
& & & & & X_9
\end{bmatrix}
$$

$$
=
\begin{bmatrix}
J_{10} & & & & & \\
& J_{11(33)} & & & & \\
& & J_{12} & & & \\
& & & J_{13} & & \\
& & & & J_{14} & \\
& & & & & J_{9(33)}
\end{bmatrix}
\begin{bmatrix}
b_{10} \\
b_{11} \\
b_{12} \\
b_{13} \\
b_{14} \\
b_9
\end{bmatrix}
+
\begin{bmatrix}
a_{10} \\
a_{11} \\
a_{12} \\
a_{13} \\
a_{14} \\
a_9
\end{bmatrix}
+
\begin{bmatrix}
u_{10} \\
u_{11} \\
u_{12} \\
u_{13} \\
u_{14} \\
u_9
\end{bmatrix}
$$

where the b_i and a_i (except in equation 12.17) are obtained by regressing each X_i on the corresponding J_i. The notation $J_{11(33)}$ and $J_{9(33)}$ indicate that J_{11} and J_9 contain one element X_{33}, in common; there are no other overlaps among the J_i's. Equation (12.17) contains two endogenous variables; the others contain only one each.

farm income are published on a quarterly basis. Estimates of the imputed rental value of farm operators' dwellings and depreciation are published only on an annual basis. Hence, interpolation is required to put these series on a quarterly basis.

(A) *Gross farm income*   Gross farm income is divided into two components. The first may be regarded as gross farm income from commodity production. It includes cash receipts from farm marketings of all commodities sold by farmers and also the value of farm products, food and fuel consumed on the farm where grown. The self-supply component of this series has been shrinking absolutely as well as relatively during 1947–1960 with the declining number of small farms and the greater reliance of farm families on commercially processed and distributed foods. The other component is the imputed rental value of farm operators' dwellings. The two equations associated with these components are shown below:

Gross farm income from commodity production [13])

$$Y_{GRS_{AF}} - RENT_{AF} = \frac{0.8532}{(1.4854)} + \frac{0.9737}{(0.0451)} \left[Y_{GRS_{AF}} - RENT_{AF} \right]_{-1}$$

$$+ \frac{25.1086}{(2.6470)} \left\{ \frac{PM_{AF}}{[PM_{AF}]_{-1}} - 1 \right\} + \frac{21.5398}{(2.0389)} \left\{ \frac{J_{Q_{AF}}}{[J_{Q_{AF}}]_{-1}} - 1 \right\} \qquad (12.12)$$

$R^2 = 0.9078$; $S_e = \$ 0.6040$ billion; $DW = 1.6142$.
Standard deviation $[Y_{GRS_{AF}} - RENT_{AF}]$: $ 1.9343$ billion.

---

[13]) An alternative version using first differences of the dependent variable yields regression coefficients very similar to those in the text, but the standard error of estimate is larger—$ 0.8182 billion. A regression in which a priori coefficients were imposed resulted as follows:

$$\Delta[Y_{GRS_{AF}} - RENT_{AF}]$$

$$= \frac{0.6098}{(0.0718)} \left[33 \left\{ \frac{PM_{AF}}{[PM_{AF}]_{-1}} - 1 \right\} + 33 \left\{ \frac{J_{Q_{AF}}}{[J_{Q_{AF}}]_{-1}} - 1 \right\} \right] \qquad (12.12a)$$

$S_e = \$ 0.8284$ billion. This would imply a regression coefficient of 20.1234 for each of the two explanatory series, prices and volume of marketings.

Imputed rental value of farm dwellings

$$RENT_{AF} = \frac{0.0550}{(0.0547)} + \frac{0.9738}{(0.0322)} [RENT_{AF}]_{-1} \qquad (12.13)$$

$R^2 = 0.9442; \quad S_e = \$ 0.0456 \text{ billion}; \quad DW = 2.2856.$

Standard deviation $RENT_{AF}$: $\$ 0.1912$ billion.

The average value of gross farm income from commodity production during 1947–1960 was about $\$ 33$ billion. The constant term and the regression coefficient with respect to last quarter's income in equation (12.12) have the effect of holding gross income nearly constant unless there are changes in one or both of the other variables.

The coefficient of the price variable implies that if the index of prices received by farmers increases 1 per cent (0.01) from the preceding quarter, the dependent variable should increase by $\$ 0.257$ billion. The remaining coefficient implies that if the physical volume of farm marketings (plus farm consumption of home-grown food and fuel) increases by 1 per cent or 0.01, the dependent variable should increase by $\$ 0.215$ billion.

A strong logical case could be made for assigning a value of 33 to each of the two coefficients, so that a 1 per cent increase in either the price or the volume component of gross income from commodity production would increase gross income by $\$ 0.33$ billion, or 1 per cent of the 1947–1960 average. But the regression coefficients imply changes in gross income only 65 to 75 per cent as large as this.

It is well-known that the product of two Laspeyres indexes, one of price and the other of quantity, will not change identically (or correlate perfectly), with a true value aggregate. PM_{AF} and $J_{Q_{AF}}$ are Laspeyres indexes and $Y_{GRS_{AF}} - RENT_{AF}$ is a true value aggregate, so there is at best an "error of closure" between the three series. PM_{AF} and $J_{Q_{AF}}$ are used essentially in first difference form; in this form their standard deviations are only 0.033 and 0.042, respectively, or 3.3 and 4.2 per cent of the previous quarter's level. Errors of measurement and "aggregation noise"—particularly the latter—could account for a significant fraction of the observed variance in each series, and the seasonal adjustment procedure applied to $J_{Q_{AF}}$ provides another somewhat arbitrary component to its observed variance.

Though some of these factors are not strictly random, their combined effect almost certainly biases the regression coefficients of the two variables toward zero. (The intercorrelation coefficient between the two series is only -0.2370, so statements about bias which are strictly applicable to simple regression coefficients will also be applicable to the multiple regression coefficients [14]).

Those income and quantity series in the farm income subset which are published on a quarterly basis are at seasonally adjusted annual rates. Most of the price components do not show substantial seasonal variations and are not seasonally adjusted. Quarterly estimates interpolated from official annual data do not, of course, require seasonal adjustment; implicitly, the adjustment is built in.

I believe it is fair to say that the official USDA quantity and value series are less accurate on a quarterly than on an annual basis. Check data are less complete on a quarterly basis, and an error in allocating sales of (say) one million hogs between December and January has a greater percentage effect on the accuracy of estimates for adjacent quarters than for adjacent years. It is also quite possible that the accuracy of the quarterly estimates and seasonal adjustments could be improved by fuller and more careful exploitation of existing basic data. The quarterly income series are relatively recent (1955) additions to USDA's published data network, and it is reasonable to expect further improvements in their accuracy relative to those of the annual series.

Equation (12.13) expresses the imputed rental value of farm operators' dwellings as a function of the previous quarter's value of the same variable. Even the official annual estimates of $RENT_{AF}$ move sluggishly, and the basic data are weak; the sluggishness of movement is to be expected, and fortunately the absolute magnitude of this variable is not large. As the quarterly values underlying equation (12.13) have been interpolated from the

---

[14]) The lagged dependent variable has little intercorrelation with the price and marketing series. The intercorrelation matrix for the three explanatory variables is

$$
\begin{array}{cccc}
 & (1) & (2) & (3) \\
[Y_{GRS_{AF}} - RENT_{AF}]_{-1} \ (1) & 1.0000 & -0.2731 & -0.1097 \\
\left\{ \dfrac{PM_{AF}}{[PM_{AF}]_{-1}} - 1 \right\} \quad (2) & -0.2731 & 1.0000 & -0.2370 \\
\left\{ \dfrac{J_{Q_{AF}}}{[J_{Q_{AF}}]_{-1}} - 1 \right\} \quad (3) & -0.1097 & -0.2370 & 1.0000
\end{array}
$$

The value of the determinant is about 0.85, compared with 1.00 for the case of zero intercorrelation and about 0.00009 for the case of extreme multicollinearity cited in connection with equations (12.2) and (12.3).

official annual series, the small standard error of the regression coefficient in equation (12.13) is more nearly an artifact than a statistical success.

(B) *Production expenditures*   The two components of farm production expenditures, current operating expenditures and depreciation, are explained by equations (12.14 and 12.15).

Production expenditures for current operations

$$\Delta XCST_{AF} = -\frac{0.1125}{(0.0618)} + \frac{0.004740}{(0.001797)} TIME + \frac{1.3557}{(0.6838)} \left\{ \frac{J_{Q_{AF}}}{[J_{Q_{AF}}]_{-1}} - 1 \right\}$$

$$+ \frac{19.2418}{(1.6768)} \left\{ \frac{PM_{PDFP}}{[PM_{PDFP}]_{-1}} - 1 \right\}$$ (12.14)

$R^2 = 0.7176$; $S_e = \$\,0.2084$ billion; $DW = 1.6870$.
Standard deviations of dependent variable:
  Original $[XCST_{AF}]$: $\$\,2.1326$ billion.
  Adjusted $[\Delta XCST_{AF}]$: $\$\,0.3813$.

Per cent of variance of $XCST_{AF}$ explained by equation (12.14):
$R^2 = 1 - (0.2084)^2/(2.1326)^2 = 0.9906$.

Depreciation

$$DPNR_{AF} = \frac{0.1596}{(0.0389)} + \frac{0.7166}{(0.0708)} [DPNR^*_{AF}]_{-1}$$

$$+ \{0.0231\, K_{PL_{AF}} + 0.159\, K_{PDE_{AF}}\}   (12.15)$$

$R^2 = 0.6550$; $S_e = \$\,0.0609$; $DW = 2.0564$ (refers to $DPNR^*_{AF}$, i.e., $DPNP_{AF} - \{0.0231\, K_{PL_{AF}} + 0.159 K_{PDE_{AF}}\}$

  Original $[DPNR_{AF}]$: $\$\,0.7637$ billion.
  Adjusted $[DPNR^*_{AF}]$: $\$\,0.1028$.

Per cent of variance of $DPNR_{AF}$ explained by equation (12.15):
$R^2 = 1 - (0.0609)^2/(0.7637)^2 = 0.9938$.

The coefficients in equation (12.14) are in close accord with a priori considerations. The average value of $XCST_{AF}$ during 1947–1960 was about $\$\,18.6$ billion. The coefficient of the term in PM_{PDFP} simply implies that if the index of prices paid by farmers for goods and services used in production increased by 1 per cent (0.01) current production expenditures would increase by $\$\,0.192$ billion, or slightly more than 1 per cent. The coefficient of the term in $J_{Q_{AF}}$ implies that if the seasonally adjusted volume of farm product marketings increases by 1 per cent (0.01) from the previous quarter, current farm production expenditures will increase by $ 0.014 billion, or less than 0.1 per cent.

The real component of farm production expenditures moves very sluggishly from one year to the next. Most inputs are planned and applied well in advance of the time at which the resulting outputs become ready for market. We may visualize farmers as purchasing a combination of inputs which, with average weather, would lead to desired levels and patterns of farm outputs.

Quarter-to-quarter changes in the seasonally adjusted volume of total farm product marketings are usually moderate. Short-term changes in aggregate crop production will stem more from changes in yields than from changes in acreage. Farmers typically plan their inputs for crop production on a per-acre basis. If favorable weather produces an abnormally high yield per acre, the increase in harvesting, hauling and other costs is quite small in relation to the preharvest production inputs. Favorable weather also improves range and pasture conditions, which affect $J_{Q_{AF}}$ through greater milk production per cow and heavier weights per animal sold. Good weather means more feed grains per acre available for feeding on the home farm; this also results (in part via a reduction in the market prices of feed grains) in increased weights per animal marketed and, with a lag of some months, an increase in numbers of broilers, turkeys and hogs produced and marketed.

$\Delta XCST_{AF}$ is a first difference and $[\{J_{Q_{AF}}/[J_{Q_{AF}}]_{-1}\}-1]$ is essentially in first-difference form. On a quarter-to-quarter change basis, it is not unreasonable to expect that the coefficient connecting them will reflect a marginal rather than an average response of production expenditures to a change in the volume of output ready for market. In view of its standard error, the true coefficient could be as high as 2.5 or 3, but would certainly not be as low as zero.

There appears to be a small time trend over and above the effects of the price and marketing variables—about $ 0.019 billion annually, or about 0.1 per cent of the 1947–1960 average value of production expenditures. The coefficient is of marginal significance, statistically and economically.

The quarterly values of depreciation in equation (12.15) were interpolated approximately linearly on the basis of the published annual data. The coefficients in brackets were based on separate simple regression analyses of these annual data, relating depreciation on buildings and machinery, respectively, to official estimates of the values of farm buildings and farm machinery (separately) at the beginning of each calender year. The first coefficient implies that depreciation on farm structures amounts to some 2.31 per cent of their fair market value per year. The second coefficient implies that farm machinery and equipment depreciates each year by approximately 15.9 per cent of the fair market value of the stock of machinery and equipment on January 1.

These figures are certainly not unreasonable; however, they might be improved upon and adjusted over time. The coefficients relating to buildings and equipment respectively are so different that it is highly important to give separate recognition to the two components of farm capital. The term in brackets evidently explains about 98 per cent of the total variance in depreciation; however, most of the movement in this variable is a strong upward trend.

The variable $DPNR_{AF}$ *minus* the items in brackets was regressed upon the lagged value of this term for the previous quarter. The regression coefficient is highly significant according to usual tests, but its real meaning is affected by the interpolation procedure used in deriving $DPNR_{AF}$.

(C) *Net change in inventories of farm products*   Equations (12.16) and (12.17) deal with net changes in inventories of farm products:

$$\Delta INV_{AF}^{54} = -\frac{0.01434}{(0.0592)} + \frac{0.6799}{(0.0993)} [\Delta INV_{AF}^{*54}]_{-1}$$

$$+ \left\{ \frac{0.6040}{(0.1090)} [\Delta X_{HAY}^{A47-9}] + \frac{1.0852}{(0.2882)} [\Delta INV_{COW}^{A53}] \right\} \quad (12.16)$$

$R^2 = 0.4645$; $S_e = \$ 0.4422$ billion   (fitted with dependent variable ΔINV_{AF}^{*54} as derived in 12.16.2).
Standard deviations of dependent variable:
Original $[\Delta INV_{AF}^{54}]$: $\$ 0.8718$.
Adjusted $[\Delta INV_{AF}^{*54}]$: $\$ 0.5988$.

Per cent of variance of ΔINV_{AF}^{54} explained by equat on 12.16:
$R^2 = 1 - (0.4422)^2/(0.8718)^2 = 0.7430$.

$$\Delta INV_{AF} = -\frac{0.4322}{(0.0880)} + \frac{1.0794}{(0.0111)} \Delta INV_{AF}^{54} + \frac{0.001377}{(0.000372)} PM_{FAN_{AF}}$$

$$+ \frac{0.00172}{(0.02810)} PM_{HAY_{AF}} \quad (12.17)$$

$R^2 = 0.9952$; $S_e = \$ 0.0678$ billion; $DW = 0.7917$.
Original standard deviation $[\Delta INV_{AF}]$: $\$ 0.9552$ billion.

Inventories of farm products include live animals and also crops harvested and stored on the farm, provided that these crops are not under the protection of the Commodity Credit Corporation price support loan program. This aspect is particularly important in connection with corn and other feed grains, most of which are fed to livestock on the farm where grown. If their storage facilities meet CCC requirements, farmers may pledge certain quantities of their feed grains to CCC as collateral for price support loans; farm structures containing exclusively corn under CCC loan are sealed by an agent of CCC. Depending on market conditions for feed grains and livestock, a farmer may later decide to repay his loan to CCC and feed the corn to his own livestock or sell it to some neighbor or dealer. For present purposes, the important point is that commodities physically on farms but pledged as collateral for CCC loans are not regarded as farm inventories in calculating the net inventory change component of farm income.

For many years, USDA's estimates of net inventory change were exclusively on an annual basis. Quarterly estimates were first published by USDA in the middle 1950's, and further improvements are possible (and needed) in them. The official quarterly estimates of net change in farm inventories at seasonally adjusted annual rates have been interpolated from the more carefully constructed annual estimates based on January 1 inventories.

As part of the Brookings-SSRC econometric project, I constructed 1947–1961 series of January 1 farm inventories of about 25 commodities valued at two alternative sets of prices: (i) those of December 15, 1953 and (ii) an average of December 15 prices in 1947, 1948 and 1949.

Regression analyses of these annual data indicated that changes in the number of cattle and hogs accounted for the great bulk of variation in the deflated value of total livestock inventories. The variance of total January 1 inventories of crops stored on farms and not under CCC loan was largely attributable to changes in the feed grains and hay component. Some major crops (including wheat) are harvested in the summer and/or moved into commercial elevators and warehouses instead of being stored on farms. Such commodities have relatively little influence on crop inventories remaining on farms as of January 1.

Equation (12.16) embodies some rather crude carpentry necessitated by lack of bona fide quarterly inventory data (as distinct from the USDA interpolations). We assume that the change in January 1 inventories of cattle and hogs is forecasted exactly—that is, ΔINV_{COW}^{A53} is taken as a predetermined variable. For both biological and institutional reasons, slaughter of some age groups and classes of cattle and hogs can be forecasted reasonably well for six to twelve months in advance. However, the accuracy with which inventory change can be forecasted for all categories of cattle and hogs combined would need to be tested empirically and checked from time to time in any practical application of equation (12.16).

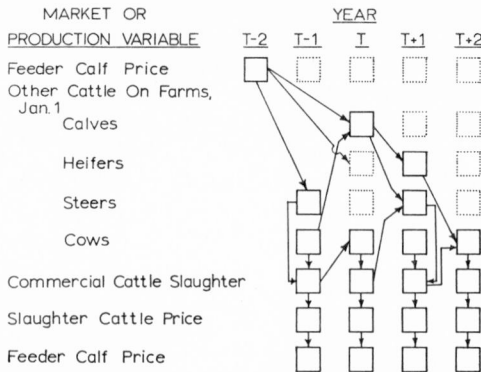

Figure 12.4. Internal mechanism of the cattle cycle.

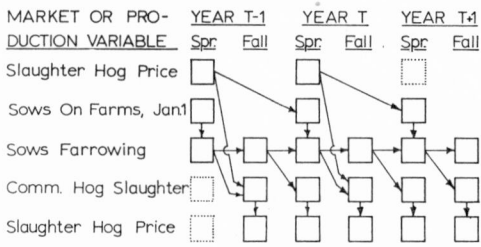

Figure 12.5. Internal mechanism of the hog cycle.

Source   Wilbur R. Maki, Decomposition of the Beef and Pork Cycles, *Journal of Farm Economics* (August, 1962) pp. 739, 741. (Reproduced by permission.)

Studies by Wilbur R. Maki [22] offer a way into the livestock inventory problem much as Brandow's 1961 study provides a bridge between equation (12.2) and (12.3) and a disaggregated set of demand functions for foods and farm products. Maki's arrow diagrams above indicate the recursive structures of his cattle and hog cycle models. These models could presumably be integrated with components based on Brandow's model and on other studies.

USDA also publishes an index of farm output by commodity groups on an annual basis. This is a Laspeyres index in which quantities of each farm commodity produced are weighted by 1947–1949 average farm prices. A large proportion of the production of feed grains and hay is fed to livestock on the farm where grown, and roughly 60 per cent of the production harvested in one calendar year is carried over into the next. The change in production of feed crops from the preceding to the current calendar year, valued at 1947–1949 prices, is held constant for all four quarters of the current calendar year. This is the definition of ΔX_{HAY}^{A47-9}; it is treated as an exogenous variable, largely determined by weather.

The coefficients in brackets in equation (12.16) were derived by means of an ancillary regression:

$$\Delta INV_{AF}^{54} = -\frac{0.0407}{(0.0908)} + \frac{0.6040}{(0.1090)}[\Delta X_{HAY}^{A47-9}] + \frac{1.0852}{(0.2882(}[\Delta INV_{COW}^{A53}]$$

$$R^2 = 0.5269; \qquad S_e = \$ \, 0.6108 \text{ billion.} \qquad\qquad (12.16.1)$$

Original standard deviation $[\Delta INV_{AF}^{54}]$ $ 0.8718 billion.

An adjusted variable,

$$\Delta INV_{AF}^{*54} = \Delta INV_{AF}^{54} - \{0.6040[\Delta X_{HAY}^{A47-9}] - 1.0852[\Delta INV_{COW}^{A53}]\} \qquad (12.16.2)$$

was computed and regressed on its own value for the preceding quarter. (The basic dependent variable, ΔINV_{AF}^{54} was computed by deflating the official quarterly estimates of net intentory change at seasonally adjusted annual rates in current dollars by the index of prices received by farmers for all commodities.) About 53 per cent of the original variance in ΔINV_{AF}^{54} was associated with changes in the bracketed term. Some 46 per cent of the remaining variation (in ΔINV_{AF}^{*54}) was associated with lagged values of the adjusted variable. The autoregressive coefficient is highly significant, but it is not clear how much of this effect derives from the methods used in constructing the other two explanatory variables and how much is characteristic of the real world.

Equation (12.17) translates inventory change in constant dollars into an estimate of inventory change in current prices corresponding to the definition of the official USDA series. The change in inventories at current prices is, of course, dominated by the change in inventories measured at 1954 prices; however, changes in farm prices of food livestock products also make a significant contribution. The coefficient with respect to farm prices of feed grains and hay, $PM_{HAY_{AF}}$, is not significant, but it is included as a reminder of its potential importance in the event of a major change in feed prices. In this case a more realistic coefficient would have to be supplied on an a priori basis.

(D) *Net farm income*   Equation (12.18) is an identity which derives an estimated value of net income of farm operators as an algebraic sum of the estimated values of the five components of farm income and expenditures described above:

$$Y_{\text{NET}_{AF}} = [Y_{\text{GRS}_{AF}} - RENT_{AF}] + RENT_{AF} - XCST_{AF} - DPNR_{AF} + \varDelta INV_{AF}.$$

(12.18)

12.4. Causal ordering and estimation in the farm price and income blocks combined

It will be recalled that in table 12.4 variables X_5 and X_8 (farm prices of food livestock products and prices received by farmers for all commodities) were treated as exogenous or predetermined variables of causal order 0 with respect to the farm income subset. Table 12.5 removes this assumption and treats variables X_1 through X_{15} as endogenous from the standpoint of the farm price and income subsets combined. This changes the causal ordering of several equations in that any variable which depends on X_5 must be of causal order 5 or higher and any variable which depends on X_8 must be of causal order 7 or higher. In the combined matrix, X_{15} (net farm income) is determined at causal order 8.

The matrix of endogenous variables is triangular in this case also. Four of the equations are identities and do not require statistical estimation. Six of the remaining endogenous variables depend exclusively on exogenous or predetermined variables, so six equations (12.6), (12.7), (12.13), (12.14), (12.15) and (12.16) can be estimated appropriately by least squares if their error terms are statistically independent of each other and of those in the other five estimated equations. Equations (12.2), (12.3), (12.10), and (12.12) include two endogenous variables and equation (12.17) includes three endogenous variables. For these equations it would be interesting to compare the least-squares results with those of two-stage least squares, but this has not been done. Thirty variables are treated as exogenous or predetermined from the standpoint of the combined farm price and farm income subsets. The matrix of regression coefficients of endogenous upon exogenous or predetermined variables is approximately though not completely block diagonal, suggesting that several quite different and relatively independent sets of variables are important in explaining movements in the various endogenous series.

It is clear that a number of the variables treated as exogenous in table 12.5

are endogenous to the Brookings-SSRC econometric model as a whole. Among these would be real disposable income per capita, retail prices of nonfoods, prices paid by farmers for commodities used in production and others.

12.5. *Ancillary equations*: *gross farm investment, agricultural employment and net acquisitions of farm products for price support purposes*

The 15 equations in the farm price and income group clearly belong in the agricultural submodel. Other participants in the Brookings-SSRC econometric project were responsible for explaining investment as it appears in the national income accounts and for explaining total employment and its subdivisions. Still other participants were responsible for the public finance and the foreign trade sectors.

The following equations were derived as a possible service to these other participants and to those responsible for integrating the model as a whole.

12.5.1. *Gross farm investment*

Theoretically, the trends in inputs of labor, farm machinery, fertilizer and other factors of production during 1947–1960 could be explained in terms of an agricultural production function which included these tangible inputs and shifted with improvements in the average level of management skills among active farm operators [15]). Over a period of years, changes in the relative prices of different farm inputs have indeed had a powerful influence on the input mix. From 1940 to 1960 hourly wage rates of farm workers increased very sharply relative to prices of land, machinery and vehicles and fertilizer, in that order. In 1960 the average unit of farm output required only 32 per cent as much labor and only 62 per cent as much land as in 1940, but the 1960 output unit utilized 2.7 times as much chemical fertilizer and was backed by 1.9 times as many farm tractors and trucks as in 1960 (table 12.6).

Although the time series on agricultural inputs and outputs are broadly consistent with classical production function concepts, during the period

---

[15]) For a comprehensive study of the demand for current agricultural inputs and for farm capital, see Heady and Tweeten [17]. 515 pp. This study uses macroeconomic data on an annual basis. An extensive treatment of the microanalytic aspects of agricultural production is contained in Heady and Dillon [16].

Determination of farm p

Causal order	Equation number	| 19	23	27	24	25	26	34	33	35	36	37	38	39	40	41	42	28
1	12.6	X	X		X	X	X											
1	12.7	X		X	X	X	X											
1	12.13							X										
1	12.14	X							X	X	X							
1	12.15											X	X	X				
1	12.16														X	X	X	
2	12.9																	X
3	12.2	X																
3	12.3	X																
4	12.8																	
5	12.10																	X
5	12.17																	
6	12.11																	
7	12.12									X								
8	12.18																	

[a]) As in tables 12.1 and 12.4, the variables are numbered as they appeared on the work she
and the endogenous variable appearing on the left-hand side of an equation is given the same nu
suggesting a considerable degree of independence among the various equations in the agricu

Variables used in equations (12.12) through (12.18) are:

$Y_{\mathrm{GRS}_{AF}}$ = gross farm income, billions of dollars

$RENT_{AF}$ = imputed rental value of farm dwellings, billions of dollars

PM_{AF} = index of prices received by farmers for all commodities, food and nonfood, 1910–1914 = 1.00

$J_{Q_{AF}}$ = index of volume of farm marketings plus farm consumption of homegrown food and fuel, 1947–1949 = 108.7 (marketing component = 100.0, farm consumption component = 8.7)

$XCST_{AF}$ = current operating expenditures for farm production, billions of dollars

$TIME$ = time trend

PM_{PDFP} = index of prices paid by farmers for goods and services used in production, 1910–1914 = 1.00.

income and expenditures ᵃ).

									Endogenous variables (causal orders 1 to 8)													
21	22	29	29a	30	30a	7a	32a	31	3	4	10	11	12	13	6	1	2	5	7	14	8	9	15
									1														
										1													
											1												
												1											
													1										
														1									
									X						1								
X	X														X	1							
X		X													X		1						
									X								X	1					
																		X	1				
	X														X			X		1			
	X	X	X	X	X	X													X		1		
					X	X															X	1	
						X	X	X													X		X	1

prepared for the Iowa State University Computing Center. The equations are numbered as in the text,
the equation. The table shows relatively little overlap among the clusters of exogenous variables,
model.

$DPNR_{AF}$ = replacement cost depreciation of farm capital, billions of dollars

$K_{PL_{AF}}$ = stock of farm buildings, billions of dollars

$K_{PDE_{AF}}$ = stock of farm machinery, billions of dollars

INV_{AF} = farm inventory stock (commodities pledged as collateral for CCC loans are excluded), billions of dollars

X_{HAY}^{A} = production of feed crops in current calender year, billions of dollars

INV_{COW}^{A} = farm inventory stock of cattle and hogs on January 1, billions of dollars

$PM_{FAN_{AF}}$ = current value at farm level of livestock component of the food market basket, dollars

$PM_{HAY_{AF}}$ = index of prices of feed grains and hay at the farm level, 1910–1914 = 1.00

$Y_{NET_{AF}}$ = net farm income, billions of dollars.

of my participation in the Brookings-SSRC econometric project there existed no comprehensive model on the production side which could be adapted to present purposes in the same fashion that I was able to adapt Brandow's consumer demand matrix. A book by Heady and Tweeten on *Resource Demand and Structure of the Agricultural Industry* was published [17] as I was engaged in the final editing of this chapter. Their book may provide the starting point for a consistent model of agricultural production as an adjunct to some later version of the complete model.

TABLE 12.6

Change in quantities of inputs per unit of total farm output and changes in prices of inputs, United States 1940 to 1960.

Input	Input per unit of farm output (1) 1960 as per cent of 1940	Price per unit of input (2) 1960 as per cent of 1940
Manhours	32	489 [a]
Cropland	62	353 [b]
Trucks	189	257 [c]
Tractors	194	250 [d]
Fertilizer	273	155 [e]

[a] Farm wage rates.
[b] Value of farm land per acre, with all improvements.
[c] Motor vehicles (price index).
[d] Farm machinery (price index).
[e] Fertilizer (price index).

The official USDA estimates of gross investment in farm buildings are alleged to rest on a weak foundation. These estimates are available only on an annual basis, and one would expect substantial seasonal fluctuations in farm construction activity.

Estimates of sales of farm machinery and equipment and purchases of automobiles, trucks and other machinery by farmers are available on a quarterly basis. It is possible to interpolate a quarterly version of the annual USDA estimates of expenditures for farm machinery and motor vehicles with the aid of a Commerce Department quarterly series which reflects a slightly different concept and level. Plausible price deflators can be derived for estimating changes in the deflated values of farm machinery purchases.

Equations (12.19), (12.20), (12.21), and (12.22) deal with gross farm

investments on the basis of these various interpolated and unofficial series.
Variables used in the investment equations are:

I_{CPL} = gross private domestic investment in plant, billions of dollars
I_{PDE} = gross private domestic investment in producers' durable equipment, billions of dollars
P_{IPDE} = implicit price deflator for investment in producers' durable equipment, 1954 = 1.00
I_{BUS} = business gross investment in plant and equipment, billions of dollars.

(A) *Gross investment in farm buildings (current prices)*

$$I_{CPL_{AF}} = \frac{0.2329}{(0.0956)} + \frac{0.8575}{(0.0592)} [I_{CPL_{AF}}]_{-4}$$

$$R^2 = 0.7986; \qquad S_e = \$ 0.0611 \text{ billion.} \tag{12.19}$$

Standard deviation $[I_{CPL_{AF}}]$: $\$ 0.1348$ billion.

(B) *Gross investment in farm machinery (1954 prices)*

$$I_{PDE_{AF}}^{54} = \frac{0.5308}{(0.2305)} + \frac{0.8042}{(0.0830)} [I_{PDE_{AF}}^{54}]_{-1}$$

$$R^2 = 0.6394; \qquad S_e = \$ 0.3216 \text{ billion.} \tag{12.20}$$

Standard deviation $[I_{PDE_{AF}}^{54}]$: $\$ 0.5306$ billion.

(C) *Gross investment in farm machinery (current prices)*

$$I_{PDE_{AF}} = P_{IPDE} \cdot I_{PDE_{AF}}^{54}. \tag{12.21}$$

Gross investment in farm buildings and machinery (current prices)

$$I_{BUS_{AF}} = I_{CPL_{AF}} + I_{PDE_{AF}}. \tag{12.22}$$

While the results of equations (12.19) and (12.20), plus the identities in equations (12.21) and (12.22), are plausible, it is not at all clear that they will be useful in the Brookings-SSRC econometric model. The only significant variable in the equations as written (and in alternative versions with two or more explanatory factors) proves to be the value of the dependent variable in the preceding quarter. Some of the inertia in the two investment series stems from the interpolation process; this is particularly true of investment in building, where the quarterly figures are interpolated from annual data.

12.5.2. Agricultural employment

It was anticipated that the Brookings-SSRC econometric model as a whole
would incorporate the official labor force and employment series published
by the U. S. Department of Labor. The dependent variable in equations
(12.23) and (12.24) is the agricultural employment component of the
monthly labor force series.

Agricultural employment

$$E_{AF} = \frac{8.121}{(0.056)} - \frac{0.0458}{(0.0017)} TIME + \frac{0.000708}{(0.00010)} [E_{AF} - E_{AF}^T]_{-1}$$

$$R^2 = 0.9431; \qquad S_e = 184.6588. \tag{12.23}$$

Standard deviation E_{AF}:   759.0867.

$$[E_{AF} - E_{AF}^T] = E_{AF} - \left[\frac{8.164}{(0.077)} - \frac{0.0471}{(0.0023)} TIME \right]$$

$$R^2 = 0.8867; \qquad S_e = 267.1560. \tag{12.24}$$

The most prominent feature of agricultural employment during this
period is a strong and relatively consistent downward trend. Equation
(12.24) implies a downward trend of 47 000 workers per quarter or 188 000
workers per year—roughly $2\frac{1}{2}$ million workers over a 13-year period.
The agricultural employment series is seasonally adjusted; nevertheless,
the standard error of estimate in equation (12.24) is 267 000 workers, or
nearly 5 per cent of the absolute level of E_{AF} as of 1960. In other words,
the uncertainty in estimating agricultural employment for any particular
quarter on the basis of trend alone would be appreciably larger than the
average 12-month decline in the trend value itself.

Equation (12.23) takes advantage of an autoregressive element in the
quarterly deviations from trend. When last quarter's deviation from trend
is included as an explanatory variable along with time itself, the standard
error of estimate is reduced to about 185 000 workers.

The official series, E_{AF} is estimated from a probability sample. The standard error of estimate attaching to this series is said to be on the order of
3 per cent, or more than 150 000 workers as of 1960.

Week-to-week fluctuations in farm employment will occur as a result
(among other things) of weather conditions. However, on a year-to-year
basis it seems clear that man-hour inputs into agriculture can be predicted
more accurately by means other than a probability sample. Specifically,

USDA publishes a carefully constructed annual series on man-hours used in farm production. The standard error of estimate associated with a regression of annual average agricultural employment E_{AF} upon the USDA annual series of man-hour inputs is 233 000 workers. The downtrends in the two series during 1947–1960 are quite similar, but the year-to-year changes in the labor force series are much more erratic than those in USDA's man-hour series.

The USDA series is a technician's series synthesized from continuous records of samples of farms, special surveys of particular farming operations and other basic sources. I believe the USDA series measures what it purports to measure with greater precision than does the agricultural employment component of the official labor force series.

In brief, the relatively large error variance in E_{AF} is a property of the sample and not of the population in which we are really interested. If more extensive work is done on the agricultural sector of the model, presumably in cooperation with USDA economists, the possibility of using USDA estimates of farm labor inputs and employment should be explored.

12.5.3. Commodity credit corporation net outlays for price support purposes

Equation (12.25) is based exclusively on annual data. For consistency with other equations, the annual figure for a given program year (approximately a fiscal year) was entered for each of the four quarters; hence, the standard errors of the regression coefficients imply approximately four times as many degrees of freedom as were actually available.

CCC net outlays for price support purposes

$$CCC^{A47-9} = -\frac{13.8227}{(1.6407)} - 1.1943 \, DMYI8^A + \frac{7.6165}{(0.7770)} \left[\frac{J^A_{QCR_{AF}}}{[J^A_{DUCR}]_{-1}} \right]$$

$$R^2 = 0.7964; \qquad S_e = \$\, 0.5030 \text{ billion.} \qquad\qquad (12.25)$$

Standard devation CCC^{A47-9}:   \$ 1.0926 billion.

The variables in equation (12.25) are:

CCC^A = annual net outlays by the Commodity Credit Corporation for supporting prices of major crops and dairy products, billions of dollars

$DMYI8^A$ = 1, 1948, 1951 and 1952;
0, all other years

$J^A_{QCR_{AF}}$ = index of the volume of output of all farm crops, 1947–1949
         = 100
J^A_{DUCR} = index of total annual domestic utilization of farm crops
         (a subaggregate of an index in which the average annual
         utilization of all U. S. farm products for all purposes, domestic
         and foreign, 1947–1949 = 100).

The variable J^A_{DUCR} is a specially tabulated series representing the total domestic utilization of farm crops during the preceding year. In other words, J^A_{DUCR} is a Laspeyres index with 1947–1949 prices as weights. However, the level of the series ranges between 50 and 65, as the base is average annual utilization of all U. S. farm products for all purposes, domestic and foreign, during 1947–1949. Domestic utilization of farm crops is equivalent to about half of total utilization of crops and livestock combined.

In equation (12.25), $[J^A_{DUCR}]_{-1}$ is a measure of a capacity of the U. S. economy to absorb farm crops. Hence, if the current year's production of farm crops, $J^A_{QCR_{AF}}$ is high relative to last year's domestic utilization, a considerable portion of the increase in crop output will move into CCC hands. During 1947–1960, the ratio in brackets ranged from about 1.9 to 2.2. Roughly speaking, the regression coefficient of the ratio variable implies that CCC's net outlay for price support purposes will increase by $ 0.76 billion if crop production increases by 5 per cent relative to domestic utilization of crops. This is consistent with a value of farm marketings of crops on the order of $ 15 billion, which is not far from reality.

The dummy variable reflects the considerable margin between the loan rate at which CCC accepts crops for price support and the minimum price at which CCC is permitted to sell its own inventories into domestic commercial channels. In years of very high demand or very short production of major crops, as in 1947–1948 and 1950–1951, CCC's net outlays for price support purposes were zero or negative.

The reasonableness of the coefficient of $DMY18^A$ should be checked further on a commodity-by-commodity basis. In any event, these two highly plausible variables accounted for nearly 80 per cent of the observed variance in CCC's annual net outlays for price support during 1947–1960. The dependent variable includes certain allowances for a new cotton price support program which was operative during 1959 and 1960.

In further interactions between USDA economists and persons responsible for the Brookings-SSRC econometric model, equation (12.25) should be interpreted and improved upon in the light of Brandow's disaggregated model of derived demands at the farm price level.

12.5.4. Total consumption of food livestock products as a function of the volume of farm marketings of livestock and livestock products

In equations (12.2) and (12.3) we treated the variable $J_{FAN/N}$, per capita consumption of food livestock products, as though it were wholly predetermined. In a logical sense, I believe this is very nearly true, but someone, presumably in USDA, must make an accurate forecast of J_{FAN} for at least one quarter ahead if equation (12.2) is to be useful in predicting $PM_{FAN_{TR}}$.

Equation (12.26) expresses J_{FAN} as a function of a seasonally adjusted index of the physical volume of livestock marketings and farm home consumption. The symbols and their definitions are:

J_{FAN} = index of total consumption of food livestock products ($J_{FAN/N}$ multiplied by total U. S. population in millions of persons)

$J_{QAN_{AF}}$ = index of physical volume of farm home consumption plus marketing of livestock, 1947–1949 = 110.5 (marketing component = 100, farm consumption component = 10.5).

$$\frac{J_{FAN}}{100} = \frac{67.1584}{(6.8428)} + \frac{0.3215}{(0.0751)} J_{QAN_{AF}} + \frac{0.3740}{(0.0717)} [J_{QAN_{AF}}]_{-1}$$

$$+ \frac{0.4110}{(0.0465)} TIME$$

$R^2 = 0.9883; \qquad S_e = 1.6403$ index points. $\qquad\qquad$ (12.26)

Standard deviation $[J_{FAN}/100]$: 14.7360 index points.

Last quarter's value of $J_{QAN_{AF}}$, is logically predetermined and should in fact be known quite accurately by the end of that period. Production, and hence marketings, of eggs, milk, broilers and turkeys can be predicted closely for three months in advance, except that favorable or unfavorable weather may affect pasture conditions and milk flow per cow. Marketings of hogs, lambs and cattle can also be anticipated fairly well for the ensuing quarter.

Nevertheless, such forecasts will be by no means perfect. The average level of $J_{FAN}/100$ during 1947–1960 was between 160 and 170. Hence, the standard error of estimate was approximately 1 per cent of the average level of the series and would be equivalent to approximately one point on the index of per capita consumption of food livestock products which appears in equations (12.2) and (12.3). This series, $J_{FAN/N}$ ranged between 100 and 110 during 1947–1960.

An error of 1 per cent in forecasting $J_{FAN/N}$ would lead to an opposite error of about 2 per cent—more specifically, \$ 11.32 over a base of about \$ 550 or \$ 600—$PM_{FAN_{TR}}$. This error is of the same order of magnitude as the standard error of estimate of $PM_{FAN_{TR}}$ from equation (12.2), namely, \$ 15.30 [16]).

---

[16]) In most econometric investigations, little attention is given to errors of measurement in variables. Unless the series are estimated from probability samples, the econometrician is usually quite reluctant to make any judgments about their measurement error components.

In 1951, while I was estimating statistical demand functions for a wide range of agricultural commodities and foods, I tried to arrive at judgment estimates of the levels of *ex post* measurement error in the time series I was using. My procedure was to interview the persons responsible for estimating each of the official published series on commodity prices and production and ask them essentially the following question: Assuming that the annual average of this series in year 1 was measured exactly, within what range do you think you have estimated the corresponding figure for year 2 in two years out of three? Conceptually, the answer to this question is a judgment estimate of the standard error of measurement in the official series.

The persons interviewed were competent applied statisticians, and they responded readily and constructively to the terms of the question. In arriving at their judgments, they took account of the availability of check data (such as regulatory reports on cotton ginnings or on livestock slaughter under federal inspection) of sample sizes and of other problems in estimating acreages and yields of different crops and numbers of different classes of livestock. The results of the 1951 interviews are summarized in Fox [10, p. 121].

In August, 1962 I interviewed some of the persons who were most familiar with a number of the time series in the agricultural submodel. I supplemented these with some judgments of my own based on knowledge of the data gained during my eight years of service (1946–1954) as associate head and head of the Bureau of Agricultural Economics' Division of Statistical and Historical Research. Some of the results, admittedly very rough, are tabulated below:

Variable	Judgment estimate of standard error of measurement (*ex post*)	Standard error of estimate in the agricultural submodel
$PM_{FAN_{TR}}$	\$ 4	\$ 15.30
$J_{FCR/N}$	0.4 index points	0.76 index points
$PM_{FAN_{TR}} - PM_{FAN_{AF}}$	\$ 5	\$ 6.17
$PM_{FCR_{TR}} - PM_{FCR_{AF}}$	\$ 4	\$ 6.01
PM_{AF}	1 index point	4.25 index points
$Y_{GRS_{AF}} - RENT_{AF}$	\$ 0.2 billion	\$ 0.60 billion
$XCST_{AF}$	\$ 0.2 billion	\$ 0.21 billion
$\Delta INV_{AF}^{54}, \Delta INV_{AF}$	\$ 0.2 billion	\$ 0.44 billion
$I_{BUS_{AF}}$	\$ 0.25 billion	\$ 0.34 billion
E_{AF}	150 000 workers	185 000 workers
$J_{FAN}/100$	0.6 index points	1.64 index points

The message of equation (12.26) is simply this: The present agricultural submodel, with its high level of aggregation relative to that at which commodity policies are actually determined, leaves much room for improvement. Some of this improvement cannot be secured without further disaggregation.

12.6. Conclusion

This chapter is already overburdened with didactic and hortatory remarks. Many of these remarks have no pragmatic significance for the first and most aggregative version of the Brookings-SSRC econometric model. Some of them should prove useful, however, if serious efforts are made in the next few years to integrate data flows, judgments and forecasts by USDA economists with descendants of the initial model. Both general and agricultural economists should profit greatly by this interaction. Also, both groups of economists should be able to advise congressmen, lay leaders and students with much greater confidence and clarity when they have explored the structure of agriculture and the strengths and weaknesses of farm policy within a comprehensive, consistent and reproducible quantitative framework.

I hope that this chapter will also provide a starting point for agricultural economists in the land-grant universities who may wish to use the Brookings-SSRC econometric model and its descendants in conjunction with some of the problems and models with which they are concerned.

REFERENCES

1. BRANDOW, GEORGE E. *Interrelation Among Demands for Farm Products and Implications for Control of Market Supplies.* Pennsylvania Agricultural Experimental Station Bulletin 680 (1961). (An interregional publication.)

If the judgment estimates of *ex post* measurement error are taken seriously, it will be difficult to reduce the standard errors of estimate of equations explaining $PM_{FAN_{TR}}$, $J_{FCR/N}$, $XCST_{AF}$, E_{AF}, $I_{BUS_{AF}}$, $PM_{FAN_{TR}} - PM_{FAN_{AF}}$, and $PM_{FCR_{TR}} - PM_{FCR_{AF}}$.

More progress should be possible (partly through disaggregation) in explaining PM_{AF}, $Y_{GRS_{AF}} - RENT_{AF}$, ΔINV_{AF}^{54}, ΔINV_{AF}, and $J_{FAN}/100$.

Some room must presumably be left for bona fide economic "disturbances", but only after we have done our best to allow for the effects of aggregation noise, errors of closure between index numbers and value aggregates, seasonal adjustment procedures and interpolation methods. In general, economic time series are combinations of true facts and artifacts. (The true facts include both exact and stochastic components.)

2. BURK, MARGUERITE C. *Measures and Procedures for Analysis of U.S. Food Consumption.* Agriculture Handbook No. 206. U.S. Department of Agriculture, Economic Research Service, June, 1961.

3. DAY, RICHARD H. *Production Response and Recursive Programming.* Amsterdam: North-Holland Publishing Company, 1963.

4. DOWNS, ANTHONY. *An Economic Theory of Democracy.* New York: Harper & Bros., 1957.

5. EGBERT, ALVIN C., and HEADY, EARL O. Interregional Competition or Spatial Equilibrium Models in Farm Supply Analysis, in *Agricultural Supply Functions.* Ames, Ia.: Iowa State University Press, 1961, 203–227.

6. FOX, KARL A. Factors Affecting Farm Income, Farm Prices and Food Consumption, *Agricultural Economics Research*, 3 (July, 1951) 65–82.

7. FOX, KARL A. *The Analysis of Demand for Farm Products.* U.S. Department of Agricultural Technical Bulletin 1081, 1953.

8. FOX, KARL A. A Spatial Equilibrium Model of the Livestock-Feed Economy in the United States, *Econometrica* 21 (October, 1953) 547–566.

9. FOX, KARL A. Structural Analysis and the Measurement of Demand for Farm Products, *Review of Economics and Statistics* (February, 1954) 55–66.

10. FOX, KARL A. *Econometric Analysis for Public Policy.* Ames, Ia.: Iowa State University Press, 1958.

11. FOX, KARL A. "Economic Models for Area Development Research". Paper presented at the Workshop on Regional Development Analysis, sponsored by the Agricultural Policy Institute and the Great Plains Resource Economics Committee, Stillwater, Oklahoma, May 8–9, 1963.

12. FOX, KARL A. Spatial Price Equilibrium and Process Analysis in the Food and Agricultural Sector, in *Studies in Process Analysis*: *Economy-Wide Production Capabilities.* Chapter 8, Cowles Foundation Monograph 18. New York: John Wiley and Sons, Inc., 1963, 215–233.

13. FOX, KARL A., and TAEUBER, RICHARD C. Spatial Equilibrium Models of the Livestock-Feed Economy, *American Economic Review* 45 (September, 1955) 584–608.

14. FRISCH, RAGNAR. A Complete Scheme for Computing all Direct and Cross Demand Elasticities in a Model with Many Sectors, *Econometrica* 27 (April, 1959) 177–196.

15. HEADY, EARL O., and EGBERT, ALVIN C. Programming Regional Adjustments in Grain Production to Eliminate Surplusis, *Journal of Farm Economics*, 41 (November, 1959) 718–733.

16. HEADY, EARL O., and DILLON, JOHN L. *Agricultural Production Functions.* Ames, Ia.: Iowa State University Press, 1961.

17. HEADY, EARL O., and TWEETEN, LUTHER G. *Resource Demand and Structure of the Agricultural Industry.* Ames, Ia.: Iowa State University Press, 1963.

18. HENDERSON, JAMES M. The Utilization of Agricultural Land: A theoretical and Empirical Inquiry, *Review of Economics and Statistics* 41 (August, 1959) 242–260.

19. HOLDREN, BOB R. *The Structure of a Retail Market and the Market Behavior of Retail Units.* Englewood Cliffs, N. J.: Prentice-Hall, Inc., 1960.

20. JUDGE, GEORGE G., and WALLACE, T. D. *Spatial Price Equilibrium Analyses of the Livestock Economy*: *Methodological Development and Annual Spatial Analyses of the Beef Marketing Sector.* Oklahoma State University Technical Bulletin TD-78, 1959.

21. MAKI, WILBUR R. Decomposition of the Beef and Pork Cycles, *Journal of Farm Economics* 44 (1962) 731–743.

22. MAKI, WILBUR R., LIU, CHARLES Y., and MOTES, WILLIAM C. *Interregional Competition and Prospective Shifts in the Location of Livestock Slaughter.* Iowa Agricultural Experimental Station Research Bulletin 511, October, 1962.

23. MEYER, JOHN R. A Survey of Regional Economics, *American Economic Review* 53 (March, 1963) 19–54.

24. MOORE, H. L. *Economic Cycles: Their Law and Cause.* New York: The Macmillan Company, 1917.

25. MOORE, H. L. *Forecasting the Yield and Price of Cotton.* New York: The Macmillan Company, 1917.

26. ROCKWELL, GEORGE R. *Income and Household Size: Their Effects on Food Consumption.* Marketing Research Report No. 340. U.S. Department of Agriculture, Agricultural Marketing Service, June, 1959.

27. SIMON, H. A. Causal Ordering and Identifiability, in *Studies in Econometric Method.* Edited by W. C. Hood and T. C. Koopmans. Cowles Commission Monograph No. 14. New York: John Wiley & Sons, Inc., 1953, 49–74.

28. SMITH, VICTOR E. Linear Programming Models for the Determination of Palatable Human Diets, *Journal of Farm Economics*, 41 (May, 1959), 272–283.

29. SMITH, VICTOR E. Measurement of Product Attributes Recognized by Consumers, in CAEA Report 5, *Seminar on Preferences and Market Development for Farm Products.* Ames, Ia.; Iowa State University, Winter Quarter, 1960, 1–27. (Mimeographed.)

30. THEIL, H. *Economic Forecasts and Policy.* Amsterdam: North-Holland Publishing Company, 2nd Rev. Ed., 1961 or 1st Ed., 1958.

31. TINBERGEN, J. *On the Theory of Economic Policy.* Amsterdam: North-Holland Publishing Company, 1952.

32. TINBERGEN, J. *Centralization and Decentralization in Economic Policy.* Amsterdam: North-Holland Publishing Company, 1954.

33. TINBERGEN, J. *Economic Policy: Principles and Design.* Amsterdam: North-Holland Publishing Company, 1956.

34. VAN EIJK, C. J., and SANDEE, J. Quantitative Determination of an Optimum Economic Policy, *Econometrica* 27 (January, 1959) 1–13.

35. WAUGH, FREDERICK V. A Partial Indifference Surface for Beef and Pork, *Journal of Farm Economics*, 38 (February, 1956) 102–112.

PART VI

Monetary and fiscal sectors

CHAPTER 13

A MODEL OF FINANCIAL BEHAVIOR

Contents

13.1. Introduction 465

13.2. Behavioral assumptions 467
    1. "Desired" relationships. 2. Stock adjustment. 3. Short-run con-
    straints. 4. Homogeneity in dollar values. 5. The "typical" equation.

13.3. Final equations 475
    1. Variables and final regressions. 2. The structure of the seven markets.

13.4. Detailed regression results 486
    1. Statistical procedures. 2. The behavior of the nonfinancial public.
    3. Behavioral equations for the banking system. 4. The behavior of
    nonbank financial institutions. 5. The four identities.

13.5. Tests and simulation plans 524
    1. Tests of individual equations against 1961–1962. 2. A test relating
    to the complete model, 1955–1962. 3. Simulation plans.

References 529

A MODEL OF FINANCIAL BEHAVIOR [1])

FRANK DE LEEUW

Division of Research and Statistics, Federal Reserve Board, Washington, D.C.

13.1. Introduction

The model below deals with quarterly demands and supplies in seven U. S. financial markets—markets for bank reserves, currency, demand deposits, time deposits, U. S. securities and two broad aggregates labeled "savings and insurance" and "private securities". The interactions of supply and demand functions in these markets determine dollar stocks and flows and levels of interest rates, just as supply and demand functions for a group of closely related goods may determine the quantities and prices of the goods. There are five broad groups of transactors in the seven markets: banks, nonbank financial institutions, the Federal Reserve, the Treasury and "the public". The model constitutes one portion of the quarterly Brookings-SSRC model of the U. S. economy.

The financial model contains a total of nineteen equations, fifteen of them behavioral relationships and four of them identities. Many of the equations involve nonfinancial variables (the main ones are personal and business income and capital expenditures) as well as financial ones, and so the model as a whole describes the behavior of financial markets *given* certain key

[1]) The model and this paper were prepared under the general direction of Daniel Brill. Ann Walka was in charge of data processing and computer operations. John Wood contributed many suggestions about the basic model and the specific relationships. Of the many other persons who furnished valuable advice, a partial list includes James Duesenberry and Lawrence Klein, Stephen Axilrod, Karl Brunner, Edwin Kuh, David Staiger and William Waldorf. The views expressed in the paper are those of the author.

"real" variables. The model does not deal with the effects of interest rates and balance-sheet positions on nonfinancial behavior; other sectors of the over-all Brookings-SSRC econometric model contain estimates of these effects. The model does, however, allow for estimation problems which these and other interactions may introduce by making use of the method of two-stage least squares.

The area of behavior which the model covers is one where theoretical foundations are weak and earlier econometric work skimpy. Most earlier work has been confined to the demand for money and the behavior of banks. Apart from these topics, there is very little to build on [2]). In the present model, demand and supply relationships for components of reserves and money involve interest rates and dollar amounts in several other financial markets and so the equations for money markets lead directly to a wider group of financial markets.

It has been possible to develop a basic framework into which most equations of the financial model fall. The typical behavioral equation of the model deals with quarterly changes in one sector's holdings of some asset or liability, expressed as a per cent of a measure of the sector's "wealth". Thus, one of the relationships of the model deals with changes in bank borrowings from the Federal Reserve System, expressed as a per cent of total bank deposits. The variables explaining these quarterly changes include the lagged stock of the asset or liability, also as a per cent of "wealth"; the interest rate on the asset or liability; yields of other assets, including in some equations a proxy variable representing the yield on real capital assets; and short-run constraint variables, such as current income for the public, again expressed as a per cent of "wealth". Not all of the equations of the model fit into this framework, but most of them do.

In spite of this common framework, the equations are rather far removed from the kind of testing of well-developed theories to which common notions about correlation and significance apply. The equations are no more than a set of preliminary empirical explorations of financial behavior. At best, they may indicate the order of magnitude of some of the effects of policy changes and nonfinancial developments on interest rates and financial stocks and may serve as a building block for future econometric studies of financial markets.

---

[2]) Johnson [13] provides a convenient survey of recent work in monetary economics. Empirical studies which have influenced the present model include Brunner and Meltzer [4], Christ [5], Duesenberry [8], Meigs [15], Meiselman [16], Morrison [18], Teigen [18], and Wood [22].

The following section of this paper, section 13.2, sets out the principal behavioral assumptions of the model. A listing of the final equations and a discussion of the structure of the seven markets appear in section 13.3. For a quick summary of the model, pp. 472–475 of section 13.2 and all of 13.3 are probably most useful. Section 13.4 presents the regression results in detail, and section 13.5 summarizes some tests relating to the behavior of the financial model as a whole and outlines plans for a full-scale simulation study of the model which will be the subject of a future paper. Tables of data and a description of data sources are available on request.

13.2. Behavioral assumptions

Put very concisely, the four principal behavioral assumptions underlying most of the equations are (1) "desired" relationships between portfolio composition and interest rates, (2) partial adjustment to "desired" composition, (3) short-run constraints and (4) homogeneity in dollar values. The paragraphs below discuss the meaning and limitations of these four assumptions.

13.2.1. "Desired" relationships

Financial institutions, households and businesses, it is assumed, have in mind long-run preferred relationships between the composition of their balance sheets and levels of interest rates. The direction of these relationships is assumed to be consistent with maximizing net worth. An increase in the yield on time deposits relative to other yields, for example, is expected to increase the proportion of its wealth which the public desires to hold in the form of time deposits.

This assumption, which offers a direct analogy with the theory of consumer behavior, passes over the question of why financial institutions and the public diversify their portfolios. Why should the public, for example, desire to hold any time deposits at all if the rate on U. S. securities is higher (and why desire to hold any U. S. securities if their yield is lower)? The answer to such questions presumably lies in transactions costs, uncertainties about yields and other characteristics of financial (and other) markets. The present model embodies all these factors in a set of preferences which are taken as fixed over time. A more complete analysis would attempt to represent these factors explicitly and thus would allow them to change over time [3]).

---

[3]) Tobin [20, 21] has analyzed some of the reasons why rational investors might diversify, their portfolios.

Since "desired" portfolio composition involves assets and liabilities as proportions of wealth, the assumption that there exist desired portfolios requires measures of wealth for the three behavioral sectors of the model: banks, nonbank financial institutions and the public. Since these measures are to serve as constraints on portfolio decisions, they should refer to wealth totals which each sector takes as given or controls to only a limited extent in short periods.

For an individual bank, deposit volume is a magnitude subject to only limited control and serves as a constraint on portfolio decisions. Deposit liabilities themselves do not actually constitute wealth, but deposit level approximately indicates the size of a bank's asset portfolio. In the portfolio of the banking sector as a whole, a more truly exogenous variable is unborrowed reserves, the size of which depends on the operations of the Federal Reserve System and the currency demand of the public. The significance of a given reserve volume for banks' portfolio behavior, however, depends on required reserve ratios, on member bank borrowing conditions and on the public's preference for demand deposits relative to time deposits. Total bank deposits (net of interbank deposits) is an approximate reflection of the combined effect of all of these factors, and so total deposits serves as a measure of the "wealth" of the banking sector in the present model.

For nonbank financial institutions, total savings by the public constrains asset holdings and is subject to only limited control in the short run. It therefore seems a plausible and simple representation of "wealth".

For the nonfinancial public, the equations of the present model make use of a weighted average of recent values of *GNP*, with weights approximating Friedman's "permanent income" weights [4]) as a measure of the public's wealth. The specific variable is

$$0.114 \sum_{i=0}^{19} (0.9)^i (GNP)_{-i}$$

with quarterly *GNP* in current dollars seasonally adjusted at annual rates. This measure of "normal" or "expected" income serves as a constraint on the borrowing capacity and asset preferences of the public.

There are other possible choices for representing the public's wealth. One is a measure of net worth—that is, net financial claims plus stocks of capital goods. A measure of net worth deals only with nonhuman wealth, that is, it does not include the wealth embodied in the labor force. Further-

---

[4]) See Friedman [9, pp. 142–147].

more, since it depends in part on savings rates it is not a variable beyond the control of the public, and it has the practical disadvantage of not being "explained" elsewhere in the over-all Brookings-SSRC econometric model. Another possible choice is a weighted average of recent incomes divided by some interest rate, on the grounds that it is wealth times some rate of return rather than wealth alone which is proportional to income. The appropriate rate of return for such a calculation is not clear; it might have very little to do with current market rates of interest. If it were related to market rates of interest the equations of the model, since they include market rates of interest as explanatory variables, should reflect this measure to some extent. The wealth measure actually used has the advantage of simplicity, but it is far from the only plausible choice.

13.2.2. Stock adjustment

The stocks of assets and liabilities held by financial institutions and the public, it is assumed, are not in general equal to desired stocks. Rather, changes in stocks from quarter to quarter are assumed to depend in part on the difference between actual and desired amounts.

Except for the words "in part", this is a familiar view of durable-goods demand [5]. The usual hypothesis is that the quarterly change is a constant fraction of the discrepancy between actual and desired stocks of durable goods, with the fraction reflecting lags in the spread of information, the making of decisions and the execution of plans. The present model assumes that some or all of these lags are present in financial markets, although the form of the equations does not preclude complete adjustment within one quarter.

The present model does not, however, assume that discrepancies between actual and "desired" stocks are the only influence on quarterly changes. The departure from a constant speed-of-adjustment fraction in the present model is due to the third basic assumption, the assumption about short-run constraints.

13.2.3. Short-run constraints

Quarterly portfolio adjustments, it is assumed, are influenced by short-run constraints as well as by actual and desired stocks. The funds readily avail-

---

[5] See Harberger, ed., [12], for some recent examples.

able to a financial institution, a business firm or a household vary from quarter to quarter, and it seems plausible to assume that the size of a sector's quarterly adjustments depends in part on the amount of these readily available funds. The public may, for example, wish to increase its stock of time deposits, but if its current income turns out to be below normal, it may postpone the increase until some more favorable quarter. Current income acts as a short-run constraint on portfolio changes by the public; it constrains changes in stocks in the short run just as wealth constrains levels of stocks [6]).

The principal short-run constraint influencing the behavior of the non-financial public in the equations below is its current gross income after federal taxes [7]). The bank and nonbank finance sectors are also assumed to take certain short-run flows as constraints. For banks, as section 13.3 of this paper will explain, changes in deposits less required reserves less loans form the principal short-run constraint. For nonbank finance, the inflow of savings from the public plus net lending by the Home Loan Bank Board forms the constraint.

Lagged as well as current values of these constraint variables are assumed to influence portfolio changes. For financial instruments with high transactions costs and undeveloped secondary markets, decisions about net changes probably depend on some average or expected inflow of funds and not on current departures from these expected inflows. Other financial instruments (in particular, money or near-moneys) might serve as buffers against unexpected short-term movements in funds—that is, might respond in part to differences between current inflows of funds and average or expected inflows. The direction of influence of lagged constraint variables can therefore be positive or negative; knowledge about financial markets permits some

---

[6]) The inclusion of a short-run constraint variable in a stock-adjustment process produces a behavioral mechanism very similar to one proposed by Meigs [15, Chapter IV, esp. pp. 49–57] although Meigs discusses his framework in slightly different terms. According to the Meigs hypothesis the change in free reserves depends on desired free reserves, actual free reserves and the rate of change of unborrowed reserves. This last factor, the rate of change of unborrowed reserves, disturbs the path from actual to desired stocks through injections or withdrawals of reserves. It affects the relationship in just the way that current short-run constraints affect the relationship of the present model. Incidentally, the specific variables affecting borrowed and excess reserves in the present model are not the same as those selected by Meigs, although they are similar.

[7] State and local taxes are not deducted because state and local authorities form part of the nonfinancial public.

judgment as to the plausibility of positive or negative influence in particular equations.

Current receipts are not the only form of short-run constraint on port-folio changes. Stocks of money or of near-moneys at the start of a period influence the ease or cost of increasing holdings of other assets or decreasing debt in the same way that flows of current receipts do. Just as it is cheaper and more convenient for the public to increase its holdings of, say, U. S. securities, when current income is high than when current income is low, it is easier to increase U. S. security holdings when initial stocks of currency, demand deposits or time deposits are high than when they are low. Although the constraints imposed by current receipts are the most important and pervasive short-run constraints in the model, stocks of money or near-moneys are important explanatory variables in a number of equations.

13.2.4. *Homogeneity in dollar values*

The final assumption about portfolio behavior is that changes in a sector's asset and liability holdings depend on the dollar "size" of the sector—that, for example, a doubling of the public's wealth, income and stock of a particular asset will, other things being equal, double the quarterly changes in its holdings of the asset. More precisely, the assumption is that all rela-tionships are homogeneous of degree one in all dollar magnitudes.

The consequence of this assumption is that the dollar variables in each equation should appear as ratios to one of the dollar variables rather than as absolute dollar amounts. The variable most easy to interpret as the de-nominator of these transformations is the wealth constraint variable. All dollar values in the behavioral equations therefore appear as proportions of wealth. Except for this homogeneity in dollar values, the equations are linear.

To justify this assumption, it is convenient to think of each dollar variable as the product of (a) the variable on a real, per capita basis, (b) a measure of the general price level and (c) total population. Homogeneity of degree one with respect to the general price level is a common assumption in monetary studies [8]. Homogeneity with respect to population is a common assumption in demand studies and surely a plausible one in relationships dealing with aggregate portfolio behavior.

Homogeneity with respect to real per capita dollar magnitudes in addition

---

[8]) See Friedman [9, p. 10], for a discussion of the assumption.

to population and prices seems less plausible. It has precedent in earlier studies [9]), but it seems likely, or at least conceivable, that a doubling of real per capita income or wealth might more than double desired holdings of some assets and less than double desired holdings of others. Instead of dividing all dollar values by wealth, an alternative procedure would therefore be to put all dollar values on a real per capita basis. Real per capita wealth would then be an explanatory variable in the behavioral equations.

The difficulty with this alternative procedure is that time series measuring wealth consist largely of trend movements in the postwar years, even after division by a price index and population. For this reason adding real per capita "permanent" income as a separate explanatory variable in the behavioral equations for the public would have all the statistical uncertainties of adding time as an explanatory variable; its coefficient might reflect a variety of trend movements having little to do with the effect of wealth on portfolio behavior. In the present study, the bias arising from dividing dollar variables by full current-dollar measures of wealth seems likely to be less than the bias which might arise from introducing real per capita wealth measures as separate explanatory variables. In a study covering a longer and more variable time period, a different procedure would probably be appropriate.

13.2.5. The "typical" equation

It seems useful at this point to write out the typical portfolio equation of the model. Let x represent the item whose holdings the equation attempts to explain, r's represent interest rates and other rates of return, f represent short-run constraints and w represent wealth. Then the typical equation reads

$$\frac{\Delta(x)_t}{w_{t-1}} = a + b_1 \frac{x_{t-1}}{w_{t-1}} + b_2 r(1)_t + b_3 r(2)_t + \ldots + b_j \frac{f(1)_t}{w_{t-1}} + b_{j+1} \frac{f(1)_{t-1}}{w_{t-1}}.$$

The change in holdings (Δx_t) depends on lagged holdings (x_{t-1}), rates of return $[r(1), r(2), \ldots]$ and current and lagged short-run constraints $[f(1)]$.

---

[9]) Friedman [9, p. 10], argues in favor of it when he suggests that demand-for-money relationships ought to be homogeneous of degree one with respect to dollar income. Studies which relate money velocity to interest rates implicitly use such an assumption.

All dollar values are divided by wealth (*w*). The unknown coefficients are
a and the *b*'s.

A comment is necessary about the fact that the wealth variable is lagged

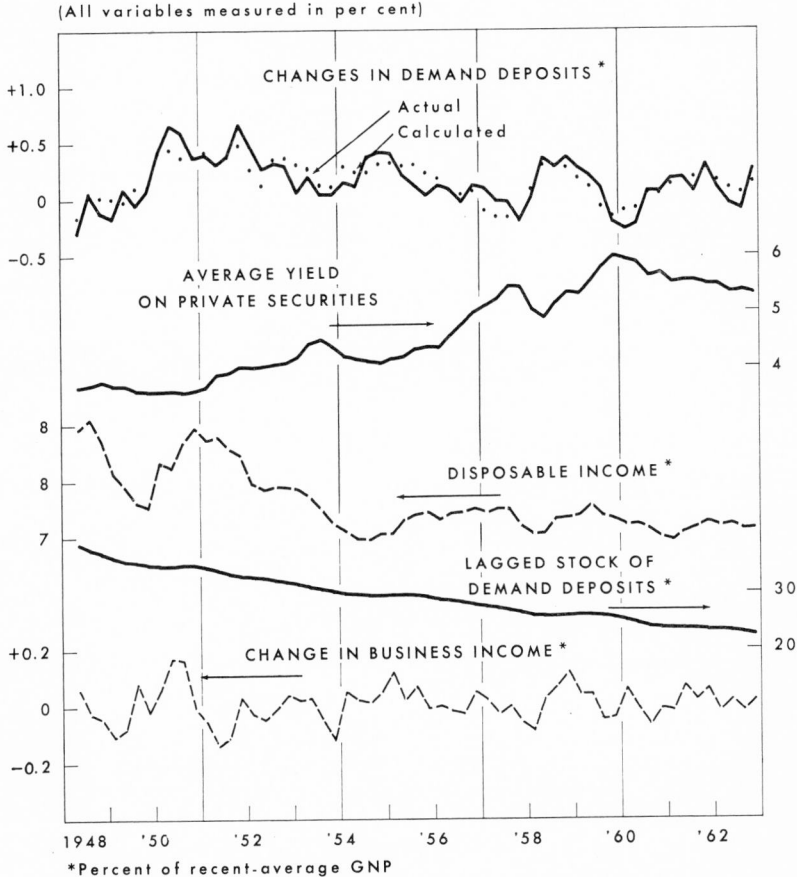

Figure 13.1. Changes in the public's holdings of demand deposits and selected explanatory variables.

one quarter. Presumably both current and lagged values of wealth influence
"desired" portfolios (this influence is the basic reason for including wealth
variables in the equations). Current values might perhaps be assumed to be
more important in many cases, but there is a strong practical reason for
choosing last quarter's wealth rather than the current quarter's wealth.

The reason is that solving and simulating the behavior of the complete model is a great deal easier if equations are linear in all current endogenous variables. Furthermore, since each of the three wealth variables in the model

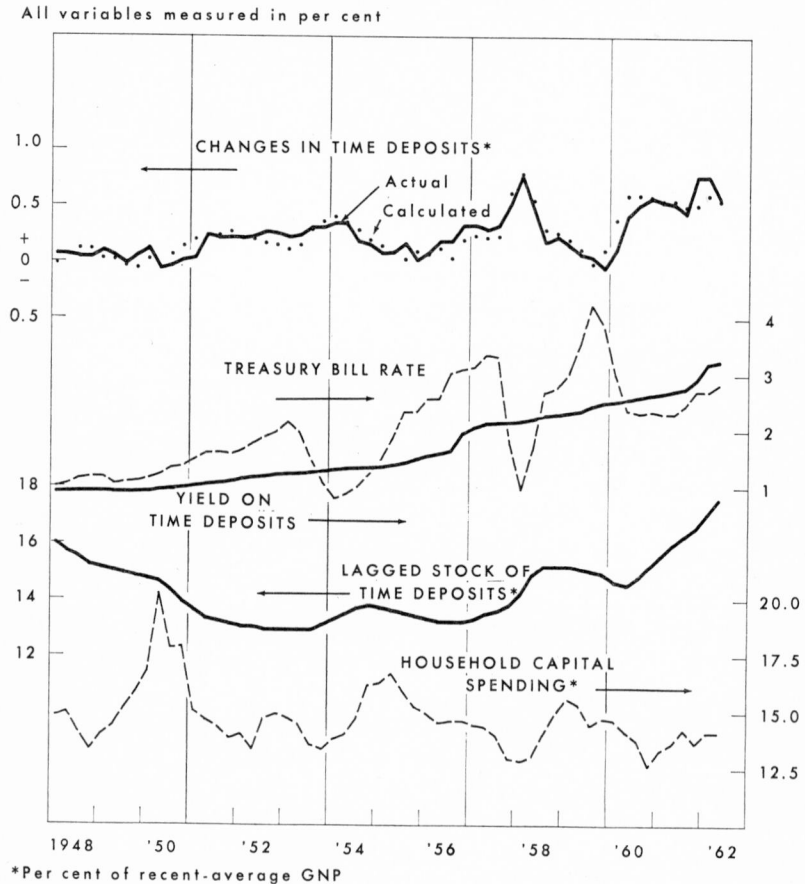

All variables measured in per cent

Figure 13.2. Changes in the public's holdings of time deposits and selected explanatory variables.

changes very smoothly over time, the effect on the estimates of a one-quarter lag is almost imperceptible.

There are twelve relationships of this form in the model, although for most of them the final equations depart from the basic form in some respects —in a few cases, in major respects. For the nonfinancial public, holdings of currency, demand deposits, time deposits, savings and insurance claims, household holdings of U. S. securities, household borrowing from financial institutions and business holdings of U. S. securities fit into the general framework. The two figures 13.1 and 13.2 show the major variables in the demand and time deposit relationships. Regressions applying the framework to business borrowing from financial institutions appear below, but as explained on p. 485, this relationship is not part of the final model. For financial institutions, holdings of U.S. securities by both banks and non-bank finance, bank holdings of excess reserves, bank borrowing from the Federal Reserve System and nonbank finance holdings of private securities also fit into the basic framework.

Of the remaining seven equations, four are identities. Two other relationships, both referring to the banking system, take quarterly changes in an interest rate rather than quarterly changes in an asset or liability as the dependent variable, on the assumption that in the markets involved (time deposits and loans) banks attempt to influence volume mainly by altering the yield and other contract terms rather than by direct decisions to borrow or lend. One final relationship, a reduced form of demand relationships for short- and long-term U. S. securities, has as its dependent variable the difference between long- and short-term interest rates on U. S. securities. Its derivation appears in section 13.4 (pp. 494–503).

13.3. Final equations

13.3.1. Variables and final regressions

This section begins with a list of the variables and final equations of the model. The final equations are two-stage least-squares estimates based on data including 1961 and 1962. After the equations comes a summary of the way in which, according to the equations, the seven financial markets behave and interact. Detailed discussion of individual relationships appears in section 13.4.

In the final equations, the interest-rate variables are percentages; an interest rate of four per cent is 4.00. Reserve ratios, however, are proportions. All dollar variables are in billions of dollars, hence, those in ratio form are proportions. The fact that a few variables are at annual rather than quarterly rates affects the equations, and the regressions are also affected by the fact that all stock variables are measured as averages during a quarter rather than as start- or end-of-quarter levels.

TABLE 13.1

Final equations (two-stage least-squares estimates through 1962)

Currency holdings $[R^2 = 0.68, S_e = 0.0032]$

$$\frac{\Delta CURR}{[WLTH]_{-1}} = 0.00861 - \frac{0.089}{(0.009)} \left\{ \frac{[CURR]_{-1}}{[WLTH]_{-1}} \right\} - \frac{0.00056}{(0.00018)} RM_{PSEC} - \frac{0.00056}{(0.00019)} RM_{BDT}$$
$$+ \frac{0.013}{(0.005)} \left\{ \frac{Y_D}{[WLTH]_{-1}} \right\} + \frac{0.017}{(0.003)} \left\{ \frac{[Y_D]_{-1}}{[WLTH]_{-2}} \right\} - \frac{0.018}{(0.005)} \left\{ \frac{[I_{CNFR} + C_D + I_{BUS}]}{[WLTH]_{-1}} \right\}$$

(13.1)

Demand deposit holdings $[R^2 = 0.71, S_e = 0.00128]$

$$\frac{\Delta DD}{[WLTH]_{-1}} = 0.00167 - \frac{0.158}{(0.029)} \left\{ \frac{[DD]_{-1}}{[WLTH]_{-1}} \right\} - \frac{0.00355}{(0.00108)} RM_{PSEC} - \frac{0.00451}{(0.00174)} RM_{BDT}$$
$$- \frac{0.140}{(0.062)} \left\{ \frac{I_{BUS}}{[WLTH]_{-1}} \right\} + \frac{0.069}{(0.035)} \left\{ \frac{Y_D}{[WLTH]_{-1}} \right\} + \frac{0.046}{(0.022)} \left\{ \frac{[Y_D]_{-1}}{[WLTH]_{-2}} \right\}$$
$$+ \frac{0.062}{(0.077)} \left\{ \frac{[RE + CCA + T_{GS}]}{[WLTH]_{-1}} \right\} - \frac{0.083}{(0.066)} \left\{ \frac{[RE + CCA + T_{GS}]_{-1}}{[WLTH]_{-2}} \right\}$$

(13.2)

Time deposit holdings $[R^2 = 0.80, S_e = 0.00101]$

$$\frac{\Delta DT}{[WLTH]_{-1}} = -0.00423 - \frac{0.102}{(0.018)} \left\{ \frac{[DT]_{-1}}{[WLTH]_{-1}} \right\} + \frac{0.00582}{(0.00056)} RM_{BDT} - \frac{0.00270}{(0.00030)} RM_{GBS3}$$
$$+ \frac{0.026}{(0.007)} \left\{ \frac{[Y_D]_{-1}}{[WLTH]_{-2}} \right\} - \frac{0.025}{(0.020)} \left\{ \frac{[I_{CNFR} + C_D]}{[WLTH]_{-1}} \right\}$$

(13.3)

Savings and insurance claims $[R^2 = 0.76, S_e = 0.00037]$

$$\frac{\Delta BNBF}{[WLTH]_{-1}} = 0.00542 + \frac{0.617}{(0.004)} \left\{ \frac{[\Delta BNBF]_{-1}}{} \right\} + \frac{0.00095}{} \left\{ \frac{1}{4} \sum_{-1}^{4} [RM_{BDT}]_{-i} \right\} - \frac{0.00071}{} \left[RM_{PSEC} \right]$$

(13.4)

$$\frac{\Delta BF_P}{[WLTH]_{-1}} = -0.01574 - \frac{0.054}{(0.025)} \left\{\frac{[BF_P]_{-1}}{[WLTH]_{-1}}\right\} + \frac{0.00303}{(0.00035)} [RM_{GBS3}] - \frac{0.00875}{(0.00129)} [RM_{BDT}] \qquad (13.5)$$

$$+ \frac{0.250}{(0.040)} \left\{\frac{[DT]_{-1}}{[WLTH]_{-1}}\right\}$$

Business holdings of U. S. securities $[R^2 = 0.64, S_e = 0.00139]$

$$\frac{\Delta BF_{ONF}}{[WLTH]_{-1}} = 0.02755 - \frac{0.103}{(0.068)} \left\{\frac{[BF_{ONF}]_{-1}}{[WLTH]_{-1}}\right\} + \frac{0.00124}{(0.00054)} [RM_{GBS3}] - \frac{0.00376}{(0.00113)} [RM_{BDT}] \qquad (13.6)$$

$$- \frac{0.111}{(0.052)} \left\{\frac{I_{BUS}}{[WLTH]_{-1}}\right\} + \frac{0.188}{(0.028)} \left\{\frac{\Delta[TC - TC_{PAY}]}{[WLTH]_{-1}}\right\}$$

Household borrowing $[R^2 = 0.79, S_e = 0.0074]$

$$\frac{\Delta BHH_F}{[WLTH]_{-1}} = -0.01333 + \frac{0.167}{(0.020)} \left\{\frac{I_{CNFR} + C_D}{[WLTH]_{-1}}\right\} - \frac{0.00144}{(0.00051)} [RM_{PSEC}] + \frac{0.00175}{(0.00049)} [RM_{BDT}] \qquad (13.7)$$

Term structure of U. S. security rates $[R^2 = 0.55, S_e = 0.376]$

$$RM_{GBL} - RM_{GBS3} = 1.399 + \frac{3.161}{(0.611)} \left\{RM_{GBL} - 0.550 \sum_{i=1}^{11} [0.45^{i-1}][RM_{GBL}]_{-i}\right\}$$

$$- \frac{4.455}{(0.511)} [RM_{GBL} - 0.261 \sum_{i=1}^{11} [0.75^{i-1}][RM_{GBL}]_{-i}] - \frac{4.8}{(2.6)} \Delta\left[\frac{BF_1}{BF_{PUB}}\right] - \frac{7.1}{(3.4)} \Delta\left[\frac{BF_{1-5}}{BF_{PUB}}\right] \qquad (13.8)$$

Bank holdings of U. S. securities $[R^2 = 0.92, S_e = 0.00313]$

$$\frac{\Delta BF_B}{[DD+DT]_{-1}} = 0.02845 - \frac{0.133}{(0.028)} \left\{\frac{[BF_B]_{-1}}{[DD+DT]_{-1}}\right\} + \frac{6.290}{(1.350)} \left\{\frac{[RES_E]_{-1}}{[DD+DT]_{-1}}\right\} + \frac{0.197}{(0.063)} \left\{\frac{\Delta[DD+DD_{GF}+DT-RES_R-ALNPS_B]}{[DD+DT]_{-1}}\right\} \qquad (13.9)$$

$$+ \frac{0.622}{(0.071)} \left\{\frac{\Delta[DD+DD_{GF}+DT-RES_R-ALNPS_B]_{-1}}{[DD+DT]_{-1}}\right\}$$

Table 13.1. (Continued)

Bank borrowing from the federal reserve $[R^2 = 0.68, \; S_e = 0.00063]$

$$\frac{\Delta RES_B}{[DD+DT]_{-1}} = 0.00226 - \frac{0.267}{(0.065)} \left\{ \frac{[RES_B]_{-1}}{[DD+DT]_{-1}} \right\} - \frac{0.033}{(0.010)} \left\{ \frac{2}{[DD+DT]_{-1}} - \frac{1}{[1000 \; RES_B]_{-1}} \right\}$$

$$\cdot \{\Delta[DD+DD_{GF}+DT-RES_R-ALNPS_B]\} - \frac{0.00191}{(0.00050)} [RM_{FRB} - RM_{GBS3}] - \frac{0.00047}{(0.00018)} RM_{GBS3} \qquad (13.10)$$

Bank holdings of excess reserves $[R^2 = 0.57, \; S_e = 0.00020]$

$$\frac{\Delta RES_E}{[DD+DT]_{-1}} = 0.00005 - \frac{0.046}{(0.045)} \left\{ \frac{[RES_E]_{-1}}{[DD+DT]_{-1}} \right\} + \frac{0.017}{(0.006)} \left\{ \frac{\Delta[DD+DD_{GF}+DT-RES_R-ALNPS_B]}{[DD+DT]_{-1}} \right\}$$

$$- \frac{0.018}{(0.004)} \left\{ \frac{\Delta[DD+DD_{GF}+DT-RES_R-ALNPS_B]_{-1}}{[DD+DT]_{-1}} \right\} + \frac{0.00019}{(0.00017)} [RM_{FRB} - RM_{GBS3}] \qquad (13.11)$$

Interest rate on private securities $[R^2 = 0.72, \; S_e = 0.074]$

$$\Delta RM_{PSEC} = 0.291 - \frac{0.199}{(0.085)} [RM_{PSEC}]_{-1} + \frac{0.088}{(0.043)} RM_{GBS3} + \frac{0.025}{(0.117)} RM_{GBL}$$

$$+ \frac{0.486}{(0.161)} \left\{ RM_{GBL} - 0.55 \sum_{i=1}^{11} [0.45^i][RM_{GBL}]_{-i} \right\} + \frac{0.64}{(0.50)} \left\{ \frac{1}{4} \sum_{i=1}^{4} \frac{[ALNPS_B]_{-i}}{[DD+DT]_{-i}} \right\} \qquad (13.12)$$

Interest rate on time deposits $[R^2 = 0.91, \; S_e = 0.042]$

$$\Delta RM_{BDT}^A = -1.390 - \frac{0.561}{(0.072)} [RM_{BDT}^A]_{-1} - \frac{0.495}{(0.055)} [RM_{GBL}^A - RM_{BDTM}^A + 1] + \frac{0.708}{(0.104)} [RM_{GBL}^A]$$

$$+ \frac{1.519}{(0.391)} \left[\frac{ALNPS_B^A}{DD^A+DT^A} \right]_{-1} \qquad (13.13a)$$

for which a quarterly approximation is

$$\Delta RM_{BDT} = -0.625 - 0.186[RM_{BDT}] + 0.166[RM_{BDTM}]_{-1} + 0.510\left[\frac{ALNPS_B}{DD+DT}\right]_{-2}$$

(13.13b)

Nonbank finance holdings of U. S. securities $[R^2 = 0.61, S_e = 0.00097]$

$$\frac{\Delta BF_{NBF}}{[BNBF]_{-1}} = -0.00047 - \frac{0.011}{(0.006)}\left\{\frac{[BF_{NBF}]_{-1}}{[BNBF]_{-1}}\right\} + \frac{0.544}{(0.258)}\left\{\frac{\Delta[BNBF+FHLB]}{[BNBF]_{-1}}\right\}$$
$$- \frac{0.337}{(0.138)}\left(\frac{1}{4}\sum_{i=1}^{4}\frac{\Delta[BNBF+FHLB]_{-i}}{[BNBF]_{-i-1}}\right) - \frac{0.00245}{(0.00191)}[RM_{PSEC}-RM_{GBL}] + \frac{0.00061}{(0.00020)}[RM_{GBS3}]$$

(13.14)

Nonbank finance holdings of private securities $[R^2 = 0.97, S_e = 0.00058]$

$$\frac{\Delta APS_{NBF}}{[BNBF]_{-1}} = 0.01194 - \frac{0.021}{(0.007)}\left\{\frac{[APS_{NBF}]_{-1}}{[BNBF]_{-1}}\right\} + \frac{0.583}{(0.262)}\left\{\frac{\Delta[BNBF+FHLB]}{[BNBF]_{-1}}\right\}$$
$$+ \frac{0.658}{(0.133)}\left(\frac{1}{4}\sum_{i=1}^{4}\frac{\Delta[BNBF+FHLB]_{-i}}{[BNBF]_{-i-1}}\right) + \frac{0.00245}{(0.00191)}[RM_{PSEC}-RM_{GBL}] - \frac{0.00061}{(0.00020)}[RM_{GBS3}]$$

(13.15)

Required reserve identity

$$RES_R = 0.84[RRR_{DD}][DD+DD_{GF}] + 0.82[RRR_{DT}][DT]$$

(13.16)

Private securities identity

$$BHH_F + BBUS_F + BFOR = ALNPS_B + APS_{NBF}$$

(13.17)

U. S. securities identity

$$BF_P + BF_{ONF} + BF_B + BF_{NBF} = BF_{DH} - RES_{NBC} + GOLD$$

(13.18)

Federal reserve open market identity

$$RES_R + RES_E - RES_B + CURR = RES_{NBC}$$

(13.19)

Endogenous financial variables in order of appearance are:

$CURR$ = currency liabilities of the Treasury and Federal Reserve less commercial banks' currency holdings, average during quarter, billions of dollars

RM_{PSEC} = weighted average yield on private securities, per cent

RM_{BDT} = yield on commercial bank time deposits, per cent

DD = private demand deposit liabilities of commercial banks less interbank deposits, cash items in process of collection and Federal Reserve float, average during quarter, billions of dollars

DT = private time deposit liabilities of commercial banks less time deposit holdings of commercial banks, average during quarter, billions of dollars

RM_{GBS3} = average market yield on three-month U. S. Treasury bills, per cent

$BNBF$ = savings and insurance claims, average during quarter, billions of dollars

BF_P = consumer and nonprofit holdings of U. S. securities, average during quarter, billions of dollars

BF_{ONF} = holdings of U. S. securities by corporations and state and local governments and finance not elsewhere classified, average during quarter, billions of dollars

BHH_F = household debt to financial institutions, average during quarter, billions of dollars

RM_{GBL} = average yield during quarter on U. S. securities maturing or callable in ten years or more, per cent

BF_B = commercial bank holdings of U. S. securities, average during quarter, billions of dollars

RES_E = excess reserves of Federal Reserve member banks, average during quarter, billions of dollars

RES_R = required reserves of Federal Reserve member banks, average during quarter, billions of dollars

$ALNPS_B$ = commercial bank holdings of loans and other private securities, average during quarter, billions of dollars

RES_B = member bank borrowing from the Federal Reserve, average during quarter, billions of dollars

BF_{NBF} = nonbank finance holdings of U. S. securities, average during quarter, billions of dollars

APS_{NBF} = nonbank finance holdings of private securities, average during quarter, billions of dollars

$BBUS_F$ = business debt to financial institutions, average during quarter, billions of dollars

Exogenous financial variables in order of appearance are:

BF_1 = U. S. marketable debt maturing within 1 year, average during quarter, billions of dollars

BF_{1-5} = U.S. marketable debt of 1- to 5-year maturity, average during quarter, billions of dollars

BF_{PUB} = marketable federal debt of all maturities outside of Federal Reserve and U.S. government agencies and trust funds, average during quarter, billions of dollars

DD_{GF} = federal government demand deposits at commercial banks, average during quarter, billions of dollars

RM_{FRB} = Federal Reserve Bank of New York discount rate, daily average during quarter, per cent

RM_{BDTM} = legal maximum rate on time deposits deposited for six months or more, per cent

$FHLB$ = Federal Home Loan Bank Board's advances to savings and loan associations, average during quarter, billions of dollars

RRR_{DD} = weighted average of required reserve ratios against demand deposits, proportion

RRR_{DT} = average reserve ratio required against time deposits, proportion

RES_{NBC} = unborrowed reserves plus currency of Federal Reserve member banks, average during quarter, billions of dollars.

Variables from nonfinancial sectors (endogenous or exogenous) in order of appearance are:

$WLTH$ = weighted average of recent values of GNP,

$$= 0.114 \sum_{i=0}^{19} (0.9)^i (GNP)_{-i}, \quad \text{billions of dollars}$$

Y_D = disposable personal income, billions of dollars

I_{CNFR} = GNP expenditures on nonfarm residential construction, billions of dollars

C_D = personal consumption expenditures on durable goods, billions of dollars

I_{BUS} = business gross investment in plant and equipment, billions of
dollars

RE = undistributed corporate profits, billions of dollars

CCA = capital consumption allowances, billions of dollars

T_{GS} = state and local government receipts, billions of dollars

TC = corporate profits tax accruals to government, billions of dollars

TC_{PAY} = current corporate profits tax payments, billions of dollars

$BFOR$ = foreign borrowings, average during quarter, billions of dollars

BF_{DH} = federal government debt, domestically held outside of federal
agencies and trust funds, average during quarter, billions of
dollars

$GOLD$ = Treasury gold stock, average during quarter, billions of dollars.

13.3.2. The structure of the seven markets

Considered as a descriptive device, the system of nineteen simultaneous equations just listed is somewhat unwieldy. To aid in the understanding of the mechanism implied in the equations, the following paragraphs will indicate verbally the way the model "works"—the way in which, according to the equations, assets and liabilities are supplied and demanded in the seven financial markets of the model. The empirical implications of the coefficients in the equations are a separate subject, on which section 13.5 of this paper and a forthcoming simulation study of the model offer some results.

It is convenient to begin a verbal description of the model by comparing it with a simpler hypothetical model. In this simpler model, one demand and one supply function for each market would determine the amount outstanding and the interest rate in that market [10]). Explanatory variables in the functions would in at least some cases include both interest rates from other markets and own interest rates; they would also include various nonfinancial and constraint variables. In some cases, a supply relationship could be replaced by defining a supply or an interest rate as exogenous. A disturbance in any one market would change the interest rate for that market and would thereby "spill over" into other markets and cause the whole system to change. As a group, the equations would determine asset amounts and interest rates, given the relevant nonfinancial and exogenous variables.

---

[10]) A demand or supply function for a particular market could, without any complication, be disaggregated into two or more equations determining two or more components of total demand or supply instead of a total alone.

The present model is similar to this simple prototype in many ways. It departs from the prototype mainly because three of the seven instruments in the model—bank reserves, currency and demand deposits—have interest rates fixed at zero [11]. These restrictions mean that three relationships must be dropped from the over-all Brookings-SSRC econometric model; financial supplies and demands must reach balance with three fewer elements to vary than in the prototype model [12].

The review of the seven financial markets in the paragraphs below will indicate which three relationships are missing in the present model. The three relationships to be dropped could include nonfinancial ones, in which case the financial equations would be determining quarterly movements in certain nonfinancial variables. For example, the financial equations could serve to determine the general level of prices if one of the price-formation equations elsewhere in the Brookings-SSRC econometric model were dropped. Or, the relationships to be dropped could all be financial ones, as in fact they are in the present model. The relationships to be dropped should be ones which are most nearly "dropped" in the economy—ones where supply or demand is either perfectly elastic or determined as a residual after other decisions are made.

On the demand side of the market for bank reserves, there are two equations. One of them (13.11) describes bank holdings of excess reserves; the other (13.16) is an identity relating required reserve holdings to demand and time deposits multiplied by required reserve ratios.

On the supply side of the reserve market, one equation (13.10) describes bank borrowing from the Federal Reserve System, an action which increases the supply of reserves [13]. The other equation on the supply side of the reserve market is one of the central equations of the model, an identity which defines unborrowed reserves plus currency ("high-powered money") as an exogenous variable determined by the open-market purchases and sales of the Federal Reserve System (13.19). Taken together, these two equations determine the supply of reserves plus currency.

---

[11] The model does not deal with service changes, compensating balance requirements and other contract terms characterizing the demand deposit market. The portion of bank reserves based on borrowing from the Federal Reserve System has an interest rate—the discount rate—but it is an exogenous variable in the model.

[12] This proposition is, of course, closely analogous to Walras' law, which would apply to an economy with one zero-interest-rate asset or one asset in terms of whose yield all other interest rates are measured.

[13] Banks participate on both the demand and the supply sides of the reserve market.

Since there is no additional supply relationship for the currency market, the open-market identity states that there is no attempt on the supply side to affect the public's choice between currency and reserves. The Federal Reserve System stands ready to trade reserves for currency in any desired amounts. This lack of Federal Reserve control over the reserve-currency allocation is one of the relationships missing from the financial model. Instead of the independent supply relationships for reserves and for currency which the prototype model would require, the equations of the present model determine only supply conditions for the sum of the two.

On the demand side of the currency market is one equation describing the public's holdings of currency (13.1). Similarly, the demand sides of the markets for demand deposits and for time deposits each consist of one equation (13.2 and 13.3) describing the public's holdings, just as they would in the prototype model.

On the supply side of the market for time deposits, there is an equation describing how the banking system sets the yield on time deposits (13.13a, b). This is the only equation describing the conditions under which banks provide deposits. The absence of a separate supply relationship for demand deposits is therefore a second relationship missing from the financial model. The Federal Reserve open-market identity, of course, sets limits to a weighted combination of currency, time deposits, excess reserves and demand deposits, but there is no additional control over the supply of demand deposits alone.

The U.S. securities equations of the model are simpler than the reserves-currency-deposits complex just described. Changes in the supply of U.S. securities held outside the Treasury and the Federal Reserve System depend, through an identity, on the Treasury's cash deficit, Federal Reserve purchases and gold movements (13.18). On the demand side of this market are separate equations for holdings by households (13.5), business (13.6), banks (13.9) and nonbank finance (13.14). There is also the term structure equation (13.8) which is a reduced form of aggregate demand equations for short- and long-term U.S. securities.

The model covers the market for savings and insurance claims in one equation (13.4), which describes holdings by the public. Instead of a supply relationship for savings and insurance claims, there is an assumption (in the absence of quarterly data) that the yield on savings and insurance claims is proportional to a moving average of the yield on time deposits. This moving average yield appears with a positive coefficient in the demand equation. Because of the assumption as to the yield, the only unknown from the savings-insurance market in the model is the amount of savings and insurance claims; it is for this reason (and not for any reason related to the three instruments with zero interest rates) that the market is covered in one equation.

Finally, four equations deal with the market for private securities. On the demand side is one equation covering nonbank finance holdings (13.15) and one dealing with bank demands (13.12). In the bank demand equation, it is the interest rate rather than bank holdings which is the dependent variable.

On the supply side of the private securities market is one equation dealing with household borrowing (13.7) and one identity defining household plus business plus foreign borrowing (exogenous to the financial sector) as equal to bank lending plus nonbank finance lending (13.17). There are five endogenous variables in this market—two components of borrowing, two components of lending and an interest rate—but there are only four equations dealing with the market. The missing equation is the business borrowing relationship, and this is third of the missing relationships corresponding to the three zero interest rates.

Regressions relating to business borrowing appear on pp. 504–505, but of all the regressions dealing with relationships close to the "money" market, these regressions yield the poorest fits. These poor fits in themselves constitute one valid reason for omitting the business borrowing relationship rather than, say, the relationship for holdings of demand deposits from the final equations of the model. The omission of a business borrowing equation forces business borrowing to be some linear combination of all the other relationships in the model. It implies that businesses use borrowing to some extent as a residual source of funds, borrowing when planned purchases and asset acquisitions exceed means of payment, and repaying in the reverse situation. Business borrowing, if this is in fact an accurate description, should respond sensitively to a whole complex of credit market forces; for this reason a regression involving a small number of explanatory variables may not go very far toward explaining its quarterly movements [14]).

As in the prototype model, a disturbance in one market of the present model rapidly affects behavior in all seven markets. An increase in the supply of unborrowed reserves and currency, for example, affects initially either bank holdings of excess or required reserves or the public's holdings of currency (or combinations of the three). In order for banks to be willing

---

[14]) Duesenberry's summary of work by Locke Anderson [8, pp. 13–14] seems consistent with the view that corporate borrowing is in large part a residual item.

to hold more excess reserves, equation (13.11) states that either the Treasury bill rate must fall, deposits must increase or bank lending must fall. If required reserves are to absorb some of the increased supply, quantities of deposits must be affected (13.16). If the amount of currency demanded is to rise, the rate on private securities must fall (13.1). In any one of these cases, effects spread further until all the endogenous variables of the financial system change.

Effects continue to spread beyond the financial system; the fact that changes in interest rates and asset positions affect markets for goods and services is, of course, the reason for dealing with financial behavior in the over-all Brookings-SSRC econometric model. These ultimate effects on markets for goods and services, however, are outside the scope of the financial equations of the model.

13.4. Detailed regression results

13.4.1. Statistical procedures

There were four steps in fitting each behavioral equation of the model. The first was fitting ordinary least-squares regressions through 1960 (starting dates vary, depending on available data and in some cases on institutional changes); the second, fitting two-stage least-squares regressions through 1960. The last two steps were testing each equation against 1961 and 1962 data and refitting the equations through 1962. Where 1961–1962 predictions were satisfactory, the refitted equations used the same variables as the pre-1960 equations. Where predictions were not satisfactory, the refitting involved some further experimentation with alternative variables and lags. The pages below discuss these steps for each of the behavioral equations. A summary of the 1961–1962 prediction results appears in section 13.5 (pp. 525–526).

A few statistical problems and procedures common to many of the equations are best outlined before the detailed discussion. First of all, in most of the equations of the model the lagged level of the dependent variable appears as one of the independent variables. The equations are thus similar to relationships in which the value of some variable in the current quarter depends in part on its value in the last quarter. They are not quite the same as these relationships, for in the present model it is the change rather than the current level of a variable which depends on the level in the last quarter. This alteration does not, however, affect the computed regression coefficients.

There are serious difficulties in interpreting equations in which the current level of a variable depends on its lagged level; the regression coefficients of the lagged level are especially sensitive to specification errors [15]). These difficulties exist for most of the equations of the present model.

Putting the dependent variable in the form of a change rather than a level does affect the coefficient of determination (R^2) and the significance of the coefficient for the lagged dependent variable. (The coefficient itself is one less than the coefficient in the "level" case, but its standard error is unchanged.) In both respects, the procedure of the present model makes it most unlikely that a good fit or a significant lag coefficient will be due simply to high serial correlation in the level of the dependent variable [16]).

A word about the two-stage least-squares procedure may be helpful in interpreting the equations. The predetermined variables used in the first stage of the two-stage estimates consist of three financial variables and five nonfinancial variables [17]). The three financial variables are: the discount rate (at the New York Federal Reserve Bank); an exogenous open-market variable equal to unborrowed reserves divided by a fixed-weight combination of required reserve ratios, plus currency; and this open-market variable lagged one quarter. The nonfinancial variables are: current population, current defense spending (in 1954 dollars), real capital stock (including inventories) at the start of each quarter, *GNP* (in 1954 dollars) lagged one quarter and new orders for durable goods (in constant dollars) lagged one quarter.

These variables far from exhaust the predetermined variables of the Brookings-SSRC econometric model. An exhaustive list would, of course, leave no degrees of freedom in the first-stage regressions and would therefore simply reproduce ordinary least-squares estimates. The list of predetermined variables was pared down by (a) excluding all lagged endogenous financial variables; (b) consolidating a number of exogenous variables—currency and unborrowed reserves and the various classes of reserve requirements—into the single open-market variables described and (c) choosing nonfinancial

---

[15]) Griliches [11] shows that a common type of specification error may make an autoregressive equation appear plausible even if underlying behavior is not autoregressive.

[16]) If the first three equations of the model were in "level" form, the high correlation of successive levels would raise values of R^2 to 1.000, 0.999 and 0.994 from the listed values of 0.68, 0.71 and 0.80. t-Ratios for the coefficients of the lagged dependent variable would be raised by 6 to 10 times.

[17]) The one exception to this procedure is that in the first-stage estimates of the yield on time deposits, the current maximum rate was added to the list of predetermined variables.

variables which intuitively seemed important in influencing financial behavior and leaving out exogenous financial variables which seemed relatively unimportant. In applying the two-stage procedure, income and capital spending as well as interest rates and financial stocks were treated as endogenous.

All equations are overidentified according to the order condition.

13.4.2. *The behavior of the nonfinancial public*

The financial balance-sheet of the public   The model deals with the following nine items in the consolidated financial balance sheet of the public.

Assets	Liabilities
Currency	Private securities; households
Demand deposits (net)	Private securities; business
Bank time deposits	Corporate tax liabilities
Savings and insurance claims	
U.S. securities; household	
U.S. securities; business	

Transactions between subsectors of the public, including common stock transactions, are not covered in the model; a more complete model would deal with these transactions and their prices also.

Savings and insurance consist claims of holdings in mutual savings banks, savings and loan associations, insurance companies and pension funds; these holdings are nearly all household rather than business assets. U.S. securities consists of debt of the U.S. Treasury, including savings bonds as well as marketable obligations. Private securities consists of lending by banks and by nonbank finance to private borrowers (including foreign borrowers and state and local governments). Time series for all items are approximations to average holdings during a quarter, though for some series the approximation is closer than for others (the statistical appendix available on request describes the various approximations used).

Corporate tax liabilities are taken to be determined outside the financial part of the model; they appear as an explanatory variable in the equation for business holdings of U.S. securities.

Currency, demand deposits and time deposits   Changes in the public's asset and liability holdings, according to the framework set out above, should be related to lagged stocks, interest rates and other yields and current income, with all dollar variables (including dependent variables) divided by a weighted average of *GNP*. Current income divided by a weighted average of *GNP*, incidentally, corresponds to the concept of "transitory" income. The yields chosen as relevant for currency and deposit holdings are those on time deposits, private securities (for currency and demand deposit holdings), Treasury bills (for time deposit holdings) and capital goods.

The expected rate of return on capital goods is represented crudely in the present model by the ratio of actual capital spending to a weighted moving average of *GNP* [18]). At least two comments on this method of representing the yield on capital goods are necessary: (i) Since actual capital spending is itself influenced by interest rates, entering it as an independent variable may distort interest rate coefficients in the equations; the coefficients may represent the influence of interest rates on financial holdings minus some fraction of their influence on capital spending. Time lags which are almost certainly present in the response of capital spending to interest rates tend to reduce such distortion as far as coefficients of current interest rates are concerned. (ii) The use of actual capital spending figures may have the advantage of reflecting any factors which influence the choice between real and financial investment but which are difficult to represent explicitly. Expectations about price changes, which may well influence shifts between financial claims and real assets, are one important example. The capital spending variable should reflect such expectations at least indirectly.

Yields on savings and loan shares and mutual savings bank deposits presumably also influence commercial bank deposits. They are omitted from the equations because of lack of quarterly data. Quarterly data are also lacking for the yield on commercial bank time deposits, but this yield seems important enough to warrant a crude representation by means of a quarterly interpolation (p. 517). Since all these yields are highly interrelated (at least annually), the coefficient of the time deposit yield probably serves to represent the net effect of all of them. In the equation for savings and insurance holdings (p. 495), a moving average of the time deposit yield serves as a proxy for savings and insurance yields.

Tables 13.2, 13.3 and 13.4 show regression results for currency and deposits through 1960 (also figures 13.1 and 13.2). Explanatory variables

---

[18]) "Capital spending" includes residential and nonresidential private construction, producers' durable equipment and consumer durables. The weighted average of *GNP* is the one described on p. 468. Other possible means of representing the rate of return on capital goods—in particular, profit rates and stock prices—seemed to present greater problems than using actual capital spending. Profits do appear as an important explanatory variable in the model, but they represent part of the current income constraint, not the expected rate of return on capital goods.

TABLE 13.2

Quarterly changes in the public's holdings of currency: $\Delta CURR/[WLTH]_{-1}$.

Equation (13.1) Period and method of estimation	$\dfrac{[CURR]_{-1}}{[WLTH]_{-1}}$	RM_{BDT}	RM_{PSEC}	$\dfrac{I_{CNFR}+C_D}{[WLTH]_{-1}}$	$\dfrac{I_{BUS}}{[WLTH]_{-1}}$	$\dfrac{Y_D}{[WLTH]_{-1}}$	$\dfrac{RE+CCA+T_{GS}}{[WLTH]}$	$\dfrac{[Y_D]_{-1}}{[WLTH]_{-2}}$	Constant term	R^2	Standard error	Durbin-Watson ratio
A. 1948–1960												
(1) OLS	−0.081 (0.009)	−0.00258 (0.00043)	0.00056 (0.00029)	—	−0.027 a) (0.005)	—	0.021 a) (0.003)	—	−0.00578	0.66	0.00034	—
(2) OLS	−0.092 (0.008)	−0.00148 (0.00017)	—	−0.014 (0.004)	−0.023 (0.007)	0.016 (0.004)	—	0.013 (0.004)	−0.00805	0.77	0.00028	1.56
(3) TSLS	−0.094 (0.009)	−0.00099 (0.00044)	−0.00029 (0.00033)	−0.026 (0.009)	−0.019 (0.010)	0.016 (0.006)	—	0.018 (0.003)	−0.00990	—	—	—
(4) TSLS	−0.091 (0.009)	−0.00134 (0.00019)	—	−0.022 (0.008)	−0.024 (0.009)	0.015 (0.005)	—	0.018 (0.003)	−0.01028	0.70	0.00032	—
B. 1948–1962												
(5) OLS	−0.089 (0.009)	−0.00064 (0.00018)	−0.00053 (0.00016)	−0.013 (0.004)	−0.016 (0.007)	0.014 (0.004)	—	0.014 (0.004)	−0.00737	0.70	0.00031	—
(6) TSLS	−0.089 (0.009)	−0.00056 (0.00019)	−0.00056 (0.00018)	—	−0.018 (0.005)	0.013 (0.005)	—	0.017 (0.003)	−0.00861	0.68	0.00032	1.25

Note A list of variables appears on pp. 480–482.

a) Coefficient refers to the sum of the two income or the two capital spending variables.

TABLE 13.3

Quarterly changes in the public's holdings of demand deposits: $\Delta DD/[WLTH]_{-1}$.

Equation (13.2) Period and method of estimation	$\dfrac{[DD]_{-1}}{[WLTH]_{-1}}$	RM_{BDT}	RM_{PSEC}	$\dfrac{I_{CNFR}+C_D}{[WLTH]_{-1}}$	$\dfrac{I_{BUS}}{[WLTH]_{-1}}$	$\dfrac{Y_D}{[WLTH]_{-1}}$	$\dfrac{RE+CCA+T_{GS}}{[WLTH]_{-1}}$	$\dfrac{[Y_D]_{-1}}{[WLTH]_{-1}}$	$\dfrac{[RE+CCA+T_{GS}]_{-1}}{[WLTH]_{-2}}$	Constant term	R^2	Standard error	Durbin-Watson ratio
A. 1948–1960													
(1) OLS	−0.143 (0.026)	−0.00229 (0.00235)	−0.00610 (0.00137)	—	−0.052 a) (0.025)	0.071 a) (0.017)		—	—	0.01923	0.57	0.00160	—
(2) OLS	−0.168 (0.019)	—	−0.00620 (0.00073)	—	−0.077 (0.029)	0.075 (0.020)	0.098 (0.032)	0.054 (0.018)	−0.153 (0.035)	−0.00117	0.76	0.00123	1.35
(3) TSLS	−0.173 (0.030)	—	−0.00643 (0.00110)	—	−0.099 (0.046)	0.096 (0.035)	0.022 (0.076)	0.033 (0.022)	−0.080 (0.069)	0.00084	0.72	0.00131	—
(4) TSLS b)	−0.151 (0.027)	—	−0.00681 (0.00110)	—	−0.103 (0.046)	0.063 (0.027)	0.070 (0.070)	0.039 (0.022)	−0.070 (0.070)	0.00095	0.71	0.00133	—
B. 1948–1962													
(5) OLS	−0.178 (0.020)	−0.00482 (0.00095)	−0.00344 (0.00063)	—	−0.113 (0.031)	0.081 (0.020)	0.105 (0.031)	0.053 (0.018)	−0.146 (0.035)	−0.00522	0.74	0.00121	—
(6) TSLS	−0.158 (0.029)	−0.00451 (0.00174)	−0.00355 (0.00108)	—	−0.140 (0.062)	0.069 (0.035)	0.062 (0.077)	0.046 (0.022)	−0.083 (0.066)	0.00167	0.71	0.00128	1.11

Note A list of variables appears on pp. 480–482.

a) Coefficient refers to the sum of the two income or the two capital spending variables.

b) In this regression the coefficients of current and lagged business income are constrained to be equal in magnitude and opposite in sign.

TABLE 13.4

Quarterly changes in the public's holdings of time deposits: $\Delta DT/[WLTH]_{-1}$.

Equation (13.3) Period and method of estimation	$\dfrac{[DT]_{-1}}{[WLTH]_{-1}}$	RM_{BDT}	RM_{GBS3}	$\dfrac{I_{CNFR}+C_D}{[WLTH]_{-1}}$	$\dfrac{I_{BUS}}{[WLTH]_{-1}}$	$\dfrac{Y_D}{[WLTH]_{-1}}$	$\dfrac{RE+CCA+T_{GS}}{[WLTH]_{-1}}$	Constant term	R^2	Standard error	Durbin-Watson ratio
A. 1948–1960											
(1) OLS	−0.115 (0.017)	0.00308 (0.00042)	−0.00160 (0.00024)		−0.044 [a] (0.012)		0.018 [a] (0.007)	0.00968	0.78	0.00081	—
(2) OLS	−0.102 (0.014)	0.00373 (0.00042)	−0.00174 (0.00020)	−0.043 (0.009)	—	0.015 (0.005)	—	0.00862	0.82	0.00073	1.36
(3) TSLS	−0.102 (0.019)	0.00408 (0.00070)	−0.00197 (0.00030)	−0.061 (0.021)	—	0.019 (0.012)	—	0.00651	0.80	0.00078	—
B. 1948–1962											
(4) OLS	−0.069 (0.017)	0.00452 (0.00050)	−0.00199 (0.00025)	−0.043 (0.011)	—	0.017 (0.007)	—	0.00210	0.82	0.00095	—
(5) TSLS	−0.102 (0.018)	0.00582 (0.00056)	−0.00270 (0.00030)	−0.025 (0.020)	—	0.026 [b] (0.007)	—	−0.00423	0.80	0.00101	0.93

Note   A list of variables appears on pp. 480–482.

[a] Coefficient refers to the sums of the two income or the two capital spending variables.

[b] Coefficient refers to household income (divided by recent average GNP) with a one-quarter lag.

have expected signs and account for a good deal of the movement in dependent variables. Lags and disaggregations into "household" and "business"
components for some of the variables improve the results. Two-stage least-
squares regressions (labeled "TSLS" in the tables) give results generally
similar to ordinary least-squares results (labeled "OLS"). Serial correlation
in the residuals is positive in these regressions, but there has been no attempt
to transform the data so as to increase the efficiency of estimation.

The coefficients of interest rates were somewhat different for the regressions
through 1962 than for the regressions through 1960. For currency regressions
through 1960, the coefficient of the yield on time deposits was several times
its standard error, but the yield on private securities was not significant.
For demand deposit regressions through 1960, just the reverse was true.
For regressions through 1962, however, both rates were important in both
relationships, as the final equations demonstrate. Behind this change in
results probably lies the divergence in yield movements during 1962, when
time deposit yields rose sharply and private security yields declined slightly.
This divergence reduces somewhat the high correlation between the two yields
which prevailed through 1960 and permits more confident estimates of the
separate effects of the two rates.

Predictions of 1961–1962 based on regressions through 1960 were poor
for demand deposits and currency and good for time deposits. A summary
of prediction results appears in section 13.5 (pp. 525–526). Predictions
are based on the two-stage least-squares regressions through 1960.

The sizeable prediction errors for currency and demand deposits are due
to the interest rate coefficients in the regressions through 1960. The revised
interest rate coefficients of the final equations greatly reduce the 1961–1962
errors. The poor predictions should serve as a reminder, however, that many
coefficients of the model even in the final equations are probably influenced
by particular historical developments and coincidences as well as by general
behavioral relationships.

Interest elasticities of the demand for currency and deposits are fairly
low according to these regressions. At 1948–1962 means, long-run elasticities
implied in the final equations are as follows:

	With respect to yield on		
Elasticity	Treasury bills	Private securities	Time deposits
Currency	—	−0.364	−0.136
Demand deposits	—	−0.352	−0.167
Time deposits	−0.374	—	0.683

Long-run or equilibrium-stock elasticities are derived by setting the quarterly changes in currency and deposits equal to zero and solving the equations for the stocks.

Savings and insurance claims and U.S. securities   Results through 1960 for these assets appear in tables 13.5, 13.6 and 13.7. U.S. security holdings are disaggregated into household and business holdings. Because there is no quarterly yield series available for savings and insurance claims, a four-quarter moving average of the yield on commercial bank time deposits serves as a proxy for the missing yield.

The basic framework does not fit these relationships as well as it does the demand relationships for currency and deposits. For savings and insurance, interest rate coefficients are the only ones which accord with expectations. Since the variance of changes in savings and insurance claims is so small that the equation has little influence on the complete model, there should be little objection to the simple expedient of relating current changes to last quarter's changes and interest rates. The resultant equation has a good fit and successfully predicts 1961–1962 (see pp. 525–526).

For holdings of U.S. securities, whether household or business, the current income constraint seems to have little influence. For households, an alternative constraint variable which improves the fit is the lagged stock of time deposits (the yield on time deposits is also an important explanatory variable). For business, quarterly changes in tax accruals greatly improve the fit. In the framework of the present model, it is helpful to think of tax liabilities as a known constraint on *future* portfolio changes which influences current portfolio behavior.

Neither U.S. security equation predicts 1961–1962 very well, but refitting greatly reduces the 1961–1962 residuals in both cases. Refitting reduces the coefficient of the time deposit yield in both equations, although the final coefficients remain high in relation to their standard errors.

Long-run elasticities with respect to the Treasury bill rate are fairly low according to the final U.S. securities equations. For households, the elasticity at 1952–1962 means is 0.75; for business, the elasticity is 0.29.

The term structure of U.S. security rates   A more detailed model than the present one might include separate demand equations for U.S. securities of different maturities instead of the equations just presented, which aggregate over-all maturities. Households would, under this more detailed procedure, have two or more demand equations for U.S. securities, and simi-

TABLE 13.5

Quarterly changes in savings and insurance claims: $\Delta BNFB/[WLTH]_{-1}$.

Equation (13.4) Period and method of estimation	$\dfrac{[BNBF]_{-1}}{[WLTH]_{-1}}$	$\dfrac{1}{4}\sum_{i=1}^{4}[RM_{BDT}]_{-i}$	RM_{PSEC}	$\dfrac{I_{CNFR}+C_D}{[WLTH]_{-1}}$	$\dfrac{Y_D}{[WLTH]_{-1}}$	$\dfrac{[\Delta BNBF]_{-1}}{[WLTH]_{-2}}$	Constant term	R^2	Standard error	Durbin-Watson ratio
A. 1952–1960										
(1) OLS	0.009 (0.009)	0.00088 (0.00074)	−0.00095 (0.00032)	0.021 (0.010)	−0.006 (0.006)	—	0.00977	0.54	0.00039	—
(2) OLS	—	0.00110 (0.00025)	−0.00081 (0.00019)	—	—	0.675 (0.091)	0.00515	0.75	0.00026	2.26
(3) TSLS	0.016 (0.012)	0.00045 (0.00091)	−0.00104 (0.00040)	0.012 (0.015)	0.000 (0.009)	—	0.00500	—	—	—
(4) TSLS	—	0.00106 (0.00027)	−0.00077 (0.00020)	—	—	0.691 (0.086)	0.00490	0.75	0.00026	—
B. 1952–1962										
(5) OLS	—	0.00088 (0.00018)	−0.00065 (0.00015)	—	—	0.641 (0.081)	0.00503	0.86	0.00028	—
(6) TSLS	—	0.00095 (0.00020)	−0.00071 (0.00017)	—	—	0.617 (0.084)	0.00542	0.76	0.00037	2.02

Note   A list of variables appears on pp. 480–482.

TABLE 13.6

Quarterly changes in household holdings of U.S. securities: $\Delta BF_P/[WLTH]_{-1}$.

Equation (13.5) Period and method of estimation	$\dfrac{[BF_P]_{-1}}{[WLTH]_{-1}}$	RM_{GBS3}	RM_{GBL}	RM_{BDT}	$\dfrac{I_{CNFR}+C_D}{[WLTH]_{-1}}$	$\dfrac{Y_D}{[WLTH]_{-1}}$	$\dfrac{[DT]_{-1}}{[WLTH]_{-1}}$	Constant term	R^2	Standard error	Durbin-Watson ratio
A. 1952–1960											
(1) OLS	−0.047 (0.026)	0.00086 (0.00035)	0.00534 (0.00117)	−0.00770 (0.00163)	0.086 (0.024)	−0.003 (0.018)	—	−0.0686	0.88	0.00088	—
(2) OLS	−0.070 (0.025)	0.00179 (0.00046)	0.00426 (0.00155)	−0.01055 (0.00140)	—	—	0.128 (0.058)	−0.00377	0.85	0.00097	1.80
(3) TSLS	−0.166 (0.045)	0.00085 (0.00060)	0.00814 (0.00246)	−0.01556 (0.00375)	−0.018 (0.047)	0.019 (0.034)	—	0.00179	—	—	—
(4) TSLS	−0.100 (0.040)	0.00178 (0.00070)	0.00496 (0.00268)	−0.01265 (0.00269)	—	—	0.140 (0.078)	0.00149	0.83	0.00102	—
B. 1952–1962											
(5) OLS	−0.039 (0.022)	0.00249 (0.00039)	0.00189 (0.00108)	−0.00918 (0.00117)	—	—	0.244 (0.034)	−0.02185	0.78	0.00113	—
(6) TSLS	−0.054 (0.026)	0.00321 (0.00061)	−0.00074 (0.00020)	−0.00829 (0.00181)	—	—	0.248 (0.040)	−0.01431	—	—	—
(7) TSLS	−0.054 (0.025)	0.00303 (0.00035)	—	−0.00875 (0.00129)	—	—	0.250 (0.040)	−0.01574	0.76	0.00116	—

Note   A list of variables appears on pp. 480–482.

TABLE 13.7

Quarterly changes in business holdings of U.S. securities: $\Delta BF_{ONF}/[WLTH]_{-1}$.

Equation (13.6) Period and method of estimation	$\dfrac{[BF_{ONF}]_{-1}}{[WLTH]_{-1}}$	RM_{GBS3}	RM_{GBL}	RM_{BDT}	$\dfrac{I_{BUS}}{[WLTH]_{-1}}$	$\dfrac{RE+CCA+T_{GS}}{[WLTH]_{-1}}$	$\dfrac{\Delta[TC-TC_{PAY}]}{[WLTH]_{-1}}$	Constant term	R^2	Standard error	Durbin-Watson ratio
A. 1952–1960											
(1) OLS	-0.100 (0.093)	0.00228 (0.00122)	0.00644 (0.00569)	-0.00877 (0.00456)	-0.079 (0.090)	0.004 (0.025)	—	0.03086	0.42	0.00200	—
(2) OLS	-0.089 (0.073)	0.00152 (0.00056)	—	-0.00424 (0.00131)	-0.117 (0.046)	—	0.158 (0.033)	0.02686	0.69	0.00143	1.02
(3) TSLS	-0.230 (0.081)	0.00076 (0.00173)	0.00755 (0.00372)	-0.01349 (0.00251)	-0.108 (0.101)	0.036 (0.050)	—	0.03049	—	—	—
(4) TSLS	-0.159 (0.065)	0.00241 (0.00063)	—	-0.00659 (0.00139)	-0.189 (0.053)	—	0.155 (0.029)	0.04370	0.64	0.00155	—
B. 1952–1962											
(5) OLS	-0.060 (0.067)	0.00105 (0.00045)	—	-0.00293 (0.00094)	-0.088 (0.040)	—	0.174 (0.029)	0.01963	0.66	0.00136	—
(6) TSLS	-0.103 (0.068)	0.00124 (0.00054)	—	-0.00375 (0.00113)	-0.111 (0.052)	—	0.188 (0.028)	0.02755	0.64	0.00139	0.98

Note   A list of variables appears on pp. 480–482.

larly with business, banks and nonbank finance. These demand relationships in combination with Treasury and Federal Reserve policies would contribute to determining long- and short-term interest rates.

The present model attempts to deal with the term structure of U.S. security yields in a single equation which is a combination of the separate demand equations for different classes of securities. The equation reflects the behavior of financial sectors as well as the behavior of the nonfinancial public. The dependent variable in the equation is the spread between the long-term rate and the Treasury bill rate—a single variable which tells a good deal about the maturity structure of rates. In deriving the equation, it is helpful to think of two categories of federal debt, "long-term" and "short-term", without specifying exactly what the boundaries of the two categories are.

In the framework of the model, separate demand equations for long- and short-term U.S. securities would involve lagged stocks interest rates and other variables, as follows:

$$\frac{\Delta g_s}{w} = -b_{11}\frac{[g_s]_{-1}}{w} + b_{12}r_s - b_{13}r_l + b_{14}z$$

$$\frac{\Delta g_l}{w} = -b_{21}\frac{[g_l]_{-1}}{w} - b_{22}r_s + b_{23}r_l + b_{24}z'$$

g_s and g_l are short- and long-term debt, r_s and r_l are short- and long-term rates of return, z and z' are weighted combinations of all the other influences on holdings and w is some measure of wealth.

To get from these behavioral equations to the single equations of the model, two key assumptions are necessary. The first is that g_s and g_l are close substitutes [19]). This assumption implies that b_{12}, b_{13}, b_{22} and b_{23} should all be large and approximately equal [20]). It also suggests that b_{14} and z should not differ greatly from b_{24} and z'. Setting $b_{12} = b_{13} = b_{22} = b_{23}$ and $b_{14}z = b_{24}z'$ and subtracting one equation from the other gives the following relationship:

$$\frac{\Delta g_s}{w} - \frac{\Delta g_l}{w} = -b_{11}\frac{[g_s]_{-1}}{w} + b_{21}\frac{[g_l]_{-1}}{w} + 2b_{12}[r_s - r_l].$$

---

[19]) The empirical work of Meiselman [16] suggests that long- and short-term securities can be treated as close substitutes.

[20]) Any income effects that might make the effects of a rise in r_s different from those of an equal fall in r_l are assumed to be reflected in z and z'.

The second key assumption is that while r_s represents the interest rate on short-term securities, the expected yield on long-term securities, r_l, is equal to the long-term interest rate plus any expected capital gains (or minus any expected capital losses) [21]. For short-term maturities only minor capital gains or losses are possible and the rate of interest measures the rate of return, but for long-term maturities expected returns due to capital gains must be added to interest returns. This assumption is the basis for identifying r_s with RM_{GBS3}, the Treasury bill rate, and r_l with $[RM_{GBL}+k]$ where RM_{GBL} is the long-term rate and k is a measure of expected rate of return due to capital gains.

Substituting $[RM_{GBS3} - RM_{GBL} - k]$ for $[r_s - r_l]$ in the equation above and letting $c = 1/2b_{12}$ leads to the following solution for the rate differential:

$$RM_{GBL} - RM_{GBS3} = -k - c\frac{\Delta g_s}{w} + c\frac{\Delta g_l}{w} - b_{11}c\frac{[g_s]_{-1}}{w} + b_{21}c\frac{[g_l]_{-1}}{w}.$$

The rate differential depends on amounts of U.S. debt outstanding in different maturity classes, on changes in these amounts and on expected capital gains.

The debt variables have been represented by flow-of-funds estimates of the proportions in various maturity classes of U.S. debt held outside the Federal Reserve and federal trust funds. These estimates show a percentage breakdown of the debt into four classes: 0 to 1 year, 1 to 5 years, 5 to 10 years, and 10 years and over. Of the four maturity classes in this representation, any one is derivable from the other three, since the figures are in the form of proportions adding to 100. In fact, nearly all the variation in maturity distribution is reflected in two classes, 0 to 1 and 1 to 5 years. The first class is definitely short term; the second is assumed to be nearer short than long term.

The variable g_s/w is accordingly represented in the model by the 0 to 1 year and 1 to 5 year proportions. The variable $\Delta g_s/w$ is represented by changes in these proportions. (It would be more precise to represent $\Delta g_s/w$ by changes in the numerator of the proportions divided by the level of the denominator, but this added precision is probably of no practical importance.) The variable g_l/w is taken to move inversely to the 0 to 1 and 1 to 5 year proportions, and $\Delta g_l/w$ is taken to move inversely to changes in the

---

[21]) Conard [6, pp. 307–308] shows that this view of rate structure is very closely related to the expectations hypothesis.

0 to 1 and 1 to 5 year proportions. Thus no additional variables are needed to represent the supply of long-term U.S. debt.

The problem in the term structure equations is choosing a variable to represent k, expected capital gains or losses. In the *General Theory* [22]) Keynes argued that investors have in mind a normal level of long-term interest rates toward which current rates are expected to move. When current rates are above normal, investors expect rates to fall and therefore capital values to rise; when current rates are below normal, investors expect capital losses. According to the Keynesian hypothesis, expected capital gains might be proportional to the difference between the current long-term rate and some moving average of past rates.

As Duesenberry has pointed out, "on a priori grounds there is no reason why the [Keynesian] argument should not be turned just the other way ... It would not ... be surprising if it turned out that a rise in rates led to an expectation of a further rise and vice versa. It is almost certainly true that most persons who take an interest in security prices will be influenced by both types of consideration ..." [23]). Empirically, then, it might be that not only the relation of the current long-term rate to a "normal" rate but also the relation of the current long-term rate to very recent long-term rates might affect expectations of capital gains. Furthermore, the coefficient of the second variable should be opposite in sign to the coefficient of the first one.

Regressions for the years 1952–1960 support the view that these two variables have some relation to term structure. The variables tested are the current long-term rate minus weighted averages of past long-term rates [24]). The expectation is that for averages spread over many past quarters the coefficient of the variable will be negative, while for averages bunched in recent quarters the coefficient will be positive. That is, when long-term rates are above "normal", capital gains are expected, the long rate tends to fall relative to the short rate and the differential between long and short rates is narrowed; at the same time, when long-term rates are rising capital losses are expected,

---

[22]) Keynes [14, pp. 201–204].

[23]) Duesenberry [7, p. 318].

[24]) More specifically, they are nine variables of the form

$$RM_{\text{GBL}} - \left[\frac{1-\lambda}{1-\lambda^{11}} \sum_{i=1}^{11} \lambda^{i-1} (RM_{\text{GBL}})_{-i} \right],$$

where λ takes on the values $0.15, 0.25, \ldots,$ up to 0.95. The variable for $\lambda = 0.15$ is practically a first difference; the variable for $\lambda = 0.95$ is the current value in relation to a much longer average.

TABLE 13.8

Term structure relationships: $RM_{GBL}-RM_{GBS3}$.

Equation (13.8) Period and method of estimation	Current U.S. long-term rate less weighted average of lagged rates						Change in 0–1 year proportion of debt	Change in 1–5 year proportion of debt	Constant term	R^2	Standard error	Durbin-Watson ratio
	Shortest lag $\lambda = 0.15$	$\lambda = 0.35$	$\lambda = 0.45$	$\lambda = 0.65$	$\lambda = 0.75$	Longest lag $\lambda = 0.95$						
A. 1952–1960												
(1) OLS	0.834 (0.490)	—	—	—	—	−1.180 (0.421)	−12.8 (4.8)	−13.6 (6.1)	1.26	0.62	0.365	—
(2) OLS	—	1.995 (0.726)	—	—	−2.332 (0.716)	—	−11.6 (4.8)	−12.2 (6.2)	1.24	0.65	0.353	—
(3) OLS	—	—	4.198 (1.382)	−4.479 (1.386)	—	—	−11.6 (4.9)	−12.3 (6.3)	1.23	0.65	0.354	—
(4) OLS	—	—	2.406 (0.846)	—	−2.777 (0.831)	—	−11.9 (4.8)	−12.8 (6.1)	1.26	0.65	0.351	0.70
(5) TSLS	—	—	2.827 (0.929)	—	−3.437 (0.832)	—	−10.1 (4.2)	−12.0 (5.3)	1.32	0.64	0.357	—
B. 1952–1962												
(6) OLS	—	—	2.702 (0.698)	—	−3.005 (6.57)	—	−10.9 (4.2)	−12.1 (5.5)	1.26	0.66	0.326	—
(7) TSLS	—	—	3.161 (0.611)	—	−4.455 (0.511)	—	−4.8 (2.6)	−7.1 (3.4)	1.40	0.55	0.376	0.62

(Quarterly, 1952-1962; per cent)

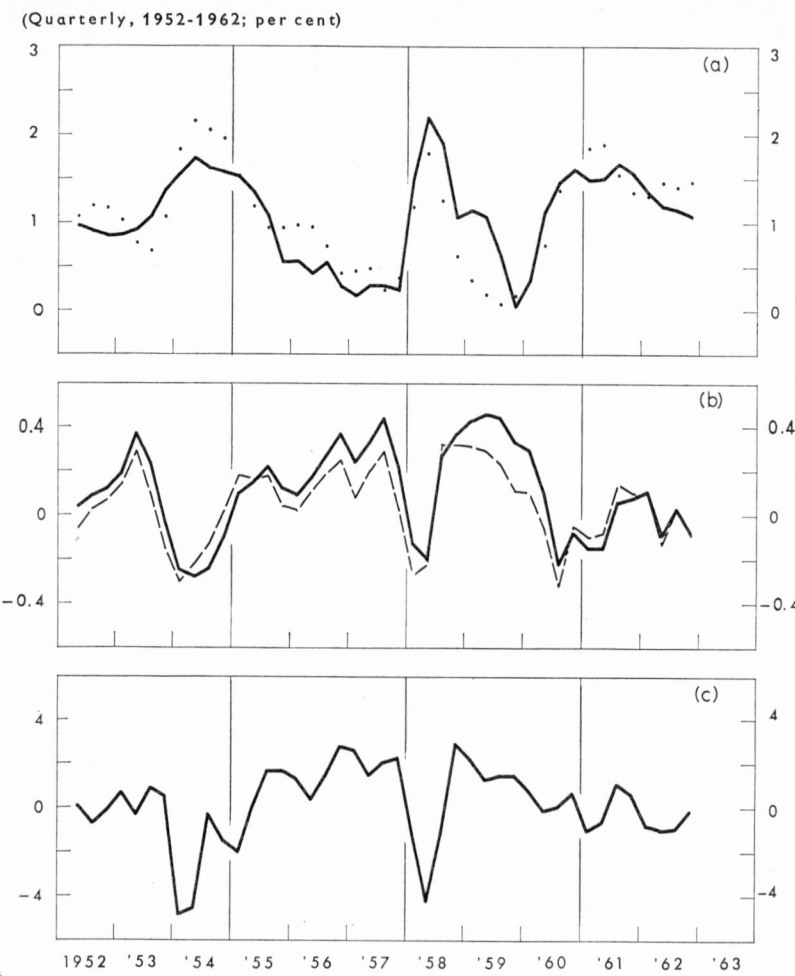

Figure 13.3. The term structure of U.S. security rates.

Key RM_{GBL} = long-term U.S. rate

RM_{GBS3} = Treasury bill rate

a) $[RM_{GBL} - RM_{GBS3}]$

.... calculated, —— actual

b) $---RM_{GBL} - 0.55 \sum_{i=1}^{11} 0.45^{i-1} [RM_{GBL}]_{-i}$

$——RM_{GBL} - 0.261 \sum_{i=1}^{11} 0.75^{i-1} [RM_{GBL}]_{-i}$

c) —— Change in 0–5 yr. proportion of U.S. debt

the long rate tends to rise relative to the short rate and the differential is widened. The equation implies that proportions of the debt in different maturity classes and changes in proportions may also influence term structure.

Table 13.8 sets out the results for four different pairs of expectational variables. In each case, as expected, the sign of the variable with the shorter lag is positive and the sign of the variable with the longer lag is negative. The values of R^2 do not discriminate sharply between different pairs of lags—by a small margin, equations (4) and (5) have the best fits. The expectational variables, together with actual and calculated values of the yield spread, are plotted in figure 13.3.

Changes in debt proportions in 0 to 1 and 1 to 5 year maturities also enter the equation with expected negative signs. The proportions themselves either had signs opposite to expectation, were small in relation to their standard errors or both. They are therefore omitted from table 13.8. The implication of the omission is that while changes in debt management operations influence interest rates for a brief period, the average composition of the debt over longer periods does not have a perceptible influence [25]).

Serial correlation of the residuals is positive and highly significant for this relationship. Roughly speaking the equation overstates the cyclical movements of yield spreads in 1952–1955 and understates them in 1957–1960. The pattern of residuals should serve as a warning that the margins of error surrounding the coefficients in table 13.7 may be very wide; 1961–1962 predictions based on the regression through 1960 are, however, quite successful [26]).

Net borrowing from financial institutions   The liabilities of households and business which appear in the model are their debts to banks and to nonbank financial institutions. Net changes in these debts, according to the framework of the model, should depend negatively on the lagged stock of debt, negatively on the interest rate on borrowing, positively on capital spending and negatively on current income. The regressions, on the whole, do not give much support to these expectations.

Household borrowing in 1952–1960 moves closely with household capital spending (which includes durable goods as well as housing), and no other

---

[25]) Wood's empirical work on the term structure of rates [22] is consistent with the same conclusion.

[26]) The "naive model" for this equation consists of the assumption that the 1961–1962 differential is equal to the 1952–1960 average differential.

TABLE 13.9

Net borrowing by households: $\Delta BHH_F/[WLTH]_{-1}$.

Equation (13.7) Period and method of estimation	$\dfrac{[BHH_F]_{-1}}{[WLTH]_{-1}}$	RM_{PSEC}	RM_{BDT}	$\dfrac{I_{CNFR}+C_D}{[WLTH]_{-1}}$	$\dfrac{Y_D}{[WLTH]_{-1}}$	Constant term	R^2	Standard error	Durbin-Watson ratio
A. 1952–1960									
(1) OLS	0.006 (0.007)	−0.00063 (0.00045)	—	0.152 (0.012)	—	−0.01331	0.85	0.00066	—
(2) OLS	—	—	—	0.156 (0.012)	—	−0.01559	0.83	0.00067	1.27
(3) TSLS	0.002 (0.014)	−0.00032 (0.00085)	—	0.168 (0.024)	0.002 (0.018)	−0.01727	—	—	—
(4) TSLS	—	—	—	0.172 (0.019)	—	−0.01788	0.82	0.00069	—
B. 1952–1962									
(5) OLS	—	−0.00158 (0.00036)	0.00179 (0.00036)	0.150 (0.013)	—	−0.01032	0.80	0.00072	—
(6) TSLS	—	−0.00144 (0.00051)	0.00175 (0.00049)	0.167 (0.020)	—	−0.01333	0.79	0.00074	1.33

Note   A list of variables appears on pp. 480–482.

TABLE 13.10

Net borrowing by business: $\Delta[BBUS_F]/[WLTH]_{-1}$

Equation (13.20) Period and method of estimation	$\dfrac{[BBUS_F]_{-1}}{[WLTH]_{-1}}$	RM_{PSEC}	$\dfrac{I_{CNFR}+C_D}{[WLTH]_{-1}}$	$\dfrac{I_{BUS}}{[WLTH]_{-1}}$	$\dfrac{RE+CCA+T_{GS}}{[WLTH]_{-1}}$	$\dfrac{\Delta[BBUS_F]_{-1}}{[WLTH]_{-2}}$	Constant term	R^2	Standard error	Durbin-Watson ratio
(1) OLS	-0.059 (0.034)	-0.00067 (0.00093)		-0.047 (0.030)	0.141 (0.065)		0.00760	0.46	0.00119	
(2) OLS	-0.005 (0.024)	-0.00040 (0.00098)	0.087 (0.024)	-0.020 (0.029)			0.00069	0.38	0.00126	
(3) OLS		-0.00039 (0.00032)	0.065 (0.024)			0.307 (0.153)	-0.00246	0.45	0.00117	1.81
(4) TSLS		-0.00037 (0.00033)	0.074 (0.029)			0.299 (0.159)	-0.00382			

Note   A list of variables appears on pp. 480–482.

variable adds anything significant to the simple borrowing-capital spending relationship. Table 13.9 contains the details. Since capital spending itself responds in some degree to financial variables, the equations do not indicate that household borrowing is unaffected by credit conditions. They indicate rather that it is difficult to find any relationship to credit conditions during 1942–1960 beyond what is already reflected in the capital spending series.

The 1952–1960 regressions predict poorly. Re-estimation including data for 1961 and 1962 suggests a significant negative response to the interest rate on private securities and a positive response to the time deposit yield as well as a positive association with capital spending. The interpretation of the response to time deposit yields is that when time deposits are attractive, households meet credit needs less by drawing on savings, and more by borrowing. The revised regression accounts for 1961–1962 borrowing movements fairly successfully.

Regressions for business borrowing are the least successful of the model. The ordinary least-squares regression through 1960 involving the lagged stock, the rate on borrowing, capital spending and current income (equation (1) of table 13.10) has an R^2 of only 0.46, most of which is attributable to the *positive*, rather than the expected negative, influence of current income divided by a weighted average of recent income. The coefficient of business capital spending also has a sign opposite the expected one. One variable which does bear some relation to business borrowing is household capital spending, probably because "business" in the present model includes certain "not elsewhere classified" financial institutions which borrow from banks and extend credit to households (for example, sales finance companies).

Equations (3) and (4) of table 13.10 utilize the same expedient for business borrowing which was used earlier for savings and insurance claims, namely, the use of lagged net borrowing (plus two other variables) to explain current net borrowing. The fit remains far from close. A number of variables not shown in the table—for example, some of the interest rate expectations variables from the term structure relationship—failed to improve the fit. It was in part because of these poor regression results that the business borrowing equation was dropped in the final model (p. 485).

13.4.3. Behavioral equations for the banking system

The balance sheet of the banking system   The model deals with the following eight balance sheet items for the consolidated commercial banking system.

Assets	Liabilities and net worth
Required reserves	Net demand deposits
Excess reserves	Net time deposits
Federal securities	Borrowing from federal reserve
Private loans and investments	Other

Two identities characterize these items. The first is the usual balance sheet identity, with the "other" item covering net worth, minor items and any statistical discrepancy. If "other" liabilities are treated as a residual, this variable and the balance-sheet identity can both be dropped from the model. The present model makes these two eliminations.

The second identity is the reserve requirement identity, which says that for member banks required reserves equal $[DD+DD_{GF}][RRR_{DD}]+[DT]$ $[RRR_{DT}]$, or the sum of the products of demand and time deposits times the required reserve ratios against them. For nonmember banks there is no such simple requirement, but for all commercial banks it is very nearly true, as equation (13.16) states, that required reserves equal $0.84[DD+DD_{GF}]$ $[RRR_{DD}]+0.82[DT][RRR_{DT}]$. The minor error involved in taking this relationship as an identity can be swept into the statistical discrepancy. The factors of 0.84 and 0.82 represent member bank proportions of total demand and time deposits. Domestic interbank deposits and federal funds, incidentally, are netted out of the consolidated system.

For three items in the balance sheet—federal securities, borrowing from the Federal Reserve, and excess reserves—banks are assumed to determine quarterly changes on the basis of interest rates, short-run constraints and other variables, just as the public determines its financial portfolio changes.

For four items in the balance sheet—demand deposits, time deposits, the required reserves which are derived from them and loans and investments—banks are assumed to accommodate any quarterly changes which the public wishes to make. Banks do attempt to control the volume of deposits and loans, but they do so, according to the present model, mainly by altering the yields they pay on time deposits and the terms on which they extend loans rather than by direct decisions to buy or sell deposits and loans.

For demand deposits there should be little dispute about this assumption, which implies no more than the willingness of banks to accept deposits and honor checks drawn against them. For time deposits, the situation is not too different. To be sure, if the market for time deposits were perfectly competitive, "the" yield on time deposits would fluctuate so as to equate demand and supply and each bank would decide what volume of time deposits to offer at the going yield. In fact, it is surely more realistic to think of a bank as setting the yield it is willing to pay on time deposits and as accepting deposits and withdrawals at the yield it has set.

Much less clear-cut is the position of loans and investments. At one extreme, the existence of credit lines under which loans are automatically granted for certain business borrowers means that some portion of the volume of loans and investments must be taken as given by the bank in the short run. The bank can set the interest rate and other contract terms of these loans, just as it sets the rate on time deposits, but at the terms it has set, short-run fluctuations in volume are beyond its control. At the other extreme, bank holdings of, say, municipal securities are a case in which the individual bank takes the yield as given and determines the extent of its participation at that yield. Disaggregation would be desirable in order to make a separation of these two categories, but disaggregation would greatly complicate the model in other respects. For the present, the variable which banks control in the loan market will be taken to be the interest rate rather than the amount outstanding [27]).

The appropriate choice of a dependent variable depends in part on the time unit of the data. In a weekly model, the choice made for the present equations would almost certainly be the appropriate one. For an annual model, on the other hand, it might be that banks can meet deposit and loan targets sufficiently precisely so that changes in deposits (at least time deposits) and loans outstanding would be appropriate dependent variables.

The short-run constraint variable for banks consists of quarterly changes in deposits less required reserves and loans. Banks adjust the other items in their portfolio and change interest rates on time deposits and loans and investments partly in response to (and in order to influence) changes in deposits and loans.

U.S. security holdings   According to the basic framework of the model, changes in bank holdings of federal securities should be related to the lagged stock of federal securities, interest rates, the short-run constraint variable

---

[27]) The interest rate in this relationship represents a whole range of contract terms and changes in screening procedures rather than interest charges alone. There is no adequate information on whether changes in interest rates actually do parallel changes in these other variables.

TABLE 13.11

Changes in bank holdings of U.S. securities: $\Delta BF_B/[DD+DT]_{-1}$.

Equation (13.9) Period and method of estimation	$\dfrac{[BF_B]_{-1}}{[DD+DT]_{-1}}$	$\dfrac{[RES_E]}{[DD+DT]_{-1}}$	RM_{GBS3}	See footnote a)	See footnote b)	Constant term	R^2	Standard error	Durbin-Watson ratio
A. 1948–1960: 3									
(1) OLS	-0.021 (0.012)		-0.00168 (0.00100)	0.790 (0.047)		0.01337	0.92	0.00310	
(2) OLS	-0.048 (0.019)	2.010 (0.876)		0.705 (0.038)	0.177 (0.035)	0.01263	0.95	0.00248	2.10
(3) TSLS	-0.037 (0.027)		-0.00290 (0.00037)	0.737 (0.112)		0.02265			
(4) TSLS	-0.135 (0.032)	6.102 (1.521)		0.627 (0.075)	0.188 (0.067)	0.03048	0.93	0.00307	
B. 1948–1962 (omitting 1960: 4)									
(5) OLS	-0.049 (0.017)	2.138 (0.817)		0.710 (0.038)	0.169 (0.035)	0.01228	0.95	0.00251	
(6) TSLS	-0.133 (0.028)	6.290 1.350		0.622 (0.071)	0.197 (0.063)	0.02845	0.92	0.00313	1.32

Note   A list of variables appears on pp. 480–482.

a) The variable is $\Delta[DD+DD_{GF}+DT-RES_R-ALNPS_B]/[DD+DT]_{-1}$. This short-run constraint variable is discussed on pp. 507–508.

b) The variable is $\Delta[DD+DD_{GF}+DT-RES_R-ALNPS_B]_{-1}/[DD+DT]_{-1}$.

TABLE 13.12

Changes in member bank borrowing and excess reserves: $\Delta RES_B/[DD+DT]_{-1}$ and $\Delta RES_E/[DD+DT]_{-1}$.

Equations (13.10) and (13.11) Period and method of estimation	$\dfrac{[RES_B]_{-1}}{[DD+DT]_{-1}}$	$\dfrac{[RES_E]_{-1}}{[DD+DT]_{-1}}$	RM_{GBS3}	$RM_{FRB}-RM_{GBS3}$	See footnote a)	See footnote b)	See footnote c)	Constant term	R^2	Standard error	Durbin-Watson ratio
A. Net borrowing, 1954–1960: 3											
(1) OLS	−0.459 (0.089)			−0.00168 (0.00043)	−0.040 (0.015)			0.00187	0.69	0.00071	1.73
(2) TSLS	−0.443 (0.108)			−0.00146 (0.00064)	−0.043 (0.020)			0.00175	0.68	0.00071	
B. Net borrowing, 1954–1962											
(3) OLS	−0.322 (0.065)			−0.00163 (0.00040)	−0.056 (0.019)		0.040×10^{-3} (0.020×10^{-3})	0.00118	0.62	0.00068	
(4) TSLS	−0.267		−0.00047	−0.00191	−0.066		0.033×10^{-3}	0.00226	0.68	0.00063	2.00

1954–1960: 3

(5) OLS	−0.102 (0.053)	0.00039 (0.00013)	0.013 (0.005)	−0.015 (0.005)	0.00023	0.68	0.00020	2.02
(6) TSLS	−0.089 (0.061)	0.00029 (0.00021)	0.016 (0.007)	−0.015 (0.006)	0.00021	0.67	0.00020	

D. Excess reserves, 1954–1962

(7) OLS	−0.060 (0.045)	0.00028 (0.00012)	0.014 (0.005)	−0.018 (0.004)	0.00007	0.58	0.00020	
(8) TSLS	−0.046 (0.045)	0.00019 (0.00017)	0.017 (0.006)	−0.018 (0.004)	0.00005	0.57	0.00020	1.95

Note A list of variables appears on p. 480.

[a] The variable is $\Delta[DD + DD_{GF} + DT - RES_R - ALNPS_B]/[DD + DT]_{-1}$. This short-run constraint variable is discussed on pp. 507–508.

[b] The variable is $\Delta[DD + DD_{GF} + DT - RES_R - ALNPS_B]_{-1}/[DD + DT]_{-1}$.

[c] The variable is $\Delta[DD + DD_{GF} + DT - RES_R - ALNPS_B]/[RES_E]_{-1}$.

for the banking system, and possibly lagged stocks of other bank assets. Table 13.11 presents regressions containing these variables [28]).

As equations (1) and (3) of the table show, the interest rate variable has a coefficient not far above its standard error and with an unexpected negative sign. The coefficient for the lagged stock of U.S. securities is negative as expected, though it indicates a rather slow speed of adjustment. The coefficient of the net change in funds is positive and many times its standard error, a reflection that most of the short-run adjustment by banks to changes in deposits and loans takes the form of purchases or sales of U.S. securities.

Of the other variables which the basic framework suggests might influence U.S. securities holdings, two—the lagged inflow of funds and the lagged stock of excess reserves, both shown in equations (2) and (4) of table 13.10 —improve the fit of the relationship. The positive coefficient for the lagged inflow of funds suggests that it is a weighted average of recent deposit and loan changes which influence sales and purchases of U.S. securities.

The positive coefficient for the stock of excess reserves suggests, plausibly enough, that other things being equal, more excess reserves lead to more purchases of U.S. securities. The size of the coefficient, however, is unexpectedly large. A coefficient of $+1.0$ would mean that a rise of, say, $100 million in excess reserves would increase purchases of U.S. securities by $100 million. A coefficient above unity seems implausible, but may indicate that excess reserve movements are serving in part as a proxy for some other influence. The absolute size of excess reserve movements, incidentally, is very small compared with the size of movements in other balance sheet items, so that even a coefficient well above unity does not mean that excess reserve changes account for an important portion of the "calculated" variation in U.S. security purchases.

Changes in member bank borrowings and excess reserves   The "basic" variables all contribute to accounting for changes in member bank borrowings, as table 13.12 shows, with very similar results for ordinary least squares and for two-stage least squares. The indicated speed of adjustment is fairly rapid, and the response to interest rate differentials moderate. (The implied long-run elasticities are -0.7 with respect to the discount rate and 0.5 with

---

[28]) The fourth quarter of 1960 was omitted in these and other banking portfolio regressions because of the influence of a 1959 Act of Congress under which banks were permitted to count vault cash as reserves. The change in treatment of vault cash took place in several steps, but a major share of the impact was in the last quarter of 1960.

respect to the bill rate, at the 1954–1962 means.) The addition of the bill rate as a separate variable improved the 1954–1962 fit; but the addition of other lagged stocks or the lagged net inflow of funds did not.

The regressions for member bank borrowing are based on data beginning in 1954. The reason for beginning in 1954 is that two structural changes—the end of the excess profits tax in 1953 and the revision of Regulation A in early 1955—make it extremely unlikely that the borrowing expansion of 1952 is explainable in the same terms as later periods of heavy borrowing. The "calculated" values of borrowing based on 1954–1960 regressions do, in fact, greatly understate the 1952 expansion in borrowings.

The final equations for member banks borrowing include an additional variable, the net inflow of funds as a per cent of lagged borrowing, which improved the rather poor fit the earlier variables gave in 1961–1962. The implication of the positive coefficient of this variable is that the negative influence of lagged borrowing—banks' "reluctance to borrow"—is greater when funds are flowing in than when banks are short of funds [29]).

Fluctuations in excess reserves have been much smaller in the postwar years than either excess reserve changes during earlier periods or changes in most other portfolio items during the postwar years. Within the postwar period, furthermore, excess reserve movements have perceptibly diminished in average amplitude from the early postwar years to more recent years, in contrast to fluctuations in loans, deposits and interest rates. Possibly the postwar growth of the federal funds market has permitted this increasing smoothness in excess reserve movements; possibly the changes in the structure of the market for bank borrowings is a factor. In any case, regressions for excess reserves, as do those for bank borrowing, begin in 1954.

These regressions, which appear in table 13.12, suggest that changes in the net inflow of funds (this quarter's inflow minus last quarter's inflow) are closely related to changes in excess reserves. Excess reserves thus appear to serve as a buffer against short-run changes in the rates at which deposits move in and loans move out. In this respect excess reserve holdings differ from U.S. security holdings, which appear to respond to a weighted average of recent net inflows of funds. The excess reserve equations also have

---

[29]) When lagged borrowing is close to zero, the positive influence of this new variable outweighs the negative influence of the short-run constraint variable with deposits as the denominator, and short-run changes in deposits and loans have the "wrong" sign. The final two-stage regression imposed the constraint that this not occur except for negligibly small levels of borrowing—less than one-twentieth of a per cent of deposits. That is, in equation (4) of table 13.12, the ratio of 0.033×10^{-3} to 0.066 was specified in advance.

TABLE 13.13

Quarterly changes in the average rate on private loans and investments: ΔRM_{PSEC}.

Equation (13.12) Period and method of estimation	$[RM_{PSEC}]_{-1}$	RM_{GBL}	RM_{GBS3}	$\dfrac{ALNPS_B}{[DD+DT]_{-1}}$	$\dfrac{1}{4}\sum_{i=1}^{4}\dfrac{[ALNPS_B]_{-i}}{[DD+DT]_{-i}}$	$RM_{GBL}-0.55$ $\times\sum_{i=1}^{11}[0.45^i][RM_{GBL}]_{-i}$	Constant term	R^2	Standard error	Durbin-Watson ratio
A. 1948–1960										
(1) OLS	-0.534 (0.054)	0.482 (0.070)	0.065 (0.023)	0.8 (0.3)			0.384	0.76	0.066	
(2) OLS	-0.614 (0.054)	0.468 (0.063)	0.085 (0.021)		1.4 (0.3)		0.401	0.81	0.059	1.47
(3) TSLS	-0.365 (0.089)	0.259 (0.134)	0.086 (0.040)	0.7 (0.5)			0.328			
(4) TSLS	-0.465 (0.095)	0.290 (0.129)	0.099 (0.039)		1.3 (0.5)		0.305	0.77	0.065	
B. 1948–1962										
(5) OLS	-0.280 (0.072)	0.136 (0.083)	0.071 (0.024)		0.7 (0.3)	0.420 (0.011)	0.332	0.73	0.073	
(6) TSLS	-0.199 (0.085)	0.025 (0.117)	0.088 (0.043)		0.64 (0.50)	0.486 (0.161)	0.291	0.72	0.074	1.91

Note   A list of variables appears on pp. 480–482.

coefficients of expected sign for the lagged stock and for the discount rate-bill rate spread, though these coefficients are not greatly above their standard errors.

Yields on private securities and on time deposits   The setting of yields is not subject to short-run constraints of the kind that enter into portfolio relationships, but otherwise the basic framework used to explain portfolio behavior extends easily to cover interest rate determination, according to calculations appearing in table 13.13.

Banks are assumed to have a desired relationship between the interest rates they determine relative to interest rates they take as given on the one hand and the composition of their portfolio on the other. Specifically, the "desired" interest rate on loans is assumed to depend positively on U.S. security yields and on loans relative to total assets or total deposits, and the quarterly change in the rate on loans is assumed to depend on the desired rate and on last quarter's actual rate. According to regression estimates in table 13.14, the change in the rate on time deposits depends on the lagged rate, U.S. security yields and the loan-deposit ratio.

For private securities, regressions through 1960 bear out these expectations, but these regressions predicted a steady rise in the rate during late 1961 and 1962 instead of the actual slight fall. The errors were not large, but since an added plausible variable reduced them it seemed desirable to change the equation. The final equation (13.12) accordingly includes the short-run interest rate expectations variable used in the term-structure equation in addition to the variables used through 1960, implying that banks raise their rates more when market rates have been rising recently than when market rates have been falling.

For time deposits, a special influence on yields is the maximum rate on time deposits set by the Federal Reserve Board. Since this rate is a ceiling, it might be expected to have no effect on a bank when it lies above the bank's "desired" yield. Considering all banks in the aggregate, it seems useful to distinguish three zones for the maximum rate: (i) If RM_{BDTM}, the maximum rate, lies above "desired" yields for all banks, it may be assumed to have no influence on bank behavior. (ii) If RM_{BDTM} lies below "desired" yields for all banks, the actual rate might be assumed to equal or approach the maximum rate. (iii) If RM_{BDTM} lies in between these two extremes—that is, above for some banks and below for others—it exercises a depressing influence on actual rates; a plausible assumption is that this influence is proportional to the difference between the top of the range of "desired"

TABLE 13.14

Annual changes in the yield on time deposits: ΔRM^A_{BDT}.

Equation (13.13a) Period and method of estimation	$[RM^A_{BDT}]_{-1}$	RM^A_{GBL}	$RM^A_{GBL} - RM^A_{BDTM} + 1$	$\dfrac{ALNPS^A_B}{DD^A + DT^A}$	$\left[\dfrac{ALNPS^A}{DD^A + DT^A}\right]_{-\frac{1}{2}}$	Constant term	R^2	Standard error	Durbin-Watson ratio
A. 1949–1960									
(1) OLS	−0.490 (0.077)	0.685 (0.123)	−0.727 (0.134)	2.2 (0.4)		−1.50	0.91	0.043	
(2) OLS	−0.534 (0.080)	0.694 (0.121)	−0.637 (0.127)		2.0 (0.4)	−1.44	0.91	0.043	1.74
(3) TSLS	−0.633 (0.078)	0.845 (0.120)	−0.679 (0.095)		1.7 (0.3)	−1.58	0.88	0.050	
B. 1949–1962									
(4) OLS	−0.523 (0.080)	0.610 (0.098)	−0.510 (0.064)		1.9 (0.4)	−1.34	0.93	0.046	
(5) TSLS	−0.561 (0.072)	0.708 (0.104)	−0.495 (0.055)		1.519 (0.391)	−1.39	0.91	0.042	1.35

Note   Time subscripts in these regressions refer to years, not quarters. The subscript "$-\frac{1}{2}$" refers to the last two quarters of the preceding year and the first two quarters of the current one. A list of variables appears on pp. 480–482.

yields and RM_{BDTM}. This difference might then be a key variable in explaining the actual yield on time deposits.

The approximation of this difference used in the model is the difference between U.S. long-term rate and the maximum rate on time deposits, plus one per cent. The implication of this representation is that the top of the range of "desired" yields on time deposits is approximately one per cent above the long-term U.S. rate. The variable has been positive throughout the postwar period, which is to say that according to this representation RM_{BDTM} has not been in "zone (i)" during the period. It is assumed, in fact, that RM_{BDTM} has been in "zone (iii)" throughout the period, and so the variable $[RM_{GBL} - RM_{BDTM} + 1]$ enters the time deposit yield equation in a simple linear fashion.

The basic yield series is available only annually, and so the equations are based on annual data. The annual regressions fit well and predict much better than a "naive model".

Values of the explanatory variables, in contrast to the time deposit yield itself, are all available quarterly. It is possible, therefore, to construct a "calculated" quarterly time deposit yield series and use this calculated series to interpolate between actual annual levels. Such a quarterly series is the time-deposit yield series used in other equations of the model. It is an imperfect substitute for actual data; a monthly or quarterly series measuring the yield in time deposits would be a useful addition to knowledge of financial markets.

A reduced-form equation for the supply of money   The banking system, in adjusting its excess, required and borrowed reserves, translates the "high-powered money" supplied by the Federal Reserve System into supplies of deposits held by the public. The money-supply equations which have appeared in other recent studies [30]) are, in terms of this model, combinations of bank portfolio equations (13.10) and (3.11), a required reserve identity (13.16) and a Federal Reserve open-market identity (13.19). It may be helpful to exhibit the reduced-form money supply equation of the present model by combining these four relationships.

The equation below is a long-run or stock-equilibrium relationship—that is, in combining equations (13.10), (13.11), (13.16), and (13.19), changes in deposits, reserves, loans, excess reserves and bank borrowing have been set equal to zero. A short-run money supply equation would be much more complex than the long-run equation. Even the stock-equilibrium equation

[30]) See Brunner [3] and Teigen [19].

requires some new symbols in addition to the ones defined on p. 480, namely:

S_M = The money supply: private demand deposits, DD, plus currency, $CURR$.

R_{DD} = The ratio of DD to S_M.

R_{DT} = The ratio of DT to S_M.

$R_{DD_{GF}}$ = The ratio of DD_{GF} to S_M.

The stock-equilibrium equation is:

$$S_M = \frac{RES_{NBC}}{1 - R_{DD} + 0.84[RRR_{DD}][R_{DD} + R_{DD_{GF}}] + 0.82[RRR_{DT}][R_{DT}] + [0.011\ RM_{FRB} - 0.010\ RM_{GBS3} - 0.007][R_{DD} + R_{DT}]}.$$

The partial elasticity with respect to RES_{NBC}, the supply of unborrowed reserves plus currency, is one. Partial elasticities with respect to the discount rate and the Treasury bill rate are, respectively:

$$-0.011\ RM_{FRB}\ \frac{[R_{DD} + R_{DT}][S_M]}{RES_{NBC}}$$

and

$$0.010\ RM_{GBS3}\ \frac{[R_{DD} + R_{DT}][S_M]}{RES_{NBC}}.$$

At postwar means, these elasticities are -0.214 and 0.172. At 1962 means, which more nearly reflect present reserve requirement ratios and other variables, the elasticities are -0.348 and 0.245. These calculations all assume no change in R_{DD} and R_{DT} in response to changes in reserves or interest rates; a planned simulation study of the model (pp. 527–529) will trace out its implied money supply responses in the short run as well as the long run and allow R_{DD} and R_{DT} to vary.

13.4.4. The behavior of nonbank financial institutions

The balance sheet of nonbank finance   The nonbank financial sector of the present model covers mutual savings banks, savings and loan associations, insurance companies and pension funds. Other nonbank financial institutions—the "finance n.e.c." subsector of the flow-of-funds accounts—are included with the business portion of "the public".

The aggregate balance sheet of the sector is condensed to the following five categories:

Assets	Liabilities and net worth

U.S. securities
Private securities
  (excluding common
  stock)
	Savings and insurance held
	  by public
	Loans from Home Loan Bank Board
	Other

"Other" includes net worth, miscellaneous liabilities less assets [31]) and any errors and discrepancies necessary to make the two sides of the balance sheet equal. Savings and insurance and Home Loan Bank Board loans are assumed to be given; the institutions determine holdings of private securities and U.S. securities. "Other" is treated as a residual derivable from the balance sheet identity.

A more detailed model would attempt to explain borrowing from the Home Loan Bank Board as a function of FHLB lending rates and other influences instead of treating it as exogenous; the present exogenous treatment simplifies the model without introducing any significant distortion. A more detailed model would also deal with how nonbank financial institutions determine the yield on their liabilities to the public, but because of lack of data, the present model simply assumes that this yield is proportional to a moving average of the yield on commercial bank time deposits.

The sector's total liabilities to the public serves as an indicator of its wealth. The short-run constraint variable for the sector is taken to be changes in these liabilities (that is, the net inflow of savings from the public) plus the net change in Home Loan Bank Board loans [32]). There are three interest rates in the equations; the rate on private securities, the rate on U.S. long-term securities and the Treasury bill rate.

The role of the Treasury bill rate warrants some comment. The nonbank finance sector holds only a small share of its portfolio in short-term U.S. securities. However, the discussion of the term structure equation above set forth the view that movements in the Treasury bill rate may serve as a representation of movements in the expected *total* return—coupon yield plus expected capital gains—on longer term securities. The bill rate will fill this role if market forces succeed in bringing total returns on securities of all

---

[31]) One of these is the common stock held by pension funds. The present model, as noted earlier, does not deal with the stock market.

[32]) An alternative constraint variable would include gross flows of funds—savings plus repayments—instead of net inflows. Lack of data rules out this possibility for the present.

TABLE 13.15

Changes in nonbank finance holdings of U.S. securities: $\Delta BF_{NBF}/[BNBF]_{-1}$.

Equation (13.14) Period and method of estimation	$\dfrac{[BF_{NBF-1}]}{[BNBF]_{-1}}$	$\dfrac{\Delta[BNBF+FHLB]}{[BNBF]_{-1}}$	$\dfrac{1}{4}\sum_{i=1}^{4}\dfrac{\Delta[BNBF+FHLB]_{-i}}{[BNBF]_{-i-1}}$	RM_{PSEC}	RM_{GBL}	RM_{GBS3}	Constant term	R^2	Standard error	Durbin-Watson ratio
A. 1952–1960										
(1) OLS unrestricted	−0.002 (0.007)	0.755 (0.197)	−0.392 (0.139)	−0.0029 (0.0019)	0.0049 (0.0018)	0.0004 (0.0003)	−0.0111	0.77	0.00081	
(2) OLS, one restriction [a]	−0.014 (0.006)	0.685 (0.214)	−0.539 (0.140)	−0.0048 (0.002)	0.0048 (0.002)	0.0010 (0.0002)	0.0043	0.71	0.00090	1.02
(3) OLS, two restrictions [a]	−0.016 (0.005)	0.736 (0.157)	−0.487 (0.121)	−0.0033 (0.0012)	0.0033 (0.0012)	0.00075 (0.00002)	0.00067	0.69	0.00101	0.96
(4) TSLS, one restriction [a]	−0.017 (0.099)	0.614 (0.486)	−0.372 (0.200)	−0.0045 (0.0048)	0.0045 (0.0048)	0.00084 (0.00039)	0.00280	0.70	0.00094	
(5) TSLS, two restrictions [a]	−0.019 (0.007)	0.701 (0.294)	−0.353 (0.150)	−0.0027 (0.0027)	0.0027 (0.0027)	0.00064 (0.00022)	−0.00169	0.66	0.00106	
B. 1952–1962										
(6) OLS, two restrictions [a]	−0.009 (0.005)	0.623 (0.142)	−0.462 (0.113)	−0.00257 (0.00100)	0.00257 (0.00100)	0.00074 (0.00014)	0.00001			
(7) TSLS, two restrictions [a]	−0.011 (0.006)	0.544 (0.258)	−0.337 (0.138)	−0.00245 (0.00191)	0.00245 (0.00191)	0.00061 (0.00020)	−0.00047	0.61	0.00097	

Note   A list of variables appears on pp. 480–482.

[a]) The restrictions referred to in the table are discussed on pp. 522–523.

TABLE 13.16

Changes in nonbank finance holdings of private securities: $\Delta APS_{NBF}/[BNBF]_{-1}$.

Equation (13.15) Period and method of estimation	$\dfrac{[APS_{NBF}]_{-1}}{[BNBF]_{-1}}$	$\dfrac{\Delta[BNBF+FHLB]}{[BNBF]_{-1}}$	$\dfrac{1}{4}\sum_{i=1}^{4}\dfrac{\Delta[BNBF+FHLB]_{-i}}{[BNBF]_{-i-1}}$	RM_{PSEC}	RM_{GBL}	RM_{GBS3}	Constant term	R^2	Standard error	Durbin-Watson ratio
A. 1952-1960										
(1) OLS, unrestricted	-0.012 (0.004)	0.465 (0.114)	0.460 (0.080)	-0.00008 (0.00111)	-0.00178 (0.00102)	0.00012 (0.00019)	0.0197	0.98	0.00046	
(2) OLS, one restriction [a]	-0.022 (0.004)	0.531 (0.144)	0.625 (0.090)	0.00175	-0.00175 (0.00131)	-0.00047 (0.00016)	0.0160	0.96	0.00060	0.88
(3) OLS, two restrictions [a]	-0.020 (0.006)	0.580 (0.159)	0.668 (0.116)	0.00327	-0.00327 (0.00122)	-0.00075 (0.00002)	0.00994	0.95	0.00071	0.88
(4) TSLS, one restriction [a]	-0.020 (0.005)	0.550 (0.241)	0.622 (0.096)	0.00094	-0.00094 (0.00237)	-0.00044 (0.00019)	0.01477	0.96	0.00060	
(5) TSLS, two restrictions [a]	-0.018 (0.008)	0.634 (0.295)	0.636 (0.145)	0.00273	-0.00273 (0.00268)	-0.00064 (0.00022)	0.00899	0.96	0.00069	
B. 1952-1962										
(6) OLS, two restrictions [a]	-0.021 (0.005)	0.517 (0.144)	0.682 (0.107)	0.00257	-0.00257 (0.00100)	-0.00074 (0.00014)	0.01328			
(7) TSLS, two restrictions [a]	-0.021 (0.007)	0.583 (0.262)	0.658 (0.133)	0.00245	-0.00245 (0.00191)	-0.00061 (0.00020)	0.01194	0.97	0.00058	

Note   A list of variables appears on pp. 480-482.

[a]) The restrictions referred to in the table are discussed on pp. 522-523.

maturities into rough equality (or into equality when corrected for possible "liquidity premiums"). The concept of total return is presumably more important for U.S. securities than for private securities.

The equations   According to the basic framework of the model, nonbank finance holdings of U.S. securities should depend negatively on the lagged stock, positively on the U.S. long-term rate and the bill rate, negatively on the rate on private securities and positively on the current inflow of savings and Home Loan Bank Board advances. For private security holdings, the expected signs are the opposite for interest rate coefficients and the same for other coefficients. Lagged savings and Home Loan Bank Board inflows may also influence holdings, either positively or negatively.

Tables 13.15 and 13.16 confirm these expectations with minor exceptions. The lagged saving-plus-FHLB-loans variable in the equations is an average of values for the four preceding quarters; this form added more to the over-all fit than a simple one-quarter lag. The coefficient of the lagged constraint is positive for private securities and negative for U.S. securities, suggesting that private security holdings depend on a weighted average of recent savings inflows, while U.S. security holdings depend on recent *changes* in savings inflows as well as on current levels.

The final equations and most of the regressions in the tables impose certain restrictions on the interest rate coefficients. Without any restrictions, multicollinearity produces high standard errors for many coefficients (equation (1) in the two tables).

The restrictions are of two kinds. The first is the restriction that coefficients of the U. S. long-term security rate and the private security rate be equal in magnitude (and of course opposite in sign) in each of the two equations [33]). The justification for this restriction is that U.S. and private securities account for nearly all of the assets of nonbank finance institutions, and therefore the differential roughly measures the yield on one asset compared with the yield on alternative assets. The restriction implies that the proportion of savings invested in private securities will be the same if the two rates are, say, 6 and 4 per cent, as they will be if the rates are 5 and 3 per cent.

The second restriction is that interest rate coefficients be of equal magni-

---

[33]) To impose this restriction, the two separate interest rate variables are replaced by one variable, the difference between the two.

tude and opposite sign as between the two equations [34]). The first restriction refers to coefficients within each equation; the second, to coefficients between the two equations. The justification for the second restriction is again that these two assets account for the great bulk of total assets, and so a decline in the proportion of funds invested in one must mean a rise in the proportion invested in the other. The restriction implies that if a given change in interest rates on private and U.S. securities causes the private security share to rise by 1 per cent it also causes the U.S. security share to fall by 1 per cent.

These restrictions would be much less plausible if there were many other assets in nonbank finance portfolios. They are more plausible if the Treasury bill rate is thought of as the rate of return including expected capital gains on securities generally than if the bill rate serves as a representation of the yield of a separate asset in the sector's portfolio.

The results of applying these restrictions appear in equations (2) to (7) of tables 13.15 and 13.16. They do improve the significance measures for many coefficients, though in the final equations the coefficient for the rate differential is only slightly above its standard error.

Two features of the nonbank finance equations are somewhat disappointing. One is the extremely slow speed of adjustment implied by the lagged stock coefficients. Surely information lags cannot be of any importance for this sector, and it seems unlikely that decision making is so slow or transactions costs and other frictions so high that the sector reduces by only 2 per cent per quarter the gap between "desired" and actual stocks. The second disappointing feature of the equations is high serial correlation in the residuals. Taken together, the two features suggest that further empirical exploration of the behavior of the nonbank finance sector may suggest some alterations in the present equations.

---

[34]) The procedure for imposing this restriction is as follows: Suppose we specify that

$$(1) \quad y_{1t} = a_1 + b_{11} x_{1t} + b_{12} x_{2t} + u_{1t}$$

$$(2) \quad y_{2t} = a_2 + b_{21} x_{1t} + b_{22} x_{2t} + u_{2t}$$

$$(3) \quad b_{11} = -b_{21}.$$

Let Y_1, X_2, etc., represent column vectors of y_{1t}, x_{1t}, etc., over n observations. Then estimate the coefficients of

$$\begin{bmatrix} Y_1 \\ Y_2 \end{bmatrix} = a_2 + \begin{bmatrix} X_1 \\ -X_1 \end{bmatrix} b_{11} + \begin{bmatrix} X_2 \\ 0 \end{bmatrix} b_{12} + \begin{bmatrix} 0 \\ X_2 \end{bmatrix} b_{22} + \begin{bmatrix} 1 \\ 0 \end{bmatrix} (a_1 - a_2) + \begin{bmatrix} U_1 \\ U_2 \end{bmatrix}$$

by least squares. The vector [1/0] is a column of n ones followed by n zeros which allows the constant terms to differ in the two equations.

13.4.5. The four identities

In addition to fifteen behavioral equations, the financial model contains four identities (13.16) through (13.19). Two of these describe portfolio changes by the Federal Reserve System and by the Treasury. A third describes the relationship of required reserves to demand and time deposits. The final identity is a market-clearing equation for private securities; total borrowing by the public (and the rest of the world) from financial institutions equals total lending to the public by financial institutions. The last two identities are already familiar.

The Federal Reserve identity (13.19) is one of the central equations of the model, but it has a number of alternative forms. The present model defines as an exogenous variable currency plus unborrowed reserves. Alternative forms would define total reserves, total reserves plus currency or free reserves as exogenous. Simulation of the model under alternative forms might throw some light on the differences between alternative open-market targets.

None of these alternative formulations defines a magnitude which the Federal Reserve System controls completely. Factors which affect reserves and currency include not only open-market purchases and sales but also gold movements, Treasury cash, float and other items which sometimes change unexpectedly in the short run. Offsetting these unexpected movements is one of the tasks of Federal Reserve policy, but it is a task which the System can perform accurately enough on a quarterly basis, and so its intricacies need not complicate the present model.

The remaining identity in the model (13.18) states that the total (domestically held) federal debt less Federal Reserve holdings (unborrowed reserves plus currency less gold stock) equals household plus business plus banking plus nonbank finance holdings of U.S. securities. Changes in the federal debt as measured in this equation are fairly close to the "consolidated cash deficit" of the U.S. Treasury.

13.5. Tests and simulation plans

This section presents the results of two kinds of tests, one referring to individual equations and the second to the model as a whole. After the description of the tests there is a brief account of plans to examine the empirical implications of the complete set of financial equations through a simulation study.

TABLE 13.17

Prediction errors 1961–1962.

	Standard error through 1960	Root-mean-square error, 1961–1962		
		Original equation	"Naive model"	Re-estimated equation
Nonfinancial public				
Currency holdings	0.032	0.066	0.035	0.026 [a])
Demand deposit holdings	0.133	0.390	0.140	0.099 [a])
Time deposit holdings	0.078	0.251	0.433	0.122 [b])
Savings and insurance	0.026	0.042	0.132	0.035 [c])
U.S. securities-households	0.102	0.342	0.218	0.115 [b])
U.S. securities-business	0.155	0.278	0.095	0.097 [c])
Borrowing-households	0.069	0.177	0.125	0.086 [a])
Term structure relationship	0.360	0.230	0.430	0.290 [c])
Commercial banks				
U.S. security holdings	0.307	0.354	0.801	0.311 [c])
Borrowing from Fed. Reserve	0.071	0.097	0.017	0.024 [a])
Excess reserves	0.020	0.022	0.012	0.013 [c])
Rate on private securities	0.065	0.085	0.114	0.073 [a])
Rate on time deposits	0.050	0.120	0.330	0.0 [c])
Nonbank finance				
U.S. security holdings	0.106	0.166	0.097	0.067 [c])
Private security holdings	0.069	0.054	0.362	0.038 [c])

ote All entries except term structure, rate on private securities and rate on time deposits have
en multiplied by 100.

he final column refers to equations refitted including 1961–1962 data. Entries marked:

[a]) indicate a major change in variables;

[b]) indicate a minor change in variables;

[c]) refer to relationships refitted with no change in variables.

For the equation for the yield on time deposits, the original regression is based on annual data through
61, and the predictions refer to the 1961–1962 change.

13.5.1. *Test of individual equations against 1961–1962*

Predictions of 1961–1962 from the two-stage least-squares regressions fit
through 1960 are a mixture of successes and failures. Not surprisingly,
prediction errors in almost all cases are greater than the standard errors
of the regression equations through 1960. Some predictions are far better
than "naive" extrapolation of the postwar average rate of growth of stocks,
while some are decidedly worse. The results of the 1961–1962 tests appear
in table 13.17.

The first two columns of the table list standard errors of the final two-stage least-squares regression fit through 1960 and root-mean-square prediction errors [35]) of these regressions for the quarters of 1961 and 1962. The expected value of the prediction errors is greater than the standard errors, and in all but one equation the prediction error is in fact greater. In 8 of the equations, the prediction error is more than 50 per cent greater; in the remainder, less.

The next column of the table presents root-mean-square errors based on a "naive" extrapolation procedure for 1961–1962. The naive procedure is to assume that stocks (divided by "wealth") or interest rates—whichever is the dependent variable in a particular equation—change at their average postwar rates during 1961–1962 [36]). In 8 of the equations, "naive model" projections were superior to predictions based on two-stage least-squares equations through 1960; in 7 of the equations, the equations through 1960 were better.

These comparisons provide a standard for evaluating the model, but in themselves they do not provide much indication of how useful the model is as a tool of current analysis. If the model had been used as a tool of current analysis during 1961 and 1962, difficulties with particular equations would soon have been apparent and some re-estimation or at least rough correction would have been undertaken. On the other hand, the same would be true of the naive models, had they been a basis for current analysis during the period. The results of table 13.13 refer only to an unchanging mechanical application of the model in this paper on the one hand and a naive model on the other.

The final column of the table refers to 1961–1962 root-mean-square errors for the fifteen relationships after fitting them to data including the quarters of 1961 and 1962. These errors refer to the final equations of the model, as listed on pp. 476–479 and discussed in section 13.4.

13.5.2. A test relating to the complete model, 1955–1962

The second test of the model is not a prediction test, since it is based on the final equations of the model during eight of the years to which they were fitted.

---

[35]) The root-mean-square error for n observation is the square root of the average of the n squared errors.

[36]) There is one exception to this procedure, namely, the term structure relationship where the dependent variable is an interest rate differential rather than changes in a stock or an interest rate. The "naive model" for this equation is to assume that the differential in 1961–1962 equals the 1952–1960 average differential.

It is a test of whether the errors in individual equations tend to offset or to cumulate in the model as a whole.

The test begins with actual predetermined variables as of the first quarter of 1955 and solves the complete model simultaneously to get calculated values of the 19 endogenous variables for that quarter. It then uses these calculated values in place of actual endogenous variables wherever there are one-quarter lags in solving for the second quarter of 1955. It continues to use actual nonfinancial and exogenous financial variables. For the third quarter of 1955 the solution is based on calculated instead of actual endogenous variables wherever there are one-quarter or two-quarter lags, and so forth through the last quarter of 1962.

The procedure differs from finding "calculated" values for individual equations in two respects: (i) the model is solved simultaneously; and (ii) estimated rather than actual values are used for lagged endogenous variables. These differences permit the errors in individual equations to combine with one another, both across equations and over time. They make it possible for actual and calculated values of an endogenous variable to drift apart or to show other systematic discrepancies not present in the separate regressions.

The present model stands up fairly well under this test. As figure 13.4 demonstrates for six major variables or groupings, most general levels, turning-points and amplitudes of fluctuation are close for actual and calculated series. The main exceptions to this close correspondence are: the levels of actual and calculated nonfinancial debt series drift apart after 1958; in 1961 and 1962 there is a minor cycle in "calculated" bill rate and bank borrowing series in contrast to actual stability; and accompanying this extra cycle is a series of discrepancies between actual and calculated holdings of U.S. securities. All of these exceptions occur after four or five years of close correspondence, suggesting that the model may be more useful for analyzing short-run changes than long-run developments.

13.5.3. Simulation plans

The nineteen financial equations as a whole can provide quantitative answers—accurate or inaccurate—to many questions about the effects of monetary policies and nonfinancial developments on credit markets. The equations do not deal with the effects of credit market developments on other markets and thus they do not by themselves have anything to say about the effects of monetary or debt management policies on aggregate income, employment, prices or foreign transactions. What they do deal with are the

effects of policy changes and of income and expenditure variations on interest
rates, money holdings and household and business debt.

The reader interested in the empirical implications of the financial model

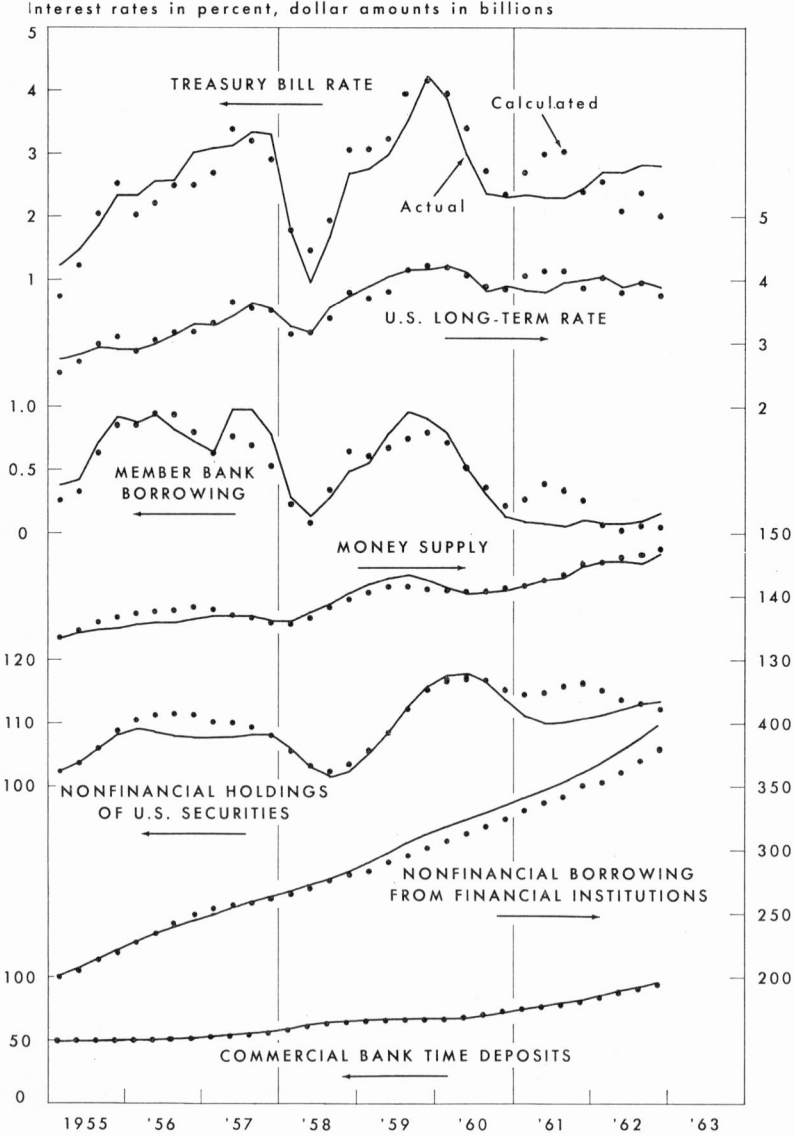

Figure 13.4. Calculated values based on simultaneous estimation, 1955–1962.

is referred to a sequel to the present study which describes a set of simulations of the model designed to show its estimates of the effects of policy changes and of nonfinancial changes on credit markets [37]). The simulations deal with the effects over time of hypothetical changes in bank reserves and currency, reserve requirements, the discount rate and levels of aggregate income and expenditure—always abstracting from the effects of credit market variables on expenditures or incomes. Space does not permit treatment of any of these matters in the present chapter.

Whether these simulations add up to a reasonably accurate portrayal of the way in which credit markets operate is highly conjectural. The simulations tell a good deal about the implications of the final equations and may well suggest useful directions for further work. It is worth repeating once more in closing that the final behavioral equations are no more than a set of empirical explorations and that further thought and testing may lead to substantial changes in the model.

REFERENCES

1. BAUMOL, WILLIAM J. Stocks, Flows and Monetary Theory, *Quarterly Journal of Economics* (February, 1962) 44–56.
2. BROWN, MURRAY, and FRIEND, IRWIN. "The Effects of Monetary Policies on Non-monetary Financial Institutions and Capital Markets." Unpublished paper prepared for Commission on Money and Credit, 1961.
3. BRUNNER, KARL. A Schema for the Supply Theory of Money, *International Economic Review* (January, 1961) 79–109.
4. BRUNNER, KARL, and MELTZER, ALLAN. Predicting Velocity: Implications for Theory and Policy, *Journal of Finance* (May, 1963) 319–354.
5. CHRIST, CARL. Interest Rates and Portfolio Selection Among Liquid Assets in the U. S., in *Measurement in Economics: Studies in Mathematical Economics and Econometrics in memory of Yehuda Grunfeld*. Stanford, Calif.: Stanford University Press, 1963.
6. CONARD, JOSEPH. *An Introduction to the Theory of Interest*. (University of California Bureau of Business and Economic Research Publication.) Berkeley: University of California Press, 1959.
7. DUESENBERRY, JAMES. Business Cycles and Economic Growth. New York: McGraw-Hill, 1958.
8. DUESENBERRY, JAMES. The Portfolio Approach to the Demand for Money and Other Assets, *Review of Economics and Statistics* (February, 1963), supplement, pp. 9–31.
9. FRIEDMAN, MILTON (ed.). *Studies in the Quantity Theory of Money*. Chicago: University of Chicago Press, 1956.

------

[37]) The sequel was presented at the December, 1963 meetings of the American Economic Association and appeared in the *American Economic Review* 54 (May, 1964) 309–323.

10. FRIEDMAN, MILTON. *A Theory of the Consumption Function.* (National Bureau of Economic Research.) Princeton, N. J.: Princeton University Press, 1957.
11. GRILICHES, ZVI. A Note on Serial Correlation Bias in Estimates of Distributed Lags *Econometrica* 29 (January, 1961) 65–73.
12. HARBERGER, ARNOLD (ed.). *The Demand for Durable Goods.* Chicago: University of Chicago Press, 1960.
13. JOHNSON, HARRY. Monetary Theory and Policy, *American Economic Review* (June, 1962) 335–384.
14. KEYNES, JOHN MAYNARD. *The General Theory of Employment, Interest and Money.* New York: Harcourt Brace and Co., 1936.
15. MEIGS, A. JAMES. *Free Reserves and the Money Supply.* Chicago: University of Chicago Press, 1962.
16. MEISELMAN, DAVID. *The Term Structure of Interest Rates.* Englewood Cliffs, N. J.: Prentice-Hall, 1962.
17. MELTZER, ALLAN H. The Demand for Money: The Evidence from Time Series, *Journal of Political Economy* (June, 1963) 219–246.
18. MORRISON, GEORGE. "Liquidity Preference of Commercial Banks." Unpublished Ph. D. dissertation, University of Chicago, 1962.
19. TEIGEN, R. L. "Demand and Supply Functions for Money in the United States". Paper presented at the December 1962 meetings of the Econometric Society. (Unpublished.)
20. TOBIN, JAMES. Liquidity Preference as Behavior Toward Risk, *Review of Economic Studies* (February, 1958) 65–86.
21. TOBIN JAMES. The Interest-Elasticity of Transactions Demand for Cash, *Review of Economics and Statistics* (August, 1956) 241–247.
22. WOOD, JOHN H. "The Term Structure of Interest Rates: A Theoretical and Empirical Study." Unpublished Ph. D. dissertation, Purdue University, 1962.

CHAPTER 14

GOVERNMENT REVENUES AND EXPENDITURES

Contents

14.1. Introduction 533

14.2. Government revenues 534
  1. Federal revenues: personal tax and nontax receipts; corporate profits tax accruals; indirect business tax and nontax accruals; contributions for social insurance. 2. State and local revenues: personal tax and nontax receipts; corporate profits tax accruals; indirect business tax and nontax accruals; contributions for social insurance.

14.3. Government expenditures 561
  1. Transfer payments: federal government; state and local governments. 2. Purchases of goods and services: federal government; state and local governments.

GOVERNMENT REVENUES AND EXPENDITURES [1])

ALBERT ANDO

University of Pennsylvania, Philadelphia, Pennsylvania

E. CARY BROWN

Massachusetts Institute of Technology, Cambridge, Massachusetts

and

EARL W. ADAMS, Jr.

Amherst College, Amherst, Massachusetts

14.1. Introduction

Government revenues and expenditures result from forces exogenous to an economic model, such as national defense requirements; from policy variables controllable by legislatures, such as tax rates or particular expenditure programs; and from endogenous forces, such as changes in unemployment, national income and consumption, which alter the amounts of actual revenues and expenditures resulting from given fiscal programs.

In economic models of moderate size, government purchases are ordinarily treated as exogenous, while taxes and transfers are dealt with in fairly aggregated form and explained by simple relationships, say, to income. We have attempted in this study to disaggregate as much as possible—to go as far as we can in explaining government revenues and expenditures by endogenous variables and fiscal-policy variables over which the government has control.

[1]) We acknowledge the assistance of M. Burton, Miss S. B. Foster, F. S. Levy, W. H. Oakland, S. A. Resnick, R. L. Teigen and Mrs. C. H. Wegman. We are indebted to the staff members of the Office of Business Economics, the U.S. Department of Commerce, particularly to Mr. Charles W. Walton and Mrs. Lillian P. Barnes of the National Income Division, for their valuable assistance in our adjustments of data used in this paper. Helpful comments by Professor Edwin Kuh of the Massachusetts Institute of Technology, Professor Lawrence Klein of the University of Pennsylvania, and Mr. Thomas Smith of the U. S. Department of Treasury, are gratefully acknowledged.

As will be seen from the results obtained, we have had to stop far short of complete disaggregation, because of both time and data limitations. It would be a monumental undertaking to explain expenditures and revenues of every governmental unit or even of every state. The diversity of excise taxes and other sources of revenue imposed severe restrictions on the detail of our inquiry. Important revenues and expenditures were given more attention than the smaller ones, and some groupings were forced on us because of lack of detail in the underlying data.

Government receipts and expenditures can be categorized in a variety of ways. Because of the over-all decision to construct the model within the framework of the national income statistics of the U.S. Department of Commerce, we have decided to follow the same classification as that used in *Income and Output* [2]), with some elaborations and modifications. The general scheme of the classification of receipts and expenditures is shown in table 14.1. In the rest of this chapter we shall discuss briefly why each of these items is or is not explained, present our preliminary statistical results, and indicate why we have adopted the specific statistical form used in our analysis.

14.2. *Government revenues*

The time pattern of government tax revenues at the federal, state and local levels depends not only on the law covering revenue liabilities but also on the administrative arrangements under which these revenues are collected and reported. These will be discussed in connection with individual revenue items.

Our general approach has been to use independent variables as closely related to the actual tax base as existing data will permit, leaving as a second and distinct step the task of relating such independent variables to other variables generated by the complete model. Tax-rate changes have been allowed for as far as possible. In some cases this has necessitated the creation of tax-rate indices which may not always capture accurately the precise effects of a rate change. However, because of the high correlation between income and rate changes in the postwar period, the absence of some rate variable in explanatory equations would lead to an unreasonably high estimate of the elasticity of tax receipts with respect to income. Introduction

---

[2]) U.S. Department of Commerce, Office of Business Economics, *U.S. Income and Output*, tables III-1 and III-2, 1958.

TABLE 14.1

Government revenues and expenditures (millions of 1960 dollars).

Item	Magnitudes for calendar year 1960
14.2 Government revenues	140 630
14.2.1. Federal revenues	96 560
(A) Personal tax and nontax receipts	44 043
(Income taxes [a])	46 602)
(Estate and gift taxes [a])	1 782)
(Nontaxes [a])	70)
(Refunds [a])	4 411)
(B) Corporate profits tax accruals	20 967
(C) Indirect business tax and nontax accruals	13 953
(1) Tobacco	1 859
(2) Alcoholic beverages	3 106
(3) Gasoline and lubricating oils	2 434
(4) Tires and tubes	299
(5) Motor vehicles and parts	1 874
(6) Transportation of persons	261
(7) Telephone and telegraph	761
(8) Electric, gas and oil appliances	124
(9) (All other excise taxes [a])	1 531)
(Customs duties [a])	1 079)
(Nontaxes [a])	851)
(Refunds [a])	226)
(D) Contributions for social insurance (Employer, employee, and self-employed persons contributions combined)	17 597
(1) Old age and survivors insurance	11 997
(2) State unemployment insurance	2 313
(Federal unemployment tax [a])	358)
(3) Railroad retirement	590
(4) Railroad unemployment insurance	165
(5) Civilian employee retirement systems	1 615
(Government life insurance [a])	559)
14.2.2. State and local revenues (Excluding federal grants-in-aid)	44 070
(A) Personal tax and nontax receipts	7 343
(1) Income taxes	2 696
(2) Other personal taxes and nontaxes (Including death and gift taxes, motor vehicle licenses, personal property taxes, other taxes, and nontaxes)	4 647

TABLE 14.1 (Continued)

Item	Magnitudes for calendar year 1960
(B) Corporate profits tax accruals	1 285
(C) Indirect business tax and nontax accruals	32 468
(1) Indirect business taxes other than property (Including sales taxes, motor vehicle licenses, other taxes and nontaxes)	16 399
(2) Property taxes	16 069
(D) Contributions for social insurance (Including state and local employee retirement systems and cash sickness compensation funds)	2 974
14.3 Government expenditures	136 784
14.3.1. Transfer payments	28 850
(A) Federal government	23 803
(1) Old age and survivors insurance benefits	11 130
(2) Other retirement and disability programs	3 991
(a) Railroad	714
(b) Civil Service	705
(c) Veterans	2 572
(3) Other survivors programs	1 237
(a) Veterans	865
(b) All other	372
(4) Unemployment compensation benefits	2 952
(a) State laws	2 729
(b) Veterans	[b])
(c) Railroad	223
(5) (Other transfer payments to persons [a])	2 837)
(Foreign transfer payments [a])	1 563)
(B) State and local government	5 045
(1) Public assistance	3 697
(a) Old age assistance	1 935
(b) Aid to dependent children	1 062
(c) Aid to the blind and aid to the permanently and totally disabled	380
(d) General assistance	320
(2) Other transfer payments	1 348
14.3.2. Purchases of goods and services	99 616
(A) Federal government	53 131
(1) Wages and salaries (Supplements are included in 14.3.2. (A) (3) below)	19 901
Civilian wages and salaries	10 007

TABLE 14.1 (Continued)

Item	Magnitudes for calendar year 1960
(Military wages and salaries – combined with 14.3.2. (A) (3) below [a]))	9 894)
(2) New construction	3 665
(a) Military and industrial facilities	1 868
(b) Conservation and development	1 050
(c) All other construction	747
(3) All other purchases of goods and services	30 145
(Government sales – combined with 14.3.2. (A) (3) above [a]))	580)
(B) State and local governments	46 485
(1) Wages and salaries (Supplements are included in 14.3.2. (B) (3) below)	23 574
(a) School	11 852
(b) Nonschool	11 722
(2) New construction	12 288
(a) Residential (Included in 14.3.2. (B) (3) below [a])	428)
(b) Nonresidential	3 979
(i) Educational	2 799
(ii) Hospital	265
(iii) Administrative and service facilities	456
(Other nonresidential construction included in 14.3.2. (B) (2) (e) below [a])	459)
(c) Highways	5 400
(d) Sewer and water systems	1 487
(e) All other construction	994
(3) All other purchases of goods and services	10 623
(Net interest paid [a])	7 761)
(Subsidies less current surplus of government enterprises [a])	521)
(Federal grants-in-aid to state and local governments [a])	6 301)

[a]) Items shown in parentheses are not explicitly and separately considered in the text.
[b]) Less than $ 1 million.

of some rate variable, even a crude proxy, reduces significantly the increase in tax yields that would have been attributed to income alone.

To ensure consistency throughout the model, the bench marks chosen have been the concepts and data, seasonally adjusted, of the Office of Business Economics (OBE), Department of Commerce. The methods by which OBE converts financial reports of government agencies into time series conforming to the national income framework are of crucial importance for determining the form of the explanatory equations reported below for each item. In particular, we have found that the way in which they make their seasonal adjustments often caused serious difficulties in our analysis.

The presentation of our results follows the OBE quarterly classification: first federal government, then state and local government. The major subdivisions are (1) personal tax and nontax receipts, (2) corporate profits tax accruals, (3) indirect business tax and nontax accruals and (4) contributions for social insurance.

14.2.1. Federal revenues

(A) *Personal tax and nontax receipts*

Personal tax receipts [3]) in the national income statistics published by OBE are not consistently based on either liabilities or collections [4]). Their procedures in estimating these revenues are not entirely satisfactory in our view and, in particular, lead to sharp steps from the fourth quarter to the first quarter of the following year through most of the period covered by our analysis. The relations we estimate below will, therefore, necessarily contain errors, and we cannot be sure whether the inadequacy lies with the model tested or the data.

We shall follow the breakdown of the tax between a withheld and non-withheld portion. The withheld part may be approximated by the relation: [5])

$$\ln TPW_{GF} = \alpha_0 + \alpha_1 \ln R_{PY1_{GF}} + \alpha_2 \ln WS + \varepsilon.$$

Greater precision could be achieved if personal exemptions were also included. However, during this period the exemptions remained at $ 600

---

[3]) In the national income statistics of OBE, quarterly figures on the personal income tax are not given separately. We have, therefore, dealt with quarterly figures called "personal tax and nontax receipts", which include, in addition to the personal income tax, estate and gift tax and nontax receipts.

[4]) For a detailed explanation and criticism of their procedures, see Wilfred Lewis, Jr., *Federal Fiscal Policy in the Postwar Recessions* (Washington, D. C.: Brookings Institution, 1961), especially chap. II and appendix B.

[5]) The OBE method of shifting back withholding receipts one quarter, however, means that what is called withholding in any quarter is in reality partly withholding in that quarter and partly withholding of the following quarter. Were interest and dividends also withheld, they would be included as are wages at the appropriate withholding rate.

per person, and the population has grown at a reasonably steady rate, so we have omitted it in the interest of simplicity.

The nonwithheld part of the personal income tax is more difficult to deal with. It consists of three parts: quarterly installments final payments, and refunds.

Quarterly installments are the least tractable items among the components of federal personal income tax payments. We shall work here with the simplest possible hypothesis, namely, that for the purposes of the first three installments, individuals base their estimates of income tax liabilities and withholding in the current year on those of the preceding year, except possibly to take account of tax-rate changes. Thus,

$$TPQI_{GF} \approx \alpha_3 [R_{PY1_{GF}}^A]_{-1}^{n_1} [Y_P^A - V^A - Y_{OL}^A]_{-1}^{n_2} + \alpha_4 [R_{PY1_{GF}}^A]^{n_3} [Y_P^A - V^A - Y_{OL}^A]_{-1}^{n_4}.$$

The final payment less refund in calendar year t should be equal to the total tax liability accrued in year $t-1$, minus withholding and quarterly installments made on account of the tax liability accrued in year $t-1$. In addition, farmers do not have to pay their first installment for year $t-1$ until January of year t, and this is a part of the item "final payment" in this context. Thus, it appears reasonable to suppose that the following relation will approximately hold:

$$TPF_{GF} \approx \alpha_5 [R_{PY1_{GF}}^A]_{-1}^{n_5} [Y_P^A - V^A - Y_{OL}^A]_{-1}^{n_6} - [TPW_{GF}^A]_{-1} - [TPQI_{GF}]_{-1}.$$

$[TPW_{GF}^A]_{-1}$ is defined as total withholding collections in March of year $t-1$ through February of year t.

The total tax payment, as defined by OBE, is then given by

$$TP_{GF} = TPW_{GF} + TPF_{GF} + TPQI_{GF},$$

where everything is measured at annual rates. The above equation, when the equations for the three components are substituted into it, is hopelessly nonlinear in its parameters and would be exceedingly difficult to estimate. We shall therefore use the following approximation [6]):

$$TP_{GF} = \beta_0 + \beta_1 \{ [R_{PY1_{GF}}][WS] \} + \beta_2 [WS] + \beta_3 \{ [R_{PY1_{GF}}^A]_{-1} [Y_P^A - V^A - Y_{OL}^A]_{-1} \}$$
$$+ \beta_4 \{ [R_{PY1_{GF}}^A][Y_P^A - V^A - Y_{OL}^A]_{-1} \} + \beta_5 [Y_P^A - V^A - Y_{OL}^A]_{-1}$$
$$+ \beta_6 [TPW_{GF}^A]_{-1} + \varepsilon.$$

---

[6]) We use as an approximation:

$$\gamma_0 R^{\gamma_1} Y^{\gamma_2} \approx \xi_1 RY + \xi_2 Y + \xi_0,$$

where R is the rate variable and Y is the tax base.

All series have very strong trends and high multicollinearity. Simple correlations between all pairs of variables are over 0.95. We have, therefore, estimated the above equation using the data in the first difference form. The least-squares regression estimate of the above equation for the period 1948:2 through 1961:4 is:

$$\Delta TP_{GF} = \frac{0.534}{(0.106)} \Delta\{[R_{PY1GF}][WS]\} + \frac{0.100}{(0.046)} \Delta WS$$

$$+ \frac{0.007}{(0.114)} \Delta\{[R^A_{PY1GF}]_{-1}[Y^A_P - V^A - Y^A_{OL}]_{-1}\}$$

$$+ \frac{0.003}{(0.006)} \Delta\{[R^A_{PY1GF}][Y^A_P - V^A - Y^A_{OL}]_{-1}\}$$

$$+ \frac{0.003}{(0.007)} \Delta[Y^A_P - V^A - Y^A_{OL}]_{-1} + \frac{0.183}{(0.287)} \Delta[TPW^A_{GF}]_{-1} - \frac{0.394}{(0.265)}$$

$$\bar{R}^2 = 0.65. \tag{14.1}$$

The standard errors of many of the coefficients are very large, and it is clear that because of the multicollinearity we cannot expect to get useful information using as many independent variables as we have in the above equation.

We have therefore dropped some of the variables and added others. Specifically, because of the OBE seasonal adjustment, the first quarter of most years was substantially larger than the predicted value, and so we have added a variable for changes in income [7]). In addition, realized capital gains and losses have been added to the relationship because their behavior does not always follow personal income. Moreover, because the first four months of 1948 were withheld at a higher rate than that used in computing final liabilities, there were abnormally high refunds in 1949:1; a dummy variable was added for that quarter. Despite these additions, the error in the first quarter of 1951 is still extremely large, and the only way this could be handled was by using a dummy variable. Its abnormality may be attributable to the sharp rise in incomes coupled with unexpected rises in tax rates

---

[7]) That is, the difference of income multiplied by the rate in the first quarter of a given year from the same variable in the first quarter of the previous year.

following the Korean War. The results of these adjustments are given below [8]):

$$\Delta TP_{GF} = \frac{0.599}{(0.046)} \Delta\{[R_{PY1_{GF}}][WS]\} + \frac{0.107}{(0.046)} \{[Y_P - V - Y_{OL}]^{Q1}[R^A_{PY1_{GF}}]$$

$$-[Y_P - V - Y_{OL}]^{Q1}_{-1}[R^A_{PY1_{GF}}]_{-1}\} - \frac{1.737}{(0.479)} DMY2 + \frac{2.316}{(0.549)} DMY3$$

$$+0.877\Delta KGAIN$$

$$\bar{R}^2 = 0.85 \qquad VN = 2.11. \tag{14.2}$$

The variables in order of appearance are:

TPW_{GF} = withholding income tax receipts of the federal government, billions of dollars

$R_{PY1_{GF}}$ = starting federal tax rate on wages and salaries, fraction [9])

WS = wage and salary disbursements, billions of dollars

$TPQI_{GF}$ = federal income tax receipts from first three quarterly installments, billions of dollars

Y_P = personal income, billions of dollars

V = transfer payments to persons, billions of dollars

Y_{OL} = other labor income, billions of dollars

TPF_{GF} = final federal income tax payments plus the fourth-quarter installment in January less refunds, billions of dollars

---

[8]) Because capital gains realized may be difficult to estimate, the equation without the last variable becomes:

$$\Delta TP_{GF} = \frac{0.646}{(0.056)} \Delta\{[R_{PY1_{GF}}][WS]\} + \frac{0.112}{(0.057)} \{[Y_P - V - Y_{OL}]^{Q1}[R^A_{PY1_{GF}}]$$

$$-[Y_P - V - Y_{OL}]^{Q1}_{-1}[R_{PY1_{GF}}]_{-1}\} - \frac{1.747}{(0.595)} DMY2 + \frac{3.357}{(0.636)} DMY3$$

$$\bar{R}^2 = 0.75 \qquad VN = 1.9.$$

[9]) Throughout this section, we approximate the movement of the effective average rate of tax by the starting rate. We feel that this is a necessary approximation, since the computation needed to obtain the over-all effective rate is quite complex. It cannot be easily calculated in advance of the year to which it applies, making it impossible to utilize it in simulation. In addition, the starting rate is a reasonably good proxy variable for the effective rate, especially since 1953. For the justification of this statement, see A. Ando, *et al.* "Lags in Monetary and Fiscal Policy", Part II, table 1, *Stabilization Policies* (Commission on Money and Credit; Englewood Cliffs, N.J.: Prentice-Hall, 1963). However, up to and including 1951, the ratio of the effective rate to the starting rate varies somewhat, and this may be one of the causes of the difficulty we encounter in explaining tax receipts for 1950 and 1951.

TP_{GF} = personal tax and nontax receipts of the federal government, billions of dollars'

$DMY2$ = 1, 1949 : 1

= 0, elsewhere

$DMY3$ = 1, 1951 : 1

= 0, elsewhere

$KGAIN$ = realized capital gains, billions of dollars.

(B) *Corporate profits tax accruals*

The concepts of profits used by the tax authorities and by OBE differ in many respects [10]). The variable available in this model closest to the base of the corporate profits tax is OBE corporate profits before taxes and before inventory valuation adjustment less state and local corporate profits tax accruals, as estimated elsewhere in this model.

The present federal tax structure is a two-bracket system consisting of a rate of 30 per cent on the first $ 25 000 of taxable income and 52 per cent of taxable income in excess of this amount [11]). The effective rate, therefore, can vary from year to year under a constant structure but has remained relatively stable after the effect of the excess profits tax disappeared, from 1955 to the present. The average of the effective rates over the period 1955–1961 is 47.5 per cent [12]). This rate can then be applied to the above profits concept. Somewhat greater precision could be achieved, and a more useful result for policy purposes, by a separate estimation of the behavior of each of the two tax brackets; this we have not undertaken.

---

[10]) The reconciliation of the OBE concept with compiled net profits of the Internal Revenue Service is given in table VII-19 of the national income statistics, OBE.

[11]) The Revenue Act of 1964 changed these rates to 20 and 50 per cent, respectively, for 1964 and 18 and 48 per cent, respctively for 1965 and subsequent years.

[12]) The effective rates in each year are as follows:

1955	47.5 per cent
1956	46.3 per cent
1957	47.4 per cent
1958	48.5 per cent
1959	47.3 per cent
1960	47.9 per cent
1961	47.4 per cent.

Survey of Current Business, July 1962, and *Income and Output*, tables I-17, III-1, and III-2. OBE Corporate profits before tax less state and local corporate profits tax accruals divided into federal corporate profits tax accruals.

(C) *Indirect business tax and nontax accruals*

Federal excise taxes, with the major exceptions of tobacco and alcoholic beverages, were reported and collected monthly prior to October, 1953. Since that time, monthly deposits are required for the first two months of the calendar quarter when more than $ 100 in tax is due, with the final payment due with the return—by the end of the month following the calendar quarter. The pattern, therefore, is a mixed one, like the personal income tax. To avoid distorting our results by the drop in receipts at the time of initiation of this new program, the third quarter of 1953 has been eliminated from the relationships.

The second general problem in this area is that, in most cases, time series are not available for the relevant tax bases, and thus we have been forced to use such data as exist, some closely related to the base but others considerably more remote.

The third general problem lies in the distinction between *specific* excises, levied per unit of output, and ad valorem excises, levied as a percentage of the value of sales or production. The first group represents the major sources of excise tax revenue at the federal level.

To avoid repetition we present our preferred relationships in table 14.2 and follow with a brief discussion of peculiarities associated with particular taxes. The equations were all estimated in logarithmic form, and in every case there has been experimentation with various lags and with alternative bases.

(1) *Tobacco*   The bulk of the revenues from this excise comes from small cigarettes, and the independent variables, both tax rates and withdrawals, refer to this commodity, although the dependent variable is the total receipts from this source.

(2) *Alcoholic beverages*   The three major components in this group are distilled spirits, beer, and wine. Wine collections were small and were merged with distilled spirits. A peculiarity of the above relationship is that the elasticity of the tax rate exceeds unity by a substantial amount. To bring it nearer unity required the introduction of lags, the coefficients of which were small and not particularly significant.

TABLE 14.2
Excise tax functions.

Specific excises

Tobacco

$$\ln TX_{\text{TB}_{GF}} = \frac{1.022}{(0.047)} \ln RX_{\text{TB}_{GF}} + \frac{0.615}{(0.072)} \ln TOB - \frac{6.056}{(0.480)}$$

$$\bar{R}^2 = 0.96 \qquad VN = 1.9 \tag{14.3}$$

Distilled spirits

$$\ln TX_{\text{LQ}_{GF}} = \frac{1.362}{(0.056)} \ln RX_{\text{LQ}_{GF}} + \frac{0.981}{(0.029)} \ln LIQ - \frac{0.451}{(0.296)}$$

$$\bar{R}^2 = 0.98 \qquad VN = 1.5 \tag{14.4}$$

Beer

$$\ln TX_{\text{BE}_{GF}} = \frac{0.947}{(0.036)} \ln RX_{\text{BE}_{GF}} + \frac{0.904}{(0.069)} \ln BEER + \frac{1.203}{(0.685)}$$

$$\bar{R}^2 = 0.95 \qquad VN = 1.6 \tag{14.5}$$

Gas and oil

$$\ln TX_{\text{GS}_{GF}} = \frac{1.072}{(0.039)} \ln RX_{\text{GS}_{GF}} + \frac{0.806}{(0.074)} \ln Q_{\text{GAS}} + \frac{8.097}{(0.728)}$$

$$\bar{R}^2 = 0.99 \qquad VN = 2.1 \tag{14.6}$$

Tires and tubes

$$\ln TX_{\text{TI}_{GF}} = \frac{0.190}{(0.143)} \ln RX_{\text{TI}_{GF}} + \frac{0.771}{(0.143)} \ln [RX_{\text{TI}_{GF}}]_{-1} + \frac{0.206}{(0.124)} \ln Q_{\text{TIRE}}$$

$$+ \frac{0.405}{(0.120)} \ln [Q_{\text{TIRE}}]_{-1} + \frac{0.973}{(1.257)}$$

$$\bar{R}^2 = 0.94 \qquad VN = 2.1 \tag{14.7}$$

Ad valorem excises

Motor vehicles and parts

$$\ln TX_{\text{AU}_{GF}} = \frac{0.918}{(0.055)} \ln [RX_{\text{AU}_{GF}}]_{-1} + \frac{0.916}{(0.108)} \ln [C_{\text{DA}}]_{-1} + \frac{6.868}{(0.375)}$$

$$\bar{R}^2 = 0.95 \qquad VN = 2.1 \tag{14.8}$$

TABLE 14.2 (Continued)

Transportation of persons

$$\ln TX_{TR_{GF}} = \frac{0.465}{(0.114)} \ln RX_{TR_{GF}} + \frac{0.425}{(0.117)} \ln [RX_{TR_{GF}}]_{-1}$$

$$+ \frac{0.262}{(0.240)} \ln REV_{TR} + \frac{0.575}{(0.241)} \ln [REV_{TR}]_{-1} + \frac{0.912}{(0.284)}$$

$$\bar{R}^2 = 0.85 \qquad VN = 2.1 \tag{14.9}$$

Telephone and telegraph

$$\ln TX_{TE_{GF}} = \frac{1.321}{(0.092)} \ln [RX_{TE_{GF}}]_{-1} + \frac{0.910}{(0.055)} \ln [REV_{TE}]_{-1} + \frac{1.459}{(0.243)}$$

$$\bar{R}^2 = 0.84 \qquad VN = 3.0 \tag{14.10}$$

Electric, gas and oil appliances

$$\ln TX_{AP_{GF}} = \frac{1.208}{(0.128)} \ln [RX_{AP_{GF}}]_{-1} + \frac{0.657}{(0.103)} \ln [I_C]_{-1} + \frac{2.697}{(0.613)}$$

$$\bar{R}^2 = 0.61 \qquad VN = 1.5 \tag{14.11}$$

The variables in order of appearance are:

$TX_{TB_{GF}}$ = collections from federal excise tax on tobacco, millions of dollars

$RX_{TB_{GF}}$ = federal excise tax rate on withdrawals of short cigarettes, dollars per thousand

TOB = taxable withdrawals of short cigarettes, millions of cigarettes

$TX_{LQ_{GF}}$ = collections from federal excise taxes on distilled spirits and wine, thousands of dollars

$RX_{LQ_{GF}}$ = federal excise tax rate on distilled spirits, dollars per proof gallon

LIQ = taxable withdrawals of distilled spirits and ethyl alcohol, thousands of gallons

$TX_{BE_{GF}}$ = collections from federal excise tax on beer, thousands of dollars

$RX_{BE_{GF}}$ = federal excise tax rate on beer, dollars per barrel

$BEER$ = taxable withdrawals of beer, thousands of barrels

$TX_{GS_{GF}}$ = collections from federal excise tax on gasoline and lubricating oil, thousands of dollars

$RX_{GS_{GF}}$ = federal excise tax rate on gasoline, dollars per gallon

Q_{GAS} = production of gasoline, hundreds of thousands of barrels

$TX_{TI_{GF}}$ = collections from federal excise tax on tires and tubes, millions of dollars

$RX_{TI_{GF}}$ = federal excise tax rate on tires, dollars per pound

Q_{TIRE} = production of pneumatic casings, thousands

$TX_{AU_{GF}}$ = collections from federal excise tax on automobiles, millions of dollars

$RX_{AU_{GF}}$ = federal excise tax rate on automobile chassis and bodies and motorcycles, fraction

C_{DA} = personal consumption expenditures on new and net used automobiles and parts, billions of dollars

$TX_{TR_{GF}}$ = collections from federal excise tax on transportation of persons, millions of dollars

$RX_{TR_{GF}}$ = federal excise rate on transportation of persons, fraction

REV_{TR} = sum of passenger revenues of domestic airlines, passenger operating revenue of class I railroads and operating revenue of class I intercity motor carriers of passengers, millions of dollars

$TX_{TE_{GF}}$ = collections from federal excise tax on local and long-distance telephone service, telegraph, cable, radio, etc. plus leased wires, millions of dollars

$RX_{TE_{GF}}$ = federal excise tax rate on local telephone service, fraction

REV_{TE} = operating revenues of telephone, wire-telegraph, ocean-cable and radiotelegraph carriers, millions of dollars

$TX_{AP_{GF}}$ = collections from federal excise tax on electric, gas and oil appliances, millions of dollars

$RX_{AP_{GF}}$ = federal excise tax rate on electric, gas and oil appliances, fraction

I_C = new construction component of gross private domestic investment, billions of dollars.

(3) *Gasoline and lubricating oils*   Lubricating oil revenues were small, and the tax rate was constant throughout the period. Lubricating oil and gasoline tax revenues were combined, and the independent variables refer to gasoline.

(4) *Tires and tubes*   Tires and tubes were combined, and the independent variables refer to the tire tax rate and tire production. The tax on tires is determined by weight. Hence, our use of number of tires produced is not a

precise measure of the tax base. The relationship is based on the period 1953 : 4 to 1961 : 4, rather than the whole period, since it gave better results.

(5) *Motor vehicles and parts*   The independent variables used were consumer expenditures on automobiles and parts and the tax rate on autos. We prefer the lagged relationship above, although the coefficients of the current independent variables were not entirely insignificant. However, for the period 1953 : 4 to 1961 : 4 when there were no rate changes, the coefficient on current purchases became negative and insignificant when lagged purchases were introduced.

(6) *Transportation of persons*   The peculiarity of this relationship is that the current tax rate is much more significant than current revenues. For the shorter period from 1953 : 4 to 1961 : 4 the coefficient on current revenues even became negative. But since this coefficient showed considerable stability for the whole period when further lags were introduced, we have retained the form in table 14.2. It should also be noted that the rate of this tax was recently changed and the base limited to airline transportation. Appropriate modification will be necessary in using this relationship in the future.

(7) *Telephone and telegraph*   The high von Neumann ratio seems to be attributable to an unsatisfactory seasonal adjustment in the tax receipts series and might be worth further investigation.

(8) *Electric, gas and oil appliances*   The relationship is not a particularly good one. We have experimented with consumer expenditures on furniture and household equipment, but it gives little additional help in explaining tax receipts. One source of difficulty may arise from the changing definitions of taxable items over this period, but adjustment of the base is not feasible.

(9) *All other indirect business taxes*   The indirect business tax and nontax accruals consist of all remaining excises, customs duties and nontaxes. The sum of these items ran around $ 2.5 billion per year in 1959. Of this total, customs duties amounted to $ 1.1 billion and are explained in the foreign sector of this model. Nontaxes amounted to $ 0.7 billion and were not separately estimated. The balance remaining consists of excise taxes on radio and television sales; other manufacturers' excise taxes not previously explained, such as on sporting goods, cameras, phonograph records, musical instru-

ments and business machines; retail excises on furs, luggage, cosmetics and jewelry; and other miscellaneous excises, such as on admissions, club dues, bowling alleys and cabarets. We have attempted to explain these various taxes by subgroups but without much success, despite the use of a wide variety of independent variables. As a consequence, it seems preferable to treat the items in this section as essentially exogenous. A naive forecast based on the assumption that next quarter's receipts would be the same as this quarter's would probably be reasonably reliable, provided rate changes are taken into consideration.

(D) *Contributions for social insurance*

Of the OBE categories under the general heading of contributions for social insurance, we shall not attempt to explain the contributions to government life insurance, since this item is largely a veterans' program and does not appear to be related to any economic variables. We shall deal with all other items below.

(1) *Old age and survivors insurance*   Old age and survivors insurance (OASI) taxes are levied on covered wages and salaries up to a fixed annual amount and, since the fourth quarter of 1950, also on proprietors' income up to a fixed amount. Hence, OASI tax liabilities can be expressed as the sum of two products: the taxable portion of wages and salaries times the appropriate tax rate plus the taxable portion of proprietors' income times its tax rate. We cannot use this procedure, however, because the tax liability and the taxable portions of incomes are not directly observable.

Monthly collections of OASI taxes are reported in the *Treasury Bulletin.* The collection and reporting procedure of the Treasury for OASI taxes is basically the same as for withholding under the personal income tax, but OBE does not derive its figures on OASI taxes from Treasury tax collection data. In the case of wages and salaries, they obtain their figure by multiplying the contribution rate by the data on total taxable wages as reported by the Department of Health, Education and Welfare. OBE then obtains the contribution of self-employed persons from the Bureau of Old Age and Survivors Insurance, on an annual basis, and makes a quarterly allocation of the latter item [13]). In order to compare the figures obtained by OBE with the collection figures reported by the Treasury, we

---

[13]) U. S. Department of Commerce, Office of Business Economics, *National Income*, 1954 edition, p. 73.

have prepared series based on the latter. Equations estimated from the two series are recorded below.

There are also difficulties associated with the measurement of the income variables. Private wages and salaries, of course, are readily available from national income statistics, but the portion of wages and salaries subject to OASI taxes depends on the income distribution and cannot be easily estimated. The same is true for proprietors' income. Under the circumstances, we have used the following approximation:

$$\ln TW_{\text{OAGF}} = \alpha_1 \ln R_{\text{OAGF}} + \alpha_2 \ln [WS_{\text{BUS}} + Y_{\text{ENT*}}] + \alpha_3 \ln J_{\text{OAMAX}} + \alpha_0 + \varepsilon.$$

The symbols used above and in the estimated equations which follow are:

TW_{OAGF} = OASI contributions by employees, employers and self-employed persons, billions of dollars

R_{OAGF} = weighted average of effective OASI contribution rates, fraction

WS_{BUS} = private wage and salary disbursements, billions of dollars

$Y_{\text{ENT*}}$ = business and professional proprietors' income from 1950 : 4 through 1954 : 3, total proprietors' income thereafter, billions of dollars [14])

J_{OAMAX} = index of maximum OASI-taxable earnings per employee, 1947–1949 = 1.00

TWC_{OAGF} = collections of OASI taxes as reported by the Treasury, billions of dollars.

We are assuming implicitly that the expression

$$\{[WS_{\text{BUS}} + Y_{\text{ENT}}]^{\alpha_2}\}\{[J_{\text{OAMAX}}]^{\alpha_3}\}$$

will serve adequately as an index of the movement of taxable income under OASI. If this assumption is reasonably accurate, we should expect our estimates of the coefficient of the tax rate, α_1, to be close to unity and of the coefficients, α_2 and α_3 to be substantially smaller than unity. The least-squares regression estimates are given below:

$$\ln TW_{\text{OAGF}} = \frac{1.006}{(0.070)} \ln R_{\text{OAGF}} + \frac{0.803}{(0.095)} \ln [WS_{\text{BUS}} + Y_{\text{ENT*}}]$$

$$+ \frac{0.421}{(0.177)} \ln J_{\text{OAMAX}} + \frac{0.600}{(0.617)}$$

$$\bar{R}^2 = 0.99 \qquad VN = 1.5. \tag{14.12}$$

---

[14]) The definition reflects the legislative broadening of the tax base and coverage.

The fit is exceedingly good, but this is not surprising, given the estimation procedure of $TW_{OA_{GF}}$ described above. More important, all the coefficients are of about the order of magnitude expected. The von Neumann statistic is a bit low, indicating that there is still a little serial correlation of the residuals left, but inspection of the residuals themselves suggests that this is not too serious. Thus, we are inclined to consider this result reasonably satisfactory [15]).

(2) *State unemployment insurance*   The provisions of the state unemployment insurance system suggest that the insurance tax liability should be given by the product of the average contribution rate and wages and salaries subject to unemployment insurance contribution. The description in *National Income* [16]) suggests that, in the case of unemployment insurance contributions (unlike that of OASI taxes), OBE bases its estimate of contributions on the figures reported by the Treasury. Discussions with the officials of the Bureau of Employment Security indicate that the figures reported under the heading "Deposits by States" in the Unemployment Insurance Trust Fund Account in the Treasury Bulletin correspond quite closely with actual collections. OBE evidently moves these figures back one quarter in order to come closer to the accrual of the liability. We have reconstructed this operation and found that they compared reasonably well with the national income statistics on a yearly basis.

The average contribution rate of employers is directly available from publications of the Bureau of Employment Security. These rates are, as far as we can ascertain, obtained by averaging rates in various states rather than by dividing total unemployment insurance contributions by covered wages and salaries. (If the latter were true, our estimating equation would be close to a tautology.) Thus, the figures on wages and salaries covered

---

[15]) The equation using collection figures assembled from the data in the *Treasury Bulletin* is:

$$\ln TWC_{OA_{GF}} = \frac{0.963}{(0.151)} \ln R_{OA_{GF}} + \frac{0.937}{(0.218)} \ln [WS_{BUS} + Y_{ENT*}]$$

$$+ \frac{0.447}{(0.404)} \ln J_{OAMAX} - \frac{0.182}{(1.409)}$$

$$\bar{R}^2 = 0.96 \qquad VN = 2.1.$$

[16]) U.S. Department of Commerce, Office of Business Economics, *National Income* (Supplement to Survey of Current Business), 1954.

by the unemployment insurance system are the hardest data to obtain in the formula above. Even if we were able to obtain or construct series representing wages and salaries subject to the unemployment insurance contribution, such a variable would not be developed in the Brookings-SSRC econometric model. Under the circumstances, we have used the following approximation:

$$\ln TW_{US_{GF}} = \alpha_1 \ln R_{US_{GF}} + \alpha_2 \ln WS_{BUS} + \alpha_3 \ln \left[\frac{L_{UIS}}{L}\right] + \alpha_0 + \varepsilon.$$

The variables are:

$TW_{US_{GF}}$ = employers' contributions for state unemployment insurance, billions of dollars

$R_{US_{GF}}$ = average employer contribution rate for state unemployment insurance, fraction

WS_{BUS} = private wage and salary disbursements, billions of dollars

L_{UIS} = labor force covered by state unemployment insurance, millions of persons

L = civilian labor force, millions of persons.

Our implicit assumption is similar to that of the preceding section and subject to the same qualifications. The least-squares regression estimates are given below:

$$\ln TW_{US_{GF}} = \frac{0.978}{(0.099)} \ln R_{US_{GF}} + \frac{0.671}{(0.107)} \ln WS_{BUS}$$

$$+ \frac{0.203}{(0.587)} \ln \left[\frac{L_{UIS}}{L}\right] - \frac{3.314}{(0.801)}$$

$$\bar{R}^2 = 0.87 \qquad VN = 2.2. \tag{14.13}$$

The multiple correlation coefficient is not as high as we expected, but the size of the regression coefficients is reasonable. The standard error of the coefficient of L_{UIS}/L, however, is very large, and this coefficient is completely unreliable. If we eliminate this variable, the result becomes

$$\ln TW_{US_{GF}} = \frac{0.974}{(0.098)} \ln R_{US_{GF}} + \frac{0.698}{(0.073)} \ln WS_{BUS} - \frac{3.56}{(0.36)}$$

$$\bar{R}^2 = 0.87 \qquad VN = 2.2. \tag{14.14}$$

Thus, the elimination of L_{UIS}/L leaves other characteristics of the estimated equation virtually unchanged. We consider equation (14.13) or (14.14) satisfactory [17]).

(3) *Railroad retirement*   Contributions to the railroad retirement system should be determined by: the rate of contribution; the maximum wage or salary per month on which the contribution is made; the number of employees in the railroad industry whose wages or salaries exceed the maximum subject to contribution; and the aggregate wages and salaries of employees earning less than the maximum subject to contribution. Unfortunately, data are not available for the number of employees whose wages or salaries exceed the maximum or for wages and salaries of employees who earn less than the maximum. We must therefore formulate the liability relation in terms of other variables which are observable.

The variables are:

$TW_{RR_{GF}}$ = contributions for railroad retirement insurance by employers and employees, billions of dollars

$R_{RR_{GF}}$ = contribution rate for railroad retirement insurance, fraction

E_{RTR} = employment in railroad transportation, thousands of persons

WSM_{RR} = maximum wage and salary per month on which railroad retirement benefit is paid, dollars

WS_{RTR} = wage and salary disbursements in railroad transportation, billions of dollars.

Our estimated equation, which takes account of the delay involved in the collections procedure, is:

$$\ln TW_{RR_{GF}} = \frac{0.824}{(0.496)} \ln [R_{RR_{GF}}]_{-1} + \frac{0.596}{(0.149)} \ln [E_{RTR}]_{-1}$$

$$+ \frac{0.688}{(0.250)} \ln [WSM_{RR}]_{-1} + \frac{0.499}{(0.162)} \ln [WS_{RTR}]_{-1} - \frac{5.948}{(2.966)}$$

$$\bar{R}^2 = 0.39 \qquad VN = 2.6. \tag{14.15}$$

---

[17]) Inspection of the data reveals that unemployment insurance contributions exhibit very erratic movements in 1948 and 1949 and have a seasonal pattern completely different from that of later years. This creates the strong suspicion that the collection procedure may have changed at the beginning of 1950, although we have not been able to verify it. The large residuals of the above regression equations are all concentrated in 1948–1949. But when these equations were reestimated excluding these years, essentially the same relationship as above was found.

The multiple correlation coefficient is extremely low, but this is to be expected to some extent because the movement of $TW_{RR_{GF}}$ is erratic. The coefficients, while somewhat low, are plausible.

(4) *Railroad unemployment insurance* The structure of this system is a relatively simple one, particularly when compared with the state unemployment system. The Railroad Retirement Board administers the unemployment insurance fund and sets the contribution rate depending upon the status of the fund.

This rate of contribution multiplied by wages and salaries subject to the contribution should give us the railroad unemployment insurance liability, but in this case also we are forced to use an approximate relation. Our data on contributions are based on collections rather than on exact liabilities, and data for wages and salaries subject to the contribution are not available.

Our least-squares estimate is:

$$\ln TW_{UR_{GF}} = \frac{0.952}{(0.038)} \ln R_{UR_{GF}} + \frac{0.262}{(0.646)} \ln WS_{RTR} - \frac{3.516}{(5.589)}$$

$$\bar{R}^2 = 0.93 \qquad VN = 2.24. \tag{14.16}$$

where

$TW_{UR_{GF}}$ = employers' contributions for railroad unemployment insurance, billions of dollars

$R_{UR_{GF}}$ = rate of contribution by employees for railroad unemployment insurance, fraction

WS_{RTR} = wages and salaries in railroad transportation, billions of dollars.

The coefficient of $R_{UR_{GF}}$ is close to unity, as expected. However, the coefficient of WS_{RTR} is insignificant and small. Inspection of the data on wages and salaries indicates that the movement of this series has been very erratic, apparently having no close relation to any other economic indicators. Furthermore, its movement over time is very small. Since WS_{RTR} is only an approximation to the wages and salaries subject to insurance contribution, we would expect the usual attenuation effect of observation of the true or approximated variable. In this case, the variance of the true variable is apparently small, and it is quite probable that the variance of WS_{RTR} is dominated by the variance of the true variable less WS_{RTR}. This may explain the unsatisfactory result.

(5) *Civilian employee retirement systems*   Receipts from civilian employee retirement programs are reported quarterly in the Social Security Bulletin and annually by OBE. The quarterly payment pattern seems to be the consequence of governmental discretionary action and varies erratically. However, it should be possible to explain the yearly contribution. Using the contribution rate and civilian wages and salaries, both current and lagged, as independent variables gave very high correlations [18]. However, the coefficient of the contribution rate is so high and that of wages and salaries so low that these regressions make little sense. In the absence of further explanation, these contributions should be treated as exogenous.

14.2.2. *State and local revenues*

(A) *Personal tax and nontax receipts*

The variables which appear in this section are:

$TP_{Y_{GS}}$ = personal income tax receipts of state and local governments, billions of dollars

$R_{PY_{GS}}$ = index of proxy state government tax rate on income, 1948 = 100

Y_P = personal income, billions of dollars

V = transfer payments to persons, billions of dollars

Y_{OL} = other labor income, billions of dollars

$TP_{O_{GS}}$ = state and local government personal tax and nontax receipts other than income tax, billions of dollars

Y_D = disposable personal income, billions of dollars.

Quarterly collections of state income taxes are not as well reported as the federal income tax. Therefore, we have estimated the annual amount of personal income tax and nontax payments and then allocated them by quarters on the basis of the coefficients computed from OBE data. However,

---

[18)] $\ln TW^A_{RCS_{GF}} = \dfrac{9.787}{(1.670)} \ln R^A_{RCS_{GF}} + \dfrac{0.187}{(0.279)} \ln WS^A_{CIV_{GF}} + \dfrac{32.367}{(6.733)}$

$\bar{R}^2 = 0.88.$

The variables are:

$TW^A_{RCS_{GF}}$ = annual contributions by employers and employees for federal civilian employee retirement systems, billions of dollars

$R^A_{RCS_{GF}}$ = contribution rate for federal civilian employee retirement systems, fraction

$WS^A_{CIV_{GF}}$ = annual federal general government wage and salary disbursements to civilians, billions of dollars.

even attempting to determine an annual relationship raises a number of difficulties.

(1) *Income taxes*　　In the first place, for the state personal income tax we wished to use essentially the same variables as for the federal income tax—rates and income. A proxy rate had to be computed for the thirty-five states with income taxes. The five states whose rate structures are used in constructing the over-all index of rates are those with the largest income tax revenues in 1962 [19]). These states accounted for two-thirds of total state income tax revenues and one-half of the personal income of all states with an income tax. Effective tax rates on personal income less other labor income less transfer payments were computed for each year based on the tax structure of each state in that year applied to the state income distribution of 1959 [20]). These effective rates for each state were combined into a weighted average, the weights being personal income in the relevant states in 1958–1960. We have chosen this latter period as a more useful one for purposes of extending the model into the future. This resulting weighted average was then converted into an index using 1948 as the base. While this procedure is arbitrary, it is doubtful if more elaborate procedures would result in major changes in this pattern.

The second problem is that some states have introduced withholding in the period under consideration. This change, which we have not taken into account, may be responsible for the instability of the coefficient of current personal income in the relationships we have computed. An alternative procedure would have been the time-consuming one of estimating these relationships for each state, but we have not undertaken this.

Using both current and lagged rates and adjusted personal income, our preferred relationship is the following:

$$\ln TP^A_{Y_{GS}} = \frac{0.356}{(0.211)} \ln \left[R^A_{PY_{GS}}\right]_{-1} + \frac{0.916}{(0.068)} \ln \left[Y^A_P - V^A - Y^A_{OL}\right]_{-1} - \frac{7.979}{(0.796)}$$

$$\bar{R}^2 = 0.99 \qquad VN = 1.9. \tag{14.17}$$

While current rates and current income yield equally good statistical results, we prefer the above relationship because the lagged coefficients are more

---

[19]) U.S. Department of Commerce, Bureau of the Census, *State Tax Collections in 1962.*

[20]) *Statistical Abstract of the United States, 1962,* table 449.

stable when combined with current variables and yield more reasonable results for income elasticities [21]).

(2) *Other personal taxes and nontaxes*   The remaining taxes in this category are death and personal property taxes, motor vehicle licenses, other taxes and nontaxes. Since the bulk of these revenues is like consumer expenditures, we use disposable income as the explanatory variable. Note that we cannot adjust for rate changes and that, therefore, we overstate the income elasticities of these revenues.

$$TP^A_{O_{GS}} = \frac{0.019}{(0.001)} Y^A_D - \frac{2.082}{(0.227)}$$

$$\bar{R}^2 = 0.97 \qquad VN = 0.6. \tag{14.18}$$

While $\bar{R}^2$ is very high, inspection of the residuals suggests that this is not a very satisfactory relationship and that this item might better be treated as exogenous.

(3) *Quarterly allocations of total*   The annual estimates can then be allocated to each quarter on the basis of the OBE quarterly allocation of state personal tax and nontax receipts. The quarterly proportions show little variation over the period 1946 to 1961 and average as follows:

Quarter	Annual receipts (per cent)
1	24.3
2	24.8
3	25.4
4	25.6

---

[21]) The current relationship is:

$$\ln TP^A_{Y_{GS}} = \frac{0.459}{(0.255)} \ln R^A_{PY_{GS}} + \frac{1.864}{(0.204)} \ln [Y^A_P - V^A - Y^A_{OL}] - \frac{13.216}{(0.895)}$$

$$\bar{R}^2 = 0.98 \qquad VN = 2.1.$$

However, when lagged income was introduced the coefficient on current income became −0.046 with a standard error of 0.502. An income elasticity of nearly 2 for current income also seems unreasonable.

(B) *Corporate profits tax accruals*

The state corporate profits tax accruals have been treated in the same way as the federal. The base of the tax is approximated by corporate profits. The tax rate variable, however, had to be constructed from state data. We have used tax rates from the three states accounting for 57 per cent of revenues from this tax in 1962 [22]). The relationship found is:

$$\ln TC_{GS} = \frac{1.285}{(0.153)} \ln R^A_{Z_{GS}} + \frac{0.693}{(0.084)} Z_{BU} - \frac{4.672}{(0.243)}$$

$$\bar{R}^2 = 0.97 \qquad VN = 0.7. \tag{14.19}$$

where

TC_{GS} = corporate profits tax accruals to state and local governments, billions of dollars

$R^A_{Z_{GS}}$ = proxy annual state tax rate on corporate profits, fraction

Z_{BU} = corporate profits before taxes and before inventory valuation adjustment, billions of dollars.

(C) *Indirect business tax and nontax accruals*

Under this heading are grouped a number of revenues. Broadly speaking, they are divided approximately equally between property taxes and all other indirect business tax and nontax accruals. We estimate these groups separately.

The symbols used in this section are:

$TX_{O_{GS}}$ = state and local government indirect business tax and nontax accruals except property taxes, billions of dollars

J_{BASE} = index of tax bases to which RX_{GS} applies

RX_{GS} = weighted average of state government alcohol, gasoline, tobacco and general excise tax rates, fraction

C = personal consumption expenditures, including imputations, billions of dollars

$TX_{PR_{GS}}$ = property taxes portion of state and local government indirect business tax and nontax accruals, billions of dollars

P_{GS} = implicit price deflator for state and local government purchases of goods and services, 1954 = 1.00

G_S = state and local government purchases of goods and services, billions of dollars

RM_{MBLM} = Moody's average long-term municipal bond yield, per cent.

---

[22]) The states were California, New York, and Pennsylvania.

(1) *Indirect business taxes other than property*   This grouping of revenues covers the following major categories: sales taxes, motor vehicle licenses, other taxes and nontaxes. Sales taxes in turn include the following major components [23]: state general sales taxes, gasoline taxes, tobacco and liquor and local sales taxes. The tax rate variable for this entire group of revenues is computed from the major state sales and excise taxes. Quarterly data are not published in this detail by OBE, but they have supplied us with quarterly property taxes, and the revenues estimated in this section represent the residuals derived by subtracting these latter amounts from the totals.

Sales and excise revenues, by definition, should be given by the formula:

$$TX_{O_{GS}} = \sum_{i,\,s} \tau_t^{is} q_t^{is} + \sum_{j,\,s} \rho_t^{js} p_t^{js} q_t^{js},$$

where τ is the specific tax rate on the ith good in the sth state in period t, ρ is the ad valorem tax rate on the jth good in the sth state in period t, q and p are corresponding quantities and prices. It is generally the case that specific taxes are imposed on gasoline, tobacco and alcoholic beverages, while the general sales tax takes the form of an ad valorem tax. To make the above relationship one that can be estimated, it must be drastically simplified to:

$$\ln TX_{O_{GS}} = \alpha_1 \ln RX_{GS} + \alpha_2 \ln J_{\text{BASE}} + \alpha_0 + \varepsilon.$$

The rate and base indices must, of course, be made consistent by being stated as ad valorem rates and money bases or as specific rates and quantity bases. Since it is almost impossible to convert ad valorem rates on general sales into specific rates, RX_{GS} must be an index that behaves like an ad valorem rate and J_{BASE} must be a current value measure. The index we have used is one in which the weights are the value of goods on which these taxes were imposed in the base period [24]. It is therefore a Laspeyres index of

---

[23] OBE includes minor state sales taxes not specified below in other taxes.

[24] Denoting the base period by 0 and assuming price differentials among states, we shall define RX_{GS} as:

$$RX_{GS} = \frac{\displaystyle\sum_{i,\,s} \frac{\tau_t^{is}}{p_t^i}\, p_0^i q_0^{is} + \sum_{j,\,s} \rho_t^{js} p_0^j q_0^{js}}{\displaystyle\sum_{i,\,s} p_0^i q_0^{is} + \sum_{j,\,s} p_0^j q_0^{js}}.$$

τ_t^{is}/p_t^i, the specific tax rate in period t divided by the unit price of the good on which the tax is applied in the same period, may be considered the ad valorem equivalent of the specific tax rate.

ad valorem rates and, as such, possesses all the properties and difficulties associated with any Laspeyres index, working exactly only when all the variables move proportionately. Also note that as the prices of goods on which specific taxes are imposed rise, the index RX_{GS} will fall.

As an index for money values we shall use aggregate consumption. We have used both current and lagged values and prefer the formulation below:

$$\ln TX_{O_{GS}} = \frac{0.764}{(0.186)} \ln [RX_{GS}]_{-1} + \frac{1.199}{(0.058)} \ln [C]_{-1} - \frac{1.753}{(0.912)}$$

$$\bar{R}^2 = 0.99 \qquad VN = 2.1. \tag{14.20}$$

The alternative relationship on current rates and consumption [25]), while having highly significant coefficients in the simple form, was rejected. When lagged rates and consumption were introduced, the current-rate coefficient became insignificant and the von Neumann ratio indicated extremely high serial correlation.

(2) *Property taxes*   Property taxes can be thought of as the residual tax in local finance. Given assessed valuations, the balance of expenditures that are not debt financed is met by an annual appropriate adjustment of the property tax rate. Unquestionably, the effective property tax rate also exerts some influence back on expenditures. However, since expenditures are reasonably well explained by other variables, we have used them as an independent variable. Ideally, we would use expenditures of local governments only, but OBE does not make this breakdown, and so we have had to use state and local expenditures combined.

The other independent variable used is the municipal bond rate. The theory underlying its use is that when borrowing is costly, property taxes will be more heavily relied on for financing local expenditures. We expect, therefore, to find positive coefficients for each of these variables.

The estimates we have made are on an annual basis because property taxes are essentially determined annually, although there are slow changes in property tax yields because of intrayear growth in assessed valuations. These annual amounts are allocated quarterly on the basis of the unpublished OBE data referred to in the previous section.

We have experimented with both current and lagged values of the variables

---

[25]) $\ln TX_{O_{GS}} = \dfrac{0.649}{(0.191)} \ln RX_{O_{GS}} + \dfrac{1.24}{(0.061)} \ln C - \dfrac{0.992}{(0.991)}$

$\bar{R}^2 = 0.98 \qquad VN = 0.8.$

in both money and real terms. The relationship which we prefer is in logarithmic form:

$$\ln\left[\frac{TX^A_{PRGS}}{P^A_{GS}}\right] = \frac{0.681}{(0.063)} \ln\left[\frac{G^A_S}{P^A_{GS}}\right] + \frac{0.113}{(0.059)} \ln RM^A_{MBLM} - \frac{0.085}{(0.159)}$$

$$\bar{R}^2 = 0.99 \qquad VN = 1.5. \tag{14.21}$$

The coefficients are significant and of the right sign. The lagged bond rate was almost always insignificant in these computations, and serial correlation was usually sharply increased when it was introduced.

The quarterly proportions of this annual total as allocated by OBE, 1946–1961, are as follows:

Quarter	Per cent of total
1	24.3
2	24.7
3	25.3
4	25.7

(D) *Contributions for social insurance*

There are two items classified under contributions for social insurance: state and local employee retirement systems and cash sickness compensation funds. The latter is a small item, and its combination with the retirement systems should not introduce much error. Because of the difficulty of determining changes in state retirement systems, we have simply used state and local government purchases of goods and services as the independent variable, having no quarterly information on wages and salaries of these governments. The regression is:

$$TW_{GS} = \frac{0.073}{(0.001)} G_S - \frac{0.460}{(0.024)} \qquad \begin{array}{l} \bar{R}^2 = 0.99 \\ VN = 1.0, \end{array} \tag{14.22}$$

where TW_{GS} and G_S are, respectively, state and local government receipts from contributions for social insurance and state and local government purchases of goods and services in billions of dollars. This expression exaggerates the importance of income fluctuations (as represented by the independent variable) because of the secular increase in contribution rates, not explicitly in the equation, which correlate highly with income. Despite this weakness, it seems more satisfactory than an autonomous treatment.

14.3. Government expenditures

We continue to follow the general classification used in the national income statistics of OBE as shown in table 14.1 in our discussion of government expenditures. Our major categories are transfer payments and purchases of goods and services. We will discuss them in turn at the federal, state and local government levels.

14.3.1. Transfer payments

(A) *Federal government*

(1) *Old age and survivors insurance benefits*　　As is the case with any transfer program, one can calculate the total amount of benefits paid by multiplying the number of people eligible to receive benefits by the relevant rates. Most OASI payments go to the demographic category, men and women over sixty-five and, since 1956, women over sixty-two. Cyclical variability in the total benefit amount, to the extent that it exists, can be accounted for largely by the early retirement of those eligible for benefits. Since people do not normally receive a full-benefit payment if they are in the labor force, we use as a representation of the recipients of OASI benefits the number of people in the age group mentioned who are not in the labor force. This variable does not take account of those who work but whose income is less than the allowable maximum; nor does it take account of younger recipients of disability benefits or survivors benefits other than widows over sixty-five.

For a variable to represent rates, we offer two alternatives: the legislated maximum-per-family benefit and the maximum "primary insurance amount" which is used as the basis for determining the size of the benefit. For example, a retired worker over sixty-five gets 100 per cent of his primary insurance amount each month, whereas a widow or widower currently receives 75 per cent each month.

Since the war there have been a number of increases in eligibility for receiving OASI benefits. Consequently, our third variable is the percentage of the population in the specified age group which is eligible for (though is not necessarily receiving) OASI benefits. The regression estimates are:

$$\ln V_{\text{OA}_{GF}} = \frac{1.243}{(0.096)} \ln \{[N_{65+}] - [L_{65+}]\} \left\{\frac{N_{\text{OASI}}}{N_{65+}}\right\}$$

$$+ \frac{1.091}{(0.213)} \ln VM_{\text{OAPI}} - \frac{12.647}{(0.817)}$$

$$\bar{R}^2 = 0.99 \qquad VN = 0.8. \tag{14.23}$$

$$\ln V_{OA_{GF}} = \frac{1.178}{(0.070)} \ln \{[N_{65+}] - [L_{65+}]\} \left\{\frac{N_{OASI}}{N_{65+}}\right\}$$

$$+ \frac{0.867}{(0.107)} \ln VM_{OA/F} - \frac{12.042}{(0.442)}$$

$$\bar{R}^2 = 0.99 \qquad VN = 0.9. \tag{14.24}$$

where

$V_{OA_{GF}}$ = OASI benefits, billions of dollars

N_{65+} = civilian population aged 65 and over (62 and over for females since 1956), millions of persons

L_{65+} = labor force aged 65 and over (62 and over for females since 1956), millions of persons

N_{OASI} = civilian population aged 65 and over (62 and over for females since 1956) eligible for OASI benefits, millions of persons

VM_{OAPI} = maximum OASI primary insurance amount, dollars

$VM_{OA/F}$ = maximum per-family OASI benefit per month, dollars.

We have constrained the coefficients of $[N_{65+}] - [L_{65+}]$ and N_{OASI} to be the same, because, in theory they should be close together. Moreover, when their coefficients were freed in estimating these equations, they were far apart and different from unity [26]. They were also altered substantially when $VM_{OA/F}$ was substituted for VM_{OAPI}.

(2) *Other retirement and disability programs*   The programs in this category are much smaller than OASI but more complicated in their rate systems.

---

[26] The equations when the coefficients were freed were:

$$\ln V_{OA_{GF}} = \frac{1.276}{(0.375)} \ln \{[N_{65+}] - [L_{65+}]\} + \frac{0.702}{(0.154)} \ln \left[\frac{N_{OASI}}{N_{65+}}\right]$$

$$+ \frac{1.865}{(0.259)} \ln VM_{OAPI} - \frac{16.647}{(1.138)}$$

$$\bar{R}^2 = 0.99 \qquad VN = 0.9.$$

$$\ln V_{OA_{GF}} = \frac{1.659}{(0.267)} \ln \{[N_{65+}] - [L_{65+}]\} + \frac{0.543}{(0.124)} \ln \left[\frac{N_{OASI}}{N_{65+}}\right]$$

$$+ \frac{1.306}{(0.121)} \ln VM_{OA/F} - \frac{15.919}{(0.798)}$$

$$\bar{R}^2 = 0.99 \qquad VN = 1.1.$$

The variables which appear in this section and in the section on other survivors programs are:

$V_{RR_{GF}}$ = railroad retirement insurance benefits, billions of dollars

N_{65+} = civilian population aged 65 and over (62 and over for females since 1956), millions of persons

L_{65+} = labor force aged 65 and over (62 and over for females since 1956), millions of persons

VM_{RR} = maximum monthly benefit from railroad retirement insurance, dollars

$V_{RCS_{GF}}$ = federal civilian pensions, billions of dollars

VM_{RCS} = maximum monthly retirement benefit for civil servants, dollars

$DMY4$ = 0, through 1955 : 3
= 1, thereafter

$DMY5$ = 0, through 1958 : 1
= 1, thereafter

$V_{RV_{GF}}$ = payments to retired and disabled veterans, billions of dollars

N_{M65+} = civilian male population aged 65 and over, average during quarter, millions of persons

L_{M65+} = male civilian labor force aged 65 and over, average during quarter, millions of persons

$DMY6$ = 0, through 1957 : 4
= 1, thereafter

$V_{SV_{GF}}$ = payments to veterans' survivors, billions of dollars

N_{F65+} = female civilian population aged 65 and over, average during quarter, millions of persons

L_{F65+} = female civilian labor force aged 65 and over (62 and over since 1956), average during quarter, millions of persons

N_{18-} = civilian population aged 18 and under, millions of persons

$V_{SNV_{GF}}$ = payments to survivors of nonveterans, billions of dollars.

(a) *Railroad*   The railroad retirement system operates on an annuity basis. The size of an employee's annuity depends on his average compensation and his years of service. When the system was established in 1937, an upper limit was set for the number of years of service which could count in the annuity determination. This limit was set at thirty years unless more years than that were served after 1937, a possibility that cannot arise until 1967. There is also an upper limit on the amount of monthly compensation which can be used in the calculation, which is changed from time to time.

We have calculated the maximum monthly annuity payment and used it and the same population variable as in OASI to explain these benefits:

$$\ln V_{\text{RR}_{GF}} = \frac{1.438}{(0.162)} \ln \{[N_{65+}] - [L_{65+}]\} + \frac{1.086}{(0.220)} \ln VM_{\text{RR}} - \frac{3.031}{(0.772)}$$

$$\bar{R}^2 = 0.96 \qquad VN = 0.69. \tag{14.25}$$

(b) *Civil service*   The civil service system is more complicated. It is also an annuity system, the pension depending on years of service and the average compensation in the highest five consecutive years with a maximum allowable percentage of the average compensation as an annual benefit. To find the maximum average compensation we have assumed that the highest five years would be the most recent five years and have used the salary for the highest grade, *GS*-15 until 1949 and *GS*-18 thereafter, to represent the movement of wages over time. We have taken the maximum percentage of this average annual salary (currently 80 per cent) and divided by twelve to get the monthly maximum annuity payment. Again we use the OASI demographic variable, although, in this case (as is also true in the case of railroad retirement), civil service employees have the option of retiring as early as age sixty without a decrease in annuity other than that resulting from the part of the formula using number of years of service and even earlier with a decrease in annuity.

Finally, in 1955 and 1958 the program was amended to give percentage increases in monthly benefits to all recipients of civil service retirement payments. We have entered dummy variables for these increases. Our period of estimation ends before the most recent change in the law, which ties the size of the monthly payments to the consumer price index.

$$\ln V_{\text{RCS}_{GF}} = \frac{1.377}{(0.225)} \ln \{[N_{65+}] - [L_{65+}]\} + \frac{1.018}{(0.156)} \ln VM_{\text{RCS}}$$

$$+ \frac{0.057}{(0.043)} DMY4 + \frac{0.175}{(0.043)} DMY5 - \frac{11.374}{(0.666)}$$

$$\bar{R}^2 = 0.99 \qquad VN = 1.1. \tag{14.26}$$

Average wages and salaries for the five preceding years were not statistically significant.

(c) *Veterans*   Veterans' retirement and disability programs are so complex as to make the straightforward construction of an index of rates impossible. Consequently, we have limited ourselves to dealing with one important rate change in 1958 in the form of a dummy variable. We use, as the demographic variable, males over sixty-five and not in the labor force. This is not entirely satisfactory, since it assumes that the number eligible for veterans benefits is a constant proportion of the population group. Inspection of the data indicates that this proportionality was far from constant until after the Korean War was terminated. Therefore, we have based our relationship on the data beginning with 1954.

$$\ln V_{RV_{GF}} = \frac{1.107}{(0.009)} \ln \{[N_{M65+}] - [L_{M65+}]\} + \frac{0.034}{(0.015)} DMY6 - \frac{0.783}{(0.134)}$$

$$\bar{R}^2 = 0.96 \qquad VN = 1.0 \tag{14.27}$$

(3) *Other survivors programs*

   (a) *Veterans*   Since benefits under this program go largely to widows and orphans of veterans, we use women over sixty-five and not in the labor force and population aged zero to eighteen as independent variables. Because of the high correlation between the two population variables, we have combined them to obtain the following relationship:

$$V_{SV_{GF}} = \frac{0.01980}{(0.00044)} \{[N_{F65+}] - [L_{F65+}] + [N_{18-}]\} - \frac{0.5908}{(0.0272)}$$

$$\bar{R}^2 = 0.99 \qquad VN = 0.53. \tag{14.28}$$

This equation, like the earlier veterans' equation, assumes that those receiving veterans' benefits constitute a constant proportion of the various demographic categories. This assumption may be inaccurate, but it should not take us too far astray in the near future, provided there is no substantial shift in the present military program.

   (b) *All other*   This category combines monthly civil service and railroad survivors programs with the lump-sum survivors program.[27] It is treated in exactly the same manner as the veterans' survivors program above. The result is:

$$V_{SNV_{GF}} = \frac{0.01280}{(0.00024)} \{[N_{F65+}] - [L_{F65+}] + [N_{18-}]\} - \frac{0.6388}{(0.0144)}$$

$$\bar{R}^2 = 0.99 \qquad VN = 0.41. \tag{14.29}$$

---

[27] There are lump-sum benefits under the civil service, railroad and veterans' programs payable when there is no survivor eligible for a monthly survivor's benefit.

(4) Unemployment compensation benefits

(a) *State laws*   The formulae for unemployment insurance benefit payments are prescribed by each state, and so the exact relation giving the aggregate payment in any period is quite complex. Approximately, aggregate benefits would be determined by (i) computing for each state the product of the average effective benefit times the number of covered unemployed who have not exhausted their benefits and (ii) summing the products. The waiting period for eligibility should also be taken into account, but even without this complicating concession to reality the relation is too unwieldy. Therefore, we approximate by:

$$\ln\left[V_{\text{US}_{GF}}\right] = \alpha_1 \ln VM_{\text{US}} + \alpha_2 \ln [RW]_{-1} + \alpha_3 \ln U$$
$$+ \alpha_4 \ln \left[\frac{L_{\text{UIS}}}{L}\right] + \alpha_5 \ln \left[\frac{U26-}{U}\right] + \alpha_0 + \varepsilon,$$

where

$V_{\text{US}_{GF}}$ = state unemployment insurance benefits paid by the federal government, billions of dollars

VM_{US} = weighted average of maximum weekly benefits under various state unemployment insurance plans, dollars

RW = average earnings per full-time equivalent employee, economy as a whole, dollars

U = unemployed civilian labor force, millions of persons

L_{UIS} = labor force covered by state unemployment insurance, millions of persons

L = civilian labor force, millions of persons

$U26-$ = number unemployed for 26 weeks or less, millions of persons.

We would expect all coefficients to be positive and the coefficients of VM_{US} and U to be near unity. The least-squares estimates accord with our expectations, except that the coefficients of RW and L_{UIS}/L are very small and insignificant. A simpler equation with these two variables eliminated is:

$$\ln V_{\text{US}_{GF}} = \frac{0.807}{(0.125)} \ln VM_{\text{US}} + \frac{1.062}{(0.099)} \ln U + \frac{1.086}{(0.750)} \ln \left[\frac{U26-}{U}\right] - \frac{3.447}{(0.379)}$$

$$\bar{R}^2 = 0.87 \qquad VN = 1.4. \tag{14.30}$$

(b) *Veterans*   The veterans' programs covered here combine unemployment compensation with readjustment for self-employed veterans, since the latter program did not last long enough to be considered separately. Because programs disappear from our series when they become smaller than

$ 1 million per quarter, these veterans' programs run from 1947 : 1 to 1951 : 1, then reappear in 1952 : 3 and end in 1959 : 4. Separate treatment was given the two periods. The first period came out reasonably well, but the second did not. Hence, we have not continued trying to improve this equation. Its current value is limited, although the most recent law changes might raise veterans' unemployment insurance benefits sufficiently high to require additional estimation.

(c) *Railroad*   Railroad unemployment compensation benefits have been explained by total unemployment, since we did not have a good series of railroad unemployment itself.

$$\ln \left[V_{UR_{GF}} \right] = \frac{1.096}{(0.118)} \ln U + \frac{1.130}{(0.138)} \ln VM_{UR} + \frac{0.041}{(0.256)}$$

$$\bar{R}^2 = 0.81 \qquad VN = 1.14, \tag{14.31}$$

where

$V_{UR_{GF}}$ = railroad unemployment insurance benefits plus sickness compensation, billions of dollars

VM_{UR} = maximum daily benefit from railroad unemployment insurance, dollars.

(5) *Other transfer payments*   The remaining transfer payments include a large number of minor miscellaneous items classified as "other" by OBE [28]). In addition, our classification includes any series not previously estimated, namely, government and national service life insurance programs. It is difficult to conceive of a small number of variables that would explain these payments. Even the use of predicted expenditures in the federal budget in each year failed to give satisfactory estimates.

(B) *State and local government*
(1) *Public assistance*   Most transfer payments of state and local governments to persons are made through the public assistance program under federal social security legislation. In the OBE transfer payments accounts, this appears as direct relief and is divided into two parts: special or categorical assistance and general assistance. The first is comprised of four programs designed for special categories of the population, old age assistance (OAA), aid to dependent children (ADC), aid to the blind (AB) and aid to the

---

[28]) See *Income and Output*, table III-7, footnote 3.

permanently and totally disabled (APTD). These programs, although financed partly by the federal government, are administered at the state and local level, and the benefit rates are set there. General assistance (GA) is entirely the responsibility of state and local governments and is usually called "relief".

(a) *Old age assistance*   Payments under the OAA program go to people over sixty-five who are not eligible to receive OASI, are unemployed or unemployable and have no other means of support. Benefit rates are set by states and localities. The complications of computing a precise rate variable lead us to use dummy variables to represent increases in the amount of federal participation in these benefits. (In the period of estimation, the federal share was increased in 1948, 1952, 1956 and 1958.) We have done this on the assumption that states increase their benefits when the federal government pays a larger share.

The estimated equation is:

$$\ln\left[\frac{V_{AO_{GS}}}{\{[N_{65+}]-N_{OASI}\}}\right] = -\frac{69.2}{(20.0)}\ln\left[\frac{E_{65+}}{N_{65+}}\right] + \frac{0.262}{(0.034)}DMY7$$
$$+\frac{0.317}{(0.024)}DMY8+\frac{0.259}{(0.030)}DMY9+\frac{0.142}{(0.037)}DMY10+\frac{3.880}{(0.285)}$$
$$\bar{R}^2 = 0.96. \tag{14.32}$$

The variables used above and in the equations for other state and local transfer payments are:

$V_{AO_{GS}}$ = state and local government old age assistance payments, billions of dollars

N_{65+} = civilian population aged 65 and over (62 and over for females since 1956), millions of persons

N_{OASI} = civilian population aged 65 and over (62 and over for females since 1956) eligible for OASI benefits, millions of persons

E_{65+} = employed persons aged 65 and over, millions

$DMY7$ = 0, through 1948 : 3
       = 1, thereafter

$DMY8$ = 0, through 1952 : 3
       = 1, thereafter

$DMY9$ = 0, through 1956 : 4
       = 1, thereafter

$DMY10$ = 0, through 1958 : 3
        = 1, thereafter

$V_{ADC_{GS}}$ = state and local government aid to dependent children, billions of dollars

N_{18-} = civilian population aged 18 and under, millions of persons

U = unemployed civilian labor force, millions of persons

U_{IS} = unemployment covered by state unemployment insurance, millions of persons

L = civilian labor force, millions of persons

L_{UIS} = labor force covered by state unemployment insurance, millions of persons

$V_{AB_{GS}}$ = state and local government aid to the blind, billions of dollars

N = civilian population including Alaska and Hawaii, millions of persons

$V_{APD_{GS}}$ = state and local government aid to the permanently and totally disabled, billions of dollars

$V_{AG_{GS}}$ = state and local government general assistance payments, billions of dollars

$DMY11$ = 0, through 1950 : 3

              = 1, thereafter

$V^{A}_{BEN_{GS}}$ = benefits from social insurance funds, billions of dollars.

(b) *Aid to dependent children*   ADC payments are largely to aid needy children under eighteen years of age who are deprived of parental support. Consequently, we have used population aged zero to eighteen as the basic determinant of the size of the payments. In addition, benefits are paid to children of unemployed parents not covered under the unemployment compensation program. Therefore, we have used as a second independent variable the uncovered unemployment rate. As before, dummy variables are used to represent changes in federal participation. The expression we have determined is:

$$\ln V_{ADC_{GS}} = \frac{1.544}{(0.144)} \ln [N_{18-}] + \frac{0.047}{(0.026)} \ln \left[\frac{U-U_{IS}}{L-L_{UIS}}\right] + \frac{0.367}{(0.031)} DMY7$$

$$+ \frac{0.097}{(0.034)} DMY9 + \frac{0.138}{(0.031)} DMY10 - \frac{0.079}{(0.570)}$$

$$\bar{R}^2 = 0.99. \tag{14.33}$$

The coefficient of the dummy variable for the 1952 amendments, $DMY8$, was negative; hence, it was excluded. The negative sign should not be interpreted as an indication that the states reduced benefit rates because the federal share in benefits was increased. It is caused, instead, by the substantial reduction in the number of recipients which occurred during the Korean War. This decrease can be explained by economic conditions during the war—labor force additions and low levels of unemployment. It is likely also that armed services allowances had an effect in making it possible for some usual ADC recipients to be supported in another manner.

(c) *Aid to the blind and aid to the permanently and totally disabled*   The remaining two categorical assistance programs are small and basically involve trends. There is little variation around the trend line (even seasonal) and no cyclical variability. The requirements for AB and APTD benefits are stringent and not subject to economic forces.

We have decided to make these payments a function only of total population. This is somewhat unsatisfactory, since in APTD there is a rising participation rate and rising rates of payment, whereas in AB there is a falling participation rate yet even more rapidly rising benefit rates. On the other hand, it is probably best to think of these programs, once started, as just growing with population. These relationships are:

$$V_{AB_{GS}} = \frac{0.00164}{(0.00003)} N - \frac{0.193}{(0.004)}$$

$$\bar{R}^2 = 0.99 \qquad VN = 0.6. \tag{14.34}$$

$$V_{APD_{GS}} = \frac{0.00841}{(0.00015)} N - \frac{1.207}{(0.024)}$$

$$\bar{R}^2 = 0.99 \qquad VN = 0.2. \tag{14.35}$$

(Equation (14.35) is estimated for 1950 : 4 through 1960 : 4.)

(d) *General assistance*   The remaining public assistance program involves no federal participation. It benefits those who are unemployed or unemployable and who are eligible for no other assistance or insurance program. Therefore, we have used uninsured unemployment as one independent variable.

Because these are state programs, benefit rates and rate changes diverge widely among states and are most difficult to determine. We have decided, therefore, to use changes in federal participation in the previous programs on the grounds that states normally would increase benefits under all their public assistance programs at the same time.

Our estimate is:

$$V_{AG_{GS}} = \frac{0.0400}{(0.0112)} [U - U_{IS}] + \frac{0.0580}{(0.0082)} [U - U_{IS}][DMY7]$$

$$- \frac{0.0465}{(0.0059)} [U - U_{IS}][DMY11] + \frac{0.0149}{(0.0061)} [U - U_{IS}][DMY9]$$

$$+ \frac{0.0249}{(0.0050)} [U - U_{IS}][DMY10] + \frac{0.1313}{(0.0105)}$$

$$\bar{R}^2 = 0.90 \qquad VN = 1.6. \tag{14.36}$$

The coefficient of *DMY11* is negative and significant. The reasons for this are quite clear. The 1950 amendment (which is not included in the earlier equations, since the rate of federal participation was not changed) established APTD and made it possible for states to receive federal funds for benefits given to the adult relative of a dependent child under ADC. Consequently, a large number of people were transferred from general assistance to these other programs.

The dummy *DMY8* representing the 1952 amendment was tried, but its coefficient was negative for the same reasons as in ADC. Therefore, we have eliminated it.

(2) *Other transfer payments*   The payments included in this category are not homogeneous, including such programs as government pensions, veterans' aid and bonuses, payments for the care of foster children and payments to nonprofit institutions, and cannot be explained satisfactorily on a quarterly or annual basis. One component of this category, which OBE entitles "benefits from social insurance funds" (government pensions and sickness compensation), is large and can be estimated somewhat better on an annual basis [29]).

14.3.2. *Purchases of goods and services*

Our discussion of the determinants of purchases of goods and services will be divided into three broad categories: wages and salaries of employees, new construction and all other. It should be borne in mind that the "all

---

[29]) $V_{BEN_{GS}}^{A} = \frac{0.100}{(0.016)} \{[N_{65+}^{A}] - [L_{65+}^{A}]\} - \frac{0.248}{(0.163)}$

$\bar{R}^2 = 0.71.$

other" category for the federal government sector includes the bulk of defense expenditures, including military personnel. Supplements of civilian employees are also included in this latter category rather than in wages and salaries.

(A) *Federal government*

(1) *Wages and salaries*   In this section, we deal only with wages and salaries of civilian employees. In estimating it we have proceeded by breaking wages and salaries down into the average annual wage and number of employees.

The average annual wage of civilian employees moves closely with average annual wages in the economy as a whole [30]). This relationship is represented by the following equations:

$$RW^{A}_{CIV_{GF}} = \frac{1.369}{(0.043)} RW^{A} - \frac{617.129}{(158.692)}$$
$$\bar{R}^2 = 0.99 \qquad VN = 1.7. \tag{14.37}$$

$$RW^{A}_{CIV_{GF}} = \frac{1.358}{(0.050)} [RW^{A}]_{-1} - \frac{346.644}{(177.737)}$$
$$\bar{R}^2 = 0.99 \qquad VN = 1.3. \tag{14.38}$$

The variables which appear in this section are:

$RW^{A}_{CIV_{GF}}$ = average annual earnings per full-time equivalent civilian employee of the federal general government, dollars

RW^{A} = average annual earnings per full-time equivalent employee, economy as a whole, dollars

$WS_{CIV_{GF}}$ = federal general government wage and salary disbursements to civilians, billions of dollars

$E_{XEC_{GF}}$ = employees in the executive branch of the federal government excluding government enterprises, thousands. [31])

---

[30]) In principle it is possible and desirable to construct a variable representing average wages and salaries in the private sector (excluding government) and use it as the independent variable. We did not attempt it, however, and the result will not be significantly different in view of very close correlation between the average wages and salaries in the private and government sector.

[31]) More precisely, $E_{XEC_{GF}}$ represents the number of paid civilian employees of the executive branch, excluding employees of the District of Columbia, C.I.A., and National Security Agency. Only employees in the U.S. are included (including Alaska and Hawaii but excluding the Canal Zone).

The annual average wage is then used to estimate total quarterly wages and salaries. We could establish no satisfactory explanation of the number of employees and so must consider them exogenous. The relationship is:

$$\ln WS_{\mathrm{CIV}_{GF}} = \frac{0.823}{(0.075)} \ln E_{\mathrm{XEC}_{GF}} + \frac{1.077}{(0.033)} \ln RW^{\mathrm{A}}_{\mathrm{CIV}_{GF}} - \frac{7.443}{(0.263)}$$

$$\bar{R}^2 = 0.99 \qquad VN = 1.0. \tag{14.39}$$

We should point out that the exogenous variable, $E_{\mathrm{XEC}_{GF}}$ is predicted in recent budget documents [32]. These predictions are available in a convenient summary form only for fiscal years 1963 and 1964 [33]. We would expect that when a sufficient number of observations of these budget predictions become available, either by tabulation from past budgets or by the passage of time, these can be used as an independent variable in making quarterly predictions along the lines used below in estimating military expenditures.

(2) *New construction*   New construction undertaken by the federal government is substantial only for military and industrial facilities (both of which are primarily for national defense purposes) and for conservation and development. We have combined all other minor categories, which include residential, educational, hospital, administrative facilities and highways. We have experimented with a number of economic variables but have been forced to conclude that none of them predicts satisfactorily these types of construction by the federal government. We have therefore resorted to the use of the budget predictions of these items and have also used the rate of unemployment as a supplementary variable when it appears to be significant.

The variables in the equations for federal government construction are:

G_{ICMI_F} = new military and industrial construction activitity by the federal government, millions of dollars

$BGT^{\mathrm{FY}}_{\mathrm{ML}}$ = national defense expenditures during fiscal year t estimated in the President's budget submission of January, year t, millions of dollars

---

[32] See, for instance, *Budget of U.S. Government, Fiscal Year 1963*, table 9, p. 41, and *Budget of U.S. Government, Fiscal Year 1964*, table 12, p. 48.

[33] These numbers can be obtained, however, by totaling items in the detailed budget for earlier years. $E_{\mathrm{XEC}_{GF}}$ as used above, differs from these budget estimates, which include employees in foreign countries (including the Canal Zone), in the District of Columbia and in government enterprises.

$BGTR_{ML}^{FY}$ = national defense expenditures requested for fiscal year $t+1$ as estimated in the President's budget submission of January, year t, millions of dollars

G_{ICO_F} = new construction activity by the federal government other than military and industrial and conservation and development, millions of dollars

RU = rate of unemployment = U/L, fraction

N = civilian population including Alaska and Hawaii, millions of persons.

(a) *Military and industrial facilities*   We have made regression estimates for each quarter separately, based on the annual budget prediction of current and prospective fiscal-year national defense expenditures. As can be seen from the relationships, the weights shift from current to prospective expenditures as one moves from the first to the fourth quarter.

$$\ln G_{ICMI_F}^{Q1} = \frac{0.613}{(0.393)} \ln BGT_{ML}^{FY} + \frac{0.913}{(0.413)} \ln BGTR_{ML}^{FY} - \frac{8.660}{(1.466)}$$

$$\bar{R}^2 = 0.91 \qquad VN = 1.4. \tag{14.40}$$

$$\ln G_{ICMI_F}^{Q2} = \frac{0.126}{(0.270)} \ln BGT_{ML}^{FY} + \frac{1.415}{(0.263)} \ln BGTR_{ML}^{FY} - \frac{8.822}{(0.985)}$$

$$\bar{R}^2 = 0.96 \qquad VN = 1.3. \tag{14.41}$$

$$\ln G_{ICMI_F}^{Q3} = \frac{1.407}{(0.099)} \ln BGTR_{ML}^{FY} - \frac{7.407}{(1.020)}$$

$$\bar{R}^2 = 0.94 \qquad VN = 2.4. \tag{14.42}$$

$$\ln G_{ICMI_F}^{Q4} = \frac{1.346}{(0.111)} \ln BGTR_{ML}^{FY} - \frac{6.736}{(1.154)}$$

$$\bar{R}^2 = 0.90 \qquad VN = 2.7. \tag{14.43}$$

There are a number of features that may be noted in these equations. The sum of the elasticities with respect to BGT_{ML}^{FY} and $BGTR_{ML}^{FY}$ are substantially more than unity in all cases, suggesting that changes in actual expenditures are underpredicted. The fact that predicted government expenditures in the future can influence the first and second quarter is attributable to build-ups or cutbacks in prospective programs which would influence the scale of current expenditures. It is surprising that the elasticity of first- and second-quarter expenditures with respect to predicted expenditures for the subsequent year is larger than that for the current fiscal year.

One would expect that higher levels of unemployment would induce an acceleration of federal construction programs, both in timing and volume, over the amount initially planned in the budget. To check this possibility, we introduced the unemployment rate as an additional independent variable. While it improved mechanically the estimates of these equations, the sign of its coefficient was uniformly negative. This fact suggests that some simultaneous equation bias may be present. While the amount of construction in this category is not large enough to influence the total unemployment level significantly, it is associated with large military expenditures, which in turn could have had a major impact on unemployment.

(b) *Conservation and development*   This category has been treated in the same manner as the construction of military and industrial facilities, but the results were uniformly unsatisfactory. Evidently, the budget process is more erratic with respect to this group of expenditures than any other that we have examined, and it is our belief that it should be treated as exogenous. It is interesting to note, however, that the coefficients of the rate of unemployment in this case are positive and not insignificant.

(c) *All other construction*   As indicated at the beginning of the section on new construction, this category includes a number of minor non-homogeneous items. We could not use the budget expenditure prediction as an independent variable because of the difficulty in aligning budget predictions with this miscellaneous group. We have therefore used population and unemployment as the major independent variables. It turned out, however, that the multiple correlation coefficient is quite low, and the serial correlation is exceedingly severe [34]). The introduction of the dependent variable in lagged form improved the serial correlation and the fit of the equation but made the population variable insignificant. The relationship is:

$$\ln G_{ICO_F} = \frac{1.047}{(0.675)} \ln \left[\frac{[RU]_{-2}+[RU]_{-3}}{2}\right] + \frac{0.055}{(0.133)} \ln N$$

$$+ \frac{0.835}{(0.080)} \ln [G_{ICO_F}]_{-1} - \frac{4.158}{(3.305)}$$

$$\bar{R}^2 = 0.85 \qquad VN = 1.8. \tag{14.44}$$

---

[34])

$$\ln G_{ICO_F} = \frac{5.413}{(0.948)} \ln N + \frac{0.454}{(0.228)} \ln \left[\frac{[RU]_{-2}+[RU]_{-3}}{2}\right] - \frac{20.252}{(5.118)}$$

$$\bar{R}^2 = 0.49 \qquad VN = 0.3.$$

We do not believe that this is a very reliable result, but it is perhaps better than treating this group of items as entirely exogenous.

(3) *All other purchases of goods and services*   The series representing this group of expenditures is obtained by subtracting the items discussed above from the total federal government purchases of goods and services reported by OBE. Its major components are national defense, including military wages and salaries, foreign aid and agriculture, less sales of government property. It also includes supplements of government civilian employees.

The major portion of this expenditure is clearly exogenous to any economic model. Instead of leaving it unexplained, however, we report its relationship to the budget estimates of expenditure on national defense and agriculture as shown in the annual budget resumé [35]).

$$\ln G_{O_F}^{Q1} = \frac{0.537}{(0.185)} \ln \left[BGT_{AG}^{FY} + BGT_{ML}^{FY} \right] + \frac{0.362}{(0.185)} \ln \left[BGTR_{AG}^{FY} + BGTR_{ML}^{FY} \right]$$

$$+ \frac{0.828}{(0.669)}$$

$$\bar{R}^2 = 0.94 \qquad VN = 1.9. \tag{14.45}$$

$$\ln G_{O_F}^{Q2} = \frac{0.872}{(0.075)} \ln \left[BGTR_{AG}^{FY} + BGTR_{ML}^{FY} \right] - \frac{1.094}{(0.790)}$$

$$\bar{R}^2 = 0.90 \qquad VN = 2.0. \tag{14.46}$$

$$\ln G_{O_F}^{Q3} = \frac{0.975}{(0.103)} \ln \left[BGTR_{AG}^{FY} + BGTR_{ML}^{FY} \right] - \frac{0.040}{(1.077)}$$

$$\bar{R}^2 = 0.92 \qquad VN = 2.0. \tag{14.47}$$

$$\ln G_{O_F}^{Q4} = \frac{0.801}{(0.064)} \ln \left[BGTR_{AG}^{FY} + BGTR_{ML}^{FY} \right] - \frac{0.186}{(0.672)}$$

$$\bar{R}^2 = 0.94 \qquad VN = 2.9. \tag{14.48}$$

The variables are:

G_{O_F} = purchases of goods and services by the federal government other than construction and civilian wages and salaries, billions of dollars

---

[35]) We excluded international affairs and finance because most expenditures in this category are classified by OBE as transfer payments. In future years, it will be important to include the category "space research and technology", although this item was quite insignificant during the period covered by our data.

BGT_{AG}^{FY} = agriculture and agricultural resources expenditures during fiscal year t estimated in the President's budget submission of January, year t, millions of dollars

BGT_{ML}^{FY} = national defense expenditures during fiscal year t estimated in the President's budget submission of January, year t, millions of dollars

$BGTR_{AG}^{FY}$ = agriculture and agricultural resources expenditures requested for fiscal year $t+1$ as estimated in the President's budget submission of January, year t, millions of dollars

$BGTR_{ML}^{FY}$ = national defense expenditures requested for fiscal year $t+1$ as estimated in the President's budget submission of January, year t, millions of dollars.

(B) *State and local governments*

(1) *Wages and salaries* (supplements are included in "other").

(a) *School*   Wages and salaries of school employees are most realistically estimated on a yearly basis because the bulk of the wage contracts cover the period of a year. This is the largest relatively homogeneous item of state and local government purchases of goods and services.

The equilibrium demand for teachers' services may be considered as a function of the number of pupils, the stock of school facilities and the wage rate of teachers [36]). The supply of teachers, on the other hand, depends upon their wage rate relative to other wage rates in the economy and the available stock of qualified teachers. Since we do not expect the supply of teachers to adjust instantaneously to the demand for them, we adopt the next simplest formulation, namely, that the proportion of the difference between the demand and supply of teachers made up in a period of a year is constant.

For statistical convenience, we approximate the available stock of teachers by the number of teachers in the previous year and the relative wage rate by the average wage for full-time equivalent employees in the total economy in the previous year and the average wage of school employees. When we write down the relationships discussed in the preceding paragraph in terms of these variables and solve them for the endogenous variables in

---

[36]) This formulation does not carry our reasoning to its logical conclusion, since it takes the existing school facilities as given. They, too, should be explained.

this context, we obtain the reduced-form equations

$$\Delta E^A_{ED_{GS}} = f_1 \left\{ [N^A_{5-18}], K^A_{ED_{GS}}, \left[\frac{RW^A}{CPI^A}\right]_{-1}, [E^A_{ED_{GS}}]_{-1} \right\}$$

$$\frac{RW^A_{ED_{GS}}}{CPI^A} = f_2 \left\{ [N^A_{5-18}], K^A_{ED_{GS}}, \left[\frac{RW^A}{CPI^A}\right]_{-1}, [E^A_{ED_{GS}}]_{-1} \right\},$$

where

$E^A_{ED_{GS}}$ = full-time equivalent employees in state and local public education, millions

N^A_{5-18} = civilian population aged 5 to 18, as of July 1, millions of persons

$K_{ED_{GS}}$ = stock of capital in state and local educational structures, billions of dollars

RW^A = average annual earnings per full-time equivalent employee, economy as a whole, dollars

CPI = consumer price index, 1954 = 1.00

$RW^A_{ED_{GS}}$ = average annual earnings per full-time equivalent employee in state and local public education, dollars.

N^A_{5-25}, which will be used in one of the following least-squares estimates, is civilian population aged 5 to 25 as of July 1, millions of persons.

We have estimated the above equations in a variety of functional forms, using all the independent variables suggested by the model developed above. However, we are dealing with yearly observations, and there are few degrees of freedom. Furthermore, the correlations among independent variables are very high (all over 0.97), and we are faced with serious multicollinearity problems.

The addition to the employment of teachers is given by:

$$\Delta \ln E^A_{ED_{GS}} = \frac{0.444}{(0.176)} \ln [N^A_{5-18}] - \frac{0.364}{(0.127)} \ln [E^A_{ED_{GS}}]_{-1}$$

$$+ \frac{0.087}{(0.109)} \ln \left[\frac{RW^A}{CPI^A}\right]_{-1} + \frac{0.013}{(0.067)} \ln K^A_{ED_{GS}} - \frac{11.060}{(0.665)}$$

$$\bar{R}^2 = 0.49 \qquad VN = 2.9. \tag{14.49}$$

It may be noted that the coefficients of $[RW/CPI]_{-1}$ and $K^A_{ED_{GS}}$ have standard errors much larger than themselves. While on theoretical grounds the above equation should not be discarded for the purpose of future structural estimation, for short-run forecasts the simpler equation below performs better [37]).

$$\Delta \ln E_{EDGS}^{A} = \frac{0.548}{(0.133)} \ln [N_{5-18}^{A}] - \frac{0.366}{(0.093)} \ln [E_{EDGS}^{A}]_{-1} - \frac{11.203}{(0.438)}$$

$$\bar{R}^2 = 0.54 \qquad VN = 3.1. \tag{14.50}$$

In the case of the wage-rate relationship, the general regression estimates yield very good fits. However, the coefficients have very large standard errors and several incorrect signs. Under the circumstances, we have approximated the influence of the three variables—stock of qualified teachers, stock of school facilities and the number of pupils—by a single variable, the first difference of the number of pupils. The estimated equation is:

$$\ln \left[\frac{RW_{EDGS}^{A}}{CPI^{A}} \right] = \frac{1.174}{(0.145)} \ln \left[\frac{RW^{A}}{CPI^{A}} \right]_{-1} + \frac{2.485}{(1.453)} \Delta \ln [N_{5-18}^{A}] - \frac{0.347}{(0.163)}$$

$$\bar{R}^2 = 0.93 \qquad VN = 1.8. \tag{14.51}$$

The total of wages and salaries is then obtained by multiplying the number of teachers by the average wage.

(b) *Nonschool*   Nonschool employees of state and local government have been treated in the same way as those of the federal government (See section 14.3.2). The annual wage rate of nonschool employees when regressed on the average annual wage in the economy as a whole for the preceding year is found to be:

$$RW_{OGS}^{A} = \frac{0.921}{(0.009)} [RW^{A}]_{-1} - \frac{123.733}{(32.927)}$$

$$\bar{R}^2 = 0.99 \qquad VN = 1.8. \tag{14.52}$$

---

[37]) The number of pupils in equations (14.49) and (14.50) is approximated by the population between ages five and eighteen inclusive. Since our other data refer to all state and local school systems, including higher education, it may be argued that the population between ages five and twenty-five inclusive is more appropriate. If this enlarged population is used, the coefficient for deflated wage rate is very close to zero and insignificant. Eliminating this variable we obtain:

$$\Delta \ln E_{EDGS}^{A} = 0.289 \ln [N_{5-25}^{A}] - \frac{0.430}{(0.121)} \ln [E_{EDGS}^{A}]_{-1} + \frac{0.157}{(0.055)} \ln K_{EDGS}^{A}$$

$$- \frac{11.805}{(0.619)}$$

$$\bar{R}^2 = 0.50 \qquad VN = 2.9.$$

We would expect the need for nonschool employees to depend on population, modified by per capita income and by federal civilian activities (as measured by its purchases of nondefense goods and services). However, in our attempt to estimate this relationship, we found real per capita personal income to be unsatisfactory and eliminated it. The resulting estimates are [38]):

$$\ln E_{O_{GS}} = \frac{1.832}{(0.090)} \ln N - \frac{0.021}{(0.021)} \ln \left[\frac{G_F - G_{MLF}}{P_G \cdot N} \right] - \frac{15.342}{(0.457)}$$

$$\bar{R}^2 = 0.92 \qquad VN = 0.3 \tag{14.53}$$

Because the number of nonschool employees is not given quarterly by OBE, we have had to use estimates which do not exactly correspond to the definition of the number of employees receiving wages and salaries. Therefore, the prediction of total quarterly wages and salaries at an annual rate cannot be obtained by direct multiplication but should be estimated by the following equation:

$$\ln WS_{O_{GS}} = \frac{0.585}{(0.124)} \ln E_{O_{GS}} + \frac{1.352}{(0.090)} \ln RW^A_{O_{GS}} - \frac{6.614}{(0.633)}$$

$$\bar{R}^2 = 0.99 \qquad VN = 2.0. \tag{14.54}$$

The variables which appear in this section are:

$RW^A_{O_{GS}}$ = average annual earnings per full-time equivalent employee, state and local nonschool except work relief and enterprises, dollars

RW^A = average annual earnings per full-time equivalent employee, economy as a whole, dollars

$E_{O_{GS}}$ = full-time equivalent employees, state and local nonschool except work relief and enterprises, millions

N = civilian population including Alaska and Hawaii, millions of persons

G_F = federal government purchases of goods and services, billions of dollars

G_{MLF} = federal government purchases of goods and services for national defense, billions of dollars

---

[38]) Since real government nondefense purchases are not very significant, equation (14.35) has been estimated, eliminating this variable.

$$\ln E_{O_{GS}} = \frac{1.885}{(0.073)} \ln N - \frac{15.638}{(0.371)} \qquad\qquad \bar{R}^2 = 0.92 \qquad VN = 0.2.$$

P_G = implicit price deflator for government purchases of goods and services, 1954 = 1.00

$WS_{O_{GS}}$ = wage and salary disbursements to nonschool (except work relief and enterprises) employees of state and local governments, billions.

(2) *New construction*   Under this heading, highways, school facilities and water and sewage systems are the major programs. While the initiative for these programs rests with state and local governments, there is substantial federal participation in many of them.

The variables in the construction equations are:

G_{ICED_S} = new educational construction activity by state and local governments, billions of dollars

$K_{ED_{GS}}$ = stock of capital in state and local educational structures, billions of dollars

N_{18-} = civilian population aged 18 and under, millions of persons

RM_{MBLM} = Moody's average long-term municipal bond yield, per cent

G_{ICHO_S} = new hospital and institutional construction activity by state and local governments, billions of dollars

$BEDSN$ = additional beds needed in state general, tubercular and mental hospitals as of January 1, thousands

$K_{HO_{GS}}$ = stock of state and local hospital assets, billions of dollars

G_{ICAD_S} = construction of administrative and service facilities by state and local governments, billions of dollars

$E_{O_{GS}}$ = full-time equivalent employees, state and local nonschool except work relief and enterprises, thousands

G_{ICHI_S} = new highway construction activity by state and local governments, billions of dollars

CAR_{REG} = stock of automobiles registered, end of quarter, millions

$HWYL$ = length of surfaced highways, including Alaskan and Hawaiian, million of miles

TX_{HWY} = highway trust fund tax revenues, millions of dollars

G_{ICWA_S} = new construction activity by state and local governments for sewer and water systems, billions of dollars

P_{GS} = implicit price deflator for state and local government purchases of goods and services, 1954 = 1.00

I_C = new construction component of gross private domestic investment, billions of dollars

I_{CO*} = petroleum and natural gas well drilling component of new construction activity, billions of dollars

P_{IC_P} = implicit price deflator for new private construction activity, 1954 = 1.00

G_{ICO_S} = all other new nonresidential construction activity by state and local governments, billions of dollars.

(a) *Residential*   Expenditures under this category move very erratically and have been combined with other purchases of goods and services (see p. 585).

(b) *Nonresidential*

(i) *Educational*   The construction of educational facilities depends quite clearly on the existing stock of school buildings as compared with the desired stock, the desired stock in turn depending on the number of school-age children and expectations as to what the school-age population is going to be in the future. In addition to these long-run determinants, the timing of construction may be affected by the cost of capital as represented by some interest rate.

$$G_{ICED_S}^{54} = \frac{0.532}{(0.092)}[N_{18-}] - \frac{0.260}{(0.096)}[K_{ED_{GS}}^{54}]_{-1} + \frac{2.3360}{(0.6028)}[RM_{MBLM}]_{-2}$$

$$- \frac{0.04556}{(0.00968)}\{[N_{18-}][RM_{MBLM}]_{-2}\} - \frac{22.252}{(3.132)}$$

$$\bar{R}^2 = 0.93 \qquad VN = 0.4. \tag{14.55}$$

Redefinition of equation (14.55) in money terms raises the coefficient of correlation substantially, but we believe the theoretical explanation should be in real terms.

As in most stock-flow adjustment models of investment, the interest rate should in theory influence the relationship between the desired stock and the variable on which the definition of the desired stock is based (N_{18-} in this case). To take account of nonlinearity in this relationship, we have introduced the product term into equation (14.55). We note that the partial derivative of construction with respect to the interest rate is negative for the range of N_{18-} in our observation. Thus, all variables have significant coefficients with correct signs.

(ii) *Hospital*   The need for total hospital facilities in a community depends upon a number of economic and demographic variables. Given this total need, the degree to which it is satisfied by public facilities depends upon the level of service provided by private hospitals. During the period with which we are concerned, there have been noticeable shifts in the relative importance of private and public hospital construction: before 1954, public hospital construction exceeded private hospital construction, whereas since that date the reverse has been true. Under the circumstances, there is no straightforward way of relating the need for public hospitals directly to the basic variables.

Fortunately, under the Hill-Burton Act, state governments are required to prepare annually their estimates of need for additional beds in state hospitals. As in the case of school construction, we hypothesize that the construction of public hospitals is some proportion of the difference between needed facilities and the existing stock. There are no precise data on the stock of hospitals, but we have approximated it by the total assets of state and local hospitals, the bulk of which we assume to be physical facilities. The resulting estimated equation is:

$$G^{54}_{ICHOs} = \frac{0.001612}{(0.000124)} BEDSN - \frac{0.000776}{(0.000012)} K^{54}_{HOGs} - \frac{0.5168}{(0.0808)}$$

$$\bar{R}^2 = 0.90 \qquad VN = 1.2. \tag{14.56}$$

The money figures are deflated by a construction cost index.

(iii) *Administrative and service facilities* We assume that the need for administrative and service facilities depends primarily on the number of nonschool employees of state and local governments. We cannot, however, directly estimate the standard stock-flow adjustment model because we have no information on the stock of administrative and service facilities. Taking the first differences of the variables and collecting terms, we get the formulation estimated below:

$$G^{54}_{ICADs} = \frac{0.14184}{(0.09724)} [\Delta E_{OGs}] + \frac{0.955}{(0.035)} [G^{54}_{ICADs}]_{-1} + \frac{0.01420}{(0.00892)}$$

$$\bar{R}^2 = 0.93 \qquad VN = 1.6. \tag{14.57}$$

(iv) *Other nonresidential construction* (see all other construction; section (e) below).

(c) *Highways* Over the long run, the need for highways depends on the economy's need for highway services. This need is a complex function of a variety of factors, and a simple way of representing it is by automobile registrations. The actual construction may be thought of as eliminating some proportion of the difference between the needed level and the existing level of highway facilities. At the same time, especially since the highway trust fund was initiated in 1956, the receipts turned over to the trust fund (gas, tire and certain excise taxes) have a substantial effect on short-run timing of highway construction. Both of these relationships are reported below:

$$\frac{G_{\text{ICHI}s}^{57-9}}{CAR_{\text{REG}}} = -\frac{2.080}{(0.712)} \left[\frac{HWYL}{CAR_{\text{REG}}}\right] + \frac{0.693}{(0.098)} \left[\frac{G_{\text{ICHI}s}^{57-9}}{CAR_{\text{REG}}}\right]_{-1} + \frac{0.116}{(0.036)}$$

$$\bar{R}^2 = 0.95 \qquad VN = 1.8. \tag{14.58}$$

$$G_{\text{ICHI}s} = \frac{0.297}{(0.135)} [TX_{\text{HWY}}]_{-1} + \frac{0.780}{(0.090)} [G_{\text{ICHI}s}]_{-1} + \frac{0.116}{(0.176)}$$

$$\bar{R}^2 = 0.92 \qquad VN = 2.1. \tag{14.59}$$

(d) *Sewer and water systems*   Construction of sewer and water systems should be closely related to other new construction which we use as the independent variable. However, there is much rebuilding of old systems and extension of service to existing communities without such facilities which may somewhat distort the relationship below:

$$\frac{G_{\text{ICWA}s}}{P_{GS}} = \frac{0.038}{(0.003)} \left[\frac{I_C - I_{CO*}}{P_{IC}}\right] + \frac{0.001004}{(0.070940)}$$

$$\bar{R}^2 = 0.81 \qquad VN = 0.5. \tag{14.60}$$

(e) *All other construction*   This series includes a wide variety of items, such as airports and terminals, crematoria, prisons, police stations, dams, fish hatcheries, street lights and parks, as well as other nonresidential construction. Clearly, there is no very satisfactory way of explaining these amounts. They may be treated as exogenous. However, they are subject to a strong trend factor, such as population growth.

We place little confidence in a reasonably close relationship using population and the unemployment rate because the category of construction includes such heterogeneous expenditure programs. In particular, the elasticity of construction on population is high, attributable, at least in part, to large airport construction. Moreover, the elasticity of construction on unemployment reflects nothing but the similar behavior of these two series during the Korean War. For future forecasting, probably the best relationship, derived for the period 1954 through 1960, is:

$$\ln\left[\frac{G_{\text{ICO}s}}{P_{GS}}\right] = \frac{0.004759}{(0.000321)} \ln N + \frac{1.3674}{(0.0016)}$$

$$\bar{R}^2 = 0.88 \qquad VN = 2.1. \tag{14.61}$$

(3) *All other purchases of goods and services*   The remaining item is quite substantial and represents the balance of purchases of goods and services, supplements and residential construction. It is closely related to the general level of current services provided by state and local governments and would be expected to have (in real terms) similar behavior over time to the number of nonschool employees of these governments (see p. 579). As in that case, we have used population, per capita personal income and federal purchases of nondefense goods and services as independent variables. We found that per capita personal income did not have much explanatory power and prefer the following relationship:

$$\ln\left[\frac{G_{Os}}{P_{GS}}\right] = \frac{0.002302}{(0.000198)} \ln N - \frac{0.083}{(0.052)} \ln\left[\frac{G_F - G_{\mathrm{ML}_F}}{P_G}\right] + \frac{1.4992}{(0.00120)}$$

$$\bar{R}^2 = 0.77 \qquad VN = 0.9. \tag{14.62}$$

PART VII

Estimation, simulation, aggregation and the complete model

DYNAMIC STRUCTURE AND ESTIMATION IN ECONOMY-WIDE ECONOMETRIC MODELS

Contents

15.1. Introduction and classification of estimators 589
    1. General introduction. 2. Classification of estimators.

15.2. Ordinary least squares. 591
    1. Assumptions and properties. 2. Recursive systems and necessary assumptions. 3. Recursive systems in economy-wide models. 4. The Proximity Theorem and near consistency. 5. Reduced form estimation.

15.3. Full-information estimators 601

15.4. Limited-information estimators 602
    1. Availability in practice. 2. Classification and large sample properties under ideal conditions. 3. Small sample properties. 4. Robustness.

15.5. Near-consistency, block-recursive systems, and the choice of eligible instrumental variables 606
    1. Introduction. 2. The theory of block-recursive systems. 3. Block-recursive assumptions in economy-wide models. 4. Reasonable properties of the disturbances. 5. Implications for the use of lagged endogenous variables.

15.6. Causality and rules for the use of eligible instrumental variables . . . 621
    1. The causal criterion for instrumental variables. 2. Available instruments and multicollinearity. 3. Rules for the use of eligible instrumental variables. 4. Discussion of the rules.

References 633

DYNAMIC STRUCTURE AND ESTIMATION IN ECONOMY-WIDE ECONOMETRIC MODELS

FRANKLIN M. FISHER [1]

Massachusetts Institute of Technology, Cambridge, Massachusetts

15.1. Introduction and classification of estimators

15.1.1. General introduction

This paper is concerned with the techniques of and the problems in the structural estimation of economy-wide econometric models. Briefly stated, the essential general features of such models which raise special problems for estimation are as follows: they tend to involve a large number of equations and variables; they are nearly closed in the sense that most of the variables of the model are endogenously determined; they are dynamic and essentially interconnected in the sense that, considered as dynamic systems, they are indecomposable; finally, the disturbances from different equations tend to be correlated with each other and with their own past values. All of these features will be discussed at greater length below, and all of them raise problems of varying magnitude for structural estimation.

As is well known, there are now a fairly large number of alternative estimation techniques available for such estimation. Such methods fall into classes which differ in the assumptions made or the amount of information taken into account. They also have different properties. In general, a great deal is known concerning the asymptotic properties under ideal conditions of most of these estimators; rather less is known of small sample properties;

[1] This paper was largely written during my tenure of a National Science Foundation Postdoctoral Fellowship at the Econometric Institute of the Netherlands School of Economics. I am indebted to T. J. Rothenberg for helpful conversations and to L. R. Klein and E. Kuh for criticism of an earlier draft, but remain responsible for errors.

and a very few results are available on their relative robustness—the relative degree to which they stand up to such things as multicollinearity, specification error and serial correlation in the disturbances of the model.

This paper begins by reviewing the known properties of the principal estimators in the context of economy-wide models. We observe that the features of such models mentioned above make even the best of such estimators rather suspect in its original form, while the size of such models makes them literally unavailable when the data involved are time series of lengths usually encountered. This leads naturally to estimation using instrumental variables in some form, and the second half of the paper is devoted in one way or another to exploring the question of how appropriate instrumental variables should be chosen. It is argued that this is best done through continual application of the a priori structural information which governs the formulation of the entire model in the first place, rather than through relatively arbitrary statistical devices.

15.1.2. *Classification of estimators*

For our purposes, the estimators which have been proposed for structural estimation may be divided into three classes. The first of these consists of ordinary least squares and its generalizations. The second includes two-stage least squares, limited-information maximum likelihood, the other members of Theil's *k*-class, Theil's *h*-class and Nagar's double *k*-class [2]. All the estimators in this group have the common property that whereas (unlike ordinary least squares) they take account of the simultaneous nature (if any) of the equations in the model to be estimated, they use a priori restrictions on only one equation at a time. Accordingly, we shall call such estimators "limited-information" methods. The last class of estimators consists of those methods which do use information on all equations at once, what we shall term "full-information" methods. Among these, of course, is full-information maximum likelihood, but the class also contains Zellner and Theil's three-stage least squares, an estimator recently proposed by Rothenberg and Leenders called "linearized maximum likelihood" and the simultaneous least-squares estimator of Brown [3].

In principle, all of the above estimators make use of all exogenous and lagged endogenous variables in the model as predetermined instruments.

---

[2]) See Theil [36, pp. 353–354] and Nagar [26].

[3]) See Zellner and Theil [41], Rothenberg and Leenders [29], and T. M. Brown [8].

As indicated above, for reasons to be discussed below, this cannot always be done or is not always desirable, and in such cases other methods which employ only some of the exogenous or lagged endogenous variables must be used. We shall discuss the problems raised in such situations below, observing here only that, given the choice of variables to be treated as predetermined, most of the estimators just classified have exact counterparts in such circumstances.

15.2. Ordinary least squares

15.2.1. Assumptions and properties

Ordinary least squares has a number of desirable properties when appropriate assumptions are satisfied. Briefly, if the explanatory variables in the equation to be estimated are either nonstochastic or distributed independently of all past, present and future values of the disturbance term in that equation; if the disturbance term is serially uncorrelated and homoscedastic; and if there are no a priori restrictions in the parameters to be estimated, ordinary least squares is the best linear unbiased estimator. In addition, if the disturbances are normally distributed, ordinary least squares is the maximum-likelihood estimator.

These assumptions can be weakened in several ways. First, if the explanatory variables are not independent of the disturbance term but are uncorrelated with it in the probability limit, ordinary least squares ceases to be unbiased but is consistent. If the disturbances are serially correlated, ordinary least squares loses efficiency but retains consistency provided such serial correlation does not affect the validity of assumptions concerning the correlation of the current disturbance term and the explanatory variables (a matter to which we shall return) [4]). Finally, ordinary least squares presents no particular difficulties of computation.

As is well known, however, the minimum assumption for the consistency of ordinary least squares—that the explanatory variables are uncorrelated with the disturbance term—cannot be maintained if the equation to be estimated is one of a system of simultaneous structural equations. In this case, ordinary least squares loses even consistency when used as an estimator of a structural equation, although not when used to estimate the equations of the reduced form.

---

[4]) See Theil [36, pp. 219–225] or Johnston [18, pp. 192–195] for a discussion of this case.

This argument is not sufficient, however, to dismiss ordinary least squares from consideration as an appropriate estimator in large econometric models. In the first place, there is the question emphasized by Wold [5] as to whether such models really should be simultaneous, given the nature of causation. Second, the issue is not of the yes-or-no variety as it is often made to appear; rather, if the model is such that correlation between the disturbance term and the explanatory variables in the given equation can be appropriately assumed to be *small* (rather than zero) or if the variance of the disturbance is known to be small, least squares will be *almost* consistent [6]. One may then be willing to accept the small inconsistencies involved for the sake of the other properties of the estimator, principally its relatively small variance around its probability limit. We must therefore go on to ask when this is likely to happen and when the assumptions of Wold's recursive model are likely to be approximately satisfied.

15.2.2. *Recursive systems and necessary assumptions*

Suppose that the model to be estimated is:

$$y_t = Ay_t + By_{t-1} + Cz_t + u_t, \tag{15.1}$$

where u_t is an m-component column vector of disturbances; y_t is an m-component column vector of current endogenous variables; z_t is an n-component column vector of exogenous variables (known at least to be uncorrelated in the probability limit with all current and past disturbances); A, B and C are constant matrices to be estimated; and $(I-A)$ is non-singular, while A has zeros everywhere on its principal diagonal. The assumption that there are no terms in $y_{t-\theta}$ for $\theta > 1$ involves no loss of generality in the present discussion, since it can always be accomplished by redefinition of y_t and expansion of the equation system and will be used only for convenience in dealing with the solution of (15.1) regarded as a system of stochastic difference equations.

If:

(R.1) A is triangular;

(R.2) the variance-covariance matrix of the current disturbances is diagonal;

(R.3) no current disturbance is correlated with any past disturbance;

[5] Wold and Juréen [38, pp. 50–51] and other writings.
[6] Wold and Faxèr [39].

the model is recursive and does not violate the assumption that in each equation the disturbance term is uncorrelated with the variables which appear therein other than the one to be explained by that equation. Ordinary least squares is then a consistent estimator and is the maximum-likelihood estimator if each element of u_t is normally distributed and homoscedastic.

To see that the no-correlation assumption is not violated, we solve the system for y_t, obtaining:

$$y_t = (I-A)^{-1}By_{t-1} + (I-A)^{-1}Cz_t + (I-A)^{-1}u_t. \tag{15.2}$$

Denote $(I-A)^{-1}$ by D and note that it is triangular by (R.1). We may take the zero elements to lie above the principal diagonal. Assuming that DB is stable, we have [7]):

$$y_t = \sum_{\theta=0}^{\infty} (DB)^{\theta}(DCz_{t-\theta} + Du_{t-\theta}). \tag{15.3}$$

Denoting the covariance matrix of u_t and $y_{t-\theta}$ by $W(\theta)$ with columns corresponding to elements of u_t and rows corresponding to elements of $y_{t-\theta}$, and that of u_t and $u_{t-\theta}$ by $V(\theta)$ (which is assumed to be independent of t) with columns corresponding to u_t and rows to $u_{t-\theta}$:

$$W(0) = \sum_{\theta=0}^{\infty} (DB)^{\theta}(DV(\theta)). \tag{15.4}$$

Since, by (R.3), $V(\theta) = 0$ for $\theta > 0$, this becomes:

$$W(0) = DV(0). \tag{15.5}$$

By (R.2), $V(0)$ is diagonal; hence, $W(0)$ is triangular with zero elements above the principal diagonal. Thus any element of y_t is uncorrelated with all higher numbered elements of u_t. Similarly,

$$W(1) = \sum_{\theta=1}^{\infty} (DB)^{\theta-1}(DV(\theta)) = 0. \tag{15.6}$$

Hence, all variables which appear in any given equation in (15.1) save that variable which is to be explained by that equation are uncorrelated with the disturbance from that equation, as stated.

---

[7]) We shall not discuss the assumption of the stability of DB in any detail at this point. If it is not stable, it suffices to assume that the model begins with nonstochastic initial conditions. Obviously, if stability fails, the assumption of no serial correlation becomes of even greater importance than if stability holds. We shall return to this and shall discuss the question of stability in general in a later section.

We have gone through this demonstration in detail partly for later purposes and partly to exhibit the way in which each of the assumptions (R.1)–(R.3) enters. We must now ask whether those assumptions can be weakened.

In the first place, it is clear that the triangularity of A is crucial. From (15.5), if A and therefore D is not triangular, $W(0)$ will not be triangular either in general and the elements of y_t cannot be taken as uncorrelated with higher-numbered disturbances. This is well known, as in this case the system (15.1) is truly simultaneous. In such a case, ordinary least squares will be inconsistent for at least one equation in the model.

What is less often realized in practice is the role played by the assumptions on the disturbances. Because of the simplicity and other advantages of ordinary least squares, there is a natural tendency to settle for a triangular A and to overlook the fact that such triangularity does not suffice to make ordinary least squares consistent [8]).

To see that such assumptions are generally required, consider first the assumption that $V(0)$ is diagonal. If this fails, (15.5) shows that $W(0)$ cannot generally be taken to be triangular whence ordinary least squares will be inconsistent. This corresponds to the intuitive idea that if a high-numbered and a low-numbered disturbance are correlated, the endogenous variable corresponding to the low-numbered disturbance cannot be taken to be uncorrelated with the high-numbered disturbance even if there is no direct influence through the explicit equations of the model. Indeed, not only is the diagonality of $V(0)$ required for the consistency of ordinary least squares, but also, if nothing more is known of the coefficients of the model save that A is triangular, such an assumption is necessary for the very identifiability of the equations [9]).

It is possible, however, to alter the assumption of no serial correlation. Clearly, this enters in both (15.5) and (15.6) because y_{t-1} appears in the model. If this were not the case, the assumption in question would not be needed for consistency. In most econometric models, however, and certainly in economy-wide ones, lagged values of the endogenous variables do in fact appear. We are nevertheless able to weaken the no-serial-correlation assumption (R.3) to:

(R.3*) B (as well as A) is triangular with zeros above the diagonal and, for all $\theta > 0$, $V(\theta)$ is triangular with the same arrangement of zeros so that

---

[8]) In fairness, it should be pointed out that Wold's theoretical writings are entirely clear on this point. See Wold [40, pp. 358–359], for example.

[9]) See Fisher [13].

high-numbered disturbances are uncorrelated with lagged values of low-numbered disturbances. Further, either B or all $V(\theta)$ ($\theta > 0$) have zeros everywhere on the principal diagonal.

If (R.1), (R.2) and (R.3*) hold, every term in (15.4) will be triangular, and so $W(0)$ will likewise be triangular as required. Further, $W(1)$ will also be triangular rather than zero and will have zeros on its principal diagonal, but this will be all that is needed, since if B is triangular no lagged endogenous variable appears in an equation of (15.1) explaining a lower-numbered current endogenous variable.

Intuitively, the general necessity of no serial correlation for the consistency of least squares is that an element of y_{t-1} is influenced by an element of u_{t-1}. If that element of u_{t-1} is itself correlated with a lower-numbered element of u_t, the corresponding element of y_{t-1} cannot be assumed to be uncorrelated with that element of u_t. Even if $V(\theta)$ is triangular for $\theta > 0$ (or even diagonal) and B is not triangular, the dynamics of the system will carry serial correlation into relations between any current disturbance and any current endogenous variable. If both $V(\theta)$ and B are triangular, however, such effects are only carried toward higher-numbered equations.

That triangularity of both $V(\theta)$ for all $\theta > 0$ and B are generally necessary in the presence of serial correlation may be seen from the fact that since D is triangular the terms in (15.4) will generally not otherwise be triangular and the fact that if B is not triangular, even triangularity of $W(1)$ will not suffice. (The condition as to the principal diagonals can be easily seen to be required by considering a single-equation model.)

Of course, as is also the case for the assumption of the diagonality of $V(0)$, even if such assumptions fail generally, similar weaker assumptions concerning certain off-diagonal elements may hold and yield the consistency of ordinary least squares for certain equations. The indicated assumptions *are* necessary for such consistency in *all* equations, however. (Such weaker conditions are fairly readily obtained from the generalization of the current discussion given in a later section.)

15.2.3. Recursive systems in economy-wide models

Are the assumptions of the recursive model just discussed likely to be valid for an economy-wide econometric model? In general, the answer appears to be in the negative.

In the first place, the argument for the triangularity of A that causation takes place sequentially in time (which, incidentally, would imply diagonality) is not conclusive if the data are collected as averages over a much longer period than the causal interval involved. It may be true that simultaneous structures are but approximations to underlying recursive ones with very short time lags; this does not make the matrices involved triangular, however, whatever it implies about appropriate estimators [10]).

Even if triangularity of the A matrix is satisfied in an economy-wide model, however, the other conditions discussed are unlikely to be fulfilled. Even the best specified econometric models inevitably omit variables the effects of which then enter the disturbance terms. If the model is well specified, these effects will not be large and systematic; rather, they will be small and random. Even so, the omitted variables appearing in the disturbances cannot all generally be expected to be different ones for different equations. Indeed, one expects there will be some events which act as shocks on many or all the equations in an economy-wide model. Such action may indeed be of different magnitudes for different equations, but it is surely extremely restrictive to assume zero correlation among the different disturbance terms. Thus it is very unlikely that $V(0)$ will be diagonal.

Similarly, it is rather unrealistic to assume no serial correlation in the disturbances. Disturbances from econometric models do in fact tend to be serially correlated, and while we shall later argue that correlation between a given element of u_t and a different element of $u_{t-\theta}$ may be small, even a diagonal $V(\theta)$ for $\theta > 0$ will not help. This is especially the case if the time lag involved in the model is small (the very situation in which triangularity of A is relatively likely), as in such a case the effects of a random shock due to an omitted variable are likely to persist for more than one time period. To put it another way, it is natural to suppose that as the time period involved goes to zero, $V(1)$ approaches $V(0)$, which is certainly not zero [11]).

Moreover, there seems little direct comfort in the points made above that it is sufficient to have $B = 0$ or to have both B and all $V(\theta)$, $\theta > 0$, triangular and either B or all such $V(\theta)$ with zero principal diagonals. Economy-wide models are generally dynamic ones, and so lagged endogenous variables do

---

[10]) Strotz [33] considers a model in which the variables are observed at discrete intervals longer than a short causal period which is allowed to approach zero—a problem not quite the same as that considered in the text. He argues that the usual estimators are not approached in the limit by the maximum likelihood estimator of his model. The status of the argument is presently in some doubt, as Gorman [14] has suggested that "natural" assumptions on the continuity of the stochastic process generating the disturbances do lead to the usual estimators in the limiting case of simultaneity.

[11]) See Gorman [14].

appear. Further, while we shall argue below that a diagonal $V(\theta)$ for $\theta > 0$ is not quite so unreasonable as it may seem, a triangular $\boldsymbol{B}$ matrix is wholly unlikely, since this would be a case in which there were *no* feedbacks (simultaneous or lagged) from one variable to another and economy-wide models simply do not have such a hierarchic structure in view of the interconnectedness of economic activity.

It is thus evident that even if one is willing to assume a triangular $\boldsymbol{A}$ matrix, the assumptions of the recursive model cannot generally be taken as valid in an economy-wide econometric model. This is especially true if triangularity has been achieved by the introduction of relatively short time lags. At the risk of overemphasis, we repeat: ordinary least squares does not become consistent when one changes a current endogenous variable to a recent past value of the same variable even if triangularity of the A matrix is achieved in this way. The assumptions which lead to the consistency of least squares require more than this, and all the same difficulties will still be encountered even if they go unrecognized.

15.2.4. *The Proximity Theorem and near consistency*

As already remarked, however, the issue of the use of ordinary least squares (or indeed of any particular estimator) is not whether the assumptions thereof are precisely satisfied. The crucial question is that of how closely they are satisfied—of how those assumptions stand up as approximations rather than as exact statements. The problem is not a discrete one; rather, it is continuous. Moreover, the question of goodness of approximation is itself dependent on the sensitivity of the properties of the estimator to variation in the assumptions thereof. In general, the less sensitive the estimator, the greater the tolerable deviation from the strict conditions under which it has desirable properties.

In the present instance, our discussion has largely run in terms of consistency. Consistency, however, is a rather weak, although desirable, property. Since ordinary least squares has several other attractive features, we might plausibly be willing to tolerate small inconsistencies to gain, for example, computational ease, small variance around probability limits, and so forth. It is thus not sufficient to ask whether the assumptions under which ordinary least squares is consistent are satisfied; we must ask whether the fact that they are not generally satisfied in economy-wide econometric models is likely to be of much importance.

This question is formally answered by the Proximity Theorem of Wold [12]). That theorem states that the inconsistency of least squares will be smaller as the correlations between the explanatory variables in the equation to be estimated and the disturbance from that equation are smaller and also as the variance of that disturbance is smaller. A perhaps more illuminating way of looking at the same thing is to consider the disturbance as made up of a linear combination of omitted variables. The inconsistencies in the parameter estimates can then be shown to be equal to the coefficients of the multiple regression of the disturbance term on the explanatory variables [13]).

For our purposes, the Proximity Theorem shows that if (R.1), (R.2) and (R.3) or (R.3*) hold approximately, the inconsistency of ordinary least squares will be small. Indeed, that inconsistency will be small in a given equation if the appropriate columns of

$$W = \begin{bmatrix} W(0) \\ W(1) \\ 0 \end{bmatrix} \tag{15.7}$$

premultiplied by the inverse of the variance-covariance matrix of the variables appearing on the right of that equation are small. Since that inverse enters the ordinary least-squares parameter estimates in precisely the same way, we can say that (roughly) *relative* inconsistencies will be small provided $W(0)$ and $W(1)$ are small. Thus, if all terms above the diagonal in A are *nearly* zero; if cross-equation covariance between contemporary disturbances is small and, if there is little serial correlation, ordinary least squares will not to do too badly.

Unfortunately, there is reason to believe that this will not generally be the case. The arguments given above for the failure of (R.2) and (R.3), in particular, are arguments that the excluded effects are likely to be substantial in practice. While one may be willing to assume that they are not so in particular cases, depending on the structure of the model to be estimated, this seems a dangerous procedure in most economy-wide models given the high degree of approximation which such models inevitably involve. The Proximity Theorem in more general form will be of considerable help to us below and is of substantial value in other contexts; for structural estimation in

---

[12]) Wold and Juréen [38, p. 189 and pp. 37–38]. The Proximity Theorem as stated by Wold is one concerning bias; we discuss inconsistency since unbiasedness is not in any case a property of least squares in models with lagged endogenous variables. See Hurwicz [17].

[13]) See Fisher [11] and Theil [35].

economy-wide models, it seems a weak reed on which to rest estimation by ordinary least squares.

15.2.5. Reduced form estimation

Our discussion thus far has run in terms of the estimation of the parameters of structural equations. The simultaneous model context in which ordinary least squares is most often thought to be appropriate, however, is not this at all, but rather the estimation of the equations of the reduced form. Here the difficulties in the use of ordinary least squares which arise from simultaneity apparently disappear as all variables on the right-hand side of reduced-form equations are either exogenous or lagged.

In this connection, the argument against the use of ordinary least squares has generally run in terms of lack of asymptotic efficiency when compared with estimates of the reduced form which are derived from structural estimates using overidentifying a priori information. Such lack of asymptotic efficiency may be particularly important in the event of a structural break or in the prediction of turning points [14]. The argument in favor of ordinary least squares estimates of reduced-form equations has been the desirability of having forecasts of the endogenous variables which are unbiased conditional on the values of the predetermined variables [15]. It has also been suggested that the added asymptotic efficiency in the use of other estimators stemming from the employment of a priori information may in fact frequently be quite illusory, as such information may be incorrect [16].

There is substantial merit in all of these arguments in various contexts. Fortunately, the issue is rather easy to decide in the context of estimation of the reduced form of a dynamic economy-wide econometric model. In the first place, such a model generally involves lagged endogenous variables. To estimate even the reduced form by ordinary least squares when such variables appear on the right-hand side does not yield consistent estimates in the presence of serial correlation, substantially as seen above. Moreover, even if the assumption of no serial correlation is made, ordinary least squares still does not give an unbiased estimate of the parameters or a conditionally unbiased forecast of the dependent variable. Nevertheless, one might plausibly be willing to accept such defects in ordinary least

---

[14]) Lesnoy [21].
[15]) Waugh [37], Fisher [12].
[16]) Liu [22].

squares for the sake of greater efficiency. Such efficiency fails asymptotically, however, if the overidentifying information on which structural estimation by other means is based is approximately correct, as the issue is again one of good approximation rather than of correctness [17]). Since restrictions on coefficients are more likely to be good approximations than are restrictions on disturbances concerning which economic theory provides relatively little information, ordinary least squares is unlikely to be asymptotically efficient.

On the other hand, such information as is available on the small sample properties of the limited-information estimators (discussed below) does suggest that asymptotic efficiency may not be remarkably important, as the small sample variances of such estimators may well be infinite. Ordinary least squares certainly does have the property of finite small sample variances under ordinary conditions, however defective it may be for other reasons. Ordinary least-squares estimates of the reduced form equations may therefore be appropriate ones to consider if one is willing to assume that serial correlation is unimportant.

Note that this is not quite the same as the situation regarding structural estimation already discussed. In that context, several strong assumptions have to be nearly satisfied in order to justify the use of ordinary least squares. In the present context, only the assumption of no serial correlation must be approximately satisfied; if it is, the remaining argument against ordinary least squares is the one of lack of asymptotic efficiency, and this may be by no means decisive in a world of relatively small samples [18]).

In practice, however, ordinary least-squares estimation of the reduced form of a large economy-wide model is simply incapable of accomplishment. If all lagged endogenous variables are treated as predetermined, the number of exogenous and predetermined variables in any but the most aggregative economy-wide model is simply too large to permit this type of estimation in the presence of the relatively low number of observations ordinarily available.

---

[17]) See Fisher [11].

[18]) All of our discussion of the effects of serial correlation has overlooked the existence of estimation techniques designed precisely to deal with that problem. See for example Johnston [18, pp. 192–195] and Theil [36, pp. 219–225]. All of these techniques, however, assume that there are no lagged endogenous variables in the model, and we have principally been concerned with the problems raised by serial correlation when there are such lagged variables.

15.3. Full-information estimators

We shall discuss the class of full-information estimators out of what is perhaps the natural order because it is relatively easy to dispose of. We shall then be free to turn our attention to the class of estimators ordinarily used in these problems—the limited-information class.

It is customary in these discussions to pay lip service to full-information maximum likelihood as the optimal estimator using all information available and then to dismiss it in practice as too difficult to compute. While it is true that such computational difficulties are still prohibitive in practice for even moderately large systems [19]), such dismissal no longer suffices. This is the case because there are now two full-information estimators which are known to have the same asymptotic distribution as full-information maximum likelihood and which are not particularly difficult to compute. These are the three-stage least-squares estimator proposed by Zellner and Theil and the linearized maximum-likelihood method of Rothenberg and Leenders [20]). Since the known virtues of full-information maximum likelihood are all asymptotic, computational difficulty can no longer be considered a valid reason for not using some such method.

As it happens, however, there are more cogent reasons than computational difficulty for the abandonment of full-information methods in practice. However desirable the properties of full-information methods may be in principle when all assumptions are met, such estimators suffer relatively heavily from a lack of robustness in the presence of common practical difficulties. Thus Klein and Nakamura have suggested that full-information maximum likelihood is more sensitive to multicollinearity than are limited-information estimators [21]). Further, it is evident that all full-information methods are rather sensitive to specification errors of the types that are unavoidable in the foreseeable state of econometric models which are only approximate. In particular, such estimators have the defects of their merits in that by using information on the entire system to estimate any single equation they carry the effects of specification error in any part of the

---

[19]) The difficulties are being overcome, however. See Eisenpress [10].

[20]) Zellner and Theil [41]; Rothenberg and Leenders [29]. Rothenberg and Leenders give the proof that these estimators have the same asymptotic distribution as full-information maximum likelihood. See also Sargan [30] and Madansky [23]. Brown's simultaneous least squares [8] (which is a member of the full-information class) is known to be consistent but is not known to have the same asymptotic distribution as the other members.

[21]) Klein and Nakamura [19].

system to the estimate of any other part. Since it is clear that some equations
may be thought to be better specified than others (as the quality of economic
information is by no means constant in an economy-wide model), this is a
highly undesirable feature. It seems clear that specification error should be
quarantined and hence that limited-information estimators which are known
to accomplish this are preferable to full-information ones in large models [22]).
While it may be desirable to use intermediate estimators which apply full-
information type methods to sectors rather than to the system as a whole,
the theory of how this should be done remains to be worked out.

15.4. *Limited-information estimators*

15.4.1. *Availability in practice*

While a great many limited-information estimators have been suggested,
in practice none of them are available for use in their original form in
estimating an economy-wide econometric model. This is the case because
all such estimators begin in one way or another with the ordinary least-
squares estimates of the reduced-form equations. As we have already seen,
such estimates are likely to be difficult or impossible to secure in all but the
most aggregate models because of the low number of observations generally
available relative to the number of predetermined variables if all lagged
endogenous variables are treated as predetermined.

In addition, as we have already seen, if lagged endogenous variables are
so treated, such treatment raises considerable difficulties in the likely presence
of serial correlation of the disturbances. On the other hand, economy-wide
models are generally sufficiently closed to make their equations unidentifiable if only truly exogenous variables are treated as instruments.

We shall discuss the problems raised by serial correlation in the next
section, which will be concerned with the question of how instrumental
variables should be chosen in practice to avoid inconsistency. In the present
section, we shall discuss the properties of the limited-information estimators
ignoring these problems. Such a discussion is not rendered irrelevant by the
practical difficulty of using all variables that are not current endogenous
ones as instruments when the number of observations is relatively limited.
This is so because, given the variables which are to be treated as predetermined, treatment of all remaining variables as endogenous results in a

---

[22]) Fisher [11, p. 155].

situation in which every known limited-information estimator has its precise counterpart [23]). Thus, for example, if only certain lagged endogenous and exogenous variables are to be used, replacing every other (save the normalized one) in a given equation by its value as computed from a multiple regression on the instruments and then regressing the normalized variable on the resulting variables provides the exact analogue of two-stage least squares.

Of course, in such a situation, and especially where serial correlation in the disturbances cannot be presumed absent, the choice of instrumental variables is likely to be of considerably greater importance than the choice of the particular limited-information method in which such instruments are to be applied. The latter choice is clearly worth discussing. Nevertheless, the major portion of our discussion will be reserved for the former one, which will be taken up in the two following sections.

15.4.2. Classification and large sample properties under ideal conditions

The limited-information estimators in common use are those of Theil's k-class. Chief among these are two-stage least squares, limited-information maximum likelihood and an estimator provided by Nagar [24]). Another class of estimators, the h-class, has also been suggested by Theil, and Nagar has recently proposed still a third class, the double k-class [25]). For our purposes such subdivisions will not be particularly important. What will be important is the fundamental distinction between limited-information maximum likelihood and all other proposed limited-information estimators. Alone among suggested members of the k-, h-, and double k-classes, the fundamental distinguishing parameter (k in this case) is stochastic in limited-information maximum likelihood, being determined as a root of a stochastic determinantal equation. As we shall see below, this distinction, aside from making limited-information maximum likelihood somewhat cumbersome to compute, leads to a lack of robustness in that estimator in the presence of multicollinearity. Such a lack is not shared by the other estimators of the limited-information class.

Indeed, when one looks only at the properties of limited-information

---

[23]) It must be admitted, however, that if different predetermined variables are used in replacing each included endogenous variable (as suggested below), it is not clear how limited-information maximum likelihood carries over to such cases. Fortunately, this will not matter for our purposes.

[24]) Theil [36, pp. 231–232]; Nagar [25].

[25]) Theil [36, pp. 353–354]; Nagar [26].

estimators under ideal conditions, there are relatively few grounds for choice among them. In the next subsection we shall consider the little which is known of their small sample properties, here we merely observe that they all have essentially the same large sample properties. It can be argued that limited-information maximum likelihood has the desirable property of treating all included endogenous variables in an equation symmetrically; indeed, Chow has shown that it is a natural generalization of ordinary least squares in the absence of a theoretically given normalization rule [26]).

On the other hand, such an argument seems rather weak, since normalization rules are in fact generally present in practice, each equation of the model being naturally associated with that particular endogenous variable which is determined by the decision-makers whose behavior is represented by the equation. The normalization rules are in a real sense part of the specification of the model, and the model is not completely specified unless every endogenous variable appears (at least implicitly) in exactly one equation in normalized form. For example, it is not enough to have price equating supply and demand, equations should also be present which explain pure quotations by sellers and buyers and which describe the equilibrating process. (For most purposes, of course, such additional equations can remain in the back of the model builder's mind, although the rules for choosing instrumental variables given below may sometimes require that they be made explicit.)

Thus, symmetry may be positively undesirable in a well-specified model where one feels relatively certain as to appropriate normalization, although it may be desirable if one wishes to remain agnostic as to appropriate normalization. So far as arguments of this type or from large sample properties under ideal conditions are concerned, there seems little or no reason for preferring one limited-information estimator to another.

15.4.3. Small sample properties

The situation is not very different at the present time when one considers small sample properties. To date, relatively little is known about these and work has proceeded largely by means of Monte Carlo experiments. Moreover, all such experiments and such analytic work as is available have been exclusively concerned with the case in which lagged endogenous variables do not appear (or at least are not used as predetermined instruments), and

---

[26]) Chow [9].

the analytic work has dealt only with those members of the k-class with non-stochastic k. In the present context, the former limitation is a severe one. Nevertheless, it seems worthwhile briefly discussing what is known about small sample properties in such cases, as the situation when lagged endogenous variables are present is probably no more promising.

The principal point that has emerged on small sample properties of limited-information estimators is that the sampling variances involved are infinite, at least in some cases. Such a conclusion is borne out both from the analytic work that has been accomplished to date and by the results of the Monte Carlo experiments that have been performed [27]). It seems idle to hope that this circumstance does not occur when lagged endogenous variables are present in the model.

In practice, this unhappy circumstance has a number of consequences, First, it is clearly the case that relatively little reliance can be placed on judgments of goodness of fit derived from consideration of asymptotic standard errors. Such asymptotic standard errors are obviously inappropriate when directly taken as approximations to an infinite sample variance and may or may not be reliable when used to derive approximations to the probability that an estimate diverges from the true parameter by more than a given amount. In general, the latter approximation is probably better for small divergences than for large ones, as the normal approximation to the small sample distribution is almost certainly worst in the tails [28]).

Second, as indicated, the absence of this property in ordinary least squares makes the latter estimator rather more attractive than would be the case if limited-information estimators always had finite variance. There is a certain amount of justification for using ordinary least squares as an approximation while building the model, provided that assumptions (R.1)–(R.3) are not too badly violated (which we have argued cannot be assumed in economy-wide models). Further, Quandt has recently suggested combining ordinary least squares and limited-information estimators to take advantage of the fact that the latter are consistent while the former has a finite variance [29]).

Furthermore, the infinite small sample variance of limited-information

[27]) See Basmann [5, 6], Bergstrom [7], Nagar [25], and Sargan [31] for the analysis. Johnston [18, pp. 275–295] summarizes most of the Monte Carlo experiments; see also Quandt [27, 28].

[28]) See Basmann [6]. Sargan [31] derives approximate expressions for the probabilities just described.

[29]) Quandt [28].

estimators casts doubt on the convergence, in some cases, of the expansions
used by Nagar to demonstrate the unbiasedness of his suggested estimator to
order $1/T$, where T is the sample size [30]). When such expansions do converge,
such unbiasedness is about the only known sample property in which one
limited-information estimator is demonstrably superior to the others. As
it happens, however, Nagar's demonstration assumes that there are no lagged
endogenous variables in the model, and so, even aside from the convergence
problem just mentioned, his results are not applicable in the present case.

15.4.4. Robustness

Thus neither large nor small sample properties under ideal conditions provide much guide for the choice of an estimator from the limited-information
class in the present state of knowledge. This is not the case with regard to
the robustness of such estimators, however. Klein and Nakamura have
shown that as a consequence of the stochastic nature of k in limited-information maximum likelihood, that estimator is more sensitive to multicollinearity than are the other members of the k-class [31]). *In the absence of
other criteria*, this seems grounds for abandoning limited-information
maximum likelihood in practice in favor of some other limited-information
estimator [32]).

There seem to be no very strong reasons, however, for choosing among
the limited-information estimators other than maximum likelihood. The
paper on robustness just mentioned indicates that these do not differ among
themselves with regard to this property. Since two-stage least squares is the
easiest of these estimators to compute, and since it does provide a natural
generalization of ordinary least squares in the presence of theoretically
given normalization rules [33]), it seems natural to choose it in the present state
of our knowledge.

15.5. Near-consistency, block-recursive systems, and the choice of eligible instrumental variables

15.5.1. Introduction

In this section we begin the discussion of the choices of predetermined

---

[30]) Nagar [25]. See Sargan [31].

[31]) Klein and Nakamura [19].

[32]) Similar grounds for choice are not presently available as regards sensitivity to
specification error.

[33]) See Chow [9].

instrumental variables which are available and the circumstances under which such choices are likely to be appropriate. Most of our discussion will be in terms of the assumptions that must be approximately satisfied if a given variable is to be eligible for inclusion as an instrument. We thus postpone to the next section the important question of how the eligible candidates ought in fact to be used. Until further notice, then, we discuss only whether and under what circumstances a given single variable ought to be treated as predetermined.

In general, we desire two things of a variable which is to be treated as predetermined in the estimation of a given equation. First, it should be uncorrelated in the probability limit with the disturbance from that equation; second, it should closely causally influence the variables which appear in that equation and should do so independently of the other predetermined variables [34]. If the first criterion is not satisfied, treating the variable as predetermined results in inconsistency; if the second fails, such treatment does not aid much in estimation—it does not reduce variances. In practice, these requirements may frequently conflict and a compromise may be needed between them. The closer the causal connection, the higher the forbidden correlation may be. Thus, in one limit, the use of ordinary least squares which treats all variables on the right-hand side of the equation as predetermined perfectly satisfies the second but not the first criterion. In the other limit, the use of instrumental variables which do not directly or indirectly causally influence any variable in the model perfectly meets the first requirement but not the second [35]. In general, one is frequently faced with the necessity of weakening the first requirement to one of low rather than of zero correlation and accepting indirect rather than direct causal relations between instruments and included variables. (Such a compromise may result in different instruments for different equations when a limited-information estimator is used; this will be the case below.)

In the present section, we discuss the circumstances under which zero or low inconsistencies can be expected, leaving explicit use of the causal criterion to the next section.

Now, two sets of candidates for treatment as instrumental variables are

---

[34] It should therefore be relatively uncorrelated with the other variables used as instruments so that lack of collinearity is not really a separate criterion. We shall return to this in the next section.

[35] If only such variables are available for use (or if an insufficient number of more interesting ones are), the equation in question is underidentified and even asymptotic variances are infinite.

obviously present. The first of these consists of those variables which one is willing to assume truly exogenous to the entire system and the lagged values thereof; the second consists of the lagged endogenous variables. The dynamic and causal structure of the system may well provide a third set, however, and may cast light on the appropriateness of the use of lagged endogenous variables. We now turn to a discussion of this.

15.5.2. The theory of block-recursive systems

A generalization of the recursive systems already discussed is provided by what I have elsewhere termed "block-recursive systems" [36]). In general, such systems have properties similar to those of recursive systems when the model is thought of as subdivided into sets of current endogenous variables and corresponding equations (which we shall call sectors) rather than into single endogenous variables and their corresponding equations.

Formally, we ask whether it is possible to partition the vectors of variables and of disturbances and the corresponding matrices (renumbering variables and equations, if necessary) to secure a system with certain properties. In such partitionings, the Ith subvector of a given vector x will be denoted as x^I. Similarly, the submatrix of a given matrix M which occurs in the Ith row and Jth column of submatrices of that matrix will be denoted by M^{IJ}. Thus:

$$M = \begin{bmatrix} M^{11} & M^{12} & \dots & M^{1N} \\ M^{21} & M^{22} & \dots & M^{2N} \\ \vdots & \vdots & & \vdots \\ M^{N1} & M^{N2} & \dots & M^{NN} \end{bmatrix}; \quad x = \begin{bmatrix} x^1 \\ x^2 \\ \vdots \\ x^N \end{bmatrix}. \tag{15.8}$$

We shall always assume the diagonal blocks, M^{II}, to be square.

If when written in this way, the matrix M has the property that $M^{IJ} = 0$ for all $I = 1, \dots, N$ and $J > I$, the matrix will be called *block-triangular*. If $M^{IJ} = 0$ for all $I = 1, \dots, N$ and $J \neq I$, the matrix will be called *block-diagonal* [37]).

Now consider the system (15.1). Suppose that there exists a partition of that system (with $N > 1$) such that:

(BR.1) A is block-triangular;
(BR.2) $V(0)$ is block-diagonal;
(BR.3) $V(\theta) = 0$ for all $\theta > 0$.

[36]) See Fisher [11].

[37]) Block-triangularity and block-diagonality are the respective canonical forms of decomposability and complete decomposability.

(Note that these are generalizations of (R.1)–(R.3).) In this case, it is easy to show that the *current* endogenous variables of any given sector are uncorrelated in the probability limit with the current disturbances of any higher-numbered sector. Such variables may thus be consistently treated as predetermined instruments in the estimation of the equations of such higher-numbered sectors.

To establish the proposition in question, observe that (15.2)–(15.4) always hold [38]). By (BR.3), (15.5) holds also, and so:

$$W(0) = DV(0). \tag{15.9}$$

By (BR.1), however, $D = (I-A)^{-1}$ is block-triangular, while $V(0)$ is block-diagonal by (BR.2). It follows that their product is block-triangular with the same partitioning. Thus:

$$W(0)^{IJ} = 0 \quad \text{for all } I, J = 1, \ldots, N \text{ and } J > I, \tag{15.10}$$

but this is equivalent to the proposition in question.

As in the special case of recursive systems, assumption (BR.3) can be replaced by a somewhat different assumption:

(BR.3*) B is block-triangular with the same partitioning as A, as is $V(\theta)$ for all $\theta > 0$. Further, either all B^{II} or all $V(\theta)^{II}$ ($\theta > 0$) are zero ($I = 1, \ldots, N$).

To see that this suffices, observe that in this case every term in (15.4) will be block-triangular.

Note, however, that whereas (BR.1)–(BR.3) patently suffice to give $W(1) = 0$ and thus to show that lagged endogenous variables are uncorrelated with current disturbances, this is not the case when (BR.3) is replaced by (BR.3*). As in the similar case for recursive systems, what is implied by (BR.1), (BR.2) and (BR.3*) in this regard is that $W(1)$ is also block-triangular with zero matrices on the principal diagonal, and so lagged endogenous variables are uncorrelated with the current disturbances of the same or *higher*-numbered blocks but not necessarily with those of *lower*-numbered ones.

If A and B are both block-triangular with the same partitioning, the matrix DB is also block-triangular and the system of difference equations given by (15.2) is decomposable. In this case, what occurs in higher-numbered sectors *never* influences what occurs in lower-numbered ones, and so there is in any case no point in using current or lagged endogenous variables as

---

[38]) Continuing to assume that DB is stable.

instruments in lower-numbered sectors. This is an unlikely circumstance to encounter in an economy-wide model in any essential way, but it may occur for partitionings which split off a small group of equations from the rest of the model. If it does not occur, (BR.3) is generally necessary for the block-triangularity of $W(0)$. Indeed, unless either (BR.3) or the first statement of (BR.3*) holds, *no* $W(0)^{IJ}$ can generally be expected to be zero if $B \neq 0$.

To see this, observe that (15.4) implies that $W(0)$ cannot generally be expected to have any zero submatrices unless every term in the sum which is not wholly zero has a zero submatrix in the same place. This cannot happen unless every matrix involved is either block-diagonal or block-triangular. Hence, if $V(\theta) \neq 0$ for all $\theta > 0$, all such $V(\theta)$ must at least be block-triangular, as must B [39]).

15.5.3. *Block-recursive assumptions in economy-wide models*

Unfortunately, while block-triangularity of A is not an unreasonable circumstance to expect to encounter in practice [40]), the assumptions on the disturbances involved in (BR.2) and (BR.3) or (BR.3*) seem rather unrealistic in economy-wide models for much the same reasons as did the parallel assumptions of the recursive model. Thus, it does not seem reasonable to assume that the omitted effects which form the disturbances in two different sectors have no common elements; nor, as already discussed, does it seem plausible to assume either that there is no serial correlation of disturbances or that the dynamic system involved is decomposable.

Note, however, that these assumptions may be better approximations than in the case of recursive systems. Thus one may be more willing to assume no correlation between contemporaneous disturbances in two different aggregate sectors than between disturbances in any two single equations. A similar assumption may be even more attractive when the disturbances in question are from different time periods, as will be seen below. Thus also, the dynamic system may be thought *close* to decomposability when broad

---

[39]) Of course, this does not show that (BR.3) or (BR.3*) is necessary, since counter-examples may easily be produced in which different nonzero terms in (15.4) just cancel out. The point is that this cannot be assumed to occur in practice. To put it another way, since such cancellation cannot be known to occur, it clearly occurs only on a set of measure zero in the parameter space. Thus (BR.3) or (BR.3*) is necessary with probability 1.

[40]) It is encountered in preliminary versions of the Brookings-SSRC econometric model. C. Holt and D. Steward have developed a computer program for organizing a model in block-triangular form.

sectors are in view and feedbacks within sectors explicitly allowed. If such assumptions are approximately satisfied, the inconsistencies involved in the use of current and lagged endogenous variables as predetermined in higher-numbered sectors will be small [41]).

Nevertheless, the assumption of no correlation between contemporaneous disturbances from different sectors, the assumption of no serial correlation in the disturbances and the assumption of decomposability of the dynamic system all seem rather strong ones to make. If these assumptions are not in fact even approximately made, the use of current endogenous variables as instruments in higher-numbered sectors leads to non-negligible inconsistencies. We shall show, however, that this need not be true of the use of *lagged* endogenous variables in higher-numbered sectors under fairly plausible assumptions as to the process generating the disturbances. We thus turn to the question of the use of lagged endogenous variables, assuming that A is known to be at least nearly block-triangular.

15.5.4. *Reasonable properties of the disturbances*

The problems which we have been discussing largely turn on the presence of common omitted variables in different equations and on the serial correlation properties of the disturbances. It seems appropriate to proceed by setting up an explicit model of the process generating the disturbances in terms of such omitted variables and such serial correlation.

We shall assume that the disturbances to any equation are made up of three sets of effects. The first of these will consist of the effects of elements common to more than one sector—in general, common to all sectors. The second will consist of the effects of elements common to more than one equation in the sector in which the given equation occurs. The third will consist of effects specific to the given equation.

Thus, let the number of equations in the Ith sector be n_I. We write:

$$u_t^I = \varphi^I e_t + \psi^I v_t^I + w_t^I \qquad (I = 1, \ldots, N) \tag{15.11}$$

where:

$$e_t = \begin{bmatrix} e_{1t} \\ \vdots \\ e_{Kt} \end{bmatrix} \tag{15.12}$$

---

[41]) See Fisher [11]. The theorems involved are generalizations of the Proximity Theorem for recursive systems.

is a vector of implicit disturbances whose effects are common (in principle) to all equations in the model and φ^I is an $n_I \times K$ constant matrix;

$$v_t^I = \begin{bmatrix} v_{1t}^I \\ \vdots \\ v_{H_I t}^I \end{bmatrix} \qquad (15.13)$$

is a vector of implicit disturbances whose effects are common (in principle) to all equations in the Ith sector but not to equations in other sectors; ψ^I is an $n_I \times H_I$ constant matrix; and

$$w_t^I = \begin{bmatrix} w_{1t}^I \\ \vdots \\ w_{n_I t}^I \end{bmatrix} \qquad (15.14)$$

is a vector of implicit disturbances the effect of each of which is specific to a given equation in the Ith sector.

Define:

$$\varphi = \begin{bmatrix} \varphi^1 \\ \vdots \\ \varphi^N \end{bmatrix}; \qquad (15.15)$$

$$v_t = \begin{bmatrix} v_t^1 \\ \vdots \\ v_t^N \end{bmatrix}; \qquad (15.16)$$

$$\psi = \begin{bmatrix} \psi^1 & 0 & \ldots & 0 \\ 0 & \psi^2 & \ldots & 0 \\ \vdots & & & \vdots \\ 0 & 0 & & \psi^N \end{bmatrix}; \qquad (15.17)$$

and

$$w_t = \begin{bmatrix} w_t^1 \\ w_t^2 \\ \vdots \\ w_t^N \end{bmatrix}. \qquad (15.18)$$

Then (15.11) may be rewritten more compactly as:

$$u_t = \varphi e_t + \psi v_t + w_t. \qquad (15.19)$$

We shall refer to the elements of e_t, v_t and w_t as *economy-wide, sector* and *equation*-implicit disturbances, respectively, noting that whether an economy-wide or sector-implicit disturbance actually affects a given equation depends on the relevant rows of φ and ψ, respectively. (The unqualified term "disturbance" will be reserved for the elements of u_t).

All elements of e_t, v_t and w_t are composites of unobservables; it is hardly restrictive to assume:

(A.1) Every element of e_t, v_t or w_t is uncorrelated in the probability limit with all present or past values of any *other* element of any of these vectors. The vectors can always be redefined to accomplish this.

We shall assume that each element of each of these implicit disturbance vectors obeys a (different) first-order autoregressive scheme [42]). Thus:

$$e_t = \Lambda_e e_{t-1} + e_t^*, \tag{15.20}$$

$$v_t = \Lambda_v v_{t-1} + v_t^*, \tag{15.21}$$

$$w_t = \Lambda_w w_{t-1} + w_t^*, \tag{15.22}$$

where Λ_e, Λ_v and Λ_w are diagonal matrices of appropriate dimension and e_t^*, v_t^* and w_t^* are vectors of non-autocorrelated random variables. Assuming that the variance of each element of e_t, v_t and w_t is constant through time, the diagonal elements of Λ_e, Λ_v and Λ_w are first-order autocorrelation coefficients and are thus each less than one in absolute value.

Let Δ_e, Δ_v and Δ_w be the diagonal variance-covariance matrices of the elements of e_t, v_t and w_t, respectively. In view of (A.1) and (15.20)–(15.22) it is easy to show that (15.19) implies:

$$V(\theta) = \varphi \Lambda_e^\theta \Delta_e \varphi' + \psi \Lambda_v^\theta \Delta_v \psi' + \Lambda_w^\theta \Delta_w \qquad (\theta \geqq 0). \tag{15.23}$$

Evidently, $V(\theta)$ will be nonzero unless a number of other assumptions are imposed. Consider, however, the question of whether $V(\theta)$ will be block-diagonal. Since all the Λ and Δ matrices are diagonal, and since ψ is itself block-diagonal by (15.17), we have:

$$V(\theta)^{IJ} = \varphi^I \Lambda_e^\theta \Delta_e \varphi^{J\prime} \qquad (\theta \geqq 0; I, J = 1, \ldots, N; J \neq I). \tag{15.24}$$

---

[42]) Autoregressive relations of higher orders could be considered in principle, but this would rather complicate the analysis. We shall thus assume that first-order relationships are sufficiently good approximations. If higher-order relationships are involved, there is no essential change in the qualitative results.

Thus the off-diagonal blocks of $V(\theta)$ depend only on the properties of the economy-wide disturbances.

This result is perhaps worth emphasizing. When applied to $\theta = 0$, it merely states formally what we have said previously, that contemporaneous disturbances from the equations of the model which occur in different sectors cannot be assumed uncorrelated if there are common elements in each of them, that is, implicit disturbance elements affecting both sectors. When applied to $\theta > 0$, however, the result is at least slightly less obvious. Here it states that despite the fact that contemporaneous disturbances from different sectors may be highly correlated, and despite the fact that every disturbance may be highly autocorrelated, a given disturbance will *not* be correlated with a lagged disturbance from another sector unless the economy-wide implicit disturbances are themselves autocorrelated. To put it another way, the presence of economy-wide implicit disturbances and the presence of substantial serial correlation do not prevent us from taking $V(\theta)$ as block-diagonal for $\theta > 0$ provided the serial correlation is entirely confined to the sector- and equation-implicit disturbances.

It is then reasonable to assume that the serial correlation is so confined? I think it is reasonable in the context of a carefully constructed economy-wide model. We argued above that any such model inevitably omits variables the effects of which are not confined within sectors. Effects which are highly autocorrelated, however, are effects which are relatively systematic over time. In an inevitably aggregate and approximate economy-wide model, there are likely to be such systematic effects influencing individual equations and even whole sectors. Systematic effects which spread over more than one sector, however, seem substantially less likely to occur, especially when we recall that the limits of a sector in our sense are likely to be rather wide [43]). Variables which give rise to such effects are not likely to be omitted variables whose influence lies in the disturbance terms. Rather they are likely to be explicitly included in the model, if at all possible. If not, if they relate to the occurrence of a war, for example, and are thus hard to specify explicitly, the time periods in which they are most important are likely to be omitted from the analysis. In short, systematic behavior of the disturbances is an indication of incomplete specification. Such incompleteness is much less likely to occur with regard to effects which are widespread than to effects which are relatively narrowly confined, especially since the former are less likely

---

[43]) As they are in the Brookings-SSRC econometric model.

to be made up of many small effects [44]). (Recall that an economy-wide implicit disturbance is one which affects more than one sector *directly*, not simply one whose effects are transmitted through the dynamic causal structure of the explicit model.) It thus does not seem unreasonable to assume that:

$$\Lambda_e = 0 \tag{15.25}$$

and therefore

$$V(\theta)^{IJ} = 0 \qquad (\theta > 0; I, J = 1, \ldots, N; J \neq I) \tag{15.26}$$

as good approximations.

15.5.5. *Implications for the use of lagged endogenous variables*

Of course, assuming (15.26) to hold is not sufficient to yield consistency when lagged endogenous variables are treated as predetermined. We have already seen that, unless $V(\theta) = 0$, the decomposability of the dynamic system must be assumed in addition to (15.26) to secure such consistency. We argued above, however, that such decomposability was rather unlikely in an interconnected economy, although the fact that (15.26) is likely to hold approximately makes it important to look for *near*-decomposability and thus secure *near*-consistency [45]).

Even if such near-decomposability of the dynamic system does not occur, however, (15.26) has interesting consequences for the treatment of lagged endogenous variables as predetermined. To these we now turn.

Consider the expression for $W(1)$ given in equation (15.6). Writing out the first few terms of the sum, we obtain:

$$W(1) = DV(1) + DBDV(2) + (DB)^2 DV(3) \ldots \tag{15.27}$$

Since D is block-triangular and $V(1)$ block-diagonal by (15.26), the first term in this expansion is also block-triangular. Hence, even if the dynamic system is not decomposable, endogenous variables lagged one period are approximately uncorrelated in the probability limit with disturbances in *higher*-numbered sectors (but not in the same or lower-numbered sectors)

---

[44]) A similar argument obviously implies that sector-implicit disturbances are less likely to be serially correlated than are equation-implicit disturbances. The analysis of the effects of this on $V(\theta)$ and the subsequent discussion is left to the reader. The assumption of no serial correlation in the sector-implicit disturbances seems considerably more dangerous than that being discussed in the text.

[45]) Near-decomposability of a dynamic system has a number of interesting consequences in addition to this. See Ando, Fisher and Simon [3], especially Ando and Fisher [2].

616 *Franklin M. Fisher* 15.5

to the extent that the right-hand terms in (15.27) other than the first can be ignored.

In what sense is it legitimate, then, to assume that such terms can in fact be ignored? Assume that the matrix DB is similar to a diagonal matrix, so that there exists a nonsingular matrix P such that [46]):

$$DB = PHP^{-1} \tag{15.28}$$

where H is diagonal and has for diagonal elements the latent roots of DB. Let:

$$\Lambda = \begin{bmatrix} \Lambda_e & 0 & 0 \\ 0 & \Lambda_v & 0 \\ 0 & 0 & \Lambda_w \end{bmatrix}, \tag{15.29}$$

$$\Delta = \begin{bmatrix} \Delta_e & 0 & 0 \\ 0 & \Delta_v & 0 \\ 0 & 0 & \Delta_w \end{bmatrix}, \tag{15.30}$$

$$Q = [\varphi \vdots \psi \vdots I]. \tag{15.31}$$

Then every such term can be written as:

$$(DB)^{\theta-1} DV(\theta) = PH^{\theta-1}P^{-1}DQ\Lambda^{\theta}\Delta Q' \qquad (\theta > 1). \tag{15.32}$$

We know that every diagonal element of the diagonal matrix Λ is less than unity in absolute value (indeed, we are assuming that some of the diagonal elements are zero). Moreover, *if we are prepared to maintain the stability assumption on DB* which was slipped in some time ago, every diagonal element of the diagonal matrix H will also be less than unity in absolute value. It follows that every element of every term in the expansion of $W(1)$ other than the first is composed of a sum of terms each of which involves at least the product of a factor less than unity and the square of another such factor. There is clearly a reasonable sense in which one may be prepared to take such terms as negligible at least when compared with the nonzero elements of the first term in the expansion for $W(1)$ which involve only the diagonal elements of Λ to the first power. If one is willing to do this, one is saying that the use of endogenous variables lagged one period as instruments in higher-numbered sectors involves only negligible inconsistency at least as compared with the use of the same variables as instruments in their own or lower-numbered sectors.

There may be considerable difficulties in accepting such a judgment, however. In the first place, it is well to be aware that there are two different

---

[46]) The assumption involved is, of course, very weak and is made for ease of exposition.

statements involved. It is one thing to say that the effects in question are negligible compared with others and quite another to say that they are negligible in a more absolute sense. If one accepts the stability assumption, there certainly is a value of θ beyond which further terms in the expansion of $W(1)$ are negligible on any given standard. These may not be all terms after the first, however; we shall discuss the case in which there are non-negligible terms after the first below.

Second (a minor point but one worth observing), even our conclusion about *relative* importance *need* not hold although other assumptions are granted. While it is true that as θ becomes large the right-hand side of (15.32) approaches zero, such approach need not be monotonic. To put it another way, every element of the matrix involved is a sum of terms. Each such term involves a diagonal element of Λ to the θ and a diagonal element of H to the $\theta - 1$. If all such diagonal elements are less than unity in absolute value, the absolute value of each separate term approaches zero monotonically as θ increases; this need not be true of the *sum* of those terms, however, and it is easy to construct counter examples. Nevertheless, there is a sense in which it seems appropriate to assume the terms in the expansion for $W(1)$ to be negligible for θ greater than some value, perhaps for $\theta > 1$.

All this, however, has leaned a bit heavily on the stability of DB. If that matrix has a latent root greater than unity in absolute value, part of the reason for assuming that the right-hand side of (15.32) is negligible even for high values of θ has disappeared. Of course, it is the case that the diagonal elements of Λ are known to be less than unity in absolute value, and so the infinite sum involved in $W(1)$ may still converge. However, such convergence is likely to be slow in an unstable case and may not occur at all, and so the effects of serial correlation are even more serious than in the stable case. Clearly, the stability assumption requires additional discussion at this point.

The usual reason for assuming stability of the dynamic model being estimated is one of convenience or of lack of knowledge of other cases. Since the unstable case tends to lead to unbounded moment matrices, the usual proofs of consistency of the limited-information estimators tend to break down in that circumstance. Indeed, maximum-likelihood estimators are presently known to be consistent only in the stable case and in rather special unstable cases [47]). It is therefore customary to assume stability in dis-

---

[47]) For example, if *all* latent roots are greater than unity in absolute value. See Anderson [1]. J. D. Sargan has privately informed me that he has constructed a proof of consistency for the general case. The classic paper in this area is that of Mann and Wald [24].

cussions of this sort. For present purposes, even if limited-information estimators are consistent in unstable cases and even if the Generalized Proximity Theorems which guarantee small inconsistencies for sufficiently good approximations also hold [48]) the approximations which we are now discussing are relatively unlikely to be good ones in such cases. Even if the existence of $W(1)$ is secured by assuming that the dynamic process (15.1) begins with nonstochastic initial conditions at some finite time in the past (and even this does not suffice for the existence of the probability limit), the effects of serial correlation will not die out (or will die out only slowly) as we consider longer and longer lags. The conclusion seems inescapable that if the model is thought to be unstable (and the more so, the more unstable it is), the use of lagged endogenous variables as instruments *anywhere* in an indecomposable dynamic system with serially correlated disturbances is likely to lead to large inconsistencies, at least for all but very high lags. The lower serial correlation and the closer the model to stability, the less dangerous is such use.

Is the stability assumption a realistic one for economy-wide models? I think it is. Remember that what is at issue is not the ability of the economy to grow but its ability to grow (or to have explosive cycles) with no help from the exogenous variables and no impulses from the random disturbances. Since the exogenous variables generally include population growth, and since technological change is generally either treated as a disturbance or as an effect which is exogenous in some way, this is by no means a hard assumption to accept. While there are growth and cycle models in economic theory which involve explosive systems, such models generally bound the explosive oscillations or growth by ceilings or floors which would be constant if the exogenous sources of growth were constant [49]). The system *as a whole* in such models is not unstable in the presence of constant exogenous variables and the absence of random shocks [50]). We shall thus continue to make the stability assumption.

Even when the stability assumption is made, however, it may not be the case, as we have seen, that one is willing to take the expression in (15.32) as negligible for all $\theta > 1$. (In particular, this will be the case if serial correlation is thought to be high so some the diagonal elements of Λ are close to unity in absolute value.) In such cases, one will not be willing to assume

---

[48]) See Fisher [11].

[49]) See, for example, Hicks [16] and Harrod [15].

[50]) Whether a linear model is a good approximation if such models are realistic is another matter.

that the use of endogenous variables lagged *one* period as instruments in higher-numbered sectors leads to only negligible inconsistencies. Accordingly, we must generalize our discussion.

Fortunately, this is easy to do. There clearly does exist such a smallest $\theta^* > 0$ that for all $\theta > \theta^*$ even the diagonal blocks of $V(\theta^*)$ are negligible on any given standard. Consider $W(\theta^*)$, the covariance matrix of the elements of u_t and those of $y_{t-\theta^*}$ with the columns corresponding to elements of u_t and the rows to elements of $y_{t-\theta^*}$. Clearly,

$$W(\theta^*) = DV(\theta^*) + \sum_{\theta=\theta^*+1}^{\infty} (DB)^{\theta-\theta^*} DV(\theta) \qquad (15.33)$$

$$= DV(\theta^*) + \sum_{\theta=\theta^*+1}^{\infty} PH^{\theta-\theta^*} P^{-1} DQ\Lambda^\theta Q'.$$

Since D is block-triangular and $V(\theta^*)$ block-diagonal by (15.26), the product, $DV(\theta^*)$, is also block-triangular. Considering $W(\theta^*)^{IJ}$ for $J > I$, it is apparent that the covariances of endogenous variables lagged θ^* periods and current disturbances from *higher-numbered sectors* are made up of only negligible terms. Not only is $V(\theta)$ negligible by assumption for $\theta > \theta^*$, but also every such term involves at least one power of H, which, by assumption, is diagonal and has diagonal elements less than unity in absolute value.

Note, however, that a similar statement is clearly false with regard to the covariances of endogenous variables lagged θ^* periods and current disturbances *from the same or lower-numbered sectors*. Such covariances involve the nonzero diagonal blocks of $V(\theta^*)$ in an essential way. It follows that the order of inconsistency, so to speak, involved in using endogenous variables lagged a given number of periods as instruments is less if such variables are used in higher-numbered sectors than if they are used in the same or lower-numbered sectors. To put it another way, the minimum lag with which it is reasonably safe to use endogenous variables as instruments is at least one less for use in higher-numbered than for use in the same or lower-numbered sectors.

As a matter of fact, our result is a bit stronger than this. It is apparent from (15.33) that the use of endogenous variables lagged θ^* periods as instruments in higher-numbered sectors involves covariances of the order of $\Lambda^{\theta^*+1} H$. Even the use of endogenous variables lagged θ^*+1 periods as instruments in the same or lower-numbered sectors, however, involves

covariances of the order of only $\Lambda^{\theta*+1}$. No positive power of H is involved
in the first term of the expansion for the latter covariances. Since H is
diagonal with diagonal elements less than unity in absolute value, the
difference between the minimum lag with which it is safe to use endogenous
variables as instruments in the same or lower-numbered sectors and the
corresponding lag for use in higher-numbered ones may be even greater
than one. This point will be stronger the more stable one believes the dynamic
system to be. It arises because the effects of serial correlation in sector- and
equation-implicit disturbances are direct in the case of lagged endogenous
variables used in the same or lower-numbered sectors and are passed through
a damped dynamic system in the case of lagged endogenous variables used
in higher-numbered sectors [51]).

To sum up, so far as inconsistency is concerned, it is likely to be safer
to use endogenous variables with a given lag as instruments in higher-
numbered sectors than to use them in the same or lower-numbered sectors.
For the latter use, the endogenous variables should be lagged by at least one
more period to achieve the same level of consistency [52]).

It may be thought that this result is a rather poor return for all the
effort we have put into securing it. While one can certainly conceive of
stronger results, the usefulness of the present one should not be under-
estimated. We remarked at the beginning of this section that one important
desideratum of an instrumental variable was a close causal connection with
the variables appearing in the equation to be estimated. In general, economy-wide (and most other) econometric models have the property that
variables with low lags are often (but not always) more closely related to
variables to be explained than are variables with high ones. There may
therefore be a considerable gain in efficiency in the use of recent rather than
relatively remote endogenous variables as instruments, and it is important
to know that in certain reasonable contexts this may be done without
increasing the likely level of resulting inconsistency. We now turn to the
discussion of the causal criterion for instrumental variables.

----

[51]) All this is subject to the minor reservation discussed above concerning sums, each
term of which approaches zero monotonically. In practice, one tends to ignore such reservations in the absence of specific information as to which way they point.

[52]) The reader should be aware of the parallel between this result and the similar result
for the use of *current* endogenous variables which emerges when (BR.1)–(BR.3) are
assumed. Essentially, we have replaced (BR.2) with (15.26) and have dropped (BR.3).

15.6. Causality and rules for the use of eligible instrumental variables

15.6.1. The causal criterion for instrumental variables

We stated above that a good instrumental variable should directly or indirectly causally influence the variables in the equation to be estimated in a way independent of the other instrumental variables, and that the more direct such influence is, the better. This statement requires some discussion. So far as the limiting example of an instrument completely unrelated to the variables of the model is concerned, the lesson to be drawn might equally well be that instrumental variables must be correlated in the probability limit with at least one of the included variables. While it is easy to see that *some* causal connection must therefore exist, the question naturally arises of why it must be one in which the instrumental variables cause the included ones. If correlation is all that matters, surely the causal link might be reversed or both variables influenced by a common third one.

This is not the case. Consider first the situation in which the proposed instrumental variable is caused in part by variables included in the model. To the extent that this is the case, no advantage is obtained by using the proposed instrumental variable over using the included variables themselves. Obviously, the included variables are more highly correlated with themselves than with the proposed instrument. Further, correlation with the disturbance will be maintained if the proposed instrument is used. To the extent that the proposed instrument is caused by variables unrelated to the included variables, correlation with the disturbances will go down, but so also will correlation with the included variables.

The situation is similar if the proposed instrumental variable and one or more of the included ones are caused in part by a third variable. In this case, it is obviously more efficient to use that third variable itself as an instrument, and, if this is done, no further advantage attaches to the use of the proposed instrumental variable in addition. (The only exception to this occurs if data on the jointly causing variable are not available. In such a case the proposed instrument could be used to advantage.)

In general, an instrumental variable should be known to cause the included variables in the equation, at least indirectly. The closer such a causal connection is, the better. As can easily be seen from our discussion of block-recursive systems, however, the closer that connection is in many cases, the greater the danger of inconsistency through high correlations with the relevant disturbances. In such systems, for example, current endogenous

variables in low-numbered sectors directly cause current endogenous variables in high-numbered sectors [53]) while the same endogenous variables
lagged are likely to be safer in terms of inconsistency but are also likely to
be more remote causes. The value of the result derived at the end of the last
section is that it provides a case in which one set of instrumental variables
is likely to dominate another set on both criteria.

15.6.2. Available instruments and multicollinearity

There is obviously one set of variables which has optimal properties on
several counts. These are the exogenous variables explicitly included in the
model. Such variables are (by assumption) uncorrelated in the probability
limit with the disturbances; they also are in close causal connection to the
current variables in any equation; indeed, they *are* some of those variables
in some cases [54]). In the happy event that such exogenous variables are
adequate in number and in the nonsingularity of their variance-covariance
matrix and no lagged endogenous variables appear, there is no need to seek
further for instrumental variables to use.

Unfortunately, this is unlikely to be the case in an economy-wide econometric model. Such models tend to be almost self-contained, with relatively
few truly exogenous variables entering at relatively few places. This is especially the case if government policies obey regular rules, following signals
from the economy; they are therefore partly endogenous for purposes of
estimation [55]). In estimating any equation, all variables not used as instruments (except the variable explained by the equation) must be replaced
by a linear combination of instruments and the dependent variable regressed
on such linear combinations. If the second stage of this procedure is not to
involve inversion of a singular matrix, there must be (counting instrumental
variables appearing in the equation) at least as many instruments used as
there are parameters to be estimated. Further, the linear combinations
employed must not be perfectly correlated. Current exogenous variables
are simply not generally sufficient to meet this requirement in economy-wide
models. Moreover, they do not cause lagged endogenous variables which
are likely to be present in a dynamic system.

---

[53]) On causation in general and in decomposable systems (or our block-recursive systems) in particular, see Simon [32].

[54]) They may not cause all such variables even indirectly if the dynamic system is decomposable. Such cases are automatically treated in the rules given below.

[55]) This is to be sharply distinguished from the question of whether governmentally
controlled variables can be used as *policy* as opposed to estimation instruments.

Clearly, however, if the system is dynamic it will be possible to use *lagged* exogenous variables as well as current ones. Such use may be especially helpful if lagged endogenous variables are to be treated as endogenous and replaced by linear combinations of instruments which can be taken as causing them in part. Indeed, if lagged endogenous variables *are* to be taken as endogenous, exclusive use of current exogenous variables as instruments will not satisfy the causal criterion for instrumental variables already discussed. Since we have already seen that lagged endogenous variables should be used as instruments only with caution, it follows that lagged exogenous variables may well provide a welcome addition to the collection of available instruments.

Unfortunately, this also is unlikely to suffice. While it is true that one can always secure a sufficient number of instruments by using exogenous variables with larger and larger lags, such a procedure runs into several difficulties. In the first place, since rather long lags may be required, there may be a serious curtailment of available observations at the beginning of the time period to be used. Second, exogenous variables in the relatively distant past will be relatively indirect causes of even the lagged endogenous variables appearing in the equation to be estimated; it follows that their use will fail the causal criterion given and that it may be better to accept some inconsistency by using endogenous variables with lower lags. Finally, after going only a few periods back, the chances are high in practice that adding an exogenous variable with a still higher lag adds a variable which is very highly correlated with the instruments already included and therefore adds little independent causal information [56]. While the use of lagged exogenous variables is therefore highly desirable, it may not be of sufficient practical help to allow the search for instrumental variables to end.

Whatever collection of current exogenous, lagged exogenous and (none, some or all) lagged endogenous variables are used, however, the multicollinearity difficulty just encountered tends to arise. Some method must be found for dealing with it.

One set of interesting suggestions in this area has been provided by Kloek and Mennes [57]. Essentially, they propose using principal component analysis in various ways on the set of eligible instruments in order to secure orthogonal linear combinations. The endogenous variables are then replaced by their regressions on these linear combinations (possibly together with

---

[56]) This is especially likely if the exogenous variables are mainly ones such as population which are mainly trends.

[57]) Kloek and Mennes [20].

the eligible instruments actually appearing in the equation to be estimated) and the dependent variable regressed on these surrogates and the instruments appearing in the equation. Variants of this proposal are also examined.

This suggestion has the clear merit of avoiding multicollinearity, as it is designed to do. However, it may eliminate such multicollinearity in an undesirable way. If multicollinearity is present in a regression equation, at least one of the variables therein is adding little causal information to that already contained in the other variables. In replacing a given endogenous variable with its regression on a set of instruments, therefore, the prime reason for avoiding multicollinearity is that the addition of an instrument which is collinear with the included ones adds little causal information while using up a degree of freedom. The elimination of such multicollinearity ought thus to proceed in such a way as to conserve causal information. The Kloek-Mennes proposals may result in orthogonal combinations of instruments which are not particularly closely causally related to the included endogenous variables. Thus such proposals may well be inferior to a procedure which eliminates multicollinearity by eliminating instruments which contribute relatively little to the causal explanation of the endogenous variable to be replaced [58]). Clearly, this may involve using different sets of instruments in the replacement of different endogenous variables. Proposals along these lines are given below.

It may be objected, however, that such a procedure may eliminate multicollinearity in the regression of the included endogenous variables (other than the left-hand one of the equation) on the chosen instruments, only to encounter it again when the dependent variable is regressed on the replaced variables and the instruments appearing in the equation. This is clearly true [59]); it is unavoidable, however. The fact that the variables to be replaced by combinations of instruments are all part of the system to be estimated guarantees that they themselves *must* be reasonably highly collinear and related to the included instruments. It is impossible to reduce *that* kind of multicollinearity without introducing as instruments noise elements which are unrelated to the included variables, and such introduction clearly gains nothing. If we can secure instrumental variables which are closely causally related to the included variables but relatively uncorrelated with the disturbance of a given equation, we have gone as far as we can.

---

[58]) This seems to have been one of the outcomes of experimentation with different forms of principal component analysis in practice. See Taylor [34].

[59]) It is also true of the Kloek-Mennes procedures.

The avoidance of multicollinearity is a necessary part of such a procedure because multicollinearity is one sort of failure of the causal criterion discussed above. To attempt to eliminate that multicollinearity which inevitably results from just those causal relations which are to be estimated, however, is self-defeating [60].

15.6.3. Rules for the use of eligible instrumental variables

We have several times pointed out that the causal criterion and that of no correlation with the given disturbance may be inconsistent and that one may only be able to satisfy one more closely by sacrificing the other to a greater extent. In principle, a fully satisfactory treatment of the use of instrumental variables in economy-wide models would involve a full-scale Bayesian analysis of the losses and gains from any particular action. Such an analysis is clearly beyond the scope of the present paper, although any recommended procedure clearly has some judgment of probable losses behind it, however vague such judgment may be.

We shall proceed by assuming that the no-correlation criterion has been used to secure a set of eligible instrumental variables whose use is judged to involve only tolerable inconsistencies in the estimation of a given equation. Note that the set may be different for different equations. Within that set are current and lagged exogenous variables and lagged endogenous variables sufficiently far in the past that the effects of serial correlation are judged to be negligible over the time period involved. As shown in the preceding section, that time period will generally be shorter for endogenous variables in sectors lower-numbered than that in which the equation to be estimated appears than for endogenous variables in the same or higher-numbered sectors [61]. Clearly, other things being equal, the use of current and lagged exogenous variables is preferable to the use of lagged endogenous variables, and the

---

[60] I want to make it clear that I am not accusing Kloek and Mennes of attempting to do this. Their proposals are designed to eliminate multicollinearity in the first stage of the procedure where it is desirable to do so. Their "Method 2" [20, pp. 51–52] does eliminate collinearity in the second stage between the replaced endogenous variables and the included predetermined ones, but this is not *necessarily* the same as the desirable and irreducible collinearity among the variables in the equation discussed in the text. It may well occur in practice that the Kloek-Mennes proposals lead to desirable results, although an approach using more structural information than does theirs seems preferable.

[61] It will not have escaped the reader's notice that very little guidance has been given as to the determination of the absolute magnitude of that time period.

use of lagged endogenous variables from lower-numbered sectors is preferable to the use of endogenous variables with the same (or possibly even a
slightly greater) lag from the same or higher-numbered sectors than that in
which the equation to be estimated occurs. We shall suggest ways of modi-
fying the use of the causal criterion to take account of this. For convenience,
we shall refer to all the eligible instrumental variables as predetermined and
to all other variables as endogenous.

Consider any particular endogenous variable in the equation to be estimated, other than the one explained by that equation. That right-hand endogenous variable will be termed of *zero causal order*. Consider the *structural*
equation (either in its original form or with all variables lagged) that explains that variable [62]). The variables other than the explained one appearing
therein will be called of *first causal order*. Next, consider the structural
equations explaining the first causal order endogenous variables [63]). All
variables appearing in those equations will be called of *second causal order*
with the exception of the *zero causal order* variable and those endogenous
variables of first causal order the equations for which have already been
considered. Note that a given predetermined variable may be of more
than one causal order. Consider now those structural equations explaining
endogenous variables of second causal order. All variables appearing in
such equations will be called of *third causal order* except for the *endogenous*
ones of lower causal order, and so forth. (Any predetermined variables never
reached in this procedure are dropped from the eligible set while dealing
with the given zero causal order variable.)

The result of this procedure is to use the a priori structural information
available to subdivide the set of predetermined variables according to closeness of causal relation to a given endogenous variable in the equation to be
estimated. Thus, predetermined variables of first causal order are known to
cause that endogenous variable directly; predetermined variables of second
causal order are known directly to cause other variables which directly
cause the given endogenous variable, and so forth. Note again that a given
predetermined variable can be of more than one causal order, and so the
subdivision need not result in disjunct sets of predetermined variables.

We now provide a complete ordering of the predetermined variables

---

[62]) There must exist such an equation if the variable in question is normalized. As
stated above, lack of such normalization is a form of incomplete specification.

[63]) Observe that endogenous variables appearing in the equation to be estimated other
than the particular one with which we begin may be of positive causal order. This includes
the endogenous variable to be explained by the equation to be estimated.

relative to the given endogenous variable of zero causal order [64]). Let p be the largest number of different causal orders to which any predetermined variable belongs. To each predetermined variable we assign a p-component vector. The first component of that vector is the lowest numbered causal order to which the given predetermined variable belongs; the second component is the next lowest causal order to which it belongs, and so forth. Vectors corresponding to variables belonging to less than p different causal orders have infinity in the unused places. Thus, for example, if $p = 5$, a predetermined variable of first, second and eighth causal order will be assigned the vector $(1, 2, 8, \infty, \infty)$. The vectors are now ordered lexicographically. That is, any vector, say f, is assigned a number, $\beta(f)$, such that, for any two vectors, say f and h:

$$\beta(f) > \beta(h) \text{ if and only if either } f_1 > h_1 \text{ or for some } j \ (1 < j \leqslant p) \quad (15.34)$$

$$f_i = h_i \quad (i = 1, \ldots, j-1) \quad \text{and} \quad f_j > h_j.$$

The predetermined variables are then ordered in ascending order of their corresponding β-numbers. This will be called the β-ordering.

Thus predetermined variables of first causal order are assigned lower numbers than predetermined variables of only higher causal orders; predetermined variables of first and second causal order are assigned lower numbers than predetermined variables of first and only causal orders higher than second (or of no higher causal order), and so forth [65]).

The procedure just described gives an a priori preference ordering on the set of instrumental variables relative to a given zero causal order endogenous variable. This ordering is in terms of closeness of causal relation. Alternatively, one may wish to modify that ordering to take further account of the danger of inconsistency. This may be done by deciding that current and lagged exogenous variables of a given causal order are always to be preferred to lagged endogenous variables of no lower causal order and that lagged endogenous variables from sectors with lower numbers than that of the equation to be estimated are always to be preferred to endogenous variables

---

[64]) I am indebted to J. C. G. Boot for aid in the construction of the following formal description.

[65]) This is only one way of constructing such an ordering. If there is specific a priori reason to believe that a given instrument is important in influencing the variable to be replaced (for example, if it is known to enter in several different ways with big coefficients), it should be given a low number. In the absence of such specific information the ordering given in the text seems a natural way of organizing the structural information.

with the same lag and causal order from the same or higher-numbered sectors. One might even go further and decide that *all* current and lagged exogenous variables of finite causal order are to be preferred to *any* lagged endogenous variables.

However the preference ordering is decided upon, its existence allows us to use a posteriori information to choose a set of instruments for the zero causal order endogenous variable in the way about to be described. Once the set has been chosen, the endogenous variable is replaced by its regression on the instruments in the set and the equation in question estimated by least-squares regression of the left-hand endogenous variable on the resulting right-hand variables [66]).

We use a posteriori information in combination with the a priori preference ordering in the following manner. Suppose that there are T observations in the sample. Regress the zero causal order endogenous variable on the first $T-2$ instruments in the preference ordering (a regression with one degree of freedom). Drop the least preferred of these instruments from the regression. Observe whether the multiple correlation of the regression drops significantly as a result. (The standard here may be the significance level of R^2 or simply its value corrected for degrees of freedom.) If correlation drops significantly, the $T-2$nd instrument contributes significantly to the causation of the zero order endogenous variable even in the presence of all instruments which are a priori more closely related to that variable than it is. It should therefore be retained. If correlation does not drop significantly, the variable in question adds nothing and should be omitted.

Now proceed to the $T-3$rd instrument. If the $T-2$nd instrument was retained at the previous step, reintroduce it; if not, leave it out. Observe whether omitting the $T-3$rd instrument reduces the multiple correlation significantly. If so, retain it; if not, omit it and proceed to the next lower-numbered instrument.

Continue in this way. At every step, a given instrument is tested to see whether it contributes significantly to multiple correlation in the presence of all instruments which are a priori preferred to it and all other instruments which have already passed the test. When all instruments have been so tested, the ones remaining are the ones to be used.

15.6.4. Discussion of the rules

The point of this procedure (or the variants described below) is to replace

---

[66]) An important modification of this procedure is described below.

the right-hand endogenous variables in the equation to be estimated by their regression-calculated values, using instruments which satisfy the causal criterion as well as possible while keeping inconsistency at a tolerable level. Certain features require discussion.

In the first place, multicollinearity at this stage of the proceedings is automatically taken care of in a way consistent with the causal criterion. If some set of instruments is highly collinear, that member of the set which is least preferred on a priori grounds will fail to reduce correlation significantly when it is tested as just described. It will then be omitted, and the procedure guarantees that it will be the *least* preferred member of the set which is so treated. If the β-ordering is used, this will be the one most distantly structurally related to the endogenous variable which is to be replaced. Multicollinearity will be tolerated where it should be, namely, where despite its presence each instrument in the collinear set adds significant causal information.

Second, it is evident that the procedure described has the property that no variable will be omitted simply because it is highly correlated with other variables already dropped. If two variables add significantly to correlation when both are present but fail to add anything when introduced separately, the first one to be tested will not be dropped from the regression, as omitting it in the presence of the other instrument will significantly reduce correlation [67]). While it is true that variables may be dropped because of correlation with variables less preferred than the $T-2$nd, which are never tested, the exclusion of the latter variables seems to be a relatively weak reliance on a priori information.

This brings us to the next point. Clearly, it is possible in principle that instruments less preferred than the $T-2$nd would in fact pass the correlation test described if that test were performed after some lower-numbered instruments were tested and dropped. Similarly, an instrument dropped at an early stage might pass the test in the absence of variables *later* dropped because of the increased number of degrees of freedom. One could, of course, repeat the entire procedure in order to test every previously dropped variable after each decision to omit; it seems preferable, however, to rely on the a priori preference ordering in practice and to insist that instruments which come late in the β-ordering pass a more stringent empirical test than those

---

[67]) This property was missing in the procedure suggested in the first draft of this paper in which variables were added in ascending order of preference and retained if they added significantly to correlation. I am indebted to Albert Ando for helpful discussions on this point.

which come early. The rationale behind the β-ordering is the belief that it is the earlier instruments in that ordering which contribute most of the causal information, and so it seems quite appropriate to calculate the degrees of freedom for testing a given instrument by subtracting the number of its place in the ordering from the total number of observations (and allowing for the constant term) [68].

Turning to another issue, it may be objected that there is no guarantee that the suggested procedures will result in a nonsingular moment matrix to be inverted at the last stage. That is, there may be some set of r endogenous variables to be replaced whose regressions together involve less than r predetermined variables. Alternatively, counting the instruments included in the equation to be estimated, there may not be as many instruments used in the final stage as there are parameters to be estimated. This can happen, of course, although it is perhaps relatively unlikely. If it does occur, it is a sign that the equation in question is unidentifiable from the sample available—that the causal information contained in the sample is insufficient to allow estimation of the equation without relaxing the inconsistency requirements. To put it another way, it can be argued that to rectify this situation, by the introduction in the first-stage regressions of variables failing the causal test as described is an *ad hoc* device which adds no causal information. While such variables may in fact appear in such regressions with nonzero coefficients in the probability limit, their use in the sample adds nothing to the quality of the estimates save the ability to secure numbers and disguise the problem.

Of course, such an argument is a bit too strong. Whether a variable adds significantly to correlation is a function of what one means by significance. The problem is thus a continuous rather than a discrete one and should be treated as such. For the criterion of significance used, in some sense, the equation in question cannot be estimated from the sample in the circumstance described; it may be estimable with a less stringent significance criterion. In practice, if the significance requirements are relaxed, the moment matrix to be inverted will pass from singularity to near-singularity, and estimated asymptotic standard errors will be large rather than infinite. The general point is that if multicollinearity cannot be sufficiently eliminated using causal information, little is to be gained by eliminating it by introducing more or less irrelevant variables.

A somewhat related point is that the use of different variables as instru-

---

[68] Admittedly, this argument loses some of its force when applied to the modifications of the β-ordering given above.

ments in the regressions for different endogenous variables in the same equation may result in a situation in which the longest lag involved in one such regression is greater than that involved in others. If data are only available from an initial date, this means that using the regressions as estimated involves eliminating some observations at the beginning of the period that would be retained if the longest-lagged instrument were dropped. In this case, some balance must be struck between the gain in efficiency from extra observations and the loss from disregarding causal information if the lagged instrument in question is dropped. It is hard to give a precise guide as to how this should be done. (My personal preference would be for retaining the instrument is most cases.) Such circumstances will fortunately be relatively infrequent, as the periods of data collection generally begin earlier than those of estimation, at least in models of developed economies. Further, the reduction in available observations attendant on the use of an instrument with a large lag renders it unlikely that the introduction of that instrument adds significantly to correlation.

Finally, the use of different instruments in the regressions replacing different endogenous variables in the equation to be estimated reintroduces the problem of inconsistency. When the equation to be estimated is rewritten with calculated values replacing some or all of the variables, the residual term includes not only the original structural disturbance but also a linear combination of the residuals from the regression equations used in such replacement. When the equation is then estimated by regressing the left-hand variable on the calculated right-hand ones and the instruments explicitly appearing, consistency requires not only zero correlation in the probability limit between the original disturbance and all the variables used in the final regression, but also zero correlation in the probability limit between the residuals from the earlier-stage regression equations and all such variables. If the same set of instruments is used when replacing every right-hand endogenous variable, and if that set includes the instruments explicitly in the equation, the latter requirement presents no problem, since the normal equations of ordinary least squares imply that such correlations are zero even in the sample [69]). When different instruments are used in the replacement of different variables, however, or when the instruments so used do not include those explicitly in the equation, the danger of inconsistency from this source does arise.

---

[69]) This is the case when the reduced-form equations are used, for example, as in the classic version of two-stage least squares.

There are several ways of handling this without sacrificing the major benefits of our procedures. One way is simply to argue that those procedures are designed to include in the regression for any right-hand endogenous variable any instrument which is correlated with the residuals from that regression computed without that instrument. The excluded instruments are either those which are known a priori not to be direct or indirect causes of the variable to be replaced or those which fail to add significantly to the correlation of the regression in question. The former instruments are known a priori not to appear in equations explaining the variable to be replaced and hence cannot be correlated in the probability limit with the residual from the regression unless both they and the replaced variable are affected by some third variable not included in that regression [70]). Such a third variable cannot be endogenous, however, since in that case the excluded instruments in question would also be endogenous; moreover, our procedure is designed to include explicitly any instrument significantly affecting the variable to be replaced. Any such third variable must therefore be one omitted from the model, and it *may* not be stretching things too far to disregard correlations between residuals and excluded instruments stemming from such a source.

As for instruments which are indirectly causally related to the endogenous variable involved but which fail to add significantly to the correlation of the regression in question, these cannot be significantly correlated with the *sample* residual from that regression. One can therefore argue that the evidence is against their being significantly correlated with that residual in the probability limit.

Such an argument can clearly be pushed too far, however. If there are strong a priori reasons to believe that the excluded instruments should be included, in view of the causal structure of the model, one may not want to reject correlation in the probability limit because multicollinearity (for the long continuance of which there may be no structural reason) leads to insignificant correlation in the sample. A modified course of action, then, is to include in the regression for any replaced variable any instrument which one believes a priori to be important in that regression *and* which appears either in the equation to be estimated or in the regression for any other replaced variable as computed by the procedures described above [71]).

---

[70]) If they were non-negligibly caused by the replaced variable itself they would be endogenous, contrary to assumption.

[71]) Omitting instruments which do *not* so appear does not cause inconsistency.

Clearly, not much is lost by doing this, since the added variables will not contribute much to the equation in the sample.

Alternatively, one may go the whole way toward guarding against inconsistency from the source under discussion and include in the regression for any replaced variable all instruments which appear in the equation to be estimated or in the regression for any other replaced variable as computed by the described procedures, whether or not such instrument is thought a priori to be important in explaining the replaced variable. This alternative clearly eliminates the danger under discussion. It may, however, reintroduce multicollinearity and may involve a serious departure from the causal criterion if a priori noncausal instruments are thus included. Nevertheless, it does retain the merit that every instrumental variable used is either explicitly included in the equation or contributes significantly to the causal explanation of at least one variable so included. In practice, there may not be a great deal of difference between these alternatives, and the last one described may then be optimal (unless it is unavailable because of the degrees of freedom required).

Whatever variant of our procedures is thought best in practice, they all have the merit of using information on the dynamic and causal structure of the model in securing estimates. The use of such information in some way is vital in the estimation of economy-wide econometric models where the ideal conditions for which most estimators are designed are unlikely to be encountered in practice [72]).

REFERENCES

1. ANDERSON, T. W. On Asymptotic Distributions of Estimates of Parameters of Stochastic Difference Equations, *Annals of Mathematical Statistics* 30 (1959) 676–687.
2. ANDO, A., and FISHER, F. M. Near-Decomposability, Partition and Aggregation, and the Relevance of Stability Discussions, *International Economic Review* 4 (1963) 53–67; reprinted as Ch. 3 of [3].
3. ANDO, A., FISHER, F. M., and SIMON, H. A. *Essays on the Structure of Social Science Models*. Cambridge, Mass.: M.I.T. Press, 1963.
4. BARGER, H., and KLEIN, L. R. A Quarterly Model for the United States Economy, *Journal of the American Statistical Association* 49 (1954) 413–437.

[72]) The use of the causal structure of the model itself to choose instrumental variables as described in the text is closely akin to the methods used by Barger and Klein to estimate a system with a triangular matrix of coefficients of current endogenous variables. See [4].

5. BASMANN, R. L. "On the Exact Finite Sample Distributions of Generalized Classical Linear Structural Estimators". Santa Barbara, Cal.: Technical Military Plannings Operation, 1960. (Mimeographed.)

6. BASMANN, R. L. A Note on the Exact Finite Sample Frequency Functions of Generalized Linear Classical Estimators in a Leading Three-Equation Case, *Journal of the American Statistical Association* 58 (1963) 161–171.

7. BERGSTROM, A. R. The Exact Sampling Distributions of Least Squares and Maximum Likelihood Estimators of the Marginal Prospensity to Consume, *Econometrica* 30 (1962) 480–490.

8. BROWN, T. M. Simultaneous Least Squares: A Distribution Free Method of Equation System Structure Estimation, *International Economic Review* 1 (1960) 173–191.

9. CHOW, G. C. A Comparison of Alternative Estimators for Simultaneous Equations, *Econometrica* 32 (1964) 532–533.

10. EISENPRESS, H. Note on the Computation of Full-Information Maximum Likelihood Estimates of Coefficients of a Simultaneous System, *Econometrica* 30 (1962) 343–348.

11. FISHER, F. M. On the Cost of Approximate Specification in Simultaneous Equation Estimation, *Econometrica* 29 (1961) 139–170; reprinted as Ch. 2 of [3].

12. FISHER, F. M. The Place of Least Squares in Econometrics: Comment, *Econometrica* 30 (1962) 565–567.

13. FISHER, F. M. Uncorrelated Disturbances and Identifiability Criteria, *Internationa Economic Review* 4, No. 2 (May, 1963) 134–152.

14. GORMAN, W. M. "Professor Strotz on a Specification Error". University of Birmingham, Faculty of Commerce and Social Science, Discussion Papers, Series A, No. 24, 1960.

15. HARROD, R. F. *Towards a Dynamic Economics*. London: Macmillan, 1948.

16. HICKS, J. R. *A Contribution to the Theory of the Trade Cycle*. Oxford: Clarendon Press, 1950.

17. HURWICZ, L. Least-Squares Bias in Time Series, Ch. 15 of *Statistical Inference in Dynamic Economic Models*. Edited by T. C. Koopmans. (Cowles Commission for Research in Economics Monograph 10.) New York: John Wiley & Sons, 1950.

18. JOHNSTON, J. *Econometric Methods*. New York: McGraw-Hill, 1963.

19. KLEIN, L. R., and NAKAMURA, M. Singularity in the Equation Systems of Econometrics: Some Aspects of the Problem of Multicollinearity, *International Economic Review* 3 (1962) 274–299.

20. KLOEK, T., and MENNES, L. B. M. Simultaneous Equations Estimation Based on Principal Components of Predetermined Variables, *Econometrica* 28 (1960) 45–61.

21. LESNOY, S. "Limited Information versus Reduced Form Least Squares in Prediction". Unpublished paper presented at Cambridge meeting of the Econometric Society, 1958.

22. LIU, T. C. Underidentification, Structural Estimation, and Forecasting, *Econometrica* 28 (1960) 855–865.

23. MADANSKY, A. On the Efficiency of Three-Stage Least-Squares Estimation. *Econometrica* 32 (1964) 51–56.

24. MANN, H. B., and WALD, A. On the Statistical Treatment of Linear Stochastic Difference Equations, *Econometrica* 11 (1943) 173–220.

25. NAGAR, A. L. The Bias and Moment Matrix of the General *k*-Class Estimators of the Parameters in Simultaneous Equations, *Econometrica* 27 (1959) 575–595.

26. NAGAR, A. L. Double k-Class Estimators of Parameters in Simultaneous Equations and Their Small Sample Properties, *International Economic Review* 3 (1962) 168–188.

27. QUANDT, R. E. "Some Small Sample Properties of Certain Structural Equation Estimators". Princeton University, Econometric Research Program, Research Memorandum No. 48, 1963.

28. QUANDT, R. E. "On Certain Small Sample Properties of k-Class Estimators". Princeton University, 1963. (Mimeographed.)

29. ROTHENBERG, T. J., and LEENDERS, C. T. Efficient Estimation of Simultaneous Equation Systems, *Econometrica* 32 (1964) 57–76.

30. SARGAN, J. D. Three-State Least Squares and Full Maximum Likelihood Estimates, *Econometrica* 32 (1964) 77–81.

31. SARGAN, J. D. "An Approximation to the Distribution Function of Two-Stage Least Squares". 1963. (Mimeographed.)

32. SIMON, H. A. Causal Ordering and Identifiability, Ch. 3 of *Studies in Econometric Method.* Edited by W. C. Hood and T. C. Koopmans. (Cowles Commission on Research in Economics Monograph 14). New York: John Wiley & Sons, 1953. Reprinted as Ch. 1 of H. A. Simon, *Models of Man.* New York: John Wiley & Sons, 1957; and as Ch. 1 of [3].

33. STROTZ, R. H. Interdependence as a Specification Error, *Econometrica* 28 (1960) 428–442.

34. TAYLOR, L. D. "The Principal-Component-Instrumental-Variable Approach to the Estimation of Systems of Simultaneous Equations". Unpublished Ph. D. dissertation, Harvard University, 1962.

35. THEIL, H. Specification Errors and the Estimation of Economic Relationships, *Review of the International Statistical Institute* 25 (1957) 45–51.

36. THEIL, H. *Economic Forecasts and Policy.* 2d ed. revised. Amsterdam: North-Holland Publishing Company, 1961.

37. WAUGH, F. The Place of Least Squares in Econometrics, *Econometrica* 29 (1961) 386–396.

38. WOLD, H. *Demand Analysis, A Study in Econometrics.* In association with L. Juréen. New York: John Wiley & Sons, 1953.

39. WOLD, H., and FAXÈR, P. On the Specification Error in Regression Analysis, *Annals of Mathematical Statistics* 28 (1957) 265–267.

40. WOLD, H. Ends and Means in Econometric Model Building, in *Probability and Statistics; The Harald Cramér Volume.* Edited by U. Grenander. New York: John Wiley & Sons, 1959, pp. 354–434.

41. ZELLNER, A., and THEIL, H. Three-State Least Squares: Simultaneous Estimation of Simultaneous Equations, *Econometrica* 30 (1962) 54–78.

CHAPTER 16

VALIDATION AND APPLICATION OF MACROECONOMIC MODELS USING COMPUTER SIMULATION

Contents

16.1. Introduction 637

16.2. Questions to be answered about and with an economic model 639
1. Fit to historical data. 2. Forecasts. 3. Structure. 4. Stability and growth. 5. Policy.

16.3. What the simulation program is designed to do 644
1. Accuracy checks. 2. Simulation calculations.

16.4. Some operating experience with the program 648

References 650

VALIDATION AND APPLICATION OF MACROECONOMIC MODELS USING COMPUTER SIMULATION [1])

CHARLES C. HOLT

The University of Wisconsin, Madison, Wisconsin

16.1. Introduction

Economists have done a great deal of theorizing about the relationships between economic variables, but only in the last thirty years have systematic efforts been made to measure these relationships. Efforts to estimate whole sets of relationships which make some pretense of yielding a model of the whole economy have appeared still more recently. The model which is presented in this book is by all odds the most ambitious effort in this direction. This chapter is devoted to the next set of questions and problems which arise, when such a model is available. Unhappily, in the past many of the models never went far beyond their initial formulation and estimation; relatively little was done with them after they were "completed". There are many reasons for this lack of follow-through, one of the important ones being the substantial difficulties that are encountered in working with large complicated systems, especially those involving nonlinear dynamic relation-

_____

[1]) The author gratefully acknowledges receiving programming support from the Social Systems Research Institute, under the leadership of Guy Orcutt, and computing support from the Numerical Analysis Laboratory, both of the University of Wisconsin. The Numerical Analysis Laboratory receives partial support from the National Science Foundation. The Brookings-SSRC econometric project also made a contribution to the programming.

The Social Systems Research Institute has received major support from funds provided by The Ford Foundation, the National Science Foundation, The Brookings Institution, The National Bureau of Economic Research, The University of Wisconsin Research Committee and The Wisconsin Alumni Research Foundation.

ships. If we are to make progress in economic analysis we shall have to face up to these problems and devise means of overcoming them.

In this chapter an effort is made to spell out the kinds of tests that need to be performed in the validation of macroeconomic models and then consider the uses to which such models may be put after they have been reasonably validated. These tests and uses indicate the requirements that should be satisfied by a computer program if the power of an electronic computer is to be brought to bear effectively upon the economist's problems in coping with complex models. The program SIMULATE, which was written to satisfy these requirements, is described briefly. Finally, some operating experience with the program is reported. Although the models which have been used to test the program are relatively small, twenty-two to forty-five equations, certain unanticipated difficulties arose. These influenced the development of the program to serve also as an aid in debugging the data and the model.

Although the present discussion is in the context of macroeconomic models, the research issues and problems often are similar for models of regions, industries, firms and even some engineering systems. Hopefully, the computer program will find a wide variety of applications.

Before proceeding further we should mention some requirements that the economic model must satisfy before it can be considered a complete system ready for simulation testing. Treating time as a discrete variable, we will need at least as many equations as there are unknown variables in the current time period; the model "explains" these endogenous variables. The exogenous variables influence the endogenous variables through the relationships in the model but are assumed not to be influenced by them. Since the model does not generate values for the exogenous variables, it may be necessary, outside the main model, to supply auxiliary relationships for forecasting their future values.

Some variables, such as survey data on expectations, are exogenous in the sense that the model does not generate them. But they are known to be strongly influenced by variables that are included in the model as endogenous. If such a model is to be used for forecasting the future (where exogenous survey data are not available), an additional relationship for each such variable must be added to the model, and the variable must be reclassified as endogenous. Finally, for variables which serve as policy instruments for government decisions, some hypothetical values or strategies must be supplied.

16.2. Questions to be answered about and with an economic model

Assuming that a set of mathematical equations is available which constitutes a model of the economy, what can we learn about the system of
equations, its ability to predict the behavior of the economy and its use in
studying policy alternatives? Before we can consider the design of a simulation program we need to examine these questions.

16.2.1. Fit to historical data

The first question to explore is how well the model fits known data. Usually
the model is estimated from historical data; the use of the same set
of data to test the model would appear somewhat questionable. However,
two important points can be explored. First, if the model was estimated as
a set of individual equations, or alternatively as subsets of equations, it
may be a significant test to solve the equations as a simultaneous system.
It is quite possible for the individual equations, or subsystems of equations,
to fit reasonably well, but when all the equations are solved jointly, errors
may accumulate and a bad fit may be obtained. Second, the parameter
estimates usually are made on the basis of "forecasting" one time period
ahead. Since many applications of the model will require forecasts for a
time horizon of several or even many time periods, it is important to test
whether the model is capable of giving reasonably good forecasts over longer
forecast spans. After the unknown endogenous variables for one time period
have been solved, time is advanced one time period and then the unknown
endogenous variables for the following period are solved, and so on. As this
process is repeated, we would anticipate that the calculated values would
gradually suffer from accumulating errors and the forecast performance
gradually worsen. This is a severe test, even when the model has the advantage of being tested against the data which were used in its estimation.
Should the model fall down badly on either of these two tests, there is clear
indication that further work is needed before any great confidence can be
placed in the model.

    Of course, no model is expected to fit the data exactly: the question is
whether the residual errors are sufficiently small to be tolerable and sufficiently unsystematic to be treated as random. For complex, nonlinear
systems we have no adequate statistical theory to provide criteria for judgment, but we can at least compute and examine the errors.

    The fit and the forecasting ability of the model are likely to be considerably better for some variables than for others, and this suggests that it may be fruitful to run tests on portions of the model in order to isolate the sources of errors. Reformulation and reestimation of portions of the model are likely to be indicated at this point.

16.2.2. Forecasts

The next step is to test the forecasting power of the model against data which were not used in the estimation process. This test might be against new observations, or a test might be made by calculating statistics which were not involved in the estimation process. For example, the National Bureau of Economic Research reference cycle analysis could be used to see if the fluctuation amplitudes of the model and the leads and lags in the turning points of its variables matched the behavior of the American economy, a procedure applied in [1] and the article by Irma Adelman [4]. Serious failure in such tests indicates a need for further work on the model.

As soon as a model has been found to yield reasonably accurate forecasts, such systematic empirical regularities can be put to practical use in making unconditional forecasts of unknown future values of the endogenous variables. However, a researcher may be justifiably uncomfortable when making predictions with a model that is not yet thoroughly studied and understood.

16.2.3. Structure

We are, of course, interested not only in knowing what the economy will do, but also in gaining insight into why it behaves as it does. Verbal analysis supplemented with geometry have been the traditional tools for obtaining such insight, but increasingly economists have resorted to advanced calculus and matrix algebra for deepening their comprehension of complex systems. Unfortunately no body of mathematics exists for adequately treating large systems of assorted nonlinear dynamic relationships, but our recently increased ability to make numerical calculations with electronic computers opens the way for the experimental study of such systems.

Equations that cannot be solved explicitly by mathematical operations to obtain an exact analytic solution often can be solved by numerical operations to obtain particular numerical solutions. This is the essence of simulation and the source of its power. However, the blind brute force search for the properties of a complex system offers us no panacea in the form of a self-sufficient methodology as the work of Balderston, Hoggatt, Jackson, Cohen, Cyert, March and Soelberg [4] shows. In a large simulation model the parameters are too many, the relationships too complex and the variables too numerous for generalizations to arise readily from the numerical exploration of a few points in a multi-dimensional space.

Parallel mathematical analysis will be needed to aid in abstracting the essential behavior of such complex systems, and essentially mathematical insights will be needed to guide experimentation on simulation models [2].

Complex nonlinear models will not, in general, be amenable to analytic solution in the forseeable future. To obtain a mathematical problem that can be solved will require extensive simplifications. By sensitivity ,studies of the simulation model a great deal can be learned about simplifications that can be made without critically affecting the behavior of the system. In this way simulation studies can guide the search for mathematical formulations that can be *both* significant and analytically solvable. The insights gained from these solutions in turn should help in guiding the experimentation on and validation of complete simulation models [2]).

In short, economists will need all the help they can get from both mathematics and computation to gain adequate understanding of economic structure and behavior. It is all too easy to become lost in a maze of complexity rather than to gain useful insights. We are familiar with this problem in looking at the real economic world, and it will face us again in looking at the behavior of a complex simulation model.

Knowledge of causal chains in an economic model would give useful insight into the system. H. A. Simon [2, chap. 2] and Herman Wold [12] have shown that there is a direct analogue between causal ordering and the ordering of the system that is needed for computation.

Some sets of equations are so strongly interrelated that they can only be solved jointly. Others can be decomposed into a recursive sequence of equations that can be solved one equation at a time. In the former case we would conclude that the variables are jointly determined; in the latter, that causality operated in the same direction as the computational ordering. Certain variables whose values can be found without consideration of other variables certainly cannot be caused by them. However, if the values of the latter variables depend on knowing the values of former variables, causality can be traced from the former to the latter variables. Where the

---

[2]) Steward, Balderston, Hoggatt and Jackson have been particularly sensitive to this largely unresolved problem.

equations can be solved one at a time, it is possible to order the list of the endogenous variables of the system in such a way that each variable may influence the variables below it in the list but cannot be influenced by them. Where a variable is jointly determined with a group of variables, an ordering may be found that applies to groups of variables. In either case, a causal interpretation can be given to such recursive orderings and block-recursive orderings, if they can be found.

Recursive ordering can be studied in the dynamic or in the static context. In the former case the influence from variable to variable is traced out within a single time period for which the solution is sought. In the latter, the influence of some variables on others is considered after sufficient time has passed for all interactions involved in the system to take place. Considered statically, an economic system is likely in large part to be jointly determined; considered dynamically with a relatively short time period, it is more likely to be recursively determined, or at least block-recursively determined. It is quite clear that the computer program for making simulation studies should, if possible, make an analysis of the recursive ordering of the equations that constitute the model.

While the recursive ordering deals with the influence of some variables on others, it does not cast light on the strength of the influence. Clearly, some influences will be negligibly small, while others will be of decisive importance. Through simulation calculations it is possible to perturb the values of certain parameters and explore their quantitative effects. Possibly some parameters can be set to zero with very little influence on the behavior of the system. In this way the ordering may be made more recursive so that the really important structural relations stand out more clearly.

Insight into parameter sensitivities hopefully will be a useful guide to improving parameter estimates. Additional work can be directed particularly to refining estimates of those parameters and relationships that prove to be most critical. Finally, insight into what might be referred to as critical structure can guide the complementary work on analytic solutions that was mentioned earlier.

16.2.4. Stability and growth

After a model has weathered the foregoing tests and studies, we would probably have enough confidence in it to want to analyze certain important characteristics, such as its growth rate and degree of stability. The growth equilibrium of a model can be observed by running it for many time periods free of exogenous disturbances. By introducing deliberate shocks to the model it is possible to observe its characteristic dynamic responses which reveal its degree of stability. Where the repercussions of a disturbance die our rapidly, a high degree of stability is indicated. A cumulative explosion or slow oscillatory decay would indicate instability and low stability, respectively. For a linear system the response to a single disturbance tells the whole story, but for a nonlinear system the stability characteristics may depend upon the region (in the variable space) in which the system is operating, being stable in some regions and unstable in others. Any tendencies for the dynamic fluctuations to influence the rate of growth of the model can be observed by resetting the model to the starting point of an earlier growth path and making a new run with random disturbances introduced. We would expect in general to find such an interaction in nonlinear systems.

In order to be able to run controlled experiments on the determinants of stability, it is important that *identical* sets of random disturbances can be reproduced under the control of the researcher.

16.2.5. Policy

After a model has been validated and insight gained into its structure and operation, we can consider its policy applications. Policy actions by government may change the values of certain instrument variables or alternatively may change the parameters of economic relationships. The model may be used to make conditional forecasts by introducing a policy change and forecasting the economic outcome. Typically this will appear more desirable in some ways and less so in others; for example, unemployment may decline but inflation increase. Thus a problem arises of *evaluating* these outcomes by some consistent measure if progress is to be made in finding improved courses of action.

At this point it may be helpful to postulate certain quantitative policy objectives in order to guide the simulation study. This can be done either in terms of a social welfare function, minimum standards or desired targets. In any case, it would be helpful to formalize the objectives in such a way that they can be incorporated into the simulation calculations so that some indices of relative desirability are obtained to aid in making comparisons.

Once both model and structure of objectives have been submitted to the computer, it is possible to make conditional forecasts contingent upon some policy action or policy strategy and evaluate the outcome in terms of desirability. Several approaches may be used in making policy studies. One is to use direct experimentation, posing alternative actions and testing them.

Another approach is to play a stabilization game [3]) in which judgmental decision methods are used to select the actions appropriate for a particular period. When the outcome of these actions is computed, the process can be repeated for the following period, and so on.

Since it is likely that we will continue, in formulating economic policy to rely on judgmental methods for some time to come, some vicarious training for governmental decision makers, using a model economy, would have much to recommend it instead of exclusively using the national economy for the learning process.

The problem of controlling a complex dynamic economy may prove to be sufficiently difficult that statistical decision theory is needed to formulate policies that improve stability. In many industrial operations research analyses, finding a good decision strategy has required quite subtle and powerful tools. However, at the present time such analyses are not available for decision problems occurring in really complex systems, and it is likely for quite some time that we will have available approximate analyses that do not take into account the full complexity of the decision. These approximate methods can be evaluated by making simulation studies of the policies which they suggest, using the full complex nonlinear model.

Since an economy and its control mechanisms operate under conditions of uncertainty, it may be desirable to make Monte Carlo experiments which will throw light upon the probability distributions of decision performances that can be anticipated. The same strategy may work very well in some circumstances but poorly in others, so it becomes necessary to take into account the probability of occurrence of the various circumstances.

Such policy studies are likely to point up deficiencies in the model formulation and the control instruments, as well as throw light on alternative policies.

16.3. What the simulation program is designed to do

In order to be prepared to make studies of the types discussed above on the Brookings-SSRC econometric model, and other models as well, we determined the program specifications implicit in the above discussion and

---

[3]) For a number of years business games have been used extensively: (1) to gain insight into judgmental decision methods and their effectiveness, (2) to train decision makers economically by exposing them to vicarious experience and (3) to obtain better understanding of the decision problems and the behavior of decision-making organizations.

proceeded to write and test the program. Clearly it was not desirable to delay the work on the program until the model was complete. A number of smaller models were used both to test the program and to improve its design specifications.

Anyone who has tried to study a sizeable model of an economy is impressed with the volume of sheer "dog work" involved in manipulating the model and data and in obtaining the mathematical solutions. The drudgery involved in these operations (not to mention the more ambitious work discussed above) undoubtedly accounts in considerable part for the tendency of under-financed researchers to study individual equations rather than estimate complete economic models, estimate models rather than test them, and test them rather than make policy analyses. Clearly, a researcher will need a great deal of help both from programmers and computers if he is to have easy, intimate and flexible interaction with his model and his data.

16.3.1. Accuracy checks

Before we consider the design of the program to aid in accomplishing the substantive research objectives, we must provide for the mundane but vitally important function of controlling the clerical accuracy of the model and the data.

Since economic data are usually collected by the government rather than the researcher, it is vitally important to double check the meaning of the data and their units of measurement. Some errors can be picked up by sub-stituting historical values into equations that are supposed to express relationships between variables. When individual relationships are studied, definitional identities play a small role, but when complete systems are assembled, definitional identities are needed as well as behavioral relation-ships. For example, if national income is used as an explanatory variable in determining consumption, a definitional identity is likely to be used to indi-cate the various components that are added to obtain national income. Historical data should satisfy the identity relationships exactly, and such tests are strongly recommended as a cross check on *both* the data and the identities.

Also, to test against misplaced decimal points and clerical errors, it is desirable to substitute the historical data into the behavioral relationships and calculate the residual errors. The calculation of such errors can be done one equation at a time without the complexities of solving the system of equations simultaneously. The program is written to perform such checks.

Routine checks are built into the program for checking the variables in the equations against a master variable list and also for checking the variable names which identify various pieces of data.

Considerable effort is justified in debugging the data and the model, because with large and complex systems the researcher's intuition cannot always be relied upon to spot nonsense results arising from errors. A great deal of effort might be wasted later if economic explanations are sought for essentially clerical mistakes.

16.3.2. Simulation calculations

We now return to the principal functions that are involved in simulation studies and consider very briefly the operations that the simulation program will perform for the researcher.

After the debugging stage, it is desirable to test the fit of the complete system of equations that constitutes the model, and various parts of it, on past historical data in order to spotlight conspicuous weaknesses. To do this, the program makes it easy for the researcher to solve the equation systems, to add or delete equations, and to make the necessary conversions of endogenous variables into exogenous variables and vice versa.

When solution of the system or a subsystem is desired, the recursive ordering of the equations needs to be determined so that simultaneous equation systems can be kept to minimum size. The program determines this ordering and prints it out using an algorithm and program by Steward [7]. This is likely to be an *essential* step toward solving the system and in any case is useful for gaining insight into its structure.

The solution for the unknown endogenous variables in the current time period must then be executed. If the simultaneous equation blocks are linear, they can be solved by matrix inversion. If they are nonlinear, they will require some iterative method of solution, such as Newton-Raphson or gradient. Since such methods require an initial trial solution, we use the values of the endogenous variables from the previous period as the first approximation to their unknown values in the current period.

Unfortunately, no numerical methods are available which guarantee solutions to arbitrary nonlinear systems, and consequently the researcher must be prepared to engage in a certain amount of experimentation. Gradient methods are very likely to converge, but they may converge slowly. The Newton-Raphson method converges at a tremendous rate once the error becomes "small". There are no panaceas that can be built into the program, so the researcher must fall back on his ingenuity in using the several alternative methods which are available. The program provides several methods which can be used individually or in sequence under the flexible control of the researcher.

It is possible that multiple solutions exist for the equations. Although Kantorovich [6] recently has extended earlier methods [3] for establishing uniqueness within a sphere and predicting Newton-Raphson convergence from a given starting point, these were not incorporated into the program initially in view of its already substantial size. If, after we have had more operating experience with the program, multiple solutions prove to be a significant problem, we can return to this matter and refine the program.

The computational desirability of a strictly recursive system that avoids the necessity for solving simultaneous nonlinear equations is obvious. However, a very short time period may be required before a strictly recursive model becomes an adequate approximation of the economy, and data problems may become acute in trying to obtain observations at shorter and shorter time intervals.

The solution is printed out by the computer with detailed labels in the researcher's notation for ready identification. Also—a point that sometimes is overlooked—the computer prints out the input to the calculation so that the researcher will know exactly what problem is being solved. The program enables the researcher to work largely with his own notation rather than forcing him to translate a familiar problem into an unfamiliar statement of it.

Insofar as is possible the researcher should be allowed to write the model in the functional forms that are most natural from the context of the problem. However, in writing the program we were unable to satisfy this requirement fully. To accommodate certain functional forms, intermediate variables and equations must be introduced.

Computer operations on the model and data are subject to easy control by specifying the time period in which the calculation is to be started and the length of the forecast horizon. Data stored on tape are automatically governed by the model which is being studied, with full indication of any missing data. Alternatively, data may be supplied from cards. The program can calculate various criteria of forecasting and policy performance, as well as calculate the solution itself, and can accommodate policy strategies in the form of additional equations. Many errors in the use of the program will be detected by the program and cause statements to be printed as aids in correcting the trouble.

Finally, the program itself is built up of modular pieces (subroutines) so that local changes can be made with a minimum of interaction with other parts of the program.

A user's manual [5] has been prepared for the researcher, and a manual for programmers has been written, hopefully, with sufficient care and detail that subsequent improvements and modifications can be made.

16.4. *Some operating experience with the program*

When the author agreed at the initiation of the Brookings-SSRC econometric project to undertake simulation studies of the model which was to be produced, neither he nor anyone else knew what the model would look like when completed. As the prospect of a large nonlinear system that was not necessarily recursive began to emerge, it was clear that we faced a formidable computing problem which probably could not be handled by available computer programs.

It was decided to start writing the needed program and to test it out on the simulation of some economic models that had already been solved. We could then proceed to make and report further simulation studies of these models in this volume. In this way we hoped to develop and test a simulation methodology as well as a computer program.

The outcome of this plan was unexpected. The magnitude of the programming effort was greater and took longer than expected for several reasons. First, programming is an activity that seems almost always to consume more man and machine time than it "ought" to. Second, to the best of our knowledge, not only had no program ever been written for rigorously determining the recursive ordering of large systems of equations, but also the necessary mathematical algorithm had not yet appeared in the literature when work on the program was started. Third, the problems of insuring clerical accuracy in large models and sets of data was not fully appreciated until the simulation of fairly large test problems was undertaken; at that point the program was revised to aid the researcher in coping with these problems.

The duration of the programming effort precluded the presentation of the simulation results that had been planned. However, the following can be reported.

A fifteen-equation subsystem of the Klein-Goldberger model [8] had been solved for two years by the authors of the model. This nonlinear annual model seemed ideal for test purposes. An analysis of its recursive ordering by the program yielded the following:

First, one linear equation can be solved.

Second, two simultaneous linear equations can be solved.

Third, twelve simultaneous nonlinear equations can be solved.

The fifteen-equation model was readily solved in this sequence, the twelve-equation nonlinear system being solved easily by the Newton-Raphson method in three iterations. Unexpectedly it was found that the computed results did not exactly check with the published ones, which were found to contain errors that were traced to rounding.

The Klein quarterly model [9] was selected as a larger test problem that, we thought initially, had been fully debugged. The recursive ordering of this system proved to be:

First, five strictly recursive linear equations can be solved.

Second, thirty-five simultaneous nonlinear equations can be solved.

Third, four strictly recursive linear equations can be solved.

Four iterations of the Newton-Raphson method reduce the sum of the squared errors in the thirty-five-equation system to 1.23×10^{-12}. Since more than half of the thirty-five errors in this sum are expressed in "billions of dollars", we see that this solution error is small indeed.

This speedy convergence was not achieved initially. Indeed, we went through a long period when we could not solve the large nonlinear system by any of a succession of methods tried. To make a long story short, we found that terms in *three* different equations were in error by a factor of a thousand. This was traced to a single decimal place error in the data. Other errors were traced to copying, keypunching, coding and an incomplete identity equation. Many of these errors were not found until we used the test of substituting into the equations one at a time the known historical values to see if they satisfied the equations. This served so well as an accuracy check that we built it into the program.

The iterative methods for solving nonlinear equations require an initial trial solution in order to start. If this is not sufficiently close to the actual solution, the computation may not converge. We finally found that our convergence problems occurred because the initial trial solution that we used, namely, the historical values from the previous period, were not sufficiently close to the actual solution of the equations due to the errors which they contained. We had been trying to debug both the test problem and the computer program at the same time. Such a situation should be avoided.

At this time (May 1965), program SIMULATE has been debugged and the recursive ordering has been calculated for a 359-equation version of the full Brookings-SSRC model:

First,   50 equations can be solved initially in arbitrary order.

Second,   13 equations can be solved individually in recursive order.

Third,   2 equations can be solved simultaneously.

Fourth,   5 equations can be solved individually in recursive order.

Fifth,   2 equations can be solved simultaneously.

Sixth,   44 equations can be solved individually in recursive order.

Seventh, 181 equations can be solved simultaneously.

Eighth,   62 equations can be solved individually in recursive order.

The large block of 181 nonlinear equations is larger than expected and some modifications of the program are under way. We hope that this simulation program will serve as a useful tool for many researchers on this model and others as well.

REFERENCES

1. ADELMAN, IRMA, and ADELMAN, FRANK L. The Dynamic Properties of the Klein-Goldberger Model, *Econometrica* 27 (October, 1959) 596–625.

2. ANDO, ALBERT, FISHER, FRANKLIN M., and SIMON, HERBERT A. *Essays on the Structure of Social Science Models*. Cambridge, Mass.: M.I.T. Press, 1963.

3. HILDEBRAND, T. H., and GRAVES, L. M. Implicit Functions and Their Differentials in General Analysis, *Transactions of American Mathematics Society* 29 (1927) 127–153.

4. HOGGATT, A. C., and BALDERSTON, F. C. (eds.). *Symposium on Simulation Models; Methodology and Applications to the Behavioral Sciences*. Cincinnati, O.: South-Western Publishing Co., 1963.

5. HOLT, CHARLES C., SHIREY, ROBERT, STEWART, DONALD V., MIDLER, JOSEPH L., and STROUD, ARTHUR H., "Program SIMULATE, a User's and Programmer's Manual". University of Wisconsin, Social Systems Research Institute, May, 1964. (Mimeographed.) The program is written in FORTRAN IV.

6. KANTOROVICH, L. V. "Functional Analysis and Applied Mathematics". Translated by C. D. Benster, U.S. Department of Commerce (NBS Rep. 1509, 202 pp., 1952; MR 14, No. 8, 766, 1953). Los Angeles, Calif.: National Bureau of Standards.

7. STEWARD, DONALD V. On an Approach to Techniques for the Analysis of the Structure of Large Systems of Equations, *Society for Industrial and Applied Mathematics Review* 4, No. 4 (October, 1962) 321–342.

8. KLEIN, L. R., and GOLDBERGER, A. S. *An Econometric Model of the United States, 1929–1952*. Amsterdam: North-Holland Publishing Company, 1955.

9. KLEIN, LAWRENCE R. A Postwar Quarterly Model: Description and Applications, in *Models of Income Determination*. National Bureau of Economic Research, Studies in Income and Wealth, vol. 28 pp. 1–58. Princeton: Princeton University Press, 1964.

10. DAVIDSON, W. C. "Variable Metric Method of Minimization". Atomic Energy Commission Research and Development Report, ANL-5990, 1959.

11. FLETCHER, R., and POWELL, M. J. D. A Rapidly Convergent Descent Method for Minimization, *Computer Journal* 6 (1963–64) 163–168.

12. WOLD, HERMAN. *Demand Analysis, A Study in Econometrics*. New York: John Wiley & Sons, 1953.

CHAPTER 17

PRICE AND OUTPUT AGGREGATION IN THE BROOKINGS ECONOMETRIC MODEL

Contents

17.1. Introduction 653

17.2. Output aggregation 654

17.3. Price aggregation 657

17.4. Estimation procedures 658
    1. Consistency with a priori constraints. 2. What estimator should be used?

17.5. Input-output conversion estimates 661

17.6. Computation of sector final demands 663
    1. Consolidation of the coefficient matrix. 2. Time series of gross sectoral outputs.

17.7. Regression of sector final demands on *GNP* components 666
    1. Variables used. 2. Regressions for the trade, regulated and residual sectors. 3. Determination of the final demand equation for the construction sector. 4. Regressions for the durable manufacturing, nondurable manufacturing and farming sectors. 5. Final demand converter.

17.8. Conversion of sector prices to *GNP* deflators 672
    1. Price conversion matrix. 2. Test of price converter. 3. Price autoregressions. 4. Concluding remarks: what should be done next.

References 678

PRICE AND OUTPUT AGGREGATION IN THE BROOKINGS ECONOMETRIC MODEL [1])

FRANKLIN M. FISHER

Massachusetts Institute of Technology, Cambridge, Massachusetts

LAWRENCE R. KLEIN

University of Pennsylvania, Philadelphia, Pennsylvania

YOICHI SHINKAI

Osaka University, Osaka, Japan

17.1. Introduction

In the Brookings-SSRC econometric model of the U.S. economy, the number and definition of final demand sectors are different from those of production sectors. Thus, final demand is broken down into sectors such as government, exports, private capital formation, automobiles, other consumer durables, consumer nondurables and services, while production is analyzed for sectors such as durables, nondurables, agriculture and so forth. In later versions of the model a far more disaggregated treatment of production is planned, the breakdown being roughly on the order of aggregation of the two-digit industry of the Standard Industrial Classification. While such different treatment is perhaps inevitable in a model constructed by different specialists and may certainly be desirable in view of differences in data availability and natural groupings of behavioral relations, it does raise the problem of reconciliation of the output and price variables used. On the one hand, the output demanded by the final demand sectors must be distributed over the production sectors; on the other hand, the prices generated by the price-formation equations in the production sectors must be aggregated to obtain prices for the final demand sectors.

---

[1]) Sections 17.1–17.4 were written by Franklin M. Fisher and sections 17.5–17.8 by Lawrence R. Klein and Yoichi Shinkai. This paper was completed during Fisher's tenure as a National Science Foundation Postdoctoral Fellow at the Econometric Institute of the Netherlands School of Economics. Arthur Okun pointed out the essential distinction between a gross-flow and a value-added model as regards this paper, but the authors retain responsibility for error.

The present paper discusses a way of performing these tasks. We first show how this can be done in principle for output aggregation and then observe that the identical equations provide the appropriate price aggregation. Finally, we discuss methods for estimating the desired equations consistent with the a priori restrictions thereon [2]).

Our discussion will be in terms both of a model in which outputs are gross flows and of one in which they are values added. The present version of the Brookings-SSRC econometric model is largely, but not entirely, in value-added terms, and it is desirable to have aggregation in terms of gross flows as well. Accordingly, two sets of aggregation equations were estimated: In the first of these, by Klein and Shinkai, value-added outputs were converted to gross flows by a base-year proportionality assumption and the aggregation equations estimated for the resulting gross-flow model. In the second, value-added outputs were used directly in securing the aggregation equations, but the proportionality assumption had to be used to obtain gross flows and market prices. As will be seen below, the gross-flow model relies on more assumptions than does the value-added model but is able to make far more efficient use of a priori information. It is thus desirable in principle to have both sets of aggregation estimates. The estimates (and the problems encountered in obtaining them) by Klein and Shinkai are reported by those responsible in the following sections of this chapter. The value-added estimates, which do not place a priori zero restrictions on the independent variables, were of such low quality because of collinearity among the eighteen explanatory variables that no estimated results will be presented. This section discusses the theory of what is involved.

17.2. *Output aggregation*

We begin with the gross-flow model. Let there be n producing sectors and m final demand sectors. Denote by f_t the n-component column vector of deliveries to final demand (including net inventory changes in final demand) at time t

---

[2]) The problems here treated were discussed at considerable length at project conferences, and a number of people made valuable contributions. While it would be impossible to pinpoint all such contributions precisely, I think it fair to state that to the best of my recollection the basic suggestion as regards output aggregation was made by Dale W. Jorgenson. In addition, it should be observed that the first part of the present paper deals with the problem at a rather abstract level and ignores a good many difficulties encountered in practice. The actual estimation of the aggregation equations was the work of Lawrence R. Klein and Yoichi Shinkai (drawing on preliminary work by Jarvis Babcock). A description thereof may be found in the later sections of this chapter.

organized by producing sector of origin. Let g_t be the m-component vector of deliveries to final demand at time t organized by final demand sector. The components of both f_t and g_t are in gross value terms, and the sum of the components of each vector is the same as that of the other, as each of them represents a different way of breaking down total final demand expenditure. Thus, if h_k denotes a k-component column vector of unit elements:

$$h_n'f_t = h_m'g_t. \tag{17.1}$$

We assume that f_t and g_t are related by:

$$f_t = Bg_t + u_t, \tag{17.2}$$

where B is an $n \times m$ constant matrix of parameters and u_t is an n-component disturbance vector. The assumption underlying (17.2) is that deliveries to final demand by producing sectors are distributed among final demand sectors in a regular and systematic way. Alternatively, one can regard (17.2) as saying that demands from final demand sectors are divided among producing sectors in a regular and systematic way. If information for only one time period is used to estimate the matrix B, this is equivalent to a fixed base-period weight aggregation. If data for all periods for which the model is estimated are used, superior aggregation is likely to be achieved, since if base-period weights are appropriate they will be generated by such a procedure.

Estimation of B will be discussed in greater detail below. Suffice it now to observe that certain elements thereof can be set equal to zero a priori, since, for example, durable manufactures presumably contribute nothing to final demand for services. Further, since each column of B represents the distribution of a particular component of final demand over consuming sectors, and since each such component must be exactly distributed, each column of B must sum to unity (and be non-negative). Thus:

$$h_n'B = h_m' \tag{17.3}$$

and, in view of (17.1):

$$h_n'u_t = h_n'(f_t - Bg_t) = h_n'f_t - h_m'g_t = 0. \tag{17.4}$$

Thus the disturbances sum to zero across all equations.

All the foregoing, however, has implicitly assumed that data are available on f_t. This is unlikely to be the case. Rather, data are available on total output by production sector. Denote the n-component vector of such outputs at time t by x_t. If A is an $n \times n$ input-output matrix (and if the assumption of a constant input-output matrix is a good one for the period studied), f_t and x_t are related by:

$$x_t = Ax_t + f_t, \tag{17.5}$$

$$f_t = (I-A)x_t. \tag{17.6}$$

We may then proceed by using (17.6) and an input-output matrix to construct estimates of f_t for substitution into (17.2). Note, however, that if (17.5), and therefore (17.6), contains an additive error term (and things are worse if A cannot be taken as approximately constant), the resulting version of (17.2) will not have disturbances satisfying (17.4).

Alternatively, we may write:

$$x_t = (I-A)^{-1}f_t = (I-A)^{-1}Bg_t + (I-A)^{-1}u_t \equiv Cg_t + v_t \tag{17.7}$$

and estimate C without using prior knowledge of A. This has the merit of avoiding dependence on a particular input-output matrix, but (even if (17.5) holds exactly) the properties of B and u_t summarized above are lost in this procedure. Thus a priori information that certain elements of B are zero and that the columns of B sum to unity is of no use if this alternative is adopted. It does seem sufficiently important, however, to avoid dependence on a particular input-output matrix [3] to lead us to disregard this defect and estimate (17.7) directly. This will free our output aggregation from dependence on input-output data; unfortunately, this cannot be done for price aggregation in a gross-flow model, as will be seen below.

Turning now to the problem of output aggregation in a value-added model, observe that in this case f_t is irrelevant and it is the components of x_t (total production in value-added terms) that sum to the total of the components of g_t (total final bill expenditure in value-added prices). It follows by an argument essentially the same as that given above that suppressing the middle member of (17.7) and simply writing

$$x_t = Cg_t + v_t, \tag{17.8}$$

the columns of C must sum to unity and the elements of v_t must sum to zero. While it is still true that a priori information on zeros in the matrix C is

---

[3] Of course, in principle, there is no reason why A need be constant in (17.5) and (17.6). In practice, however, input-output matrices for the U. S. economy are available in the postwar period only for 1947 and for 1958 (the matrix for the latter year has just recently been released). Presumably some interpolation will be possible.

unlikely to be available, it is the case that estimation of C directly yields the appropriate aggregation equations *without* transformation by an input-output relationship.

17.3. Price aggregation

Price formation in the Brookings-SSRC econometric model takes place at the level of the n production sectors, but prices for the m final demand sectors are used in the analysis of final demand. Accordingly, production-sector prices must be transformed to obtain final demand prices. Fortunately, the means are at hand to do this.

Clearly, one obvious choice of a price index for each final demand sector will be composed of a weighted average of the prices of the production sectors, the weights being the average expenditures made by the final demand sector in the different productive sectors over the sample period [4]). A moment's thought, however, reveals that these weights are just the elements of the appropriate column of the matrix B of (17.2) in the gross-flow model or the elements of the appropriate column of the matrix C of (17.8) in the value-added model. Price aggregation is thus the dual of output aggregation in the model.

Unfortunately, as observed above, estimates of B for the gross-flow model (which are essential for price if not for output aggregation) depend rather heavily on specific input-output information. If output aggregation is performed by using (17.7) and price aggregation by using (17.2), these may not be quite compatible if such information is unreliable [5]). Nevertheless, it seems worth putting up with this and estimating output aggregators from (17.7) and price aggregators from (17.2) and (17.6). No such problem arises in estimating the matrix C of (17.8) in the value-added model.

Before proceeding to a discussion of estimation methods, one point needs discussing. The output of an estimate of B or C, as just discussed, is a set of weights for price aggregation. The input to such an estimate, however, includes data for the components of g_t which have been constructed using

---

[4]) I am ignoring nonlinear indices. As before, using a single observation to obtain expenditure weights is obviously inferior to the proposal in the text, which includes it as a special case if weights do not change.

[5]) Even if (17.5) holds exactly and A is known correctly, there will be a minor incompatibility if (17.2) is estimated using a priori information. If no restrictions are placed on B, it is trivial to show that (17.7) and (17.2) with $(I-A)x_t$ substituted for f_t imply the same estimate of B for any estimator linear in the left-hand variable.

aggregated prices. It is clearly likely to be the case that the aggregation weights implied by the results are different from those used to construct the data. If this discrepancy is large, it may be desirable to iterate the estimation until reasonable consistency is maintained, assuming that such a process converges. The problem is not likely to be more than minor, however.

17.4. *Estimation procedures*

17.4.1. *Consistency with a priori constraints*

We begin our discussion of estimation procedures for the aggregation equations by ignoring all the problems raised above and assuming that (17.2) or (17.8) is to be estimated directly. [If (17.6) holds exactly, our remarks will apply when $(I-A)x_t$ is substituted for f_t in (17.2).] We shall be concerned with the restrictions on B or C imposed by (17.3) and shall show that such restrictions will be automatically satisfied by the sample estimate of B or C obtained using a wide variety of estimators. It follows that the seriousness of the problems raised above for the gross-flow model can be evaluated in practice by observing how far the column sums of B as estimated deviate from unity. As these problems do not arise in the value-added model, we shall concentrate on the estimation of (17.8).

Assume that (17.8) is estimated by ordinary least squares applied to each equation or (more generally) by substituting for g_t its expected value estimated by regression on a set of instrumental variables and then by least-squares regression applied to each of the resulting equations [6]. Denote the expected value in question by $\bar{g}_t$, so that:

$$g_t = \bar{g}_t + w_t \qquad (17.9)$$

and observe that in the sample period the elements of w_t are uncorrelated with those of $\bar{g}_t$ [7]. Substituting in (17.8), we obtain:

$$x_t = C\bar{g}_t + Cw_t + v_t. \qquad (17.10)$$

Denote by x (without the time subscript) the $n \times T$ matrix of T sample values

---

[6] As discussed below, certain other methods are not available in the case under discussion, since (17.4) (*mutatis mutandis*) implies that the variance-covariance matrix of the elements of v_t is singular.

[7] If ordinary least squares is used (which in a simultaneous system will lead to inconsistent estimates), $\bar{g}_t = g_t$ and $w_t = 0$.

of x_t and similarly for $\bar{g}$, w and v [8]). The estimate of C, say $\hat{C}$, obtained by least squares applied to each equation of (17.10) is given by:

$$\hat{C} = x\bar{g}'(\bar{g}\bar{g}')^{-1} = C+(Cw+v)\bar{g}'(\bar{g}\bar{g}')^{-1} = C+v\bar{g}'(\bar{g}\bar{g}')^{-1}, \quad (17.11)$$

since

$$w\bar{g}' = 0. \tag{17.12}$$

Using (17.3) and (17.4) with C and v_t substituted for B and u_t, respectively, this implies:

$$h_n'\hat{C} = h_n'C+h_n'v\bar{g}'(\bar{g}\bar{g}')^{-1} = h_m' \tag{17.13}$$

and so the *sample* estimate of C has all its column sums equal to unity, as stated. It follows that (17.3) need not be separately imposed in the pure case under consideration.

17.4.2. What estimator should be used?

We must now proceed to consider the question of what estimator to use in estimating (17.8) or (17.2). The first issue we must discuss is that of whether the objections usually raised to the use of ordinary least squares in simultaneous systems apply in the present case.

This issue appears to turn on the question of what one thinks he is doing in estimating the aggregation equations discussed above. If those equations are considered to be of real structural validity, ordinary least squares is no more appropriate when applied to them than when applied to any structural equation [9]). There does seem to be a strong case, however, for not pretending that (17.2) or (17.8) are structural equations; rather, they are artificial contrivances for linking up different sections of the model. As such, they are composites of a wealth of different and unspecified effects which they summarize in a special and convenient form. The weights obtained from them should be close approximations to the average distribution of expenditure by final demand sectors over production sectors for the sample period, and such an approximation can best be obtained by using ordinary least squares. To put it another way, what is involved here is data-splicing rather than structural estimation. Ordinary least squares is a convenient way of accomplishing this. The usual objection that ordinary least squares estimates will

---

[8]) We have conformed to the usual notation for input-output matrices above which has led to the transpose of the usual notation for regression theory.

[9]) For a discussion of such issues, see Fisher [2].

only continue to stand up if all the interconnections of the system remain the same loses much of its force in this context, since *any* estimate of the equations under discussion rests on such continuity in view of the non-structural nature of those equations.

On the other hand, this seems to be pushing the argument a bit far. While it is true that the validity of any estimate of the equations involved rests on the continuance of a number of unspecified regularities, the same is true to a degree of any equation in an aggregate model. The use of ordinary least squares is objectionable from this point of view because it *adds* certain interrelationships implied by the model itself between the left-hand and the right-hand variables to the collection of regularities which must be expected to continue. This is unnecessary in the presence of other available esti-mators with some superior properties.

In short, while there does seem to be a better case for using ordinary least squares here than in the estimation of better-specified structural relations (at least as a first approximation), that case *may* not seem sufficiently con-vincing in spite of the minimum variance properties of ordinary least squares which are of particular importance in data splicing. We turn then to the subject of estimation with a consistent estimator [10].

What that estimator should be requires a little discussion beyond the general one given in [2]. This is the case because one is naturally tempted to estimate all equations of (17.2) or (17.8) simultaneously, using some full-information procedure such as three-stage least squares [11]. As it happens, however, this does not seem a particularly fruitful procedure unless the entire model or some subsection including these equations under discussion is to be so estimated.

Consider first estimation of (17.8) by three-stage least squares. If three-stage least squares is to be applied *only* to the equations of (17.8), the esti-mates obtained will be identical with those of two-stage least squares, since the a priori restrictions on those equations (only that a different variable appears on the left-hand side of each) are just sufficient to identify them when

---

[10] Note, however, that the result derived above for the simple case applies to ordinary least squares. This means that the biases of that estimator should sum approximately to zero across equations so that the deviation of the sum from unity can be used to determine the magnitude of the problems involved in the general case.

[11] See Zellner and Theil [8]. All remarks given will apply if the consistency question is ignored and Zellner's method for estimating seemingly unrelated regressions is used. See Zellner [9].

considered as the complete system [12]). It follows that there is no gain from using three-stage least squares or other full-information methods here [13]).

On the other hand, it seems at first sight that three-stage least squares will promote asymptotic efficiency if applied to the estimation of (17.2) in the gross-flow model where there is a priori information on the elements of B [14]). Unfortunately, this is not the case. If (17.6) holds exactly and is substituted in (17.2), the variance-covariance matrix of the error terms (which must be inverted in three-stage least squares) will be singular in view of (17.4). If (17.6) does not hold exactly, this difficulty will not arise; in this case, however, the a priori restrictions on B which give three-stage least squares its increased asymptotic efficiency over two-stage least squares will not generally be correct when the components of $(I-A)x_t$ are used in place of those of f_t with a constant A assumed. The closer (17.6) is to holding exactly, the closer will be those restrictions to correctness, but then the closer the matrix to be inverted will be to singularity [15]). On the whole it seems best not to use three-stage least squares or other full-information methods in practice to estimate (17.2) and (17.8), but to use an instrumental variable technique [16]).

17.5. *Input-output conversion estimates*

The Brookings-SSRC econometric model, though much more detailed than any existing econometric model of a whole economy, has one characteristic in common with others: It is an aggregative demand model. In its simplest form, an aggregative demand model has an equation:

---

[12]) See Zellner and Theil [8, p. 62] and cf. Zellner [9, p. 351]. Another way of saying the same thing is to observe in Zellner and Theil's notation that the present case is one in which all Z_μ are identical and so $A^*=0$.

[13]) Three-stage least squares is known to have the same asymptotic distribution as full-information maximum likelihood. See Madansky [3], Rothenberg and Leenders [4] and Sargan [5].

[14]) On using the restrictions that the column sums of B are unity (which will not be automatically satisfied in the general case now being considered), see Zellner and Theil [8, p. 78] and Theil [7, pp. 536–538].

[15]) One exception should be noted. If (17.6) holds with additive disturbances, the a priori restrictions in question will be preserved and singularity avoided. This still requires a constant input-output matrix, however. Even if this were the case, near singularity would be a large problem unless the additive error terms in question had relatively large variances.

[16]) As is well known, two-stage least squares and other limited-information methods can be thought of as instrumental variable techniques. On choosing appropriate instruments, see Fisher [2].

Aggregate demand = Gross national product,

and several price equations that determine deflators of demand items, possibly as functions of the *GNP* deflator. The same kind of relationships should hold in the Brookings-SSRC econometric model, but a complication arises because of the fact that there are several production sectors and as many output deflators. Thus, instead of a single identity we must define

$$x = Ag$$

where x and g are, respectively, vectors of sector outputs and of expenditure items, and A a conversion matrix. Price equations will take the form

$$p = Bq$$

where p and q are, respectively, vectors of deflators of expenditure items and of outputs and B another conversion matrix. One matrix shows how aggregate demand determines sector outputs to meet that demand. The other shows how prices determined in production sectors of the economy are transformed into price aggregates for *GNP* components. It is the purpose of this section to estimate these two conversion matrices.

Expenditure items are the deflated *GNP* components published by the Office of Business Economics (OBE), together with their deflators. In the aggregated version of the Brookings-SSRC econometric model there are seven production sectors; outputs (or *GNP* originating in the respective sectors) and their deflators were compiled by C. Schultze and J. Tryon. Our purpose, therefore, is to distribute the *GNP* expenditure items among originating sectors and link the *GNP* deflators with the sectoral output deflators. A natural procedure that suggests itself would be to regress sector outputs on *GNP* components and use the identity that sector final demands add up to the total *GNP* to obtain weights for deflator conversion. This line of attack was, in fact, taken at first by J. Babcock, who discussed the difficulties involved and how they were overcome [17]).

The main difficulty arises from the fact that there is no a priori information that serves to connect sector outputs to *GNP* components. So far as our notion of interindustry relations is correct, it must be assumed that some amount of nearly every output goes into nearly every *GNP* component. If instead we could use sector final demands in the regression analysis, we would be much better off, inasmuch as we are reasonably sure that output of a certain

---

[17]) This presentation was made at the second Dartmouth conference of the project.

sector will not be delivered to a certain *GNP* component as a final product. As it is, time series of sector final demands are not available and regression technique in the ordinary sense cannot be used.

After some experimental computations, F. Fisher suggested, as in the preceding section of this chapter, that we compute estimated time series of sector final demands and regress these on *GNP* components. This is the procedure we have followed, and we shall discuss in some detail the method and results of our analysis.

17.6. Computation of sector final demands

Our main problem in this section is to work out a formula that relates final expenditure items (*GNP* components) to the sector final demands. We will use regression techniques for this purpose, but since time series of sector final demands are not available, we have decided to compute them by a reverse application of the input-output relation. We have started with the 1947 Bureau of Labor Statistics interindustry table and OBE estimates of annual *GNP* by major industries [18]). The interindustry data satisfy the relationship

$$f = (I - A)x$$

where f is the vector of sector final demands, $(I - A)$ the input coefficient matrix and x the vector of gross sector outputs. If we assume that $(I - A)$ is reasonably stable over the sample period (in this case, from 1947 to 1960), the same relationship should hold approximately for each year. Thus, given the time series of x, we can compute the time series of f by matrix multiplication [19]).

17.6.1. Consolidation of the coefficient matrix

In the aggregative version of the model, there are seven production sectors. For output and price conversion, we used (1) farming, (2) durable manufacturing, (3) nondurable manufacturing, (4) wholesale and retail trade,

---

[18]) We use OBE annual figures instead of our own quarterly *GNP* originating. The reason will be indicated presently. The 1947 BLS input-output table can be found in [1]. The OBE estimates of *GNP* by industries are in [6].

[19]) Note that even if the $(I - A)$ matrix is well-behaved, the non-negativity of f is not guaranteed for any non-negative x. However, for the actual values of x we should obtain reasonably good estimates of f.

TABLE 17.1

Consolidated input coefficient matrix, I-A.

	AF	MD	MN	T	R	C	O
AF	0.7304	−0.0025	−0.1758	−0.0134	−0.0005	−0.0032	−0.0015
MD	−0.0112	0.6318	−0.0281	−0.0341	−0.0361	−0.3276	−0.0310
MN	−0.0908	−0.0684	0.6786	−0.0912	−0.0558	−0.0529	−0.0670
T	−0.0399	−0.0200	−0.0171	0.9597	−0.0216	−0.0995	−0.0205
R	−0.0260	−0.0376	−0.0348	−0.0324	0.9239	−0.0467	−0.0559
C	−0.0059	−0.0031	−0.0022	−0.0046	−0.0550	0.9998	−0.0554
O	−0.0709	−0.0377	−0.0364	−0.1164	−0.0575	−0.0498	0.9075

(5) regulated industries including transportation, communications, and public utilities, (6) contract construction, and (7) residual industries including mining, finance, insurance, real estate, and services. This industrial classification differs in two respects from the classification used by Schultze and Tyron in preparing quarterly estimates of gross product originating. First, Schultze and Tyron combine nondurable manufacturing and mining of crude petroleum and natural gas. Second, real estate and household and institutional services are not included in their estimates.

Consolidation of the input coefficient matrix was done mainly by J. Babcock. His procedure was to aggregate the original transactions matrix to a 32×32 matrix (which will be used in the disaggregated version of the model) and divide their columns by the aggregated gross outputs (net of inventory depletions and competitive imports). We followed the same procedure to make a further aggregation and obtained a 7×7 coefficient matrix, which can be found in table 17.1.

17.6.2. Time series of gross sectoral outputs

For the basic time series of sector outputs we used the OBE annual estimates of *GNP* by industrial sectors. They cover the period from 1947 to 1960 and are nearly of the same aggregation level as our seven sectors. We might have used the Schultze-Tryon quarterly estimates of *GNP* originating in sectors; they are so constructed that the annual average figures agree with the OBE estimates (except for the differences noted above). However, since our purpose is to estimate the weights of conversion of *GNP* components to sector final demands that are not likely to change from quarter to quarter, we thought that annual data would give sufficient information.

TABLE 17.2

Ratios of sector gross outputs to GNP originating by industries, 1947.

AF	MD	MN	T	R	C	O
1.8716	2.4310	3.2344	1.2684	1.4564	3.1893	1.4391

TABLE 17.3

1947 Values of implicit deflators of GNP originating by sectors (1954 = 1.00).

AF	MD	MN	T	R	C	O
1.225	0.752	0.859	0.866	0.821	0.738	0.734

TABLE 17.4

Computed sector final demands (billions of 1954 dollars).

	F_{AF}	F_{MD}	F_{MN}	F_T	F_R	F_C	F_O
1947	7.9	44.6	57.7	53.7	16.2	29.9	61.3
1948	10.6	45.3	59.4	53.9	16.4	33.3	63.8
1949	9.5	39.2	59.6	54.3	15.1	34.3	66.1
1950	10.0	50.5	60.4	61.3	18.0	37.3	69.2
1951	7.5	62.1	62.7	60.3	21.3	43.4	72.1
1952	8.0	61.6	65.1	62.3	20.5	43.6	73.0
1953	8.3	69.7	66.6	64.8	20.4	43.6	74.5
1954	10.3	59.7	63.6	64.1	21.2	43.8	77.2
1955	9.7	69.8	70.3	69.9	24.7	47.0	81.1
1956	8.7	66.2	72.1	71.6	27.3	49.3	86.8
1957	7.6	66.5	74.7	71.5	28.1	47.9	91.9
1958	7.7	54.3	78.5	70.5	27.8	45.4	95.0
1959	5.3	63.2	87.3	76.2	30.7	48.3	98.5
1960	6.3	65.7	88.5	77.3	32.6	45.2	104.1

The OBE estimates consist of constant price *GNP* (in 1954 dollars) by sectors, the sectors being agriculture (but only farming was used here); durable manufacturing; nondurable manufacturing [20]); wholesale and retail

---

[20]) For 1959 and 1960 only total manufacturing figures are published. We allocated them to durable and nondurable sectors by means of the Schultze-Tryon data.

trade; finance, insurance and real estate; transportation; communications; public utilities; and services. To obtain the regulated and the residual series, we simply added the relevant OBE figures [21]). We then converted the seven series to 1947 dollars, using the implicit deflators published with the *GNP* series. We assumed that *GNP* by sectors and gross sector outputs (gross of intermediate products used up in production) change proportionately. We therefore computed the ratios of *GNP* by sectors to gross outputs for 1947 and inflated the *GNP* series by these ratios. The resultant figures were postmultiplied into $(I - A)$ to obtain the computed sector final demands in 1947 dollars. Finally, they were converted back to 1954 dollars. Tables 17.2 – 17.4 list the 1947 ratios of *GNP* to gross outputs by sector, 1947 values of implicit deflators (1954 = 1.00), and the computed final demands in 1954 dollars.

17.7. *Regression of sector final demands on GNP components*

Once series of computed final demands are given, we can apply regression techniques to explain them by relevant *GNP* components. Unlike the regression problems in the other chapters, we are working with annual data consisting of fourteen observations (1947–1960). With samples of this size, it was felt that we should keep the number of explanatory variables as small as possible. This consideration led, after some experimental computations, to a procedure in which we used whatever a priori information was available for each equation, and we ignored minor inaccuracies in the specification of equations. Thus we assumed that no delivery was made from the nondurable manufacturing sector to the *GNP* expenditure on consumers' durables and automobiles, whereas this is not strictly true, since expenditures on autos include purchase of tires and other parts that come from the nondurable manufacturing sector.

17.7.1. *Variables used*

Data on *GNP* components are mostly the standard series published by OBE. We shall briefly describe the definition of the variables used and indicate departures from the standard series. All expenditures are measured in billions of 1954 dollars. The variables are listed alphabetically.

---

[21]) Sector compositions are defined on pp. 667–68.

C = personal consumption expenditures

C_{DA} = personal consumption expenditures for new and net used automobiles and parts

C_{DEA} = personal consumption expenditures for durable goods other than new and net used automobiles and parts

$C_{NEF} - C_{INEF}$ = personal consumption expenditures for nondurable goods other than food, excluding imputations

$C_{NF} - C_{INF}$ = personal consumption expenditures for food, excluding imputations

$C_S - C_{IS}$ = personal consumption expenditures for services, excluding imputations

C_{SR} = personal consumption expenditures for rent, including rent of owner-occupied nonfarm residences

$DMY12$ = 1, 1953 through 1955
              = 0, other years

$DMY13$ = 0, 1947 through 1957
              = 1, elsewhere

EX = exports of goods and services

F = estimated final demand

G = government purchases of goods and services

G_{CD} = government purchases of durable goods

G_{CS} = government purchases of services

G_{CN} = government purchases of nondurable goods

G_{IC} = government construction

GNP = gross national product

I_{CNFR} = GNP expenditures on nonfarm residential construction

I_{CO} = private, nonresidential, nonbusiness construction

I_{CPL} = gross private domestic investment in plant

I_{PDE} = gross private domestic investment in producers' durable equipment

INV = business inventory stocks (unpublished data for durable and nondurable manufacturing and trade were supplied by the Office of Business Economics of the Department of Commerce)

M = imports of goods and services

$TIME$ = time trend.

Sector subscripts are:

AF = farming

C = contract construction
M = manufacturing
MD = durable manufacturing
MN = nondurable manufacturing
O = residual industries: mining; finance, insurance and real estate; and all services
R = regulated industries: transportation, communications and public utilities
T = wholesale and retail trade.

17.7.2. Regressions for the trade, regulated and residual sectors

Trade, regulated and residual sectors have one characteristic in common, namely, that their "outputs" are delivered to nearly all the *GNP* expenditure items. For example, the final demand in the trade sector, which is the total traders' margin paid by final purchasers, enters all *GNP* expenditures except producers' inventory investment and exports. This is also the case with the final demand in the regulated industries, which consists of transportation cost, advertising cost, cost of gas and electricity, and so on. Therefore, F_T and F_R are made functions of nearly all the *GNP* expenditures.

The estimated equations are:

$$F_T^{A54} = \frac{0.250}{(0.024)} [C^{A54} - C_{DA}^{A54}] + \frac{0.359}{(0.239)} C_{DA}^{A54}$$

$$+ \frac{0.0761}{(0.0423)} [GNP^{A54} - C^{A54} - EX^{A54} - \Delta INV_{AF}^{A54} - \Delta INV_M^{A54}]$$

$$\bar{R}^2 = 0.958. \tag{17.14}$$

$$F_R^{A54} = \frac{0.0640}{(0.0019)} [GNP^{A54} - \Delta INV_{AF}^{A54} - \Delta INV_M^{A54}]$$

$$\bar{R}^2 = 0.781. \tag{17.15}$$

The trade margins for automobiles, other consumer goods and nonconsumption items are evidently different. Though the coefficient of automobile consumption is not statistically significant, all the coefficients seem to be of reasonable order of magnitude. We are more or less uncertain as to what is the right order of magnitude for the markup coefficient of the regulated sector. Several experiments to separate *GNP* into components were unsuccessful. Here we included exports in the explanatory variables because they are certainly marked up over domestic transportation costs.

Constant terms are deliberately left out. It is our general procedure to force the regression line to pass through the origin. This results in a little poorer fit than otherwise, but equations that are homogeneous of first degree are theoretically superior to nonhomogeneous equations when they are supposed to represent the relation between final purchases and sector final demands.

The residual sector is very heterogeneous, comprising mining, finance, insurance, real estate and services. The real estate component of the final demand is rent, that actually paid by tenants and that imputed for owner-occupied dwellings. This component was taken out of F_O before running the regression. By doing this, we implicitly made its regression coefficient unity, showing that all such final demand goes directly to the residual sector's output. The bulk of the service component of F_O goes to consumers' expenditure on services. We assumed that the only other deliveries to $[C_S - C_{IS}]$ come from the trade and regulated sectors and used the respective markup coefficients of $[C_S - C_{IS}]$ in F_T and F_R to determine the coefficient of $[C_S - C_{IS}]$ in the residual sector $(0.6865 = 1 - 0.2495 - 0.0640)$. This component was also taken from F_O. We then regressed the residual, $F_O - C_{SR} - 0.6865[C_S - C_{IS}]$, on the rest of GNP:

$$F_O^{A54} = C_{SR}^{A54} + 0.6865[C_S^{A54} - C_{IS}^{A54}]$$

$$+ \frac{0.0222}{(0.0014)} \{GNP^{A54} - C_{SR}^{A54} - [C_S^{54} - C_{IS}^{A54}]\}$$

$$\bar{R}^2 = 0.990. \tag{17.16}$$

It should be noted that $[C_S - C_{IS}]$ includes rent paid by tenants (though not imputed rent); rent paid is about 10 per cent of total services expenditures. This results in some double counting; ideally, rent should be totally excluded from $[C_S - C_{IS}]$ in the equation. In that case, since both $[C_S - C_{IS}]$ and rent are fairly smooth trend variables, the result would be a 10 per cent lower coefficient of $[C_S - C_{IS}]$ and a slight change in the coefficient of GNP. However, the coefficient of $[C_S - C_{IS}]$ does not affect any other equations, and the effect of a small change in the GNP coefficient, itself a small markup factor, will be negligible. The present treatment may be justifiable in view of the fact that no equation that explains paid rent is or will be provided in the whole model. On the other hand, total rent C_{SR}^{54} may be defined as the real rent index times total available dwelling units, both generated in the construction submodel; this product must, of course, be multiplied by an absolute, average 1954 rental figure.

17.7.3. Determination of the final demand equation for the construction sector

Output of the construction sector is delivered entirely as final demands to the construction components of *GNP* after whatever markups are allowed for the trade margin, transportation cost, finance cost, etc. Therefore, the coefficient of the construction sector was determined a priori as $1-0.0761-0.0640-0.0222 = 0.8377$. In this particular case we use a constant term to make the residuals add to zero. Thus

$$F_C^{A54} = 9.68+0.8377[I_{CNFR}^{A54}+I_{CPL}^{A54}+I_{CO}^{A54}+G_{IC}^{A54}]$$

$$\bar{R}^2 = 0.857. \tag{17.17}$$

The correlation coefficient, though somewhat artificial, is computed to give a rough idea of the fit of this equation.

17.7.4. Regressions for the durable manufacturing, nondurable manufacturing and farming sectors

Final demands of the durable and nondurable manufacturing sectors show relatively large variations over time and have proved to be most difficult to explain. Durable final demand is unusually high in 1953, 1954 and 1955, and nondurable final demand shows a sudden jump after 1958. After some experimental computations, we decided to explain these unusual movements by dummy variables so as not to distort the usual pattern of relationship. Estimated equations are:

$$F_{MD}^{A54} = 0.555C_{DA}^{A54}+0.664C_{DEA}^{A54}+0.8377[I_{PDE}^{A54}+G_{CD}^{A54}]+\Delta INV_{MD}^{A54}$$

$$+ \frac{0.3170}{(0.0287)}[EX^{A54}+\Delta INV_T^{A54}]+ \frac{5.288}{(1.25)}DMY12$$

$$\bar{R}^2 = 0.963. \tag{17.18}$$

$$F_{MN}^{A54} = 0.664[C_{NEF}^{A54}-C_{INEF}^{A54}]+0.838G_{CN}^{A54}+\Delta INV_{MN}^{A54}$$

$$+ \frac{0.379}{(0.007)}[C_{NF}^{A54}-C_{INF}^{A54}+\Delta INV_T^{A54}+EX^{A54}-M^{A54}]$$

$$+ \frac{0.651}{(0.085)}[DMY13][TIME]$$

$$\bar{R}^2 = 0.972. \tag{17.19}$$

As before, coefficients recorded without sampling error were determined by deducting from 1 the markup factors estimated in equations for final demand in the trade, regulated and residual sectors. It is assumed that the durable manufacturing sector delivers its output only to the durable GNP components, and the same is true of the nondurable manufacturing sector. It is also assumed that manufacturing inventories are all held by producers, and so ΔINV_{MD} and ΔINV_{MN} have unit coefficients. In the equation for F_{MN} the difference of exports and imports is entered. This may be justified by noting that, of the total U.S. imports, nondurable goods occupy a substantial proportion but durable goods do not.

Agricultural final demand has a declining trend over time, which suggests that some structural change of the input-output coefficients has occurred. Lacking information as to the nature and extent of this change, and also lacking explanatory variables with downward trends, we had no choice but to include a time trend variable. With the time trend variable entering the whole sample period, there is no reason why the equation for F_{AF} should be homogeneous of the first degree. Therefore, we estimated it with a constant term.

$$F_{AF}^{A54} = 0.2801[C_{NF}^{A54} - C_{INF}^{A54}] + \Delta INV_{AF}^{A54} - \frac{7.76}{(1.75)} + \frac{0.0440}{(0.0384)} G^{A54}$$

$$- \frac{0.756}{(0.150)} TIME$$

$$\bar{R}^2 = 0.344. \tag{17.20}$$

This is by far the poorest equation, but the standard error of estimate, which is 1.24 (in billions of dollars), is not so large as might be suspected from the correlation coefficient. Most of agricultural output is delivered to other sectors, and relatively little goes directly to final demands. Government programs are of extreme importance in final demand and are reflected in our use of G as an explanatory variable. Some agricultural production goes into exports, but we could not determine a satisfactory relationship with this kind of variable in our sample.

17.7.5. Final demand converter

These seven equations serve as a converter that distributes different components of GNP expenditures among seven production sectors as final demands. We may call the matrix of coefficients a final demand converter, and it is listed in table 17.5. It will be noted that the column sums of exports and

TABLE 17.5

Coefficients of final demand conversion.

F_j	C_{DEA}	C_{DA}	$C_{NEF}-C_{INEF}$	$C_{NF}-C_{INF}$	C_S-C_{IS}	C_{SR}	I_{CPL}	I_{PDE}
AF				0.2856				
MD	0.6643	0.5550						0.8377
MN			0.6643	0.3787		0.3787		
T	0.2495	0.3588	0.2495	0.2495	0.2495	0.2495	0.0761	0.0761
R	0.0640	0.0640	0.0640	0.0640	0.0640	0.0640	0.0640	0.0640
C							0.8377	
O	0.0222	0.0222	0.0222	0.0222	0.6865	0.0222	0.0222	0.0222

F_j	I_{CNFR}	ΔINV_{MD}	ΔINV_{MN}	ΔINV_T	ΔINV_{AF}	EX	M	G_{CD}
AF					1.0000			0.0440
MD		1.0000		0.3170		0.3170		0.8377
MN			1.0000	0.3787		0.3787	−0.3787	
T	0.0761			0.0761				0.0761
R	0.0640			0.0640		0.0640	−0.0640	0.0640
C	0.8377							
O	0.0222	0.0222	0.0222	0.0222	0.0222	0.0222	−0.0222	0.0222

F_j	G_{CN}	G_{IC}	G_{CS}	Constant term	$TIME$	$DMY12$	$[DMY13]\,[TIME]$
AF	0.0440	0.0440	0.0440	−7.7600	−0.7556		
MD						5.2880	
MN	0.8377						0.6514
T	0.0761	0.0761	0.0761				
R	0.0640	0.0640	0.0640				
C		0.8377		9.6800			
O	0.0222	0.0222	0.0222				

Note   All monetary variables are measured in billions of 1954 dollars.

government expenditures are not equal to unity. This is mainly due to the unsatisfactory treatment of the agriculture equation. Column sums of inventory coefficients also differ from unity, though the differences are trivial.

17.8. *Conversion of sector prices to GNP deflators*

The regression coefficients estimated in the previous section will also serve to convert sectoral prices to *GNP* deflators. For this purpose minor scaling up or down of coefficients and aggregation of *GNP* expenditure items are necessary, which will be discussed shortly. However, the principle can best be stated without going into details.

In the input-output system for production sectors we have seven final demands and as many gross outputs. The main sectors that are excluded from the input-output network are government and household-institutional, both viewed as originators of outputs. "Outputs" in these two sectors consist mainly of labor services for which wages are paid. Evidently, they are delivered directly to final demands corresponding to these two sectors. Therefore, we may think of an augmented input-output system that includes government and household-institutional superimposed on the seven production sectors without invalidating the analysis of the previous section.

Now the value of total final demands is identical to *GNP* in current prices. This may be expressed as

$$\sum P_j F_j^{54} = \sum P_k GNP_k^{54}$$

where P_j is the price for the jth sector, F_j^{54} is the final demand (in constant dollars) of the jth sector, P_k is the deflator of the kth *GNP* component and GNP_k^{54} is the constant-price value of the kth *GNP* component. Our purpose is to find a relationship between P_j and P_k. This can be accomplished if we can replace the F_j's by some linear functions of GNP_k's. A natural choice would be to use the regression equations of final demand conversion.

Let us write the regression coefficients as w_{jk}, where j stands for a production sector and k for a *GNP* component. The identity becomes

$$\sum_j P_j \sum_k [w_{jk}][GNP_k^{54}] = \sum_k [P_k][GNP_k^{54}],$$

or

$$\sum_k [\sum_j P_j w_{jk}] GNP_k^{54} = \sum_k [P_k][GNP_k^{54}].$$

For this identity to hold, we must have

$$\sum_j P_j w_{jk} = P_k \quad \text{for any } k.$$

Thus the regression coefficients estimated in the previous section are themselves the necessary weights, and what little remains to be done is to ascertain that in each set the weights add up to unity.

17.8.1. Price conversion matrix

At this writing, nine *GNP* component deflators are generated by the model. They are five consumer-goods deflators (automobiles, other durables,

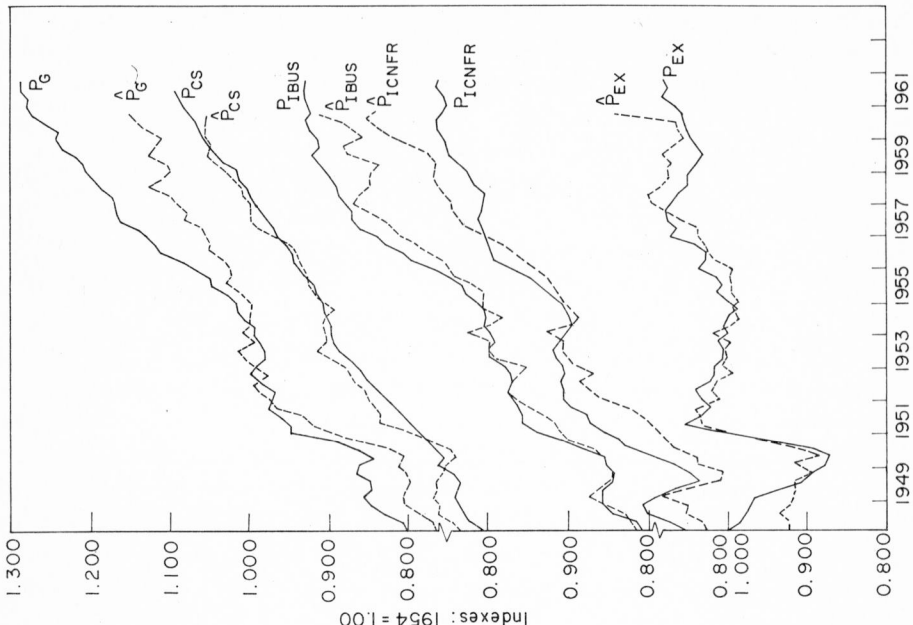

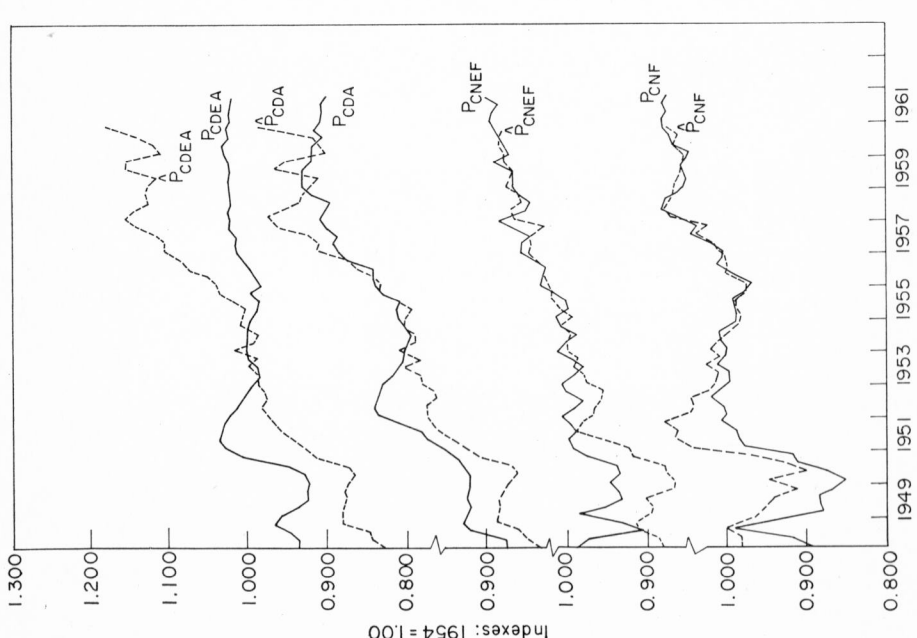

Figure 17.1. Actual and computed price conversion indexes.

foods, other nondurables and services), two producer-goods deflators (producers' plant and equipment and residential construction), exports and government. Deflators for inventories are assumed to be equal to the (respective) sector prices.

For deflators of consumer goods and producer goods, weights of the final-demand converter can be applied without any modification. To combine producers' plant and equipment, we may use the ratio of the two expenditures in the base year, 1954. Export weights do not add up to unity, and we assigned the residual value to the agricultural sector. This is somewhat arbitrary, but possibly justifiable in view of the good result. For these eight deflators, zero weights are assigned to the government and household-institutional sectors.

We cannot pinpoint *GNP* components to which deliveries of output from the household-institutional sector are made. Since there is no sector price corresponding to it, we may ignore the household-institutional sector, understanding that, in the identity, deliveries from this sector are made to total *GNP*. On the other hand, it is evident that output of the government sector is delivered directly to G_{CS}, government purchases of services. In the final-demand conversion matrix G_{CS} receives some weight from several production sectors, and it is natural to assign the residual weight to the government sector. We may then proceed to aggregate weights for four government expenditure items, using ratios of base-year expenditures and scaling the result so that the final weights add up to unity. In this way we can obtain a

TABLE 17.6

Weights for price conversion.

	Equation								
	(17.21)	(17.22)	(17.23)	(17.24)	(17.25)	(17.26)	(17.27)	(17.28)	(17.29)
	$\hat{P}_{CDEA}$	$\hat{P}_{CDA}$	$\hat{P}_{CNEF}$	$\hat{P}_{CNF}$	$\hat{P}_{CS}$	$\hat{P}_{IBUS}$	$\hat{P}_{ICNFR}$	$\hat{P}_{EX}$	$\hat{P}_{G}$
PV_{AF}				0.2856				0.2181	0.0420
PV_{MD}	0.6643	0.5550				0.4964		0.3170	0.1886
PV_{MN}			0.6643	0.3787				0.3787	0.0703
PV_{T}	0.2495	0.3588	0.2495	0.2495	0.2495	0.0761	0.0761		0.0728
PV_{R}	0.0640	0.0640	0.0640	0.0640	0.0640	0.0640	0.0640	0.0640	0.0612
PV_{C}						0.3413	0.8377		0.1247
PV_{O}	0.0222	0.0222	0.0222	0.0222	0.6865	0.0222	0.0222	0.0222	0.0213
$J_{RW_{G}}$									0.4188

Note   See pp. 754–56 for definition of symbols.

matrix of weights that converts sector prices to *GNP* deflators, as listed in table 17.6.

17.8.2. Test of price converter

In order to assess the reasonableness of the conversion weights, we computed *GNP* deflators over the sample period. Prices of production sectors were supplied by Schultze-Tryon and K. Fox. For the government sector we used an index of the average wage of government employees.

Except for deflators of consumers' durables and government, the computed deflators behave more or less in line with the observed deflators. But the "fit" is not satisfactory enough to warrant the use of the converter in the model without modification, and certainly in the case of consumers' durables and government something must be done to close the gap between the computed and observed deflators (see figure 17.1, p. 674).

It was suggested by J. Duesenberry that in the case of consumers' durables, the gap is caused by a gradual deterioration in retail margins, due mainly to the expansion of discount-house operations. This implies a structural change over time of the input-output coefficients, but, lacking appropriate information, we were unable to incorporate this idea.

17.8.3. Price autoregressions

Improvement of the conversion weights, though desirable, seemed to require much more than the research time available. Instead, we decided to compute regression equations connecting the observed and computed prices. These would be empirical relationships that were supposed to exist between the observed prices on the one hand and the computed prices and the lagged values of the observed prices on the other. Three different versions were tried, namely,

$$P_k = \alpha_0 + \alpha_1 \hat{P}_k + \alpha_2 (P_k)_{-1}$$

$$P_k = \beta_0 + \beta_1 \hat{P}_k + \beta_2 (P_k - \hat{P}_k)_{-1}$$

$$P_k = \hat{P}_k + \gamma_0 + \gamma_1 (P_k - \hat{P}_k)_{-1},$$

where P_k is the observed price of the kth *GNP* component and $\hat{P}_k$ the computed price.

On the whole, the second version gave the most satisfactory result. Regression coefficients, their estimated standard errors and estimated standard errors of residuals are listed below.

$$P_{CDEA} = \frac{0.117}{(0.070)} + \frac{0.877}{(0.070)} \hat{P}_{CDEA} + \frac{0.834}{(0.089)} [P_{CDEA} - \hat{P}_{CDEA}]_{-1}$$

$$S_e = 0.0154. \tag{17.30}$$

$$P_{CDA} = \frac{0.121}{(0.045)} + \frac{0.884}{(0.042)} \hat{P}_{CDA} + \frac{0.624}{(0.120)} [P_{CDA} - \hat{P}_{CDA}]_{-1}$$

$$S_e = 0.0175. \tag{17.31}$$

$$P_{CNEF} = \frac{0.250}{(0.059)} + \frac{0.761}{(0.057)} \hat{P}_{CNEF} + \frac{0.229}{(0.121)} [P_{CNEF} - \hat{P}_{CNEF}]_{-1}$$

$$S_e = 0.0181. \tag{17.32}$$

$$P_{CNF} = -\frac{0.0637}{(0.0627)} + \frac{1.059}{(0.061)} \hat{P}_{CNF} + \frac{0.709}{(0.092)} [P_{CNF} - \hat{P}_{CNF}]_{-1}$$

$$S_e = 0.0183. \tag{17.33}$$

$$P_{CS} = -\frac{0.0204}{(0.0136)} + \frac{1.019}{(0.013)} \hat{P}_{CS} + \frac{0.783}{(0.096)} [P_{CS} - \hat{P}_{CS}]_{-1}$$

$$S_e = 0.0087. \tag{17.34}$$

$$P_{IBUS} = -\frac{0.0435}{(0.0233)} + \frac{1.052}{(0.025)} \hat{P}_{IBUS} + \frac{0.534}{(0.136)} [P_{IBUS} - \hat{P}_{IBUS}]_{-1}$$

$$S_e = 0.0138. \tag{17.35}$$

$$P_{ICNFR} = \frac{0.0958}{(0.0254)} + \frac{0.906}{(0.024)} \hat{P}_{ICNFR} + \frac{0.741}{(0.076)} [P_{ICNFR} - \hat{P}_{ICNFR}]_{-1}$$

$$S_e = 0.0123. \tag{17.36}$$

$$P_{EX} = \frac{0.0672}{(0.0495)} + \frac{0.933}{(0.049)} \hat{P}_{EX} + \frac{0.630}{(0.102)} [P_{EX} - \hat{P}_{EX}]_{-1}$$

$$S_e = 0.0177. \tag{17.37}$$

$$P_G = -\frac{0.0208}{(0.0173)} + \frac{1.025}{(0.018)} \hat{P}_G + \frac{0.958}{(0.049)} [P_G - \hat{P}_G]_{-1}$$

$$S_e = 0.0130. \tag{17.38}$$

The coefficients were estimated by the limited-information maximum-likelihood method. It is noted that almost all the coefficients are statistically significant and that standard errors of estimate are fairly small, considering that the average values of the dependent variables are approximately 1.000.

This result suggests that though there are some discrepancies between the observed prices and the prices computed from our conversion weights, those discrepancies are fairly regular and a simple autoregressive scheme works well to eliminate the discrepancies. We might conjecture that our conversion weights are basically correct but change over time in more or less systematic fashion and that the autoregressive equations serve to explain the movements of the weights over time.

17.8.4. Concluding remarks: what should be done next

Before concluding this chapter we should like to emphasize the tentative nature of our empirical results. Aside from the question of further disaggregating the sectors, knowledge of the 1958 input-output table should be incorporated. We might simply replace the 1947 table by the 1958 table, or we might interpolate annual input-output tables from the two tables and use interpolated values to compute annual estimates of sector final demands.

It should be remembered that the final demand regressions were estimated by ordinary least squares. They should presumably be reestimated by one of the instrumental variables methods, but this would be a delicate job because of the small size of the sample. Reestimation would result in a somewhat different set of conversion weights, and it would then be necessary to recompute the price autoregression equations.

REFERENCES

1. EVANS, W. D., and HOFFENBERG, M. The Interindustry Relations Study for 1947, *Review of Economics and Statistics* 34 (1952) 97–142.
2. FISHER, F. M. "Dynamic Structure and Estimation in Economy-wide Econometric Models," Ch. 15 of the present volume.
3. MADANSKY, A. On the Efficiency of Three-Stage Least Squares Estimation, *Econometrica* 32 (1964) 51–56.
4. ROTHENBERG, T. J., and LEENDERS, C. T. Efficient Estimation of Simultaneous Equation Systems, *Econometrica* 32 (1964) 57–76.
5. SARGAN J. D. Three-Stage Least Squares and Full Maximum Likelihood Estimates, *Econometrica* 32 (1964) 77–86.
6. U. S. Office of Business Economics, *Survey of Current Business*, October, 1962.

7. THEIL, H. *Economic Forecasts and Policy*. 2nd ed. revised. Amsterdam: North-Holland Publishing Company, 1961.
8. ZELLNER, A., and THEIL, H. Three-Stage Least Squares: Simultaneous Estimation of Simultaneous Equations, *Econometrica* 30 (1962) 54–78.
9. ZELLNER, A. An Efficient Method of Estimating Seemingly Unrelated Regressions and Tests for Aggregation Bias, *Journal of the American Statistical Association* 57 (1962) 348–368.

CHAPTER 18

THE COMPLETE MODEL: A FIRST APPROXIMATION

Contents

18.1. The aggregative model 681

18.2. Discussion of the model. 722
    1. Some observations in retrospect.

18.3. Appendix: preliminary estimation and predetermined variables . . 736

THE COMPLETE MODEL: A FIRST APPROXIMATION

GARY FROMM

The Brookings Institution, Washington, D.C.

and

LAWRENCE R. KLEIN

University of Pennsylvania, Philadelphia, Pennsylvania

Each of the individual members of our research team has faithfully pursued his work assignment in comparative isolation (except for the summer seminars and occasional meetings) and produced the separate equation estimates shown in the preceding chapters. Any of these estimates is defensible by itself and represents a careful theoretical and statistical consideration of relationships in a sector of the economy. We now turn to the difficult task of fitting all these separate pieces together in a single model. The model is nearly complete, but, as can be expected from the research coordination of so many individual investigations, there are "loose ends". All the major variables are covered by structural equations or identities, but since there were time limitations and this is a continuing research project, small gaps were left for future work. Some rather trivial identities that essentially define combinations of variables may have escaped our attention. We may have omitted some identities but not behavioral or technical equations, unless the deletion was deliberate.

18.1. The aggregative model

A system of equations, constructed from the guide lines established in the preceding chapters, is set out below. Since this is a large system, even though aggregated into seven production sectors, it makes for easier comprehension to list the equations by economic groupings and to define variables at the end of each grouping [1]). The equations (except where otherwise noted)

---

[1]) As noted in the preface, equations in the volume are numbered consecutively by chapter. In what follows, original equation numbers are used if the equation specification is identical to that appearing in a preceding chapter (the coefficients of the variables may differ from the original if consistent estimates have been made). Equations which do not appear elsewhere in the volume are numbered in this chapter.

have been estimated by the method of limited-information maximum likelihood or two-stage least squares [2]).

Unless otherwise indicated, all monetary variables are in billions of current dollars seasonally adjusted; monetary flow variables are at annual rates; and stock variables are end-of-period. Lags or leads in variables are indicated by the general subscript i or plus or minus numbers; e.g., a lag of one period is $t - i$ with $i = 1$, or simply (without t) -1. The subscript j indicates that the variable to which it applies is generated by production sector. The subscript k refers to *GNP* components.

Other modifiers of the variables are:

Superscripts

47–9	= constant 1947–1949 dollars
53	= constant 1953 dollars
54	= constant 1954 dollars
57–9	= constant 1957–1959 dollars
A	= annual data
N	= "normal" value of the variable as defined in each instance
NS	= not adjusted for seasonal variation
Q1, Q2, etc.	= first quarter, etc.
T	= trend value of the variable.

Subscripts   Subscripts are defined with the variables to which they apply.

Sector subscripts   These refer only to producing sectors and government.

A	= agriculture, forestry and fisheries
AF	= farming
AO	= agriculture, forestry and fisheries except farming
C	= contract construction
EA	= all private industries except agriculture, forestry and fisheries
EAF	= nonfarm business
F	= federal government (used only as subscript for government expenditure variables)
G	= government and government enterprises

---

[2]) Our general procedure has been to use limited-information estimates where possible. These estimates are sensitive to multicollinearity and other complications; therefore, we have substituted two-stage least-squares estimates in cases where limited-information estimates became "explosive". In pure regressions, with only one unlagged endogenous variable, we have used ordinary least-squares estimates.

GE	=	government enterprises
GEF	=	federal government enterprises
GES	=	state and local government enterprises
GF	=	federal government
GS	=	state and local governments
M	=	manufacturing
M*	=	manufacturing plus mining of crude petroleum and natural gas
MD	=	durable manufacturing
MN	=	nondurable manufacturing
MN*	=	nondurable manufacturing plus mining of crude petroleum and natural gas
O	=	residual industries: mining; finance, insurance and real estate; and all services
O*1	=	residual industries *O* excluding: mining of crude petroleum and natural gas, real estate and household and institutional services
O*2	=	trade and contract construction plus residual industries *O* excluding: banking, insurance carriers, real estate, medical services, legal services and household and institutional services
O*3	=	residual industries *O*2* plus communications less mining
O*4	=	residual industries *O* plus contract construction and regulated industries
O*5	=	residual industries *O*2* less trade and contract construction
OFR	=	real estate
OSH	=	household and institutional services
P	=	private
R	=	regulated industries: transportation, communications, public utilities
RP	=	public utilities
S	=	state and local governments (used only as a subscript for government expenditure variables)
T	=	wholesale and retail trade
T*	=	wholesale and retail trade excluding the retail automotive group
TR	=	retail trade
TRDA	=	automotive group of retail trade
W	=	rest of the world
491	=	electric companies and systems.

Consumer demand

$$C_{DEA}^{54} = -\frac{22.93}{(11.97)} + \frac{0.2415}{(0.0372)} Y_D^{54} - \frac{10.62}{(8.16)} \left[\frac{P_{CDEA}}{P_C}\right]$$
$$-\frac{0.07405}{(0.0170)} [K_{CDEA}^{54}]_{-1}.$$
(18.1)

$$K_{CDEA}^{54} = [K_{CDEA}^{54}]_{-1} + C_{DEA}^{54} - \frac{1}{48}\{\sum_{i=-48}^{-1} [C_{DEA}^{54}]_i\}.$$
(18.2)

$$C_{DA}^{54} = -\frac{21.19}{(12.9)} + \frac{0.0501}{(0.0053)} Y_D^{54} - \frac{8.333}{(11.7)} \left[\frac{P_{CDA}}{P_C}\right]$$
$$+\frac{0.2950}{(0.0411)} [ATT]_{-1}.$$
(18.3)

$$C_{NF}^{54} - C_{INF}^{54} = \frac{30.57}{(12.4)} + \frac{0.08701}{(0.0155)} Y_D^{54} - \frac{15.76}{(10.6)} \left[\frac{P_{CNF}}{P_C}\right]$$
$$+\frac{0.4154}{(0.0984)} \{\frac{1}{4} \sum_{i=-4}^{-1} [C_{NF}^{54} - C_{INF}^{54}]_i\}.$$
(18.4)

$$C_{NEF}^{54} - C_{INEF}^{54} = \frac{7.31}{(12.5)} + \frac{0.1457}{(0.0287)} Y_D^{54} - \frac{5.345}{(1.04)} \left[\frac{P_{CNEF}}{P_C}\right]$$
$$+\frac{0.2697}{(0.137)} \{\frac{1}{4} \sum_{i=-4}^{-1} [C_{NEF}^{54} - C_{INEF}^{54}]_i\}.$$
(18.5)

$$C_S^{54} - C_{IS}^{54} = -\frac{25.25}{(9.01)} + \frac{0.0193}{(0.0144)} Y_D^{54} - \frac{6.096}{(8.17)} \left[\frac{P_{CS}}{P_C}\right]$$
$$+\frac{0.6994}{(0.101)} \{\frac{1}{4} \sum_{i=-4}^{-1} [C_S^{54} - C_{IS}^{54}]_i\} + \frac{0.0562}{(0.0197)} \left[\frac{ALQD^*}{P_C}\right]_{-1}$$
$$+\frac{0.2297}{(0.126)} [N + N_{ML}].$$
(18.6)

The variables in order of appearance are:

C_{DEA} = personal consumption expenditures for durable goods other than new and net used automobiles and parts, billions of dollars

Y_D = disposable personal income, billions of dollars

P_{CDEA} = implicit price deflator for personal consumption expenditures on durable goods other than new and net used automobiles and parts, 1954 = 1.00

P_{C} = implicit price deflator for personal consumption expenditures, 1954 = 1.00

K_{CDEA} = stock of consumer durable goods excluding automobiles and parts, billions of dollars

C_{DA} = personal consumption expenditures for new and net used automobiles and parts, billions of dollars

P_{CDA} = implicit price deflator for personal consumption expenditures on new and net used automobiles and parts, 1954 = 1.00

ATT = index of consumer attitudes and inclinations to buy, 1954 = 100

C_{NF} = personal consumption expenditures for food, including imputations, billions of dollars

C_{INF} = personal consumption expenditures for food, imputed or in kind, billions of dollars

P_{CNF} = implicit price deflator for personal consumption expenditures on food, 1954 = 1.00

C_{NEF} = personal consumption expenditures for nondurable goods other than food, including imputations, billions of dollars

C_{INEF} = personal consumption expenditures for nondurable goods other than food, imputed or in kind, billions of dollars

P_{CNEF} = implicit price deflator for personal consumption expenditures on nondurable goods other than food, 1954 = 1.00

C_{S} = personal consumption expenditures on services including imputations, billions of dollars

C_{IS} = imputed personal consumption expenditures on services, billions of dollars

P_{CS} = implicit price deflator for personal consumption expenditures on services, 1954 = 1.00

$ALQD^{*}$ = end-of-quarter holdings of currency and adjusted time and demand deposits, billions of dollars

N = civilian population including Alaska and Hawaii, millions of persons

N_{ML} = military population including armed forces overseas, millions of persons.

Residential construction

$$HU_{STS} = -\frac{168.84}{(107.0)} + \frac{0.426}{(0.344)}[\Delta HH] + \frac{1.876}{(1.53)}HU_{REM}$$

$$-\frac{0.1222}{(0.0361)}[HU_{VAC*}]_{-1} + \frac{2.853}{(0.839)}\left[\frac{CPI_{SR}}{P_{ICNFR}}\right]_{-1} - \frac{18.54}{(6.69)}\{\tfrac{1}{3}\sum_{i=-4}^{-2}[RM_{GBS3}]_i\}$$

$$+\frac{0.3944}{(0.145)}[HU_{STS}]_{-1} - \frac{0.2384}{(0.0728)}[HU_{STS}]_{-3}. \tag{6.4}$$

$$\frac{PM_{ICRD}}{P_{ICNFR}} = -5555.31 + \frac{29.35}{(3.28)}\{\tfrac{1}{3}\sum_{i=-4}^{-2}\left[\frac{Y_D}{P_{GNP}\cdot HH}\right]_i\}\times 10^5$$

$$-\frac{296.4}{(119.4)}\{\tfrac{1}{3}\sum_{i=-4}^{-2}[RM_{GBS3}]_i\}. \tag{6.5}$$

$$\Delta HH = \left[\frac{MAR}{MARE}\right][\Delta HHE]^3). \tag{6.7a}$$

$$HU_{REM} = \frac{21.46}{(0.14)} + \frac{0.000999}{(0.000003)}HU_{AVL}. \tag{6.8}$$

$$HU_{AVL} = [HU_{AVL}]_{-1} + [HU_{FIN}] - [HU_{REM}]. \tag{6.12}$$
$$HU_{FIN} = [HU_{STS}]_{-2}. \tag{18.7}$$
$$HU_{VAC} = [HU_{VAC}]_{-1} + \Delta HU_{AVL} - \Delta HH. \tag{6.13a}$$
$$HU_{VAC*} = HU_{VAC} - 26.73\ TIME. \tag{6.13b}$$
$$CPI_{SR} = 0.7441 + \frac{0.00226}{(0.00008)}\left[\frac{Y_D}{P_{GNP}}\right]_{-1} - \frac{0.00005}{(0.00002)}[HU_{VAC*}]_{-1}. \tag{6.9}$$

$$I^{54}_{CNFRD*} = \left[0.41\left\{\left[\frac{PM_{ICRD}}{P_{ICNFR}}\right][HU_{STS}]\right\} + 0.49\left\{\left[\frac{PM_{ICRD}}{P_{ICNFR}}\right][HU_{STS}]\right\}_{-1}\right. \tag{6.1}$$

$$\left. +0.10\left\{\left[\frac{PM_{ICRD}}{P_{ICNFR}}\right][HU_{STS}]\right\}_{-2}\right]\times 10^{-6}.$$

$$I^{54}_{CNFRO*} = \left[-\frac{458.18}{(392.4)} + \frac{0.05240}{(0.00182)}[HU_{AVL}] - \frac{1143.55}{(386.7)}\left[\frac{P_{ICNFR}}{P_{GNP}}\right]_{-2}\right]\times 10^{-3}. \tag{6.2}$$

$$I^{54}_{CNFR*} = [I^{54}_{CNFRD*} + I^{54}_{CNFRO*}]. \tag{6.10b}$$
$$I^{54}_{CNFR} = [I^{54}_{CNFR*}][DMY15]. \tag{6.10a}$$

[3]) An equation to explain marriages is developed in a later section.

$$I_{CO}^{54} = -\frac{157.55}{(32.9)} + \frac{0.4019}{(0.0710)}\left[\sum_{i=-4}^{0} w_i IP_{CO_i}^{54}\right] + \frac{2.013}{(0.173)}\left\{\frac{1}{3}\sum_{i=-4}^{-2}\left[\frac{Y_D}{P_{GNP}}\right]_i\right\}.$$

$$(6.3)$$

$$IP_{CO}^{54} = -52.53 + \frac{0.7873}{(0.0866)}\left[IP_{CO}^{54}\right]_{-1} + \frac{0.5294}{(0.247)}\left\{\frac{1}{3}\sum_{i=-4}^{-2}\left[\frac{Y_D}{P_{GNP}}\right]_i\right\}. \quad (6.6b)$$

$$\left[\sum_{i=-4}^{0} w_i IP_{CO_i}^{54}\right] = 0.129\, IP_{CO}^{54} + 0.294\left[IP_{CO}^{54}\right]_{-1} + 0.281\left[IP_{CO}^{54}\right]_{-2}$$

$$+ 0.181\left[IP_{CO}^{54}\right]_{-3} + 0.115\left[IP_{CO}^{54}\right]_{-4}. \quad (6.6a)$$

New variables in order of appearance are:

HU_{STS} = number of private housing units started, thousands

HH = number of households, thousands

HU_{REM} = net removals of housing units, thousands

HU_{VAC*} = adjusted vacant available housing units, thousands

CPI_{SR} = rent component of consumer price index, 1947–1949 = 100

P_{ICNFR} = implicit price deflator for GNP expenditures on nonfarm residential construction, 1954 = 1.00

RM_{GBS3} = average market yield on three-month U.S. Treasury bills, per cent

PM_{ICRD} = average cost per unit of private housing starts, dollars

P_{GNP} = implicit price deflator for GNP, 1954 = 1.00

MAR = number of marriages, thousands

$MARE$ = number of expected marriages, thousands

HHE = expected households based on population cohorts, thousands

HU_{AVL} = total available housing units, thousands

HU_{FIN} = housing units completed, thousands

HU_{VAC} = vacant available housing units, thousands

$TIME$ = time trend.

I_{CNFRD*} = current level expenditures on new, nonfarm dwelling units, quarterly rate, billions of dollars

I_{CNFRO*} = current level expenditures on residential, nonfarm construction other than new dwelling units, quarterly rate, billions of dollars

I_{CNFR*} = current level expenditures on nonfarm, residential construction, quarterly rate, billions of dollars

I_{CNFR} = GNP expenditures on nonfarm, residential construction, billions of dollars

$DMY15$ = converter from quarterly rate current level expenditures on residential construction to GNP expenditures on residential construction at annual rate

I_{CO} = private, nonresidential, nonbusiness construction, quarterly rate, billions of dollars

IP_{CO}^{54} = value of building permits for private, nonresidential, nonbusiness construction, quarterly rate, deflated by price of private, nonbusiness construction other than residential nonfarm, billions of 1954 dollars.

Inventory investment

$$\Delta INV_{MD}^{54} = -\frac{15.48}{(42.80)} + \frac{0.0544}{(0.0375)} \Delta O_{UMD}^{54} + \frac{0.0300}{(0.0300)} O_{UMD}^{54} + \frac{73.860}{(33.432)} J_{HP_{MD}}$$

$$-\frac{58.088}{(34.400)} \left\{ \frac{WPI_{MD}}{[WPI_{MD}]_{-1}} \right\} + \frac{0.0904}{(0.0772)} [GNP_D^{54} - \Delta INV_D^{54} + GNP_{IC}^{54}]$$

$$-\frac{0.440}{(0.344)} [INV_{MD}^{54}]_{-1}. \tag{18.8}$$

$$\Delta INV_{MN}^{54} = -\frac{7.580}{(1.772)} - \frac{0.288}{(0.074)} \Delta O_{UMN}^{54} + \frac{1.264}{(0.196)} O_{UMN}^{54}$$

$$+\frac{0.120}{(0.040)} [GNP_N^{54} - \Delta INV_N^{54}] - \frac{0.512}{(0.236)} [INV_{MN}^{54}]_{-1}. \tag{18.9}$$

$$\Delta INV_{T*}^{54} = -\frac{0.4208}{(2.9920)} + \frac{0.2104}{(0.1084)} \Delta RM_{GBS3}$$

$$+\frac{0.0600}{(0.0364)} \left[GNP^{54} - \Delta INV^{54} - C_S^{54} - \frac{WS_G}{P_G} \right]$$

$$+\frac{55.80}{(15.20)} \left\{ \frac{\Delta WPI_{EAF}}{[WPI_{EAF}]_{-1}} \right\} - \frac{0.416}{(0.248)} [INV_{T*}^{54}]_{-1}. \tag{18.10}$$

$$\Delta INV_{O*4}^{54} = \frac{0.2205}{(0.9480)} - \frac{0.1497}{(0.2800)} \Delta RM_{GBS3}$$

$$-\frac{0.0026}{(0.0027)} \left[GNP^{54} - \Delta INV^{54} - \frac{WS_G}{P_G} \right]$$

$$+\frac{82.8}{(42.4)} \left\{ \frac{\Delta WPI_{EAF}}{[WPI_{EAF}]_{-1}} \right\} - \frac{0.1676}{(0.2160)} [INV_{O*4}^{54}]_{-1}. \tag{18.11}$$

$$\Delta INV^{54} = \Delta INV_{AF}^{54} + \Delta INV_{AO}^{54} + \Delta INV_{MD}^{54} + \Delta INV_{MN}^{54} + \Delta INV_{T*}^{54}$$
$$+ \Delta INV_{TRDA}^{54} + \Delta INV_{O*4}^{54}. \tag{18.12}$$

The variables in order of appearance are:

INV = business inventory stock, billions of dollars
O_U = manufacturers' unfilled orders, billions of dollars
$J_{HP_{MD}}$ = index of hours worked by production workers in durable manufacturing, $1954 = 1.00$
WPI = wholesale price index, $1954 = 1.00$
GNP_D = durable goods component of gross national product, billions of
= dollars
INV_D = inventory stock of durable goods, billions of dollars
GNP_{IC} = construction component of gross national product, billions of dollars
GNP_N = nondurable goods component of gross national product, billions of dollars
INV_N = inventory stock of nondurable goods, billions of dollars
GNP = gross national product, billions of dollars
C_S = personal consumption expenditures for services, including imputations, billions of dollars
WS_G = government wage and salary disbursements, billions of dollars
P_G = implicit price deflator for government purchases of goods and services, $1954 = 1.00$.

Orders

$$O_{MD}^{54} = -\frac{1712.28}{(476.28)} + \frac{2.964}{(0.660)}[GNP_D^{54} - \Delta INV_D^{54} + GNP_{IC}^{54}]$$

$$-\frac{1.168}{(0.612)}[GNP_D^{54} - \Delta INV_D^{54} + GNP_{IC}^{54}]_{-2} + \frac{1648.68}{(463.44)}\left\{\frac{WPI_{MD}}{[WPI_{MD}]_{-1}}\right\}$$

$$+\frac{3.336}{(1.428)}\left\{\Delta\left[\frac{G_{ML_F}}{P_{GF}}\right]\right\}. \tag{5.1b}$$

$$O_{MN}^{54} = -\frac{186.12}{(69.60)} + \frac{1.584}{(0.060)}[GNP_N^{54} - \Delta INV_N^{54}]$$

$$+\frac{135.6}{(72.0)}\left\{\frac{WPI_{MN}}{[WPI_{MN}]_{-1}}\right\} + \frac{7.320}{(4.824)}DMYI. \tag{5.2}$$

$$O_{U_{MD}} = [O_{U_{MD}}]_{-1} + O_{MD}^{NS} - [2.4310 X_{MD}^{NS} - \Delta INV_{MD}^{NS}]. \tag{18.13}$$

$$O_{U_{MN}} = [O_{U_{MN}}]_{-1} + O_{MN}^{NS} - [3.2344 X_{MN}^{NS} - \Delta INV_{MN}^{NS}]. \tag{18.14}$$

Seasonal coefficients

Quarter	$\dfrac{O_{MD}^{NS54}}{O_{MD}^{54}}$	$\dfrac{O_{MN}^{NS54}}{O_{MN}^{54}}$	$\dfrac{2.4310\,X_{MD}^{NS54}-\Delta INV_{MD}^{NS54}}{2.4310\,X_{MD}^{54}-\Delta INV_{MD}^{54}}$	$\dfrac{3.2344\,X_{MN}^{NS54}-\Delta INV_{MN}^{NS54}}{3.2344\,X_{MN}^{54}-\Delta INV_{MN}^{54}}$
1	1.0145	0.9936	0.9952	0.9935
2	1.0123	0.9893	1.0257	0.9824
3	0.9724	1.0051	0.9625	1.0078
4	0.9870	1.0081	1.0138	1.0176

New variables in order of appearance are:

O = manufacturers' net new orders, billions of dollars

G_{ML_F} = federal government purchases of goods and services for national defense, billions of dollars

P_{GF} = implicit price deflator for federal government purchases of goods and services, 1954 = 1.00

$DMY1$ = 1, 1950 : 3 through 1951 : 2

          = 0, all other quarters

X = gross product originating, billions of dollars.

Investment realization

$$\Delta\left[\frac{I_{BUS_{MD}}^{54}-IA_{MD}^{54}}{IA_{MD}^{54}}\right] = -0.0004 + \frac{0.119}{(0.224)}\left\{\frac{[\Delta S_{MD}^{54}]_{-1}}{[S_{MD}^{54}]_{-2}}\right\}$$

$$+ \frac{0.222}{(0.198)}\left\{\frac{[\Delta S_{MD}^{54}]_{-2}}{[S_{MD}^{54}]_{-3}}\right\} + \frac{0.079}{(0.069)}\left\{\frac{[\Delta Z_{AU_{MD}}^{NS54}]_{-1}}{[Z_{AU_{MD}}^{NS54}]_{-2}}\right\}$$

$$+ \frac{0.005}{(0.069)}\left\{\frac{[\Delta Z_{AU_{MD}}^{NS54}]_{-2}}{[Z_{AU_{MD}}^{NS54}]_{-3}}\right\} + \frac{0.423}{(0.108)}\left\{\frac{[I_{BUS_{MD}}^{54}]_{-1}-IA_{MD}^{54}}{[I_{BUS_{MD}}^{54}]_{-1}}\right\}$$

$$- \frac{0.541}{(0.108)}\left[\frac{I_{BUS_{MD}}^{54}-IA_{MD}^{54}}{IA_{MD}^{54}}\right]_{-1}. \tag{3.8}$$

$$\Delta\left[\frac{I_{BUS_{MN}}^{54}-IA_{MN}^{54}}{IA_{MN}^{54}}\right] = -0.018 + \frac{0.664}{(0.316)}\left\{\frac{[\Delta S_{MN}^{54}]_{-1}}{[S_{MN}^{54}]_{-2}}\right\}$$

$$+ \frac{0.797}{(0.325)}\left\{\frac{[\Delta S_{MN}^{54}]_{-2}}{[S_{MN}^{54}]_{-3}}\right\} + \frac{0.012}{(0.064)}\left\{\frac{[\Delta Z_{AU_{MN}}^{NS54}]_{-1}}{[Z_{AU_{MN}}^{NS54}]_{-2}}\right\} + \frac{0.014}{(0.063)}\left\{\frac{[\Delta Z_{AU_{MN}}^{NS54}]_{-2}}{[Z_{AU_{MN}}^{NS54}]_{-3}}\right\}$$

$$+ \frac{0.533}{(0.088)}\left\{\frac{[I_{BUS_{MN}}^{54}]_{-1}-IA_{MN}^{54}}{[I_{BUS_{MN}}^{54}]_{-1}}\right\} - \frac{0.825}{(0.093)}\left[\frac{I_{BUS_{MN}}^{54}-IA_{MN}^{54}}{IA_{MN}^{54}}\right]_{-1}. \tag{3.9}$$

$$\Delta \left[\frac{I^{54}_{BUS_{RP}} - IA^{54}_{RP}}{IA^{54}_{RP}} \right] = -0.013 + \frac{0.377}{(0.288)} \left\{ \frac{[\Delta S^{NS54}_{491}]_{-1}}{[S^{NS54}_{491}]_{-2}} \right\}$$

$$+ \frac{0.165}{(0.247)} \left\{ \frac{[\Delta S^{NS54}_{491}]_{-2}}{[S^{NS54}_{491}]_{-3}} \right\} - \frac{0.105}{(0.062)} \left\{ \frac{[\Delta Z^{NS54}_{AU_{RP}}]_{-1}}{[Z^{NS54}_{AU_{RP}}]_{-2}} \right\} + \frac{0.008}{(0.061)} \left\{ \frac{[\Delta Z^{NS54}_{AU_{RP}}]_{-2}}{[Z^{NS54}_{AU_{RP}}]_{-3}} \right\}$$

$$+ \frac{0.395}{(0.090)} \left\{ \frac{[I^{54}_{BUS_{RP}}]_{-1} - IA^{54}_{RP}}{[I^{54}_{BUS_{RP}}]_{-1}} \right\} - \frac{0.719}{(0.112)} \left[\frac{I^{54}_{BUS_{RP}} - IA^{54}_{RP}}{IA^{54}_{RP}} \right]_{-1}. \qquad (3.10)$$

$$\Delta \left[\frac{I^{54}_{BUS_{O*3}} - IA^{54}_{O*3}}{IA^{54}_{O*3}} \right] = 0.002 + \frac{0.254}{(0.220)} \left\{ \frac{[\Delta S^{54}_{TR}]_{-1}}{[S^{54}_{TR}]_{-2}} \right\} - \frac{0.052}{(0.219)} \left\{ \frac{[\Delta S^{54}_{TR}]_{-2}}{[S^{54}_{TR}]_{-3}} \right\}$$

$$+ \frac{0.109}{(0.058)} \left\{ \frac{[\Delta Z^{54}_{AU_{O*3}}]_{-1}}{[Z^{54}_{AU_{O*3}}]_{-2}} \right\} + \frac{0.064}{(0.059)} \left\{ \frac{[\Delta Z^{54}_{AU_{O*3}}]_{-2}}{[Z^{54}_{AU_{O*3}}]_{-3}} \right\}$$

$$+ \frac{0.696}{(0.090)} \left\{ \frac{[I^{54}_{BUS_{O*3}}]_{-1} - IA^{54}_{O*3}}{[I^{54}_{BUS_{O*3}}]_{-1}} \right\} - \frac{0.953}{(0.086)} \left[\frac{I^{54}_{BUS_{O*3}} - IA^{54}_{O*3}}{IA^{54}_{O*3}} \right]_{-1}. \qquad (3.11)$$

New variables in order of appearance are:

I_{BUS} = business gross investment in plant and equipment, billions of dollars

IA = current anticipated investment expenditure reported by business in the prior quarter, billions of dollars

S = shipments by manufacturers and sales by other industries, billions of dollars

Z_{AU} = corporate profits after tax but before inventory valuation adjustment, billions of dollars.

Investment intentions

$$IA^{54}_{MD} = \frac{0.00099}{(0.00040)} \left\{ \Delta \left[\frac{S^{54}_{MD} + \Delta INV^{54}_{MD}}{UKC_{MD}} \right]_{-3} \right\}$$

$$+ \frac{0.00079}{(0.00043)} \left\{ \Delta \left[\frac{S^{54}_{MD} + \Delta INV^{54}_{MD}}{UKC_{MD}} \right]_{-4} \right\} + \frac{0.00054}{(0.00040)} \Delta \left[\frac{S^{54}_{MD} + \Delta INV^{54}_{MD}}{UKC_{MD}} \right]_{-5}$$

$$+ \frac{1.2422}{(0.142)} \left\{ [IA^{54}_{MD}]_{-1} - 0.0279 [K^{54}_{MD}]_{-4} \right\}$$

$$- \frac{0.3938}{(0.139)} \left\{ [IA^{54}_{MD}]_{-2} - 0.0279 [K^{54}_{MD}]_{-5} \right\} + \frac{0.02561}{(0.00309)} [K^{54}_{MD}]_{-3}. \qquad (2.3)$$

$$IA_{MN}^{54} = \frac{0.00058}{(0.00029)} \left\{ \Delta \left[\frac{S_{MN}^{54} + \Delta INV_{MN}^{54}}{UKC_{MN}} \right]_{-6} \right\}$$

$$- \frac{1.2195}{(0.1364)} \{[IA_{MN}^{54}]_{-1} - 0.02648[K_{MN}^{54}]_{-4}\}$$

$$- \frac{0.4198}{(0.1335)} \{[IA_{MN}^{54}]_{-2} - 0.02648[K_{MN}^{54}]_{-5}\} + \frac{0.01835}{(0.00438)} [K_{MN}^{54}]_{-3}. \quad (2.15)$$

$$IA_R^{54} = \frac{0.00105}{(0.00172)} \left\{ \Delta \left[\frac{S_R^{54}}{UKC_R} \right]_{-5} \right\} + \frac{0.00420}{(0.00163)} \left\{ \Delta \left[\frac{S_R^{54}}{UKC_R} \right]_{-6} \right\}$$

$$+ \frac{0.00355}{(0.00177)} \left\{ \Delta \left[\frac{S_R^{54}}{UKC_R} \right]_{-7} \right\} + \frac{0.8406}{(0.1383)} \{[IA_R^{54}]_{-1} - 0.01147[K_R^{54}]_{-4}\}$$

$$+ \frac{0.1228}{(0.1379)} \{[IA_R^{54}]_{-2} - 0.01147[K_R^{54}]_{-5}\} + \frac{0.01029}{(0.00112)} [K_R^{54}]_{-3}. \quad (2.27)$$

$$IA_{O*2}^{54} = \frac{0.00033}{(0.00016)} \left\{ \Delta \left[\frac{S_{O*2}^{54} + \Delta INV_T^{54}}{UKC_{O*2}} \right]_{-3} \right\} + \frac{0.00024}{(0.00016)} \left\{ \Delta \left[\frac{S_{O*2}^{54} + \Delta INV_T^{54}}{UKC_{O*2}} \right]_{-4} \right\}$$

$$- \frac{0.8028}{(0.0810)} \{[IA_{O*2}^{54}]_{-1} - 0.0246[K_{O*2}^{54}]_{-4}\} + \frac{0.02216}{(0.00217)} [K_{O*2}^{54}]_{-3} \quad (2.39)$$

New variables are:

UKC = user cost of capital goods, billions of dollars
K = stock of business capital, billions of dollars.

Foreign trade

$$M_{FIN}^{54} = \frac{1.19}{(3.22)} + \frac{0.0263}{(0.0079)} \left[\frac{Y_D}{P_C} \right] - \frac{4.428}{(2.41)} \left[\frac{PM_{MFIN}}{P_{GOOD}} \right] + \frac{0.6527}{(0.0872)} [M_{FIN}^{54}]_{-1}.$$
$$(18.15)$$

$$M_{EFIN}^{54} = \frac{2.87}{(0.794)} + \frac{0.0269}{(0.0151)} \Delta INV_{EAF}^{54} + \frac{0.0176}{(0.0052)} X_{M*}^{54}$$

$$- \frac{1.011}{(0.576)} \left[\frac{PM_{MEFIN}}{P_{GOOD}} \right] + \frac{0.4705}{(0.119)} [M_{EFIN}^{54}]_{-1}. \quad (18.16)$$

$$EX^{54} = \frac{22.99}{(4.36)} - \frac{24.95}{(4.93)} \left[\frac{P_{EX}}{PM_{EXW}} \right] + \frac{0.5821}{(0.0705)} [EX^{54}]_{-1}$$

$$+ \frac{0.0945}{(0.0129)} EX_W^{54}. \quad (11.3)$$

New variables are:

M_{FIN} = imports of finished goods and services, billions of dollars

PM_{MFIN} = unit value index of imports of finished goods and services, 1954 = 1.00

P_{GOOD} = implicit price deflator for *GNP* goods, 1954 = 1.00

M_{EFIN} = imports of crude materials, crude foodstuffs and semimanufactures, billions of dollars

PM_{MEFIN} = unit value index of imports of semimanufactures, crude materials, and crude foodstuffs, 1954 = 1.00

EX = U.S. exports of goods and services, billions of dollars

P_{EX} = implicit price deflator for exports of goods and services, 1954 = 1.00

PM_{EXW} = unit value index of world exports excluding U.S. components, 1954 = 1.00

EX_{W} = world exports excluding U.S. exports, billions of dollars.

Government receipts and expenditures

$$\Delta TP_{GF} = \frac{0.599}{(0.046)} \Delta\{[WS][R_{\text{PY1}_{GF}}]\} + \frac{0.107}{(0.046)} \{[Y_{\text{P}} - Y_{\text{OL}} - V]^{Q1}[R^{\text{A}}_{\text{PY1}_{GF}}]$$

$$- [Y_{\text{P}} - Y_{\text{OL}} - V]^{Q1}_{-1}[R^{\text{A}}_{\text{PY1}_{GF}}]_{-1}\}$$

$$+ \frac{0.877}{(0.165)} \Delta KGAIN - \frac{1.737}{(0.479)} DMY2 + \frac{2.316}{(0.539)} DMY3. \tag{14.2}$$

$$TC_{GF} = 0.475[Z_{\text{BU}} - TC_{GS}]. \tag{18.17}$$

$$TC = TC_{GF} + TC_{GS}. \tag{18.18}$$

$$\ln TW_{\text{OA}_{GF}} = \frac{0.600}{(0.617)} + \frac{1.006}{(0.070)} \ln R_{\text{OA}_{GF}} + \frac{0.803}{(0.095)} \ln [WS_{\text{BUS}} + Y_{\text{ENT}*}]$$

$$+ \frac{0.421}{(0.177)} \ln J_{\text{OAMAX}}. \tag{14.12}$$

$$\ln TW_{\text{US}_{GF}} = -\frac{3.314}{(0.801)} + \frac{0.978}{(0.099)} \ln R_{\text{US}_{GF}} + \frac{0.671}{(0.107)} \ln WS_{\text{BUS}}$$

$$+ \frac{0.203}{(0.587)} \ln \left[\frac{L_{\text{UIS}}}{L}\right]. \tag{14.13}$$

$$\ln TP^A_{Y_{GS}} = -\frac{7.979}{(0.796)} + \frac{0.356}{(0.211)} \ln [R^A_{PY_{GS}}]_{-1}$$

$$+ \frac{0.916}{(0.068)} \ln [Y_P - Y_{OL} - V]^A_{-1}. \tag{14.17}$$

$$0.971[TP_{Y_{GS}} + TP_{O_{GS}}]^A = TP^{Q1}_{GS}. \tag{14.17.1}$$

$$0.991[TP_{Y_{GS}} + TP_{O_{GS}}]^A = TP^{Q2}_{GS}. \tag{14.17.2}$$

$$1.015[TP_{Y_{GS}} + TP_{O_{GS}}]^A = TP^{Q3}_{GS}. \tag{14.17.3}$$

$$1.023[TP_{Y_{GS}} + TP_{O_{GS}}]^A = TP^{Q4}_{GS}. \tag{14.17.4}$$

$$\ln TC_{GS} = -\frac{4.672}{(0.243)} + \frac{1.285}{(0.153)} \ln R^A_{Z_{GS}} + \frac{0.693}{(0.084)} \ln Z_{BU}. \tag{14.19}$$

$$\ln TX_{O_{GS}} = -\frac{1.753}{(0.912)} + \frac{0.764}{(0.186)} \ln [RX_{GS}]_{-1} + \frac{1.199}{(0.058)} \ln [C]_{-1}. \tag{14.20}$$

$$\ln \left[\frac{TX^A_{PR_{GS}}}{P^A_{GS}}\right] = -\frac{0.085}{(0.159)} + \frac{0.681}{(0.063)} \ln \left[\frac{G^A_S}{P^A_{GS}}\right] + \frac{0.113}{(0.059)} \ln RM^A_{MBLM}. \tag{14.21}$$

$$0.972 TX^A_{PR_{GS}} = TX^{Q1}_{PR_{GS}} \tag{14.21.1}$$

$$0.988 TX^A_{PR_{GS}} = TX^{Q2}_{PR_{GS}}. \tag{14.21.2}$$

$$1.012 TX^A_{PR_{GS}} = TX^{Q3}_{PR_{GS}}. \tag{14.21.3}$$

$$1.028 TX^A_{PR_{GS}} = TX^{Q4}_{PR_{GS}}. \tag{14.21.4}$$

$$\ln V_{OA_{GF}} = -\frac{12.042}{(0.442)} + \frac{1.178}{(0.070)} \ln \left\{\frac{N_{OASI}}{N_{65+}}\right\} \{[N_{65+}] - [L_{65+}]\}$$

$$+ \frac{0.867}{(0.107)} \ln VM_{OA/F}. \tag{14.24}$$

$$\ln V_{US_{GF}} = -\frac{3.447}{(0.379)} + \frac{1.062}{(0.099)} \ln U + \frac{1.086}{(0.750)} \ln \left[\frac{U26-}{U}\right]$$

$$+ \frac{0.807}{(0.125)} \ln VM_{US}. \tag{14.30}$$

$$\ln\left[\frac{V_{\mathrm{AO}_{GS}}}{\{[N_{65+}]-[N_{\mathrm{OASI}}]\}}\right] = \frac{3.880}{(0.285)} - \frac{69.2}{(20.0)}\ln\left[\frac{E_{65+}}{N_{65+}}\right] + \frac{0.262}{(0.034)}DMY7$$

$$+ \frac{0.317}{(0.024)}DMY8 + \frac{0.259}{(0.030)}DMY9 + \frac{0.142}{(0.037)}DMY10. \tag{14.32}$$

$$\ln V_{\mathrm{ADC}_{GS}} = -\frac{0.079}{(0.570)} + \frac{1.544}{(0.144)}\ln[N_{18-}] + \frac{0.047}{(0.026)}\ln\left[\frac{U-U_{\mathrm{IS}}}{L-L_{\mathrm{UIS}}}\right]$$

$$+ \frac{0.367}{(0.031)}DMY7 + \frac{0.097}{(0.034)}DMY9 + \frac{0.138}{(0.031)}DMY10. \tag{14.33}$$

$$RW^{\mathrm{A}}_{\mathrm{CIV}_{GF}} = -\frac{346.64}{(117.74)} + \frac{1.358}{(0.050)}[RW^{\mathrm{A}}]_{-1}. \tag{14.38}$$

$$\ln WS_{\mathrm{CIV}_{GF}} = -\frac{7.443}{(0.263)} + \frac{0.823}{(0.075)}\ln E_{\mathrm{XEC}_{GF}} + \frac{1.077}{(0.033)}\ln RW^{\mathrm{A}}_{\mathrm{CIV}_{GF}}. \tag{14.39}$$

$$\Delta\ln E^{\mathrm{A}}_{\mathrm{ED}_{GS}} = -\frac{11.203}{(0.438)} + \frac{0.548}{(0.133)}\ln[N^{\mathrm{A}}_{5-18}]$$

$$-\frac{0.366}{(0.093)}\ln[E^{\mathrm{A}}_{\mathrm{ED}_{GS}}]_{-1}. \tag{14.50}$$

$$\ln\left[\frac{RW^{\mathrm{A}}_{\mathrm{ED}_{GS}}}{CPI^{\mathrm{A}}}\right] = -\frac{0.347}{(0.163)} + \frac{1.174}{(0.145)}\ln\left[\frac{RW^{\mathrm{A}}}{CPI^{\mathrm{A}}}\right]_{-1} + \frac{2.485}{(1.453)}\Delta\ln[N^{\mathrm{A}}_{5-18}].$$

$$\tag{14.51}$$

$$WS^{\mathrm{A}}_{\mathrm{ED}_{GS}} = [RW^{\mathrm{A}}_{\mathrm{ED}_{GS}}][E^{\mathrm{A}}_{\mathrm{ED}_{GS}}] \times 10^{-3}. \tag{18.19}$$

$$RW^{\mathrm{A}}_{\mathrm{O}_{GS}} = -\frac{123.73}{(32.93)} + \frac{0.921}{(0.009)}[RW^{\mathrm{A}}]_{-1}. \tag{14.52}$$

$$\ln E_{\mathrm{O}_{GS}} = -\frac{15.342}{(0.457)} + \frac{1.832}{(0.090)}\ln N - \frac{0.021}{(0.021)}\ln\left[\frac{G_F-G_{\mathrm{ML}_F}}{P_G}\right]. \tag{14.53}$$

$$\ln WS_{\mathrm{O}_{GS}} = -\frac{6.614}{(0.633)} + \frac{0.585}{(0.124)}\ln E_{\mathrm{O}_{GS}} + \frac{1.352}{(0.090)}\ln RW^{\mathrm{A}}_{\mathrm{O}_{GS}}. \tag{14.54}$$

$$G^{54}_{\mathrm{ICED}_S} = \frac{0.260}{(0.096)}[K^{54}_{\mathrm{ED}_{GS}}]_{-1} + \frac{0.532}{(0.092)}[N_{18-}] + \frac{2.3360}{(0.6028)}[RM_{\mathrm{MBLM}}]_{-2}$$

$$- \frac{0.04556}{(0.00968)}\{[N_{18-}][RM_{\mathrm{MBLM}}]_{-2}\} - \frac{22.252}{(3.132)}. \tag{14.55}$$

$$\frac{G^{57-9}_{\text{ICHI}_S}}{CAR_{\text{REG}}} = -\frac{2.080}{(0.712)}\frac{HWYL}{CAR_{\text{REG}}} + \frac{0.693}{(0.098)}\left[\frac{G^{57-9}_{\text{ICHI}_S}}{CAR_{\text{REG}}}\right]_{-1} + \frac{0.116}{(0.036)}. \quad (14.58)$$

$$\frac{G_{\text{ICWA}_S}}{P_{GS}} = \frac{0.038}{(0.003)}\left[\frac{I_C - I_{\text{CO}*}}{P_{\text{IC}_P}}\right] + \frac{0.001004}{(0.070940)}. \quad (14.60)$$

New variables in order of appearance are:

TP_{GF} = personal tax and nontax receipts of the federal government, billions of dollars

WS = wage and salary disbursements, billions of dollars

$R_{\text{PY}1_{GF}}$ = starting federal tax rate on wages and salaries, fraction

Y_P = personal income, billions of dollars

Y_{OL} = other labor income, billions of dollars

V = transfer payments to persons, billions of dollars

$KGAIN$ = realized capital gains, billions of dollars

$DMY2$ = 1, 1949 : 1
  = 0, elsewhere

$DMY3$ = 1, 1951 : 1
  = 0, elsewhere

TC_{GF} = corporate profits tax accruals to the federal government, billions of dollars

TC_{GS} = corporate profits tax accruals to state and local governments, billions of dollars

Z_{BU} = corporate profits before taxes and before inventory valuation adjustment, billions of dollars

TC = corporate profits tax accruals to government, billions of dollars

$TW_{\text{OA}_{GF}}$ = OASI contributions by employees, employers and self-employed persons, billions of dollars

$R_{\text{OA}_{GF}}$ = weighted average of effective OASI contribution rates, fraction

WS_{BUS} = private wage and salary disbursements, billions of dollars

$Y_{\text{ENT}*}$ = nonfarm proprietors' income beginning 1950 : 4, total proprietors' income beginning 1954 : 4, billions of dollars

J_{OAMAX} = index of maximum OASI-taxable earnings per employee, 1947–1949 = 1.00

$TW_{\text{US}_{GF}}$ = employers' contributions for state unemployment insurance, billions of dollars

$R_{\text{US}_{GF}}$ = average employer contribution rate for state unemployment insurance, fraction

L_{UIS} = labor force covered by state unemployment insurance, millions of persons

L = civilian labor force, millions of persons

$TP_{Y_{GS}}$ = personal income tax receipts of state and local governments, billions of dollars

$R^{\text{A}}_{\text{PY}_{GS}}$ = index of proxy state government tax rate on income, 1948 = 100

$TP_{O_{GS}}$ = state and local government personal tax and nontax receipts other than income tax, billions of dollars

TP_{GS} = personal tax and nontax receipts of state and local governments, billions of dollars

$R^{\text{A}}_{Z_{GS}}$ = proxy state tax rate on corporate profits, fraction

$TX_{O_{GS}}$ = state and local government indirect business tax and nontax accruals other than property taxes, billions of dollars

RX_{GS} = weighted average of state government alcohol, gasoline, tobacco and general excise tax rates, fraction

C = personal consumption expenditures including imputations, billions of dollars

$TX_{\text{PR}_{GS}}$ = property-taxes portion of state and local government indirect business tax and nontax accruals, billions of dollars

P_{GS} = implicit price deflator for state and local government purchases of goods and services, 1954 = 1.00

G_S = state and local government purchases of goods and services, billions of dollars

RM_{MBLM} = Moody's average long-term municipal bond yield, per cent

$V_{\text{OA}_{GF}}$ = old-age and survivors insurance benefits, billions of dollars

N_{OASI} = civilian population aged 65 and over [62 and over for females since 1956] eligible for OASI benefits, millions of persons

N_{65+} = civilian population aged 65 and over [62 and over for females since 1956], millions of persons

L_{65+} = labor force aged 65 and over [62 and over for females since 1956], millions of persons

$VM_{\text{OA/F}}$ = maximum per-family OASI benefit per month, dollars

$V_{\text{US}_{GF}}$ = state unemployment insurance benefits paid by the federal government, billions of dollars

U = unemployed civilian labor force, millions of persons

$U26-$ = number unemployed for 26 weeks or less, millions of persons

VM_{US} = weighted average of maximum weekly benefit under various state unemployment insurance plans, dollars

$V_{\text{AO}_{GS}}$ = state and local government old age assistance payments, billions of dollars

E_{65+} = employed persons aged 65 and over, millions of persons

$DMY7$ = 0, through 1948 : 3
           = 1, thereafter

$DMY8$ = 0, through 1952 : 3
           = 1, thereafter

$DMY9$ = 0, through 1956 : 4
           = 1, thereafter

$DMY10$ = 0, through 1958 : 3
           = 1, thereafter

$V_{\text{ADC}_{GS}}$ = state and local government aid to dependent children, billions of dollars

N_{18-} = civilian population aged 18 and under, millions of persons

U_{IS} = unemployment covered by state unemployment insurance, millions of persons

$RW_{\text{CIV}_{GF}}$ = average earnings per full-time equivalent civilian employee of the federal general government, dollars

RW = average earnings per full-time equivalent employee, economy as a whole, dollars

$WS_{\text{CIV}_{GF}}$ = federal general government wage and salary disbursements to civilians, billions of dollars

$E_{\text{XEC}_{GF}}$ = employees in the executive branch of the federal government excluding government enterprises, thousands of persons

$E_{\text{ED}_{GS}}$ = full-time equivalent employees in state and local public education, millions of persons

N^{A}_{5-18} = civilian population aged 5 to 18, as of July 1, millions of persons

$RW_{\text{ED}_{GS}}$ = average earnings per full-time equivalent employee in state and local public education, dollars

CPI = consumer price index, 1954 = 1.00

$WS_{\text{ED}_{GS}}$ = wage and salary disbursements to employees in state and local public education, billions of dollars

$RW_{\text{O}_{GS}}$ = average earnings per full-time equivalent employee, state and local nonschool except work relief and enterprises, dollars

$E_{\text{O}_{GS}}$ = full-time equivalent employees, state and local nonschool except work relief and enterprises, millions

G_F = federal government purchases of goods and services, billions of dollars

G_{ML_F} = federal government purchases of goods and services for

P_G national defense, billions of dollars
   = implicit price deflator for government purchases of goods and services, 1954 = 1.00

$WS_{O_{GS}}$ = wage and salary disbursements to nonschool (except work relief and enterprises) employees of state and local governments, billions of dollars

G_{ICED_S} = new educational construction activity by state and local governments, billions of dollars

$K_{ED_{GS}}$ = stock of capital in state and local educational structures, billions of dollars

G_{ICHI_S} = new highway construction activity by state and local governments, billions of dollars

CAR_{REG} = end-of-quarter stock of automobiles registered, millions

$HWYL$ = length of surfaced highways, including Alaskan and Hawaiian, millions of miles

G_{ICWA_S} = new construction activity by state and local governments for sewer and water systems, billions of dollars

I_C = new construction component of gross private domestic investment, billions of dollars

I_{CO*} = petroleum and natural gas well drilling component of new construction activity, billions of dollars

P_{IC_P} = implicit price deflator for new private construction activity, 1954 = 1.00.

Production functions (labor requirements) and *income distribution* (factor shares)

$$E_{P_{MD}} = \frac{0.6886}{(0.3189)} + \frac{0.0535}{(0.0052)} X_{MD}^{54} - \frac{0.0342}{(0.0064)} [X_{MD}^{54}]_{-1} - \frac{0.0246}{(0.0065)} [K_{MD}^{54}]_{-1}$$
$$+ \frac{0.1402}{(0.0496)} [\Delta H_{P_{MD}}]_{-1} + \frac{0.8616}{(0.0554)} [E_{P_{MD}}]_{-1}. \tag{8.10}$$

$$E_{P_{MN*}} = \frac{0.2261}{(0.2975)} + \frac{0.0378}{(0.0049)} X_{MN*}^{54} - \frac{0.0326}{(0.0051)} [X_{MN*}^{54}]_{-1} - \frac{0.0097}{(0.0037)} [K_{MN}^{54}]_{-1}$$
$$+ \frac{0.0961}{(0.0169)} [\Delta H_{P_{MN*}}]_{-1} + \frac{0.9866}{(0.0394)} [E_{P_{MN*}}]_{-1}. \tag{8.11}$$

$$E_T = -\frac{0.2174}{(0.3981)} + \frac{0.0219}{(0.0038)} X_T^{54} + \frac{0.0053}{(0.0041)} [X_T^{54}]_{-1} - \frac{0.0065}{(0.0023)} TIME$$
$$+ \frac{0.8599}{(0.0457)} [E_T]_{-1}. \tag{8.13}$$

$$MH_R = -\frac{0.3529}{(0.7161)} + \frac{0.1465}{(0.0365)} X_R^{54} - \frac{0.0814}{(0.0416)} [X_R^{54}]_{-1} - \frac{0.0278}{(0.0077)} TIME$$

$$+ \frac{0.8548}{(0.0933)} [MH_R]_{-1}. \tag{8.16}$$

$$E_c = \frac{0.1425}{(0.1197)} + \frac{0.0503}{(0.0107)} X_c^{54} - \frac{0.0016}{(0.0009)} TIME + \frac{0.6370}{(0.0818)} [E_c]_{-1}. \tag{8.12}$$

$$MH_{O*1} = -\frac{0.0687}{(0.4601)} + \frac{0.2101}{(0.0319)} X_{O*1}^{54} - \frac{0.1612}{(0.0421)} [X_{O*1}^{54}]_{-1}$$

$$- \frac{0.0056}{(0.0038)} TIME + \frac{0.8476}{(0.0891)} [MH_{O*1}]_{-1}. \tag{8.17}$$

$$E_{OMD} = \frac{0.1646}{(0.0530)} + \frac{0.0052}{(0.0008)} X_{MD}^{54} + \frac{0.0076}{(0.0040)} [K_{MD}^{54}]_{-1} + \frac{0.7910}{(0.0686)} [E_{OMD}]_{-1}.$$

$$\tag{8.14}$$

$$E_{OMN*} = \frac{0.0680}{(0.0232)} + \frac{0.0023}{(0.0005)} X_{MN*}^{54} - \frac{0.0038}{(0.0019)} [K_{MN}^{54}]_{-1} + \frac{0.9972}{(0.0534)} [E_{OMN*}]_{-1}.$$

$$\tag{8.15}$$

$$H_{PMD} = \frac{5.0918}{(1.6113)} + \frac{5.61}{(0.53)} \left\{ \frac{\varDelta X_{MD}^{54}}{[X_{MD}^{54}]_{-1}} \right\} + \frac{0.8731}{(0.0396)} [H_{PMD}]_{-1}. \tag{8.18}$$

$$H_{PMN*} = \frac{11.1846}{(2.4602)} + \frac{11.20}{(1.50)} \left\{ \frac{\varDelta X_{MN*}^{54}}{[X_{MN*}^{54}]_{-1}} \right\} + \frac{0.7135}{(0.0623)} [H_{PMN*}]_{-1}. \tag{8.19}$$

$$H_{Pc} = \frac{4.7027}{(2.8250)} + \frac{2.62}{(0.71)} \left\{ \frac{\varDelta X_c^{54}}{[X_c^{54}]_{-1}} \right\} + \frac{0.8719}{(0.0756)} [H_{Pc}]_{-1}. \tag{8.20}$$

$$H_{PT} = \frac{1.0656}{(1.6506)} + \frac{0.9718}{(0.0417)} [H_{PT}]_{-1}. \tag{18.20}$$

$$\varDelta INT_G = \frac{0.1167}{(0.0267)} + \frac{0.5880}{(0.4813)} [RM_{GBS3}][\varDelta BF]$$

$$+ \frac{0.0661}{(0.0231)} [BF][\varDelta RM_{GBS3}]. \tag{8.22}$$

$$\varDelta INT_{BUS} = \frac{0.0427}{(0.0530)} + \frac{1.19}{(0.25)} [RM_{GBL}][I_{CNFR} + \varDelta K_{CD}]$$

$$+ \frac{0.17}{(0.08)} [\varDelta RM_{GBL}][K_{CD}]. \tag{8.23}$$

$$\Delta K_{CD}^{54} = C_D^{54} - \tfrac{1}{48} \sum_{i=-48}^{-1} [C_D^{54}]_i. \tag{18.21}$$

$$K_{CD} = [K_{CD}^{54}][P_{CD}]. \tag{18.22}$$

$$P_{CD} = \frac{[P_{CDA}][C_{DA}^{54}] + [P_{CDEA}][C_{DEA}^{54}]}{C_{DA}^{54} + C_{DEA}^{54}}. \tag{18.23}$$

$$PIVA = -\frac{1.5350}{(3.8088)} + \frac{1.0090}{(0.1753)} \left\{ \left[1 - \frac{\Delta INV_{EAF}^{54}}{X_{M*}^{54}} \right] [WPI_{EAF}] \right\}$$
$$- \frac{0.9100}{(0.1545)} \left\{ \left[1 - \frac{\Delta INV_{EAF}^{54}}{X_{M*}^{54}} \right] [WPI_{EAF}]_{-1} \right\} + \frac{0.9204}{(0.0559)} [PIVA]_{-1}. \tag{8.28}$$

$$-IVA = [\Delta INV_{EAF}^{54}][\Delta PIVA]. \tag{8.26}$$

$$\Delta DIV = \frac{0.2601}{(0.2846)} + \frac{0.09935}{(0.02166)} [Z_A + CCAC] - \frac{0.3545}{(0.0767)} [DIV]_{-1}. \tag{8.33}$$

$$Y_{ENT_{EAFj}} = \lambda_j X_j. \tag{18.24}$$

$$Y_{ENT_{EAF}} = \sum_j Y_{ENT_{EAF_j}} \tag{18.25}$$

New variables in the production functions are:

E_P = employment of production workers, millions of persons
X = gross product originating, billions of dollars
H_P = average workweek of production workers, hours
E = employment, millions of persons
MH = manhours, billions per year
E_O = employment of overhead workers, millions of persons

New variables in the factor shares equations are:

INT_G = personal interest income paid by government, billions of dollars
BF = total federal government debt, billions of dollars
INT_{BUS} = personal interest income paid by business, billions of dollars
RM_{GBL} = average yield during quarter on U.S. securities maturing or callable in 10 years or more, per cent
K_{CD} = stock of consumer durable goods measured at original cost, billions of dollars
C_D = personal consumption expenditures on durable goods, billions of dollars
P_{CD} = implicit price deflator for personal consumption expenditures on durable goods, 1954 = 1.00

$PIVA$ = price index used to estimate inventory valuation adjustment, 1954 = 1.00

IVA = inventory valuation adjustment, billions of dollars

DIV = dividends, billions of dollars

Z_A = corporate profits after taxes and after inventory valuation adjustment, billions of dollars

$CCAC$ = corporate capital consumption allowances, billions of dollars

$Y_{ENT_{EAF}}$ = business and professional proprietors' income, billions of dollars.

Labor force and marriage rate

$$\frac{L_{F20+}}{N_{F20+}} = 0.5595 + \frac{0.840}{(0.265)}\left[\frac{DRFT}{N_{M14+}}\right] + \frac{0.03713}{(0.01496)}E_{F15_{AF}} - \frac{0.007624}{(0.001831)}H_{MD}$$

$$+ \frac{0.7928}{(0.2891)}\left[\frac{U27+}{L_{M14+}}\right]_{-1} + \frac{0.00169}{(0.00015)}\left[\frac{CDTE_P}{P_{CD}}\right]. \tag{10.1}$$

$$\frac{L_{F1419}}{N_{F1419}} = 0.2573 + \frac{0.07612}{(0.02038)}E_{F15_{AF}} - \frac{1.134}{(0.412)}\left[\frac{U27+}{L_{M14+}}\right]. \tag{10.16}$$

$$\frac{L_{M20+}}{N_{M20+}} = 0.9634 - \frac{0.48}{(0.10)}\left[\frac{U27+}{L_{M14+}}\right]_{-1} + \frac{0.001512}{(0.000500)}H_{MD}$$

$$- \frac{0.4188}{(0.0271)}\left[\frac{L_{F20+}}{N_{F20+}}\right]_{-1}. \tag{10.19}$$

$$\frac{L_{M1419}}{N_{M1419}} = 0.2405 - \frac{0.76}{(0.64)}\left[\frac{U27+}{L_{M14+}}\right] - \frac{0.292}{(0.533)}\left[\frac{DRFT}{N_{M14+}}\right] + \frac{0.1235}{(0.0303)}E_{F15_{AF}}$$

$$- \frac{0.0017}{(0.0003)}\left[\frac{CDTE_P}{P_{CD}}\right] + \frac{0.00500}{(0.00358)}H_{MD}. \tag{10.21}$$

$$MAR = 1450.8 + \frac{9580.}{(1560.)}\Delta\left[\frac{DRFT}{N_{M14+}}\right] - \frac{1336.8}{(201.6)}[RU_{M2024}]$$

$$+ \frac{306.12}{(54.48)}\left[\frac{N_{M2024}}{N_{F1419}}\right]_{-1}. \tag{10.22}$$

New variables in order of appearance are:

L_{F20+} = female civilian labor force aged 20 and over, millions of persons

N_{F20+} = civilian noninstitutional female population aged 20 and over, millions of persons

$DRFT$ = U.S. armed forces military personnel procurement, millions of persons

N_{M14+} = civilian noninstitutional male population aged 14 and over, millions of persons

$E_{F15_{AF}}$ = unpaid females employed 15 or more hours per week in agriculture, millions

H_{MD} = average workweek in durable manufacturing, hours

$U27+$ = number unemployed for 27 or more weeks, millions of persons

L_{M14+} = total male labor force aged 14 and over, millions of persons

$CDTE_P$ = consumer credit extensions, billions of dollars

L_{F1419} = female civilian labor force aged 14 through 19, millions of persons

N_{F1419} = civilian noninstitutional female population aged 14 through 19, millions of persons

L_{M20+} = male civilian labor force aged 20 and over, millions of persons

N_{M20+} = civilian noninstitutional male population aged 20 and over, millions of persons

L_{M1419} = male civilian labor force aged 14 through 19, millions of persons

N_{M1419} = civilian noninstitutional male population aged 14 through 19, millions of persons

MAR = number of marriages, thousands

N_{M2024} = civilian noninstitutional male population aged 20 through 24, millions of persons

RU_{M2024} = rate of unemployment among males aged 20 through 24, fraction.

Agriculture

$$J_{\text{FCR/N}} = \frac{27.33}{(10.11)} + \frac{0.016163}{(0.010021)}\, TIME + \frac{0.3533}{(0.3519)}\, DMY16$$

$$+ \frac{0.7600}{(0.0878)}\, [J^*_{\text{FCR/N}}]_{-1} + \left\{ -0.15952\, J_{\text{FAN/N}} - 0.0677\, PM_{\text{FCR}_{TR}} \right.$$

$$\left. + 0.000753\, P_{\text{CEF}} + 0.01397\, \frac{Y_{\text{D}}}{[P_{\text{C}}][N + N_{\text{ML}}]} \right\}. \tag{12.3}$$

$$PM_{\text{FCR}_{TR}} - PM_{\text{FCR}_{AF}} = \frac{49.88}{(11.22)} + \frac{0.4419}{(0.1219)}\, TIME$$

$$+ \frac{0.4917}{(0.1182)}\, [PM_{\text{FCR}_{TR}} - PM_{\text{FCR}_{AF}}]_{-1} - \frac{7.1672}{(3.6806)}\, DMY17$$

$$+ [1.5\, ULC_{\text{FM}} + 50\, PM_{\text{PDFS}}]. \tag{12.7}$$

$$J^*_{FCR/N} = J_{FCR/N} - \left\{ -0.15952 \, J_{FAN/N} - 0.06776 \, PM_{FCR_{TR}} \right.$$

$$\left. +0.000753 \, P_{CEF} + 0.01397 \, \frac{Y_D}{[P_C][N+N_{ML}]} \right\}. \qquad (12.3.2)$$

$$CCC^{A47-9} = -\frac{13.82}{(1.64)} - \frac{1.1943}{(0.1711)} \, DMYI8^A + \frac{7.6165}{(0.7770)} \left\{ \frac{J^A_{QCR_{AF}}}{[J^A_{DUCR}]_{-1}} \right\}. \qquad (12.25)$$

$$PM_{AF} = [PM_{AF}]_{-1} + \frac{0.00357}{(0.00037)} \, \Delta PM_{F_{AF}} + \frac{0.1015}{(0.0348)} \, \Delta PM_{HAY_{AF}}$$

$$+ \frac{0.0080}{(0.0026)} \, \Delta PM_{COT_{AF}}. \qquad (12.11)$$

$$Y_{GRS_{AF}} - RENT_{AF} = \frac{0.8532}{(1.4854)} + \frac{0.9737}{(0.0451)} \, [Y_{GRS_{AF}} - RENT_{AF}]_{-1}$$

$$+ \frac{25.1086}{(2.6470)} \left\{ \frac{PM_{AF}}{[PM_{AF}]_{-1}} - 1 \right\} + \frac{21.5398}{(2.0389)} \left\{ \frac{J_{Q_{AF}}}{[J_{Q_{AF}}]_{-1}} - 1 \right\}. \qquad (12.12)$$

$$XCST_{AF} = [XCST_{AF}]_{-1} - \frac{0.1125}{(0.0618)} + \frac{19.2418}{(1.6786)} \left\{ \frac{PM_{PDFP}}{[PM_{PDFP}]_{-1}} - 1 \right\}$$

$$+ \frac{1.3557}{(0.6838)} \left\{ \frac{J_{Q_{AF}}}{[J_{Q_{AF}}]_{-1}} - 1 \right\} + \frac{0.00474}{(0.00180)} \, TIME. \qquad (12.14)$$

$$DPNR_{AF} = \frac{0.1596}{(0.0389)} + \frac{0.7166}{(0.0708)} \, [DPNR^*_{AF}]_{-1}$$

$$+ [0.159 \, K_{PDE_{AF}} + 0.0231 \, K_{PL_{AF}}]. \qquad (12.15)$$

$$\Delta INV^{54}_{AF} = -\frac{0.01434}{(0.0592)} + \frac{0.6799}{(0.0993)} \, [\Delta INV^{*54}_{AF}]_{-1}$$

$$+ \left\{ \frac{0.6040}{(0.1090)} \, \Delta X^{A47-9}_{HAY} + \frac{1.0852}{(0.2882)} \, \Delta INV^{A53}_{COW} \right\}. \qquad (12.16)$$

$$Y_{NET_{AF}} = Y_{GRS_{AF}} - XCST_{AF} - DPNR_{AF} + \Delta INV_{AF}. \qquad (12.18)$$

$$E_{AF} = \frac{8.121}{(0.056)} - \frac{0.0458}{(0.0017)} \, TIME + \frac{0.000708}{(0.00010)} \, [E_{AF} - E^T_{AF}]_{-1}. \qquad (12.23)$$

$$[E_{AF} - E^T_{AF}] = E_{AF} - \left[\frac{8.164}{(0.077)} - \frac{0.0471}{(0.0023)} \, TIME \right]. \qquad (12.24)$$

New variables in order of appearance are:

$J_{FCR/N}$ = index of per capita consumption of food crop products, 1947–1949 = 100

$DMY16$ = 1, 1947 : 1 through 1948 : 3
= 1, 1950 : 3 through 1952 : 4
= 0, all other quarters

$J^*_{FCR/N}$ = adjusted index of per capita consumption of food crop products, 1947–1949 = 100

$J_{FAN/N}$ = index of per capita consumption of food livestock products, 1947–1949 = 100

$PM_{FCR_{TR}}$ = retail value of crop component of the food market basket, dollars

P_{CEF} = implicit price deflator for personal consumption expenditures on goods and services except food, 1954 = 1.00

$PM_{FCR_{AF}}$ = current value at farm level of crop component of the food market basket, dollars

$DMY17$ = 1, in 1949 : 3 through 1950 : 1
= 0, all other quarters

ULC_{FM} = index of unit labor costs in food marketing operations, 1957–1959 = 100

PM_{PDFS} = price index of purchased materials and services used in food marketing, 1947–1949 = 1.00

CCC^A = annual net outlays by the Commodity Credit Corporation for supporting prices of major crops and dairy products, billions of dollars

$DMY18^A$ = 1, in 1948, 1951 and 1952
= 0, in all other years

$J^A_{QCR_{AF}}$ = index of the volume of output of all farm crops, 1947–1949 = 100

J^A_{DUCR} = index of total annual domestic utilization of farm crops (a subaggregate of an index in which the average annual utilization of all U.S. farm products for all purposes, domestic and foreign, 1947–1949 = 100)

PM_{AF} = index of prices received by farmers for all commodities, food and nonfood, 1910–1914 = 1.00

$PM_{F_{AF}}$ = current value at farm level of the food market basket, livestock and crop components combined, dollars

$PM_{HAY_{AF}}$ = index of prices of feed grains and hay at the farm level, 1910–1914 = 1.00

$PM_{COT_{AF}}$ = U.S. average price of cotton at the farm level, cents per pound

$Y_{GRS_{AF}}$ = gross farm income, billions of dollars

$RENT_{AF}$ = imputed rental value of farm dwellings, billions of dollars

$J_{Q_{AF}}$ = index of volume of farm marketings plus farm consumption of home-grown food and fuel, 1947–1949 = 108.7 (marketing component = 100.0, farm consumption component = 8.7)

$XCST_{AF}$ = current operating expenditures for farm production, billions of dollars

PM_{PDFP} = index of prices paid by farmers for goods and services used in production, 1910–1914 = 1.00

$DPNR$ = replacement-cost depreciation, billions of dollars

$DPNR^*_{AF}$ = adjusted replacement-cost depreciation of farm capital, billions of dollars

K_{PDE} = stock of producers' durable equipment, billions of dollars

K_{PL} = stock of plant, billions of dollars

INV_{AF} = farm business inventory stock (commodities pledged as collateral for CCC loans are excluded), billions of dollars

INV^*_{AF} = adjusted farm business inventory stock, billions of dollars

X^A_{HAY} = production of feed crops in current calendar year, billions of dollars

INV^A_{COW} = farm inventory stock of cattle and hogs on January 1, billions of dollars

$Y_{NET_{AF}}$ = net farm income, billions of dollars

E = employment, millions of persons

E^T_{AF} = trend of employment in agriculture, millions of persons.

Depreciation (accounting prices)

$$DPN_{MD} = -\frac{0.2165}{(0.0081)} + \frac{0.02501}{(0.00024)} \sum_{i=1}^{80} [I_{BUS_{MD}}]_{-i} + \frac{0.6404}{(0.0147)} DMY14$$

$$-\frac{0.0126}{(0.0003)} \{DMY14\} \{\sum_{i=1}^{80} [I_{BUS_{MD}}]_{-i}\}. \qquad (18.26)$$

$$DPN_{MN} = -\frac{0.1742}{(0.0106)} + \frac{0.01574}{(0.00023)} \sum_{i=1}^{80} [I_{BUS_{MN}}]_{-i} + \frac{0.1569}{(0.0194)} DMY14$$

$$-\frac{0.00168}{(0.00030)} \{DMY14\} \{\sum_{i=1}^{80} [I_{BUS_{MN}}]_{-i}\}. \qquad (18.27)$$

$$DPN_R = -\frac{0.1925}{(0.0125)} + \frac{0.01735}{(0.00024)}\sum_{i=1}^{80}[I_{\text{BUS}_R}]_{-i} + \frac{0.3098}{(0.0209)}DMY14$$

$$-\frac{0.00339}{(0.00030)}\{DMY14\}\{\sum_{i=1}^{80}[I_{\text{BUS}_R}]_{-i}\}. \tag{18.28}$$

The variables are:

DPN = depreciation in accounting prices, billions of dollars
I_{BUS} = business gross investment in plant and equipment, billions of dollars
$DMY14$ = 0, 1948 : 1 through 1955 : 1
= 1, thereafter.

Depreciation (replacement costs)

$$DPNR_{MD}^{54} = 0.0279[K_{MD}^{54}]_{-1}. \tag{18.29}$$

$$DPNR_{MN}^{54} = 0.02648[K_{MN}^{54}]_{-1}. \tag{18.30}$$

$$DPNR_R^{54} = 0.01147[K_R^{54}]_{-1}. \tag{18.31}$$

$$DPNR_{O*2}^{54} = 0.02460[K_{O*2}^{54}]_{-1}. \tag{18.32}$$

$$DPNR_T^{54} = \left[\frac{DPNR_T^{54}}{DPNR_{O*2}^{54}}\right]_{-1}[DPNR_{O*2}^{54}]. \tag{18.33}$$

$$DPNR_C^{54} = \left[\frac{DPNR_C^{54}}{DPNR_{O*2}^{54}}\right]_{-1}[DPNR_{O*2}^{54}]. \tag{18.34}$$

$$DPNR_{O*5} = \left[\frac{DPNR_{O*5}^{54}}{DPNR_{O*2}^{54}}\right]_{-1}[DPNR_{O*2}^{54}]. \tag{18.35}$$

The variables are:

$DPNR$ = replacement-cost depreciation, billions of dollars
K = stock of business capital, billions of dollars.

Prices and wage rates

$$WPI_{MD} = -0.0226 + \frac{1.845}{(0.042)}ULC_{MD}^N + \frac{0.371}{(0.151)}[ULC_{MD} - ULC_{MD}^N]$$

$$-\frac{0.059}{(0.012)}\left\{\left[\frac{INV_{MD}^{54}}{X_{MD}^{54}}\right] - \left[\frac{INV_{MD}^{54}}{X_{MD}^{54}}\right]^T\right\}_{-1}. \tag{9.7}$$

$$WPI_{MN*} = -0.0627 + \frac{1.490}{(0.072)} ULC^N_{MN*} + \frac{0.279}{(0.018)} P_{AF}$$

$$- \frac{0.098}{(0.013)} \left\{ \left[\frac{INV^{54}_{MN*}}{X^{54}_{MN*}} \right] - \left[\frac{INV^{54}_{MN*}}{X^{54}_{MN*}} \right]^T \right\}_{-1}. \tag{9.8}$$

$$PV_T = 0.3461 + \frac{1.159}{(0.037)} ULC^N_T + \frac{1.423}{(0.164)} [ULC_T - ULC^N_T]$$

$$- \frac{0.028}{(0.009)} \left\{ \left[\frac{INV_T}{X_T} \right] - \left[\frac{INV_T}{X_T} \right]^T \right\}_{-1}. \tag{9.9}$$

$$PV_R = -0.0605 + \frac{1.556}{(0.041)} [ULC^N_R + UCCA^N_R] + \frac{0.956}{(0.155)} \{[ULC_R + UCCA_R]$$

$$- [ULC^N_R + UCCA^N_R]\}.$$

$$P_{IC} = 0.0603 + \frac{0.858}{(0.052)} ULC^N_C + \frac{0.349}{(0.095)} [ULC - ULC^N_C]$$

$$+ \frac{0.036}{(0.006)} WPIS_{CM}. \tag{9.11}$$

$$PV_{O*1} = 0.1070 + \frac{1.701}{(0.027)} ULC^N_{O*1} + \frac{1.748}{(0.395)} [ULC_{O*1} - ULC^N_{O*1}]. \tag{9.12}$$

$$\frac{RWSS_C - RWSS_{C,-4}}{RWSS_{C,-4}} = -0.041 + \frac{0.146}{(0.209)} \frac{1}{4} \sum_{i=-3}^{0} \left\{ \left[\frac{CPI - CPI_{-4}}{CPI_{-4}} \right]_i \right\}$$

$$+ \frac{2.33}{(0.75)} \left\{ \frac{1}{4} \sum_{i=-3}^{0} \left[\frac{Z_{Bc}}{X_C} \right]_i \right\} + \frac{0.00192}{(0.00056)} \left[\frac{1}{RU^*} \right]$$

$$- \frac{0.337}{(0.117)} \left[\frac{RWSS_{C,-4} - RWSS_{C,-8}}{RWSS_{C,-8}} \right]. \tag{9.13}$$

$$\frac{RWSS_{MD} - RWSS_{MD,-4}}{RWSS_{MD,-4}} = 0.0187 + \frac{0.883}{(0.109)} \left\{ \frac{1}{4} \sum_{i=-3}^{0} \left[\frac{CPI - CPI_{-4}}{CPI_{-4}} \right]_i \right\}$$

$$+ \frac{0.132}{(0.049)} \left\{ \frac{1}{4} \sum_{i=-3}^{0} \left[\frac{Z_{BMD}}{X_{MD}} \right]_i \right\} + \frac{0.00106}{(0.00034)} \left[\frac{1}{RU^*} \right]$$

$$- \frac{0.430}{(0.101)} \left[\frac{RWSS_{MD,-4} - RWSS_{MD,-8}}{RWSS_{MD,-8}} \right]. \tag{9.14}$$

$$\frac{RWSS_{MN*}-RWSS_{MN*,-4}}{RWSS_{MN*,-4}} = 0.0390 + \frac{0.763}{(0.108)}\left\{\frac{1}{4}\sum_{i=-3}^{0}\left[\frac{CPI-CPI_{-4}}{CPI_{-4}}\right]_i\right\}$$

$$+\frac{0.036}{(0.079)}\left\{\frac{1}{4}\sum_{i=-3}^{0}\left[\frac{Z_{B_{MN*}}}{X_{MN*}}\right]_i\right\}+\frac{0.000698}{(0.000289)}\left[\frac{1}{RU*}\right]$$

$$-\frac{0.559}{(0.088)}\left[\frac{RWSS_{MN*,-4}-RWSS_{MN*,-8}}{RWSS_{MN*,-8}}\right]. \tag{9.15}$$

$$\frac{RWSS_{T}-RWSS_{T,-4}}{RWSS_{T,-4}} = 0.0445 + \frac{0.068}{(0.099)}\left\{\frac{1}{4}\sum_{i=-3}^{0}\left[\frac{CPI-CPI_{-4}}{CPI_{-4}}\right]_i\right\}$$

$$+\frac{0.001129}{(0.000270)}\left[\frac{1}{RU*}\right]-\frac{0.556}{(0.119)}\left[\frac{RWSS_{T,-4}-RWSS_{T,-8}}{RWSS_{T,-8}}\right]. \tag{9.16}$$

$$\frac{RWSS_{R}-RWSS_{R,-4}}{RWSS_{R,-4}} = -0.044 + \frac{0.359}{(0.157)}\left\{\frac{1}{4}\sum_{i=-3}^{0}\left[\frac{CPI-CPI_{-4}}{CPI_{-4}}\right]_i\right\}$$

$$+\frac{0.534}{(0.308)}\left\{\frac{1}{4}\sum_{i=-3}^{0}\left[\frac{Z_{B_R}}{X_R}\right]\right\}+\frac{95.10^{-6}}{(45.10^{-6})}\left[\frac{1}{RU*}\right]$$

$$-\frac{0.109}{(0.151)}\left[\frac{RWSS_{R,-4}-RWSS_{R,-8}}{RWSS_{R,-8}}\right]. \tag{9.17}$$

$$\frac{RWSS_{O*1}-RWSS_{O*1,-4}}{RWSS_{O*1,-4}} = -0.022 + \frac{0.521}{(0.118)}\left\{\frac{1}{4}\sum_{i=-3}^{0}\left[\frac{CPI-CPI_{-4}}{CPI_{-4}}\right]_i\right\}$$

$$+\frac{0.592}{(0.328)}\left\{\frac{1}{4}\sum_{i=-3}^{0}\left[\frac{Z_{B_{O*1}}}{X_{O*1}}\right]_i\right\}+\frac{0.000513}{(0.000413)}\left[\frac{1}{RU*}\right]$$

$$-\frac{0.498}{(0.106)}\left[\frac{RWSS_{O*1,-4}-RWSS_{O*1,-8}}{RWSS_{O*1,-8}}\right]. \tag{9.18}$$

New variables in order of appearance are:

ULC^N = normal unit labor costs, dollars per dollar

$$= \frac{WSS}{MH} \div \frac{1}{12}\sum_{i=-11}^{0}\left[\frac{X}{MH}\right]_i$$

ULC = unit labor cost [compensation of employees per unit of gross product originating], dollars per dollar

$\left[\dfrac{INV}{X}\right]^T$ = trend of ratio of inventory stock to gross product originating, fraction

P_{AF} = implicit price deflator for farm gross product, 1954 = 1.00

PV = implicit price deflator for gross product originating, 1954 = 1.00

$UCCA^N$ = normal unit capital consumption allowances [smoothed ratio of CCA to capacity output], dollars per dollar

$UCCA$ = unit capital consumption allowances [capital consumption allowance per unit of gross product originating], dollars per dollar

P_{IC} = implicit price deflator for construction component of *GNP*, 1954 = 1.00

$WPIS_{CM}$ = special wholesale price index for construction materials, 1954 = 1.00

$RWSS$ = compensation of employees per man-hour, dollars per hour

Z_B = corporate profits before taxes including inventory valuation adjustment, billions of dollars

RU^* = five-quarter average of *RU* centered on $t-2$, fraction
= $\frac{1}{8}RU_{-4}+\frac{1}{4}RU_{-3}+\frac{1}{4}RU_{-2}+\frac{1}{4}RU_{-1}+\frac{1}{8}RU$

RU = rate of unemployment, fraction.

Final demand and price conversion (annual data) [4])

$$F_{AF}^{A54} = 0.2801[C_{NF}^{A54} - C_{INF}^{A54}] + \Delta INV_{AF}^{A54} - \frac{7.76}{(1.75)} + \frac{0.044}{(0.0384)} G^{A54}$$
$$- \frac{0.756}{(0.150)} TIME. \tag{17.20}$$

$$F_{MD}^{A54} = 0.555 C_{DA}^{A54} + 0.664 C_{DEA}^{A54} + 0.8377[I_{PDE}^{A54} + G_{CD}^{A54}] + \Delta INV_{MD}^{A54}$$
$$+ \frac{0.3170}{(0.0287)} [EX^{A54} + \Delta INV_T^{A54}] + \frac{5.288}{(1.25)} DMY12. \tag{17.18}$$

$$F_{MN}^{A54} = 0.664[C_{NEF}^{A54} - C_{INEF}^{A54}] + 0.838 G_{CN}^{A54} + \Delta INV_{MN}^{A54}$$
$$+ \frac{0.379}{(0.007)} [C_{NF}^{A54} - C_{INF}^{A54} + \Delta INV_T^{A54} + EX^{A54} - M^{A54}]$$
$$+ \frac{0.651}{(0.085)} [DMY13][TIME]. \tag{17.19}$$

$$F_T^{A54} = \frac{0.250}{(0.024)} [C^{A54} - C_{DA}^{A54}] + \frac{0.359}{(0.239)} C_{DA}^{A54}$$
$$+ \frac{0.0761}{(0.0423)} [GNP^{A54} - C^{A54} - EX^{A54} - \Delta INV_{AF}^{A54} - \Delta INV_M^{A54}]. \tag{17.14}$$

---

[4]) One equation is redundant by the basic *GNP* definition.

$$F_R^{A54} = \frac{0.0640}{(0.0019)} \left[GNP^{A54} - \varDelta INV_{AF}^{A54} - \varDelta INV_M^{A54}\right]. \tag{17.15}$$

$$F_C^{A54} = 9.68 + 0.8377[I_{CNFR}^{A54} + I_{CPL}^{A54} + I_{CO}^{A54} + G_{IC}^{A54}]. \tag{17.17}$$

$$F_O^{A54} = C_{SR}^{A54} + 0.686[C_S^{A54} - C_{IS}^{A54}]$$

$$+ \frac{0.0222}{(0.0014)} \{[GNP^{A54} - C_{SR}^{A54}] - [C_S^{54} - C_{IS}^{A54}]\}. \tag{17.16}$$

(Quarterly data)

$$\hat{P}_{CDEA} = 0.6643PV_{MD} + 0.2495PV_T + 0.0640PV_R + 0.0222PV_{O*1}. \tag{17.21}$$

$$\hat{P}_{CDA} = 0.5550PV_{MD} + 0.3588PV_T + 0.0640PV_R + 0.0222PV_{O*1}. \tag{17.22}$$

$$\hat{P}_{CNEF} = 0.6643PV_{MN*} + 0.2495PV_T + 0.0640PV_R + 0.0222PV_{O*1}. \tag{17.23}$$

$$\hat{P}_{CNF} = 0.2856PV_{AF} + 0.3787PV_{MN*} + 0.2495PV_T + 0.0640PV_R$$

$$+ 0.0222PV_{O*1}. \tag{17.24}$$

$$\hat{P}_{CS} = 0.2495PV_T + 0.0640PV_R + 0.6865PV_{O*1}. \tag{17.25}$$

$$\hat{P}_{IBUS} = 0.4964PV_{MD} + 0.0761PV_T + 0.0640PV_R + 0.3413PV_C + 0.0222PV_{O*1}. \tag{17.26}$$

$$\hat{P}_{ICNFR} = 0.0761PV_T + 0.0640PV_R + 0.8377PV_C + 0.0222PV_{O*1}. \tag{17.27}$$

$$\hat{P}_{EX} = 0.2181PV_{AF} + 0.3170PV_{MD} + 0.3787PV_{MN*} + 0.0640PV_R + 0.0222PV_{O*1}. \tag{17.28}$$

$$\hat{P}_G = 0.0420PV_{AF} + 0.1886PV_{MD} + 0.0703PV_{MN*} + 0.0728PV_T$$

$$+ 0.0612PV_R + 0.1247PV_C + 0.0213PV_{O*1} + 0.4188J_{RWG}. \tag{17.29}$$

$$P_{CDEA} = \frac{0.117}{(0.070)} + \frac{0.877}{(0.070)} \hat{P}_{CDEA} + \frac{0.834}{(0.089)} [P_{CDEA} - \hat{P}_{CDEA}]_{-1}. \tag{17.30}$$

$$P_{CDA} = \frac{0.121}{(0.045)} + \frac{0.884}{(0.042)} \hat{P}_{CDA} + \frac{0.624}{(0.120)} [P_{CDA} - \hat{P}_{CDA}]_{-1}. \tag{17.31}$$

$$P_{CNEF} = \frac{0.250}{(0.059)} + \frac{0.761}{(0.057)} \hat{P}_{CNEF} + \frac{0.229}{(0.121)} [P_{CNEF} - \hat{P}_{CNEF}]_{-1}. \tag{17.32}$$

$$P_{CNF} = -\frac{0.0637}{(0.0627)} + \frac{1.059}{(0.061)} \hat{P}_{CNF} + \frac{0.709}{(0.092)} [P_{CNF} - \hat{P}_{CNF}]_{-1}. \tag{17.33}$$

$$P_{CS} = - \frac{0.0204}{(0.0136)} + \frac{1.019}{(0.013)} \hat{P}_{CS} + \frac{0.783}{(0.096)} [P_{CS} - \hat{P}_{CS}]_{-1} . \tag{17.34}$$

$$P_{IBUS} = - \frac{0.0435}{(0.0233)} + \frac{1.052}{(0.024)} \hat{P}_{IBUS} + \frac{0.534}{(0.136)} [P_{IBUS} - \hat{P}_{IBUS}] \tag{17.35}$$

$$P_{ICNFR} = \frac{0.0958}{(0.0254)} + \frac{0.906}{(0.024)} \hat{P}_{ICNFR} + \frac{0.741}{(0.076)} [P_{ICNFR} - \hat{P}_{ICNFR}]_{-1} . \tag{17.36}$$

$$P_{EX} = \frac{0.0672}{(0.0495)} + \frac{0.933}{(0.049)} \hat{P}_{EX} + \frac{0.630}{(0.102)} [P_{EX} - \hat{P}_{EX}]_{-1} . \tag{17.37}$$

$$P_{G} = - \frac{0.0208}{(0.0173)} + \frac{1.025}{(0.018)} \hat{P}_{G} + \frac{0.958}{(0.049)} [P_{G} - \hat{P}_{G}]_{-1} . \tag{17.38}$$

(Annual data)

$$
\begin{bmatrix}
0.7304 & -0.0025 & -0.1758 & -0.0134 & -0.0005 & -0.0032 & -0.0015 \\
-0.0112 & 0.6318 & -0.0281 & -0.0341 & -0.0361 & -0.3276 & -0.0310 \\
-0.0908 & -0.0684 & 0.6786 & -0.0912 & -0.0558 & -0.0529 & -0.0670 \\
-0.0399 & -0.0200 & -0.0171 & 0.9597 & -0.0216 & -0.0995 & -0.0205 \\
-0.0260 & -0.0376 & -0.0348 & -0.0324 & 0.9239 & -0.0467 & -0.0559 \\
-0.0059 & -0.0031 & -0.0022 & -0.0046 & -0.0550 & 0.9998 & -0.0554 \\
-0.0709 & -0.0377 & -0.0364 & -0.1164 & -0.0575 & -0.0498 & 0.9075
\end{bmatrix}
$$

$$
\begin{bmatrix}
X_{AF}^{A54}(1.8716)(1.225) \\
X_{MD}^{A54}(2.4310)(0.752) \\
X_{MN}^{A54}(3.2344)(0.859) \\
X_{T}^{A54}(1.2684)(0.866) \\
X_{R}^{A54}(1.4564)(0.821) \\
X_{C}^{A54}(3.1893)(0.738) \\
X_{O}^{A54}(1.4391)(0.734)
\end{bmatrix}
=
\begin{bmatrix}
F_{AF}^{A54}(1.225) \\
F_{MD}^{A54}(0.752) \\
F_{MN}^{A54}(0.859) \\
F_{T}^{A54}(0.866) \\
F_{R}^{A54}(0.821) \\
F_{C}^{A54}(0.738) \\
F_{O}^{A54}(0.734)
\end{bmatrix}
$$

New variables in order of appearance are:

F^A = estimated annual final demand, billions of dollars

G = government purchases of goods and services, billions of dollars

I_{PDE} = gross private domestic investment in producers' durable equipment, billions of dollars

G_{CD} = government purchases of durable goods, billions of dollars

$DMY12$ = 1, 1953 through 1955

          = 0, other years

G_{CN} = government purchases of nondurable goods, billions of dollars

M = imports of goods and services, billions of dollars

$DMY13$ = 0, 1947 through 1957

= 1, other years

I_{CPL} = gross private domestic investment in plant, billions of dollars

G_{IC} = government construction, billions of dollars

C_{SR} = personal consumption expenditures for rent, billions of dollars

P_{IBUS} = implicit price deflator for busines gross investment in plant and equipment, 1954 = 1.00

J_{RW_G} = index of average wage of government employees, 1954 = 1.00.

Financial sector

$$\left\{\frac{\Delta DD}{[WLTH]_{-1}}\right\} = -0.01676 - \frac{0.178}{(0.030)}\left\{\frac{[DD]_{-1}}{[WLTH]_{-1}}\right\} - \frac{0.00553}{(0.00147)}RM_{GBL}$$

$$- \frac{0.00372}{(0.00176)}RM_{BDT} - \frac{0.171}{(0.058)}\left\{\frac{I_{BUS}}{[WLTH]_{-1}}\right\} + \frac{0.105}{(0.036)}\left\{\frac{Y_D}{[WLTH]_{-1}}\right\}$$

$$+ \frac{0.047}{(0.022)}\left\{\frac{[Y_D]_{-1}}{[WLTH]_{-2}}\right\} + \frac{0.044}{(0.076)}\left\{\frac{[RE+CCA+T_{GS}]}{[WLTH]_{-1}}\right\}$$

$$- \frac{0.071}{(0.064)}\left\{\frac{[RE+CCA+T_{GS}]_{-1}}{[WLTH]_{-2}}\right\}. \tag{18.36}$$

$$\left\{\frac{\Delta DT}{[WLTH]_{-1}}\right\} = -0.00423 - \frac{0.102}{(0.018)}\left\{\frac{[DT]_{-1}}{[WLTH]_{-1}}\right\} + \frac{0.00582}{(0.00056)}RM_{BDT}$$

$$- \frac{0.00270}{(0.00030)}RM_{GBS3} + \frac{0.026}{(0.007)}\left\{\frac{[Y_D]_{-1}}{[WLTH]_{-2}}\right\} - \frac{0.025}{(0.020)}\left\{\frac{I_{CNFR}+C_D}{[WLTH]_{-1}}\right\}. \tag{13.3}$$

$$\tfrac{1}{4}\{\sum_{i=0}^{3}[RM_{BDT}]_{-i} - \sum_{i=4}^{7}[RM_{BDT}]_{-i}\} = -0.01192 - \frac{0.515}{(0.110)}\{\tfrac{1}{4}\sum_{i=4}^{7}[RM_{BDT}]_{-i}\}$$

$$- \frac{0.493}{(0.085)}\{\tfrac{1}{4}\sum_{i=0}^{3}[RM_{GBL}-RM_{BDTM}+1]_{-i}\}$$

$$+ \frac{0.904}{(0.141)}\{\tfrac{1}{4}\sum_{i=0}^{3}[RM_{GBL}]_{-i}\}. \tag{18.37}$$

$$RES_R = 0.84[RRR_{DD}][DD+DD_{GF}] + 0.82[RRR_{DT}][DT]. \tag{13.16}$$

$$RM_{\text{GBL}} - RM_{\text{GBS3}} = \frac{3.161}{(0.611)} \{RM_{\text{GBL}} - 0.550 \sum_{i=1}^{11} [0.45^{i-1}][RM_{\text{GBL}}]_{-i}\}$$

$$- \frac{4.455}{(0.511)} \{RM_{\text{GBL}} - 0.261 \sum_{i=1}^{11} [0.75^{i-1}][RM_{\text{GBL}}]_{-i}\}$$

$$- \frac{4.8}{(2.6)} \varDelta \left[\frac{BF_1}{BF_{\text{PUB}}} \right] - \frac{7.1}{(3.4)} \varDelta \left[\frac{BF_{1-5}}{BF_{\text{PUB}}} \right] + 1.399. \tag{13.8}$$

New variables in order of appearance are:

DD = private demand deposit liabilities of commercial banks less interbank deposits, cash items in process of collection and Federal Reserve float, average during quarter, billions of dollars

$WLTH$ = weighted average of recent values of GNP, billions of dollars

$$= 0.114 \sum_{i=0}^{19} [0.9]^i [GNP]_{-i}$$

RM_{BDT} = yield on commercial bank time deposits, per cent

RE = undistributed corporate profits, billions of dollars

CCA = capital consumption allowances, billions of dollars

T_{GS} = state and local government receipts, billions of dollars

DT = private time deposit liabilities of commercial banks less time deposits holdings of commercial banks, average during quarter, billions of dollars

RM_{BDTM} = legal maximum rate on time deposits deposited for 6 months or more, per cent

RES_{R} = reserves required of Federal Reserve member banks, average during quarter, billions of dollars

RRR_{DD} = weighted average of required reserve ratios against demand deposits, proportion

DD_{GF} = federal government demand deposits at commercial banks, average during quarter, billions of dollars

RRR_{DT} = average reserve ratio required against time deposits, proportion

BF_1 = U.S. marketable debt maturing within 1 year, average during quarter, billions of dollars

BF_{PUB} = marketable federal debt of all maturities outside of Federal Reserve and U.S. government agencies and trust funds, average during quarter, billions of dollars

BF_{1-5} = U.S. marketable debt of 1- to 5-year maturity, average during quarter, billions of dollars.

Alternative investment functions

$$I^{54}_{\text{BUS}_{MD}} = -0.071 - \frac{0.02609}{(0.0136)} \left[K^{54}_{MD}\right]_{-1} + \frac{0.01153}{(0.00670)} \left[X^{54}_{MD}\right]_{-1}$$

$$+ \frac{0.00948}{(0.00671)} \left[X^{54}_{MD}\right]_{-2} + \frac{0.2434}{(0.125)} \left[RM_{\text{GBL}}\right]_{-1} + \frac{0.02353}{(0.00561)} \left[X^{54}_{MD}\right]_{-5}$$

$$- \frac{0.3732}{(0.111)} \left[RM_{\text{GBL}}\right]_{-5}. \qquad (18.38)$$

$$I^{54}_{\text{BUS}_{MN}} = 0.414 - \frac{0.08977}{(0.0154)} \left[K^{54}_{MN}\right]_{-1} + \frac{0.04209}{(0.0125)} \left[X^{54}_{MN*}\right]_{-1}$$

$$+ \frac{0.02331}{(0.0144)} \left[X^{54}_{MN*}\right]_{-2} - \frac{0.3119}{(0.0736)} \left[RM_{\text{GBL}}\right]_{-1}$$

$$+ \frac{0.06085}{(0.0144)} \left[X^{54}_{MN*}\right]_{-5} + \frac{0.02173}{(0.0149)} \left[X^{54}_{MN*}\right]_{-6} - \frac{0.0637}{(0.0795)} \left[RM_{\text{GBL}}\right]_{-5}.$$

$$\qquad (18.39)$$

$$I^{54}_{\text{BUS}_{R}} = 2.248 - \frac{0.02512}{(0.00950)} \left[K^{54}_{R}\right]_{-1} + \frac{0.01959}{(0.0307)} \left[X^{54}_{R}\right]_{-1}$$

$$+ \frac{0.01896}{(0.0372)} \left[X^{54}_{R}\right]_{-2} + \frac{0.09970}{(0.0790)} \left[RM_{\text{GBL}}\right]_{-1} + \frac{0.00808}{(0.0357)} \left[X^{54}_{R}\right]_{-5}$$

$$+ \frac{0.06269}{(0.0317)} \left[X^{54}_{R}\right]_{-6} - \frac{0.3964}{(0.0801)} \left[RM_{\text{GBL}}\right]_{-5}. \qquad (18.40)$$

$$I^{54}_{\text{BUS}_{O*2}} = 0.073 + \frac{0.03105}{(0.00743)} \left[X^{54}_{O*1}\right]_{-1} + \frac{0.00988}{(0.00815)} \left[X^{54}_{O*1}\right]_{-2}$$

$$- \frac{0.04156}{(0.0105)} \left[K^{54}_{O*2}\right]_{-1} - \frac{0.3299}{(0.0619)} \left[RM_{\text{GBL}}\right]_{-1}. \qquad (18.41)$$

$$I^{54}_{\text{BUS}_{T}} = \left[\frac{I^{54}_{\text{BUS}_{T}}}{I^{54}_{\text{BUS}_{O*2}}}\right]_{-1} \left[I^{54}_{\text{BUS}_{O*2}}\right]. \qquad (18.42)$$

$$I^{54}_{\text{BUS}_{C}} = \left[\frac{I^{54}_{\text{BUS}_{C}}}{I^{54}_{\text{BUS}_{O*2}}}\right]_{-1} \left[I^{54}_{\text{BUS}_{O*2}}\right]. \qquad (18.43)$$

$$I^{54}_{\text{BUS}_{O*5}} = \left[\frac{I^{54}_{\text{BUS}_{O*5}}}{I^{54}_{\text{BUS}_{O*2}}}\right]_{-1} \left[I^{54}_{\text{BUS}_{O*2}}\right]. \qquad (18.44)$$

Identities

Gross national product or expenditures

$$GNP = \sum_k P_k GNP_k^{54} + \varepsilon_1 = [P_C][C^{54}] + [P_{ICNFR}][4I_{CO}^{54} + I_{CNFR}^{54}]$$

$$+ [PM_{AF}][\Delta INV_{AF}^{54} + \Delta INV_{AO}^{54}] + [WPI_{MD}][\Delta INV_{MD}^{54}]$$

$$+ [WPI_{MN*}][\Delta INV_{MN}^{54}]$$

$$+ [PV_T][\Delta INV_{T*}^{54} + \Delta INV_{TRDA}^{54}] + [\alpha P_{IC} + \beta PV_R + \gamma PV_{O*1}][\Delta INV_{O*4}^{54}]$$

$$+ [P_{IBUS}][I_{BUS_{MD}}^{54} + I_{BUS_{MN}}^{54} + I_{BUS_R}^{54} + I_{BUS_{O*2}}^{54} + I_{BUS_A}^{54}]$$

$$+ [P_{EX}][EX^{54}] - [P_M][M^{54}] + [P_G][G^{54}] + \varepsilon_1$$

$$= [PM_{AF}][X_{AF}^{54}] + [WPI_{MD}][X_{MD}^{54}] + [WPI_{MN*}][X_{MN}^{54}] + [PV_T][X_T^{54}]$$

$$+ [PV_R][X_R^{54}] + [P_{IC}][X_C^{54}] + [PV_{O*1}][X_O^{54}] + WSS_G + X_{AO} - SUB$$

$$+ X_W + \varepsilon_2 . \tag{18.45}$$

$$GNP^{54} = \sum_k GNP_k^{54}. \tag{18.46}$$

$$P_{GNP} = \frac{\sum_k P_k GNP_k^{54} + \varepsilon_1}{\sum_k GNP_k^{54}}. \tag{18.47}$$

$$[P_C][C^{54}] = [P_{CDEA}][C_{DEA}^{54}] + [P_{CDA}][C_{DA}^{54}] + [P_{CNF}][C_{NF}^{54} - C_{INF}^{54}]$$

$$+ [P_{CNEF}][C_{NEF}^{54} - C_{INEF}^{54}] + [P_{CS}][C_S^{54} - C_{IS}^{54}] + C_{IS} + C_{INF} + C_{INEF}. \tag{18.48}$$

$$C^{54} = C_{DEA}^{54} + C_{DA}^{54} + C_{NF}^{54} + C_{NEF}^{54} + C_S^{54}. \tag{18.49}$$

$$C_D^{54} = C_{DA}^{54} + C_{DEA}^{54}. \tag{18.50}$$

$$C_S^{54} = [C_S^{54} - C_{IS}^{54}] + \left[\frac{C_{IS}}{P_{CS}}\right]. \tag{18.51}$$

$$C_{NF}^{54} = [C_{NF}^{54} - C_{INF}^{54}] + \left[\frac{C_{INF}}{P_{CNF}}\right]. \tag{18.52}$$

$$C_{NEF}^{54} = [C_{NEF}^{54} - C_{INEF}^{54}] + \left[\frac{C_{INEF}}{P_{CNEF}}\right]. \tag{18.53}$$

$$C_N^{54} = C_{NF}^{54} + C_{NEF}^{54}. \tag{18.54}$$

$$M^{54} = M_{FIN}^{54} + M_{EFIN}^{54}. \tag{18.55}$$

$$GNP^{54} = GNP_{\mathrm{D}}^{54} + GNP_{\mathrm{N}}^{54} + GNP_{\mathrm{S}}^{54} + GNP_{\mathrm{IC}}^{54}. \tag{18.56}$$

$$GNP_{\mathrm{D}}^{54} = C_{\mathrm{D}}^{54} + I_{\mathrm{PDE}}^{54} + \varDelta INV_{\mathrm{D}}^{54} + G_{\mathrm{CD}}^{54} + EX_{\mathrm{D}}^{54} - M_{\mathrm{D}}^{54}. \tag{18.57}$$

$$GNP_{\mathrm{N}}^{54} = C_{\mathrm{N}}^{54} + \varDelta INV_{\mathrm{N}}^{54} + G_{\mathrm{CN}}^{54} + EX_{\mathrm{N}}^{54} - M_{\mathrm{N}}^{54}. \tag{18.58}$$

$$GNP_{\mathrm{S}}^{54} = C_{\mathrm{S}}^{54} + G_{\mathrm{CS}}^{54} + EX_{\mathrm{S}}^{54} - M_{\mathrm{S}}^{54}. \tag{18.59}$$

$$GNP_{\mathrm{IC}}^{54} = I_{\mathrm{CPL}}^{54} + I_{\mathrm{CNFR}}^{54} + 4I_{\mathrm{CO}}^{54} + G_{\mathrm{IC}}^{54}. \tag{18.60}$$

$$I_{\mathrm{BUS}}^{54} = I_{\mathrm{CPL}}^{54} + I_{\mathrm{PDE}}^{54}. \tag{18.61}$$

$$I_{\mathrm{BUS}}^{54} = \sum_j I_{\mathrm{BUS}_j}^{54}. \tag{18.62}$$

Relation of gross national product, national income, personal income and disposable income

$$Y_{\mathrm{N}} = GNP - STAT + SUB - CCA - TX_{GF} - TX_{GS} - V_{\mathrm{BUS}}. \tag{18.63}$$

$$WS_G = WS_{\mathrm{CIV}_{GF}} + WS_{\mathrm{ML}_{GF}} + WS_{\mathrm{ED}_{GS}} + WS_{\mathrm{O}_{GS}} + WS_{GE}. \tag{18.64}$$

$$\begin{aligned}
WSS = &\{[RWSS_C][E_C][H_{\mathrm{P}_C}] + RWSS_{MD}\{[E_{\mathrm{P}_{MD}}][H_{\mathrm{P}_{MD}}] + 40E_{\mathrm{O}_{MD}}\} \\
&+ RWSS_{MN*}\{[E_{\mathrm{P}_{MN*}}][H_{\mathrm{P}_{MN*}}] + 40E_{\mathrm{O}_{MN*}}\} \\
&+ [RWSS_T][E_T][H_{\mathrm{P}_T}]\}52 \times 10^{-3} \\
&+ [RWSS_R][MH_R] + [RWSS_{O*1}][MH_{O*1}] + WSS_A + WSS_{OFR} \\
&+ WSS_{OSH} + WSS_W + WS_G + SUPP_G. \tag{18.65}
\end{aligned}$$

$$Z_{\mathrm{BU}} = Y_{\mathrm{N}} - WSS - Y_{\mathrm{ENT}_{EAF}} - Y_{\mathrm{NET}_{AF}} - Y_{\mathrm{RENT}} - IVAC - INT_{\mathrm{BUS}} + WALD. \tag{18.66}$$

$$Z_{\mathrm{AU}} = Z_{\mathrm{BU}} - TC. \tag{18.67}$$

$$Z_{\mathrm{A}} = Z_{\mathrm{AU}} + IVAC. \tag{18.68}$$

$$RE = Z_{\mathrm{A}} - DIV. \tag{18.69}$$

$$TW = TW_{\mathrm{OA}_{GF}} + TW_{\mathrm{US}_{GF}} + TW_{\mathrm{O}_{GF}} + TW_{GS}. \tag{18.70}$$

$$V_G = V_{\mathrm{OA}_{GF}} + V_{\mathrm{US}_{GF}} + V_{\mathrm{AO}_{GS}} + V_{\mathrm{ADC}_{GS}} + V_{\mathrm{O}_{GF}} + V_{\mathrm{O}_{GS}}. \tag{18.71}$$

$$V = V_G + V_{\mathrm{BUS}}. \tag{18.72}$$

$$Y_{\mathrm{P}} = Y_{\mathrm{N}} - RE - TC - IVAC - TW - WALD + INT_G + V. \tag{18.73}$$

$$TP = TP_{GF} + TP_{Y_{GS}} + TP_{O_{GS}}. \tag{18.74}$$

$$Y_D = Y_P - TP. \tag{18.75}$$

Profits by sector

$$Z_{BU_j} = PV_j X_j^{54} - WSS_j - Y_{ENT_j} - Y_{RENT_j} - IVAC_j - INT_{BUS_j} - CCA_j$$
$$- TX_j - V_{BUS_j}. \tag{18.76}$$

$$Z_{BU} = \sum_j Z_{BU_j} - STAT + Z_{BU_W}. \tag{18.77}$$

$$Z_{AU_j} = Z_{BU_j} - TC_j. \tag{18.78}$$

$$Z_{AU} = \sum_j Z_{AU_j} - STAT + Z_{AU_W}. \tag{18.79}$$

Government receipts and expenditures

$$T = T_{GF} + T_{GS}. \tag{18.80}$$

$$T_{GF} = TP_{GF} + TC_{GF} + TX_{GF} + TW_{OA_{GF}} + TW_{US_{GF}} + TW_{O_{GF}}. \tag{18.81}$$

$$T_{GS} = TP_{Y_{GS}} + TP_{O_{GS}} + TC_{GS} + TX_{PR_{GS}} + TX_{O_{GS}} + TW_{GS} + V_{AID}. \tag{18.82}$$

$$[P_G][G^{54}] = WS_G + SUPP_G + P_{IC_{GS}}[G_{ICED_S}^{54} + G_{ICHI_S}^{54} + G_{ICWA_S}^{54}] + G_O. \tag{18.83}$$

$$G = G_F + G_S. \tag{18.84}$$

$$G_F = WS_{CIV_{GF}} + WS_{ML_{GF}} + G_{IC_F} + G_{O*_F}. \tag{18.85}$$

$$G_S = WS_{ED_{GS}} + WS_{O_{GS}} + G_{O*_S} + G_{IC_S}. \tag{18.86}$$

$$G_{IC_S} = G_{ICED_S} + G_{ICHI_S} + G_{ICWA_S} + G_{ICO*_S}. \tag{18.87}$$

$$G_{IC} = G_{IC_S} + G_{IC_F}. \tag{18.88}$$

$$G = G_{CD} + G_{CN} + G_{CS} + G_{IC}. \tag{18.89}$$

$$DEF_{GF} = T_{GF} - V_{OA_{GF}} - V_{US_{GF}} - V_{O*_{GF}} - V_{FOR_{GF}} - V_{AID} - INT_{GF}$$
$$- SUB_{GF} - G. \tag{18.90}$$

Labor force and unemployment

$$L = L_{F1419} + [L_{F20+}] + L_{M1419} + [L_{M20+}]. \tag{18.91}$$

$$L = L_{UIS} + L_{EUIS}. \tag{18.92}$$

$$U = U_{IS} + U_{EIS}. \tag{18.93}$$

$$U = L - E_{AF} - E_{AO} - E_{MD} - E_{MN*} - E_T - E_R - E_C - E_{O*1} - E_{OSH} - E_{OFR}$$
$$- [E_{ED_{GS}} + E_{O_{GS}} + E_{GES} + E_{CIV_{GF}} + E_{GEF}] - E_W. \tag{18.94}$$

$$U = [U26-] + [U27+]. \tag{18.95}$$

Capital stock

$$K_j^{54} = [K_j^{54}]_{-1} + \tfrac{1}{4}[I_{BUS_j}^{54} - DPNR_j^{54}]. \tag{18.96}$$

$$UKC_j = \alpha_j[RM_{GBL}] + \beta_j[RDR_{K_j}]. \tag{18.97}$$

Miscellaneous

$$ALQD^* = [DD^* + CURR^*] + DT^*. \tag{18.98}$$

$$X_{M*}^{54} = X_{MD}^{54} + X_{MN*}^{54}. \tag{18.99}$$

$$\Delta INV_M^{54} = \Delta INV_{MD}^{54} + \Delta INV_{MN}^{54}. \tag{18.100}$$

New variables in order of appearance are:

P_M = implicit price deflator for imports of goods and services, 1954 = 1.00

WSS = compensation of employees, billions of dollars

SUB = subsidies less current surplus of government enterprises, billions of dollars

X_W = gross product originating in rest-of-the-world sector, billions of dollars

C_N = personal consumption expenditures on nondurable goods, billions of dollars

GNP_S = services component of gross national product, billions of dollars

EX_D = U.S. exports of durable goods, billions of dollars

M_D = U.S. imports of durable goods, billions of dollars

EX_N = U.S. exports of nondurable goods, billions of dollars

M_N = U.S. imports of nondurable goods, billions of dollars

G_{CS} = government purchases of services, billions of dollars

EX_S = U.S. exports of services, billions of dollars

M_S = U.S. imports of services, billions of dollars

Y_N = national income, billions of dollars

$STAT$ = statistical discrepancy, billions of dollars

TX_{GF} = indirect business tax and nontax accruals to the federal government, billions of dollars

TX_{GS} = indirect business tax and nontax accruals to state and local governments, billions of dollars

V_{BUS} = business transfer payments to persons, billions of dollars

$WS_{ML_{GF}}$ = federal government wage and salary disbursements to military persons, billions of dollars

WS_{GE} = wage and salary disbursements to employees of government enterprises, billions of dollars

$SUPP$ = supplements to wages and salaries, billions of dollars

Z_{BU} = corporate profits before taxes and before inventory valuation adjustment, billions of dollars

$Y_{ENT_{EAF}}$ = business and professional proprietors' income, billions of dollars

$Y_{NET_{AF}}$ = net farm income, billions of dollars

Y_{RENT} = rental income of persons, billions of dollars

$IVAC$ = corporate inventory valuation adjustment, billions of dollars

$WALD$ = excess of wage accruals over disbursements, billions of dollars

Z_{AU} = corporate profits after taxes but before inventory valuation adjustment, billions of dollars

Z_A = corporate profits after taxes and after inventory valuation adjustment, billions of dollars

TW = contributions for social insurance, billions of dollars

$TW_{O_{GF}}$ = federal government receipts from contributions for social insurance other than OASI and state unemployment insurance, billions of dollars

TW_{GS} = state and local government receipts from contributions for social insurance, billions of dollars

V_G = government transfer payments to persons, billions of dollars

$V_{O_{GF}}$ = federal government transfer payments to persons other than OASI and state unemployment insurance benefits, billions of dollars

$V_{O_{GS}}$ = state and local government transfer payments to persons other than old age assistance and aid to dependent children, billions of dollars

V = transfer payments to persons, billions of dollars

Y_P = personal income, billions of dollars

TP = personal tax and nontax receipts (or payments), billions of dollars

T = government receipts, billions of dollars

T_{GF} = federal government receipts, billions of dollars

T_{GS} = state and local government receipts, billions of dollars

V_{AID} = federal grants-in-aid to state and local governments, billions of dollars

$P_{\text{IC}_{GS}}$ = implicit price deflator for new construction activity by state and local governments, $1954 = 1.00$

G_O = government purchases of goods and services other than compensation of employees and state and local government construction of educational structures, highways, and sewer and water systems, billions of dollars

G_F = federal government purchases of goods and services, billions of dollars

G_S = state and local government purchases of goods and services, billions of dollars

WS_{GEF} = wage and salary disbursements to employees of federal government enterprises, billions of dollars

G_{IC_F} = new construction activity by the federal government, billions of dollars

G_{O*_F} = federal government purchases of goods and services other than compensation of employees and new construction activity, billions of dollars

WS_{GES} = wage and salary disbursements to employees of state and local government enterprises, billions of dollars

G_{IC_S} = state and local government new construction activity, billions of dollars

G_{O*_S} = state and local government purchases of goods and services other than compensation of employees and new construction activity, billions of dollars

$G_{\text{ICO}*_S}$ = new construction activity by state and local governments other than construction of educational facilities, highways and sewer and water systems, billions of dollars

G_{IC} = new public construction, billions of dollars

DEF_{GF} = federal government deficit or surplus on income and product account, billions of dollars

$V_{\text{FOR}_{GF}}$ = net foreign transfer payments, billions of dollars

L_{EUIS} = labor force not covered by state unemployment insurance, millions of persons

U_{EIS} = unemployed not covered by state unemployment insurance, millions of persons

$E_{CIV_{GF}}$ = civilian employees of federal general government, millions of persons

RDR_K = rate of depreciation of business capital stock, fraction

$ALQD^*$ = holdings of currency and adjusted time and demand deposits, end of quarter, billions of dollars

DD^* = private demand deposit liabilities of commercial banks less interbank deposits, cash items in process of collection and Federal Reserve float, end of quarter, billions of dollars

DT^* = private time deposit liabilities of commercial banks less time deposit holdings of commercial banks, end of quarter, billions of dollars

$CURR^*$ = currency liabilities of the Treasury and Federal Reserve less commercial banks' currency holdings, end of quarter, billions of dollars

18.2. Discussion of the model

The system of equations, when put together in a consistent way as we have done here, comes to more than 150 equations. The exact number is not easy to state because there are many trivial and definitional equations that we refrain from eliminating by substitution, for matters of convenience. That is to say, it is much simpler to use *GNP* for gross national product or Y_D for disposable income in various equations of the system instead of writing out the long chain of plus-minus components that make up these popular aggregative concepts. Many seasonal conversions, depreciation calculations and other equations with simple a priori coefficients are essentially trivial in the econometric sense that they are not inferred from our standard samples of data by the usual estimation techniques. Approximately 150 of our equations are genuinely estimated, and this is why we say, roughly, that our system is of this size.

    In order to achieve consistency, some of the individual sector results given in the supporting chapters by the specialists have been modified to fit into the system as a whole. All the consumption equations were considered as potentially related to disposable income, relative price, real liquid assets, population and lagged consumption. In the final results presented here, some of these variables did not appear to give sensible statistical results and were deleted. In the case of durables, cars and other, we considered asset stocks and consumer attitudes or buying plans as special additional variables. Of these, stocks appear to have some influence on spending in the nonautomotive group, while consumer buying plans and attitudes are statistically significant for car buying. Generally speaking, these are ordinary consumer demand functions, but it is odd that liquid asset and population effects are more discernible in services demand than among other consumption components.

The housing equations are essentially like those presented by Maisel in his chapter, but the estimates are obtained by a consistent method. The equation for marriage rate, needed by Maisel in developing his households variable, is not used here. Instead, we have selected the marriage equation developed by Lebergott in connection with labor supply.

The inventory investment equations are of a modified stock adjustment type. Some price change and unfilled orders variables are included. The unfilled orders variable was found by Lovell in his chapter to be overshadowed in the case of durables by military orders. We have instead used the form with the unfilled orders variable to obtain symmetry in treatment with inventory change for nondurables. The orders equations complete this sector of the model and are used as explained in the chapter on orders.

In the case of capital formation, we have selected the best equation estimates of Eisner and Jorgenson. It is to be noted that their data sources (U.S. Department of Commerce—S.E.C. series on investment and anticipations) did not permit separate estimation of equations for I_{BUS_T}, I_{BUS_C}, and I_{BUS_O}.

Jorgenson's equations could be used, with actual investment as dependent variables, to determine capital formation without using Eisner's realization equations. We have not listed those in this consistent system, but we have included some plausible estimates of linear investment functions of a very ordinary type that could be used in lieu of the Eisner-Jorgenson combination, and these might be fairly reliable for simulation studies.

It should be noted that all the investment functions, those of Eisner and Jorgenson as well as the alternative set, are pure lag relationships; therefore, consistent estimates are obtained directly from the least-squares regressions.

The equations for exports and two types of imports differ from Rhomberg's formulation in that consistent estimates were obtained for the final model and that, after the consistent estimates were computed, Rhomberg redefined his import variables slightly.

The equations associated with the government sector have been condensed from the more elaborate versions given in the chapter by Ando, Brown and Adams. Their equations have not been basically changed, but some poor relationships or pure autoregressions have been replaced by treating the associated dependent variable as exogenous. The large number of excise tax relationships associated with specific commodities (whiskey, tires and tubes, gasoline, motor vehicles, etc.) has been reduced. Similarly, specific items of government expenditures have been classified as exogenous, and equations for them have been dropped.

In the national accounting definitions, there are three types of government accounts. On the expenditure side, there are purchases of goods and services. Reconciling various income and expenditure accounts, we have taxes (direct and indirect) and transfers. The transfers are expenditures but not elements of *GNP*. Transfers are made in large part as payments out of un-employment and retirement accounts. Receipts for these accounts are treated as tax collections.

Our equations first deal with tax collections from persons and business (federal and state and local). Then we have receipts for unemployment and social insurance funds. On the expenditure side, we have transfer payments from these funds and government expenditures. A major expenditure is for wages and salaries of government employees. Others are for school construction, highways and local services (sewer and water). Military expenditures are a major exogenous variable.

The production functions are normalized as labor requirement functions, expressing labor input as a function of output and capital stock. This is the treatment introduced by Kuh and splits the requirements, where possible, into production workers, overhead workers and hours of work. We have not modified the form of his final set of estimates and have also followed his selections for the remaining nonfarm factor shares. From wage equations and the employment-hours equations we can determine labor's factor income. Other factor incomes are interest payments (public and private), rent, inventory valuation adjustment and dividend payments. Profits will be a residual, but corporate profits may be divided between dividends and corpo-rate savings. This is why we need the dividend equation.

Farm income is also a factor payment and is determined in Fox's sector as the difference between farm receipts and expenses. Farm receipts come from food sales and nonfood sales. The latter are sales of feed crops, cotton and similar products. Fox builds a total of food sales from two types—those of crop and those of livestock origin. There may be some inconsistency between the total of these and the food consumption equation of the model in the consumption sector; therefore, we use his equations for food consumption of crop origin with our total food consumption function, implying a residual that will cover consumption of food livestock products. Similarly, we use his marketing margin equation for crop foods and not for livestock foods. An over-all marketing margin for all food crops is implied by our price-conversion equations discussed below.

Through the government price support program, crop prices are determined by government policy. We therefore make these prices exogenous. This is the form in which government policy affects the agricultural sector directly. In the food consumption equation for items of crop origin, quantity is the dependent variable. Price to the farmer is exogenous and marked up through the marketing system according to the equation of spread between farm and retail price.

Farm inventory demand is expressed in a stock adjustment equation like those for nonfarm inventories. Suitable relations for farm investment in buildings and machines are not given. Rather than use Fox's pure autoregressions, we have classified this investment variable as exogenous. We do the same with rent income from farm dwellings.

Depreciation occurs in two forms in our model: as a physical measure for replacement investment and as an accounting measure for completing the national income and product identities. We therefore need two sets of depreciation equations. The physical functions are those of Jorgenson and are the same ones used by him in constructing estimates of capital stock and replacement investment in his demand equations. The other set of equations follows customary business practices in evaluating depreciation by straight-line accounting methods [5]). An average 20-year (80-quarter) lifetime is assumed for capital equipment, and accounting-value capital consumption is made a linear function of the current value of the preceding 80 quarters of gross investment. With changes in U.S. Treasury rules for allowable write-off rates, we found need for dummy variables to change the levels and slopes of these functions.

The accounting measures of depreciation are taken from the U.S. national income accounts and are used essentially to complete identities among elements of these accounts. Since agricultural depreciation is treated only on a replacement cost basis in these accounts, we do not need an equation for agricultural depreciation in accounting prices.

---

[5]) These equations were estimated by Dr. A. Hirsch, formerly of the University of Pennsylvania.

The conversion of prices from sector of production origin to elements of *GNP* final demand requires a set of regressions of estimated final demand, $[I-A]x = f$, on selected elements of *GNP*. In this notation, $[I-A]$ is an input-output matrix $[7 \times 7]$, x is a seven-element vector of gross sector outputs and f is a seven-element vector of estimated final demands. Our final demand regressions of f on elements of *GNP* are built up sequentially so that restrictions on coefficients are met. We first determine coefficients for the trade and regulated sectors to allow for marketing margins. We then fix some coefficients by a restriction on their sum in all the regressions and estimate the remaining ones. At this stage, we found it cumbersome and inconvenient to rely on consistent methods of estimation and simply used least-squares regression coefficients. Having used these biased coefficients and the input-output coefficients to determine the matrix of conversions from PV_{AF}, PV_{MD}, PV_{MN*}, PV_T, PV_R, PV_C, PV_{O*1} to P_{CDEA}, P_{CDA}, P_{CNEF}, P_{CNF}, P_{CS}, P_{IBUS}, P_{ICNFR}, P_{EX}, P_G, we then used consistent methods to improve the correlations between computed values of *GNP* deflators and the observed values.

The financial sector, estimated by de Leeuw, has many equations to deal with several types of financial assets and holders. In the aggregative version of our model, we are concentrating attention on three financial variables: short and long rates of interest and total cash holdings. These three variables can be estimated fairly well from a compact system of four equations and some definitions. De Leeuw's model has been condensed by him, and that is the form we are using here. The short-term rate appears in equations for housing construction demand and government interest income; the long rate is in the investment functions and business interest income equations; and cash balances affect consumer demand. These variables, and others that are necessary, are in de Leeuw's condensed model. His equations show the influence of monetary policy on the money market variables through reserve requirement coefficients, time deposit maximum rates and maturity structure of the public debt.

From Lebergott's several equations, we have selected four covering labor force participation by an exhaustive set of age-sex groups; females 14 to 19 years, females 20 years and over, males 14 to 19 years and males 20 years and over. These participation rate equations all involve indicators of labor market conditions. In some cases, Lebergott obtained reasonable results for a traditional form of labor supply function, dependent on wage rates, but he was suspicious of the structural validity of these equations, and we followed him in not selecting them. His unemployment variable, one of the indicators of labor market conditions, is a measure of long-term unemployment—the number unemployed for twenty-seven weeks or more. The identity relation connecting labor force, employment and unemployment does not give us this particular variable, and our system is not closed in the sense that we do not explain the time duration of unemployment.

Lebergott's equations explain labor force participation but not pure demographic variables, such as population numbers in age-sex classifications. These are exogenous in our model. He does, however, provide us with an equation to explain the number of marriages. This variable is also needed for the housing sector.

The equations for the agricultural sector explain farm prices, partly through direct government support and partly through markup over farm costs. Feed grain costs may also be supported. The remaining prices, by producing sectors, are explained by equations estimated by Schultze and Tryon. These are mainly markup equations over wage and other costs, although some weight is given to inventory positions in the price-determination equations.

The identities or definitional equations are needed to close the system. Many of these are identities from national accounting. Some are stock-flow definitions, and some are clearly statements that a whole is the sum of its component parts. Some simple relations of assumed fixed proportions or assumed exogeneity are also needed in order to tie the system together because of differences in decompositions in different parts of the model or because of the use of specialized variables, e.g., total unemployment, unemployment of 27 weeks or more and unemployment of males between the ages of 20 and 24 years.

In this highly interrelated system, it is not always easy to see what determines what, but it is informative to associate an endogenous variable with each equation of the model. All variables that are not so associated are regarded as exogenous. In some cases, this is nothing more than an assumption of convenience. Tables 18.1, 18.2, and 18.3 present a partial list of endogenous variables (with equation numbers for reference) in the format of the national income accounts. A list of predetermined variables for relationships that were estimated by simultaneous equation techniques are shown in an appendix.

18.2.1. *Some observations in retrospect*

Having progressed through an introduction outlining the philosophy of constructing this model, having studied the sectoral analyses of the

Table 18.1

Gross national product or expenditure.

	Constant 1954 dollars — Equation	Price inflator — Series	Price inflator — Equation	Current dollars — Series	Current dollars — Equation	Current dollars — Remarks
Gross national product	18.46	P_{GNP}	18.47	GNP	18.45	Identity
Personal consumption expenditures	18.49	P_C	18.48	C	18.48	Identity
Automobiles and parts	18.3	P_{CDA}	17.31	C_{DA}	18.48	
Other durable goods	18.1	P_{CDEA}	17.30	C_{DEA}	18.48	
Food excluding imputations	18.4	P_{CNF}	17.33	$[C_{NF}\!-\!C_{INF}]$	18.48	
Imputed				C_{INF}		Missing
Other nondurable goods excluding imputations	18.5	P_{CNEF}	17.32	$[C_{NEF}\!-\!C_{INEF}]$	18.48	
Imputed				C_{INEF}		Missing
Services excluding imputations	18.6	P_{CS}	17.34	$[C_S\!-\!C_{IS}]$	18.48	
Imputed				C_{IS}		Missing
Gross private domestic investment				I		
Nonbusiness construction						
Residential nonfarm	6.10a	P_{ICNFR}	17.36	I_{CNFR}	18.45	
New housing units	6.1			I_{CNFRD*}		
Other residential nonfarm	6.2			I_{CNFRO*}		
Other nonbusiness	6.3	P_{ICNFR}	17.36	I_{CO}	18.45	
Business investment in plant and equipment						
All industries except agriculture, forestry and fisheries	18.45	P_{IBUS}	17.35	I_{BUS}	18.62	Identity
				I_{BUSEA}	18.45	Identity
Durable manufacturing Anticipations	2.3			(IA_{MD})		
Realization	3.8			I_{BUSMD}		
Nondurable manufacturing Anticipations	2.15			(IA_{MN})		
Realization	3.9			I_{BUSMN}		
Regulated industries Anticipations	2.27			(IA_R)		
Realization [a]	3.10			I_{BUSRP}		
Residual industries [b] Anticipations	2.39			(IA_{O*2})		
Realization	3.11			I_{BUSo*2}		
Farm buildings				I_{CPLAF}		Missing
Farm machinery				I_{PDEAF}		Missing
Agricultural services				$I_{\ldots}$		Missing

Description	Eq.	Symbol	Eq.	Symbol	Eq.	Remarks
Changes in business inventories	18.12			ΔINV	18.45	Identity
Nonfarm				ΔINV_{EAF}	18.45	
Durable manufacturing	18.8	WPI_{MD}	9.7	ΔINV_{MD}	18.45	
Nondurable manufacturing	18.9	WPI_{MN*}	9.8	ΔINV_{MN}	18.45	Identity
Wholesale and retail trade		PV_T	9.9	ΔINV_T	18.45	
Excluding retail automotive group	18.10	PV_T	9.9	ΔINV_{T*}	18.45	Missing
Retail automotive group			9.10	ΔINV_{TRDA}		
Residual industries	18.11	PV_{O*4} [c]	9.11, 9.12	ΔINV_{O*4}	18.45	
Farm	12.16	PM_{AF}	12.11	ΔINV_{AF}	18.45	
Agricultural services				ΔINV_{AO}		Exogenous
Net exports of goods and services				$EX-M$		
Exports	11.3	P_{EX}	17.37	EX	18.45	Identity
Imports	18.55	P_M	Exogenous	M	18.45	Identity
Finished goods and services	18.15	PM_{MFIN}	Exogenous	M_{FIN}		
Unfinished goods	18.16	PM_{MEFIN}	Exogenous	M_{EFIN}		
Government purchases of goods and services		P_G	17.38	G	18.84	Identity
Federal				G_F	18.85	Identity
Civilian wages and salaries				$WS_{CIV_{GF}}$	14.39	
Other purchases				G_{O**_F}		Missing and exogenous
State and local				G_S	18.86	Identity
Public education wages and salaries	14.55 ⎫			$WS^A_{ED_{Gs}}$	18.19	
Nonschool wages and salaries	14.58 ⎬ $P_{IC_{Gs}}$		Missing	$WS_{O_{Gs}}$	14.54	
Educational construction	14.60 ⎭			G_{ICED_s} ⎫		
Highway construction				G_{ICHI_s} ⎬	18.83	Identity
Sewer and water construction				G_{ICWA_s} ⎭		
Other purchases				G_{O**_s}		Missing and exogenous

Note   The equations selected for this table are, with few exceptions, of a structural nature; forecasting and purely autoregressive relationships generally have been excluded. Where no equation number is shown, the variable is not endogenously derived in the model. The word "missing" in the remarks column indicates that an endogenous function is contemplated but has as yet not been estimated. Where "missing and exogenous" appears, some components of the variable will be specified exogenously while other components will be estimated endogenously.

a) For public utilities only   b) Industry content differs. See list of symbols   c) Industry content differs. See list of symbols $PV_{O*4} = \alpha P_{IC} + \beta PV_R + \gamma PV_{O*1}$

TABLE 18.2

National income, by type of income.

	Component series	Current dollars		
	Equation	Series	Equation	Remarks
National Income		Y_N	18.63	Identity
Compensation of employees		WSS	18.65	Identity
Private		WSS_{BUS}		
Durable manufacturing:				
$RWSS_{MD}[E_{P_{MD}} \cdot H_{P_{MD}} + 40E_{O_{MD}}] 52 \times 10^{-3}$	8.10, 8.14, 8.18, 9.14	WSS_{MD}	18.65	
Nondurable manufacturing: with integrated petroleum:				
$RWSS_{MN*}[E_{P_{MN*}} \cdot H_{P_{MN*}} + 4OE_{O_{MN*}}] 52 \times 10^{-3}$	8.11, 8.15, 8.19, 9.15	WSS_{MN*}	18.65	
Wholesale and retail trade: $RWSS_T[E_T \cdot H_{P_T}] 52 \times 10^{-3}$	8.13, 18.20	WSS_T	18.65	
Contract construction: $RWSS_C[E_c \cdot H_{P_c}] 52 \times 10^{-3}$	8.12, 8.20, 9.13	WSS_C	18.65	
Regulated industries: $RWSS_R \cdot MH_R$	8.16, 9.17	WSS_R	18.65	
Residual industries: $RWSS_{O*1} \cdot MH_{O*1}$	8.17, 9.18	WSS_{O*1}	18.65	
Agriculture, forestry, fisheries		WSS_A		Missing
Real estate		WSS_{OFR}		Missing from WSS_{O*1}
Household and institutional services		WSS_{OSH}		Missing from WSS_{O*1}
Rest of the world		WSS_W		Missing
Military		$WSS_{ML_{GF}}$		Exogenous
Government civilian		WSS_{CIV_G}		Identity
Wages and salaries		WS_{CIV_G}		

Federal civilian		$WS_{\text{CIV}_{GF}}$	14.39
State and local public education: $[RW_{\text{ED}_{GS}}^{A}]^{\text{a})}$ $[E_{\text{ED}_{GS}}^{A}]$ 14.50 14.51		$WS_{\text{ED}_{GS}}^{A}$	18.19
State and local other		$WS_{\text{O}_{GS}}$	14.54
Other government		WS_{GE}	Missing or exogenous
Supplements to wages and salaries		$SUPP_{\text{CIV}_{G}}$	Missing
Proprietors income		Y_{ENT}	
Business and professional (by industry)		$Y_{\text{ENT}_{EAF}}$	18.25
Farm		$Y_{\text{NET}_{AF}}$	12.18
Rental income of persons		Y_{RENT}	Missing
Corporate profits and inventory valuation adjustment		Z_B	
Profits before tax		Z_{BU}	18.66 Identities (also by industry)
Profits tax liabilities		TC	18.18 Identity
Federal		TC_{GF}	18.17
State and local		TC_{GS}	14.19
Profits after tax		Z_{AU}	18.67 Identities (also by industry)
Dividends		DIV	8.33
Undistributed profits		RE	18.69 Identity
Inventory valuation adjustment		$IVAC$	Included in IVA, 8.26
Net interest		INT_{BUS}	8.23

Note See note on table 18.1.

a) Deflated by consumer price index

TABLE 18.3

Relation of gross national product, national income, personal income, and disposable income.

		Current Dollar		
		Series	Equation	Remarks
Gross national product		GNP	18.45	Identity
Less:	Capital consumption allowances	CCA		Partially missing;
				Depreciation 18.26, 18.27, 18.28
Equals:	Net national product	NNP		
Less:	Indirect business tax and nontax liability	TX		
	Federal	TX_{GF}		Missing
	State and local	TX_{GS}		
	Property taxes	$TX_{PR_{GS}}$	14.21	
	Other liabilities	$TX_{O_{GS}}$	14.20	
	Business transfer payments	V_{BUS}		Exogenous
	Statistical discrepancy	$STAT$		Missing and exogenous
Plus:	Subsidies minus current surplus of government enterprises	SUB		Exogenous
Equals:	National income	Y_N	18.63	Identity
Less:	Undistributed corporate profits	RE	18.69	Identity
	Corporate profits tax liability	TC	18.18	Identity
	Federal	TC_{GF}	18.17	
	State and local	TC		

733

Corporate inventory valuation adjustment	$IVAC$		Included in IVA, 8.26
	TW	18.70	Identity
Contributions for social insurance			
Old-age and survivors insurance	$TW_{OA_{GF}}$	14.12	
State unemployment insurance (employers contributions only)	$TW_{US_{GF}}$	14.13	
Other payments	TW_{O_G}		Missing and exogenous
Excess of wage accruals over disbursements	$WALD$		Zero or exogneous
Plus: Net interest paid by government	INT_G	8.22	
	V_G	18.71	Identity
Government transfer payments to persons			
Old-age and survivors insurance benefits	$V_{OA_{GF}}$	14.24	
State unemployment insurance benefits	$V_{US_{GF}}$	14.30	
Old age assistance	$V_{AO_{GS}}$	14.32	
Aid to dependent children	$V_{ADC_{GS}}$	14.33	
Other payments	V_{O_G}		Missing and exogenous
Business transfer payments	V_{BUS}		Exogenous
Equals: Personal income	Y_P	18.73	Identity
Less: Personal tax and nontax payments	TP	18.74	Identity
Federal	TP_{GF}	14.2	
State and local	TP_{GS}		
Income taxes	$TP_{Y_{GS}}$	14.17	
Other payments	$TP_{O_{GS}}$		Missing
Equals: Disposable personal income	Y_D	18.75	Identity

Note   See note on table 18.1.

various contributors, and having examined the composite equation system, it should be clear to the reader that the task of building a large-scale, quarterly econometric model of the U.S. economy has only begun. Although the present model is significantly more advanced than its predecessors—in size, detail and finesse—some of its equation specifications need improvement, its internal compatibility between and within sectors is imperfect, and its statistical performance is unknown. These difficulties are recognized and their correction has already begun. However, to assist potential users of the present version of the model, an indication of some of the most important incompatibilities will be given.

It was Emerson who noted that "a foolish consistency is the hobgoblin of little minds". Certainly this is true for structural specifications for particular sectors. On the other hand, a complete system model without internal consistency in its definition of variables and sectors is of little use. It is apparent that the comparative isolation of the individual specialists has resulted in a sizable number of incompatibilities and gaps that remain to be closed. Tables 18.1, 18.2 and 18.3 illustrate these difficulties.

The components of gross national product, as derived in the model, are shown in table 18.1. It can readily be seen that functions for imputed consumption services, the agricultural services industry's investment, and inventory investment for the retail automotive group, agricultural services, and a part of the residual industry are missing. Also, the production sector definitions of the business investment anticipations and realizations functions are incompatible with one another. The regulated sector for anticipations includes the railroad, non-rail transportation, communications and public utility industries; for realizations in this sector, only public utilities are included. Moreover, rail and non-rail transportation and mining investment expenditures are missing from the realizations functions altogether, thus causing an understatement of *GNP*. It might also be noted that the industry investment data are drawn from the quarterly Department of Commerce, Office of Business Economics (OBE) anticipations surveys, and therefore do not reconcile, when summed, with the total expenditure figures used in the *GNP* accounts estimated from sales of producers' durable equipment and construction outlays.

Another set of incompatibilities arises between a number of the constant dollar series and their price deflators. The implicit price for nonfarm residential construction is a poor deflator for other private nonresidential building, especially since OBE deflates the current dollar series separately and the price deflators exhibit disparate trends.

More seriously, the inventory inflators largely are inappropriate. Any current period final price is a biased deflator for work-in-process inventories. This poses a particular problem for durable manufacturing where the production lead times are long and the only endogenously generated price is a wholesale price index (*WPI*) for current period sales and contracts. The inflator for nondurable manufacturing is also affected by this consideration. Moreover, the industry definition of the endogenous price variable for this sector differs from that for inventory change. A similar discrepancy exists in the trade area.

Depending upon whether corporate profits are estimated in the aggregate or by production sector, price inflation difficulties may also plague the items of tables 18.2 and 18.3. If the latter technique is employed (cf. identities 18.76–18.79), then profits will probably be biased downwards. This arises from the use of market rather than value added prices. For example, in the manufacturing sector, wholesale prices are not output originating prices. The former prices overstate the latter in absolute form; however, on an index basis, there is no a priori basis for stating whether the bias is negative or positive. Nevertheless, a comparison of Marimont's implicit price deflator for total manufacturing output originating with the *WPI* for all commodities other than farm products indicates that the bias is probably negative and not insignificant [6]). With 1954 = 100, the Marimont index was 114.5 for 1960 manufacturing output and the *WPI* for all commodities other than farm products was 110.6 (this index is analogous to the production sector price series generated in chapter 9). Thus, the understatement in current dollar *GNP* (and profits) by sector originating would have been $ 4.8 billion from this source. [7]) Obviously, since price indexes for the cost of purchased inputs are not explicitly determined, value added price indexes are preferred to market price indexes for the purpose of sector profits estimation in the present model.

At present, too, the endogenous determination of sector profits is hampered by the absence of functions for a number of appropriate variables (rental income, business transfers, entrepreneurial income, and capital

---

[6]) Martin L. Marimont, *GNP* by Major Industries: Comparative Patterns of Postwar Growth, *Survey of Current Business*, (October, 1962), p. 16; and *GNP* by Major Industries, 1958–1962-Revised and Updated, *Survey of Current Business*, (September, 1963), p. 10. The *WPI* for all commodities other than farm products was derived by weighting the *WPI* for all commodities other than farm products and foods and the *WPI* for processed foods by 1958 weights.

[7]) $ 122.0 (114.5–110.6)/100 = $ 4.8 billion.

consumption allowances) and the unavailability of quarterly data for the majority of each sector's value added components. Although dummy series may be employed to interpolate the annual statistics, the equations derived from these data may introduce bias and inconsistency (because of nonlinearities) in complete model simulations. The probability of this outcome might also be heightened by missing structural relationships (only a few of which are listed in the preceding tables) for other endogenous variables.

It is evident, given the problems just mentioned, and others that might be cited, that we do not view the present model as a finished product. Truly, although significant advances have been achieved, we have only completed the preliminary phases of constructing a large-scale quarterly model of the economy that accurately reflects its true structure and is useful for forecasting purposes, for the evaluation of government policy alternatives, and for the examination of cycle and growth theories. Our continuing efforts are dedicated toward achieving that goal.

18.3. Appendix: preliminary estimation and predetermined variables

Most of the equations listed in this chapter were estimated by the methods of limited-information maximum likelihood or two-stage least squares, i.e., consistently in the statistical sense. Those equations that contained only one unlagged endogenous variable, with all others being predetermined, were estimated as ordinary least-squares regressions (single stage).

The limited-information or two-state estimates for each equation required the use of predetermined variables from other equations in the system in the first stage of estimation. Considering all the lagged variables in the system, we would have had more predetermined variables to use for each first-stage regression than there were degrees of freedom available. There appear to be many exogenous variables, but several are closely related to one another. We have actually gone so far in expanding the scope of endogenous explanation within this system that there are not many important, mutually independent and genuinely exogenous variables. Our problem has been to find a good number of exogenous variables outside the equation being estimated and a limited number of lagged variables. In choosing the lagged variables we have grouped the equations according to the block-recursive layouts discussed by Fisher and have tried to follow his general criteria for choosing lagged or other predetermined variables from equations in blocks of a lower order in the recursive scheme.

For all equations in the system, exogenous variables from government (expenditures, tax rates, subsidies, debt, monetary control) and the external world were used in the first-stage regressions.

Consumption and foreign trade were estimated in a single block together. This required the use of all the predetermined variables actually appearing in the two groups of equations to be estimated and, in addition:

RRR_{DD} = weighted average of required reserve ratios against demand deposits

RRR_{DT} = average reserve ratio required against time deposits

RM_{BDTM} = legal maximum rate on time deposits deposited for six months or more

BF = total federal government debt

CCC = net outlays by the Commodity Credit Corporation for price support programs

BGT_{GF} = federal government budget

$G_{ML_F}^{54}$ = federal government purchases of goods and services for national defense

$R_{PY1_{GF}}$ = starting federal tax rate on wages and salaries

$\left\{\dfrac{WPI-[WPI]_{-1}}{[WPI]_{-1}}\right\}_{-1}$ = lagged proportionate change in wholesale price index

HU_{REM} = net removals of housing units.

The housing equations were estimated in a separate block which made use of all the predetermined variables appearing in this group of equations and some of those appearing in the preceding group on consumption and foreign trade. Variables used which have already been defined are: RRR_{DD}, RRR_{DT}, RM_{BDTM}, BF, CCC, BGT_{GF}, $R_{PY1_{GF}}$, $\{(WPI-[WPI]_{-1})/([WPI]_{-1}\}_{-1})$. Other variables used are:

ATT = index of consumer attitudes and inclinations to buy

$\left[\dfrac{ALQD^*}{P_C}\right]_{-1}$ = lagged beginning-of-quarter holdings of currency and adjusted time and demand deposits deflated by implicit price deflator for personal consumption expenditures.

The external predetermined variables used in estimating the inventory-orders block of equations were ATT, $\{ALQD^*/P_C\}_{-1}$, RRR_{DD}, RRR_{DT}, RM_{BDTM}, BF, BGT_{GF}, $R_{PY1_{GF}}$, $\{(WPI-[WPI]_{-1})/([WPI]_{-1}\}_{-1})$, HU_{REM}, as defined above, and

$N+N_{ML}$ = population, including Alaska and Hawaii and armed forces overseas.

For the price autoregressions, we used RRR_{DD}, RRR_{DT}, BF, CCC, BGT_{GF}, $R_{PY1_{GF}}$, $N+N_{ML}$, ATT, HU_{REM}, $G^{54}_{ML_F}$ and

PM_{MEFIN} = unit value index of imports of semimanufactures, crude materials and crude foodstuffs

EX^{54}_W = world exports including U.S. exports.

In the financial sector equations, the predetermined variables used, in addition to those already in the equations, were $N+N_{ML}$, $G^{54}_{ML_F}$, and RM_{FRB} = Federal Reserve Bank of New York discount rate.

$\dfrac{RES_{NB}}{[0.7RRR_{DD}+0.3RRR_{DT}]} + CURR$ = unborrowed reserves of Federal Reserve member banks divided by weighted required reserve ratio plus currency

$\left\{ \dfrac{RES_{NB}}{[0.7RRR_{DD}+0.3RRR_{DT}]} + CURR \right\}_{-1}$ = lagged value of preceding variable

$[K^{54}]_{-1} + \sum\limits_{i=1}^{\infty} \Delta INV^{54}_{-i}$ = beginning-of-quarter stock of fixed capital and inventories

$[O^{54}_{MD}]_{-1}$ = lagged value of durable goods manufacturers' net new orders

$[GNP^{54}]_{-1}$ = lagged value of GNP.

KEY TO ABBREVIATIONS

Brookings econometric model

List of variables, symbols and definitions

Unless otherwise indicated by superscripts or their definitions, all monetary variables are in billions of current dollars, seasonally adjusted. Monetary flow variables are at annual rates; stock variables are end-of-period. Lags or leads in variables are indicated by the general subscript i or plus or minus numbers; e.g., a lag of one period is $t-i$ with $i = 1$, or simply (without t) -1. The subscript j indicates a variable is by production sector. The subscript k indicates a *GNP* component.

Superscripts

47–9	= constant 1947–1949 dollars
53	= constant 1953 dollars
54	= constant 1954 dollars
57–9	= constant 1957–1959 dollars
A	= annual data
E	= equilibrium level
FY	= fiscal year
N	= "normal" value of the variable as defined in each instance
NS	= not adjusted for seasonal variation
PRO	= "projections" value of the variable as defined in each instance
Q1, Q2, etc.	= first quarter, etc.
T	= trend value of the variable.

Subscripts   Subscripts are defined with the variables to which they apply.

Sector subscripts   These refer only to producing sectors and government. At the two-digit manufacturing level and higher degrees of disaggregation,

1957 Standard Industrial Classifications numbers are used, and the SIC's
which appear in this volume are given below. For levels below or other
than the two-digit manufacturing level, subscripts are as follows:

A	= agriculture, forestry and fisheries
AF	= farming
AO	= agriculture, forestry and fisheries except farming
C	= contract construction
EA	= all private industries except agriculture, forestry and fisheries
EAF	= nonfarm business
F	= federal government (used only as subscript for government expenditure variables)
G	= government and government enterprises
GE	= government enterprises
GEF	= federal government enterprises
GES	= state and local government enterprises
GF	= federal government
GS	= state and local governments
M	= manufacturing
M^*	= manufacturing plus mining of crude petroleum and natural gas
MD	= durable manufacturing
MN	= nondurable manufacturing
MN^*	= nondurable manufacturing plus mining of crude petroleum and natural gas
O	= residual industries: mining, finance, insurance, and real estate and all services
O^*1	= residual industries O excluding: mining of crude petroleum and natural gas, real estate, and household and institutional services
O^*2	= trade and contract construction plus residual industries O excluding: banking, insurance carriers, real estate, medical services, legal services, and household and institutional services
O^*3	= residual industries O^*2 plus communications less mining
O^*4	= residual industries O plus contract construction and regulated industries
O^*5	= residual industries O^*2 less trade and contract construction
OFO	= finance and insurance
OFR	= real estate
OM	= mining
OM^*	= mining except crude petroleum and natural gas

OS	=	services
OSH	=	household and institutional services
OSO	=	services other than household and institutional
P	=	private
R	=	regulated industries: transportation, communications and public utilities
RC	=	communications
RP	=	public utilities
RT	=	transportation industry
RTN	=	nonrail transportation
RTR	=	railroad transportation
S	=	state and local governments (used only as a subscript for government expenditure variables)
T	=	wholesale and retail trade
T*	=	wholesale and retail trade excluding the retail automotive group
TR	=	retail trade
TR*	=	retail trade excluding the retail automotive group
TRD*	=	durable goods retail stores excluding the retail automotive group
TRDA	=	automotive group of retail trade
TRN	=	nondurable goods retail stores
TW	=	wholesale trade
W	=	rest of the world

SIC numbers

13	=	mining crude petroleum and natural gas
19	=	ordnance and accessories
21	=	tobacco manufactures
24	=	lumber and wood products, except furniture
25	=	furniture and fixtures
26	=	paper and allied products
27	=	printing, publishing, and allied industries
28	=	chemicals and allied products
29	=	petroleum refining and related industries
30	=	rubber and miscellaneous plastics products
31	=	leather and leather products
32	=	stone, clay, and glass products
325	=	structural clay products
33	=	primary metal industries

34	= fabricated metal products, except ordnance, machinery, and transportation equipment
35	≐ machinery, except electrical
36	= electrical machinery, equipment, and supplies
37	= transportation equipment
371	= motor vehicles and motor vehicle equipment
3711	= motor vehicles
38	= professional, scientific, and controlling instruments; photographic and optical goods; watches and clocks
39	= miscellaneous manufacturing industries
491	= electric companies and systems
531	= department stores

AGE_{CDA}	= average age of cars scrapped, quarters of years
$ALNPS_B$	= commercial bank holdings of loans and other private securities, average during quarter, billions of dollars
$ALQD^*$	= holdings of currency and adjusted time and demand deposits, end-of-quarter, billions of dollars
$ALQD_{HH}$	= stock of liquid assets held by households: currency, demand deposits, and fixed-value redeemable claims, end of quarter, billions of dollars
APS_{NBF}	= nonbank finance holdings of private securities, average during quarter, billions of dollars
ATT	= index of consumer attitudes and inclinations to buy, 1954 = 100
$BBUS_F$	= business debt to financial institutions, average during quarter, billions of dollars
$BEDSN$	= additional beds needed in state general, tubercular, and mental hospitals as of January 1, thousands
$BEER$	= taxable withdrawals of beer, thousands of barrels
BF	= total federal government debt, billions of dollars
BF_1	= U.S. marketable debt maturing within 1 year, average during quarter, billions of dollars
BF_{1-5}	= U.S. marketable debt of 1 to 5 year maturity, average during quarter, billions of dollars
BF_B	= commercial bank holdings of U.S. securities, average during quarter, billions of dollars
BF_{DH}	= federal government debt domestically held outside of federal

agencies and trust funds, average during quarter, billions of dollars

BF_{NBF} = nonbank finance holdings of U.S. securities, average during quarter, billions of dollars

BF_{ONF} = holdings of U.S. securities by corporations, state and local governments, and finance not elsewhere classified, average during quarter, billions of dollars

BF_{P} = consumer and nonprofit holdings of U.S. securities, average during quarter, billions of dollars

BF_{PUB} = marketable federal debt of all maturities outside Federal Reserve and U.S. government agencies and trust funds, average during quarter, billions of dollars

$BFOR$ = foreign borrowings, average during quarter, billions of dollars

$BGT_{\text{AG}}^{\text{FY}}$ = agriculture and agricultural resources expenditures during fiscal year t estimated in the President's budget submission of January, year t, millions of dollars

$BGT_{\text{ML}}^{\text{FY}}$ = national defense expenditures during fiscal year t estimated in the President's budget submission of January, year t, millions of dollars

$BGTR_{\text{AG}}^{\text{FY}}$ = agriculture and agricultural resources expenditures requested for fiscal year $t+1$ as estimated in the President's budget submission of January, year t, millions of dollars

$BGTR_{\text{ML}}^{\text{FY}}$ = national defense expenditures requested for fiscal year $t+1$ as estimated in the President's budget submission of January, year t, millions of dollars

BHH_{F} = household debt to financial institutions, average during quarter, billions of dollars

$BNBF$ = savings and insurance claims, average during quarter, billions of dollars

C = personal consumption expenditures, including imputations, billions of dollars

C_{D} = personal consumption expenditures on durable goods, billions of dollars

C_{DA} = personal consumption expenditures for new and net used automobiles and parts, billions of dollars

C_{DEA} = personal consumption expenditures for durable goods other than new and net used automobiles and parts, billions of dollars

C_{INEF} = personal consumption expenditures for nondurable goods other than food, imputed or in kind, billions of dollars

C_{INF} = personal consumption expenditures for food, imputed or in kind, billions of dollars

C_{IS} = personal consumption expenditures for services, imputed, billions of dollars

C_N = personal consumption expenditures on nondurable goods, billions of dollars

C_{NEF} = personal consumption expenditures for nondurable goods other than food, including imputations, billions of dollars

C_{NF} = personal consumption expenditures for food, including imputations, billions of dollars

C_S = personal consumption expenditures for services including imputations, billions of dollars

C_{SR} = personal consumption expenditures for rent, billions of dollars

CAR_{REG} = stock of automobiles registered, end of quarter, millions

$CARS$ = end-of-quarter stock of new cars and new car equivalents of used cars, millions

CCA = capital consumption allowances, billions of dollars

$CCAC$ = corporate capital consumption allowances, billions of dollars

CCC^A = annual net outlays by the Commodity Credit Corporation for supporting prices of major crops and dairy products, billions of dollars

$CDTE_P$ = consumer credit extensions, billions of dollars

CPI = consumer price index, 1954 = 1.00

CPI_{DEA} = durable-commodities-less-automobiles component of consumer price index, 1954 = 1.00

CPI_N = nondurable-commodities component of consumer price index, 1954 = 1.00

CPI_{SR} = rent component of consumer price index, 1947–1949 = 100

$CURR$ = currency liabilities of the Treasury and Federal Reserve, less commercial banks' currency holdings, average during quarter, billions of dollars

$CURR^*$ = currency liabilities of the Treasury and Federal Reserve, less commercial banks' currency holdings, end of quarter, billions of dollars

DD = private demand deposit liabilities of commercial banks less interbank deposits, cash items in process of collection, and

	Federal Reserve float, average during quarter, billions of dollars
DD^*	= private demand deposit liabilities of commercial banks less interbank deposits, cash items in process of collection, and Federal Reserve float, end of quarter, billions of dollars
DD_{GF}	= federal government demand deposits at commercial banks, average during quarter, billions of dollars
DEF_{GF}	= federal government deficit or surplus on income and product account, billions of dollars
DIV	= dividends, billions of dollars
$DMY1$	= 1, 1950 : 3 through 1951 : 2
	= 0, all other quarters
$DMY2$	= 1, 1949 : 1
	= 0, elsewhere
$DMY3$	= 1, 1951 : 1
	= 0, elsewhere
$DMY4$	= 0, through 1955 : 3
	= 1, thereafter
$DMY5$	= 0, through 1958 : 1
	= 1, thereafter
$DMY6$	= 0, through 1957 : 4
	= 1, thereafter
$DMY7$	= 0, through 1948 : 3
	= 1, thereafter
$DMY8$	= 0, through 1952 : 3
	= 1, thereafter
$DMY9$	= 0, through 1956 : 4
	= 1, thereafter
$DMY10$	= 0, through 1958 : 3
	= 1, thereafter
$DMY11$	= 0, through 1950 : 3
	= 1, thereafter
$DMY12$	= 1, 1953 through 1955
	= 0, other years
$DMY13$	= 0, 1947 through 1957
	= 1, other years
$DMY14$	= 0, 1948 : 1 through 1955 : 1
	= 1, thereafter
$DMY15$	= converter from quarterly rate current level expenditures on

residential construction to *GNP* expenditures on residential construction at annual rate

$DMY16$ = 1, 1947 : 1 through 1948 : 3

           = 1, 1950 : 3 through 1952 : 4

           = 0, all other quarters

$DMY17$ = 1, in 1949 : 3 through 1950 : 1

           = 0, all other quarters

$DMY18^{A}$ = 1, in 1948, 1951, and 1952

           = 0, all other years

DOD_{OBE} = Department of Defense obligations, billions of dollars

DPN = depreciation in accounting prices, billions of dollars

$DPNR$ = replacement cost depreciation, billions of dollars

$DPNR^{*}_{AF}$ = adjusted replacement-cost depreciation of farm capital, billions of dollars

$DRFT$ = U.S. armed forces military personnel procurement, millions of persons

DT = private time deposit liabilities of commercial banks less time deposit holdings of commercial banks, average during quarter, billions of dollars

DT^{*} = private time deposit liabilities of commercial banks less time deposit holdings of commercial banks, end of quarter, billions of dollars

DW = *Durbin* = *Watson* statistic

E = employment, millions of persons

E_{AF}^{T} = trend of employment in agriculture, thousands of persons

E_{65+} = employed persons aged 65 and over, millions

$E_{CIV_{GF}}$ = civilian employees of the federal general government, millions of persons

$E_{ED_{GS}}$ = full-time equivalent employees in state and local public education, millions of persons

$E_{F15_{AF}}$ = unpaid females employed 15 or more hours per week in farming, millions of persons

E_{O} = employment of overhead workers, millions

$E_{O_{GS}}$ = full-time equivalent employees, state and local nonschool except work relief and enterprises, millions

E_{P} = employment of production workers, millions

$E_{XEC_{GF}}$ = employees in the executive branch of the federal government excluding government enterprises, thousands

EX = U.S. exports of goods and services, billions of dollars

EX_D	= U.S. exports of durable goods, billions of dollars
EX_N	= U.S. exports of nondurable goods, billions of dollars
EX_S	= U.S. exports of services, billions of dollars
EX_W	= world exports excluding U.S. exports, billions of dollars
F^A	= estimated annual final demand, billions of dollars
$FHLB$	= Federal Home Loan Bank Board's advances to savings and loan associations, average during quarter, billions of dollars
G	= government purchases of goods and services, billions of dollars
G_F	= federal government purchases of goods and services, billions of dollars
G_S	= state and local government purchases of goods and services, billions of dollars
G_{CD}	= government purchases of durable goods, billions of dollars
G_{CN}	= government purchases of nondurable goods, billions of dollars
G_{CS}	= government purchases of services, billions of dollars
G_{IC}	= new public construction, billions of dollars
G_{IC_F}	= new construction activity by the federal government, billions of dollars
G_{IC_S}	= state and local government new construction activity, billions of dollars
G_{ICAD_S}	= construction of administrative and service facilities by state and local governments, billions of dollars
G_{ICED_S}	= new educational construction activity by state and local governments, billions of dollars
G_{ICHI_S}	= new highway construction activity by state and local governments, billions of dollars
G_{ICHO_S}	= new hospital and institutional construction activity by state and local governments, billions of dollars
G_{ICMI_F}	= new military and industrial construction activity by the federal government, millions of dollars
G_{ICO_F}	= new construction activity by the federal government other than military and industrial and conservation and development, millions of dollars
G_{ICO_S}	= new nonresidential construction activity by state and local governments, other than for educational structures, hospitals, administrative and service facilities, highways, and sewer and water systems, billions of dollars

$G_{ICO^*_S}$ = new construction activity by state and local governments other than construction of educational facilities, highways, and sewer and water systems, billions of dollars

G_{ICWA_S} = new construction activitity by state and local governments for sewer and water systems, billions of dollars

G_{ML_F} = federal government purchases of goods and services for national defense, billions of dollars

G_{MLDV_F} = Department of Defense net expenditures for development, procurement, research, test and evaluation, billions of dollars

G_O = government purchases of goods and services other than compensation of employees and state and local government construction of educational structures, highways, and sewer and water systems, billions of dollars

G_{O_F} = purchases of goods and services by the federal government other than construction expenditures and civilian wage and salary disbursements, billions of dollars

$G_{O^*_F}$ = federal government purchases of goods and services other than compensation of employees and new construction activity, billions of dollars

$G_{O^{**}_F}$ = federal government purchases of goods and services other than wage and salary disbursements to civilian employees of general government, billions of dollars

G_{O_S} = purchases of goods and services by state and local governments except wage and salary disbursements and non-residential construction expenditures, billions of dollars

$G_{O^*_S}$ = state and local government purchases of goods and services other than compensation of employees and new construction activity, billions of dollars

$G_{O^{**}_S}$ = state and local government purchases of goods and services other than wage and salary disbursements to employees of general government and construction of educational facilities, highways, and sewer and water systems, billions of dollars

GNP = gross national product, billions of dollars

GNP_D = durable goods component of gross national product, billions of dollars

GNP_{IC} = construction component of gross national product, billions of dollars

GNP_N = nondurable goods component of gross national product, billions of dollars

GNP_S = services component of gross national product, billions of dollars

$GOLD$ = Treasury gold stock, average during quarter, billions of dollars

H = average workweek, hours

H_P = average workweek of production workers, hours

HH = number of households, thousands

HHE = expected households based on population cohorts, thousands

HU_{AVL} = total available housing units, thousands

HU_{FIN} = housing units completed, thousands

HU_{REM} = net removals of housing units, thousands

HU_{STS} = number of private housing units started, thousands

HU_{STS}^M = number of multi-family private housing units started, thousands

HU_{STS}^S = number of single-family private housing units started, thousands

HU_{UC} = stock of housing units under construction, thousands

HU_{VAC} = vacant available housing units, thousands

HU_{VAC*} = adjusted vacant available housing units, thousands

$HWYL$ = length of surfaced highways, including Alaskan and Hawaiian, millions of miles

I = gross private domestic investment, billions of dollars

I_{BUS} = business gross investment in plant and equipment, billions of dollars

I_C = new construction component of gross private domestic investment, billions of dollars

I_{CNFR} = *GNP* expenditures on nonfarm residential construction, billions of dollars

I_{CNFR*} = current level expenditures on nonfarm residential construction, quarterly rate, billions of dollars

I_{CNFRD*} = current level expenditures on new, nonfarm dwelling units, quarterly rate, billions of dollars

I_{CNFRO*} = current level expenditures on residential, nonfarm construction other than new dwelling units, quarterly rate, billions of dollars

I_{CO} = private nonresidential, nonbusiness construction, quarterly rate, billions of dollars

I_{CO*} = petroleum and natural gas well drilling component of new construction activity, billions of dollars

I_{CPL} = gross private domestic investment in plant, billions of dollars

I_{PDE} = gross private domestic investment in producers' durable equipment, billions of dollars

IA = current anticipated investment expenditures reported by business in the prior quarter, billions of dollars

$IA1$ = current anticipated investment expenditures reported by business in the current quarter, billions of dollars

INT_G = personal interest income paid by government, billions of dollars

INT_{BUS} = personal interest income paid by business, billions of dollars

INV = business inventory stock, billions of dollars

INV_{AF} = farm inventory stock (commodities pledged as collateral for CCC loans are excluded), billions of dollars

INV_{AF}^* = adjusted farm business inventory stock, billions of dollars

$INV_{\text{COW}}^{\text{A}}$ = farm inventory stock of cattle and hogs on January 1, billions of dollars

INV_{D} = inventory stock of durable goods, billions of dollars

INV_{N} = inventory stock of nondurable goods, billions of dollars

$\left[\dfrac{INV}{X}\right]^{\text{T}}$ = trend of ratio of inventory stock to gross product originating, fraction

IP_{CO} = value of building permits for private, nonresidential, nonbusiness construction, quarterly rate, billions of dollars

IVA = inventory valuation adjustment, billions of dollars

$IVAC$ = corporate inventory valuation adjustment, billions of dollars

J_{BASE} = index of tax bases to which RX_{GS} applies

$J_{\text{DUCR}}^{\text{A}}$ = index of total annual domestic utilization of farm crops (a subaggregate of an index in which the average annual utilization of all U.S. farm products for all purposes, domestic and foreign, 1947–1949 = 100)

J_{FAN} = index of total consumption of food livestock products ($J_{\text{FAN/N}}$ multiplied by total U.S. population in millions of persons)

$J_{\text{FAN/N}}$ = index of per capita consumption of food livestock products, 1947–1949 = 100

$J_{\text{FCR/N}}$ = index of per capita consumption of food crop products, 1947–1949 = 100

$J_{\text{FCR/N}}^*$ = adjusted index of per capita consumption of food crop products, 1947–1949 = 100

J_{HP} = index of hours worked by production workers, 1954 = 1.00

J_{OAMAX} = index of maximum OASI-taxable earnings per employee, 1947–1949 = 1.00

$J_{Q_{AF}}$ = index of volume of farm marketings plus farm consumption of home-grown food and fuel, 1947–1949 = 108.7 (marketing component = 100.0, farm consumption component = 8.7)

$J_{\mathrm{QAN}_{AF}}$ = index of physical volume of farm home consumption plus marketings of livestock, 1947–1949 = 110.5 (marketing component = 100, farm consumption component = 10.5)

$J_{\mathrm{QCR}_{AF}}^{\mathrm{A}}$ = index of the volume of output of all farm crops, 1947–1949 = 100

J_{RW_G} = index of average wage of government employees, 1954 = 1.00

K = stock of business capital, billions of dollars

K_{CD} = stock of consumer durable goods measured at original cost, billions of dollars

K_{CDEA} = stock of consumer durable goods excluding automobiles and parts, billions of dollars

$K_{\mathrm{ED}_{GS}}$ = stock of capital in state and local educational structures, billions of dollars

$K_{\mathrm{HO}_{GS}}$ = stock of state and local hospital assets, billions of dollars

K_{PDE} = stock of producers' durable equipment, billions of dollars

K_{PL} = stock of plant, billions of dollars

$KGAIN$ = realized capital gains, billions of dollars

KU_{FR_M} = manufacturing output as a per cent of capacity (de Leeuw)

KU_{MH_M} = per cent of capacity output utilized in manufacturing (Mc-Graw-Hill)

L = civilian labor force, millions of persons

L_{65+} = labor force aged 65 and over (62 and over for females since 1956), millions of persons

L_{EUIS} = labor force not covered by state unemployment insurance, millions of dollars

$L_{\mathrm{F14}+}$ = female civilian labor force aged 14 and over, millions of persons

L_{F1419} = female civilian labor force aged 14 through 19, millions of persons

$L_{\mathrm{F20}+}$ = female civilian labor force aged 20 and over, millions of persons

$[L_{\mathrm{F20}+}]^{\mathrm{PRO}}$ = John Durand's projection of female labor force aged 20 and over, millions of persons

$[L_{F20+}]^T$ = trend of female labor force aged 20 and over, millions of persons

L_{F65+} = female labor force aged 65 and over (62 and over since 1956), average during quarter, millions of persons

L_{M14+} = total male labor force aged 14 and over, millions of persons

L_{M1419} = male civilian labor force aged 14 through 19, millions of persons

L_{M20+} = male civilian labor force aged 20 and over, millions of persons

L_{M2024} = male civilian labor force aged 20 through 24, millions of persons

L_{M2534} = male civilian labor force aged 25 through 34, millions of persons

L_{M65+} = male labor force aged 65 and over, average during quarter, millions of persons

L_{UIS} = labor force covered by state unemployment insurance, millions of persons

LIQ = taxable withdrawals of distilled spirits and ethyl alcohol, thousands of gallons

M = U.S. imports of goods and services, billions of dollars

M_{COF} = imports of coffee, billions of dollars

M_D = U.S. imports of durable goods, billions of dollars

M_{DA} = imports of automobiles, billions of dollars

M_{EFIN} = imports of crude materials, crude foodstuffs, and semi-manufactures, billions of dollars

M_{EFIN*} = imports of crude materials and semimanufactures, billions of dollars

M_{FIN} = imports of finished goods and services, billions of dollars

M_{FIN*} = imports of finished goods and services and crude foodstuffs, billions of dollars

M_{FINF} = imports of manufactured foodstuffs and beverages, billions of dollars

M_{FINM} = imports of finished manufactures, billions of dollars

M_N = U.S. imports of nondurable goods, billions of dollars

M_S = U.S. imports of services, billions of dollars

MAR = number of marriages, thousands

$MARE$ = number of expected marriages, thousands

MH = manhours, billions per year

MH_O = manhours of overhead workers, billions per year

MH_P = manhours of production workers, billions per year

N	= civilian population including Alaska and Hawaii, millions of persons
N^A_{5-18}	= civilian population aged 5 to 18, as of July 1, millions of persons
N^A_{5-25}	= civilian population aged 5 to 25, as of July 1, millions of persons
N_{14+}	= noninstitutional population aged 14 and over, billions of persons
N_{18-}	= civilian population aged 18 and under, millions of persons
N_{65+}	= civilian population aged 65 and over (62 and over for women since 1956), millions of persons
N_{F14+}	= civilian noninstitutional female population aged 14 and over, millions of persons
N_{F1419}	= civilian noninstitutional female population aged 14 through 19, millions of persons
N_{F20+}	= civilian noninstitutional female population aged 20 and over, millions of persons
N_{F2024}	= civilian noninstitutional female population aged 20 through 24, millions of persons
N_{F65+}	= female civilian population aged 65 and over (62 and over since 1956), average during quarter, millions of persons
N_{FS14+}	= unmarried civilian females aged 14 and over, millions of persons
N_M	= noninstitutional male population, millions of persons
N_{M14+}	= civilian noninstitutional male population aged 14 and over, millions of persons
N_{M1419}	= civilian noninstitutional male population aged 14 through 19, millions of persons
N_{M20+}	= civilian noninstitutional male population aged 20 and over, millions of persons
N_{M2024}	= civilian noninstitutional male population aged 20 through 24, millions of persons
N_{M2534}	= civilian noninstitutional male population aged 25 through 34, millions of persons
N_{M65+}	= civilian male population aged 65 and over, millions of persons
N_{ML}	= military population including armed forces overseas, millions of persons
N_{OASI}	= civilian population aged 65 and over (62 and over for females since 1956) eligible for OASI benefits, millions of persons

NNP	= net national product, billions of dollars
O	= manufacturers' net new orders, billions of dollars
O_U	= manufacturers' unfilled orders, billions of dollars
OBM_M	= months of orders backlog in manufacturing
P_{AF}	= implicit price deflator for farm gross product, $1954 = 1.00$
P_G	= implicit price deflator for government purchases of goods and services, $1954 = 1.00$
P_{GF}	= implicit price deflator for federal government purchases of goods and services, $1954 = 1.00$
P_{GS}	= implicit price deflator for state and local government purchases of goods and services, $1954 = 1.00$
P_C	= implicit price deflator for personal consumption expenditures, $1954 = 1.00$
P_{CD}	= implicit price deflator for personal consumption expenditures on durable goods, $1954 = 1.00$
P_{CDA}	= implicit price deflator for personal consumption expenditures on new and net used automobiles and parts, $1954 = 1.00$
P_{CDEA}	= implicit price deflator for personal consumption expenditures on durable goods other than new and net used automobiles and parts, $1954 = 1.00$
P_{CEF}	= implicit price deflator for personal consumption expenditures on goods and services except food, $1954 = 1.00$
P_{CN}	= implicit price deflator for personal consumption expenditures on nondurable goods, $1954 = 1.00$
P_{CNEF}	= implicit price deflator for personal consumption expenditures on nondurable goods other than food, $1954 = 1.00$
P_{CNF}	= implicit price deflator for personal consumption expenditures on food, $1954 = 1.00$
P_{CS}	= implicit price deflator for personal consumption expenditures on services, $1954 = 1.00$
P_{EX}	= implicit price deflator for exports of goods and services, $1954 = 1.00$
P_{GNP}	= implicit price deflator for GNP, $1954 = 1.00$
P_{GOOD}	= implicit price deflator for GNP goods, $1954 = 1.00$
P_{IBUS}	= implicit price deflator for business gross investment in plant and equipment, $1954 = 1.00$
P_{IC}	= implicit price deflator for construction component of GNP, $1954 = 1.00$
$P_{IC_{GS}}$	= implicit price deflator for new construction activity by state

and local governments, 1954 = 1.00

P_{IC_P} = implicit price deflator for new private construction activity, 1954 = 1.00

P_{ICNFR} = implicit price deflator for *GNP* expenditures on nonfarm residential construction, 1954 = 1.00

P_{IPDE} = implicit price deflator for investment in producers' durable equipment, 1954 = 1.00

P_M = implicit price deflator for imports of goods and services, 1954 = 1.00

$PIVA$ = price index used to estimate inventory valuation adjustment, 1954 = 1.00

PM = market price or index thereof

PM_{AF} = index of prices received by farmers for all commodities, food and nonfood, 1910–1914 = 1.00

$PM_{COT_{AF}}$ = U.S. average price of cotton at the farm level, cents per pound

PM_{EXW} = unit value index of world exports excluding U.S. components, 1954 = 1.00

$PM_{F_{AF}}$ = current value at farm level of the food market basket, livestock and crop components combined, dollars

$PM_{FAN_{AF}}$ = current value at farm level of livestock component of the food market basket, dollars

$PM_{FAN_{TR}}$ = retail value of livestock component of the food market basket, dollars

$PM^*_{FAN_{TR}}$ = adjusted retail value of livestock component of the food market basket, dollars

$PM_{FCR_{AF}}$ = current value at farm level of crop component of the food market basket, dollars

$PM_{FCR_{TR}}$ = retail value of crop component of the food market basket, dollars

$PM_{HAY_{AF}}$ = index of prices of feed grains and hay at the farm level, 1910–1914 = 1.00

PM_{ICRD} = average cost per unit of private housing starts, dollars

PM_{MCOF} = unit value index of coffee imports, 1954 = 1.00

PM_{MDA} = unit value index of imported automobiles, 1954 = 1.00

PM_{MEFIN} = unit value index of imports of semimanufactures, crude materials, and crude foodstuffs, 1954 = 1.00

PM_{MEFIN*} = unit value index of imports of semimanufactures and crude materials, 1954 = 1.00

PM_{MFIN} = unit value index of imports of finished goods and services, 1954 = 1.00

$PM_{\text{MFIN}*}$ = unit value index of imports of finished goods and services and crude foodstuffs, 1954 = 1.00

PM_{PDFP} = index of prices paid by farmers for goods and services used in production, 1910–1914 = 1.00

PM_{PDFS} = price index of purchased materials and services used in food marketing, 1947–1949 = 1.00

PR = price of raw materials

PR^{N} = normal price of raw materials (four-quarter moving average of PR)

PV = implicit price deflator for gross product originating, 1954 = 1.00

$Q^{\text{A}}_{\text{CASUG}}$ = anticipated consumption of sugar (consumption during the preceding year inflated by the ratio of population growth from the preceding year to the current year), millions of short tons per year

Q_{GAS} = production of gasoline, hundreds of thousands of barrels

$Q^{\text{A}}_{\text{MSUG}}$ = imports of sugar, millions of short tons per year

Q_{TIRE} = production of pneumatic casings, thousands

$Q^{\text{A}}_{\text{XASUG}}$ = available supply of sugar (domestic, including offshore, production of the preceding crop year plus the deviation of sugar stocks from linear trend, 1948–1962, thereof), millions of short tons per year

R^{2} = coefficient of determination (proportion of explained variance)

$\bar{R}^{2}$ = coefficient of determination (proportion of explained variance) corrected for degree of freedom

$R_{\text{OA}_{GF}}$ = weighted average of effective OASI contribution rates, fraction

$R^{\text{A}}_{\text{PY}_{GS}}$ = index of proxy state government tax rate on income, 1948 = 100

$R_{\text{PY1}_{GF}}$ = starting federal tax rate on wages and salaries, fraction

$R^{\text{A}}_{\text{RCS}_{GF}}$ = contribution rate for federal civilian employee retirement systems, fraction

$R_{\text{RR}_{GF}}$ = contribution rate for railroad retirement insurance, fraction

$R_{\text{UR}_{GF}}$ = rate of contribution by employers for railroad unemployment insurance, fraction

$R_{\text{US}_{GF}}$ = average employer contribution rate for state unemployment insurance, fraction

$R_{Z_{GF}}$ = average effective federal tax rate on corporate profits, fraction

$R^{A}_{Z_{GS}}$ = proxy state tax rate on corporate profits, fraction

$RDPN_{DA}$ = rate of depreciation of automobiles, per cent

RDR_{K} = rate of depreciation of business capital stock, fraction

RE = undistributed corporate profits, billions of dollars

$REGS$ = registration of new passenger cars, quarterly rate, millions

$REGS_{COM}$ = new compact cars registered in the U.S., millions

$REGS_{DOM}$ = new domestically produced cars registered in the U.S., millions

$REMS$ = removals of automobiles, quarterly rate, millions

$RENT_{AF}$ = imputed rental value of farm dwellings, billions of dollars

RES_{B} = member-bank borrowing from the Federal Reserve, average during quarter, billions of dollars

RES_{E} = excess reserves of Federal Reserve member banks, average during quarter, billions of dollars

RES_{NBC} = unborrowed reserves plus currency of Federal Reserve member banks, average during quarter, billions of dollars

RES_{R} = required reserves of Federal Reserve member banks, average during quarter, billions of dollars

REV_{TE} = operating revenues of telephone, wire-telegraph, ocean-cable, and radio-telegraph carriers, millions of dollars

REV_{TR} = sum of passenger revenues of domestic airlines, passenger revenue of class I railroads, and operating revenues of class I intercity motorcarriers of passengers, millions of dollars

RM_{BDT} = yield on commercial bank time deposits, per cent

RM_{BDTM} = legal maximum rate on time deposits deposited for six months or more, per cent

RM_{BLS} = bank rate of interest on short-term business loans, average for 19 large cities, per cent

RM_{FRB} = Federal Reserve Bank of New York discount rate, daily average during quarter, per cent

RM_{GBL} = average yield during quarter on U.S. securities maturing or callable in ten years or more, per cent

RM_{GBS3} = average market yield on three-month U.S. Treasury bills, per cent

RM_{MBLM} = Moody's average long-term municipal bond yield, per cent

RM_{PSEC} = weighted average yield on private securities, per cent

RRR_{DD} = weighted average of required reserve ratios against demand deposits, proportion

RRR_{DT} = average reserve ratio required against time deposits, proportion

RU = rate of unemployment, fraction

RU^* = five-quarter average of RU centered on $t-2$, fraction. $RU^* = \frac{1}{8}RU_{-4}+\frac{1}{4}RU_{-3}+\frac{1}{4}RU_{-2}+\frac{1}{4}RU_{-1}+\frac{1}{8}RU$

RU_{M1824} = rate of unemployment among males aged 18 through 24, fraction

RU_{M2024} = rate of unemployment among males aged 20 through 24, fraction

RW = average earnings per full-time equivalent employee, economy as a whole, dollars

$RW_{CIV_{GF}}$ = average earnings per full-time equivalent civilian employee of the federal general government, dollars

$RW_{ED_{GS}}$ = average earnings per full-time equivalent employee in state and local public education, dollars

$RW_{O_{GS}}$ = average earnings per full-time equivalent employee, state and local nonschool except work relief and enterprises, dollars

RWS = wages and salaries per manhour, dollars per hour

$RWSS$ = compensation of employees per manhour, dollars per hour

RX_{GS} = weighted average of state government alcohol, gasoline, tobacco, and general excise tax rates, fraction

$RX_{AP_{GF}}$ = federal excise tax rate on electric, gas and oil appliances, fraction

$RX_{AU_{GF}}$ = federal excise tax rate on automobile chassis and bodies and motorcycles, fraction

$RX_{BE_{GF}}$ = federal excise tax rate on beer, dollars per barrel

$RX_{GS_{GF}}$ = federal excise tax rate on gasoline, dollars per gallon

$RX_{LQ_{GF}}$ = federal excise tax rate on distilled spirits, dollars per proof gallon

$RX_{TB_{GF}}$ = federal excise tax rate on withdrawals of short cigarettes, dollars per thousand

$RX_{TE_{GF}}$ = federal excise tax rate on local telephone service, fraction

$RX_{TI_{GF}}$ = federal excise tax rate on tires, dollars per pound

$RX_{TR_{GF}}$ = federal excise tax rate on transportation of persons, fraction

S = shipments by manufacturers or sales by other industries, billions of dollars

S_e = standard error of estimate

$STAT$	= statistical discrepancy, billions of dollars
SUB	= subsidies less current surplus of government enterprises, billions of dollars
$SUPP$	= supplements to wages and salaries, billions of dollars
$SUPP_{CIV_G}$	= supplements to wages and salaries of civilian government employees, billions of dollars
T	= government receipts, billions of dollars
T_{GF}	= federal government receipts, billions of dollars
T_{GS}	= state and local government receipts, billions of dollars
TC	= corporate profits tax accruals to government, billions of dollars
TC_{GF}	= corporate profits tax accruals to the federal government, billions of dollars
TC_{GS}	= corporate profits tax accruals to state and local governments, billions of dollars
TC_{PAY}	= current corporate profits tax payments, billions of dollars
$TIME$	= time trend
TOB	= taxable withdrawals of short cigarettes, millions of cigarettes
TP	= personal tax and nontax receipts (or payments), billions of dollars
TP_{GF}	= personal tax and nontax receipts of the federal government, billions of dollars
TP_{GS}	= personal tax and nontax receipts of state and local governments, billions of dollars
$TP_{O_{GS}}$	= state and local government personal tax and nontax receipts other than income tax, billions of dollars
$TP_{Y_{GS}}$	= personal income tax receipts of state and local governments, billions of dollars
TPF_{GF}	= final federal income tax payments plus the fourth-quarter installment in January less refunds, billions of dollars
$TPQI_{GF}$	= federal income tax receipts from first three quarterly installments, billions of dollars
TPW_{GF}	= withholding income tax receipts of the federal government, billions of dollars
TW	= contributions for social insurance, billions of dollars
TW_{GS}	= state and local government receipts from contributions for social insurance, billions of dollars
TW_{O_G}	= contributions for social insurance other than OASI and employers, contribution for state unemployment insurance,

billions of dollars

TW_{OGF} = federal government receipts from contributions for social insurance other than OASI and employers' contribution for state unemployment insurance, billions of dollars

TW_{OAGF} = OASI contributions by employers, employees, and self-employed persons, billions of dollars

TW_{RCSGF} = contributions by employers and employees for federal civilian employee retirement systems, billions of dollars

TW_{RRGF} = contributions for railroad retirement insurance by employers and employees, billions of dollars

TW_{URGF} = employers' contribution for railroad unemployment insurance, billions of dollars

TW_{USGF} = employers' contributions for state unemployment insurance, billions of dollars

TWC_{OAGF} = collections of OASI taxes as reported by the Treasury, billions of dollars

TX = indirect business tax and nontax accruals, billions of dollars

TX_{GF} = indirect business tax and nontax accruals to the federal government, billions of dollars

TX_{GS} = indirect business tax and nontax accruals to state and local governments, billions of dollars

TX_{APGF} = collections from federal excise tax on electric, gas, and oil appliances, millions of dollars

TX_{AUGF} = collections from federal excise tax on automobiles, millions of dollars

TX_{BEGF} = collections from federal excise tax on beer, thousands of dollars

TX_{CUGF} = U.S. customs duties as published by the Treasury, billions of dollars

TX_{GSGF} = collections from federal excise tax on gasoline and lubricating oil, thousands of dollars

TX_{HWY} = highway trust fund tax revenues, millions of dollars

TX_{LQGF} = collections from federal excise taxes on distilled spirits and wine, thousands of dollars

TX_{OGS} = state and local government indirect business tax and nontax accruals other than property taxes, billions of dollars

TX_{PRGS} = property taxes portion of state and local indirect business tax and nontax accruals, billions of dollars

TX_{TBGF} = collections from federal excise tax on tobacco, millions of dollars

$TX_{TE_{GF}}$ = collections from federal excise tax on local and long-distance telephone service, telegraph, cable, radio, etc., plus leased wires, millions of dollars

$TX_{TI_{GF}}$ = collections from federal excise tax on tires and tubes, millions of dollars

$TX_{TR_{GF}}$ = collections from federal excise tax on transportation of persons, millions of dollars

U = unemployed civilian labor force, millions of persons

U_{EIS} = unemployed not covered by state unemployment insurance, millions of persons

U_{IS} = unemployed covered by state unemployment insurance, millions of persons

$U15+$ = number unemployed for 15 or more weeks, millions of persons

$U26-$ = number unemployed for 26 weeks or less, millions of persons

$U27+$ = number unemployed for 27 or more weeks, millions of persons

$UCCA$ = unit capital consumption allowances (capital consumption allowance per unit of gross product originating), dollars per dollar

$UCCA^N$ = normal unit capital consumption allowances, (smoothed ratio of CCA to capacity output), dollars per dollar

UKC = user cost of capital goods, billions of dollars

ULC = unit labor cost (compensation of employees per unit of gross product originating), dollars per dollar

ULC^N = normal unit labor cost, dollars per dollar.
$$\left(\frac{WSS}{MH} \div \tfrac{1}{12} \sum_{i=-11}^{0} \left[\frac{X}{MH} \right]_i \right)$$

ULC_{FM} = index of unit labor costs in food marketing operations, 1957–1959 = 100

V = transfer payments to persons, billions of dollars

V_G = government transfer payments to persons, billions of dollars

$V_{AB_{GS}}$ = state and local government aid to the blind, billions of dollars

$V_{ADC_{GS}}$ = state and local government aid to dependent children, billions of dollars

$V_{AG_{GS}}$ = state and local government general assistance payments, billions of dollars

V_{AID} = federal grants-in-aid to state and local governments, billions of dollars

$V_{AO_{GS}}$ = state and local government old age assistance payments,

	billions of dollars
$V_{\mathrm{APD}_{GS}}$	= state and local government aid to the permanently and totally disabled, billions of dollars
$V_{\mathrm{BEN}_{GS}}$	= benefits from social insurance funds, billions of dollars
V_{BUS}	= business transfer payments to persons, billions of dollars
$V_{\mathrm{FOR}_{GF}}$	= net foreign transfer payments, billions of dollars
$V_{\mathrm{INS}_{GF}}$	= servicemen's insurance dividend component of transfer payments to persons, billions of dollars
V_{O_G}	= government transfer payments to persons other than OASI benefits, state unemployment insurance benefits, old age assistance, and aid to dependent children, billions of dollars
$V_{\mathrm{O}_{GF}}$	= federal government transfer payments to persons other than OASI and state unemployment insurance benefits, billions of dollars
$V_{\mathrm{O}_{GS}}$	= state and local government transfer payments to persons other than old age assistance and aid to dependent children, billions of dollars
$V_{\mathrm{OA}_{GF}}$	= old-age and survivors insurance benefits, billions of dollars
$V_{\mathrm{RCS}_{GF}}$	= federal civilian pensions, billions of dollars
$V_{\mathrm{RR}_{GF}}$	= railroad retirement insurance benefits, billions of dollars
$V_{\mathrm{RV}_{GF}}$	= payments to retired and disabled veterans, billions of dollars
$V_{\mathrm{SNV}_{GF}}$	= payment to survivors of nonveterans, billions of dollars
$V_{\mathrm{SV}_{GF}}$	= payments to veterans' survivors, billions of dollars
$V_{\mathrm{UR}_{GF}}$	= railroad unemployment insurance benefits plus sickness compensation, billions of dollars
$V_{\mathrm{US}_{GF}}$	= state unemployment insurance benefits paid by the federal government, billions of dollars
$VM_{\mathrm{OA/F}}$	= maximum per-family OASI benefit per month, dollars
VM_{OAPI}	= maximum OASI primary insurance amount, dollars
VM_{RCS}	= maximum monthly retirement benefit for civil servants, dollars
VM_{RR}	= maximum monthly benefit from railroad retirement insurance, dollars
VM_{UR}	= maximum daily benefits from railroad unemployment insurance, dollars
VM_{US}	= weighted average of maximum weekly benefits under various state unemployment insurance plans, dollars
VN	= von Neumann statistic
$WALD$	= excess of wage accruals over disbursements, billions of dollars
$WLTH$	= weighted average of recent values of GNP

$$= 0.114 \sum_{i=0}^{19} (0.9)^i [GNP]_{-i}, \text{ billions of dollars}$$

WPI	= wholesale price index, 1954 = 1.00
WPI_{CNEF}	= wholesale price index for consumer nondurable goods except food, 1954 = 1.00
$WPIS_{\text{CM}}$	= special wholesale price index for construction materials, 1954 = 1.00
WS	= wage and salary disbursements, billions of dollars
WS_{BUS}	= private wage and salary disbursements, billions of dollars
$WS_{\text{CIV}_{GF}}$	= federal general government wage and salary disbursements to civilians, billions of dollars
$WS_{\text{ED}_{GS}}$	= wage and salary disbursements to employees in state and local public education, thousands of dollars
$WS_{\text{ML}_{GF}}$	= federal government wage and salary disbursements to military personnel, billions of dollars
$WS_{\text{O}_{GS}}$	= wage and salary disbursements to nonschool (except work relief and enterprises) employees of state and local governments, billions of dollars
WSM_{RR}	= maximum wage and salary per month on which railroad retirement benefit is paid, dollars
WSS	= compensation of employees, billions of dollars
X	= gross product originating, billions of dollars
$X^{\text{A}}_{\text{HAY}}$	= production of feed crops in current calendar year, billions of dollars
X_{K}	= capacity output, billions of dollars
X_{KS}	= capacity output of principal supplying industry, billions of dollars
X_{S}	= output of principal supplying industry, billions of dollars
$\left[\dfrac{X}{X_{\text{K}}}\right]^{\text{N}}$	= normal capacity utilization rate, fraction
$\left[\dfrac{X_{\text{S}}}{X_{\text{KS}}}\right]^{\text{N}}$	= normal capacity utilization rate of principal supplying industry, fraction
$XCST_{AF}$	= current operating expenditures for farm production, billions of dollars
Y_{D}	= disposable personal income, billions of dollars
Y_{ENT}	= proprietors' income, billions of dollars
$Y_{\text{ENT*}}$	= business and professional proprietors' income from 1950 : 4 through 1954 : 3, total proprietors' income thereafter, billions of dollars

$Y_{\text{ENT}_{EAF}}$ = business and professional proprietors' income, billions of dollars

$Y_{\text{GRS}_{AF}}$ = gross farm income, billions of dollars

Y_{N} = national income, billions of dollars

$Y_{\text{NET}_{AF}}$ = net farm income, billions of dollars

Y_{OL} = other labor income, billions of dollars

Y_{P} = personal income, billions of dollars

Y_{RENT} = rental income of persons, billions of dollars

Z_{A} = corporate profits after taxes and after inventory valuation adjustment, billions of dollars

Z_{AU} = corporate profits after tax but before inventory valuation adjustment, billions of dollars

Z_{B} = corporate profits before taxes including inventory valuation adjustment, billions of dollars

Z_{BU} = corporate profits before taxes and before inventory valuation adjustment, billions of dollars.

AUTHOR INDEX

Abramovitz, M., 132n, 160, 235n

Ackley, G., 204, 223

Adams, E. W., Jr., 17, 533, 724

Adelman, F., 13, 32, 650

Adelman, I., 13, 32, 640, 650

Åkerman, G., 92

Allen, J. W., 160

Anderson, L., 485n

Anderson, T. W., 617n, 633

Anderson, W. H. L., 37n, 89

Ando, A., 17, 142n, 160, 204, 223, 533, 541n, 615n, 629n, 633, 650, 724

Axilrod, S., 465n

Babcock, J., 20, 21, 654n, 662, 664

Bailey, M. J., 41n, 89

Balderston, F. C., 641, 650

Ball, R. J., 316, 401

Barger, H., 633

Barnes, L. P., 533n

Barry, C. A., 240n, 241

Basmann, R. L., 605n, 634

Bauman, J., 229n

Baumol, W. J., 529

Bell, P. W., 380n

Bergstrom, A. R., 605n, 634

Boissonneault, L., 375, 379, 385n, 386n, 405n

Boles, R., 409n

Boot, J. C. G., 627n

Bowman, M. J., 89, 96n

Brandow, G. E., 409n, 418, 420, 423, 426ff, 446, 452, 456, 459n

Bridge, L., 126

Brill, D., 465n

Bronfenbrenner, J., 37n, 90

Brookings Institution, vi, vii

Brown, E. C., 17, 142n, 160, 533, 724

Brown, M., 529

Brown, T. M., 590, 601n, 634

Brumberg, R., 204

Brunner, K., 465n, 466n, 517n, 529

Bry, G., 239

Burk, M. C., 418, 423, 460

Burton, M., 533n

Burton, T., 335n

Butler, R. D., 409n

Campagna, A. S., 163

Chenery, H. B., 40, 52, 89

Cheng, H. S., 401n

Chiang, C. L., 55n, 89

Chow, G. C., 210, 223, 604, 634

Christ, C., 466n, 529

Clem, M., 409n

Coen, R. M., 95n

Cohen, B. I., 380n

Cohen, K. J., 38, 91, 95n, 641

Conard, J., 499n, 529

Copeland, M., 227n

Cornwall, J., 13, 32

Craig, J. A., vii

Cyert, R., 641

Daly, R. F., 409n

Darling, P. G., 15, 16, 13lff, 143n, 160, 275, 276

Dartmouth College, v, vi

Davidson, W. C., 650

Day, R. H., 460

de Leeuw, F., 20, 137, 157, 160, 465, 726

Debs, E. V., 362n

Dedrick, C., 339n

Denison, E. F., vii

Dicks–Mireaux, L. A., 316

Dillon, T. L., 449n, 451n, 460

Douglas, P. H., 53n, 89
Dow, J. C. R., 316
Downs, A., 460
Duesenberry, J. S., v, vi, 3, 205, 223, 227n, 265n, 335n, 465n, 466n, 485n, 500, 529, 676
Durand, J., 348, 357, 751
Durbin, J., 89
Durost, D. D., 409n
Dutta, M., 16, 17, 163

Eckstein, O., 265n, 314, 316
Egbert, A. C., 460
Eisenhower, D. D., 336
Eisenpress, H., 601n, 634
Eisner, R., 16, 17, 37, 89, 90, 95, 96n, 723
Eklund, H., 409n
Evans, W. D., 678

Farr, W., 359
Faxer, P., 592n, 635
Federal Reserve Board, vii
Ferber, R., 223
Ferguson, T., 55n, 90
Fisher, F. M., 20, 21, 27, 29, 589, 594n, 598n, 599n, 600n, 602n, 606n, 608n, 611n, 615n, 618n, 633, 634, 650, 653, 659n, 661n, 663, 678, 736
Fisher, I., 41, 54, 90
Fletcher, R., 650
Foss, M. F., 37n, 90, 98
Foster, S. B., 533
Fox, K. A., 19, 20, 21, 206, 304n, 409, 419n, 458, 460, 676, 724, 725
Friedman, M., 204, 223, 285, 468, 471n, 472n, 529, 530
Friend, I., 37n, 90, 529
Frisch, R., 418, 420, 460
Fromm, G., vi, 265n, 285n, 331, 681

Gentry, R. H., 160
Goldberger, A. S., 375n, 648, 650
Goldsmith, R., 58, 90
Goldstein, H., 335n
Gordon, R. A., vii
Gorman, W. M., 596n, 634
Graham, R. E., Jr., 229n

Graves, L. M., 650
Grebler, L., 185n
Grenander, U., 635
Griliches, Z,. 39n, 90, 487n, 530
Groze, L., 57n, 90

Haavelmo, T., 90
Hansen, M., 339n
Harberger, A., 469, 530
Harding, W., 336
Harrod, R. F., 618n, 634
Heady, E. O., 409n, 449n, 452, 460
Hecht, R., 409n
Hempstead, J. C., 42n, 91
Henderson, J. M., 460
Hickman, B., vii
Hicks, J. R., 618n, 634
Hildebrand, T. H., 650
Hirsch, A., 725n
Hirshleifer, J., 41n, 90
Hitch, C. J., 157, 165n
Hoffenberg, M., 678
Hoggatt, A. C., 641, 650
Holdren, B. R., 409n, 460
Holt, C. C., 12, 21, 160, 238, 610n, 637, 650
Hood, W. C., 461, 635
Howe, J., 227n
Humphrey, D., 337
Humphreys, N. A., 359n
Hurwicz, L., 598n, 634

International Monetary Fund, vii

Jackson, E. L., 641
Jaszi, G., 57n, 90
Jesperson, H., 409n
Johnson, H., 466n, 530
Johnston, J., 591n, 600n, 605n, 634
Jorgenson, D. W., 16, 17, 21, 35, 90, 235, 242, 654n, 723, 725
Judge, G. G., 460
Juréen, L., 592n, 598n

Kalecki, M., 235
Kantorovich, L. V., 647, 650
Kareken, J., 142n, 160

Katona, G., 206, 223
Katz, A., 340
Kendrick, J. W., 236
Kenen, P. B., 380n
Keynes, J. M., 40n, 90, 203, 204, 223, 359, 500, 530
Kirk, D., 359
Klein, L. R., v, vi, 3, 20, 21, 39, 40, 55n, 90, 137, 160, 163n, 214, 227n, 314, 316, 336, 375, 465n, 533n, 589n, 601, 606, 633, 634, 648, 649, 650, 653, 654, 681
Kloek, T., 623ff, 634
Koopmans, T. C., 91, 461, 634, 635
Kosobud, R. F., 336
Koyck, L. M., 40, 52, 54, 91, 100n
Kravis, I. B., 227n, 336
Kuh, E., vi, 18, 29, 42, 75, 91, 227, 234n, 235n, 265n, 465n, 553n, 589n, 724
Kuhn, A., 315
Kurtz, E. B., 42n, 91
Kurtz, T., 335n
Kuznets, P., 142n

Ladd, G. W., 149n, 150n, 160
Lebergott, S., 20, 335, 347n, 357n, 723, 726, 727
Leenders, C. T., 590, 601, 635, 661n, 678
Leipnik, R. B., 91
Lerner, A. P., 40n, 91
Lesnoy, S., 599n, 634
Levine, R. A., 37n, 91
Levy, F. S., 533n
Lewis, W., Jr., 538n
Lewis, W. A., 40n, 91
Linter, J., 236, 275, 277
Lipsey, R. G., 314
Liu, C. Y., 461
Liu, T. C., 142n, 160, 599n, 634
Long, C., 336n, 339n
Lovell, M., 15, 16, 131ff, 144, 156n, 160, 723
Lutz, F., 40n, 91
Lutz, V., 40n, 91

McCarthy, M. D., vii
McCullough, J. R., 359

McGraw–Hill, 17n, 158, 335n
McKinley, W., 336
Madansky, A., 601n, 634, 661n, 678
Maisel, S. J., 15, 17, 179, 185n, 723
Maki, W. R., 409n, 446, 461
Malinvaud, E., 91
Malthus, T., 359
Mann, H. B., 91, 617n, 634
March, J., 641
Marimont, M. L., 260, 735
Marshall, A., 359
Marston, A., 42n, 91
Marwah, K., 401
Massachusetts Institute of Technology, vii
Masucci, R., 409n
Meigs, J. A., 466n, 470n, 530
Meiselman, D., 466n, 498n, 530
Meltzer, A., 466n, 529, 530
Mennes, L. B. M., 623ff, 634
Meredith, G., 362n
Meyer, J. R., 42, 75, 91, 461
Midler, J. L., 650
Mihaltse, W., 227n
Mill, J. S., 359
Mills, E., 137, 160
Milne, J., 359
Modigliani, F., 37, 38, 91, 95n, 160, 204, 205, 223, 238, 379
Moore, H. L., 418, 461
Moriguchi, C., 134n, 160
Morrison, G., 466n, 530
Motes, W. C., 461
Mueller, E., 206, 223
Muth, J. F., 163n, 175, 238

Nagar, A. L., 590, 603, 605n, 606, 634, 635
Nakamura, M., 601, 606, 634
Nassimbene, R., 37n, 56n, 91
National Science Foundation, v, vi
Natrella, V., 37n, 90, 91
Neisser, H., 379
Newton, I., 646, 647, 649
Neyman, J., 55n, 91
Nield, R. R., 228n

Oakland, W. H., 533n
Office of Business Economics, vii

OBE–SEC, 17n, 37, 56, 57, 73, 91, 98
Ogburn, W., 359
Oi, W., 237n
Okun, A. M., vii, 37, 91, 653n
Olson, R., 409n
Orcutt, G. H., vii, 401n, 637

Park, S. Y., 131n
Pascal, B., 53
Pashigian, P., 102n
Phillips, W., 227n
Polak, J. J., 379
Powell, M. J. D., 650
Prais, S. J., 401n
Prescott, J. R., 409n

Quandt, R. E., 605, 635

Randall, C. K., 409n
Raman, C. S., vii
Raphson, J., 646, 647, 649
Reder, M., 235n
Resnick, S. A., 533n
Rhomberg, R. R., 17, 375, 379, 380n, 385n,
    386n, 405n, 723
Robinson, J., 335, 336n
Rockwell, G. R., 418, 423, 461
Roos, C. R., 39, 40, 91, 92
Rosenthal, S., 227n
Rothenberg, T. J., 589n, 590, 601, 635,
    661n, 678
Rubin, H., 91
Ryckoff, A., vii

Salter, W. E. G., 236
Sandee, J., 461
Sargan, J. D., 601n, 605n, 606n, 617n, 635,
    661n, 678
Sastry, M. V. R., 409n
Schultze, C. L., 19, 21, 227n, 235, 242, 281,
    282n, 315, 348, 662, 664, 665n, 676, 727
Schwartz, M. H., 143n
Scott, A. D., 40n, 92
Sengupta, J. K., 409n
Shinkai, Y., 20, 21, 653, 654
Shirey, R., 650
Simon, H. A., 238, 461, 615n, 622n, 633,
    635, 641, 650

Smith, R., 533n
Smith, V. E., 461
Soelberg, A., 641,
Solow, R. M., 54, 92, 142n, 160
Sparks, G. R., 15, 203, 390n, 428
Staiger, D., 465n
Stanback, T., Jr., 132n, 135ff., 160, 161
Stein, R., 335n
Steinberg, R., 335n
Steuer, M. D., 314
Steward, D. V., 610n, 641n, 646, 650
Strotz, R. H., 32, 89, 596n, 635
Stroud, A. H., 650
Suits, D. B., 15, 203, 204, 223, 390, 428
Sweeney, T. D., 388n
Szeliski, Von, V. S., 91, 92

Taeuber, R. C., 460
Taylor, L. D., 624n, 635
Teeter, B. T., 37n, 56n, 91
Teigen, R. L., 466n, 517n, 530, 533n
Theil, H., 37n, 77, 92, 461, 590, 591, 598n,
    600n, 601, 603, 635, 660n, 661n, 679
Thomas, D., 359
Thomas, R. W., 409n
Tinbergen, J., 5, 13, 39, 40, 92, 461
Tobin, J., 467n, 530
Tryon, J. L., 19, 235, 242, 260, 281, 662,
    664, 665n, 676, 727
Tweeten, L. G., 449n, 452, 460

Van Eijk, C. J., 461

Wald, A., 91, 617n, 634
Waldorf, W., 465n
Walka, A., 465n
Wallace, T. D., 460
Walton, C. W., 533n
Wasson, R., 57n, 90
Waugh, F. V., 461, 599n, 635
Webb, S., 359n
Webbink, P., v, vii
Wegman, C. H., 533n
Weidenbaum,, M. L., 135n, 140, 161
Weingartner, H. M., 37, 91
Whitaker, G. R., 137n, 161
Wicksell, K., 53n, 92

Wilson, T. A., 314, 316
Winfrey, R., 42n, 91
Wold, H., 27, 32, 592, 594n, 598, 635, 641,
650
Wolf, K., 227n
Wood, J. H., 465n, 466n, 503n, 530
Wood, L., 348

Wool, H., 344n
Woytinsky, V., 337

Zarnowitz, V., 163, 175
Zellner, A., 223, 590, 601, 635, 660n, 661n,
679

SUBJECT INDEX

A priori information, 418, 425, 590, 591, 599, 626, 654ff

Acceleration, 133: theory of fixed investment, 40ff. *See also* Flexible accelerator.

Aggregation: degree of, 7ff, 150, 155, 203, 251, 261, 290, 310, 427, 459; estimation procedures, 658ff; price and output, 653ff; value–added vs. gross flow, 654ff

Agricultural sector, 7, 19–20, 409ff, 703ff, 727: employment 449, 454; and foreign trade sector, 411; government policy, 725. *See also* Farm.

Anticipatory demand: business orders, 163ff; investment, 35ff, 723; realization of, 95ff. *See also* Intentions, Consumer attitudes, Consumer buying plans.

Asset preferences, 468, 723. *See also* Portfolio composition.

Asymptotic efficiency, 599, 600

Autocorrelation, 73. *See also* Serial correlation.

Automobile demand, 15, 144, 205, 207ff, 395, 684–685. *See also* Car demand.

Autoregressive equation, 20

Banking system: balance sheet, 506; behavioral equations, 506ff

Balance of payments, 200, 375ff. *See also* Foreign trade.

Bank reserves, 483ff

Bayesian analysis, 625

Bias, 14. *See also* Estimators.

Block recursive systems, 21, 27, 29, 606ff, 642, 736

Borrowing: and capital spending, 506; and excess reserves, 512ff; by business, 485, 505, 528; by household, 503, 504, 528; from financial institutions, 503; member bank, 510ff

Budget predictions, federal government 573, 575

Business cycle and growth theories, 12ff

Capacity, expansion of, 51, 108

Capacity principle, 39

Capacity utilization, 5, 16, 137, 140, 143, 144, 148, 153, 156–157, 287ff, 310

Capital accumulation, neoclassical theory of optimal, 38ff. *See also* Investment behavior.

Capital consumption. *See* Depreciation, Replacement investment.

Capital gains: component of user cost, 58–59; expected, 499, 500; realized, 540. *See also* Price speculation.

Capital goods, price of, 40

Capital–output ratio, 96

Capital stock: desired and actual, 47, 48, 52, 96; measurement of, 56–57

Capital spending, 489: household 503

Car demand, 15, 703. *See also* Automobile demand.

Cash flow, 5

Causal chains, 641. *See also* Recursive ordering.

Collinearity, 14, 152, 654. *See also* Multicollinearity.

Commodity Credit Corporation, 445, 455–456

Construction, non–business: 179ff: airport 584; effect on unemployment, 584; flow diagram of, 183, 184; government expenditure on, 573, 581; planning and contracting of,183; residential, 686–688. *See also* Investment.

Consumer: attitudes, 206, 211, 684–685, 723; buying plans, 15, 684–685, 723. *See also* Anticipatory demand.

Consumer demand for food, 15, 215, 416ff, 684–685, 725

Consumption regress'ons, 203ff, 684, 722

Contract curve, 315

Corporate profit taxes, 488: federal, 542, 693; state, 557, 694

Costs: farm, 442, normal or standard, 284–285, 290; temporary, 284–285, 290; unit labor, 290, 304–310, 707–709

Credit rationing, 153

"Critical structure", 642

Currency, 475, 484, 488ff

Customs duties 393

Cycles, 156: cyclical changes, 132; 148, 277, 283, 306; endogenously generated, 13; peaks and troughs, 131, 134n, short-run, 133; yields spreads, 503. *See also* Business cycle.

Data splicing, 659

Decision theory, statistical, 644

Defense, Department of, procurement, 135, 140, 157, 175, *See also* Government military.

Degrees of freedom, 26ff, 117, 136, 262, 629, 633, 736

Demand deposits, 473, 475, 488ff, 524, 713–714

Demographic variables, 7, 15. *See also* Labor force, Marriages, Population growth.

Department of Defense, 135, 139, 140. *See also* Military expenditures.

Depreciation, 42–44, 57, 87, 113, 230, 275, 286, 706–707, 725: agricultural, 442–444, 704–706; manufacturing, 297–303; regulated industries, 286, 294–296. *See also* Replacement investment.

Distributed lag, 38, 40, 47, 48, 52, 59, 60ff, 78, 83, 103, 150, 194, 199, 245: estimates of, 63ff; Koyck–type, 40, 100; Pascal form, 53ff; "restricted form", 62. *See also* Flexible accelerator, Stock adjustment mechanism.

Disturbances: economy–wide, 613ff; equation–implicit, 613; properties of, 12, 14, 611ff; sectorimplicit, 613. *See also* Errors.

Dividends, 275–277, 701–702, 724

Dummy variable, 30, 134n, 165, 166, 307, 540, 564, 569, 670

Durables: consumer demand for, 205ff, 684–685, 722–723; price of, 674–676

Dynamic programming, 238

"Echo effect", 42, 75, 78

Economic policy, 4, 7, 21. *See also* Federal Reserve policy, Policy simulation.

Elasticities: food demand, 420; foreign trade, 17, 384ff, 400, 692; money demand, 493ff

Employment: error structure of manhour estimates, 261ff; labor requirements, 699–701, 724; over business cycle, 227ff; production functions, 237ff, 699–701, 724. *See also* Labor force, Unemployment.

Endogenous variables, 6, 10, 18, 23, 638, 727: lagged, 6, 29, 609, 611, 615, 618, 623, 625

Equilibrium stocks, 134. *See also* Stock adjustment mechanism.

Errors: anticipations, 115ff, 127; in equations, 11, 55; measurement in variables, 55, 458n; residual, 639. *See also* Disturbances, Serial correlation, Specification.

Estimators: best linear unbiased, 59, 591; classification of, 23–27, 31, 589ff; consistency of, 23,31,55; full information 26, 27, 590, 601; large–sample properties, 603; limited information, 26, 602, 682, 736–738; Nagar's double *k*–class, 590, 603; Theil's *h*–class, 590, 603; Theil's *k*–class, 590, 603

Euler condition necessary for maximum, 45, 46

Excess profit tax, 542

Excess reserves, 484, 512ff. *See also* Reserves.

Exchange restrictions, 389

Excise taxes, 543ff, 694–697, 724: specific, 544, 545, 724

Exogenous variables, 10, 17, 18, 20, 29, 638, 727, 736: lagged, 29, 623, 625. *See also* Predetermined variables.
Explosive systems, 618
Export demand, 17, 380ff, 692–693, 723. *See also* Foreign trade.
Extrapolation, 30, 31

Factor income payments, 18, 227ff, 700–702, 724, 730–733. *See also* Farm income, Interest rate, Profit, Rent index, Wage determination.
Farm: depreciation on buildings and machinery, 443; dwellings, imputed rental value of, 440ff; gross investment, 449ff; income, 19, 410, 436, 437ff, 448, 450–451, 724; inventory change, 438, 444ff; policy, 459; product prices, 410ff, 425; production expenditures, 438, 442ff; support programs, 19, 427, 445, 449, 455. *See also* Agricultural sector.
Federal debt, 524
Federal Reserve policy, 200, 524
Federal revenues, 538ff: corporate profit tax accruals, 542; excise taxes on alcoholic beverages, 543, 544; excise taxes on tobacco, 543; indirect business tax and nontax receipts, 543; other specific excises, 544, 545; personal tax and nontax receipts, 538. *See also* Government sector.
Feedback, 5, 18, 23, 132, 156, 307, 379, 597, 611. *See also* Endogenous variable, Recursive ordering.
Final demand sectors, 653, 655, 710–712: computation of, 663ff
Financial: behavior, model of, 465ff: expectations, 489; sectoral equations, 713, 714, 626. *See also* Monetary sector.
Financial intermediaries, 269
Fiscal policy, 533
Flexible accelerator, 40, 41, 52, 53, 134. *See also* Accelerator, Stock adjustment mechanism.
Flow chart: nonbusiness construction. 183–185; whole system, 22–25
Food demand, 15, 215, 416ff, 684–685, 725

Food products: livestock, 457; marketing charges, 431ff; marketing services, 430
Forecasting, 13, 21, 31, 73, 121, 200, 389. 599, 638ff, 647, 736: conditional, 643; efficiency, 390ff, 402; error, 150; naive, 14, 74, 124; one–quarter, 10; unconditional, 10
Foreign trade elasticities, 17, 384ff, 400
Foreign sector, 375ff, 547: forecasts, commodity groups, 401

GNP price deflators, 21, 99, 283, 734: conversion of sector prices to, 21, 672–678, 711–712, 726; fixed investment, 57; output deflators, 662. *See also* Price.
Goods–in–process, 146
Government military: expenditures, 165–167, 169–174, 689–690; orders, 16. *See also* Defense procurement.
Government sector, 7, 17, 533, 724, 736: magnitudes, 534; purchases of goods and services, 571; revenues and expenditures, 533ff, 693–699, 718; state and local, 577ff
"Great ratios" in economics, 336
Hill–Burton Act, 583
Home Loan Bank Board, 519, 522
Homogeneity condition, 421, 467, 471
Homoscedasticity, 591, 593
Household formation, 183, 191ff, 686–687
Housing: demand, 7, 15, 723. *See also* Nonbusiness construction, Residential construction.
Housing starts, 15, 195ff: changes in interest rates, 197; and inventory changes, 197; reaction time of inventories, 197; shifts in number of starts, 201; stock of housing, 267; vacancies, 197

Identification, 14, 594, 602
Identities, 681, 716–719: financial, 524
Import demand, 380ff, 692–693, 723: automobiles, 404–406; coffee, 403; commodity groups, 395ff; sugar, 403–404. *See also* Foreign trade.
Income: entrepreneurial, 269; expectations, long–run, 285; farm, 437ff; interest, 269–271; national, 717, 730–733; "nor-

mal" or "expected", 468; permanent, 472; transitory, 489. *See also* Factor income payments.

Income distribution, 699ff: factor shares, 227ff, 699ff, 724; over business cycle, 227ff; secular, 234

Initial conditions, 10

Input–output, 19ff, 23, 29, 234, 411, 656, 657: conversion of prices, 661ff, 710–711, 726; structural change, 672

Instrumental variables, 590, 602ff, 661, 678: and causality, 621ff; and multicollinearity, 622

Interest elasticities, money demand, 493

Interest rates: financial behavior, 465ff, 713–714; fixed investment, 44ff, 86–89, 691–692, 715; interest income, 269–271, 700–701; inventory investment, 145, 148–156, 688–689; residential construction, 187, 197, 200, 686–687; state and local construction, 581–582, 695–697. *See also* Rate of interest.

Inter–temporal utility function, 41

Inventory: actual and planned change, 145, 149, 157; behavior, 15, 16; cost of holding, 146, 148; determinants of, 147, 148; durable and nondurable manufacturing, 142, 150, 155; farm, 444–447, 704–706; investment in, 131ff, 688–689, 723; theory of, 145; trade, 143, 155

Inventory valuation adjustment, 18, 269, 271–275, 277, 701–702.

Investment: actual and anticipated, 16, 17, 691–692, 715, 723; allowances, 85; appropriation of funds for, 36, 49; behavior, 35ff, 84, 715; demand function, 121, 235; for expansion, 77, 80, 81, 85; farm, 393, 449–453; in farm tractors 39n; long-term response, 80, 89; realization of anticipations, 38, 95ff, 114ff, 690–691, 723; short–term and long–term responses to changes in tax structure, 89; short–term response of, 80, 87, 88, 89; survey of OBE–SEC, 37; tests of theory, 74ff; theory and econometrics of, 43; time pattern of response, 17, 79, 81, 83ff. *See also* Replacement investment.

Jacobian determinant, 27

Klein–Goldberger model, 13, 19, 32, 375, 648

Korean war, 30, 166, 271, 286, 307, 332, 389, 541, 565, 570, 584: aid to dependent children, 570; construction and unemployment, 584; depreciation allowances, 286; foreign trade elasticities, 389; inventory valuation adjustment, 271; major disturbances, 30; new orders manufacturing, 166; profit margins in trade, 307; tax receipts, 540; veterans' benefits, 565

Koyck lag distributions, 40, 52, 54, 100ff

Kronecker delta, 55

Labor force, 20, 335ff, 702–703, 726–727. *See also* Employment, Population, Unemployment

Labor productivity, cyclical changes, in, 228, 233, 234, 241, 267

Lag operator, 51, 54, 60ff

Lag structure, 17, 28, 36, 40, 165, 237, 244, 281, 308, 332: distribution of in investment, 38, 40, 47–55, 74–85. *See also* Koyck lag distributions, Pascal distributed lag function.

Lagged dependent variables, 205–206, 243, 252

Lagrangian expression, 45

Laspeyres price index, 427, 440, 446

Learning process, 644

Least squares, estimation method, 23, 55, 115, 590ff, 659–661, 678. *See also* Estimators.

Liquid assets, effects in consumption, 204–205, 214, 216, 684–685. *See also* Monetary sector.

Liquidity principle, 39

Long–run projections, 133

Marginal productivity, conditions of, 46, 53

Mark–up equations, 19, 281, 284, 287

Marriages: housing market, 194–195, 723; labor force, 359ff, 702–703

Marshallian partial equilibrium theory, 86

Maximum–likelihood: full information,

26, 238, 590; limited information, 26, 29, 590, 682; linearized, 590, 601
Military expenditure, 165–167, 169–174
Minimum chi–squared, principle of, 55
Model-building, 4ff: applications, 9ff, 639ff; as cumulative and collective process, 9; dynamic elements, 5; estimation of, 589ff; group research, 14, 22
Monetary sector, 7, 20. *See also* Financial.
Monetary policy, 20, 527, 726
Money holdings, 528
Money–supply, equations of, 20, 517–518
Monte Carlo experiments, 11, 604, 605, 644
Multicollinearity, 26, 29, 145, 153n, 156, 410, 424, 441n, 522, 540, 578, 590, 601, 603, 606, 622ff

Naive models, 72, 73, 124ff
Near consistency, 597–599, 615
Near money, 471
Net worth, 41, 78, 467, 468: maximization of, 43ff
Newton–Raphson iterative solution, 646ff
"Noise" level, 145
Noise–to–signal ratio, 8
Nonbank financial sector, 518ff
Nonbusiness construction, 179ff. *See also* Housing demand, Residential construction.
Non financial public, behavior of in financial sector, 488ff
Nonfinancial variables, in financial sector equations, 482, 487, 527
Nonlinearities, 14, 21, 145, 637, 641, 644, 646ff, 736: stability of, 643

OBE Capital Goods Study, 57, 98
OBE–SEC Investment Survey, 56, 73
OBE Monthly Survey, 58
Open–market purchases and sales, 483
Ordering, causal, 28, 411ff, 437, 448, 641: farm prices, 412; two–stage least squares, 414. *See also* Block recursive systems, Recursive ordering.
Orders: in inventory analyses, 15, 135ff, 148, 688–689, 723; new, 16, 163ff, 689–

690, 723; unfilled, 16, 97, 101ff, 127, 163ff, 689–690, 723
Ordinary least squares, 590ff, 659–661, 678. *See also* Estimators.

Parameters, continuous and discrete, 44n
Pascal distributed lag function, 53ff, 59ff. *See also* Distributed lag.
Phillips curve, 314
Policy instruments, 11, 12, 18, 414, 638: parameters, 18, 377; simulation, 21, 389, 647; variables, 133, 200, 201, 533
Population growth, 618. *See also* Employment, Labor force, Marriage, Unemployment.
Portfolio composition: changes, 494; desired, 467ff
Precautionary motives, inventory holdings, 146
Predetermined instruments, 26–27, 590, 626, 727, 736, 737. *See also* Exogenous variables.
Price: aggregation, 657–658; autoregressions, 676, 711; changes and business new orders, 169, 174; conversion matrix, 673, 710, 726; determination, 19, 235, 281ff, 707ff; indexes for producers' durable equipment, 57; investment goods, 57; market price concept, 284; received by farmers, 432ff; shadow or accounting, 46, 58; speculation in inventory demand, 144, 146, 148, 152, 153; value-added, 282ff. *See also GNP* price deflator.
Principal component analysis, 26, 623–624
Private loans and investments, 514
Private securities, 485, 488, 489, 523, 524; nonbank finance holdings of, 521, yields on, 515
Production functions, 18, 29, 234, 235, 246ff, 699–700, 724: Cobb–Douglas, 53, 235; cyclical, 227n, 235, 237ff
Production smoothing, 140
Profit taxes: corporate, 488; federal, 542, 693; state, 557, 694
Profits, 104, 111, 124, 127. 241, 267, 284, 717–718: maximization of, 135
"Profits" principle, 39

Proximity theorem, 597, 598, 611: generalized, 618
Proxy variable, 165, 169, 175

Railroad: retirement insurance, 552, 563;
unemployment insurance, 553, 567
Ratchet effect, 290
Rate of interest, 40, 87, 88, 89, 156
Realizations function, 38, 95ff, 115ff, 127–
128, 188, 690–691, 723
Recursive ordering, 21, 27ff, 411, 642, 646,
647: necessary assumptions for, 592ff;
triangular matrix of 27, 28, 413. *See also*
Block recursive systems, Causal chains.
Reduced form equations, 10, 26: estimation
599–600, 602
Renewal theory, 51
Rent index, 183, 193, 267
Rentier income, 18
Replacement investment, 41, 50ff, 77, 81,
84, 85: geometric form of distribution of,
42, 51. *See also* Depreciation.
Reserves, required, 507, 713–714. *See also*
Excess reserves.
Residential construction, 187ff, 686–688
Retirement systems: civilian employee,
554; railroad, 552
Robustness of estimators, 590, 601, 603,
606
Root mean square error, 117

Sales expectations, 101, 137: long–run 285
Savings and insurance claims, 475, 484,
485, 488, 489, 494ff
Seasonal variation, 23, 59, 136ff, 682: ad-
justment coefficient, 29, 168, 538, 547
Sensitivity analysis, 11, 641
Serial correlation, 14, 121, 590, 600, 610,
614
Services demand, 209, 216, 219, 684–685:
effect of liquid assets and population, 723
Simulation, 10ff, 21, 31, 278, 308, 524ff, 723:
computer, 637ff; Monte Carlo, 11; pol-
icy, 11; sensitivity, 641
Simultaneous equation estimation, 23ff,
142, 143, 156, 589ff
Simultaneous least–squares estimator, 590

Single equation least–squares regression,
23, 27, 30ff. *See also* Least squares.
Small sample properties, 589, 600, 604ff
Social insurance, contributions for, 548ff
Social welfare function, 643
Specification error, 14, 55, 251, 487, 590,
601, 602, 606n, 614, 734
Stabilization game, 644
Stabilization policy, 4, 80, 84ff
Standard Industrial Classification, 56
State revenues, 554ff: corporate profit tax,
557; expenditure, 578ff; indirect busi-
ness taxes, 558; personal tax and nontax,
554; property taxes, 559; social insur-
ance, 560
State unemployment insurance, 550
Steel strike, 30
Stochastic disturbances, 137. *See also* Dis-
turbances and errors.
Stock adjustment mechanism, 205, 212ff,
469, 582. *See also* Flexible accelerator.
Stock equilibrium, 517
Stocks, 526
Stocks, auto dealers', 144, 150
Structural break, 599. *See also* Korean war
Structural estimation, problems and tech-
niques, 589ff

Target variable, 11
Tax accruals, 494
Tax rate indices, 537
Tax revenue, 537ff
Tax structure, 41, 43, 44, 87, 89
Technical change, 241ff, 618
Three–stage least–squares, 590, 601, 660,
661. *See also* Simultaneous equation es-
timation.
Time deposits, 474ff, 488ff, 494, 506, 515ff,
713–714, 726
Time lags, effect on simultaneous equation
estimation, 596
Transactions motive, inventory holdings
for, 145, 148
Transfer payments, 561: federal, 561ff; old–
age and survivors' insurance, 561; other
retirement and disability programs, 562;
state and local, 567ff

Two–digit manufacturing industries, 19, 310

Two–stage least–squares, 26, 29, 238, 590, 682. *See also* Simultaneous equation estimation.

Unemployment insurance, 550ff: benefits for compensation, 566

Unemployment rate and federal expenditure, 573ff: and military expenditures, 575

Unfilled orders, 16, 97, 101ff, 116, 118, 124, 127, 135ff, 142, 148, 163ff, 688–690, 723

Unit labor cost, 304–310

U.S. securities, 494, 496, 523: bank holdings of, 508ff; nonbank finance holdings of, 520, 522; rates, term structure of, 494, 501ff

User cost, 40, 46, 56, 58, 59, 87

Variance–covariance matrix, 11

Von Neumann: ratio, 72, 173, 252; system, 335

Wage determination, 19, 281ff, 707–710; and profits, 314; and unemployment, 312; wage inflation, 329

Wealth, 466, 471ff, 526

Wharton School model, 375

World War II, impact on population shifts, 431